W9-BBH-432

Partisan Journalism

Communication, Media, and Politics
Series Editor: Robert E. Denton, Jr., Virginia Tech

This series features a range of work dealing with the role and function of communication in the realm of politics, broadly defined. Including general academic books and texts for use in graduate and advanced undergraduate courses, the series encompasses humanistic, critical, historical, and empirical studies in political communication in the United States. Primary subject areas include campaigns and elections, media, and political institutions. Communication, Media, and Politics books will be of interest to students, teachers, and scholars of political communication from the disciplines of communication, rhetorical studies, political science, journalism, and political sociology.

Titles in the Series

The 2004 Presidential Campaign: A Communication Perspective, Edited by Robert E. Denton, Jr.

Transforming Conflict: Communication and Ethnopolitical Conflict, by Donald G. Ellis

Bush's War: Media Bias and Justifications for War in a Terrorist Age, by Jim A. Kuypers

Center Stage: Media and the Performance of American Politics, by Gary C. Woodward

Message Control: How News Is Made on the Campaign Trail, by Elizabeth A. Skewes

Tag Teaming the Press: How Bill and Hillary Clinton Work Together to Handle the Media, by James E. Mueller

The 2008 Presidential Campaign: A Communication Perspective, Edited by Robert E. Denton, Jr.

Political Campaign Communication: Principles and Practices, Seventh Edition, Judith S. Trent, Robert V. Friedenberg, and Robert E. Denton, Jr.

The 2012 Presidential Campaign: A Communication Perspective, Edited by Robert E. Denton, Jr.

Last Man Standing: Media, Framing, and the 2012 Republican Primaries, Danielle Sarver Coombs

Partisan Journalism: A History of Media Bias in the United States, by Jim A. Kuypers

Partisan Journalism

A History of Media Bias in the United States

Jim A. Kuypers

HUMBER LIBRARIES LAKESHORE CAMPUS
3199 Lakeshore Blvd West
TORONTO, ON. M8V 1K8

ROWMAN & LITTLEFIELD
Lanham • Boulder • New York • Toronto • Plymouth, UK

Published by Rowman & Littlefield
4501 Forbes Boulevard, Suite 200, Lanham, Maryland 20706
www.rowman.com

10 Thornbury Road, Plymouth PL6 7PP, United Kingdom

Copyright © 2014 by Rowman & Littlefield

All rights reserved. No part of this book may be reproduced in any form or by any electronic or mechanical means, including information storage and retrieval systems, without written permission from the publisher, except by a reviewer who may quote passages in a review.

British Library Cataloguing in Publication Information Available

Library of Congress Cataloging-in-Publication Data

Kuypers, Jim A.
Partisan journalism : a history of media bias in the United States / Jim A. Kuypers ; foreword by Larry Schweikart.
pages cm. — (Communication, media, and politics)
Includes bibliographical references and index.
ISBN 978-1-4422-2593-0 (cloth : alk. paper) — ISBN 978-1-4422-2594-7 (electronic)
1. Journalism—Objectivity—United States—History. 2. Press and politics—United States. I. Title.
PN4888.O25K84 2013
302.230973 (—dc23
2013026883

∞™ The paper used in this publication meets the minimum requirements of American National Standard for Information Sciences Permanence of Paper for Printed Library Materials, ANSI/NISO Z39.48-1992.

Printed in the United States of America

Contents

Foreword

Perhaps the two most frequent questions audiences ask me as a speaker on the conservative circuit are "Why are colleges so liberal?" and "Why is the media so liberal?" This book is about the latter question, and while it assumes that there has been a historical change, it seeks to analyze that shift in a historical light, applying journalistic tests, rather than document it using social science methods. That has already been done well by Tim Groseclose in his book *Left Turn*. What Groseclose did was to apply *both* the accepted measurements of the left and the right to establish a common index, then prove by that index that the media was not only well to the left of the American public, but by its constant, biased reporting has shifted anyone exposed to its reports significantly to the left as well. Even the supposedly "right-wing" Fox News is slightly to the left of the typical American.[1]

Groseclose's work has been somewhat harder for liberals to dismiss than an earlier book by CBS insider Bernard Goldberg (*Bias*) as anecdotal or even sour grapes. Goldberg used an insider's viewpoint at CBS News to expose the distortion of the news by liberals—an act that sealed his fate as a respected journalist once and for all.[2] Over time, there had been snippets of truth leak out about the media, but Goldberg's book was one of the first to catalog the details from inside the newsroom itself.

But none of these books—or many of the others on the market, whether left or right—have sought to place journalism and its liberal bias in a historical perspective. Enter Jim Kuypers, a professor of communication at Virginia Tech. I first came across Jim's work with his excellent *Press Bias and Politics*, published in 2002. He demonstrated that what politicians said is often not what the press reported they said. Quite the contrary, Kuypers, by examining over 800 reports on hot-button issues across 116 different newspapers showed that in four separate ways, the "Mainstream" press ignored arguments or positions that it simply did not agree with. He concluded that this was not a healthy development for a democracy.[3]

Kuypers followed this with a study of George W. Bush's speeches on terrorism, Iraq, and weapons of mass destruction (WMDs) and found that, again, what Bush actually said was seldom what was reported. Rather, the media filtered and altered his words, turning the argument that Iraq *might* have WMDs, and that it was entirely irresponsible to continue to act as though it didn't in a terrorist age, into a certainty that

Bush used the *certainty* of WMDs—and only that argument—to convince the American public and legislators to support the invasion in 2003.[4] While the event occurred after Jim's book came out, it was not surprising that the press virtually ignored the news that 550 *tons* of "yellowcake" uranium had been quietly shipped out of Iraq since 2003! CNN carried the story on July 7, 2008, but completely unlike the stories about Abu Ghrab, there were no relentless headlines in the *New York Times*. This was the same "yellowcake" that sparked the controversy over Joe Wilson— who had insisted that the Iraqis were not trying to acquire it from Niger. Apparently, they found it somewhere else, or Wilson was incredibly inept as a detective. At any rate, probably the single most important event of Operation Iraqi Freedom, other than the capture of Saddam Hussein and the killing of Abu al-Zarqawi (an al-Qaeda terrorist—another example of something that was "not" in Iraq), Operation McCall and its transfer of the uranium out of Iraq was the most important news story of the war. Yet it might as well have never happened.[5]

Yet both of Kuypers's books (and several others he did on similar subjects in the first decade of the 21st century) stayed pretty much in the present. What was lacking was an explanation of how we got here, for most journalism-history books were written by liberals scarcely different than the reporters themselves. That's what *Partisan Journalism: A History of Media Bias in the United States* is about. Has journalism always been this way? If not, when did it change? Was it ever "fair and balanced," or even moderately objective?

It might surprise the reader to know that aside from the earliest era of "broadsides," when a large portion of the public was still illiterate and "readers" in public settings would read (mostly local) news stories aloud, the press was horribly biased at birth. This was by design. Martin van Buren, the founder of the modern-day Democratic Party, revolutionized the political system in the mid-1820s by creating a "spoils system" to reward political supporters. His goal was to prevent a civil war. It was noble in itself, but the means by which he sought to avoid war was reprehensible. He intended to stifle all public debate about slavery by essentially buying supporters. Of course, he couldn't bribe everyone, but through the Democratic Party, he and his successors could reward loyal organizers who got out the vote. There was no concern about why people voted or what the issues were. The only concern was that they voted, in Van Buren's case, for his candidate Andrew Jackson.

He quickly perfected the system, also known as *patronage*, to the point that by the 1850s it was a science. Although a creation of Hollywood, the film *Gangs of New York* perfectly captures the process of herding drunks out to vote, revoting the same person again and again, and corralling non-English speakers to cast their ballots. It would be funny had it not been so tragic.

But Van Buren's success in preventing a war by avoiding any discussion of slavery needed some other pieces for the system to work. First and foremost, he needed a good propaganda machine, which he created in the form of newspapers. These early papers, as is made clear in the work of Thomas Leonard, were nearly universally "partisan," meaning they were not only outlets for a particular political party, but were almost always owned by them. Van Buren even hand-picked the editors. None of them could make a profit in the free market, and at least 80 percent by Leonard's count relied entirely on subsidies from their political patrons. Thus, no one *ever* got the "news." What they got was a huge dose of Andy Jackson or, if in a Whig paper (later a Republican paper), Henry Clay. It must be emphatically noted, though, that the Whigs and Republicans only played on the field already established by Van Buren, and there is no evidence whatsoever that propaganda-type newspapers would have emerged if not for his desire to protect slavery. And that was exactly what the early Democratic Party's founding was about: protecting slavery.

As Kuypers notes, a massive change occurred during the Civil War, brought about in part by the public's unrelenting demand for accurate—not biased—information, and by the business revolution that required newspapers to actually make a profit. To do so, publishers suddenly had to appeal to a large majority of the people, not just Democrats, Whigs, or Republicans. These publishers were also impressed by the success of the "penny press," which catered to the public's appetite for nonpolitical news. Thus by the mid-1800s, the purely partisan newspaper disappeared, replaced by the "objective" newspaper which had a partisan editorial page. But the assumption was that the "news" part of the paper was unbiased.

Despite some notable exceptions, such as the Hearst and Scripps papers, journalism began a shift toward objectivity, to the point that by the early part of the 20th century, journalists actually drafted a code of ethics whose regulations would appear entirely foreign to most modern so-called journalists. All sources were to be named—there was to be no such thing as an anonymous source. All issues were to receive a fair debate explaining both sides of the story—from each side's own point of view, not the perspective of the reporter. All claims were to require multiple sources, not a single "insider." There were many others, but in these three guidelines alone, one could expect to see something of "objective" news.

To see how far we have drifted from these principles, look at any political story (or, for that matter, almost any story) in a major paper today, or on television news. How many times are "sources close to the administration" or "high ranking officials in the campaign" cited? How often is the other side of the story told fairly, and from the other side's viewpoint, without ridicule or code words?

The objective model held, more or less, for almost 100 years, and did not begin to break down until the early 1960s. In one of *Partisan Journalism*'s most important contributions to the debate, Kuypers analyzes five major newspapers over a 12-year period (1958–1970) using accepted journalistic analysis tools to prove the steady leftward march of the nation's major news sources. Rather than a single smoking gun event, Kuypers discovers a continual drift, but one that is unmistakable.

Worse, however, he documents a radically leftward lurch after 1970, despite the rise of decidedly conservative news platforms, such as the "Rush Limbaugh Show," conservative talk radio, Fox News, and the Internet. However, the advent of new conservative voices came as the entire universe of "news" was expanding almost exponentially, and the cacophony of voices tended to now overwhelm even the more partisan outlets with a slow drip of cultural leftism. According to Markus Prior's paper "Media and Political Polarization," it was true that broadcast outlets were more likely to report rising poll numbers for Bill Clinton and lower poll numbers for George W. Bush.[6] But more distressingly, Prior finds that once the "glory days" of network news—with its three main networks showing their major news programs at the dinner hour—died, the opportunity for people with little interest in the news to see the day's events (even if slanted leftward by the three networks) also vanished. Today, we have a name for them: "low information voters." Whether these voters are ignorant or genuinely stupid demands further analysis. But there is little doubt that they do not receive political news through Fox News or CBS or any other major news outlet, but rather absorb it through osmosis from the culture at large. Or, at least, from the media's coverage of the culture at large.

And that brings us back to Van Buren and a partisan press, but with a twist. While we may be rapidly approaching a time when almost all news outlets will be blatantly partisan and subsidized by political parties, this will not restore balance because the rest of the media from which voters get their entertainment, sports, and business stories are as dominated by the left as the "mainstream" news used to be. One only has to watch commentary on ESPN or *Entertainment Tonight* to pick up the subtle, but steady drip of leftist viewpoints. It may well be, therefore, that so much damage has already been done that even competition in a free market will no longer balance the scales.

This is not to argue for greater regulation, which inherently moves society leftward by positioning government as the "fair" referee, leading to still more public indoctrination that government is the solution, not the problem. It may mean, however, that a major, society-altering event is necessary to reshape the journalistic landscape. As Kuypers shows, this occurred once with the American Civil War, which came at the cost of over a half-million lives.

Jim Kuypers's effort here has not been to predict the future, but to explain and analyze the past. He therefore has blended history with the skills of an academician steeped in journalism and communication. Before we can know where we're going, we better know where we've been.

Larry Schweikart
Professor of History
University of Dayton

NOTES

1. Tim Groseclose, *Left Turn: How Liberal Media Bias Distorts the American Mind* (New York: St. Martin's, 2011).

2. Bernard Goldberg, *Bias: A CBS Insider Exposes How the Media Distort the News* (Washington, DC: Regnery, 2001).

3. Jim Kuypers, *Press Bias and Politics: How the Media Frame Controversial Issues* (New York: Praeger, 2002).

4. Jim Kuypers, *Bush's War: Media Bias and Justifications for War in a Terrorist Age* (New York: Rowman & Littlefield, 2006).

5. "About that 500 Tons of Yellowcake . . ." *American Thinker*, July 20, 2005.

6. Markus Prior, "Media and Political Polarization," February 2013, www.princeton.edu/~mprior/Prior%20MediaPolarization.pdf.

Preface

This book is an argument, ending with the conclusion that America today has all but returned to a partisan press. I reach that conclusion after reviewing four key periods of press history: the early days of the Republic; the growth of the objective period of the American press, particularly its growth after World War I; the transitional years following President Kennedy and Watergate; and the rise of the partisan press, up to and through the press treatment of the campaigns and presidency of Barack Obama. In writing about this last section I emphasize in particular the rise of alternative news media voices in AM radio, cable TV, and the Internet, voices slowly acting to add a competitive nature to the press today.

I have always believed that a good argument takes the form of "state your case, then prove it." You will certainly find assertions in this book. You will also find "proof" taken from a wide variety of sources: academic books and articles, mainstream press sources, Internet sources, alternate press sources, and liberal, conservative, and alternate political sources. In the last chapters I draw heavily on alternative sources of news to better demonstrate the charged partisan and competitive atmosphere in which a news consumer today encounters the news. In writing this book, I drew upon the disciplines of communication, history, journalism, and political science; in that sense it is part politics, part history, and part critique. Through it all is a simple purpose: to better understand where we started, how we got to where we are today, and to see where we are going. American Democracy is inextricably linked with a strong, competitive press. The country started in that situation, and, I argue, we are again returning to such a situation—but perhaps just don't know it.

Acknowledgments

I thank my family for their unreserved and continual support of my writing. It is with gratitude that I mention Virginia Tech, which paid my salary and also funded library services such as interlibrary loan, Ebscohost, and Lexis-Nexis, all absolutely necessary to the completion of this project. The value Virginia Tech places on research allows projects such as this book to be undertaken and completed. My department head, Robert E. Denton, provided steadfast support, which I greatly appreciated.

I also wish to acknowledge the encouragement and strong support of Larry Schweikart. His generous gifting of ideas, material, and the foreword for this book deserve far more credit than he was willing to accept.

Introduction

No sooner had the curtain descended on the 2009 presidential inauguration of Barack Obama—following an amazing Democrat election triumph in both the House and Senate—than the president singled out conservative radio talk show host Rush Limbaugh for criticism. According to reporter Jim Meyers, "Obama told the lawmakers they shouldn't be listening to Limbaugh if they plan on getting along with him: 'You can't just listen to Rush Limbaugh and get things done,' he told the GOP leaders during a discussion about his planned stimulus package."[1] This was the first time a sitting president had publicly singled out a lone American citizen for political attack. Months following this personal attack, in August 2009, Speaker of the House Nancy Pelosi (D-CA) along with House Majority Leader Steny Hoyer (D-MD) singled out those protesting the House bill on health care reform, saying "such behavior is 'simply un-American.'"[2] Just a month later, Bill Clinton disinterred his wife's 1998 "vast right-wing conspiracy" comments while being interviewed on NBC's *Meet the Press*. Is the vast right-wing conspiracy still there? asked David Gregory: "'Oh, you bet. Sure it is. It's not as strong as it was, because America's changed demographically, but it's as virulent as it was,'" the former president replied. 'I mean, they're saying things about him [Obama]—you know, it's like when they accused me of murder and all that stuff they did.'"[3]

Obama, Pelosi, Hoyer, and Clinton intended to cast doubt on the notion that average, everyday Americans could possibly disagree with their views—hence, un-American, or a "conspiracy." They did so, moreover, with full confidence that a waiting and willing press would convey and amplify approvingly their criticisms. Yet ironically, they might be close to the truth, but in ways they could scarcely imagine: over the last 50 years there has indeed been a conspiracy at work, though not of the type that Pelosi and Clinton assert. Since the 1960s, journalism in America has suffered from "a conspiracy of shared values," which has colored and prejudiced much of the reporting.

More than a few people have noticed this slant. Books such as *Bias* by Bernard Goldberg and *Slander* by Ann Coulter have made the case that a liberal bias exists in the news media. Polemical in nature, these nevertheless important best-selling works failed to provide detailed academic studies supporting a claim of liberal bias—despite abundant evidence that it exists. Research surveying press treatments of volatile public is-

1

sues has found that "there is a demonstrable liberal bias to the mainstream press in America."[4] Other studies have found the same bias operating, to even a greater extent.[5] Studies by journalism researchers Brigitte
Lebens Nacos, Gladys Lang, Kurt Lang, and others, using a variety of
testing methods and investigating bias on specific issues and in individual elections, have discovered bias operating as well.[6]

Progressives and leftist activists do not deny the presence of bias,
although they do deny the presence of left-leaning political bias; instead,
Eric Alterman, Al Franken, Pelosi, and others complain about a conservative dominance of AM radio, and, to a lesser degree, of Fox News airing
other than progressive points of view.[7] They cite anecdotal evidence
from newscasters, such as Tom Brokaw, who have bristled at Goldberg's
allegations of bias: "The idea that we [journalists] would set out, consciously or unconsciously, to put some kind of an ideological framework
over what we're doing is nonsense," Brokaw stated to C-SPAN's Brian
Lamb.[8] How Brokaw would know if he was guilty of "unconsciously"
imposing a framework on his reporting was not explained. Contrary to
Brokaw's assertions, journalists are increasingly admitting their prejudices. For instance, CBS's Andy Rooney acknowledged, "There is just no
question that I, among others, have a liberal bias. I mean, I'm consistently
liberal in my opinions."[9] Commenting on his colleague Dan Rather, Rooney said, "I think Dan is transparently liberal. Now, he might not like to
hear me say that."[10] *Washington Post* Book World editor Marie Arana
provides another example: "The elephant in the newsroom is our nar-
rowness. Too often, we wear liberalism on our sleeve and are intolerant
of other lifestyles and opinions. . . . We're not very subtle about it at this
paper: If you work here, you must be one of us. You must be liberal,
progressive, a Democrat. I've been in communal gatherings in *The Post*,
watching election returns, and have been flabbergasted to see my colleagues cheer unabashedly for the Democrats."[11] These are but a few of
the numerous insider claims of a left-leaning political bias in the news.

These accusations and admissions of bias are troubling to some journalists. For instance, from 1997 to 1999 the Committee of Concerned Journalists organized "the most sustained, systematic, and comprehensive
examination ever conducted by journalists of news gathering and its responsibilities."[12] Other panels and symposia have been convened on
journalistic ethics and professionalism, all with the objective of reassuring the public that the mainstream media is addressing its "bias problem." One reason these journalists began to investigate themselves was
that their ideological predispositions had already been exposed by alternate news sources that had begun to appear in the 1980s—news outlets
that challenged the facts and interpretations offered by the mainstream
press. Those alternative new sources, followed a decade later by Internet-
based alternate news sources and blogs, offered the public evidence that
other viewpoints existed, many of which were not expressed in the main-

stream news media. This, in turn, only further confirmed the presence of a liberal slant.

Not surprisingly, when alternative sources of news first appeared, they were aggressively attacked by the mainstream (establishment) news media as illegitimate. The Internet, which has allowed an explosion of alternate news voices, has been denounced as "too democratic," and one critic claimed that Internet news reporting had weakened "the methodology of verification journalists have developed."[13] "Facts have become a commodity, easily acquired, repackaged, and repurposed," wrote supposed media reformers Bill Kovach and Tom Rosensteil. What, exactly, is their complaint? One can surmise that it is that "facts have become a commodity, easily acquired."[14] A troubling implication is that people should not acquire facts, lest they come to a conclusion different from that of Kovach and Rosensteil.

For example, the *Washington Times*, which began publication in 1982, was the first serious challenger to what I will argue in later chapters was the mainstream/liberal media monopoly. Whereas other papers competed against the liberal slant in smaller markets, the *Washington Times* set up shop in Washington, DC, itself, and made a name for itself in scooping the "majors" on important stories, especially those dealing with national security. It went head-to-head with the *Washington Post*, one of the two most important dailies in the nation. Within a few years, Rush Limbaugh arrived to pose a much different challenge to the establishment news media by offering sound clips and instant analysis of comments that evening newscasts or the major papers tried to ignore or bury. A generation of conservative talk-radio hosts soon followed Limbaugh, while liberal talk hosts virtually disappeared in this competitive market. The Internet as a news source followed the appearance of Limbaugh, fostering the rapid transmission of facts and providing instant verification of mainstream news accounts. Finally, Fox News appeared in 1996, offering for the first time a competing set of images as well as commentary that presented viewers with new perspectives. Presenting news incorporating various "sides" of any issue, Fox is often villianized by the left as a conservative bull horn, yet recent studies have shown it to be the most ideologically balanced of the major news outlets.[15]

One would think that an accurate news service would welcome such a dispersion of facts—in essence, a means by which millions of people could verify in an instant journalistic integrity and accuracy. Instead, the mainstream press reacted negatively to the presence of such fact-checking. Media critic Howard Kurtz bemoaned the "shackles of objectivity," and Max Frankel of the *New York Times Magazine* claimed that reporting "just the facts" amounted to "objective misrepresentation."[16] "Aggressive interpretation," Frankel added, is necessary "for accuracy and fairness,"[17] implying, perhaps, that the presentation of facts without a mainstream journalistic interpretation meant that the public could not acquire the truth.

Journalism's lean to the left did not occur slowly over time, but rather rapidly in the 1960s, followed by a steady growth of issue-oriented activism culminating in what I see today as a return to the old partisan press of the Jacksonian era. This new partisan press, however, differs greatly from the Jacksonian newspapers in that mainstream journalists today pretend to operate behind a veil of objectivity. They present opinion under the guise of an objective journalism that took root during the years following World War I and especially following the rise of European fascists—what some call the objective turn in journalism. This objective period was short-lived and came apart fairly rapidly after 1960; in a sense, journalists evoke a memory as they practice a new history.

Throughout American history reporters and editors have ranged the spectrum of left and right. During partisan periods these political tendencies showed, but during the objective turn the profession of journalism operated under a set of practices that attenuated the bias of most journalists. Within short order, though, a rapid shift occurred in which several factors coalesced: the decline of professional standards; a rebellion against the concept of "fairness"; and a new emphasis on "progressive" reporting. Journalists informally rewrote the rules by which they operated, measuring "fairness" by word counts or an equal number of interview subjects, while ignoring slant, labeling, and tone. Story selectivity (agenda-setting) itself became part of the slant (framing)—and it grew so pervasive that many journalists sincerely did not notice it.

Put another way, progressive journalists freed themselves from the constraint of "facts," thus indulging the bias that solid journalistic practices had kept in check for so many decades. This is how veteran CBS newsman Bernard Goldberg could write in his May 2001 *Wall Street Journal* editorial that mainstream news anchors were so biased that they "don't even know what liberal bias is."[18] "Liberal bias," Goldberg contended, "is the result of how they see the world."[19] As Stuart Garner, CEO of Thomson Newspapers, put it, most modern reporters "want to save the world, whether the world wants to be saved or not."[20] A reporter for the *New York Daily News* confirmed this worldview: "I want to give voices to people who need the voice . . . [and to] people who are powerless."[21] Such a view assumes that people who "need the voice" have a point, or a genuine grievance. But is that true? One would hardly argue that in American society today the Ku Klux Klan has much of a "voice." But should it have one, based on the views of the *Daily News* reporter? If so, should not also the Nazis—truly a "voiceless" group in the United States—also be given "a voice" by a journalist acting as advocate?

How does one square the above worldview with a Pew Research Center survey in 1999 in which journalists unanimously responded that "getting the facts right" was the paramount value in the profession?[22] Interestingly, a 2008 Pew survey suggests that the number of journalists who think getting the facts right is a paramount value is steadily dropping; journalists today "are much less concerned than . . . eight years earlier about issues of quality and credibility."[23] Which is it? Should journalists give voice to the voiceless or report the facts? The answer is that in the minds of many journalists, they are one and the same because journalists do not today recognize the fundamental biases involving selectivity and labeling, which, among other journalistic practices, slant and distort the facts that they seek to "get right."

Prior to the 1990s, to the "average American" bias in the press would suggest an image of a spokesman for the Democratic or Republican National Committee, replete with lapel pin, conducting the newscast. But the bias Goldberg observed, and which scholarship confirms exists, is far more troubling, because it involves slanting stories through a shared worldview of the reporters, a "conspiracy of shared values." This worldview reveals itself in many ways, two of which are the selectivity of stories covered and the labeling of sources. Selectivity of coverage is a particularly popular and covert means for journalists to present their bias while appearing superficially to be "fair" and "objective" in their coverage of an *event*.[24] They can therefore at the same time know that they are biased in the events they choose to cover as "news," yet with a clear conscience offer an "objective" report of that biased selectivity.

Labeling is another source of "hidden bias" in the mainstream news. Whether someone is "right-wing" or "left-wing," "ultra-conservative" or "ultra-liberal" is itself something of a value judgment. What stands out, however, is that extreme labels are applied to conservatives and Republicans in much higher percentages than to liberals and Democrats. For example, during the 2000 Democratic primaries, Bill Bradley, a liberal Democrat by most standards, was so labeled by the three major networks—"exactly one time." In a similar vein, Al Gore was not called a "liberal" even once during the same period under review.[25] On the other hand, Fox News Channel's Bill O'Reilly pointed out to a roomful of television critics that he was constantly referred to as "conservative" while Bill Moyers, a liberal PBS journalist, was never labeled a "liberal."[26] There are numerous other examples. During the 2008 election, for instance, one found McCain labeled "conservative" up to ten times as often as Obama was labeled "liberal," even though prior to this campaign McCain was labeled by the mainstream media as a "moderate" Republican.[27] During coverage of the vice presidential picks of Biden and Palin, the networks never labeled Biden as liberal, but did label Palin, multiple times, as a conservative. Biden was depicted in nonideological ways, but Palin was described in ideological terms.[28] The major networks seemed to have a ban on the use of the term "liberal" to describe Obama, Biden, Gore, and other top politicians with a leftist tilt: "The only exception to the liberal label blackout included references by NBC's 'Today' and

CBS's 'Early Show' . . . when various reporters affectionately referred to Ted Kennedy as the 'liberal lion,' of the Senate, a clear term of endearment."[29] In sharp contrast, the major networks described many top Republicans as conservatives during the Republican National Convention.

Unfortunately, rather than accept such criticisms and address the issue, the mainstream news media has entrenched, denied, and resisted change. Instead of admitting its errors, it has, as will be demonstrated in later chapters, swung further to the left. This has, however, opened the door in a free market for a wide array of competitors since the early 1980s, including the *Washington Times*, talk radio, cable news, and, most recently, Internet sources. Despite establishment press claims that these competing sources lack credibility, the sustained success of papers such as the *Washington Times*, and websites and blogs such as Drudgereport.com and Hotair.com, continues to force the mainstream media to assess its own viability in a changing news and market landscape.

I argue in later chapters that the mainstream press today is liberal/progressive in both its composition and in its reportorial practices. This is not, however, the central focus of this book, although it will be amply demonstrated. Rather, my interest is in how the American news media changed over the course of over 235 years—how it transformed itself first from a partisan press to professional, objective, fact-based journalism, then how it changed yet again back into a biased and overwhelmingly liberal press, then again transitioned into a "partisan" press with new conservative competition. When did these changes occur, and why? Why did the press commit itself to "objective" journalism in the first place, and why did that become the mark of "professionalism"? Why has "fact-based journalism" faced a constant struggle against "progressive" or "value-based" journalism? Why did journalism suddenly abandon a long-standing commitment to "objective," nonpartisan reporting to again start revealing its biases—and even publicly justifying them? And how did the consumers of news respond to all of this?

I am inclined to believe that as public trust in government began to slide in the 1960s, so too began to slide the norms of journalistic objectivity. Though this is often linked to dissatisfaction over the Vietnam War, I suggest there were other forces at work—forces within journalism itself. Distrust of government soared well before Watergate or the end of the Vietnam War, marking a rapid decline from attitudes of the previous decade when 57 percent of Americans "trusted" the government in Washington to "do the right thing" most of the time, and 14 percent trusted it to do the right thing almost all the time.[30] Partly out of a feeling they had been betrayed by the military and by the Johnson and Nixon administrations during Vietnam, and partly out of a new focus in journalism on "investigative journalism," mainstream journalists became much more aggressive in their coverage of subsequent presidents and policies. In fact, the myth of investigative reporters bringing down a president in

Watergate accelerated the shift from "objective" to "progressive" journalism, leading publisher Jack Fuller to observe, "Watergate may have damaged journalism more than it did the presidency."[31] Following Watergate, journalists sought to buttress their own credibility by asking "hard questions" about government, and the law of unintended consequences went to work: *both* government and the news media lost credibility in the eyes of the public. However, backing these hard questions was a particular perspective. As demonstrated in chapter 3, from 1958 to 1970 editors showed a growing willingness to look to the federal government to foster social progress, yet during this period the same editors evinced a growing distrust of the federal government. This seemingly contradictory position is further complicated when one considers that during this same period there was a major ideological shift from the right to the left among these editors, coinciding with the slow abandonment of a "balanced" presentation of facts in favor of advocacy.

Liberal/Progressive bias in the media was so obvious by the late 1980s that apologists sought to deflect analysis of "a liberal media" by challenging definitions and by attacking definitions of an "establishment" or "liberal" media. Of course, defining such terms always poses pitfalls. When using these terms here, I refer primarily to the television news divisions of ABC, CBS, NBC, MSNBC, and CNN; news magazines such as *Time*, *U.S. News & World Report*, and *Newsweek*; and major metropolitan papers such as the *New York Times*, the *Washington Post*, the *Los Angeles Times*, and also *USA Today*. Such a definition also applies to television "news magazines" such as *60 Minutes* and *20/20* in most cases; to NPR (National Public Radio); and to news- or history-related programs on PBS (the Public Broadcasting System). There are exceptions to everything, of course. The *Washington Post* did, for instance, initially take a substantially "conservative" position on the war with Iraq; PBS has on more than one occasion aired fair and balanced programs dealing with President Ronald Reagan; and NPR recently aired a balanced program on the federal government's disability-awards process. Likewise, there are "outlier" publications, such as the *Christian Science Monitor*, that have an established record for objectivity. My focus here, then, is on the "mainstream" or "establishment" news media, both press and television news divisions.

Part of the reason the books of Goldberg, Coulter, and others raced to the top of the bestseller lists is that a large number of Americans—those born in the Baby Boom generation and before—had clung to the notion that "news" reporting is, or at least should be, fair, accurate, and balanced. When it became apparent to the Boomers that the mainstream media no longer fulfilled those objectives, these books struck a chord. Many citizens still expected "news" to be "factual" as opposed to political. At one time, CBS newsman Walter Cronkite was called the "most trusted man in America" because of the perception that he delivered fair, accurate, and unvarnished facts. It was a common badge of honor in the early 1960s that no reader or viewer could tell from the commentary a reporter or news anchor's politics. To be "outed" politically was considered a job failure.

Contrary to some claims, the view of the news media as "unbiased" is not a romantic fantasy of things that never were. While acknowledging that "pure" objectivity is elusive, nevertheless there is a history of American journalistic practice that supports the notion of a fair, balanced, objective press. A veteran reporter at the Cleveland *Plain Dealer*, Lou Guzzo, reminiscing about breaking into the profession in the mid-twentieth century, recalled "the devotion there to balanced and truthful reporting, regardless of the issues or persons involved."[32] Journalists adhered to the principles found in the "The Journalist's Creed," written by Walter Williams, dean of the University of Missouri School of Journalism, in the early twentieth century. Here are a few of Williams's points:

> In the Profession of Journalism
> I believe that the public journal is a public trust; that all connected with it are, to the full measure of their responsibility, trustees for the public; that acceptance of a lesser service than the public service is a betrayal of this trust.
>
> I believe that clear thinking and clear statement, accuracy, and fairness, are fundamental to good journalism.
>
> I believe that suppression of the news, for any consideration other than the welfare of society, is indefensible.
>
> I believe that the journalism which succeeds best—and best deserves success—fears god and honors man; is stoutly independent, unmoved by pride of opinion or greed of power, constructive, tolerant but never careless, self-controlled, patient, always respectful of its readers but always unafraid, is quickly indignant at injustice; is unswayed by the appeal of privilege or the clamor of the mob; seeks to give every man a chance, and, as far as law and honest wage and recognition of human brotherhood can make it so, an equal chance; is profoundly patriotic while sincerely promoting international goodwill and cementing world-comradeship; is a journalism of humanity, of and for today's world.[33]

"Fears God"? One of the men formerly in charge of one of the largest news-gathering institutions in the world, Ted Turner, referred to Christians as weak and called Catholics "religious zealots" for observing Ash Wednesday. Does this expression "Fears God" apply to the near gag-rule that has shackled nearly all major and local papers and television news shows regarding the name Jesus Christ in any "news" story? As one *Dayton Daily News* reporter stated, that name was *verboten* except on the "religion" page. Does the expression "Fears God" apply to the producer of CBS's *60 Minutes*, Don Hewitt, who, according to the *New York Post* "Page Six," was at an event at 21 where he "railed against born-again Christians, likening them to recovering alcoholics."[34] "Profoundly patriotic"? Does this phrase apply to modern news-media figures such as Jonathan Alter, Peter Arnett, Katie Couric, Aaron Brown, Keith Olbermann, or Bryant Gumbel? In the years following 9/11, the image of most journalists as being "profoundly patriotic" does not readily spring to mind, especially considering that at CNN reporters were not allowed to use the term "terrorist," and American flag pins on the lapels of news readers was viewed as "compromising their objectivity."

If mainstream journalism cannot easily be termed "profoundly patriotic," or "God-fearing," what about Williams's requirement that it consist of "clear statement, accuracy, and fairness?" As we will see, not only are "clear statement" and "fairness" problematic, but "fairness" is a goal that most reporters fall short of attaining. In later chapters I discuss how the very lifestyle and personal values of reporters, editors, and anchors is in sharp contrast to those of the public they claim to serve, and greatly shape the way they report the news.[35] They have fundamentally different experiences and lifestyles that create within them a "template" through which to present all news. Their tainting of the supply of the news has not gone unnoticed, however, and when news consumers had an opportunity to choose otherwise, they did so. When alternative sources began to appear, first in talk radio, then the Internet and Fox, audiences enthusiastically embraced the change.

"Journalistically," said James Carey of Columbia University, "the twentieth century can be defined as the struggle for democracy against propaganda, a struggle inevitably waged by an 'objective' and 'independent' press."[36] Although the "objective" journalists won, the "progressives" still sought to define reporting as "deciding what needs to be changed or fixed in our society."[37] This countercurrent grew in the 1960s, and today many journalists not only fail to recognize their own bias, but insist that they are taking courageous stands for the principle of "objectivity" at the very same time that the news media is dangerously close to a return to the age of propaganda.

The 1960s present an interesting era for the mainstream press: "progressives" clearly were ascendant, their success further enhanced by a new medium, television. During the 1960s, television news surpassed newspapers as the public's main source of "facts," delivering a monopoly over information into the hands of the three major television networks, ABC, NBC, and CBS. In an era before the 24-hour news program, the average American increasingly looked to the evening news for the important stories of the day. Joined later by morning "news/talk" format shows and "news magazine" specials, such as *60 Minutes* and *20/20*, the "big three" television networks wielded an inordinate amount of influence over what news Americans heard—and how they heard it—for nearly two decades. Of course, these news broadcasts witnessed the same cultural and political fallout as did print, and as two historians of journalism suggest, "After Vietnam and Watergate . . . journalism became noticeably more subjective and judgmental."[38]

This post–objective phase press existed virtually unchallenged from the 1960s to 1980. With a monopoly over content in two of the three major national newspapers, all three national television networks, two of the three major national "news" magazines (with *U.S. News & World Report* remaining relatively objective until the 1980s), and national taxpayer-based PBS and NPR, the left controlled the interpretation of the news, if not the news itself. However, nothing better illustrated the maxim that in a free market a monopoly is virtually impossible to maintain than did the news media monopoly of the early 1980s. It took a president whose communication skills went over the intermediaries in the press, a radio raconteur who singlehandedly revived AM radio, and the computer to crack the left's dominance over news and to meet the growing demand for alternative voices (notably conservative) and also for fact-based, fair reporting. During the 1980s, for example, Rush Limbaugh overcame the barriers to entry and provided an alternative conservative voice. As he frequently noted, "I don't need balance, I *am* balance." Importantly, the rise of Limbaugh and other alternative sources of news did not so much mark a return to the partisan press, but rather a return to a *competitive* press.

An analysis of the reemergence of a partisan press suggests that the best defense against tyranny—whether of ideas, products, or people—is competition. Liberals dominated the news media for more than 25 years, during which time journalists became entrenched in their reportorial practices. Ironically, this was a time in which the United States was winning the Cold War, and the collapse of both the liberal media and the Soviet Union coincidentally came at about the same time. Tellingly, at that time in the Soviet Union there were only three major papers, all controlled and censored by the government, *Pravda* (Truth), *Izvestia* (News), and *Krasnaya zvezda* (Red Star). Soviet citizens had a saying, "*V Pravde ni izvestiia i v Izvestiia ni pravda,*" or, loosely translated, "In the Truth there is no news, and in the News there is no truth."

What follows is a brief history of journalism; it is not intended as a thorough investigation of every twist and turn in the profession. I focus instead on the transformation of journalism from the highly partisan newspapers of the Jacksonian era to a postbellum journalism business oriented toward large circulations, and then its transformation into the situation in which we find ourselves today. The emphasis on large circulation in part brought an end to the partisan press, although papers certainly still had political views represented on their editorial pages.[39] A number of factors produced this transformation, which held for nearly a century (with periodic, but highly visible, exceptions), including the adoption of journalistic codes of ethics, the appearance of new practices and methodologies in reporting, and the influence of Progressive era trends that brought about a separation of "facts" from "values." All these factors institutionalized "objective" reporting by the early twentieth century. The 1960s brought change yet again.

The remainder of this book is organized into four major sections, each of which corresponds with four major periods of press practices in the United States. First, I discuss the early days of the Republic, and the partisan press that was so common until the early twentieth century, particularly during the Jacksonian era. Second, I overview the development of the objective period of the American press, particularly focusing on its growth in response to the rise of networks of propaganda and the development of totalitarian states in Europe. Third, I explore the transition period of the American press, the years following Kennedy, and also Watergate. Finally, I comment on the rise of the partisan press, the era of the liberal press; here I focus especially on the press treatment of the campaigns and presidency of Barack Obama.

NOTES

1. Jim Meyers, "Rush Limbaugh Responds to Obama Attack," *Newsmax*, January 26, 2009, www.newsmax.com/insidecover/limbaugh_obama_attack/2009/01/26/175268.html.

2. "In a Tight Spot, Pelosi Calls Health Care Critics 'Un-American,'" *Foxnews*, August 10, 2009, www.foxnews.com/politics/2009/08/10/tight-spot-pelosi-calls-health-care-critics-american/.

3. "Bill Clinton: 'Vast Right-Wing Conspiracy' as 'Virulent' as Ever," *CNN*, September 27, 2009, www.cnn.com/2009/POLITICS/09/27/clinton.conspiracy/index.html.

4. Jim A. Kuypers, *Press Bias and Politics* (New York: Praeger, 2002), 202.

5. For both an overview of such studies and original research into this issue, see Jim A. Kuypers, *Bush's War: Media Bias and Justifications for War in a Terrorist Age* (Lanham, MD: Rowman & Littlefield, 2006); Robert E. Denton and Jim A. Kuypers, *Politics and Communication in America: Campaigns, Media, and Governing in the 21st Century* (Carbondale, IL: Waveland Press, 2008); and Jim A. Kuypers, Stephen Cooper, and Matthew Althouse, "The President and the Press: A Rhetorical Framing Analysis of George W. Bush's Speech to the United Nations on November 10, 2001," *American Communication Journal* 10, no. 3 (2008), www.ac-journal.org/?page_id=37.

6. Daniel Sutter ("Can the Media Be So Liberal? The Economics of Media Bias," *CATO Journal* 20, Winter 2001, 431–51) never seriously addresses content analysis done by Lichter and others that overwhelmingly proves such bias. See also Ben Bagdikian, *The Media Monopoly*, 6th ed. (Boston: Beacon Press, 2000); L. Brent Bozell and B. H. Baker, eds., *That's the Way It Isn't: A Reference Guide to Media Bias* (Alexandria, VA: Media Research Center, 1990); B. Goff and R. D. Tollison, "Why Is the Media So Liberal?" *Journal of Public Finance and Public Choice* 1, 1990, 13–21; Timur Kuran, *Private Truths, Public Lies* (Cambridge, MA: Harvard University Press, 1995); and Paul H. Weaver, *News and the Culture of Lying* (New York: Free Press, 1994).

7. Eric Alterman, *What Liberal Media? The Truth about Bias and the News* (New York: Basic Books, 2003); James Fallows, *Breaking the News: How the Media Undermine American Democracy* (New York: Vintage Books, 1997 [1996]); Bill Kovach and Tom Rosenstiel, *Warp Speed: America in the Age of Mixed Media* (New York: Century Foundation, 1999); Peter Stoler, *The War against the Press: Politics, Pressure and Intimidation in the 80s* (New York: Dodd, Mead and Company, 1986); Tom Rosensteil, *Strange Bedfellows: How Television and the Presidential Candidates Changed American Politics, 1992* (New

York: Hyperion, 1994); and Martin A. Lee and Norman Solomon, *Unreliable Sources: A Guide to Detecting Bias in the News Media* (New York: Carol Publishing, 1991).

8. "Brokaw Denies 'Ideological Framework,'" Media Research Center Cyber Alert, May 25, 2001.

9. Rooney quoted from the "Larry King Live" show, in the "Quote of the Week," *Washington Times*, June 10, 2002.

10. Rooney.

11. Marie Arana, quoted in Howard Kurtz, "Suddenly Everyone's a Critic," *Washington Post*, October 3, 2005, www.washingtonpost.com/wp-dyn/content/article/2005/10/02/AR2005100201296.html.

12. Bill Kovach and Tom Rosensteil, *The Elements of Journalism: What Newspeople Should Know and the Public Should Expect* (New York: Crown, 2001), 11; Committee of Concerned Journalists (CCJ) and the Pew Research Center for the People & the Press, "Striking the Balance: Audience Interests, Business Pressures and Journalists' Values," March 1999, 79.

13. Kovach and Rosensteil, 75.

14. Kovach and Rosensteil, 75.

15. See, for example, S. Robert Lichter, "Fox News: Fair and Balanced?" Forbes.com, November 16, 2009, www.forbes.com/2009/11/14/fox-news-barack-obama-media-opinions-contributors-s-robert-lichter.html.

16. Howard Kurtz, *Media Circus: The Trouble with America's Newspapers* (New York: Times Books, 1993), 41, 48; Max Frankel, "Journalism 101," *New York Times Magazine*, January 22, 1995, 18.

17. Frankel, 18.

18. Bernard Goldberg, "On Media Bias, Network Stars Are Rather Clueless," *Wall Street Journal*, May 24, 2001; and Bernard Goldberg, *Bias: A CBS Insider Exposes How the Media Distort the News* (Washington: Regnery, 2002), 5.

19. Goldberg, 5.

20. Quoted in Tim Jones, "A Simple Formula: Writing What People Will Read," *Chicago Tribune*, November 15, 1999.

21. Yuen Ying Chan, quoted in Kovach and Rosensteil, *Elements of Journalism*, 18.

22. Pew Research Center for the People & the Press, "Striking the Balance," 79.

23. Pew Research Center for the People & the Press, "The Web: Alarming, Appealing and a Challenge to Journalistic Values," March 17, 2008. http://people-press.org/report/403/financial-woes-now-overshadow-all-other-concerns-for-journalists.

24. Liberals also complain about this tactic. Chris Geovanis, a freelance journalist in Chicago, maintained that the Chicago mainstream press routinely covers "crime on the West Side" without putting it in the context of overall crime rates among blacks falling (Interview with Chris Geovanis, August 12, 2003).

25. Eric Burns, "Study Finds Bias in Media Labels," *Fox News*, June 28, 2002, www.foxnews.com/story/0,2933,56524,00.html.

26. Burns.

27. For one example of this see Noel Sheppard, "MSNBC Says 'Conservative' 10 Times as Much as 'Liberal' on Tuesday," newsbusters.com, February 7, 2008, http://newsbusters.org/blogs/noel-sheppard/2008/02/07/msnbc-says-conservative-10-times-much-liberal-tuesday.

28. Brent Baker, "CBS & NBC Label Palin 'Conservative,' Didn't Tag Biden as Liberal," Newsbusters.com, August 29, 2008, http://newsbusters.org/blogs/brent-baker/2008/08/29/cbs-nbc-label-palin-conservative-didnt-tag-biden-liberal.

29. Scott Whitlock, "Networks Skip Liberal Labels for Dem Convention," newsbusters.com, August 29, 2008, http://newsbusters.org/blogs/scott-whitlock/2008/08/29/networks-skip-liberal-labels-dem-convention.

30. Study cited in David Frum, *How We Got Here: The 70s, the Decade That Brought You Modern Life (for Better or Worse)* (New York: Basic Books, 2000), 4.

31. Jack Fuller, *News Values* (Chicago: University of Chicago Press, 1996), 192.

32. Personal E-mail exchanges between Larry Schweikart and Lou Guzzo, various dates, 2001; provided by Larry Schweikart.

33. Walter Williams, dean, School of Journalism, University of Missouri, 1908–1935, found at www.press.org.

34. Richard Johnson, "Page Six," *New York Post*, September 11, 2003.

35. David Shaw, "Journalists Losing Touch with the Man on the Street," www.latimes.com, December 8, 2002. Kuypers, *Press Bias and Politics*.

36. James Carey, *James Carey: A Critical Reader*, ed. Eve Stryker Munson and Catherine A. Warren (Minneapolis: University of Minnesota Press, 1997), 233.

37. Kuypers, 15.

38. Kovach and Rosensteil, 55.

39. Ronald Shilen, "The Concept of Objectivity in Journalism in the United States," Ph.D. dissertation, New York University, 1956.

ONE

The Rise of a Partisan Press: News Was Not Always "News"

It is common today for Americans to assume that the purpose of newspapers or journalism is, and has always been, to transmit "news" to a reading public. Certainly reader tastes and values play a role in shaping journalism in a free market *if* a newspaper's purpose is to make a profit. It is also true, however, that the tastes and values of readers will not be a consideration if a newspaper exists for other purposes, such as to incite rebellion or to advance a political party's ideological agenda—often the case in the early 1800s. As one study showed, the "press was not particularly responsive to its audience during the 1820–1860 years."[1] If people expect truth in news, truth becomes the standard by which news is measured if the purpose of a newspaper is to make profits.[2] Yet truth can become a casualty quite quickly when editors and publishers possess motivations other than supplying a for-profit product for a reading public. The key to understanding American newspapers in the Jacksonian era is recognizing that they were not necessarily profit-driven organizations but instead political creatures whose central purpose was to elect a party's candidates.

Well before the Jacksonians introduced a highly partisan press, journalism consisted of mostly broadsides and small-circulation newspapers whose political roots went back to the American Revolution. Political tracts had circulated widely in the metropolitan areas of the American colonies, making a critical contribution to stirring up the rebellion against England.[3] These tracts, or even accounts of local events, lacked widespread circulation due to cost and technology, and by modern standards they were pitifully tiny: one Massachusetts paper sold only about 300 copies per issue even after existing for 15 years.[4] By 1719, Boston had only two weekly papers, making news irregular at best, even when a town had a paper. Moreover, papers were not printed in all areas, tending to appear in only the major metropolitan regions. Even at that, distribution remained poor. For example, New York City had, for every 32 residents, only one copy of the daily paper. As one historian observed, "If *all* the newspapers published in 1790 had been evenly distributed, each American would have received just one issue that year."[5] Even so, the number of papers published saw continued growth: "The *Boston News-Letter* began publication in 1704 and is generally regarded as the first continuously published American Newspaper. Then the *Boston Gazette* in 1719. By 1730 there were seven newspapers published regularly in four colonies and by 1800 there were 180 newspapers."[6]

Counteracting the low official circulation numbers was the practice of individuals sharing newspapers after they read them, meaning that a substantial second-hand circulation, not counted in official sales statistics, existed. Keep in mind, too, that by 1840 the urban areas of America had a literacy rate approaching 90 percent.[7] For comparison, consider that in England at the same time the literacy rate was around 75 percent.[8] Americans were hungry for news and for literature. Through the early 1700s and into the 1800s a tradition of reading news in taverns developed, in which the readers embellished and enhanced the tales with their own interpretations, and in which patrons discussed and debated the meaning of the news.[9] This, of course, helped spread the content of the news much further into areas with considerably lower literacy rates. The *Bible*, by far, was read by more people, and was found in more homes, than all the newspapers put together, putting the comment of a Victorian writer who referred to the average American as a "newspaper reading animal" into perspective.[10] Even then, such comments exaggerated the news literacy of many Americans, who often *acted* as though they read the news, or even carried papers as props to convince others of their literacy.

Distribution of news tracts and papers depended on "exchanges," or a process in which printers were permitted by postal law to exchange their papers without postage through the mails.[11] This policy, first codified in 1758 by Benjamin Franklin and William Hunter, deputy postmasters general for the American colonies, locked together the post office and the early newspapers in a relationship that would dramatically reshape the way Americans read. Moreover, it resulted in a channel of communication that went out from the printers in New York City, Boston, Philadelphia, and Baltimore to secondary cities such as Albany, Hartford, and New Haven, before then penetrating to the hinterland around these more urban areas. Eventually, cities on postal routes further inland, such as Cincinnati and Detroit, would receive the news. At each step of the journey, local papers were free to "cut and paste" from the original source, thus standardizing information as it was transmitted inland.[12]

Consequently, it is true to some extent that a somewhat hierarchical structure of information transmission existed in early America.[13] That did not make the system elitist, however. At each stop along the way, a grass-roots news-reading culture (think back to taverns) took whatever information existed and made it interactive, immediately taking it out of the hands of the elites, much the way Internet bulletin-board news sites function. Discussing news events that at one point or another had appeared in print constituted a major pastime for many early Americans, especially in more remote towns and villages, where the arrival of papers sparked celebrations. Even the Indians noticed that reading newspapers so preoccupied Americans that natives would welcome white visitors by holding up buffalo robes and pretending to read them.[14]

What, exactly, did these early American news junkies pore over? Journalism in the United States had evolved from an emphasis in colonial times on local developments to, by the time of the Revolution, virtual advertisements for the commercial activities in towns; whatever "news" did appear in print often represented a cross-section of the opinions of the townspeople.[15] One study of Revolutionary era papers, for example, showed that of the seven papers in Boston, four were "loyalist" papers, two were "patriot" papers, and one, Thomas Fleet's *Boston Evening Post*, attempted to remain neutral during the crisis.[16] Taking circulation into account, the above ratio roughly resembled popular sentiment during the war, wherein about one-third of the colonists were loyalists, one-third were patriots, and one-third sat on the sidelines. Fleet tried to maintain objectivity through balancing the number of articles in each issue supporting the loyalist and patriot perspectives and by enforcing strict guidelines on language. Although both John and Thomas Fleet were supporters of the patriot cause, they nevertheless thought impartiality was "a worthy goal in and of itself."[17] Even after Lexington and Concord, the paper attempted to maintain objectivity, impressing patriot printer Isaiah Thomas, who wrote that "the impartiality with which the paper was conducted, in those most crucial times . . . gained [the Fleets] great and deserved reputation."[18]

The Fleets aside, during the Revolutionary War, the press took clear sides and played a crucial role in the founding of the new nation when the participants in the Continental Congress realized that they needed to keep a record of the events of their body. Purely from the fact that the Congress had to move frequently to avoid the British (10 times during its existence), the Founders concluded that they needed to maintain an account of what they said and did and to make that account open to the public so as to allay suspicions of a secretive and oppressive government. Actual speeches themselves remained unrecorded—both houses distrusted reporters—and the Founders expressed the view that by *not* recording each speech, delegates would be more likely to make sound decisions. Such fears gained credence with the writings of Anti-Federalist papers such as the *Aurora*, which "celebrated Washington's departure, actually prayed for his imminent death," and contemptuously concluded that the world would have to decide "whether you are an apostate or an impostor, whether you have abandoned good principles or whether you ever had any." [19]

Philip Freneau, the leading opposition journalist of the Anti-Federalist and anti-Washington crowd, established and edited the *National Gazette* in 1791 with the support of Thomas Jefferson. The secretary of state used all of his patronage power to provide cash flow to the *Gazette*, "including a steady stream of sources which he not only delivered but also on occasion edited and even translated for the paper." [20] Jefferson's view was that Freneau merely provided balance to John Fenno's Federalist *Gazette of the United States*, arguing, "The two papers will show you both sides of our politics." [21] Freneau later infuriated Washington with an editorial titled "The Funeral of George Washington"; that, and his attack on Alexander Hamilton's economic program, left the *National Gazette* as an unmistakable mouthpiece for Republican views. Jefferson himself was targeted for equally vicious slanders by journalist James T. Callender, who afflicted politicians of all stripes, including Jefferson's *bete noir* Alexander Hamilton and his old friend John Adams, leading one modern-day writer to refer to Callender as "Jefferson's Matt Drudge." [22]

Partly to ensure some degree of accuracy (or, perhaps, favorable interpretation of language), Congress contracted to have its proceedings recorded by the *National Intelligencer* newspaper. The *Intelligencer*'s status constituted a political monopoly, and the paper's reporters refused to allow the lawmakers to edit their own remarks, supposedly ensuring accuracy and objectivity. In fact, this policy represented an attempt by the infant press to interpose its own views with actual events and comments. These alterations did not go unnoticed by the principle orators of the day: Davy Crockett—a man known for his storytelling—noted that one reporter "made me a much better speech than I made . . . or ever could make." [23] Martin Van Buren, among other politicians, viewed as one of his greatest successes that he managed to keep his speeches unreported. On one occasion, Van Buren collected all the reporters' notes of the Senate speeches, destroyed them, and substituted his own version of the proceedings as official record. [24] Van Buren certainly was not alone: it was a common practice of politicians to hold up publication of their remarks until they, or their party, could edit them. Daniel Webster apparently mastered this technique. At other times, sympathetic editors allowed lawmakers of their own persuasion extensive leeway in adding to, or subtracting from, published remarks and speeches.

This certainly suggests that when the *Intelligencer*'s reports saw print and reached the taverns and reading rooms, they were a mere shadow of the reality they purported to capture. Regardless, people devoured newspapers, with both foreign and domestic politics especially capturing the attention of most discussants in local newsrooms, who made their views known in full voice to all other "readers" in a tavern or hotel. Thus, rather than reading and analyzing "news" for themselves, many people absorbed a regurgitated version of publicly accepted "news" that had been edited by literate (and loud) locals. All of which misses the point that from an early date in American history, printed matter originated from presses that had clear political biases, and which usually made those biases clear, brazenly proclaiming themselves the house organ of one "party" or another.[25]

EARLY MINGLING OF PRESS AND POLITICS: AN EXAMPLE

By the time of the 1820 Missouri Crisis, both the Federalists and the Jeffersonian Republicans had disappeared as viable political entities. Jefferson himself saw the Missouri Crisis, as did many others, as an event that would precipitate disunion, secession, and possibly a civil war. Calling it the "knell of the Union," Jefferson noted that news of the compromise awoke him like a "firebell in the night."

Jefferson wasn't alone. New York politician Martin Van Buren and Georgian William Crawford knew that the compromise, which admitted Maine as a free state and Missouri as a slave state, threatened to destroy the union because of several dynamics built into the agreement. First, an imaginary line was drawn at the 36°30′ parallel, which prohibited slavery above that line (where all the open land lay), while permitting new states below the line (a tiny section of Oklahoma, at the time) to choose to be free or slave states. Southerners could count: in a matter of years, the North would have far more seats in the House of Representatives and Senators than the South, to the point of having a "supermajority" that could legislate slavery out of existence and, more importantly, impose its will on the South. Southerners would not tolerate such a situation, and they raised the specter of disunion and war should such a situation arise.

Second, the compromise shifted the balance of power in the electoral college to the North, endangering the executive branch as well as Congress in the eyes of Southerners. Rather than deal with slavery itself or with the impending Northern political dominance, Van Buren and Crawford sought to restructure the system so they could control the mechanisms of government through a new creation, the political party. In Van Buren's system, the party would have as its unstated rule that it would not bring up the issue of slavery in the national debate. As historian Richard Brown observed, "Perceptive Southerners saw (1) that unless effective means were taken to quiet discussion of the question, slavery might be used at any time in the future to force the South into permanent minority in the Union . . . and (2) that if the loose constitutional construction of the day were allowed to prevail, the time might come when the government would be held to have the power to deal with slavery."[26] The supreme irony of Van Buren's position, though, was that he thought (consistent with Jeffersonian views) that the "majority was strongest where it was purest, least subject to the corrupting power of money.... That was in the South."[27] Because Southern security demanded creation of a party that would depend on the South for any election, the Democratic Party at its inception could have no principles that might divide the sections. Put another way, "national parties and slavery agitation were mutually exclusive," and the Jacksonians kept slavery "at a respectful and practical distance."[28] Consequently, the Democratic Party was born without a principle other than simply to gain office. That was hardly the kind of stuff to excite supporters to devote time and money to the effort. How, then, to ensure that a core of "true believers" would exist where there was nothing to believe in except getting elected?

Van Buren concluded that the answer lay in offering employment, both in the organization and in the government. Party faithful would be rewarded through "patronage," or jobs in government, the party, or in party-related functions—in other words, a bribe. Van Buren's party, known for its first presidential candidate, Andrew Jackson, took the name "Jacksonians," "Jacksonian Democrats," or, as they eventually were known, simply "Democrats." In short, Van Buren and Crawford founded the modern party system, but the Democratic Party in particular, on the principle that no principle was worth fighting for—certainly not slavery—and that voters could be "bought" through party favors and spoils. Still, spoils could only be granted to a relative handful of loyal supporters, although certainly those most active in the party. To win elections, however, required a completely new structure of politics and a new function for the press.

GETTING OUT THE VOTE

Getting out the vote made up a critical element in Van Buren's strategy. At this time, property qualifications restricted the privilege of voting. Women, slaves, and Indians did not receive the franchise in national elections; under any circumstances, only a small portion of the population was ever qualified to vote, although a remarkably large percentage of free males did meet the property requirements. In Pennsylvania, for example, 92 percent of the males met the property requirement, and 88 percent of those eligible actually voted in the 1800 election; and in Delaware, 88 percent met the requirement in 1800, while 86 percent of those eligible actually voted. Presidential electors were not subject to a statewide popular vote, but were elected by state legislators in all but two states; by 1832, all but one state had instituted popular votes for the electors.

Once voters had a stake in the outcome, they demanded participation, to the extent that by the mid-1820s the property requirements were virtually eliminated until almost all adult males, except as noted above, could vote. Supposedly, this favored the Democrats (and thus the South), yet that had ironic results in another context, in that after the property requirements were eliminated, participation rates fell below the rates prior to 1824. From 1800 to 1820, with property requirements in place, participation rates soared to stratospheric levels: in some states, such as New Hampshire in 1814, the number of adult males voting exceeded 80 percent of those eligible to cast ballots, while Alabama had an astonishing 96.7 percent of eligible voters actually participating in 1819.[29]

Van Buren and Crawford had already decided to base their new party on "volume." They created a sophisticated political organization that divided responsibility for getting out the vote into state, district, ward, and precinct committees, with those responsible for putting a ward, precinct, or district into the "win" column for the Democrats rewarded with a promotion to a position of more responsibility (and, at the district level, pay) or with government spoils. Although it took more than a decade, by 1840 an entire state and national structure was in place that featured a national party convention.[30] This greatly reduced the power of the state caucuses, which had "acquired the stigma of aristocracy."[31]

A POLITICIZED PRESS

Because the system was novel, getting out the vote required new strategies. Energizing the electorate required selling the message to the citizens, and that task required mass publications faithful to the party's ideology—newspapers.[32] Historian Robert Remini contended that this was "perhaps the single most important accomplishment" of the Jacksonians—the "creation of a vast, nationwide newspaper system" that supported their ideology.[33] The Jacksonians blatantly established their own party organs, such as Duff Green's Washington, DC–based *U.S. Telegraph* (1826), by lending the editor the money to start the paper. Green obediently repaid his political masters with pro-Jackson editorials, and obligingly turned out a special extra paper during the 1828 election with a circulation of 40,000 issues.[34] He also played "Johnny Appleseed" to the Jacksonian news nexus, helping to set up other Jacksonian papers around the country. Defenders of Green point to the fact that he was "struggling financially" and thus could not possibly have been "on the take"; he in fact relied on increasing sales to distant subscribers, and like all other papers of the era, his fell victim to the reluctance of subscribers to actually pay for the paper.[35] The evidence, though, suggests that Green was every bit as partisan as his accusers have claimed, and that he likely was a poor businessman. Printing profits, for example, averaged 40 percent a year during one ten-year stretch, and an official paper could incur tremendous lithographing, printing, and engraving fees.[36] For a paper whose motto was "Power Is Always Stealing from the Many to the Few," this description of what Green and his friends were doing seemed apt. Not only did he receive official monies, but Jacksonian loyalists endorsed Green's personal notes and funneled "soft money" to him on a regular basis.

Surprisingly, Green himself recognized the dangers of the politicized press. In 1826, he wrote that "it is in vain to talk of a free press when the *favor of power* is essential to the support of editors, and the money of the people, by passing through the hands of the Executive, is made to operate as a bribe against liberty . . . [I]f liberty shall ever expire in our country, it will die of the poisonous draught of corrupt patronage."[37] Nor was Green alone in his concerns about a politicized press. Thomas Ritchie, editor of the Richmond *Enquirer*, warned that "showering patronage too much on Editors of newspapers and on Members of Congress, and the rights of the people themselves are exposed to imminent danger."[38] Of course, with patronage dollars flowing in, such concerns tended to be fleeting. Francis Preston Blair's paper, the *Congressional Globe*, supported initially by the State Department to publish session laws, perhaps even exceeded Green's *Telegraph* in its loyalty to the party. The *Globe* functioned solely as an organ of the Jackson administration, and Blair's attitude on given current issues was "determined by Jackson's stand on them."[39] Simply put, the *Globe* served as the political handbook for the party, printing marching orders for other editors around the country to follow.

Unwilling to consider the dangers of a politicized press, or unable to contemplate the political results, political parties propelled newspaper circulation upward. Consider that circulation in the early 1800s was roughly equal to population growth, but by 1840 it was growing more than five times as fast as the population. This tsunami of newspapers had little to do with market forces and everything to do with political patronage. Publishers carried delinquent customers for months, their deficits offset through political contributions, "loans," and even subsidies from the U.S. Congress.[40] Gerald Baldasty found that in 1830 the state of Georgia had 11 newspapers, "all of them embroiled in political fights," and the party had at least three patronage papers in each state, with the *Globe* serving as their pilot for editorial policy.[41] By 1850, political bias so dominated the newspaper industry that the U.S. Census estimated nearly 80 percent of American papers were partisan, while other estimates have put the number of partisan papers at close to 100 percent.[42]

Thus, at the time that "newspapers" emerged as a driving force in American political life, they had little to do with objective news. Quite the contrary, they deliberately reported everything with a political slant, and were intended to be biased. Nor did they hide their purpose: it was in their names, such as the *Arkansas Democrat-Gazette*, or the *Arizona Republican* (which later dropped the "an" to appear less partisan). Partisanship was their primary raison d'etre.[43] Editors viewed readers as voters who needed to be guided to appropriate views, then mobilized to vote.[44] Green's *Telegraph* flatly condemned neutrality as an absence of principles, and overall, editors increasingly inserted their points of view into papers.[45] A Louisville paper criticized an Indiana paper for its neutrality, noting that "in this State, people have more respect for an open, independent adversary than for dumb partisans . . . who are too imbecile to form an opinion."[46] One Jacksonian editor stated, "We most of all abhor and detest . . . a neutral paper. It pretends to be all things to all men."[47] Various studies of content have confirmed this attitude, finding that the percentage of editorial comment in "news" stories increased, then nearly doubled between 1847 and 1860.

Many editors owed their jobs directly and specifically to the Jacksonians, frequently slipping back and forth between editor positions and postmaster jobs. Jackson himself appointed numerous editors to salaried political positions, including many postmasters, while nationally it is estimated that 50–60 editors had been given plum political jobs.[48] Rewarding political friends was nothing new—the Federalists had appointed nearly 1,000 editors to postmaster positions over a 12-year period—but the Jacksonians transformed an ad hoc approach to appointments to a strategic political plan.[49] Under such circumstances, few readers of "news" doubted where a paper stood on particular positions, nor did people think they were receiving objective facts upon which to make reasoned decisions.

Ironically—keeping in mind that the entire purpose behind founding the Democratic Party was to exclude slavery from the political debate—newspapers for more than a century provided a cheap and reliable way of catching runaway slaves and overcoming the cost barriers of distance.[50] Eighteenth-century owners used "print to counter the mobility of the unfree, to establish or reestablish confidence in slavery and servitude."[51] This aspect of the public discussion of slavery apparently went unnoticed in Van Buren and Crawford's schemes, but it reflected a truth about slavery and the press, namely, not to take a stand against slavery was to facilitate its existence.[52] Put another way, at the local level, "printers and postmasters . . . served as agents for masters. They were go-betweens" who supported the slave structure through the dissemination of information needed to reacquire runaways.[53] This fact clashed on the most profound level with the Jacksonian imperative requiring slavery to remain absent from the public sphere, while subtly and consistently pushing maintenance of "the peculiar institution" into the public sphere. Over time, as Northern states ended slavery, even pro-Jacksonian papers that ran ads about runaways began to vanish, further distinguishing

Northern and Southern papers, "free" and "slave" papers, all in stark contrast to what Van Buren had hoped would occur.

Southern Democrats attempted to manipulate and control the press even more over time, seeking to stem the influx of hostile, abolitionist literature between 1820 and 1860. This affected the nature of news-gathering itself as editors depended less on "clipped news" (which fell from 54 percent of the stories in 1820 to just 30 percent by 1860) because of the potential for pro- or anti-slave views to surface in the text.[54] Instead, reporter-generated stories doubled between 1820 and 1860, a trend that shifted the location of stories to a geographical area within the editor's reach, allowing him to tell the slavery story as he saw fit.[55] For example, from 1820 to 1860, news emanating from Washington, DC, fell by 3 percent as a share of total news at a time when the federal government played an increasingly important role in the lives of ordinary citizens. On the other hand, news originating in the city in which it was published rose by 4 percent—and shot up 8 percent just between 1847 and 1860.[56] One particular study of content showed that discussion of sectional problems "increased steadily [between 1820 and 1860], from 5% of the coverage in the early years to 12% at the end."[57] Even that sharp increase in sectional issues did not adequately reflect the profound impact slavery had on the party system and the press due to the understanding of a "gag" on all discussion of slavery on the part of Southern editors. In essence, the increasing sectional tone of newspaper discussions occurred even while a gag on debate over slavery was imposed in the South.

Meanwhile, the "news" greatly benefitted those politicians in both parties who won office, providing free advertising at unprecedented levels and favorable coverage of their speeches. Newspapers profited from cozy connections with city governments and state legislatures. State printing contracts were firmly entrenched as political weapons by the early 1820s, although it would become epidemic during the reign of New York's infamous Tweed Ring in the 1850s (when pet presses received hundreds of thousands of dollars in public printing contracts for such inane items as the roster of militia units).[58] New York state printing contracts with the Van Buren–controlled *Albany Argus*, for example, totaled more than $15,000 per year—around $85,000,000 today expressed as a relative share of GDP. Pennsylvania state contracts with sympathetic editors averaged about the same amount.[59] Even so, the most important link between the government and the newspapers occurred in the use, and abuse, of the post office to transmit newspapers.

POST OFFICES AND POLITICS: THE NEWS MEETS THE MAIL

At the national level, both the executive branch and Congress utilized federal largesse as inducements to gain favorable newspaper coverage.

The federal government, through contracts issued by the treasury and other executive departments, passed out contracts to partisan editors that boasted profit margins of 20–55 percent. Editors of the *National Intelligencer* received nearly $300,000 for their federal work in the 1820s. [60] Printing expenditures by the executive branch rose by almost 75 percent between 1831 and 1841. Overall dollar amounts may have been relatively small as a share of federal, state, or local budgets, yet because newspapers were relatively inexpensive to establish and to run, a little money for a newspaper went a long way, leaving the newspapers beholden to their patrons.

Congress also wielded the important contracts for the proceedings of the House and Senate. However, Congress's main support for friendly papers came not through direct contracts but rather through the use, and abuse, of the U.S. Post Office. By 1850, the Post Office represented an enormous source of patronage with its 18,468 branches, or, unbelievably, an office for every 1,300 people. Although virtually all mail delivery functions failed to make a profit—even when the Post Office had revenues of $5.5 million in 1850—as a political organization the Post Office brandished considerable clout. As early as 1831, the postal system controlled 8,700 postmaster jobs alone—over three-fourths of the entire federal civilian workforce and larger than the army! Clearly, the marriage between politics, jobs, and publicity was obvious to even the most casual observer. Since the postal system shipped newspapers for only a fraction of the cost of transporting them, a strong incentive arose to print—and mail—more newspapers. Between 1800 and 1840, the number of newspapers shipped through the mails rose from just under 2 million to almost 40 million. If the newspapers had paid the same rate as other publications for postage, their transmission costs would have been *700 times higher*.

Books, on the other hand, received no such subsidies. This had important ramifications for the entire society's political awareness, both good and bad. Richard John, a historian of the postal system, concluded that the subsidization of newspapers through the public mails constituted an important economic choice by favoring the transmission of less thoughtful, less considered, and shorter newspapers at the expense of longer and more costly books. By the 1830s, "the news made up roughly 95 percent of the total messages" and equaled the number of letters that passed through an average post office. [61] Considering that more than half of that news was stridently partisan, one could estimate that around 25 percent of all postal deliveries was partisan propaganda.

An even more insidious connection between the mail and the newspapers had taken root, though. By identifying the recipients of papers, local postmasters brought together "clubs" of readers (i.e., political groups), and with each new member of the club, the postmaster's power and influence grew with the added postage he collected from those receiving the mail. Still more threatening uses of the news/mail nexus could be seen in the actions of Thomas Ritchie, who "used postmasters as intelligence agents to check up on subscribers who did not pick up the Richmond *Enquirer*," turning the postmaster into a highly paid political snitch.[62]

Allowing the news such a (subsidized) central place in American life had other, hidden ramifications. A government-newspaper nexus moved Americans from the well-reasoned arguments that the Founders had studied—the writings of Locke, Montesquieu, Hobbes, Cato, and others—to a pulp format of "politics lite." An emphasis on catchy phrases, clever campaign slogans, or simplistic concepts drove more serious discussions from the realm of the public and pubs into colleges and intellectually oriented parlors. Perhaps that is why the tariff debate at times seemed to threaten the Union with utter destruction, and yet at other times it barely caused a stir. Only when the tariff could be specifically painted as benefiting Northern interests, and thus could be subject to sloganeering, did it generate measurable regional reaction. Whatever may have been gained in having larger numbers of Americans exposed to the news was lost in wide but shallow reporting and analysis. When it came to politics, Americans knew a little about a lot. That, of course, fit Van Buren's purposes to perfection, leaving him with a populace that could be easily subjected to propaganda. Even the Jacksonians, though, failed to appreciate the close connection between emotion and news, and they still endeavored to describe their positions with intellectual arguments. Not until television, with its immediacy and, most important, pictures, did news make the transition from intellectual to purely emotional appeal.

Meanwhile, politicians made exquisite use of the new alliance between the Post Office and newspapers to exploit the system to their own ends. Whenever lawmakers spotted a column in which they were quoted, they purchased or collected as many copies as they could, which then were sent free (via the franking privilege) through public mails to constituents. For example, Stephen Douglas, in his campaign against Lincoln for a U.S. Senate seat in 1858, mailed more than 350,000 news clippings containing his speeches back to Illinois.

FROM A FREE MARKET TOWARD A FREE PRESS

Only the free market and the First Amendment prevented the government from manipulating the news to suit its own purposes more frequently, and the challenge of the market took two distinct forms. First, despite their patronage powers, the Jacksonians could not exclude competitors from the news business. In 1840, there were 138 *daily* papers in America, and by 1850, there were 254—a number that "accounted for more than half of the annual circulation for all the periodicals in America."[63] Many of these adopted the radical views of the new utopian movements, the most important of which was William Lloyd Garrison's paper, the *Liberator* (1831), which, despite its position as a stalwart abolitionist paper, encouraged and published dissenting (pro-slave) views.[64] The *Liberator* was striking in "its devotion to reader participation through correspondence and to the interchange of information and opinions on abolition and all other reform questions that the paper pursued."[65] Garrison reveled in receiving correspondence from his enemies, thinking that publication of their views would discredit their position.

If "independent" papers such as the *New York Herald* (see below) interpreted "objectivity" as "a middle ground between parties," the *Liberator* favored an appeal directly to the people above the parties.[66] Frederick Douglass's paper, *North Star*, which started publication in 1827 as the nation's first paper published and edited by black Americans, echoed many of Garrison's sentiments, but unlike Garrison, Douglass supported the "Free Soil" party, then the Republicans, without hesitation. His *North Star* broke with Garrison, who endorsed no political party, and the *New York Herald*, who sided with the slave owners in that its editors thought it best if slavery remained outside the national discussion. Essentially, then, three leading independent papers possessed very different thoughts on the slavery debate.

A second source of opposition to the partisan press came from free-market entrepreneurs' challenges to the partisan postal monopoly. Private carriers found themselves hopelessly underpriced by the government subsidy, effectively sealing off the postal system from competition until the 1970s, when Federal Express employed jet aircraft technology to shatter the government's monopoly.[67] If news-gatherers could not compete directly with the postal system, though, technology provided another alternative, the telegraph, which forced greater objectivity into the news by bringing partisan papers into competition with the wire services.[68]

THE SEEDS OF OBJECTIVITY: THE SEARCH FOR PROFIT

Whatever their take on the political leanings of the press, modern critics simply obsess over the fact that the news has become commercialized, ignoring the fact that the search for profits contributed heavily to the partial depoliticization of newspapers by the late 1800s. Commenting on the commercialization of the newspaper industry, Gerald Baldasty pointed out, "The measure of success in journalism [by the 1850s] was no longer political wisdom or advocacy but the ability to entertain, the acquisition of large circulations, and the generation of large revenues."[69] As powerful as the partisan presses were, they were not exempt from competition from "objective" newspapers.

James Gordon Bennett's *New York Herald* (founded 1836) led the way in the new "commercial and objective" journalism, proclaiming, "We shall support no party—be the organ of no faction."[70] He announced that his paper would "record facts on every public and proper subject, stripped of verbiage and coloring."[71] The *Herald* represented a new wave of "penny presses," the first of which, the *New York Sun*, had appeared three years earlier. Many of the "alternate" presses of the day were genuine commercial papers, often with the name "Mercantile," "Advertiser," or "Commercial" in the title. These papers usually sold for a penny, whereas partisan, subsidized competitors, such as James Watson Webb's *Courier and Enquirer*, charged a hefty six cents for each issue. The "pennies" relied exclusively on sales by newsboys who peddled the papers from door to door; and, to attract a larger circulation, they covered a wide range of topics across a larger region of the nation. Above all, they were strictly nonpartisan. The *New York Transcript* stated its political views in three words: "We have none."[72] Likewise, the *Herald*'s popularity, noted a competitor, succeeded because "it offended all parties and all creeds."[73] Bennett's paper certainly found a receptive market, for within five years it had a combined circulation of 51,000, or 14,000 more than Webb's *Enquirer*. Webb and Bennett (who had worked for Webb) engaged in a ferocious competition for consumers of "objective" news, viciously attacking each other's business practices in their columns.

Webb and Bennett personified the differences in the two publishing models. Webb "worked short days, took time off, traveled, and engaged in politics. Bennett, in contrast, was surrounded by strangers and was supported by no one, the ultimate 'independent' journalist."[74] Differences in the papers ran far deeper than work habits or the cost of an issue: Webb, loyal to the Democratic cause, joined a mob that sacked Charles Grandison Finney's church. Bennett had no love for the abolitionists, but clung to an optimistic view of America. Nevertheless, his paper's goading of Webb induced Webb to physically attack Bennett on three separate occasions. In a sense, by making enemies of all, Bennett achieved a certain degree of "objectivity" and "detachment" praised by journalism reformers.[75] It is worth noting that of the major editors, only Bennett endorsed both Democrat and Whig presidential candidates.

By themselves, the "pennies" could not crack the monolith of partisan journalism, but several other factors were also at work during the next few decades. In an effort to save money, in August 1846 Congress decided to give printing contracts to the lowest bidder instead of a partisan organ, and, at the same time, ended most printing contracts with partisan papers. That year also, the Mexican War—the first national conflict fought with a widely circulating press—intruded on partisanship. In 1860, the final official link between the government and the press was severed when the Government Printing Office was founded.

Meanwhile, a nascent transformation within the ranks of journalists themselves took root, in which reporters began to adopt a new image of themselves as, on the one hand, social crusaders and, on the other, as professional, detached reporters. Papers sought to cover other aspects of life for the first time, including sports, entertainment, crime, and cultural events. Competition increasingly drove papers to greater accuracy as the number of newspapers in the nation soared between 1840 and 1860.[76] As circulation rose, so did profits: by 1865, the *New York Times* reported gross income of more than $380,000 (that's $564,000,000 in today's dollars, measured as percentage of GDP), and all three of New York's major papers had incomes of more than a quarter of a million dollars.[77]

Competition continued to make it more difficult to slant news by omitting facts or by ignoring them altogether. Publishers' thirst for funding drove them to temper their public stances on a variety of issues so as not to offend advertisers, while direct political contributions gradually came to be seen as unseemly. As one editor noted, accepting money for a paper's political influence constituted "the lowest . . . of editorial degradations" and was "a coarse and groveling form of corruption."[78]

Papers also underwent a transformation common to almost all large-scale business enterprises of the day by becoming modern corporations replete with "managerial hierarchies."[79] As the speed of business and the scope of industrial activities expanded, individual owners could no longer manage the firms, requiring them to hire professionals, and this forced a separation of ownership and management. These new professional managers favored long-term growth over short-term profits, making the businesses increasingly risk averse.[80] Larger papers, seeking constantly growing circulations, reduced political coverage by more than half in big cities, although in smaller markets the level of political coverage remained high.[81] Where large metropolitan markets flourished, the papers increasingly attempted to appear nonpartisan.

"Independent" became the favored term. By 1877, according to a newspaper registry of the era, in 25 leading cities, nearly 40 percent of the papers claimed to be independent, and by the early 1900s, those calling themselves independent had increased to 50 percent. Papers began to identify customers not as voters, but as consumers of advertising; thus, "many publishers had come to believe that overt partisanship was a financial liability."[82] Insofar as it related to their advertisers, papers even became advocates for business.

A MOVE TO "FACTS"

Some experts attribute the decline in political coverage to the market decisions to cover other topics, which is true to some extent. Consumers of news also wanted more coverage of sports, cooking, social activities, and local news, while the effort to broaden the subscription base led publishers to excise partisan rhetoric from their "news" sections and confine it to their editorial pages. Other changes, however, also muted the partisanship of the papers. A quiet modification in the concept of objectivity had taken place between 1800 and 1860, and had actually accelerated after about 1840. Prior to 1850, most journalists viewed the world in a biblical context, understanding that man had fallen and needed salvation and regeneration.[83] After 1850, journalists in larger numbers gravitated to a standard of scientific measurement of facts: "Facts; facts; nothing but facts. So many peas at so much a peck; so much molasses at so much a quart."[84] These changes held tremendous implications for discerning what constituted facts, creating as they did a conflict between fact-based (or what might be called "value-free") reporting and partisan and/or reform-oriented ("value-laden") journalism. Thus we see a movement toward objectivity had already started when the cataclysmic event of the century, the Civil War, accelerated the transformation.

NOTES

1. Donald Lewis Shaw, "At the Crossroads: Change and Continuity in American Press News, 1820–1860," *Journalism History*, 8 (1981), 48.

2. Hazel Dicken-Garcia, *Journalistic Standards in Nineteenth-Century America* (Madison: University of Wisconsin Press, 1989), 6.

3. See Thomas C. Leonard, *The Power of the Press: The Birth of American Political Reporting* (New York: Oxford University Press, 1996); Charles E. Clark, *The Public Prints: The Newspaper in Anglo-American Culture, 1665–1740* (New York: Oxford University Press, 1994); and Michael Warner, *The Letters of the Republic: Publication and the Public Sphere in Eighteenth-Century America* (Cambridge, MA: Harvard University Press, 1990).

4. Richard D. Brown, *Knowledge Is Power: The Diffusion of Information in Early America, 1700–1865* (New York: Oxford University Press, 1989), 37.

5. Leonard, 4.

6. "A History of Literacy Initiatives in the United States and the Role of the American Literacy Council," American Literary Council, www.americanliteracy.com/Archives/lit-history(a).htm.

7. "A History of Literacy Initiatives in the United States."

8. "Illiteracy," *The Oxford Companion to British History*, 2002. www.encyclopedia.com/doc/1O110-literacy.html.

9. Leonard, 6–12.

10. Edward Dicey, quoted in Leonard, *Power of the Press*, xii.

11. Richard B. Kielbowicz, "Newsgathering by Printers' Exchanges before the Telegraph," *Journalism History*, 9 (Summer 1982), 42–48.

12. Allan R. Pred, *Urban Growth and the Circulation of Information* (Cambridge, MA: Harvard University Press, 1973), 32–34.

13. Brown, 36.

14. Thomas C. Leonard, *News for All: America's Coming of Age with the Press* (New York: Oxford University Press, 1995), xii.

15. Leonard, 18–20.

16. James L. Moses, "Journalistic Impartiality on the Eve of Revolution: The *Boston Evening Post*, 1770–1775," *Journalism History*, 20 (Autumn–Winter 1994), 125–30. See

also Bernard Bailyn and John Hench, eds., *The Press and the American Revolution* (Boston: Northeastern University Press, 1981).

17. Moses, 126.

18. Quoted in Moses, 129.

19. Joseph Ellis, *Founding Brothers* (New York: Vintage, 2002), 126.

20. Michael Lienesch, "Thomas Jefferson and the American Democratic Experience: The Origins of the Partisan Press, Popular Political Parties, and Public Opinion," in Peter Onuf, ed., *Jeffersonian Legacies* (Charlottesville: University of Virginia Press, 1993), 316–339, quotation on 319.

21. Quoted in Lienesch, 321. Original spelling changed.

22. Evan Cornog, "Jefferson's Matt Drudge," quoted online at www.cjr.org/year/00/1/cornog.asp, reviewing William Safire's book on Callender, *Scandalmonger* (New York: Simon & Schuster, 2000). See also Jeffrey L. Pasley, *"The Tyranny of Printers": Newspaper Politics in the Early American Republic* (Charlottesville: University of Virginia Press, 2001).

23. Crockett quoted in Leonard, 74.

24. Leonard, 77.

25. It is historically inaccurate to call either the Federalists or the Jeffersonian Republican/Democrats a "party" in the modern sense, and most historians date the formation of the "second American party system" as the origin of modern political parties.

26. Richard H. Brown, "The Missouri Crisis, Slavery, and the Politics of Jacksonianism," in Stanley N. Katz and Stanley I. Kutler, *New Perspectives on the American Past*, vol. 1 (Boston: Little Brown, 1969), 241–256, quotation on 244.

27. Brown, 248.

28. John McFaul, "Expediency vs. Morality: Jacksonian Politics and Slavery," *Journal of American History*, 62 (June 1975), 24–39, quotation on 27.

29. William N. Chambers and Philip C. Davis, "Party, Competition and Mass Participation: The Case of the Democratizing Party System, 1824–1852," in Joel H. Silbey, Allan G. Bogue, and William H. Flanigan, eds., *The History of American Electoral Behavior* (Princeton, NJ: Princeton University Press, 1978), 174–197. Voting percentages appear in Richard P. McCormick, "New Perspectives on Jacksonian Politics," *American Historical Review*, 14 (January 1960), 288–301.

30. Richard P. McCormick, *The Second American Party System: Party Formation in the Jacksonian Era* (New York: W. W. Norton, 1973 [1966]), and his "New Perspectives on Jacksonian Politics," *American Historical Review*, 65 (1960), 288–301.

31. James Staton Chase, "Jacksonian Democracy and the Rise of the Nominating Convention, *Mid-America*, 45 (October 1963), 239–249, quotation on 239; and his *Emergence of the Presidential Nominating Convention, 1789–1832* (Urbana: University of Illinois Press, 1973).

32. The genius of this system can be seen in Lynn L. Marshall, "The Strange Stillbirth of the Whig Party," *American Historical Review* (January 1967), 445–468.

33. Robert V. Remini, *The Election of Andrew Jackson* (Philadelphia: J.B. Lippincott, 1963), 77.

34. Remini, 49.

35. Gretchen Garst Eweing, "Duff Green, Independent Editor of a Party Press," *Journalism Quarterly*, 54 (Winter 1977), 733–739, quotation on 736.

36. Erik McKinley Eriksson, "President Jackson's Propaganda Agencies," *Pacific Historical Review*, 7 (January 1937), 47–57.

37. Green in the *United States Telegraph*, February 7, 1826, quoted in Culver H. Smith, "Propaganda Technique in the Jackson Campaign of 1828," *East Tennessee Historical Society Publications*, 6 (1934), 53. See also Fletcher M. Green, "Duff Green, Militant Journalist of the Old School," *American Historical Review*, 52 (January 1947), 247–264.

38. Thomas Ritchie to Martin Van Buren, March 27, 1829, quoted in John Spencer Bassett, ed., *The Correspondence of Andrew Jackson*, 7 vols. (Washington, DC: Carnegie Institution, 1929), 4:17.

39. Culver H. Smith, *The Press, Politics, and Patronage: The American Government's Use of Newspapers, 1789–1875* (Athens: University of Georgia Press, 1977), 131.

40. Richard B. Lielbowicz, *News in the Mail: The Press, Post Office and Public Information* (New York: Greenwood Press, 1989).

41. Gerald J. Baldasty, *The Commercialization of News in the Nineteenth Century* (Madison: University of Wisconsin Press, 1992), 7.

42. See Gerald J. Baldasty's dissertation, for example: "The Political Press in the Second American Party System: The 1832 Election," Ph.D. dissertation, University of Washington, 1978, 140–170. He performed a content analysis of five metropolitan newspapers and four non-metropolitan newspapers in which he found that political topics made up more than one-half of all stories in the city papers, and in the non-metropolitan publications, nearly 70 percent (Baldasty, *Commercialization of News*, table 1.1., 23).

43. Brown, 280.

44. Smith, *Press, Politics and Patronage*, 131.

45. Washington, DC, *U.S. Telegraph*, October 7, 1828.

46. *Louisville Public Advertiser*, July 9, 1828.

47. New York, *Lyons Western Argus*, August 1, 1832.

48. Carolyn Steward Dyer, "Political Patronage of the Wisconsin Press, 1849–1861: New Perspectives on the Economics of Patronage," *Journalism Monographs*, 109 (February 1989), 1–40; Milton Hamilton, *The Country Printer: New York State, 1785–1830* (New York: Columbia University Press, 1936),120; and Baldasty, *Commercialization of News*, 20.

49. Carl E. Prince, "The Federalist Party and the Creation of a Court Press, 1789–1801," *Journalism Quarterly*, 53 (Summer 1976), 238–241; Michael Emery and Edwin Emery, *The Press and America: An Interpretive History of the Mass Media*, 6th ed. (Englewood Cliffs, NJ: Prentice Hall, 1988); and Frank Luther Mott, *American Journalism: A History of Newspapers in the United States through 160 Years: 1690–1950*, rev. ed. (New York: Macmillan, 1950).

50. David Waldstreicher, "Reading the Runaways: Self-Fashioning, Print Culture, and Confidence in Slavery in the Eighteenth-Century Mid-Atlantic," *William and Mary Quarterly* (April 1999), 243–272.

51. Waldstreicher, 247.

52. As Shane White, pointed out, print remained an effective means of enforcing the slave system (*Somewhat More Independent: The End of Slavery in New York City, 1770–1810* [Athens: University of Georgia Press, 1991], 114–149).

53. Waldstreicher, 269.

54. Shaw, 41.

55. Shaw, 41.

56. See table 3 in Shaw, 42.

57. Shaw, 41.

58. See Alexander B. Callow, Jr., *The Tweed Ring* (New York: Oxford University Press, 1966).

59. Baldasty, 21.

60. William Ames, *A History of the "National Intelligencer"* (Chapel Hill: University of North Carolina Press, 1972), 111–112, 153, 281–283, and Erik McKinley Eriksson, "President Jackson's Propaganda Agencies," *Pacific Historical Review*, 6 (1937), 47–57.

61. Leonard, 13, 43.

62. Leonard, 15.

63. David Paul Nord, "Tocqueville, Garrison and the Perfection of Journalism," *Journalism History*, 13 (Summer 1986), 56–63; J. D. B. Debow, *Statistical View of the United States*, Compendium of the Seventh Census (Washington, DC: Beverley Tucker,

1854); Clarence S. Briham, *History and Bibliography of American Newspapers, 1690–1820,* 2 vols. (Worcester, MA: American Antiquarian Society, 1947).

64. Nord, 60.

65. Nord, 60.

66. Mindich, 50.

67. Larry Schweikart, *The Entrepreneurial Adventure: A History of American Business* (Ft. Worth, TX: Harcourt Brace, 2000), 439–440.

68. Donald L. Shaw, "News Bias and the Telegraph: A Study of Historical Change," *Journalism Quarterly,* 44 (1967), 3–12.

69. Baldasty, 46.

70. Quoted in Baldasty, 47. See also Frederic Hudson, *Journalism in the United States from 1690 to 1872* (New York: Harper and Bros., 1873), 432–433.

71. *New York Herald,* May 6, 1835.

72. Quoted in David T. Z. Mindich, *Just the Facts* (New York: New York University Press, 1998), 18.

73. *New York Tribune,* June 3, 1872.

74. Mindich, 25.

75. Mindich, 36.

76. William Dill, *Growth of Newspapers in the United States* (Lawrence: University of Kansas Press, 1928).

77. Francis Brown, *Raymond of the "Times"* (New York: W. W. Norton, 1951), 275–276.

78. Richard Grant White, "The Morals and Manners of Journalism," *The Galaxy,* 8 (December 1869), 840–848 (quotations on 845–848).

79. See Schweikart, ch. 7–10.

80. Alfred D. Chandler, Jr., *Visible Hand: The Managerial Revolution in American Business* (Cambridge, MA: Belknap Press, 1977). Also see Gerald J. Baldasty.

81. Baldasty, 123.

82. Baldasty, 129.

83. Marvin Olasky, *Prodigal Press: The Anti-Christian Bias of the American News Media* (Wheaton, IL: Crossway Books, 1988), 62.

84. Michael Schudson, *Discovering the News* (New York: Basic Books, 1978), 78, 86.

paying for the papers in the readers' hands, not the hands of political hacks. If their ideas had no currency, penny papers flopped; if they were legitimate, they soared.

At the same time, a broader transformation in American enterprise unfolded that encompassed the news business. In the 1850s, railroads had seen a "managerial revolution" in which management of companies became separated from ownership, and creation of a permanent, professional management caste followed.[22] With the founding of the first industry-wide professional publication, the *Journalist*, in 1884, journalism joined the revolution.

Professional managers applied scientific principles to business, including new accounting practices (such as a regular use of depreciation), and, as noted, gradually came to seek steady growth over rapid. Managers' quest for efficiency rested on planning, especially controlling costs through the cultivation of reliable markets. Sales, distribution, and advertising dominated the strategy of these new managerial hierarchies. Publishers learned these business lessons, finding that alienation of readers of any political stripe resulted in loss of revenue. Advertising had to appeal across the spectrum, and for an increasing number of papers, circulation triumphed over partisan ideology. Newspapers likewise had to control print and labor costs by cutting lines of text, which saved both paper and ink, forcing publishers to impose a rigid wire-service-type discipline over word economy.

A DETOUR: THE GROWTH OF SENSATIONALISM

When it came to paring labor costs, however, the industry took a strange detour during the transition to objective reporting by encouraging sensationalism. Paradoxically, this began with low salaries for reporters: a novice New York City reporter made about $15 per week in the 1880s,[23] when other skilled workers in comparable positions received up to two times that amount. Papers in smaller cities paid even less. Often, low wages stemmed from the "space and time rates" adopted by many papers, in which a reporter received a fixed rate per column for any copy that was printed, but if he wrote a story on assignment that the editors chose not to run, the reporter received an hourly rate for the time he spent working on the piece. (This practice was also referred to as "space and detail.")[24] Recalling his younger days, reporter Samuel G. Blythe observed of his counterparts covering a local trial,

> What an underpaid, happy-go-lucky, careless, and in the case of several, brilliant crowd. . . . Not one of them had a cent, or expected to have one, except on payday. All lived from hand to mouth. All worked fourteen, sixteen, seventeen hours a day at the most grueling work,

reporting on a paper in a small city where many yawning columns
must be filled each day whether there is anything going on or not. [25]

Working against the fact-driven, telegraph-based reporting of the war,
the space system motivated reporters to fill columns and encouraged the
use of literary license if enough facts weren't available, tempting reporters to create stories when there was no real news. [26] One publication
claimed the space system explained 90 percent of the sensationalistic exaggeration in newspapers. [27] Even so, by the late 1800s, the inexorable
power of marketplace competition started to impose intellectual honesty
on journalists. No paper could for long offer unsubstantiated scribbling
without being made to look foolish by competitors.

Professional journalists themselves called for standards to purge the
profession's excesses. This was nothing new: as early as 1843, editors had
called for a national convention for the purpose of establishing standards,
"enter[ing] into mutual pledges . . . [and] form[ing] a virtuous resolution,
that they will hereafter control their passions, moderate their language,"
in order to "pursue truth." [28] Horace Greeley, editor of the *New York
Tribune*, established rules for contributors to his paper, ensuring that "all
sides" of an argument received attention. [29] Greeley's objective approach
to journalism was not universal: Edwin Godkin of the *Nation* suggested
in 1869 that daily newspapers could "mould public opinion completely
[with] their mode of reporting" and could determine whether a community's laws were "nullified or enforced." [30] Of course, Godkin maintained,
the masses could not be counted on for wise policy; and the columns of
newspapers should be "gentlemen writing for gentlemen." [31] The God-
kin/Greeley debate over the nature of journalism lasted through much of
the late 19th century, and some publishers, such as Richard White, strad-
dled the fence between the two camps. In 1869, White explained that a
journalist was "the advocate of a party" and should make the "strongest
argument" he could, but he was not "at liberty to make intentionally a
single erroneous assertion, or to warp a single fact." [32] As long as news
remained factually accurate, White maintained, political bias was acceptable. Pure objectivity without consideration of the consequences "to parties, schools, to corporations, to individuals" would leave a paper little
more than "a second sun." [33]

Many journalists simply went with the flow, and although Godkin
still had acolytes, a growing number of editors favored objectivity. One
neat solution was to separate news columns from editorial columns and
emphasize local stories that appealed to mass audiences—a practice
called the "new journalism." [34] Although traditional journalism could
command high advertising fees, the "new journalism," evident in Pulitzer's *New York World*, reached a broader audience. The *World* attained a
readership of nearly 300,000 by 1893, generating advertising revenues
proportional to its circulation. Papers such as the *San Francisco Examiner*

published massive special editions, such as a "World's Fair" edition in 1893 that brought in $70,000 in revenues.[35]

Objectivity may have been a goal in the "new journalism," but the reality was that the "new journalists" still thrived on stories about train wrecks, runaway buggies, fires, crime of all sorts, and local scandal; and of course, if the actual news did not produce sufficient interest, the reporters continued to invent stories. Lamenting such fictional accounts, the *Journalist* claimed, "Old men mating with maidens of sweet seventeen, and aged spinsters taking to themselves husbands from the ranks of schoolboys. Not one in a hundred of these paragraphs is anything but pure fiction, coined at the point of the writer's pen."[36] Many of those who had ushered in the "new journalism" were troubled by its new, distinctly nonprofessional direction. John Cockerill, former managing editor of the *World*, who resigned after disagreeing with Pulitzer over the paper's direction, said, "The crying and constantly pressing necessity is for sensation, scandal, crime, something to sell papers, something to attract more readers and so bring in more advertisements at higher rates. It is a mighty maelstrom, whose vortex centers over the counter of the business office."[37] Arthur Dodge of the *Madison* [Wisconsin] *State Journal* likewise warned, "News is not gossip, nor romance, nor history, nor literature, nor opinion," and noted that newspapers could not perform their civic duty to educate citizens merely by holding up a "mirror to social life."[38]

In 1889, for the first time, an article criticizing the press used the word "ethics" in the title, and a year later a code of conduct for journalists first appeared.[39] Adolph Ochs, who bought the struggling *New York Times*, symbolized the ascent of objectivity over partisanship when he arrived in New York in 1896 and instructed his staff "to give the news impartially, without fear or favor, regardless of party, sect or interests involved."[40] Oswald Garrison Villard, publisher of the *Nation* and the *New York Evening Post*, reiterated the concept of fairness, emphasizing that the objective journalist had to report "both sides of every issue."[41] Subjects besides politics were increasingly covered, and whatever interested "any one hundred people" merited reporting, but the centrality of fact was first established.[42]

The market alone, then, could not have transformed journalism from pure partisanship to an emphasis on fact were it not for two other contributing factors. First, a common assumption existed that truth was a concept that could be apprehended, and, further, that a consensus about what constituted truth came from religion. Americans may have differed over doctrine and dogma, but they overwhelmingly shared a Christian heritage and a set of moral beliefs that transcended Quaker and Baptist, Congregationalist and Presbyterian.[43] Permeating American society was an almost universal agreement that scriptural truth existed, and that to some extent it was knowable.[44] By the late 1800s, a more secular consensus on ethics and morality supplanted specific denominational religion in public life.[45] Generic Christian morality, rather than specific sectarian doctrine, assumed center stage in public life, within which even the extremely small minority of non-Christians could be subsumed into a national ethical framework. That ethical/moral generic Christianity persuaded most citizens that moral and, hence, factual truth existed, and that it was discernable with proper spiritual guidance. But regardless of whether any particular sect claimed the truth, virtually everyone acknowledged that truth, somewhere, in some form, was ascertainable. In other words, whatever else they believed, Americans rejected relativism.

Adoption of the new inverted-pyramid style, however, posed dangers for the concept of a public truth because a scientific objectivity devoid of specific connections to God tended to push moralistic writing into the background, even though, as one analyst observed, three-quarters of all the issues covered by the press were theological or religious in some sense.[46] Religion was soon separated from mainstream journalism, with a few powerful non-Christian editors such as E. W. Scripps and William Randolph Hearst outwardly hostile to religious news. Scripps, a city editor for the *Detroit Evening News* who founded an effective chain of papers, was a self-admitted atheist whose leftist secular religion rested on the premise that "whatever is, is wrong."[47]

As the discipline imposed by spiritual values faded, the increasing use of wire services, which imposed a rigor much different from that of religion, introduced a different type of discipline. Wire service reporting required an abbreviated journalistic style. The AP, United Press, and others served dozens of newspapers each, of every political slant, requiring that the wire service itself remain as "value-free" as possible.[48] The demands of brevity meant that "wire service journalists focused on crafting stories without overt bias or a strong political point of view."[49] This jibed well with the growing reliance on science and fact, which, when combined with the demise of spiritual constraints, the discipline of brevity imposed by the wire services, and the financial constraints of publishing, resulted in fact-based journalism emerging as the dominant form of print reporting by the late 1890s.[50] Consequently, the free market, business changes, and the rise of scientific professionalism all combined to force the news business to provide the basic building blocks of truth: facts. As part of its commitment to facts, the press placed new emphasis on balance, by which journalists did not mean "telling both sides" in an equally sympathetic way, but rather explaining why one side was right and the other wrong. Put another way, balance meant explaining to the public why one set of views was factual, or "news." Even Greeley—supposedly a reformer for fairness and objectivity—insisted that several topics be excluded from discussion, including revival of the slave trade, spiritualism, and material he considered "immoral."[51] "Objective" and "scientific" soon became buzz-words that spread throughout society, leading to an intersection of academics and journalists.

JOURNALISTS, MEET ACADEMICS

As journalism crawled toward objectivity, the notion that facts could be separated from values found a powerful ally in American universities. Over the course of more than a century, the scientific method insinuated itself into the study of history and politics, spawning new academic areas generally lumped into what today we call the social sciences. Those disciplines sought to eliminate all values and focus only on objective data, or facts. Led by Herbert Baxter Adams, these scientific historians struggled to root out bias and subjectivity, and to define facts as existing apart from the values of the time. Understanding objective (or scientific) facts required historians to rid themselves of all personal biases.[52] On the other extreme, so-called progressive historians engaged in "presentism," in which history offered a means to comment on, and shape, the present.[53] These academics maintained that the simple act of fact selection—whether in a history book or a news article—engaged the bias of the selector, thus tainting all facts as "unobjective," which, in turn, made all facts relative.[54]

Consequently, these two streams of methodology, or ways of dealing with facts, saw parallel development. The "value-free" approach strove to eliminate bias, while the "value-laden/progressive" practitioners embraced it. Many journalists attempted to rigorously separate facts and values, which became the essence of objectivity, while others became the muckrakers and fostered the development of partisan (value-laden) and negative reporting. Although facts could be tested scientifically, values could not. This simple truth led to the flawed idea that all values had to be treated equally, adding further weight to the increasingly popular methodology of interviewing and "getting both sides."[55] However, once either an academic or a journalist accepted this point of view, it took on a life of its own, and often called for a commitment to liberal, egalitarian democracy, or, more generally, an "open society."[56] Explained another way, despite their best efforts to be value-free and objective, journalists had unwittingly embraced a system that ultimately required them to be critical of society at all times. After all, society was never perfect. This, in turn, created an inherent bias against good news, or the qualification of every piece of positive reporting with a dark "but" or "however." In pursuit of objectivity, journalists had adopted a worldview in which no news was good enough, and where there had to be a downside to everything.

Reporters found themselves subscribing to another old adage—that they should "comfort the afflicted and afflict the comfortable." But why? What did either have to do with truth? As modern publisher Jack Fuller asked, "Should journalists *always* afflict the comfortable even when the comfortable are doing no harm? And what about the afflicted? What if telling the truth to and about them would cause them discomfort?"[57] The importance of such questions was pushed aside, and the impact of this logic over time inevitably corralled objective journalism further and further into the field of value-laden or progressive reporting. James Carey was one of the first to take this to its logical extreme when he lamented the rise of objective reporting ("a fetish" of journalism, and "thumbsucker journalism," as he called it), which converted "independent interpreters" of events into mere "reporters."[58]

Of course, hindsight is 20/20, so it is unsurprising that in the late 1800s these trends were not obvious to most journalists, whereas the desirability of objective reporting was. The American Society of Newspaper Editors, established in 1912, adopted a code of ethics which stated, "Partisanship, in editorial comment which knowingly departs from the truth, does violence to the best spirit of American journalism; in the news columns it is subversive of a fundamental principle of the profession."[59] Journalists thought the oral interview supplied a key tool to ensure objectivity. After 1900, interviewing as a source of most news increased, accelerating the ascension of value-free reporting. However, fairness and balance required only that the journalist interview subjects "on both sides" of the issue, regardless of how legitimate or sensible either's position or claims might be.[60] The technique became so prominent it has become a staple in journalism ethics textbooks: the "Get-the-Other-Side-of-the-Story Rule."[61] Essentially, not only did this boil down all questions to only two points of view, it suggested that there were always *at least* two points of view, implying that truth might not exist. After all, who was to say which side was right or wrong?[62] Muckrakers, meanwhile, still hewed to the adversarial press position—essentially the value-laden position—which presumed that a community's values needed to be challenged. There, again, arose a problem: What if a community has the "right" values? Do those also need to be challenged? Increasingly, as will be discussed in later chapters, reporters become *less* attuned to the values of their readers, and more attuned to the promulgation of their own values and views.

Proponents of objectivity in the 19th century argued that "getting-the-other-side-of-the-story" constituted basic fairness. But a new group of social-reformer journalists called for more: they wanted journalism to be "ahead of the times . . . foreshadowing future values, whereas some will be at one with established values, or even somewhat behind, holding to receding values."[63] In *The Art of Newspaper Making*, which illustrated this reformist attitude, Charles Dana wrote, "Humanity is advancing; and there is progress in human life and human affairs; and . . . the future will be greater and better than the present or the past."[64] Exposing social ills became a central mission of some journalism. The status quo was not to be reported so much as a fact, but as a fact *to be changed*.[65] Thus, the reformer-journalist, the "muckraker," was at odds with reporting good news about the status quo (even if it was true).

MUCKRAKERS UNITE: ADVOCACY JOURNALISM VS. PROFESSIONALIZATION

The concept of objectivity may have increasingly influenced the nation's newsrooms at the turn of the century, yet it was by no means an unchallenged assumption. Practitioners who wanted to use journalism for social reform still controlled important papers with large circulations. Gradually there was a shift from notions such as "the public's right to know" and "change society for the better" to once again embracing ideological support for certain political positions. The move toward professionalization was intertwined with muckraking and open advocacy. The most extreme and widely read of these reformer journalists were known as "muckrakers" for their penchant to "dig in the mud" for a story. Muckraking became "an insistent trade practice" in the early 1900s, when investigation of social problems seemed "to be everywhere in the press."[66] Some historians of journalism have labeled the first decade of the 1900s as "the golden age of muckraking," or have credited the muckrakers with changing journalistic standards with their "adversarial, critical and anti-authoritarian stance."[67] Some muckrakers did motivate citizens and government to act in a positive manner—changes in the meatpacking industry stand out, for instance.

For the most part, though, muckrakers were not high-profile Pulitzers and Hearsts, nor were they the moral critics of society they portrayed themselves as being. Rather, in many cases, they were sensationalists. Of course, sensationalism sold newspapers; this was obvious in the size of their publications: John Speed, a civil engineer who conducted the first content analysis of newspapers in the 1890s, found that in four papers he examined, the amount of space devoted to sensationalism had tripled in just over a decade.[68] Speed counted columns, finding just 4.5 columns of gossip and scandal per paper in 1881, while in 1893 the same papers contained 116 columns of gossip and 7.5 columns of scandal.

Other reporters, however, took a dim view of dredging up the worst on society. Some took a higher ground, viewing their work as a "moral force" for the betterment of humanity.[69] For these practitioners of the "new journalism," the news existed to advance their view of human progress. Oliver Bovard of the influential *St. Louis Post-Dispatch*, for instance, favored a constitutional amendment to abolish private property, so as to institute socialism more rapidly; many others became brazen activists.[70] The newspaper-reading public, however, gradually but steadily sided with the objective journalists. Letter writers to prominent papers equated "public service" with truth-telling and fairness, which readers distinguished sharply from "moral force."[71] Significantly, from 1900 to 1912, readers demanded a fair and balanced approach to news reporting, and were very much concerned with getting objective news. The ratio between letters written about reporting and articles or editorials written about reporting shifted sharply toward getting the facts about public concerns.[72] *Collier's* magazine, considered a muckraking publication, tried to have it both ways, reminding journalists of a broader "truth, fogged by the imperfections of human sight [which] stands the final aim of a reporter. . . . Truth is the very kernel of the reporter's art."[73] Still, *Collier 's* could not help but imply that the journalists' truth was better than that of the public they served. Journalists, the magazine noted, cast their beam of light "forward up on the way that must be followed."[74]

Partly in response to the muckrakers, the Society of Professional Journalists was founded in 1909, followed by a more serious response in 1922 when Malcolm Bingay, of the *Detroit Free Press*, organized the American Society of Newspaper Editors (ASNE) to unite editors "on the common ground of high purpose."[75] Bingay and Casper S. Yost of the *St. Louis Globe* feared that "general attacks upon the integrity of journalism as a whole reflect upon every newspaper and every newspaperman."[76] Editors responded, initially, with ASNE's membership swelling to 100,000 (including editors and editorial page writers) before the numbers started to shrink due to internal ASNE disagreements over policy.

One key to establishing the news business as a profession was a code of ethics or conduct, which ASNE established as the "Canons of Journalism." The Canons embraced the objective position by stating that the "primary purpose of gathering and distributing news and opinion is to serve the general welfare by informing the people and enabling them to make judgements on the issues." *Editor & Publisher* magazine (itself launched in 1901 and merged with the *Journalist* in 1907) boasted the new standards would eliminate the "Typhoid Marys of Journalism."[77]

The reporters' counterpart to ASNE, the Society of Professional Journalists, joined in the call for standards, stating that "public enlightenment is the forerunner of justice and the foundation of democracy," and that journalists should further those ends by "seeking truth and providing a fair and comprehensive account of events and issues."[78] As if to underscore the point about "seeking truth," the society insisted journalists be "honest, fair, and courageous in gathering, reporting and interpreting information," and that they test the accuracy of their information to avoid inadvertent error. "Deliberate distortion," the code of ethics added, "is never permissible."[79]

The AP's "Managing Editors' Code of Ethics" reflected similar concerns with fairness, accuracy, and truth-telling:

- The good newspaper is fair, accurate, honest, responsible, independent, and decent.
- Truth is its guiding principle.
- It avoids practices that would conflict with the ability to report and present news in a fair, accurate, and unbiased manner.[80]

Nevertheless, the code also embraced the muckraking impulse since it called for a paper to be a "constructive critic" of society—a requirement that would clash with both imperatives that papers tell the truth and be fair because it presumed a bias against the status quo. Present in the tension between truth-seeking and "constructive criticism" lay the notion that to be credible, the press had to be critical, and that any affirmative reporting about business, government, or religious institutions, or indeed any good news, constituted "un-critical" reporting. Journalists had slipped into a quagmire of requiring truth *and* criticism, when in fact the nature of news events might demand that if something was true, it should be reported *without* criticism.

ASNE initially lacked any enforcement mechanism for its code, which raised anew the role of values in the news.[81] Boiled down to its essentials, the editors worried that *any* charge of "unprofessional conduct" could be viewed as a matter of opinion—the ASNE equivalent of "value-free" relativism. After a decade's worth of wrangling, ASNE approved a murky sanction clause that empowered its board of directors to expel a journalist for "due cause." In general, enforcement of journalistic ethics increasingly fell to the new class of professional managers. Whitelaw Reid, a politician who had worked in newspapers, announced, "The age of Bohemia is gone."[82] These journalistic professionals brought with them a certain elitism, wherein journalists "entered the thriving ranks of professional elites by subscribing to the prevailing tenet that political decision making required insulation from 'mobbish' and 'irrational' voters."[83] In that vein, Joseph Pulitzer hoped his creation of a journalism school at Columbia would "create a class distinction between the fit and the unfit."[84] Cornell had created a "certificate of journalism" in 1874, and 20 years later, the University of Pennsylvania established its degree program in journalism, coinciding with publication of the first real journalism textbook, Edwin Shuman's *Steps into Journalism*.

WALTER LIPPMANN AND THE GROWTH OF THE ADVOCACY PRESS

Journalism also became intertwined with a portion of the new study of communication with the appearance of Walter Lippmann's influential 1922 book, *Public Opinion*.[85] With this and subsequent publications, Lippmann effectively breathed new life into the waning ideologically oriented press. *Public Opinion* grew out of Lippmann's experience at the Versailles Peace Conference, where he assisted Woodrow Wilson in writing the Fourteen Points. Disgusted by the negotiations at Versailles, Lippmann blamed reporters for inundating their readers with "gossip and frantic explanation," and he concluded that the public was incapable either of being properly informed or of making sensible judgments.[86] Lippmann argued that democracy was fundamentally flawed, and that people could not be trusted with facts. He called for a "new order of samurai" to "mold the public mind and character."[87] Lippmann actually took matters a step further, contending that the news and news-gathering industry, not the state, was the greatest threat to human freedom. Making a case for media-controlled propaganda, Lippmann argued that only his "samurai" journalists were competent enough to "mold the public mind," leading to his conclusion that "you could have democracy without citizens."[88]

Lippmann's elitism led him to embrace a value-laden, progressive approach to the news: "News and truth are not the same thing. . . . The function of news is to bring to light the hidden facts, to set them into relation with each other, and make a picture of reality upon which men can act."[89] This seems to sound fine so far. Of course, it would be Lippmann's reality upon which men acted. Lippmann's influence was extensive, and his arguments persuaded many editors. Casper Yost, for example, the first president of ASNE, wrote, "No people have ever progressed morally who did not have conceptions of right impressed upon them by moral leadership."[90] By "moral leadership," Yost meant himself and his colleagues. George Harvey, of *Harper's Weekly*, lectured to other journalists that the "true mission" of journalism was to "protect people from themselves."[91] Over the next 20 years, journalistic textbooks questioned whether the news could ever present the truth, and as early as 1947, the Hutchins Commission, establishing the obligations of journalism, said, "It is no longer enough to report *the fact* truthfully. It is now necessary to report *the truth about the fact*."[92] Merely allowing facts to establish the truth wasn't sufficient: journalists had to establish the truth before they could present the facts.[93] Of course, the question became "Whose truth?" and the answer was "The journalists' truth."[94]

Despite the best efforts of reformers such as Lippmann, news consumers continued to prefer objectivity, forcing journalists to tread lightly when it came to sanitizing facts. As one historian of journalism noted, "Even during the most polarized period of the early twentieth century, the *ideal* of unitary truth with universal application continued to be uncontested."[95] Of course, the introduction of journalistic standards of objectivity in the late 19th century *itself* originated partly in a moralistic crusading; partisan presses were viewed as the status quo, and thus overturning them contributed toward improving society. Objectivity helped create a "good press" that had the best interests of the public at heart, as opposed to a partisan press, which was concerned with narrow ideological interests.

Just before America's entry into World War II, most mainstream papers in America had published their own statements of principle and codes of ethical conduct. These codes placed a premium on objective standards of reporting. For instance, the *Washington Post* in 1935 published principles to which the paper still gives lip service today. Several point particularly to an objective standard:

> The first mission of a newspaper is to tell the truth as nearly as the truth can be ascertained. The newspaper shall tell ALL the truth so far as it can learn it, concerning the important affairs of America and the World. The newspaper's duty is to its readers and to the public at large, and not to the private interests of its owners. The newspaper shall not be the ally of any special interest, but shall be fair and free and wholesome in its outlook on public affairs and public men.[96]

As mentioned already, in 1922 ASNE published its statement of principles. Two articles in particular support an objective approach:

> ARTICLE I: The primary purpose of gathering and distributing news and opinion is to serve the general welfare by informing the people and enabling them to make judgments on the issues of the time.
>
> ARTICLE IV: Every effort must be made to assure that the news content is accurate, free from bias and in context, and that all sides are presented fairly. Editorials, analytical articles and commentary should be held to the same standards of accuracy with respect to facts as news reports. Significant errors of fact, as well as errors of omission, should be corrected promptly and prominently.[97]

By adhering to such codes, the press made it clear that it voluntarily committed to provide the "American public with the *full details* of important issues within an *unbiased context.*" In short, the press was saying that it would act to "serve *all Americans* regardless of political position."[98]

But if editors and writers did "mold" public opinion, did they not shape it to their own political biases?[99] This dilemma concerned the late-19th-century editors and journalists as they struggled to maintain objectivity, a problem they attempted to solve by separating editorial and reportorial functions, in the attempt to present "all sides," and by seeking to alienate as few as possible so as to maintain large circulations. This is not to say that overt partisanship disappeared from all papers at this time. For example, George Lanphere, editor of the Minnesota-based *Moorhead News*, addressing the Minnesota Editorial Association in 1888 on ethics said, "The fact is, a newspaper does not amount to anything politically unless it is partisan," but he somehow concluded that every editor need not be partisan.[100] These tensions were not fully resolved, merely temporarily buried as America moved into the 20th century and through two world wars. Journalism had, for the most part, committed itself to objectivity, but as we have seen, a very powerful undercurrent of elite, moralistic progressivism ran under the surface, contained only minimally by loosely constructed concepts of professionalism. This would, of course, not last long.

NOTES

1. L. Edward Carter, "The Revolution in Journalism during the Civil War," *Lincoln Herald*, 73 (Winter 1971), 229–224, quotation on 230. See also J. C. Andrews, *The North Reports the Civil War* (Pittsburgh, PA: University of Pittsburgh Press, 1955), 6–34; Edwin Emery and Henry Ladd Smith, *The Press and America* (New York: Prentice-Hall, 1954); and Havilah Babcock, "The Press and the Civil War," *Journalism Quarterly* 6, 1–5.

2. Carter, 231.

3. Jeffery Alan Smith, *War and Press Freedom: The Problem of Prerogative Power* (New York: Oxford University Press, 1999), 103.

4. Smith, 104–105. See also David T. Z. Mindich, "Edwin M. Stanton, the Inverted Pyramid, and Information Control," *Journalism Monographs*, 140 (August 1999).

5. Abraham Lincoln to John M. Schofield, October 1, 1863, in Roy P. Basler, ed., *The Collected Works of Abraham Lincoln* (New Brunswick, NJ: Rutgers University Press, 1953), 6:452.

6. Robert S. Harper, *Lincoln and the Press* (New York: McGraw-Hill, 1951), 303–324.

7. Dan Schiller, *Objectivity and the News: The Public and the Rise of Commercial Journalism* (Philadelphia: University of Pennsylvania Press, 1981), 4.

8. James Carey, "The Dark Continent of American Journalism," 144–190, quotation on 161, in Evea Stryker Munson and Catherine A. Warren, eds., *James Carey: A Critical Reader* (Minneapolis: University of Minnesota Press, 1997).

9. Robert W. Jones, *Journalism in the United States* (New York: Dutton, 1947), 322.

10. Ford Risley, "The Confederate Press Association: Cooperative News Reporting of the War," *Civil War History*, 47 (September 2001), 222–239.

11. Thrasher quoted in Risley, 231.

12. Quoted in Risley, 231.

13. Mindich, 78–79.

14. Mindich, "Edwin M. Stanton, the Inverted Pyramid, and Information Control."

15. Stephens, 254.

16. Mindich, 88.

17. Brown, 258.

18. Mindich, *Just the Facts*, 67–68. Also see Donald L. Shaw, "At the Crossroads: Change and Continuity in American Press News, 1820–1860," *Journalism History*, 8 (Summer 1981), 38–50 and "News Bias and the Telegraph: A Study of Historical Change," *Journalism Quarterly*, 44 (Spring 1967), 3–31; and Michael Schudson, *Discovering the News* (New York: Basic Books, 1978).

19. Gobright quoted in Mindich, 109.

20. Harlan S. Stensaas, "Development of the Objectivity Ethic in U.S. Daily Newspapers," *Journal of Mass Media Ethics*, 2 (Fall/Winter 1986–1987), 50–60, and Donald L. Shaw, "At the Crossroads: Change and Continuity in American Press News, 1820–1860," *Journalism History*, 8 (Summer 1981), 38–50.

21. Quoted in Ted Curtis Smythe, "The Reporter, 1880–1900: Working Conditions and Their Influence on the News," *Journalism History*, 7 (Spring 1980), 1–10, quotation on 1.

22. Alfred D. Chandler, *Visible Hand* (Cambridge, MA: Belknap, 1977).

23. This is roughly $375 gross per week based on the consumer price index for 2010.

24. Smythe, 2.

25. Samuel G. Blythe, *The Making of a Newspaper Man* (Philadelphia, PA: Henry Altemus Co., 1912), 4.

26. Smythe, 8.

27. *The Journalist*, August 1887, quoted in Smythe, 7.

28. "American and British Newspaper Press," *Southern Quarterly Review*, 4 (July 1843), 235–238.

29. William G. Bovee, "Horace Greeley and Social Responsibility," *Journalism Quarterly*, 63 (Summer 1986), 251–259.

30. Edwin L. Godkin, "Opinion-Moulding," *The Nation*, 9 (August 12, 1869), 126.

31. "Edwin Lawrence Godkin," *The Journalist*, July 11, 1891.

32. Richard Grant White, "The Morals and Manners of Journalism," *The Galaxy*, 8 (December 1869), 844.

33. White, 843.

34. "Gathering Local News," *Harper's Weekly*, January 9, 1891; Eugene M. Camp, "What's the News?" *Century Magazine*, June 1890, 260–262; and William Henry Smith, "The Press as News Gatherer," *Century Magazine*, August 1891, 524–536.

35. See, Randall S. Sumpter, "News about News: John G. Speed and the First Newspaper Content Analysis," *Journalism History*, 27 (Summer 2001), 65. Also see, "About Mammoth Newspapers," *Newspaperdom*, June–July 1893, 152, and "By-the-Bye," *The Journalist*, April 22, 1893. The amount is roughly $1,750,000 based on the consumer price index for 2010.

36. "Sensational Journalism," *The Journalist*, August 20, 1892, 12.

37. John A. Cockerill, "Some Phases of Contemporary Journalism," *The Journalist*, October 22, 1892, 5, 12–13, quotation on 12.

38. Arthur J. Dodge, "What Is News—Should the People Get It All?" *Newspaperdom*, June–July 1893; "Col. M'Clure Discusses the Virtues of Journalism," *The Journalist*, June 10, 1893.

39. W. S. Lilly, "The Ethics of Journalism," *The Forum*, 4 (July 1889), 503–512; George Henry Payne, *History of Journalism in the United States* (New York: D. Appleton, 1925), 251–253. Also see standards in the *Minnesota Newspaper Association Confidential Bulletin*, no. 20 (May 17, 1988), 4–5, and those adopted by Will Irwin, published in *Collier's Magazine* (1911), reprinted in Clifford F. Weigle and David G. Clark, eds., *The American Newspaper by Will Irwin* (Ames: Iowa State University Press, 1969).

40. Quoted in Bill Kovach and Tom Rosenstiel, *The Elements of Journalism: What Newspeople Should Know and the Public Should Expect* (New York: Crown, 2001), 53.

41. Oswald Garrison Villard, "Press Tendencies and Dangers," in Willard G. Bleyer, *The Profession of Journalism* (Boston: Atlantic Monthly Press, 1918), 23.

42. Richard Grant White, "The Pest of the Period: A Chapter in the Morals and Manners of Journalism," *The Galaxy*, 9 (January 1870), 102–112, quotation on 107, responding to Edwin Godkin, "Opinion-Moulding," *The Nation*, 9 (August 12, 1869), 126–127.

43. Paul Johnson, "God and the Americans," *Commentary* (January 1995), 25–45.

44. Johnson, 33.

45. Johnson, 33. See also Paul Johnson, *A History of the American People* (New York: HarperCollins, 1997), 28–62, 79–88, 296–307.

46. See David P. Nord, "The Evangelical Origins of Mass Media in America, 1815–1835," *Journalism Monographs*, 88 (May 1984), 1–31, and Marvin Olasky, *Prodigal Press* (Wheaton, IL: Crossway Books, 1988), 17.

47. Olasky, 52.

48. See Jonathan Fenby, *The International News Services* (New York: Shocken Books, 1986), 25.

49. Sheldon R. Gawiser and G. Evans Witt, *A Journalist's Guide to Public Opinion Polls* (Westport, CT: Praeger, 1994), 13.

50. Hazel Dicken-Garcia, *Journalistic Standards in Nineteenth-Century America* (Madison: University of Wisconsin Press, 1989), 89.

51. Bovee, 256–258.

52. For a summary of these views, See Robert J. Loewenberg, "'Value-Free' vs. 'Value-Laden' History: A Distinction without a Difference," *Historian* (May 1976), 439–454.

53. Edward S. Shapiro, "Liberalism and the College History Textbook: A Case Study," *Continuity* (Fall 1992), 27–45, quotation on 28.

54. See, for example, Charles and Mary Beard, *The Rise of American Civilization* (New York: Macmillan, 1927).

55. Michael Schudson, "Question Authority: A History of the News Interview in American Journalism, 1860s–1930s," *Media, Culture, and Society*, 16 (1994), 97–112, and Schudson, *The Power of News* (Cambridge, MA: Harvard University Press, 1995).

56. Edward A. Purcell, Jr., *The Crisis of Democratic Theory: Scientific Naturalism and the Problem of Value* (Lexington: University of Kentucky Press, 1972), 205.

57. Jack Fuller, *News Values: Ideas for an Information Age* (Chicago: University of Chicago Press, 1996), 33; Dicken-Garcia, 7. The notion that all values are "imposed" is reflected in modern scholarship on journalism that claims "notions of right and wrong journalistic conduct at any given time are products of dominant cultural strains." See Schiller, *Objectivity and the News*, 87. See also Gaye Tuchman, "Objectivity as Strategic Ritual: An Examination of Newsmen's Notions of Objectivity," *American Journal of Sociology*, 77 (1972), 660–679.

58. James Carey, "The Communications Revolution and the Professional Communicator," in Munson and Warren, 128–143, quotation on 137; and Carey, 163.

59. See Paul Alfred Pratte, *Gods within the Machine* (Westport, CT: Praeger, 1995), 3.

60. The dangers of relying on interviews was not lost on early journalism critics. See George T. Rider, "The Pretensions of Journalism," *North American Review*, 135 (November 1882), 471–483.

61. Philip Meyer, *Ethical Journalism* (New York: Longman, 1987), 51.

62. Meyer, 51.

63. Dicken-Garcia, 16.

64. Charles A. Dana, *The Art of Newspaper Making* (New York: D. Appleton, 1895), 18–20.

65. This is because "the status quo is not the open society" (Loewenberg, "'Value-Free' vs. 'Value-Laden' History," 451).

66. Thomas C. Leonard, *The Power of the Press* (New York: Oxford University Press, 1986), 216.

67. W. L. Rivers and C. Matthews, *Ethics for the Media* (Englewood Cliffs, NJ: Prentice Hall, 1988), 99; W. Irwin, "The American Newspaper: A Study of Journalism in Its Relation to the Public," part 8, "All the News That's Fit to Print," *Collier's Magazine*, May 6, 1911, p. 17.

68. Randall S. Sumpter, "News about News: John G. Speed and the First Newspaper Content Analysis," *Journalism History*, 27 (Summer 2001), 64–72.

69. Brian Thornton, "Moral Force Or Just the Facts: The Debate over the Standards of Journalism in the Muckraking Era," *New Jersey Journal of Communication*, 3 (Fall 1995), 83–102.

70. James Markham, *Bovard of the Post-Dispatch* (Baton Rouge: Louisiana State University Press, 1954).

71. Thornton, 86–87.

72. Thornton, 93.

73. *Collier's* quoted in W. Irwin, *The American Newspaper*, part 7, April 22, 1911, 21.

74. Richard Grant White, "The Morals and Manners of Journalism," *The Galaxy*, 8 (December 1869), 840–867, quotation on 840.

75. Frederick L. Allen, "Newspapers and the Truth," *Atlantic Monthly*, January 1922, 44–54; quotation on the ASNE website, www.asne.org/index.cfm?ID=3460.

76. Quoted in Bruce J. Evensen, "Journalism's Struggle over Ethics and Professionalism during America's Jazz Age," *Journalism History*, 16 (Autumn-Winter 1989), 54–63, quotation on 55.

77. Cited in Evensen, 54.

78. Cited in Jim A. Kuypers, *Press Bias and Politics* (New York: Praeger, 2002), 201.

79. "Code of Ethics," Society of Professional Journalists, http://spj.org/ethics/code/htm.

80. "Associated Press, Code of Ethics," www.asne.org/ideas/codes/apme.htm.

81. Cited in Evensen, 58.

82. Whitelaw Reid, *American and English Studies*, vol. 2, *Biography, History, and Journalism* (Freeport, NY: Books for Libraries Press, 1968), 2:219.

83. Summers, 848.

84. Joseph Pulitzer, "The College of Journalism," *North American Review*, May 1904, 649.

85. Walter Lippmann, *Public Opinion* (New York: Free Press, 1965 [1922]).

86. Quoted in Munson and Warren, 22.

87. Lippmann quoted in Carey's essay, "The Chicago School and the History of Mass Communication Research," in Munson and Warren, 23.

88. Munson and Warren, 24.

89. Lippmann quoted in Kovach and Rosenstiel, 40.

90. Casper S. Yost, *The Principles of Journalism* (New York: D. Appleton, 1924), 110, 154.

91. George Harvey, *Journalism, Politics, and the University* (n.p., 1908), 1–8. See also Merle Thorpe, *The Coming Newspaper* (New York: Henry Holt, 1915), 223–238.

92. Robert D. Leigh, ed., *A Free and Responsible Press* (Chicago: University of Chicago Press, 1947), 23.

93. Richard Grant White, "The Pest of the Period: A Chapter in the Morals and Manners of Journalism," *The Galaxy*, 9 (January 1870), 106–108.

94. As historian Robert Loewenberg observed, this resulted in a situation in which facts become interpretations (Loewenberg, "'Value-Free' vs. 'Value-Laden' History," 451). CNN reporter Christianne Amanpour echoed Loewenberg's assessment: Objectivity meant "giving all sides a fair hearing, but not treating all sides equally. . . . So 'objectivity' must go hand in hand with morality." (Christiane Amanpour, "Television's Role in Foreign Policy," *Quill*, 84 [April 1996], 16–17).

95. Schiller, 193.

96. "Eugene Meyer's Principles for the *Washington Post*," *Washington Post*, www.washpost.com/gen_info/principles/.

97. American Society of Newspaper Editors Statement of Principles. "ASNE's Statement of Principles was originally adopted in 1922 as the 'Canons of Journalism.' The document was revised and renamed 'Statement of Principles' in 1975." The full document can be obtained at www.asne.org/kiosk/archive/principl.htm.

98. Kuypers, *Press Bias*.

99. For example, if everything must be open to free speech, then is not the concept of free speech subject to inquiry and debate? See Loewenberg, "Journalism and 'Free Speech,'" 13.

100. Dicken-Garcia, 178.

THREE

A Golden Age of Objective Journalism

By the end of World War II, the objectivity school had sufficiently suppressed muckraking to reign as the industry standard.[1] One only has to look at individual journalists to find a commitment to facts and fairness. Lou Guzzo, a reporter for the Cleveland *Plain Dealer* from 1937 to 1942, then again after the war, recalled the near-dogmatic commitment to objective reporting at his paper: "When a reporter on any beat dared fracture the barrier of objective reporting, his copy was tossed back to him for immediate revision."[2] "Neither city editor tolerated even the slightest hint of bias in news reporting," Guzzo noted, and "the newspaper itself espoused so subtle an editorial stance that virtually no one could state with authority that the *Plain Dealer* editorial board or the staff was conservative, liberal, or whatever."[3] "Balance in reporting," he concluded, "was not simply a textbook venture for the entire *Plain Dealer* staff; it was a badge of honor."[4] Guzzo recalled "the devotion there to balanced and truthful reporting, regardless of the issues or persons involved," an expectation made clear in the "Journalist's Creed."[5]

Modern critics, looking back, complain that in the age of objectivity, "the mainstream press downplayed or 'buried' news of business leaders and other elites who reaped unfair advantages or benefits."[6] One historian suggested that newspapers saw themselves as little more than "note-takers"—an obvious swipe at objectivity.[7] These sentiments echoed complaints of radicals in the 1950s who asserted that American journalists had "become . . . infatuated with the great god GNP," implying that good news alone simply was intolerable.[8] These modern critics attempted to blame journalists for failing to challenge social and political mores, pointing to a "sense of inferiority" among reporters of the era that resulted from their "low social status."[9] I am inclined to believe that this criticism falls flat since the same ideological restraint of editors and publishers resulted from no such "sense of inferiority." Rather, a different motivation had to account for the reporters' adherence to fact-based reporting, one that recognizes that the majority of journalists in the 1950s saw themselves as professionals who dealt in facts, not interpretation of news events. In this chapter we will see the effect of World War II and the introduction of television on journalism. After this, we'll look at the rise of liberal/progressive journalists in the late 1950s and explore the roots of this rise.

WORLD WAR II

The coverage of World War II gave journalists the best of both worlds: they could freely report what they wanted, while at the same time knowing that War Department censors would remove anything that could compromise troop safety. Critics of wartime censorship consistently fail to understand the necessity for restricting information in wartime, often failing to grasp even the simplest techniques used by friend and foe alike to determine force size and direction of movement. For example, in early 1942, news about Col. Jimmy Doolittle's raid on Tokyo, launched from a single aircraft carrier at maximum range, was released, but the press was prohibited from describing the details of the operation, including the fact that the planes came from a carrier, even though it was widely assumed that the public knew this fact. One critic of wartime censorship, Jeffrey Smith, complained that "a year passed before censors would allow the news media to say that the raid was launched from a carrier," and President Roosevelt joked that the B-25s had launched from the mythical Shangri-La.[10] Yet although the Japanese suspected the planes came from a carrier, they could not be entirely certain without confirmation. That uncertainty played a significant role in Japan's decision to attack Midway Island in May 1942. As late as 1945, many Japanese officers remained convinced that Midway played a role in the attack. Censorship, therefore, contributed to luring the Japanese fleet into an ambush that turned the tide of war in the Pacific.[11] Disgruntled reporters whose dispatches contained information about low morale or supply shortages may have thought they served a higher purpose by bringing such news to the reading public, but they would have alerted enemy intelligence—which *did* read American and British papers—of the same information. That information could easily prove deadly for the American troops the journalists sought to "protect" if acted upon by Nazi or Japanese commanders.

Following World War II, however, the threat was gone, and reporters and editors grew concerned that they had been too patriotic in their wartime coverage. They were also concerned about what we had learned in Europe about fascist and communist control of the news media. The year 1947 saw a formal response to these concerns as editors and reporters supported the formation of the Commission on Freedom of the Press, headed by Robert M. Hutchins, the president of the University of Chicago, to address problems in journalism. The commission published *A Free and Responsible Press,* in which it expressed concern that ownership of the media, in particular, had become too concentrated and that unpopular ideas did not get a fair hearing (this at a time when virtually every major city had at least two major newspapers, usually of different editorial stripes). The commission's basic thought was that "the power and near monopoly position of the media impose on them an obligation to be socially responsible."[12] The Hutchins Commission again raised the progressive standard, arguing that journalists should "serve society" rather than merely report news.[13] This idea of "social responsibility" is summed up by Theodore Peterson: "Freedom carries concomitant obligations; and the press, which enjoys a privileged position under our government, is obliged to be responsible to society for carrying out certain essential functions of mass communication in contemporary society."[14] The commission advanced an interesting mix of objective and activist principles in listing the standards for press performance.

1. The press must provide "a truthful, comprehensive, and intelligent account of the day's events in a context which gives them meaning."
2. The press must serve as a "forum for the exchange of comment and criticism."
3. The press must project "a representative picture of the constituent groups in society."
4. The press must assume responsibility for "the presentation and clarification of the goals and values of the society" in which it operates.
5. The press must provide "full access to the day's intelligence."[15]

In short, the Hutchins Commission reflected the Golden Age of objective journalism, but also the emerging activist voice in the press. Nevertheless, reporters and editors continued to endorse objective rather than progressive journalism.

ENTER TELEVISION

Following World War II, journalism faced a challenge from the new medium of television news, which relied heavily on imagery. By nature, images invoke an emotional response rather than a rational reaction. Thus even the most balanced television news report—whose words could be counted and found "fair and balanced"—could tilt the table dramatically in favor of whatever position the broadcaster chose merely through the selection of some images over others.

Even the most optimistic proponents of television news could not help but have been surprised by its success. Although its first broadcast was in the 1930s, television news primarily developed from the radio broadcasts of World War II, combined with wartime newsreel footage featuring a voice-over announcer, but it was hampered by the fact that the AP and United Press International (UPI; then UP) could not provide news bulletins directly to networks. CBS's Edward R. Murrow had already done radio documentaries—the famous *Hear It Now* programs—but it was NBC that pioneered the first real newscast with a 15-minute program called the *Esso Newsreel* on Sundays (10 minutes on Mondays and Thursdays) beginning in 1946, and a year later, CBS introduced a news broadcast twice a week. But the first nightly television news did not appear until 1948 with *CBS TV-News*, again programmed for only 15 minutes. Frequently, these news shows featured specific sponsors, such as Camel cigarettes, with titles reflecting their sponsor—for example, *The Camel News Caravan*, hosted by John Cameron Swayze in 1949.[16]

Television news established itself as a presence during the political conventions in 1952, where, for the first time, newspaper editors started to complain about it—a sure sign that television was making inroads. Felix McKnight, editor of the *Dallas Morning News*, declared television was "big, rude and somewhat of a bully at [the Republican convention in] Chicago."[17] The clash between the two mediums was illustrated when Jay Hayden, the Washington bureau chief of the *Detroit News*, stood up to ask a question at a news conference at the convention. Someone in the camera crew behind him tugged on his jacket and said, "You're in the way of the camera." Hayden refused to budge, and said in a voice loud enough to be picked up on the air, "Then turn the goddamn thing off."[18]

If some of the old-guard newspaper journalists did not appreciate the power of pictures, the younger generation did. Ben Bagdikian, a young reporter for the *Providence Journal*, observed that "people were talking about what they had seen on television, not, as previously, about what they had read in the newspapers."[19] Dale Stafford of the *Detroit News* likewise warned that "too many newspapers are being presented in the vintage of 1902. They must wake up."[20] It was celebrated journalist Edward R. Murrow who issued that wake-up call. He inaugurated his *See It Now* series (derived from his radio *Hear It Now* programs) with CBS—no inexpensive show to produce. *See It Now* received more of a budget share than any news broadcast, and it never operated in the black. CBS had anticipated this, concluding that "network news would be free-spending, in spite of the fact that at the time no one foresaw that news could ever turn a profit."[21] CBS hoped to keep advertisers' influence minimal, which also kept profits low. Murrow showed CBS that the face of news and its delivery were as important as content; hence, the first "news anchor," even though Murrow never actually delivered the nightly news. Instead, he offered a multi-story format that in 1953 evolved into a single-story documentary with his *Christmas in Korea* broadcast.

That year, CBS allowed Murrow to do a story called *The Case against Milo Radulovich*, about an Air Force reserve officer classified as a security risk because he had family members who had links to communist Yugoslavia. Murrow hosted the program, using it to soften up the public in preparation for the network's impending attack on Senator Joseph McCarthy. The Air Force, seeing it had a weak case, retained Radulovich, and Air Force Secretary Harold Talbott made an announcement just before the program that the Air Force had decided Radulovich was no security risk. Television news had its first triumph over the U.S. government and had entered the realm of activist journalism: pushing interpretation of the news to support a specific political outcome.

Emboldened, Murrow unleashed CBS's campaign against Senator McCarthy in March 1954. He encountered, however, an opponent who himself had figured out how to manipulate the press. Milt Kelly of the AP and Warren Duffee of UP found that they could go to McCarthy and say, "'I must have a story,' and McCarthy would go through his files until he found something. And what he did say also could be counted on to draw a stinging rebuke from every Democrat from President Truman on down, also on the front page."[22] McCarthy posed a dilemma for the reputation of journalists. On the one hand, too much emphasis on journalists' acquiescence in McCarthy's agenda, and unwillingness to challenge his claims, painted reporters and editors as powerless. On the other hand, an emphasis on journalists' crusading "role" in blocking McCarthy leads to the question "Why did they wait so long?" It also raises an important issue: Were McCarthy's so-called victims, in fact, communist agents—an issue few reporters cared to tackle, then or now?[23]

There was also a sense that the reporters resented McCarthy for catching on to their style, their internal rhythms. He understood the timing of wire service releases, finding that if he dropped a critical piece of information on the right desks just ahead of the 11:00 a.m. deadline, the news services did not have time to check the facts or sources that day. They either ran the story, or took the risk that someone else would if they pushed it back to confirm the key elements of the report.[24] As a UP reporter noted, "He really had the press figured out," and Edwin Bayley, in *Joe McCarthy and the Press*, concluded McCarthy was "able to generate massive publicity because he understood the press, its practices, and its values; he knew what made news."[25] Which is to say that McCarthy perceived that for all their talk about accuracy, most members of the press valued the scoop more than reliable reporting, and that having a story *now* was more important than having a story *right*. Yet the McCarthy episode also underscored the trust in government officials held by most in the public.[26] Far from assuming McCarthy was lying, most Americans suspected he indeed had evidence of communist infiltrators (as subsequent Soviet documents confirm he did).[27]

Murrow was determined to stop McCarthy, whom he blamed for a "situation of fear" in America.[28] Offered an opportunity to respond, McCarthy used his television time to call Murrow "the leader and the cleverest of the jackal pack which is always found at the throat of anyone who dares to expose individual communists and traitors."[29] Polling showed that at least one-third of those surveyed sided with McCarthy in thinking that Murrow was himself a communist.

Murrow despised the "equal time" requirement at CBS, where if politician x were given a minute of free air time, opposing politician z had to be given the same; Murrow saw this as a compromise with the objects of his investigation. Behind the scenes, sponsors liked his numbers, but his constant criticism of the government horrified them. The equal time issue finally forced CBS to cancel Murrow's show. Murrow had wanted his brand of journalism alone to stand as fair and balanced; he wanted no criticism or questioning of his stories. On October 15, 1958, Murrow gave a speech in which he blasted not just CBS management but all news organizations by complaining about the growing need to reach viewers: "I am frightened by the imbalance, the constant striving to reach the largest possible audience for everything."[30] His great concern was always about the relationship between profits and news, never about the relationship between the *truth* and the news.

So what began as a novelty abruptly took off, and by the end of the 1950s, television news had supplanted radio broadcasts as the source from which most Americans obtained their news, surpassing print news in the early 1960s. During the decade of the 1950s, the number of stations in the United States broadcasting news leaped tenfold, while television news went from attracting print reporters in the early 1950s to becoming a specialized subfield of television broadcasting at the time of Kennedy's election.[31] From 1948 to 1956, the percentage of American homes with a television rose from 4 percent to about 65 percent. Television news, once irrelevant, gained almost instant legitimacy. One estimate found that 45 percent of all television owners watched the weekend news in 1950–1951.

As noted, an important advantage television news had that its print contemporaries lacked was the power of images, both static and moving. Although the term "framing" was not yet in vogue, clever producers found that images "framed" stories far better than words. Want to do a piece on the threat of nuclear war? Show images of atomic bombs exploding, coupled with the devastation of Hiroshima. Need a story on the inequities of wealth? Contrast images of wealthy people getting out of their limos with images of migrant workers' shanty houses. Yes, television certainly had serious limitations: the depth to which any reporter or newscast could cover an issue in a few minutes of airtime per night forced television news into the most superficial types of coverage. Nevertheless, images provoked emotions, whereas words engaged the intellect. Television, therefore, could appeal to the unintellectual as well as the learned, and, if the producers so chose, it could manipulate emotions without substantive backing.

For example, images played a central role in the televised news coverage of the civil rights movement, where, as David S. Broder maintained, the first real adversarial relationship between government and the press appeared.[32] Some have argued that journalism "changed the definition of news by turning social justice issues into daily news stories for both the print and broadcast media."[33] George Hunt, managing editor of *Life* magazine, credited the news media with the success of the civil rights movement, and to an extent he was right: Martin Luther King, Jr., among others, perceived that the key to the movement's success lay in appealing to the moral rectitude of the majority outside the South.[34]

THE LEFTWARD LURCH: NEWSPAPER EDITORIALS
FROM 1958 TO 1970

During the 1950s, fissures in the edifice of objectivity started to appear. For instance, James B. Reston, the Washington bureau chief for the *New York Times*, started to write "news" columns in 1953 that "clearly reflected his own judgments."[35] Although the prevailing notion still was that news columns would contain only facts, and the editorial page would contain opinions, Reston broke tradition, and "in time similar articles were written occasionally by other *Times* reporters."[36] Even here, however, some see television as provoking the change. Clifton Daniel of the *New York Times* claimed, "There is no doubt that television news accelerated acceptance of the news analysis articles."[37]

It has been asserted that between the late 1950s and late 1970s there began an editorial trend toward endorsing progressive policies. Most of these assertions are well-supported by circumstantial evidence, even to the point of overwhelming one with their strength. To actually test these assertions, I examined the domestic policy and foreign affairs editorials written by five major U.S. papers during a 13-year period, 1958 through 1970. I examined the *Los Angeles Times*, the Cleveland *Plain Dealer*, the *Washington Post*, the *New York Times*, and the *Atlanta Constitution*. From these papers I randomly selected one editorial with a foreign affairs focus and one editorial with a domestic focus for each month of each year between 1958 and 1970. This yielded 24 editorials for each paper for every year for a total of 1,560 editorials. After culling out those editorials that were deficient in some manner (poor copy quality, original microfilm damage, etc.) I was left with a total of 1,484 editorials spanning the 13 years.

I subjected these editorials to a close textual analysis; that is to say, they were slowly, carefully, and repeatedly read and analyzed to see if specific information concerning political lean was embedded within the editorial. The idea was to look for editorial policies and assertions that would suggest a left or right political leaning. In general, specific stances on a particular political policy were not taken into consideration because determining general political leanings from any given political issue can be difficult, but even more so when one adds the patina of age: some of the minor political issues in these editorials were over 50 years old. Instead, I focused on discovering philosophical leanings associated with liberal or conservative political positions.

I looked for certain key liberal and progressive values or a lack thereof. Liberalism and progressivism are distinct yet related concepts, but for the purposes of this analysis I relied on key aspects of each since they are both popularly considered on the left of the political spectrum.[38] One key element of each involves the political attitude of using the federal government to shape, through law, changes to culture, society, and the economy. In terms of the study, for example, a statement in support of a stronger federal presence in domestic policy would suggest a liberal political orientation. In contrast, a statement in support of states' rights would suggest a conservative political orientation. In terms of looking for conservative thought, I was guided by the work of conservative scholar Russell Kirk. For instance, if an editorial suggested the principle of prudence—of which Russell Kirk writes, "Any public measure ought to be judged by its probable long-run consequences, not merely by temporary advantage or popularity"[39]—it would be considered as offering a conservative political orientation. Likewise, in foreign policy, if an editorial was opposed in principle to communism, it was associated with a conservative political orientation.

If an editorial exhibited a conservative slant, it was marked as 0.00; if it exhibited a liberal slant, it was marked as 1.00; if no slant could be detected, or if the editorial was balanced, it was marked as 0.50. In this manner each editorial was assigned either a 0.00, a 0.50, or a 1.00. This was done for all editorials from each paper in a given year. All the editorial numbers for a given year were then added together and divided by the total number of editorials to produce an aggregate value for that year, a number ranging from a perfect conservative score of 0.00 to a perfect liberal score of 1.00. This was done for domestic and foreign editorials, with the average of the two also determined. The results are charted on the graphs in figures 3.1 and 3.2.[40]

The row of horizontal numbers at the bottom of each graph represents each year between 1958 and 1973. The row of vertical numbers at the left of each graph represents the conservative/liberal influence found in each paper. The closer the graph point for each year is to 0.00, the more conservative the editorials for that year; and the higher it rises toward 1.00, the greater the liberal influence that year. There is a line representing all domestic editorials, a line representing all foreign affairs editorials, and one representing the average of the two. They begin close to 0.35, representing a conservative influence in 1958, and quickly rise with each passing year.

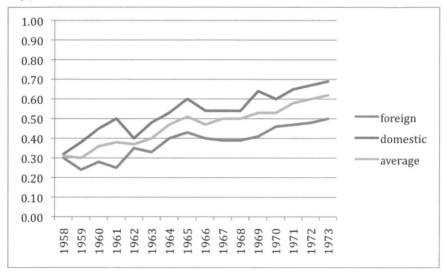

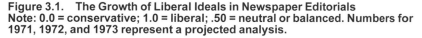

Figure 3.1. The Growth of Liberal Ideals in Newspaper Editorials
Note: 0.0 = conservative; 1.0 = liberal; .50 = neutral or balanced. Numbers for 1971, 1972, and 1973 represent a projected analysis.

Figure 3.2 offers a slightly different take on the results of the study. At the time, the notion of balance was still prevalent in the writing style of editors. Additionally, there was strong anticommunist sentiment across the nation, and this certainly included many news editors. I weighted the results of the study to account for these tendencies. Take away these two influences, and the results reveal an even greater liberal influence. This is speculative information, but of interest nonetheless.

Looking at the data either way, it is clear that during the 1960s the editorial boards of these major papers (and I suggest that they represent a national trend) lurched hard to the left. In terms of the modified averages in the second chart, the papers began with a conservative influence (around 0.39), and by the early 1970s, they had flipped to a progressive/ liberal influence (around 0.65). Although foreign policy was much slower to change, domestic issues saw an incredible change, swinging an amazing 0.35 points to the left, from 0.37 to 0.72. Even when removing the nonprojected numbers and looking at the first chart, the trend is clear. American newspapers shifted quickly to the left after 1958. Of note then is that the worldview of editors began to shift from a more conservative or neutral orientation to a progressive/liberal orientation. Additionally, this study reveals as well that the editorials started to move beyond pro-

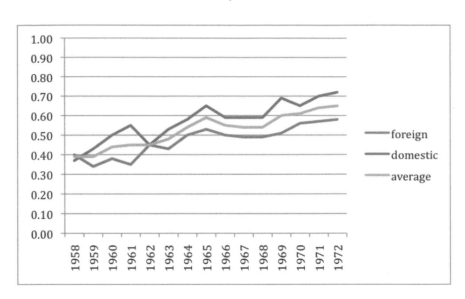

Figure 3.2.   The Growth of Liberal Ideals in Newspaper Editorials
Note: 0.0 = conservative; 1.0 = liberal; .50 = neutral or balanced. Numbers for
1971 and 1972 represent a projected analysis. Additionally, numbers are
weighted for anticommunist sentiment and non-prescriptive style of editorials.

viding a nonpartisan news information approach—that is, giving the public food for thought so that it could make up its own mind; instead, *they increasingly felt free to advocate a particular policy position.* Thus the leftward turn was coupled to a return of the partisan press.

RISE OF A JOURNALISTIC ELITE: WHY THE LIBERAL TURN?

Journalism itself seemed exempt from the consumer-oriented mandates that demanded accountability from producers: sources were still protected; due to the First Amendment, virtually anything could be printed (even blatant falsehoods) if no malice or intent to do harm could be proven; and editors increasingly shaped the policies that disciplined the writers and reporters. There are several interrelated factors that contributed to the leftward shift. One significant factor in the media's political and social shift involved a broader phenomenon of inbreeding among journalism departments and schools. At one time the nation's elite colleges and universities featured a cross-section of students whose parents had the means to pay for their education. From one perspective, this produced a homogenous student body as it related to ability to pay. Although it was rare, Catholics, Jews, farm boys, and Southerners could migrate into the best schools as long as their parents had the financial wherewithal to send them. The students reflected extensive diversity in some areas. Few minority students or women were admitted, but those who did attend represented a wide range of worldviews, geographic regions, work backgrounds, and religious sects. Keep in mind that prior to the 1940s, the road to wealth did not necessarily travel through institutions of higher education. During the 20th century, the prevalence of a four-year college degree went from 1 in 50 to a little over 1 in 4 Americans.

By the 1950s, the American Dream and the G.I. Bill had made it increasingly easier for middle-class families to send a child (or several) to college, forcing elite universities to tighten admission policies, whereas public universities went on building sprees. In the early part of the century the students came from families of self-made men who started banks and railroads, soap companies and slaughterhouses; by mid-century, students at elite schools more than ever came from parents who themselves held degrees from elite schools, and they were in some ways less ideologically diverse than ever.

For journalism, this growth meant journalism schools such as Columbia's gained an inordinate degree of influence over those aspiring to careers in the news. One cannot underestimate the influence on the media of swimming in this self-selecting gene pool. Sociological studies confirm that "political choices . . . [are] dominated more by active personal influence and face-to-face communications than by the mass media."[41] When those influencing aspiring journalists' political choices were members of elite journalism schools, followed by working members of the news media, a significant inbreeding started to develop. Contrary to the notion that the elites were always "conservative," in journalism the predominance of the peer group ensured that primarily liberal views would triumph.

As important as either the educational elitism or social exclusiveness that developed, an unusual concept of professionalism had thoroughly entrenched itself, one that also contributed to the change in political orientation. Journalism was a self-regulating community, not responsible to outside accreditation agencies or boards, and not constantly rebelling against control by management or ownership. This tended to diminish, or even eliminate, distinctions between strata of journalists (beat reporters, columnists, network anchors, and so on) as they all viewed themselves as "an interpretive community."[42] Reporting provided not only a sense of importance as messengers, but allowed journalists to maintain a source of authority, credibility, and power. Although not all young novice reporters who joined this group had already gone through liberal journalism programs, they all would enter a profession in which the majority of those around them were liberal, taking a progressive turn, and expecting new recruits to get with the program. One would learn quickly that to keep his job, he would have to either adopt the worldview of those around him or keep his mouth shut.

This homogenization was evidenced in numerous ways. From 1964 to 1976, for instance, the percentage of journalists voting for the Democratic candidate in national elections *never fell below 81 percent*. ABC reporter Frank Reynolds, in an attempt to refute the notion that the network news reflected the attitudes of a group of Eastern elites, wound up confirming the fact: "Sure, I suppose there is an Eastern Establishment, left-wing bias. But that just happens to be because the people who are in [news reporting] feel that way."[43] In truth, however, much of the bias was self-reinforcing because it *was* the worldview undergirding the profession. At the human level, further self-selection occurred to weed out those who did not accept this worldview. Theodore H. White commented on the exclusionary social milieu in which the Eastern journalists operated: "These people drink together, talk together, read the same esoteric and mad reviews . . . [and] they control the cultural heights. . . . [O]ne who does not agree with them has enormous difficulty in breaking through."[44] Such a bias could prove critical in 1969 when 90 percent of the population watched a television news show regularly.

One cannot overstate the similarity in the worldview of the top leadership of the nation's top papers. In a study of the leadership since the 1960s at four major papers—the *New York Times* (seven subjects), the *Washington Post* (two), the *Boston Globe* (six), and the *Los Angeles Times* (five)—the biographies reveal that there "is not a single graduate degree among them outside of journalism, and only a handful of years spent doing anything other than reporting and editing."[45] They have, in the process, been "thoroughly inculcated in the creed of newspapermen. They are important. They are privileged."[46] Virtually none had military experience, and aside from running a magazine or two, none had ever had to meet a real payroll where profits counted. Increasingly, they all came from the same narrow strip, the New York–Washington corridor, that accounted for some 40 percent of Columbia Journalism School students.[47] The effect is felt even today. When Hugh Hewitt recently surveyed a Columbia Journalism School class, of the sixteen students, none owned a gun, all supported same-sex marriage, and only three had been in a house of worship the previous week. One of the twelve eligible to vote had voted for George W. Bush, eleven had voted for John Kerry. By the 20th century's end, the American Society of Newspaper Editors found that "the typical newspaper journalist is still a liberal, college-educated, white-male baby boomer."[48]

ROOTS OF THE LIBERAL TURN

Another factor pushing journalism to the left was the founding of the America Newspaper Guild in 1933, in which journalists "opted for pay over romance." This had the effect of moving journalists from an objective and neutral news role into the position of supporting one side—labor's—against management.[49] As veteran newsman Lou Guzzo recalled, "I was a charter member of the Guild [in Cleveland] and Labor's suddenly powerful position in America [was] a decisive factor in turning media people's sentiments towards liberal causes. Now they had another, more personal set of principles to guide them than their onetime obedience to the muse of journalism."[50]

In addition to ideological and labor trends, certain industry practices also accelerated the impact of any bias that crept in, liberal or otherwise. Beginning in 1933, the *Albuquerque Journal* and the *Albuquerque Tribune*—two supposed competitors—merged their editorial operations.[51] These joint-operating agreements picked up steam over the next few decades, ensuring that a single editorial view would dominate locally. Then in 1970, seeking to turn this into an institutional monopoly, the newspaper industry successfully pleaded for the Newspaper Preservation Act, which offered an exemption to violations of antitrust law for newspapers that would allow joint pricing, pooling, and allocation of market territories.[52] Typically, however, critics of the joint-operating agreements looked at the financial side—the downward spiral caused when one of two newspapers gets a slight circulation edge, then gets the advertising revenue—rather than the cause of one paper getting or maintaining an edge in the first place. Certainly with both papers sharing an editorial view, customers obviously did not care if one of them died.

Often touted as the result of conservative policies, the decline of competition in the news actually solidified a dominant liberal ideology even further. It could take years for a second paper, usually a newcomer, to convince the reading public, regardless of its accuracy, to switch.[53] With joint-operating agreements in place, by the 1960s most major cities were subject to a monolithic political view coming from their major source of printed news.

A final element in the rise of a journalistic elite came from the relatively new medium of television, where the position of anchor gained in prestige and respect. CBS producer Don Hewitt recalled that the term "anchor" originated with the 1952 Republican convention in Chicago, where reporters would hand off stories to the next reporter until the best reporter—likened to the fastest man on a relay team, or the anchor—would bring the story home.[54] Murrow, Swayze, then later Walter Cronkite all stood apart from other reporters when it came to the anchorman's popularity. Eventually, Chet Huntley and David Brinkley at NBC, with their famous sign-off, "Good night, Chet. Good night, David," would also emerge as network news stars.[55]

As of 1960, though, even the most prominent of anchors still did not approach the star status they would have a decade later. Television news remained second to print journalism, but both print and television journalists started to exhibit a remarkable homogeneity—a liberal/progressive worldview tempered and constrained by the still-dominant ideology of objectivity. The inauguration of John Kennedy, however, marked a turning point in journalism, reviving the long-dormant partisan press that had slept since the days of Lincoln.

NOTES

1. James L. Aucoin, "The Re-emergence of American Investigative Journalism, 1960–1975," *Journalism History*, 21 (Spring 1995): 3–13, quotation on 3.

2. Lou Guzzo to Larry Schweikart, January 27, 2001, via e-mail. Used with permission.

3. Guzzo, January 27, 2001.

4. Guzzo, January 27, 2001.

5. Guzzo, various dates, 2001.

6. Aucoin, 4. Also see Warren Breed, "Mass Communication and Sociocultural Integration," in Lewis Dexter and David Manning White, eds., *People, Society, and Mass Communications* (New York: Free Press, 1964), 183–201, quotation on 191.

7. James L. Baughman, *The Republic of Mass Culture: Journalism, Filmmaking, and Broadcasting in America since 1991* (Baltimore: Johns Hopkins University Press, 1992), 14–21; James Boylan, "Declarations of Independence: A Historian Reflects on an Era in Which Reporters Rose Up to Challenge—and Change—the Rules of the Game," *Columbia Journalism Review*, November/December 1986, 29–45.

8. Quoted in Carey McWilliams, "Is Muckraking Coming Back?" *Columbia Journalism Review*, Fall 1970, 8–15, quotation on 10. See also Carey McWilliams, "The Continuing Tradition of Reform Journalism," in John M. Harrison and Harry H. Stein, eds., *Muckraking: Past Present and Future* (University Park: Pennsylvania State University Press, 1973).

9. Aucoin, 5.

10. Jeffery A. Smith, *War and Press Freedom: The Problem of Prerogative Power* (New York: Oxford University Press, 1999), 160.

11. See Gordon Prange, *Miracle at Midway* (New York: Penguin, 1983).

12. See Fred S. Siebert, Theodore Peterson, and Wilbur Schramm, *Four Theories of the Press* (Urbana: University of Illinois Press, 1956), 5.

13. Aucoin, 8.

14. Siebert, Peterson, and Schramm, 74.

15. Siebert, Peterson, and Schramm, 87, 89, and 91.

16. Steve M. Barkin, *American Television News* (London: M.E. Sharpe, 2003), 28.

17. Robert J. Donovan and Raymond L. Scherer, *Unsilent Revolution: Television News and American Public Life, 1948–199* (Cambridge: Cambridge University Press, 1992), 258.

18. Donovan and Scherer, 258.

19. Donovan and Scherer, 258.

20. *Proceedings of the American Society of Newspaper Editors (ASNE)*, 1951, 147.

21. Harry Reasoner, *Before the Colors Fade* (New York: Alfred A. Knopf, 1981), 82.

22. Quoted in Edwin R. Bayley, *McCarthy and the Press* (Madison: University of Wisconsin Press, 1981), 70.

23. The guilt or innocence of those named by McCarthy is dealt with in Arthur Herman's biography, *Joseph McCarthy* (New York: Free Press, 2000) and in Ann Coulter's *Treason* (New York: Crown Forum, 2003). See also Rodger Streitmatter, *Mightier Than the Sword* (Boulder, CO: Westview Press, 1997); Barkin; and Aucoin.

24. Streitmatter, 158.

25. Streitmatter, 157.

26. Louis M. Lyons, "Introduction: *Nieman Reports* and Nieman Fellowships," in Louis Lyons, ed., *Reporting the News: Selections from Nieman Reports* (New York: Atheneum, 1968), 30.

27. See, for instance, Jon Utley, "Most-Hated Senator was Right: Scholars: Joseph McCarthy's Charges 'now accepted as fact,'" *WND*, February 8, 2000, www.wnd.com/2000/02/4020/

28. Eric Barnouw, *The Image Empire: A History of Broadcasting in the United States*, vol. 3 (New York: Oxford University Press, 1970), 52.

29. Barnouw, 52.

30. Edward Bliss, Jr., *Now the News: The Story of Broadcast Journalism* (New York: Columbia University Press, 1991), 364.

31. Sig Mickelson, *The Decade that Shaped Television News* (Westport, CT: Praeger, 1998), 3–5.

32. David S. Broder, *Behind the Front Page* (New York: Simon & Schuster, 2000), 140.

33. Aucoin, 6.

34. George P. Hunt, "The Racial Crisis and the News Media: An Overview," in Paul L. Fisher and Ralph L. Lowenstein, *Race and the News Media* (New York: Anti-Defamation League of B'nai B'Right, 1967), 7.

35. Donovan and Scherer, 266.

36. Donovan and Scherer, 266.

37. Donovan and Scherer, 266.

38. One difficulty in pinning down a definition of liberal thought is that its contemporary meaning flows from so many streams of thought. There is classic liberalism: www.associatedcontent.com/article/2370160/ten_principles_of_classical_liberalism_pg2.html?cat=4; there is socialism: www.socialistinternational.org/viewArticle.cfm?ArticleID=3; and there is also more radical versions of liberal thought: www2.iath.virginia.edu/sixties/HTML_docs/Resources/Primary/Manifestos/SDS_Port_Huron.html. In general, if greater involvement of the federal government, redistribution of wealth, or an egalitarian attitude were present, I classified that editorial as potentially leaning left.

39. All 10 of Kirk's principles were looked for. They can be found here: www.kirkcenter.org/index.php/detail/ten-conservative-principles/.

40. For those wishing to know about the reliability of this study, I performed a reliability test (essentially testing how well I agreed with myself; or, put another way, how consistent I was in my observations). The coefficient produced using percentage of agreement was 98 percent and using Scott's Pi was 0.966.

41. Gabriel Weimann, *The Influentials: People Who Influence People* (Albany: State University of New York Press, 1994), 91.

42. Barbie Zelizer, *Covering the Body* (Chicago: University of Chicago Press, 1992), 9.

43. Joseph Charles Keeley, *The Left-Leaning Antenna: Political Bias in Television* (New Rochelle, NY: Arlington House Publishers, 1971), 28.

44. Theodore H. White, on William F. Buckley's "Firing Line," quoted in Keeley, 47.

45. Hugh Hewitt, "'Inbreeding' Among Royals, Pitbulls and Editors," July 12, 2006, www.townhall.com/Columnists/HughHewitt/2006/07/12/inbreeding_among_royals,_pitbulls,_and_editors.

46. Hewitt.

47. Hugh Hewitt, "The Media's Ancien Regime: Columbia Journalism School Tries to Save the Old Order," January 30, 2006, www.weeklystandard.com/Content/Public/Articles/000/000/006/619njpsr.asp.

48. "The Newspaper Journalists of the '90s," A Survey Report of the American Society of Newspaper Editors, April 1997, 5.

49. James Boylan, "Declarations of Independence," *Columbia Journalism Review*, November/December 1986, 29–45, quotation on 30.

50. E-mail from Lou Guzzo to Larry Scheikart, January 28, 2001. Used with permission.

51. See John C. Busterna and Robert G. Picard, *Joint Operating Agreements* (Norwood, NJ: Ablex Publishing Company, 1993).

52. Stephen R. Barnett, "The JOA Scam," *Columbia Journalism Review*, November–December 1991, 47–48.

53. This could be observed in the demise of the New York *Herald Tribune*, which, despite ideologically conservative leadership, closed in 1966 after a massive infusion of cash. Christopher D. McKenna, "Two Strikes and You're Out: The Demise of the New York *Herald Tribune*," *Historian*, 63 (Winter 2001), 287–308.

54. Don Hewitt, *Tell Me a Story* (New York: PublicAffairs, 2001), 51.

55. Barbara Matusow, *The Evening Stars* (Boston: Houghton-Mifflin, 1983), 66–78.

FOUR

Three Presidents and a War

Pollster George Gallup, speaking to the Public Relations Symposium in September 1968, summarized the public's view of journalism: "Never in my time has journalism of all types—book publishing, television, radio, newspapers, magazines, movies—been held in such low esteem."[1] Although sad, it is true that American confidence in all institutions eroded beginning in the 1960s; however, the public's opinion of the press simply plummeted.[2] Coincidentally, the same year journalism hit new lows, CBS premiered its new "gotcha" news show, *60 Minutes*, and as David Frum noted, "nothing on television worked harder to spread mistrust" than *60 Minutes*.[3]

The press seemed oblivious to its credibility problem as it scoured the landscape to expose scandals. Even squeaky-clean evangelist Billy Graham was subjected to a meritless hit piece by the *Charlotte Observer*.[4] Yet journalists' frantic attempts to show the public that reporters were doing their job failed to convince anyone: Gallup's survey revealed the public's strong suspicion that the press had covered up elements of the Kennedy assassination, had concealed foreign policy intrigue in Cuba and Vietnam, and had failed to reveal significant aspects of Kennedy's life and administration. Perhaps it was the description of the "job" of the press that was the sticking point. While the press saw itself increasingly as moral crusaders out to expose and fix society's ills, the public simply wanted the facts so it could make up its own mind about issues and events.

The history of journalism in the 1960s has frequently been misinterpreted. David Broder claimed that "events in the 1960s and 1970s increased the clashes [between the press and the government and] established the investigative role for reporters."[5] Historians Michael Schudson and James Boylan likewise asserted that investigative journalism surged because of the Vietnam War.[6] The real reaction was already under way, though, and it had more to do with than just the war. In the wake of President Kennedy's assassination, the press's loss of credibility and the subsequent questions surrounding the Warren Commission report demanded instant attention if the media had any hope of reclaiming its perch atop the pre-Kennedy pedestal of fact and truth. To do so required a dramatic display—something that would demonstrate that journalists could ferret out uncomfortable facts after all.

Independent assassination researchers had already started to publish material that challenged the Warren Report as soon as it appeared. Astonishingly enough, the Warren Report did not even have an index, making it automatically suspicious in the minds of some. It was up to Sylvia Meagher, a left-wing activist, who later would produce her own book, *Accessories after the Fact* (1976), to catalogue and index the entire Warren Report.[7] Among the earliest books published critical of the Warren Report (and hence the mainstream press that, almost unanimously, supported it) was one by Mark Lane, an attorney. His *Rush to Judgment* (1966) challenged the "magic bullet" theory and succeeded in raising doubt and generating controversy.[8] *Rush to Judgment* leaped up the best-seller lists even as mainstream journalists denounced it.[9] Lane was soon joined by Josiah Thompson, who managed to get a conspiracy piece into the *Saturday Evening Post*—but not until late 1967, four full years after the assassination and at a time that the nation had shifted its gaze from the eternal flame of Kennedy's grave to burning villages in Vietnam.[10] Even at that, defenders of the Warren Report's conclusions, including William Manchester (*Death of a President*; 1967) and James Bishop (*The Day Kennedy Was Shot*; 1968) failed to counter the growing perception that both the Warren Report and journalists had failed to examine credible and relevant evidence.[11] A four-part CBS news inquiry into the Warren Report in June 1967, culminating in its defense, failed to sway the public: Gallup found that two-thirds of all Americans surveyed still did not believe the Warren Report's conclusions.

Already a stream of conspiracy books and articles had started to appear, most of them penned by investigators well outside the fraternity of journalism. Edward Jay Epstein, a political scientist who taught at Harvard, published *Inquest* in 1966; his critique of journalism, *Between Fact and Fiction*, followed in 1967.[12] David Lifton, an engineering student working on NASA programs, started his research into *Best Evidence* at about that time.[13] Harold Weisberg, whose four-volume *Whitewash* began appearing in 1965, was a poultry farmer and former intelligence analyst for the State Department. He had done some writing, making him probably the closest of any of the critics to a mainstream reporter. Jim Garrison, a New Orleans district attorney, contributed grist for the conspiracy-minded with a 1967 investigation of businessman Clay Shaw. Garrison's claims of a massive conspiracy produced nothing and culminated in

Shaw's 1969 acquittal, but he managed to uncover odd and unexplained relationships between Oswald and shady figures in New Orleans that the mainstream press ignored.[14]

Various articles appeared between 1969 and 1975, but the real break-throughs came when the press finally showed some interest in the incon-sistencies of the assassination record. Both the *Saturday Evening Post* and the *New York Review of Books* broke rank to question the Warren Report's conclusions, as did counterculture publications such as *Rolling Stone*.[15] *New York Times Magazine* now referred to "The Assassination That Will Not Die," presumably a reference to the efforts the paper had made to close the coffin for more than a decade.[16]

All of this, though, was hindsight and covering one's tail. In 1963–1964, the media had simply missed the boat, due almost entirely to the ideological and methodological preconditions it put on its reporting during the years while Kennedy was alive and Camelot hummed. When uncomfortable facts surfaced from independent researchers, the press generally ignored them. Certainly there was no major effort prior to 1975 by anyone in the mainstream press to incorporate or synthesize all the revelations by nonprofessional researchers. I suspect, though, that the journalists knew they had allowed their personal attraction to Kennedy to get in the way of reporting the news. Now, to some degree to show they were on the job, reporters had to challenge government-sourced information. It certainly didn't hurt that the main policy issue of the Johnson years, the war in Vietnam, was particularly vulnerable to an assault by journalistic investigation because the Johnson administration had engaged in a campaign of disinformation. This contributed to a re-newal of investigative reporting now coupled with an increasing sense of being misled on American Vietnam policy. By the time of Nixon's second term, the press had assumed an antagonistic role with the White House.

PRESIDENTS, THE PRESS, AND VIETNAM

Media treatment of Vietnam is an area of contentious debate. A common view, especially among conservatives, is that "media coverage of the war and the anti-war protestors at home turned overwhelmingly antagonistic toward the government."[17] The media coverage was actually much more complex than this. Although overt anti-administration reporting was less common than believed, reporters nevertheless framed stories against the war by giving more coverage to critics within the government and the military[18] —an understandable, although unprofessional, response to criticism of Kennedy reporting and concern with administration disinfor-mation. An equally persistent myth has portrayed the press as pursuing its responsible obligation to criticize the military because the military was lying about progress in the war. Initially, press coverage of Vietnam was dualistic: journalists, whether deliberately or subconsciously, segregated war news from the Kennedy administration and from Kennedy himself. In part, this contributed to conspiracy notions that the Pentagon "set up" Kennedy through secrecy and manipulation of statistics, and that "had Jack only known" what was happening in Vietnam, he would have pulled the plug.[19] Johnson, considerably less charismatic, inherited a slowly escalating war and a policy of providing disinformation to the press. In some senses, it was natural, then, for the press to have been much less generous with Johnson than it had been with Kennedy.

It is true that military relations with journalists reached an all-time low during the Vietnam war. Some 500 journalists covered the war—200 more than covered either Korea or World War II, for a ratio of one journalist for every 2,800 soldiers (see table 4.1). William Hammond observed, "There were . . . no precedents for what happened [between the military and the news media]."[20] Prior to 1965 in Vietnam, journalists "showed great sympathy for the American fighting man" even as they criticized policy.[21]

Much of the pre-1965 media criticism was focused not on the American military but on South Vietnamese premier Ngo Dinh Diem. Despite the commonly presented American media portrait of Diem as an

Table 4.1. Reporters With the Troops

Conflict/Ratio	Troops	Journalists
World War I 53,694:1	2.040	38
World War II 8,667:1	2.600	300
Korea 2,667:1	.800	300
Vietnam 2,800:1	1.400	500
Gulf War 577:1	.750	1,300
Iraq War 293:1*	.176	600*

Key: Figures are for millions of personnel involved in the indicated operation and have been rounded. Those for World War I and the Iraq War are for U.S. Troops only, those for other conflicts include Allied forces as well. *Ratio* is the number of troops per journalist in theater. For some more recent smaller American military operations, the ratio has tended to be even lower: Grenada (39:1) and Panama (69:1). * Denotes only embedded reporters with both US and British troops.
Sources: James F. Dunnigan and Albert A. Nofi, *Dirty Little Secrets of the Vietnam War* (New York: St. Martins, 1999), 259. USF-I Press Briefing, June 14, 2010.

abject failure, the North Vietnamese communists had a much different appraisal of Diem in 1958, when party commissar Le Doan visited South Vietnam. He issued an alarming report that the economic and political conditions for the majority of the South Vietnamese were improving so fast that within a few years it would be impossible for the North to instigate a revolution there. In their effort to halt progress in the South, the communists attempted to thwart government malaria-spraying operations by killing the spraying teams, or butchering medical teams on their way from hospitals to jungle-hedged villages. Villagers who resisted the communists were found with their heads impaled on poles—a lesson to others not to side with the government.[22] Traditional estimates of the number of troops needed to resist guerillas meant that defeating the 2,000 or so committed communist guerillas would have required an armed force of 30 times that many soldiers, or an army far larger than Diem could put in the field. That the journalists were slowly tending toward criticism of Diem over criticism of the communists fit in with the growing countercultural movement among American intellectual elites during this time. Diem was by no means a perfect creature, and charges of corruption and nepotism should have been, and were, reported. However, much progress for Vietnam was also seen during Diem's time, progress alarming to the North, although this aspect was increasingly ignored by the American press.

Of course, journalists also tried to portray Diem as unwilling to use the forces he had. *New York Times* reporter Neil Sheehan, relying heavily on the experiences of Army Lt. Col. John Paul Vann (assigned to advise the South Vietnam guerilla resistance forces), claimed Diem had his generals preserve their forces for internal security purposes. Yet Vann (and by extension Sheehan) was hardly an objective source. Press analyst William Kennedy argued that Vann had "launched what, in effect, was a mutiny, using his young and impressionable news reporters as the lever with which to subvert [his superior, Gen. Paul D.] Harkins's policy of working within the Diem regime, and, ultimately, to depose Diem."[23] Such reporting mitigated against the arguments of some advisors, who believed that a few thousand modern rifles and radios in the hands of the local defense forces might have shifted the balance completely against the Viet Cong who, deprived of their terror weapon, would have been unable to bring large numbers of villages under their sway.

Well-off American reporters missed the central reality in Vietnam, that the war first and foremost involved not political progress for the Vietnamese but their physical security. Nothing could improve the lives of the peasants as long as the Viet Cong engaged in random killing. Terror methods allowed groups of guerrillas numbering as few as 200 to dominate 40 square miles of territory. Unfortunately, journalists frequently huddled in Saigon, where their stories assumed a monolithic character because they shared information regularly, especially as it was fed to them by Vann. At the battle of Ap Bac in January 1963, which essentially founded the myth of Vietnamese helplessness and corruption, Vann ignored intelligence that warned that the Vietnamese troops would be dropping into a highly defended zone. Reporters did not interview or cross-check Vann's post-combat rant against the ARVN (Army of the Republic of Vietnam) with Col. Andrew P. O'Meara, who was in the battle and who was available to reporters. Instead, journalists based their reports entirely on Vann, who personally fed his version of the story to David Halberstam of the *New York Times*.[24] This is, of course, not at all dissimilar to how reporters behaved during the Iraq War, when Baghdad-based American journalists routinely and uncritically included the pronouncements of the Iraqi Minister of Information, Muhammed Saeed al-Sahaf: "Only when the combat reached Baghdad itself did some journalists began to question the veracity of al-Sahaf's statements, particularly when al-Sahaf denied the presence of Allied forces which were visible from the hotel in which the reporters were staying."[25]

Additionally, reporters' stories attained a certain uniformity because Halberstam and other reporters constantly exchanged notes, "creat[ing] a small . . . intelligence network."[26] Thus the Saigon group submitted stories that seldom offered alternative viewpoints of the political and military situations. This same group formed the "Diem-must-go" clique that helped to convince Kennedy that Diem was a liability. When *New York Times* military correspondent Hanson Baldwin arrived in Vietnam in 1965, he said, "I was appalled by the bias I found in the *Times* reporters," and Liz Trotta of NBC, also newly arrived, saw Charles Mohr of the *Times* threaten to beat up another reporter who voiced his support for the war.[27] Naturally, American war planners "expressed their frustration with the ease with which reporters wrote stories based on the comments of individuals such as Vann."[28]

For almost a year, journalists struggled with what to report. On the one hand, the Kennedy administration was actively deceiving them whenever possible. When the Vietnam journalists did get accurate information, they were pressured not to use it. Kennedy and the journalists came to a fork in the road, and, as Yogi Berra said, they took it. Kennedy went one direction, and the press pretended he didn't. Less than a month before he was shot, Kennedy approved a CIA plan to fund General "Big" Minh to overthrow Diem. Kennedy would later say that he did not know this would result in Diem's death—highly unlikely given the well-understood nature of coups in the Third World. Yet the press absolved Kennedy of all involvement in the assassination, and certainly celebrated the demise of the regime. As one Kennedy staff member said, Diem's assassination "nailed the American flag to the pole in Saigon."[29]

Early coverage of the war came from reporters accompanying U.S. troops on support missions, but, unlike World War II, there was no Bill Mauldin or Ernie Pyle to empathize with the troops or tell their stories on the home front. Quite the contrary, journalists at home paid little attention to the conflict and even less to the troops, instead covering the Kennedy/Johnson social programs at home: "especially after LBJ's 1964 landslide, the . . . Great Society programs were highly exciting to *Post* editors, reporters, and editorial writers. The war . . . was an annoying distraction."[30]

Johnson ran for re-election in 1964 against a conservative Republican, Barry Goldwater of Arizona, a figure journalists disliked. They made no attempt to challenge the most famous ad in the campaign, the "Daisy Girl" television ad, as dirty or unfair politics. The now infamous "Daisy Girl" spot featured a young girl picking petals from a daisy and ended with an atomic explosion and mushroom cloud. Johnson's voiceover said, "These are the stakes," and the implication was unmistakable: elect Goldwater, get a nuclear war. As an advisor to Johnson admitted, "We would saturate prime-time viewing hours for a few days (or more if we could get away with it) and then respond to the inevitable protests by withdrawing the spot."[31] Reporters did nothing to challenge or question that atomic image. Although as many newspapers endorsed Goldwater as Johnson (actually representing a decline in the number of newspapers that in the past had supported Republican presidential candidates), many of the editorial boards thought Goldwater "too conservative."[32] The unwillingness to treat Goldwater's candidacy seriously, or to investigate the Kennedy/Johnson policies, whether in Cuba, Laos, or Vietnam, continued to move journalism away from objectivity and fairness.

By March 1965, though, changes were in the wind—Johnson was no Kennedy. Russell Baker in the *New York Times*, admitting to being befuddled over America's Vietnam policy, opened up one of the first cracks in the dam, clearly tying whatever happened in Vietnam to President Johnson (though not, it is worth noting, to President Kennedy).[33] That year, CBS's Morley Safer broadcast a report from Cam Ne that showed American soldiers burning the huts of villagers suspected of supporting the Vietcong. As Lois Liebovich noted, "For many Americans, naive about the savagery of war, the graphic pictures were horrifying."[34] Johnson's inept handling of the war—failing, for example, to define Ho Chi Minh and the North Vietnamese communists as the brutal thugs that they were—allowed the press to set the definitions.

A few intermittent articles attempted to portray reality, including Don Moser's *Life* magazine piece "Eight Dedicated Men Marked for Death," which recounted the stand taken by a group of leaders in the town of Loc Dien in the summer of 1965, or Bernard Fall's article in the *New Republic* in which he argued that the United States was winning *despite* its mistakes.[35] Occasionally, the press even covered Viet Cong atrocities.[36] Images counted more than words, however, and the only images available to American newsmen were of operations from the American side. That ensured that only American casualties and mistakes were shown, never the savage brutality of the communist enemy.

ABC, CBS, and NBC nightly news shows had continued to gain viewers, attracting in 1965 some 35 million a night. As long as television news remained positive, or even neutral, toward the war, the Johnson administration was safe. A general perception of television news is that until the end of 1967, it "was overwhelmingly favorable to American policy."[37] In part, this is true: television had only started to undergo the change from objective news to advocacy and editorializing (i.e., partisanship) that could already be seen in print journalism. The limited 30 minutes (with commercials) allotted for television news imposed, like the telegraph, a certain discipline of objectivity on television news. However, as the antiwar movement picked up steam, the question arose of what to cover: the war, or opposition to it?

Television news had a more significant impact on war views than the major news magazines, which according to one study, dedicated only about 7 percent of their coverage to the war.[38] Another study found the press failed to sufficiently investigate the conditions that prompted the war in the first place and certainly did not cover the North Vietnamese/ Viet Cong atrocities or the military disadvantages under which American forces operated.[39] Former correspondent Robert Elegant wrote, "For the first time in modern history, the outcome of a war was determined not on a battlefield, but on the printed page and, above all, on the television screen."[40]

Meanwhile, nearly three-quarters of people surveyed in 1966 agreed that the United States should either "Keep our soldiers in Vietnam but try to end the fighting" or "Take a stronger stand even if it means invading North Vietnam," with the respondents split evenly over which course to take. Significantly, "Pull out of Vietnam entirely" was favored by only 9 percent of the respondents.[41] Support remained strong through 1967— and (depending on how the question was worded) the percentage of those favoring "escalation" as opposed to "withdrawal" actually increased from 36 percent in 1966 to 55 percent in 1967.[42] Therefore, one must take care with the pollster's term "opposition," in that "take a stronger stand" can be interpreted as opposition; actually, there is some evidence that the opposition movement was increasingly growing, enhanced by those who thought the United States was not being aggressive enough. As late as October 1967, 53 percent agreed with the statement that the United States should "increase the strength of its attacks on North Vietnam," and another 10 percent favored keeping the present troop levels. By then, however, 31 percent favored withdrawal.[43] In 1970, when Richard Nixon ordered the bombing of Cambodia, the opposition fell while support for the war rose.[44] So, which story to cover? The two-thirds of the public who wanted to increase the U.S. effort (or keep it the same) or the one-third who either did not know or who wanted to withdraw?

Keeping in mind press concern with their Kennedy coverage, their growing unease with White House obfuscations, and their growing tendency toward a liberal worldview, I think you will already know the choice the media made. Coverage of the opposition, of the growing number of antiwar demonstrators, combined with press reporting on Johnson's lack of strategy, started to produce substantial unease among the voters. Johnson felt it when, in a surprise announcement in 1968, he told the public he would not run for another term. This opened the door for Eugene McCarthy of Minnesota and Robert F. Kennedy of New York, two prominent antiwar politicians (despite the fact that Kennedy had "converted" only recently from the strong support he had given his brother's Vietnam policies). Increasingly the "doves" gravitated toward Kennedy until his assassination in June 1968. This threw the antiwar candidacy open to McCarthy, who had little hope of unseating Hubert Humphrey, the sitting vice president and anointed of the Democratic Party regulars. Already, though, antiwar sentiment, especially among Democrats, had surged due to a shocking turn of events in Southeast Asia.

SNATCHING DEFEAT FROM THE JAWS OF VICTORY: THE TET OFFENSIVE

In January 1968, the Viet Cong, with extensive North Vietnamese logistical support, orchestrated a massive offensive that included simultaneous assaults on some 100 targets including the U.S. Embassy in Saigon and almost every military base in the South. In the Tet Offensive, Viet Cong troops reached the U.S. Embassy in Saigon where they (contrary to popular movie renditions) were killed to a man, stormed the old capital of Hue, and surrounded the U.S. base at Khe Sanh. Although they made spectacular gains, through this pyrrhic victory the Viet Cong removed themselves permanently from the playing field. They suffered phenomenally high casualties of 60,000 dead and three times that many wounded, and they lost most of their heavy artillery. From that point on, any pretense that Vietnam was a civil war was over: now, the only hope for the communists to win had to come from direct, and heavy, infusions of troops from Hanoi.

The battle at Khe Sanh saw nearly 25,000 air sorties that subjected the seasoned attackers to a merciless bombardment, killing 10,000 communists compared to 205 Americans killed.[45] One senior American general called Khe Sanh the first major ground battle won almost entirely by air power.[46] Yet at the very time that a mere three bombers "blanketed a one-by-two kilometer box every ninety minutes, around the clock, with explosives and napalm . . . destroy[ing] nearly every living thing within one kilometer of the marine ramparts," the American news media was telling a completely different story and prophesying doom. *Life* magazine, for instance, predicted a "looming bloodbath at Khe Sanh."[47] Journalism critic James Boylan admitted to the singularity of Tet coverage: "There dawned one of those mysterious moments of press agreement, the kind of thing that makes paranoids believe that a grand conspiratorial directorate must meet in a skyscraper somewhere and issue instructions to the media."[48] To the press, Tet was an American defeat.

That was news to American forces who were, in popular vernacular, "kicking butt." In the provincial capital of Hue, surprised and outnumbered U.S. Marines expelled 10,000 enemy from "a fortified urban center in just over three weeks at the cost of fewer than 150 dead."[49] U.S. military historian Robert Leckie referred to Tet as "the most appalling defeat in the history of the war" for Hanoi—an "unmitigated military disaster."[50] Yet Walter Cronkite, without waiting for the battle damage assessments or enemy casualties to be evaluated, exclaimed, "I thought we were *winning* this war."[51] He promptly departed for Vietnam to produce a CBS special, called *Report from Vietnam by Walter Cronkite*, which began filming during the third week of the offensive.[52] When he returned, he announced the U.S. was in a quagmire, and "the only rational way out . . . would be to negotiate, not as victors, but as honorable people."[53] At that point, Johnson reportedly said that if he had lost Walter Cronkite, he'd lost the American people, although this statement is thought now to be apocryphal. Regardless, he had hardly "lost the American people," as polls after Tet showed more than 70 percent of the public preferred military victory to withdrawal.

The very failure of the communists' Tet Offensive did, however, illustrate the flawed nature of U.S. strategy. It was impossible to deter the North by mere casualties. Without invading the North, capturing or killing Ho Chi Minh, and otherwise cutting off the Ho Chi Minh trail, simply killing Northern communists sent south was a long-term proposition in which no public relations victory could be achieved because the majority of visible casualties were Americans, while the thousands of dead North Vietnamese were simply ignored or glossed over by the American press. Consequently, in a single battle, Americans had achieved a 50-to-1 kill ratio, and yet the media reported this *as a Communist victory*. Scenes were cut and spliced in the studios into 30-second clips of Marines and body bags, with an accompanying text, "American troops mauled."

Instead of reporting the phenomenal kill ratios and success of the American troops, pundits emphasized the possibility of a "military disaster."[54] Some uttering these gloomy prognostications were Kennedy supporters and former staffers. "Court historian" Arthur Schlesinger, Jr., in March warned the United States "not [to] re-enact Dien Bien Phu," or "sacrifice our brave men to the folly of generals and the obstinance of

Presidents."[55] Even *Newsweek* admitted that for the first time in history the American press was more friendly to its country's enemies than to the United States. In terms of a journalistic coup, the communists could not have achieved a greater victory. Tet occurred at a time when the administration had come to believe—and had successfully sold the American press on the view—that the ground war was nearly over. Worse, the news media bungled the reporting, giving the communists victories they did not achieve. For example, NBC's Chet Huntley reported that the Viet Cong had "seized part of the United States Embassy" and that twenty suicide commandos held the first floor of the embassy.[56] Although the Viet Cong had entered the compound, they had never held any part of the embassy itself. Nevertheless, instead of covering the decisive destruction of the Viet Cong in the fields, the journalists found themselves, just as they had in the Diem episode, locked into events in Saigon, with television crews filming gun battles around the embassy, and nightly coverage running as long as 2 minutes of a 26-minute newscast.[57]

Both CBS and NBC produced half-hour news specials, "alarmist in tone" and negative in approach, which "strongly reinforced the message that Tet was a devastating defeat for the United States."[58] One CBS reporter, impervious to reality, stated, "The Viet Cong proved they could take and hold almost any area they chose."[59] He neglected to say that taking and holding any area they chose had cost the Viet Cong their entire army. Likewise, ABC reporter Joseph Harsch concluded, "Best estimates here are that the enemy has not yet, and *probably never will*, run out of the manpower to keep his effort going."[60] Certainly he could not have received such information from American officers, who had a pretty good idea how many Viet Cong had been eliminated, or from North Vietnamese officers who told Ho Chi Minh that after a few more such "victories," the war was over.

More than any other image, the televised execution by South Vietnamese general Nguyen Loan of a Viet Cong prisoner exemplifies the press's utter disregard for proper context. Standing just a few feet from the prisoner, who was bound, Gen. Loan raised his pistol to the man's head and killed him while the cameras rolled. NBC, which filmed the execution, ran the film up to the point when blood splattered out of the Viet Cong's head, and critics immediately hailed the "courage" of the network to broadcast such "reality." One *Washington Post* reporter said the pictures "shocked the world" (although it is doubtful that in nations where such killings were routine, anyone even saw it); NBC's Edwin Newman said that the "film revolted the nation . . . Public opinion was moving. Television caused the change."[61] One study of the film asserted that "formal composition helps to explain the photograph's impact. In the symmetry of Loan's sinewy arm and his pearl-handled revolver, the muscles in the forearm seem to approximate the bulge of the gun chamber. The gun becomes an extension of Loan's arm."[62] The North Vietnamese also thought the pictures powerful, and promptly used them as a propaganda tool—what Peter Baestrup later called "super-pornography that tells us nothing about policy." One North Vietnamese journalist told photographer Edie Adams, "We have your photograph in the center of our War Museum."[63] When the film was shown in America, no proper context was provided: the Vietnamese had declared martial law in that town, and anyone who was armed and walking the streets under martial law was automatically a VC suspect who could be shot on sight.

For several months the American media portrayed Tet both as a communist victory and as evidence of deliberate lies on the part of the administration. Even after evidence rolled in that Tet had been a disaster for the Viet Cong and the North, the media continued to propagate the myth of American defeat. Only later in 1968 did field producer Jack Fern recommend a three-part series describing Tet as a debacle for the Viet Cong, but, as NBC executives told Fern, "Tet was already established in the public's mind as a defeat, and, therefore, it *was* an American defeat."[64] At least one journalist, however, knew the truth. ABC anchorman Howard K. Smith resigned in February 1968 because he thought the coverage was completely lacking in context. His own son, "left for dead in Vietnam in 1965, had watched the North Vietnamese execute a dozen American soldiers in uniform," and Smith recoiled at the fact that "not even a perfunctory acknowledgment was made of the fact that such executions en masse are the Viet Cong way of war."[65]

Fern's recollections and Smith's actions confirm that not only did the media shape policy in Vietnam, but that it—and not the military—participated in the more serious distortions of facts. Don Oberdorfer's analysis of the Tet Offensive further attests to the role of the press in turning victory into a defeat:

> It says something about this war that the great picture of the Tet Offensive was Eddie Adam's photograph of a South Vietnamese general shooting a man with his arms tied behind his back, that the most memorable quotation was Peter Arnett's damning epigram from Ben Tre, "It became necessary to destroy the town to save it" and that the only Pulitzer Prize awarded specifically for reporting an event . . . was given two years later to Seymour M. Hersh, who never set foot in Vietnam, for exposing a U.S. Army massacre of more than a hundred civilians at My Lai.[66]

Television coverage, by its very nature, was even worse. As Gen. William Westmoreland said, "Television's unique requirements contributed to a distorted view of the war," because the footage almost always came from the American side, showing, inevitably, casualties, while it could not possibly show enemy losses.[67] Likewise, whereas every American decision was subject to question, television could not reveal the confusion and frustration of enemy leaders, the fact that their troops were on the verge of starvation, or the decimation of their units by American firepower. It is an unpleasant fact that television is drawn to the action—the initiative—which meant that from 1965 to 1968, the troop landings, air strikes, and search-and-destroy operations received the brunt of coverage. Thus, when the enemy launched his suicidal offensive, television reporters turned their attention to that story.[68]

Since the end of the war, there has been an ongoing effort to reconstruct the image of journalists for their role in the defeat. Within this context, George Herring insisted that "a direct link between television reporting and public opinion cannot be established."[69] We now know, of course, what numerous agenda-setting studies have told us, that the opposite is in fact true: the greater the concentration of news stories on an issue, the greater that issue's importance in the minds of news consumers. In Vietnam, the media's coverage had repeated and damaging effects. James Reston, of the *New York Times*, toward the end of the war, admitted that "maybe the historians will agree that the reporters and cameras were decisive in the end. They brought the issue of the war to the people . . . and forced the withdrawal of American power from Vietnam."[70]

Perhaps the real story of the war was that only American hesitation, indecision, and weakness kept the North Vietnamese from being obliterated on several occasions. A new study of the defense of Hanoi during the 1967 Linebacker Offensive, for example, shows that American technological developments (particularly radar-jamming aircraft) threatened to overwhelm Vietnamese defenses.[71] Using North Vietnamese documents, Merle Pribbenow found that American bombing pauses gave the communists the critical time they needed to assess the attacks and develop new tactics. Each time the United States had the North Vietnamese on the ropes, Johnson called a bombing halt and gave Hanoi the room it needed to reorganize.

Other scholars have not absolved the media of undercutting American policy. Daniel Hallin's study of televised editorial comments revealed interesting biases in the press.[72] Comments about the North Vietnamese, for example, plunged from 100 percent unfavorable before Tet to only 29 percent unfavorable afterward. Negative editorial comments about administration supporters rose 71 percent after Tet, and negative references to democracy in South Vietnam rose sixfold. Likewise, negative references to troop morale went from 0 pre-Tet to 15 percent, while critiques of administration policy—of which there were only four segments, or stories, in the period under study before Tet—suddenly shot up 26 percent after Tet. At the same time, the press stopped using military spokesmen as sources. Quotations from American soldiers in the field shrank by half after Tet, and the number of quotations from North Vietnamese/communist officials, while small in number, increased threefold over the same period. Television reporters quoted North Vietnamese officials eight times as frequently after Tet than before, while relying on American officers only slightly more than before, and the number of critical comments per hour of coverage started to eclipse the number of editorial comments about U.S. activities overall.[73]

DEMONSTRATING FOR THE MEDIA

A now traditional account of the Vietnam era goes something like this: The war was popular at first, but as the flawed nature of U.S. strategy became apparent, most Americans wanted out. These "average Americans" who wanted out were represented in a vocal way by demonstrators and "student" protestors who staged massive marches; eventually, their actions "forced" the United States out of the war by the sheer weight of their moral position.

Little of that is true, however. A wave of massive protests had been building since the early 1960s, and virtually none of it had to do with the war until roughly 1964. Only later did Vietnam stand out as unique in rallying a large core of opponents. Perhaps an even greater missed story involved the infiltration and manipulation of the student movement by Soviet agents. At least some of the unrest emanated from Moscow, which trained and supported an extensive network of radical leaders for the purposes of disrupting American society and alienating youth from "bourgeois" ideas. Sit-in protests and mass demonstrations on California campuses appeared as early as 1958, usually directed at a specific incident or university policies. After 1964, however, at the University of California, Berkeley, the demonstrations grew increasingly violent under the Free Speech Movement. According to the history of the American Communist movement, "Communists and other varieties of Marxists and Marxist-Leninists were among the organizers and leaders" of the Free Speech Movement.[74] FBI head J. Edgar Hoover, testifying before Congress, identified several members of the Communist Party of the United States as "leading organizers," including Bettina Kurzweil, daughter of Herbert Aptheker, considered the Communist Party's leading theoretician.[75] Students for a Democratic Society (SDS) leaders, such as Carl Davidson, proudly proclaimed their Marxist-Leninist sympathies, and Bernardine Dohrn, leader of SDS in 1968, when asked if she was a socialist, answered, "I consider myself a revolutionary Communist."[76]

Whether to even admit communists constituted a key decision in the early history of the radical movement.[77] Others in the peace movement discouraged a communist presence, arguing that it linked the movement to totalitarian governments.[78] At the very time that SDS had established itself on 350–400 campuses across the country, claiming perhaps 100,000 members, communist elements within the organization tore it apart, achieving the goal of the more militant communists of pushing the radical movement toward street violence.[79] Thus campus violence was not a case of emotions getting out of hand, as the mainstream press characterized it. Rather, it represented a predictable evolution of events when a radical minority steeped in revolutionary tactics and filled with an ideology of terror attempted to impose its worldview on the (paying) majority by shutting down facilities.

Main Street America, which often received skewed news reports of the ostensible causes of the disruption—over 450 college campuses were closed at some point in the 1960s due to demonstrations—read stories emphasizing nonthreatening student issues. Students were portrayed as seeking only to challenge unreasonable dress codes, or to have a say in curriculum design, or to protest unpopular dorm policies. These stated reasons for protest masked the true objective, which was to use any initial demand as a starting point for closing the university.[80] Radical leaders themselves later admitted they practiced a strategy of constantly escalating demands so that no compromise could ever be reached with them. Jerry Rubin, who drafted many of these early tactics, explained, "Satisfy our demands and we go twelve more . . . All we want from these meetings are demands that the Establishment can never satisfy . . . Demonstrators are never 'reasonable.'"[81]

Even at the time, it was unrealistic and illogical to assume that such propaganda events did not have an affect, either on American morale or by boosting the spirits of the enemy. But with the advantage of historical hindsight, and subsequent publications, the destructive role of these antiwar offensives becomes startlingly clear. One North Vietnamese official later confessed,

> Every day our leadership would listen to world news over the radio . . . to follow the growth of the American antiwar movement. Visits to Hanoi by people like Jane Fonda and former Attorney General Ramsey Clark and ministers gave us confidence that we should hold on in the face of battlefield reverses. We were elated when Jane Fonda, wearing a red Vietnamese dress, said at a press conference that she was ashamed of American actions in the war and that she would struggle along with us.[82]

Interestingly, at a time when the press was distancing itself from its past anticommunist stances, it was also ignoring the very real communist sympathies and influences that were part of student protests nationwide.

As with other aspects of reporting, what was not reported was as important as what was covered. French journalist Jean Lacouture published *Ho Chi Minh* in 1968, which later served as the basis for Halberstam's biography of Ho Chi Minh. Lacouture admitted that he "dissimulated certain defects of North Vietnam at war against the Americans, because I believed that the cause of the North Vietnamese was good and just [and] I believed it was not opportune to expose the Stalinist nature of the North Vietnamese regime . . . at the time Nixon was bombing Hanoi." [83]

Yet Halberstam duly regurgitated what Lacouture had fed him, writing a favorable biography of an enemy leader in the midst of the conflict. (For comparison's sake, would any reporter have even contemplated writing an intentionally complimentary piece on Mussolini, Hitler, or Tojo in the middle of World War II?) Veteran reporter Keyes Breech supported the view that such antics by the media "helped lose the war . . . because of the way the war was reported." [84] Defenders of the press unwittingly have confirmed the negative impact of coverage. Lavishing praise on "courageous" journalists, Jeffrey Smith noted that after CBS correspondent Morley Safer's report on Marines burning the huts of suspected Viet Cong at Cam Ne, Safer "feared being killed by angry soldiers." [85] It did not occur to Smith that the soldiers saw Safer's reporting as a direct threat to their mission and morale.

ENTER NIXON

Media coverage of the war unraveled the Johnson administration. Sniped at by reporters, demonized by protestors, and abandoned by many within his own party, Lyndon Johnson announced in 1968 that he would not run for re-election. That left his vice president, Hubert Humphrey, to ward off antiwar messengers such as Eugene McCarthy and the Republican challenger, Richard Nixon. Humphrey could not appeal to large portions of the Democratic base by appearing too hawkish, and thus he substantially ceded the war issue to Nixon, who won a close election (thanks to the presence of a third-party candidate, former Alabama governor George Wallace, viewed also as a hawk).

Using the low turnout (61 percent of registered voters) as a reason to deny Nixon's legitimacy, the press was immediately hostile. Nixon did not carry a single large city. Reporter David Broder observed that "the men and the movement that broke Lyndon Johnson's authority in 1968 are out to break Richard Nixon in 1969 . . . breaking a president is, like most feats, easier to accomplish the second time around." [86] Nixon had felt ill-treated by a hostile press in his failed California gubernatorial race, warning his staff, "The press is the enemy . . . [N]obody in the press is a friend. They are all enemies." [87] Nixon's history with vile press treatment dated back to his Checkers speech in the 1952 campaign when the *New York Post* ran the subheadline "Secret Rich Man's Trust Fund Keeps Nixon in Style Far Beyond His Salary." [88]

When it came to Vietnam, Nixon wanted to withdraw without appearing weak. Combining a policy of heavy bombing of the North with generous arms support for the South Vietnamese, Nixon reduced American forces in Vietnam by 526,000 in four years and slashed Vietnam-related spending from $25 billion to $3 billion. Nor did he hesitate to negotiate with the North in secret talks in Paris. Carefully controlling information given to the press through his press secretary, Ron Ziegler, Nixon held fewer press conferences than his predecessors. Nevertheless, in 1972, he had seven, more than twice the number Bill Clinton had in his last *two* years in office. Mostly, Nixon relied on radio addresses, where the media could not interpret his remarks. This was especially effective at the time because neither the automatic opposition response nor the endless media analysis of presidential speeches had yet become a normal practice.[89]

Reporters, especially television news anchors, attempted to conceal their contempt for Nixon by claiming that they opposed conservative politicians on other grounds. For example, Chet Huntley, of NBC's *Nightly News*, claimed to oppose Nixon because of the president's limited intellectual capacities. Huntley, demonstrating his own conceit, told *Life* magazine in 1970, "The shallowness of the man overwhelms me; the fact that he is President frightens me."[90] Journalists in general admitted their loathing of Nixon in unguarded moments. Tribune Publishing Company president Jack Fuller recalled that "some journalists made their reputations simply by showing hostility to the President and his men."[91] After attending a White House correspondents' dinner in 1970, an event Nixon described as "three hours of pure boredom and insults," he told Bob Haldeman that from that point on "everybody on my staff has a responsibility to protect the office of the Presidency from such insulting incidents."[92] Despite admissions by Fuller, Huntly, and others, journalists viewed Nixon as paranoid for stating the obvious: most journalists were "just waiting for the chance to stick the knife in deep and twist it."[93]

Coverage of Nixon got so negative on the three major networks that Vice President Spiro Agnew gave a speech attacking the fairness of network news. Although CBS and NBC sharply criticized Agnew, ABC actually promised it would seek greater fairness in its coverage. The network conducted "attitudinal surveys" of its viewers, hired Harry Reasoner to team up with Howard K. Smith, and gave Avram Westin the power to create a "news concept."[94] Westin promised a "different type of fairness, a different type of balance," taking a story from the perspective of "middle America" rather than the "Eastern liberal" perspective. He observed that this required "a conscious policy of reversing perspectives," essentially admitting that the networks did not see things the way "middle America" did.[95]

LINEBACKER COVERAGE DROPS THE BALL

As the war continued, Nixon kept his promise to withdraw American troops from Vietnam. The press ignored or distorted this rather significant achievement—one which liberal elites presumably would support—and only grew more defensive. In May 1969, Nixon announced a new eight-point plan to withdraw all foreign troops from Vietnam and hold internationally supervised elections. Under the new plan, the United States agreed to talk directly to the National Liberation Front (NLF), while behind the scenes sending Kissinger to work the Soviet Union to pressure the North. That June, Nixon also withdrew the first large number of troops from Vietnam, some 25,000. Using the stick with the carrot was a renewed commitment to bombing North Vietnam.

Nixon's one serious attempt at bringing the North to the bargaining table through bombing involved the April–August 1972 Linebacker Offensive. Linebacker proved extremely successful: more than 70 percent of enemy tanks were destroyed or damaged by tactical aircraft and gunships, and by August, allied air power had destroyed nearly 300 North Vietnamese tanks, virtually eliminating any armored capability in the North.[96] Linebacker II, unleashed in December after Hanoi grew intransigent, consisted of an eleven-day bombing. According to one analyst of air power, "The effect of the . . . campaign on Hanoi's ability to resist was crushing . . . the rail system around Hanoi was attacked with such persistence and intensity that poststrike reconnaissance showed that repair crews were making no effort to restore even token rail traffic."[97] Another source concluded that North Vietnam was "laid open for terminal destruction."[98] Prisoners of war in Hanoi confirmed that the North Vietnamese were nearly on the verge of collapse during the bombing, a view supported by the British and other foreign ambassadors there.

Nevertheless, even with the bombing pauses, Ho Chi Minh and the communist warlords in the North realized that they could not take much more punishment, and certainly could not afford any more "successes" such as Tet. There is considerable evidence that until that time the North counted on American antiwar protestors to coerce America out; but Nixon had gone over the media's heads in November 1969 in his speech to the "great, silent majority," which was followed by a January 1970 Gallup poll showing him with a 65 percent approval rating on his handling of the war. The protestors and their allies in the media had lost, and the worst was yet to come. With the bombings in 1972, followed by the abolishment of the draft in 1973 that almost overnight destroyed student protests, the North had little to rely on.

In the 1972 election, the Democrats again nominated an antiwar politician, George McGovern of South Dakota. His extreme positions included a $1,000 cash giveaway to every American family; legalization of marijuana; and immediate and unconditional withdrawal of all U.S. forces from Vietnam. The South Dakota senator had made his own efforts to gain favorable press coverage: during the primary, Senator Gary Hart advised McGovern to have his aides look as happy as possible at all times, sending signals that their internal polling carried good news for their candidate. In fact, however, he did not have to do much. McGovern routinely got good press because the journalists' views closely resembled his own, as seen in *Time* magazine's claim that McGovern's support was "astonishingly broad, bracketing liberals, conservatives, blue-collar workers, farmers, suburbanites, and the young."[99] McGovern's "astonishingly broad" support won him exactly one state in the general election.

Nixon realized what the Democrats had handed him with the nomination of McGovern, telling his staff, "Here is a situation where the Eastern Establishment media finally has a candidate who almost totally shares their views."[100] The president noted that the nation would "find out whether what the media has been standing for during these last five years really represents majority thinking."[101] Nixon won a crushing landslide over McGovern, who carried only the District of Columbia and Massachusetts. The magnitude of Nixon's victory stunned and terrified elite journalists. McGovern's popular vote total—29.1 percent—was the lowest ever by a major party's candidate.

If Nixon was right, namely, that McGovern almost totally represented the views of the liberal media in America, it meant that the American public had utterly rebuked the media and its candidate. The reaction was predictable, and chilling: one powerful editor responded to Nixon's election, "There's got to be a bloodletting. We've got to make sure that nobody ever thinks of doing anything like this again."[102] When he referred to "anything like this," he meant *winning an election*. Historian Paul Johnson described the aim of the powerful editors and publishers was "to use the power of the press and TV to reverse the electoral verdict of 1972 which was felt to be, in some metaphorical sense, illegitimate."[103] Soon they had their issue, which would send them into a moral frenzy: the break-in of Democratic Party Headquarters at the Watergate Hotel in Washington, DC. If the Kennedy assassination was a seminal event in causing the press to abandon its objectivity, Watergate was its public "coming out" party.

PIRANHAS IN THE POOL

No event in journalism history is romanticized more than the Watergate scandal, ostensibly "broken" by two *Washington Post* reporters, Carl Bernstein and Bob Woodward. The affair featured a president hated by the press and easily demonized by journalists, cover-ups and exposés of abuse of power, and crusading journalists who brought down an administration. As much as journalists loved Kennedy, they despised Nixon.

Contrary to many portrayals, especially the romanticized view of journalism made popular by Hollywood movies such as *All the President' s Men*, Watergate represented the culmination of the profession's return to partisanship, not the beginning. As one novelist described the journalistic setting, "Then came Watergate . . . [and] we threw the bum out. And who pulled it off? Two journalists. All of a sudden, journalism had a new image . . . Journalists were movers and shakers, shapers of public opinion. Now we had power to dethrone people."[104] Apparently many young Americans accepted this image of the media, as enrollments in journalism schools quadrupled between 1968 and 1978.

The Watergate break-in did not figure in the campaign itself. Although journalists covered some of the news about the break-in, "it was defined primarily as a partisan clash between Democrats and Republicans."[105] Those familiar with the "dirty tricks" of the Kennedy and Johnson administrations would have agreed that, while laws were broken, certainly the Watergate affair simply perpetuated political espionage carried out by the two previous Democratic administrations. What differed in Watergate was that for the first time, Congress, dominated by the opposing (and adversarial) party, was determined to make such political hijinks a political and legal issue. Additionally, an adversarial and openly partisan press was out to hurt the president. Looking specifically at Watergate coverage, Gladys Lang and Kurt Lang discovered that coverage was first provided within the framework of the presidential election campaign; the public thought it simply partisan politics. Yet as soon as the press switched contextual frames, moving from the framework of the 1972 presidential campaign to the framework of continual Washington corruption, the nation became obsessed and Nixon's fortunes tumbled.[106]

Apologists for the media's behavior during the period dismiss the charge that Watergate coverage was unfair or distorted, arguing that the "same publicity that was effectively utilized by his opponents was available to Nixon whenever he chose to make use of it."[107] Quite the contrary, despite Nixon's "bully pulpit" of the presidency—which is only as good as the post-speech coverage allows it to be—willing accomplices in the press greatly aided the Democrats by wall-to-wall coverage of what would otherwise have been irrelevant hearings. No number of presidential appearances could offset the nonstop coverage of the Senate hearings controlled by the Democrats (and later, House impeachment hearings), whose intent from the outset was nothing less than to remove Nixon from power.

While Woodward and Bernstein conducted their journalistic sleuthing, though, the key breakthroughs came not from reporters but from evidence introduced during the Senate investigation. This was especially true of the revelation in Senate hearings that Oval Office conversations were taped. Someone in the administration leaked the tapes to the *New York Times*, which published the contents, encouraging rumors that Nixon's staff had doctored the tapes. (Subsequent research proved they were not tampered with.) Searching desperately for a "smoking gun"—some comment that would show Nixon knew about and planned the break-in—newspapers printed the transcripts and commented on them daily, all with a tone of moral indignation.

By that time, of course, congressional machinery had already been oiled and the gears of impeachment started to whirr. Given a substantial Democratic advantage in the House, Nixon faced certain impeachment, and he embarked on a "race for public support" to survive a Senate trial. Whether Nixon ever placed any faith in a vindication by public opinion, filtered through the media, is another question. One analyst claimed Nixon saw public opinion as an "ever-present danger" which could be "stirred up by the media, deliberately manipulated by his enemies, and tracked by pollsters."[108] On the other hand, Nixon's fairly steady popularity until nearly the end may have tempered the media's coverage. When it changed, though, public opinion shifted rapidly, and by November 1973, when Nixon looked straight at the camera and told the American people their president was "not a crook," nearly 60 percent of Americans did not believe "much of what the president says these days," according to an ABC poll.[109]

Those who would exculpate the media do admit that "coverage reached saturation levels, with Watergate on the front page and on the evening news day after day."[110] More important, if framing was a key, then the framing of Watergate was already done for the journalists before their stories ever appeared by the Senate Democrats, whose hearings determined witnesses, topics, and even the timing of testimony. As Nicholas von Hoffman wrote, "It wasn't journalism; it was lynching. Not only were the pretentious canons of the trade chucked overboard; so were fairness and common sense."[111] Moreover, journalists apparently never came close to the actual origins of the break-in order, which apparently came from John Dean in an effort to determine if his then-fiancée's name was listed in the address book of a recently arrested DC madam.[112]

Nixon never forgot, or forgave, his treatment by the press. In 1989, when advising the newly elected president, George H. W. Bush, Nixon warned him that reporters were "inherently adversarial": "TV reporters always claim to be 'speaking for the people,' but they are really speaking primarily for themselves. In many ways, they are political actors, just like the President, mindful of their ratings, careful of preserving and building. A President must respect them for that power, but he can never entirely trust them."[113] Ripping the facade off objective journalism, Nixon told Bush, through a "memo" published in *TV Guide*, the "media don't have to be convinced. They have to be outfoxed, outflanked and outperformed . . . [and] will use his [Bush's] failures to pursue [their own agendas]."[114]

DEPARTURE OF TRUST

Far from recovering their credibility, the media, with its vicious attacks on Nixon, continued to fall further in the public eye. The public may not have trusted the fallen president, but it certainly did not trust journalists either.[115] Neither the government nor the news media recovered its credibility. It was not economic conditions that caused the loss in confidence in "all institutions," including the media, as some have argued. A survey measuring confidence in government from 1958 to 1980 shows two distinct shifts. Following six years (1958–1964) of widespread trust in government (approximately 80 percent), there was a sharp rise in those saying they "cannot trust the government to do right most of the time," with the percentage nearly doubling in six years. The survey reveals that confidence in government fell steadily during the Vietnam era, but then held steady for about two years, from 1970 to 1972.[116]

At the same time, public attitudes toward business reflected a decade's worth of media attacks. Although more than 80 percent of respondents admitted that "large companies are essential for the nation's growth and expansion," the number seeing the profits of large companies as making "things better for everyone" dropped nearly 30 percent in just over a decade. In other survey questions, the respondents saw business as cold, impersonal, and monopolistic. Nevertheless, over time, as analysts Seymour Martin Lipset and William Schneider observed, antigovernment sentiment exceeded even the hostility toward business.[117] The press's decade-long campaign against the institution of government had paid off. Other polls showed faith in Congress falling from 42 percent to 19 percent between 1966 and 1971, and faith in military leaders falling from 62 percent to 27 percent in the same five-year span, while faith in the presidency dropped from 41 percent to 23 percent.[118]

If, however, the intention of the media's new adversarial relationship with government (with business thrown in as a class enemy on general principle) was to bolster its own credibility as purveyor of fact and truth, then that effort was a monumental defeat. And here is an irony, as the media was so successful in helping to lower faith in business and government, no group fell lower in confidence than the news media itself. It was already held in low regard in 1966 (with only 29 percent of Americans having faith in the media), falling still further to 18 percent by 1971, and by 1980 the "respect levels" of news media leaders had plummeted to 16 percent.[119] A similar Gallup poll revealed that journalists and reporters ranked below pollsters and funeral directors as having honest and ethical standards, although reporters came in ahead of lawyers and sellers of insurance. Yet it was hardly a joking matter: overall, the composite surveys used by Harris in all institutional leadership showed a complete collapse after the Kennedy assassination.[120]

Journalists' assault on Nixon had come at a great cost: the integrity of journalism itself. But rather than working to reestablish its credibility, the establishment press pushed on, seemingly oblivious to the loss of the trust of the public. Although journalists had succeeded in tarnishing the credibility of government, that had not rebounded to the credit of the press.

NOTES

1. Joseph Charles Keeley, *The Left-Leaning Antenna: Political Bias in Television* (New Rochelle, NY: Arlington House Publishers, 1971), 45.

2. See Arthur Miller, Thad Brown, and Alden Raine, "Social Conflict and Political Estrangement, 1958–1972," paper presented at the Midwest Political Science Association Convention, May 1973, and Norman H. Nie, Sidney Verba, and John R. Petrocik, *The Changing American Voter* (Cambridge, MA: Harvard University Press, 1976).

3. David Frum, *How We Got Here* (New York: Basic Books, 2000), 36.

4. *Charlotte Observer*, June 26, 1977.

5. David S. Broder, *Behind the Front Page* (New York: Simon & Schuster, 1987), 139–140.

6. Michael Schudson, *Discovering the News* (New York: Guilford, 1991); James Boylan, "Declarations of Independence: A Historian Reflects on an Era in which Reporters Rose Up to Challenge—and Change—the Rules of the Game," *Columbia Journalism Review*, November/December 1986, 29–45.

7. Sylvia Meagher, *Accessories after the Fact* (New York: Vintage, 1976), and her *Subject Index to the Warren Report and Hearing and Exhibits* (New York: Scarecrow, 1966).

8. Michael Kurtz, *The Crime of the Century*, 2nd ed. (Knoxville: University of Tennessee Press, 1996 [1982]), 157.

9. Examine the responses of the *New York Times*, November 24, 1966; "A Primer of Assassination Theories," *Esquire*, 66 (1966), 51–62, 206–211; Fred J. Cook, "The Warren Report," *Nation*, October 1966, 38–54; Fletcher Knebel, "A New Wave of Doubt," *Look*, July 12, 1966, 31–43; "JFK's Murder: Sowers of Doubt," *Newsweek*, December 1966, 25–26. *Esquire* appropriately captured the perspective of the mainstream press: "Who's Afraid of the Warren Report?" *Esquire*, December 1966, 204, 330–332, 334; "Death of a President: The Established Facts," *Atlantic Monthly*, March 1965, 112–118; "Truth about Kennedy Assassination: Questions Raised and Answered," *U. S. News & World Report*, October 1966, 44–50.

10. Josiah Thompson, "The Cross Fire that Killed President Kennedy," *Saturday Evening Post*, December 2, 1967, 27–31.

11. James A Bishop, *The Day Kennedy Was Shot* (New York: Funk and Wagnalls, 1968).

12. Edward Jay Epstein, *Inquest: The Warren Commission and the Establishment of Truth* (New York: Viking, 1966), and Edward Jay Epstein, *Between Fact and Fiction* (New York: Vintage, 1975 [1967]).

13. Mark Lane, *A Citizen's Dissent* (New York: Holt, Rinehart, 1968).

14. Jim Garrison, *On the Trail of the Assassins* (New York: Sheridan Square Press, 1988) served as the basis for the Oliver Stone movie *JFK* (1991).

15. "The Question That Won't Go Away," *Saturday Evening Post*, December 1975, 38–39; Robert Blair Kaiser, "The JFK Assassination: Why Congress Should Reopen the Investigation," *Rolling Stone*, April 24, 1975, 27–28, 30–31, 33, 37–38; Daniel Schorr, "The Assassins," *New York Review of Books*, October 3, 1977, 14–22.

16. James Phelan, "The Assassination That Will Not Die," *New York Times Magazine*, November 23, 1975, 27–28, 109–111, 119–123, 126, 132–133.

17. James L. Aucoin, "The Re-emergence of American Investigative Journalism, 1960–1975," *Journalism History*, 21 (Spring 1995), 7.

18. Daniel C. Hallin, *The "Uncensored War": The Media and Vietnam* (New York: Oxford University Press, 1986); Clarence R. Wyatt, *Paper Soldiers* (New York: W. W. Norton, 1993); and Robert J. Donovan and Ray Scherer, *Unsilent Revolution* (Cambridge: Cambridge University Press, 1992).

19. This is the argument in John M. Newman, *JFK and Vietnam: Deception, Intrigue, and the Struggle for Power* (New York: Warner Books, 1992).

20. William H. Hammond, *Reporting Vietnam* (Lawrence, KS: University Press of Kansas, 1998), ix.

21. Hammond, ix; William H. Hammond, "The News Media and the Military," in *Encyclopedia of the American Military*, ed. John E. Jessup and Louis B. Ketz (New York: Scribner, 1994).

22. Guenther Lewy, *America in Vietnam* (New York: Oxford University Press, 1978), and Edward Lansdale, *In the Midst of Wars* (New York: Fordham University Press, 1991).

23. William V. Kennedy, *The Military and the Media* (Westport, CT: Praeger, 1993), 96.

24. Kennedy, 96.

25. Stephen Cooper and Jim A. Kuypers, "Embedded versus Behind-the-Lines Reporting on the Second Gulf War," in Ralph D. Berenger, ed., *The Global Media Goes to War* (Spokane, WA: Marquette Books, 2004).

26. Russ Braley, *Bad News: The Foreign Policy of the* New York Times (Washington, DC: Regnery Gateway, 1984), 212.

27. Kennedy, 102.

28. Newman, 206.

29. John P. Roche, "The Death of Liberal Internationalism," *National Review*, May 3, 1985, 26–35, 40–44, quotation on 32.

30. Chalmers McGeagh Roberts, *The Washington Post: The First 100 Years* (New York: Houghton Mifflin, 1977), 373.

31. Donovan and Scherer, 228.

32. Louis W. Liebovich, *The Press and the Modern Presidency* (Westport, CT: Praeger, 1998), 39.

33. Russell, Baker, "Befuddled in Asia," *New York Times*, March 2, 1965, in Hammond, 138–139.

34. Liebovich, 58.

35. Don Moser, "Eight Dedicated Men Marked for Death," *Life*, September 3, 1965, 28–33, 68–70, 72, 75–76; Bernard B. Fall, "Vietnam Blitz: A Report on the Impersonal War," *New Republic*, October 9, 1965, 17–21.

36. William Tuohy, "A Big 'Dirty Little War,'" *New York Times Magazine*, November 28, 1965, 43–43, 177, 186–188.

37. Rodger Streitmatter, *Mightier Than The Sword: How the News Media Have Shaped American History* (Boulder, CO: Westview Press, 1998), 191.

38. Oscar Patterson, III, "Television's Living Room War in Print: Vietnam in the News Magazines," *Journalism Quarterly*, 61 (Spring 1984), 35–39, 136.

39. Patterson, 39.

40. Robert Elegant, "How to Lose a War: Reflections of a War Correspondent," *Encounter*, August 1981, 73–90, quotation on 73.

41. John E. Mueller, *War, Presidents and Public Opinion* (New York: John Wiley, 1973), 87.

42. William L. Lunch and Peter W. Sperlich, "American Public Opinion and the War in Vietnam," *Western Political Quarterly*, 32 (March 1979), 21–44.

43. Mueller, 89.

44. Mueller, 56.

45. Phillip B. Davidson, *Vietnam at War* (New York: Oxford University Press, 1988), 552.

46. Benjamin S. Lambeth, *The Transformation of American Air Power* (Ithaca, NY: Cornell University Press, 2000), 23.

47. Victor Davis Hanson, *Carnage and Culture* (New York: Doubleday, 2001), 401.

48. Boylan, 36.

49. Hanson, 398.

50. Robert Leckie, *The Wars of America, Vol. 2: From 1900 to 1992* (New York: Perennial, 1993), 1006–1007.

51. Don Oberdorfer, *Tet!* (New York: Doubleday, 1978), 158.

52. Norman Graebner, "The Scholar's View of Vietnam," in Dennis E. Showalter and John G. Albert, eds., *An American Dilemma: Vietnam, 1964–1973* (Chicago: Imprint Publications, 1993), 29.

53. Graebner, 29.

54. Bernard Nalty, *Air Power and the Fight for Khe Sanh* (Washington, DC: U.S. Air Force History Office, 1973), 39–40.

55. Hanson, 401.

56. Streitmatter,194.

57. Streitmatter, 194.

58. Streitmatter, 194.

59. Streitmatter, 194.

60. Streitmatter, 194–195; emphasis added.

61. Oberdorfer, 248–249; Streitmatter, 197. Also see "Tet: The Turning Point," *Washington Post Magazine*, January 29, 1978.

62. David Culbert, "Television's Visual Impact on Decision-making in the USA, 1968: The Tet Offensive and Chicago's Democratic National Convention," *Journal of Contemporary History*, 33 (July 1998), 419–449, quotation on 424.

63. Culbert, 426. Baestrup's quotation is on 433.

64. Edward Jay Epstein, *Between Fact and Fiction* (New York: Vintage, 1975), 225.

65. Baestrup, 1:654–656; Culbert, 436.

66. Oberdorfer, 332.

67. William Westmoreland, *A Soldier Reports* (Garden City, NY: Doubleday, 1976), 420.

68. Edward J. Epstein, "Changing Focus," *TV Guide*, October 13, 1973, 49.

69. George Herring, *America's Longest War*, 2nd ed. (New York: Afred A. Knopf, 1986), 203.

70. "Vietnam and Electronic Journalism," *Broadcasting*, May 19, 1975, 26.

71. Merle L. Pribbenow, II, "The -Ology War: Technology and Ideology in the Vietnamese Defense of Hanoi, 1967," *Journal of Military History*, January 2003, 175–200.

72. Daniel Hallin, "The Media, the War in Vietnam, and Political Support; A Critique of the Thesis of an Oppositional Media," *Journal of Politics*, 46 (February 1984), 2–24, table on 8.

73. Hallin, 8.

74. Harvey Klehr and John Earl Haynes, *American Communist Movement* (New York: Twayne, 1992), 151.

75. Joseph Kelley, *The Left-Leaning Antenna* (New Rochelle, NY: Arlington House, 1971), 107.

76. Klehr and Haynes, 159; Peter Collier and David Horowitz, *Destructive Generation* (New York: Summit, 1989), 74.

77. Thomas S. Powers, *The War at Home* (New York: Grossman, 1973), 75–76.

78. Kirkpatrick Sale, *SDS* (New York: Random House, 1973), 466.

79. Guenter Lewy, *The Cause That Failed* (New York: Oxford University Press, 1990), 250–276.

80. For an extensive discussion of these tactics, see Larry Schweikart and Michael Allen, *A Patriot's History of the United States* (New York: Sentinel, 2004), ch. 19.

81. Jerry Rubin, *Do It: Scenarios of the Revolution* (New York: Simon & Schuster, 1970), 125.

82. Lewis Sorley, *A Better War* (New York: Harcourt, 1999), 93.

83. Grace Sevy, ed., *The American Experience in Vietnam: A Reader* (Norman, OK: University of Oklahoma Press, 1989), 262.

84. Keyes Breech, "How to Lose a War: A Response from an 'Old Asia Hand,'" in Harrison Salisbury, ed., *Vietnam Reconsidered: Lessons from a War* (New York: Harper & Row, 1984), 152.

85. Jeffery A. Smith, *War and Press Freedom: The Problem of Prerogative Power* (New York: Oxford University Press, 1999), 182.

86. Paul Johnson, *A History of the American People* (New York: HarperCollins, 1997), 888.

87. Johnson, 888.

88. Donovan and Scherer, 38.

89. Robert Shogan, *Bad News: Where the Press Goes Wrong in the Making of the President* (Chicago: Ivan R. Dee, 2001), 64.

90. Keeley, 148.

91. Jack Fuller, *News Values* (Chicago: University of Chicago Press, 1996), 192.

92. Smith, 185.

93. Smith, 185.

94. Ron Cram, "Toward More Conservative News Coverage," www.MediaWars.com, June 18, 2000.

95. Cram.

96. Major A. J. C. Lavalle, ed., *Air Power and the 1972 Spring Invasion* (Washington, DC: United States Air Force Southeast Asia Monograph Series, 1985), 57.

97. Lambeth, 29.

98. Alan Gropman, "The Air War in Vietnam, 1961–73," in R. A. Mason, ed., *War in the Third Dimension: Essays in Contemporary Air Power* (London: Brassey's, 1986), 57.

99. Robert Shogan, *Bad News: Where the Press Goes Wrong in the Making of the President* (Chicago: Ivan R. Dee, 2001), 56.

100. Johnson, 895.

101. Johnson, 895.

102. Johnson, 895.

103. Johnson, 895.

104. Randy Alcorn, *Deadline* (Portland, OR: Multnomah Books, 1996), 263.

105. Gladys Engel Lang and Kurt Lang, "The Media and Watergate," in Doris A. Graber, ed., *Media Power in Politics* (Washington, DC: Congressional Quarterly Press, 1984), 202–209, quotation on 206.

106. Lang and Lang, 202–209.

107. Lang and Lang, 207.

108. Lang and Lang reject the notion that public opinion drove Nixon from office (203).

109. Frum, 26.

110. Lang and Lang, 204.

111. Von Hoffman quoted in Boylan, 41. The "frame" was ideological, not financial: Fred McChesney found no significant effects on the stock value of the *Washington Post* as a result of the investigation. See Fred S. McChesney, "Sensationalism, Newspaper Profits and the Marginal Value of Watergate," *Economic Inquiry*, 25 (January 1987), 135–144.

112. Len Colodny and Robert Gettlin, *Silent Coup: The Removal of a President* (New York: St. Martins Press, 1991).

113. Richard Nixon, "Memo to President Bush: How to Use TV—And Keep from Being Abused by It," *TV Guide*, January 14, 1989, 26–30.

114. Nixon.

115. William G. Mayer, *The Changing of the American Mind* (Ann Arbor, MI: University of Michigan Press, 1992).

116. Ballard C. Campbell, *The Growth of American Government* (Bloomington, IN: Indiana University Press, 1995); and David Brian Robertson and Dennis R. Judd, *The Development of American Public Policy* (Glenview, IL: Scott, Foresman, 1989).

117. Seymour Martin Lipset and William Schneider, *The Confidence Gap* (New York: Free Press, 1983), 33.

118. Lipset and Schneider, 43.

119. Lipset and Schneider, 48–49.

120. Lipset and Schneider, 55.

FIVE

Beyond Nixon: Growth of the Partisan Press

Bolstered by Nixon's resignation, the attendant journalistic braggadocio, followed in the Hollywood culture with the inevitable movie, *All the President's Men*, attempting to make journalists into the new American heroes. After all, who would ever have thought that relatively unimportant reporters could "bring down" a company, a union leader, a general, or a president? In retrospect, much of the news media had initially ignored the Watergate story, largely because it was too much work and because the public sensed that "there was nothing exceptional about the Watergate incident except that the perpetrators got caught."[1] Max Frankel of the *New York Times*, explaining his paper's struggles to stay abreast of Woodward and Bernstein, said, "This is the kind of story that may take ten people to move a couple of inches."[2]

For all its self-congratulations, though, the news media failed even when it managed to report the specifics of the Watergate story. Journalists' blind hatred of Richard Nixon never allowed them to properly place the Watergate break-in within the context of other political "dirty tricks" by Kennedy or Johnson. (Kennedy's Justice Department, for instance, was notorious for bugging the headquarters of political opponents.) The chief difference between Nixon and some of his predecessors was that he, indeed, got caught and, worse, denied it to the American people. Nevertheless, the press had not benefited from the affair. Quite the contrary, the media's credibility sank, and in its place rose a dangerous new distortion of news in the form of conspiracy theories.

The demise of journalistic credibility came on the heels of the five-year informal campaign of the press to erode public trust in government credibility. However, with both government and press credibility declining, a sudden proliferation of conspiracy theories started to appear in the 1970s surrounding almost any controversial issue. Instead of journalists replacing government as a perceived source of truth for certain types of news, the credibility decline of both institutions resulted in the increased willingness of average citizens to turn to unverified, groundless, and often outrageous explanations of events.

Americans have always loved a good juicy conspiracy theory: the First and Second Banks of the United States were assailed as being in the clutches of the British monarchy; Masons periodically came under suspicion; and of course the decade prior to the Civil War spawned competing conspiracy interpretations of the nation's schism: the "slave power conspiracy" and the "abolitionist plot."[3] Over the next 100 years, Americans entertained notions that the *Lusitania* was sunk deliberately to draw the United States into World War I; that Franklin Roosevelt knew in advance about the Japanese attack on Pearl Harbor; and that mysterious groups of international power-brokers controlled the world.[4] After the 1960s, conspiracy notions gained wider circulation because *neither* the government *nor* the media could be trusted. The explosion of conspiracy theories after 1970 was a symptom that journalism still had not restored its reputation, even after Watergate.

Oblivious to this trend, journalists continued to drift away from objectivity and toward increasingly "progressive" or "interpretational" journalism. A potent new way to detect how journalists used the new value-laden/progressive reporting is a research tool called "framing analysis," which allows us to delve behind the facade of objectivity to discover how journalists introduce bias. In the pages that follow, I look at this notion of framing as it relates to a new nonobjectivity of the press. Following this, I look at six other areas that highlight important concerns following Watergate: the growth of news as entertainment, the Carter years, how Reagan exposed a leftward tilt, the 24-hour news cycle, Christian bashing, and Willie Horton.

FRAMING AND THE NEW NONOBJECTIVITY: WHAT MAKES NEWS THE "NEWS"?

News reports following Watergate increasingly saw the introduction of value-laden/progressive elements. This shift was both subtle and difficult to detect. Ostensibly, reporters still appeared fair, covering both sides of an issue. Yet when their stories are looked at through a notion of framing, we can see how they could be cast in a light of the journalist's choosing. Framing goes on around us everyday. It is *how* something is framed that is important. Reporters can frame in a way that reflects a balanced, fair interpretation of issues and events, one that presents the facts in a more neutral sense. Or reporters can frame in such a manner that their own biases and predilections guide their reporting. This may occur intentionally or unintentionally. At its core, framing

> is the process whereby communicators act—consciously or not—to construct a particular point of view that encourages the facts of a given situation to be viewed in a particular manner, with some facts made more or less noticeable (even ignored) than others.
>
> When highlighting some aspect of reality over other aspects, frames act to define problems, diagnose causes, make moral judgments, and suggest remedies. They are located in the communicator, the text, the receiver, and the culture at large. Frames are central organizing ideas within a narrative account of an issue or event; they provide the interpretive cues for otherwise neutral facts.[5]

Framing takes place through "the presence or absence of certain keywords, stock phrases, stereotyped images, sources of information, and sentences that provide thematically reinforcing clusters of fact or judgments."[6] The press frames issues through selectivity of language. Not only are frames "composed of certain keywords, metaphors, concepts, and symbols; they work by highlighting some features of reality over others."[7] How often are terms such as "budget cuts" versus "reining in costs," for instance, used across time? Such an inherent bias—which springs from a "conspiracy of shared values"—requires no memos, no e-mails, no faxes, no phone calls. It operates purely by the collective worldview of reporters.

There are other ways framing can work. For example, by seeking quotations from individuals who promote certain views, journalists can ensure framing a story the way they want it told. Likewise, by moving quotations unfavorable to the reporter's thesis to the bottom of the article, contrary views are stripped of their punch, while placing sources who support the journalist's position toward the top of the story adds weight to the position. Polls, another new tool for the press, can also be effective in framing, especially when a poll result supportive of the desired position can be quoted or posted at the beginning of the article with a phrase such as "According to a recent poll, x number of Americans favor/oppose" a given position. On the other hand, polls that do not support the desired position can be buried or simply ignored.

The elements involved in framing a story include basic journalistic decisions such as "What makes news, the 'news'?" and "What constitutes fairness?" Journalists themselves, though, establish the criteria that certain stories merit coverage (say, for example, homosexual rights or pro-choice marches) and which do not (large-scale meetings of traditional religious groups or Promise Keepers). In this manner, journalists can provide superficially fair and unbiased coverage of a subject already framed as important by its very selection over other news. Story selection became an increasingly important part of the shift to value-laden/progressive reporting. By the late 1970s, news reporting had congealed in its attitudes of what constituted news, while becoming thoroughly self-deluded about its own bias. Herbert Gans, in his study of television news in 1967 and news magazines from 1967 to 1975, identified four factors that made news the "news" during this period of time. Echoes of these four elements are seen even today.

Gans's first factor is that stories on government decisions, policy, and personnel dwarfed all other issues combined except for crime.[8] By 1970, the federal government had grown to such a point that its activities, particularly those of the president, the Congress, and the Supreme Court, constituted newsworthy topics at almost any time. Just as editors in the early 1800s assumed that their own party's political events constituted the news, at the time Watergate began to unfold, the media (especially television) had developed a set of criteria that defined news events, and not surprisingly government activities dominated the selection process.

Gans's survey included *CBS Evening News*, *NBC Nightly News*, *Newsweek*, and *Time*, and Gans found that the most important consideration in whether or not a story was suitable or important was the rank in government or other hierarchies of the person involved in the story.[9] Incumbent presidents, presidential candidates, and other government officials were covered by news sources at a rate more than five times higher than any other category of person. Any statement or activity by a president had a greater likelihood of getting news coverage than similar speeches or activities by other government officials or people in the private sector. At the same time, editors and reporters tended to place statements or activities of nongovernmental actors in the context of their contact with the government. This rather stunning rank-ordering of the importance of sources thus tied everything back to the federal government—another way of reinforcing the media's preoccupation with the notion that all problems had a solution that lay in Washington.

It also meant that a malcontent activist who had the ear of a high-ranking public official was much more likely to get news coverage than a person outside of government who might, in reality, be responsible for genuine accomplishments. Yet these activities "don't count" because they are not linked to a clearly defined government hierarchy. Similarly, "approved" organizations receive attention in story selection. As a contemporary example, see how statements from the National Association of Women (NOW) routinely get news coverage, despite the fact that the membership of NOW is considerably smaller than some conservative women's organizations, such as the Conservative Women's Forum (CWF). But NOW is "approved" as a "source" for women's issues (as defined by the news media), while CWF is not. In similar manner, the Heritage Foundation is the token right-leaning organization most often quoted. Its close association with policy makers in Washington, DC, gives it an advantage over others.

Although Gans's discovery is critically important, one must keep in mind that story selection itself is governed by a hierarchy, or pecking order. Both left-wing media critic Noam Chomsky and conservative radio host Rush Limbaugh agree on the impact of the mainstream media. Chomsky has said the "elite media," meaning the *New York Times*, *Washington Post*, CBS, NBC, and ABC "set the framework in which everyone else operates" by producing the equivalent of a "notice to editors" that the next day's edition will have certain stories on the front page.[10] Thus if "you're an editor of a newspaper in Denver, Colorado, or Dayton, Ohio," Chomsky argued, "and you don't have the resources to figure out what the news is . . . this tells you what the news is."[11] Likewise, Limbaugh has argued that the mainstream media has a "template," with daily stories originated by the *New York Times*.

Certainly this appears to be the case if one looks at the labels provided to the local press by the national media. Looking for labels is one of the main ways to detect the framing of news issues. For example, the *New York Times*, in any given year, will use the terms "Christian conservatives" and "religious right" nearly 200 times but will not once use the terms "religious left," "atheist left," or "atheist liberals."[12] Despite decrying the power of the "religious right," the *Times* and other papers have constantly run articles reporting the demise of the "religious right." Through the 1970s to 1981, the national media could not seem to decide if the "religious right" was growing in power (and was thus a "threat" to other Americans' freedoms) or whether it was shrinking and was therefore irrelevant.[13] So which was it? Was the "religious right" gaining or losing ground? Two years later, in 1983, *Newsweek* claimed that religious conservatives had suffered local electoral losses and had to "rebuild their influence."[14] Obviously the "religious right" was no threat. Except that a 1984 article discovered religious conservatives were "a powerful force" and were better organized and funded than in 1980, when the *Washington Post* had wondered if the Moral Majority would "have much impact" at all![15] Regardless of whether the press derided the "religious right" as ineffectual fools or pronounced dire warnings about the political "threat" posed by "Christian conservatives," the media had its label, which it used to denigrate a sizable portion of Americans with whom they disagreed.

Gans's second factor for determining what constitutes news is the impact on the nation and the national interest of an event. Again, this has the effect of elevating any events associated with the federal government, or government action, above other events that initiate with the private sector. Measuring such an "impact" of an event required applying a set of values by the story selector. As one editor noted of story selection, "interesting" stories are, "prototypically, 'people stories' which focus on 'ordinary' people being acted on or oppressed."[16] Walter Cronkite once claimed that journalism had to side with "humanity against authority." Jack Fuller, president of Tribune Publishing, agreed that the "humanity" versus "authority" dichotomy was prevalent, problematic, and an influence on how reporters wrote their stories:

> No journalist I know would favor lying to give the weaker party a more even chance of prevailing in the debate. Far more likely would a journalist shade his report of a valuative debate to favor an individual suffering under a disadvantage. Somebody, he might say, has to speak up for the flood victims, or the physically handicapped, or the urban underclass. [17]

Even more often, though, story selection involves clear-cut bias about issues important to liberals, and framed in ways advantageous to their cause. A classic case involves the gun-control debate. One can ask, Which is more relevant news—that a deranged gunman shoots a handful of shoppers at a suburban mall, or that 1.5 to 3.4 million Americans use guns to protect themselves or their businesses each year? National news organizations have an operational policy of seldom reporting incidents when a citizen other than police officers uses a gun to save lives. Yet publications by the National Rifle Association, including *American Rifleman* and *American Hunter*, regularly devote space to what the mainstream news ignores: items from around the country where armed citizens save lives or defend themselves against human or animal attackers. These columns average 10–15 entries, or enough to run one story every two days, yet such incidents are rarely mentioned in mainstream newspapers. Certainly this bias in reporting, using the criteria of being "more relevant in its impact on the nation," only is reasonable if the bias is *toward* gun control legislation and *against* Second Amendment rights.

This "impact"-oriented journalism has led to the assumption, according to one insider and newsroom critic, that "if it bleeds, it leads." [18] Using specific and widespread news examples, Matthew Kerbel followed a typical day of television reporting. He documented the tendencies of television news to hype violence (even when none exists), to always lead with bloodshed and destruction (if possible), and to measure "impact" according to whether or not one has pictures to accompany the story. [19] As just one example, a local *Eyewitness News* broadcast began with a report that "officers in riot gear [cleared] the streets around South Mountain High School after a fight between several students escalated into a rock-throwing melee." Kerbel provides an accurate translation of what happened: "What started as an ordinary fight among several students in a matter of moments became—an ordinary fight among several students." [20]

Story language in such reports is not only inaccurate, but inane. Violence, Kerbel points out, seems to happen only at "popular restaurants," leading one to conclude that the safest place to eat is somewhere unpopular! So-called eyewitnesses are, in fact, only *specially selected* eyewitnesses who provide the best sound bites. In a school shooting in 2001, one savvy teenager offered herself for interviews, claiming to know the participants, and noted to a friend that she had to change clothes between filming so that she did not appear the same on every channel. Victims must evoke a reaction from the viewer, whether the labels apply or not. Terms such as "desperate" or "tragic" find their way into reports frequently. Kerbel, only half-joking, provides a formula for a do-it-yourself story in which the writer can select a word or phrase from each of several columns ("In broad daylight today . . . hundreds of . . . homeless persons . . . were found"). Yellow police tape is almost essential to a story, he notes, as is blood.

Kerbel provides interesting food for thought: If it bleeds (and supports the causes of the press), it leads. For example, readers might notice that while the killing of Matthew Shepard, a homosexual young man in Wyoming, made national news and virtually every national front page, the horrific bondage/sodomy killing by two homosexuals of 13-year-old Jesse Dirkhising, which came to trial in 2001, went almost unreported. Only those stories that both bleed and fit the value-laden/progressive template rate media attention. Even the editorially conservative *Washington Times* did not cover the Dirkhising trial.

It is here that market capitalism, which provides the competitive need for news in a broad sense, often supports as newsworthy anti-market and antidemocratic events or positions. As Gans points out, "Story selectors fasten on the laws of the land, which are beyond argument most of the time."[21] To appreciate the liberal/progressive bias in the media, it is worthwhile to consider Gans's proposition that "the more highly ranked the target of protest or violence, the more important the story becomes."[22] But this clearly is not true, in that the major media and publishing institutions by the 1980s had unwritten, fast rules against reporting pro-life marches, even though abortion would be considered one of the most important issues in the country. A longer-term dialectic was at work as well: since laws only constitute news when they change, the bias in coverage is against the status quo and in favor of constant change. Thus the law is worth discussing when it is being undermined or reversed, not when it is upheld, or, as one producer said, "when things go awry, when institutions are not functioning normally."[23]

The mindset of the producers, editors, and reporters is critical here: what is meant, in their view, by "functioning normally?" The preoccupation with Cronkite's "humanity against authority" alternative seems to affect many journalists. If journalists in America speak on behalf of "humanity," why (as we will see in detail in chapter 8) are they so often on the opposite side of most humans in America? And what constitutes "the world of humanity"? Is any rebellion against any authority, including that of God, automatically included? One must assume so. The implication is that if this view of journalism reflects that of most journalists, reporting *always* is opposed to the status quo, even when the status quo is morally right.

Gans's third factor, deciding what stories make the airwaves or see print, involves the subject's impact on large numbers of people—and the larger the number, the better. Yet again, journalists and broadcasters tend to view an event's impact through the prism of their own social and cultural class. "One news magazine," Gans reported, "often evaluated stories by the extent to which they were thought to affect 'our kinds of people,' the well-educated upper middle-class to which journalists belong."[24] Joel Kotkin and David Friedman observe,

> The media's leftward bent often obscures an even more compelling fact: its physical concentration in a single New York borough that is one of the least representative places in modern America. All four national news networks . . . are headquartered within walking distance of each other. The nation's two most dominant papers, the *Wall Street Journal* and the *New York Times*, are published within a subway ride of opinion-shaping magazines like *Time*, *Newsweek*, *Business Week*, and *Fortune*.[25]

Increasingly, reporters and editors had become less diverse, with one survey of hundreds of media elites showing that by 1984 they came disproportionately from three states—New York, Pennsylvania, and New Jersey—and that 40 percent came from approximately one-third of the country encompassing the northeast and Atlantic coast.[26] In 1981 Robert Lichter published survey data generated from media self-descriptions. He found that at "least 81% of the news media had voted for the liberal Democrat for President in every election going back to 1964. He found that 90% favored abortion; 83% found nothing wrong with homosexuality; only 47% believed adultery to be wrong; 50% had no religious affiliation; and 85% seldom or never attended church or synagogue."[27] Even today, 30 years later, the leftward lean of this stance is pronounced. In Ronald Reagan's day, media elites were overwhelmingly to the left of the political spectrum according to their own views of themselves, and when measured using a "litmus test" list of key issues, they fell into the far-left segment of the political spectrum. Gans's studies confirmed that journalists' attitudes shaped the news: "Journalists believe that people ought to be interested in *important news* . . . even if the news does not directly affect them."[28]

Yet even when reporting news that did "directly affect" the public, the networks adopted a paternalistic, "this-is-what-you-need-to-know" attitude. CBS, for example, moved from "hard news" to "soft news," or a type of tabloid journalism, in the 1980s under Gordon Sauter. Coming to CBS in 1981, Sauter was convinced that the network was out of touch with the country—which was correct, except not in the way Sauter thought. His executive team made major programming changes that dropped "serious coverage of things like public affairs and foreign news in favor of more personality-oriented, celebrity-oriented, crime-oriented coverage."[29] Unfortunately, such coverage rewarded "gotcha" journalism at the expense of solid, fact-based reporting. CBS's competitor, NBC, fared the worst in this genre with its sinking show *Dateline*, when the network staged a fuel-tank explosion of a General Motors truck to "expose" a fuel-tank problem. However, *Dateline* producers installed igniting devices under the gas tanks to ensure a sensational explosion. Several staff members quit, the network apologized to General Motors, and *Dateline* continued to languish near the bottom of the ratings.[30]

There was no arguing that by the late 1980s, news had shifted from election/political/foreign affairs news to science, lifestyle, and "other national" stories. A study by Steve Barkin comparing the evening news on ABC, CBS, and NBC during roughly similar weeks in April twenty years apart, in 1976 and 1996, found that election news fell 900 percent, but science, other national, and lifestyle news all increased.[31] Although "hard-news" was still focused narrowly on federal government decisions, polices, and so forth, the percentage of "soft-news" as entertainment was growing.

As a final factor in what constituted news, Gans cited "significance for the past and future" as a criterion for news selection. Again, determining what is significant "for the past and future" relies substantially on a person's political, social, and religious values. With similar results to the Lichter study mentioned above, a 1980 Media Research survey of hundreds of editors, broadcasters, and publishers found that only 8 percent of the media elites attended church or synagogue regularly—compared to more than half of the American public—and that some 86 percent seldom or never attended church services. Almost 30 percent agreed with the statement that America needed a "complete restructuring" of its basic institutions; 49 percent said that the structure of our society caused people to feel alienated; and more than half thought the United States had contributed to Third World poverty.[32] When almost 61 percent of the voters selected Republican Richard Nixon in 1972, giving him every state except Massachusetts, 81 percent of the media voted for Democrat George McGovern.

Gans's extensive study of CBS, NBC, *Newsweek*, and *Time* from 1967 to 1975 suggested that journalists claimed to disdain ideology, with many seeing "ideology to be an obstacle to story selection and production."[33] He found that top editors and producers claimed ignorance of the political values held by colleagues, and that journalists did not share their politics with each other. Yet, showing evidence of blinders or hypocrisy, when asked to place their colleagues on a political continuum, journalists, editors, and producers came within 2 percent of accurately identifying their cohorts with the labels the individuals gave themselves. Even on the surface, the fact that any profession that claimed objectivity could produce a population that voted between 81 percent and 91 percent for the candidates of the Democratic Party suggests either a shocking malfunction in the hiring and promotion processes of the major news organizations, a self-delusion on the part of the elites, or a bald-faced fabrication. If true, this "objectivity" would suggest that, without knowing that their peers and subordinates were liberals, the news industry somehow managed to hire liberals over conservatives at a rate of seven to one.

ENTERTAINMENT AS NEWS

As hinted at above, there is some truth to the liberal criticism that corporate pressure for news to become more "entertaining" entrenched itself in the 1970s. Ron Powers, for example, lamented that "the biggest heist of the 1970s [was] the five o' clock news. The salesmen took it. They took it away from the journalists."[34] Of course, newspapers have always had to face sales realities, and either a customer or an advertiser had to pay for the publication. Trends in television news in the 1970s and early 1980s largely tracked the paths of three ABC employees, Roone Arledge, Geraldo Rivera, and Barbara Walters, each of whom in his or her own way moved the news business closer to entertainment.

Roone Arledge pioneered sports coverage at ABC, inventing *Monday Night Football*. His techniques of slow-motion, close-ups, and instant replays added to the drama of the game itself. More importantly, he joined three diverse personalities (Frank Gifford, Don Meredith, and Howard Cosell) in the announcing booth so that they could carry poor games. Arledge set the stage for other mainstream news anchors and reporters to "become" the news, and, at the same time, he helped make sports part of the mainstream news coverage.[35] Both Walters, who became a personality doing featured reports in 1980 with ABC's *20/20* television news magazine, and Geraldo Rivera, who (along with Morton Downey, Jr.) introduced "shock," or "reality," television that appealed to raw emotion, brought new emphasis to the face in front of the camera. Walters, especially, debunked the long-held notion that only the young could attract viewers. Walters, who gained a reputation for asking softball questions, was middle-aged by the time she hit her peak in television.

Rivera, who also worked on *20/20* before a dispute over details of Marilyn Monroe's sexual relationships with the Kennedys led to his departure, merged "tabloid journalism" with news. Half-Jewish, half–Puerto Rican, Rivera was raised on Long Island and educated at Brooklyn Law School, and he practiced as a storefront attorney before joining WABC in 1968. Contrasting himself with the anonymous reporter who merely writes the story, Rivera put himself in the middle of his stories, some of which exposed shocking details of government or corporate corruption. Rivera perfected "ambush journalism," and willingly took big risks. (Once he staged a much-ballyhooed opening of Al Capone's "vault," with no idea what was inside. The vault was empty.) After a stint with his own "trash talk" show, featuring every type of outrageous character, Rivera eventually landed with Fox News, where he covered combat in Afghanistan and Iraq before he inadvertently revealed the location of a combat unit, causing his removal from the front.[36]

Only slightly less influential than Arledge, Walters, and Rivera was Don Hewitt, who conceived of an alternative to the traditional documentary that would be broken up into three 15-minute segments. (This idea, with only slight variations, was soon adapted to television dramas and comedies in such shows as *The Love Boat*, *Hotel*, *Fantasy Island*, and *Hill Street Blues*, where three or four story lines, each receiving an equal amount of time, were interwoven.) Hewitt balanced a "hard-hitting," investigative journalism piece with lighter fare, such as a celebrity interview or humorous segment. According to one history of television broadcasting, "*60 Minutes* . . . demonstrated that television journalism could be massively profitable," "cast reporters as the protagonists in . . . minidramas," "accelerated the demise of the hour-long, single-subject television documentary," and "introduced effective and dramatic techniques in editing and investigative reporting."[37] Although the program, which debuted in 1968, struggled against traditional television dramas, it found a viable time slot on Sundays at 6:00 p.m., then, some time later, 7:00 p.m., until it finally led all shows in that time slot in 1978.

One of the techniques involved the use, and abuse, of the interview. If Hewitt or his segment directors wanted to make someone look bad, they did an extreme close-up that accentuated facial flaws and revealed the sweat from the lighting; but if they wanted to soften the image of the interviewee, they used longer shots that made the person more human. CBS's "unbiased" interviewers—Mike Wallace, Harry Reasoner, Roger Mudd, Ed Bradley, and Morley Safer—were only shown in their best moments, when they were in control of the interview. This led to the introduction of another new technique, which involved employing new interview footage with a subject interspersed with film of the location shot after the event to "place" the person back in the context of the event. Although Rivera perfected it, it was *60 Minutes* that pioneered "ambush journalism," which surprised principals involved in the issue (a government or military official, for example, or a business leader) when they had not had a chance to review the questions or think about the answers. Supposedly this got real answers, but in fact, it constituted an underhanded attempt at demonizing otherwise ethical or capable people who did not think fast on their feet. Although the program routinely ambushed *safe* small-time business criminals and white collar criminals, it seldom went after murderers, dope pushers, or organized crime figures. Each segment "starred" the correspondent, accentuating the trend of "journalist-as-personality." Some reporters objected to this practice.

Meredith Vieira, for example, "hated being the center of a story and purposefully kept herself out" of segments, to the chagrin of the producers.[38] Most correspondents, however, appeared to relish their starring roles.

Increasingly, the "cheater-gets-caught" theme dominated *60 Minutes*, although, as newsman Sander Vanocur of NBC aptly observed, the major themes of *60 Minutes* or any other news "magazine" consisted of "only a limited number of plots—'Black versus White,' 'War is Hell,' 'America is Falling Apart,' 'Man against the Elements,' 'The Generation Gap,' etc.— which we seem to be constantly redoing with different casts of characters."[39] Notice the extent of the "plots" that a mainstream journalist thought possible: division among races and ages (but, apparently, not racial harmony or intergenerational cooperation); the evils of war (but not the tangible positive results from necessary wars); and the decline of America (but not America's successes). Here again is the mindset of the establishment journalist—the conspiracy of shared values—that what mattered was not progress but lack thereof; not the success of the large majority, but the failures of a few; and not the necessity of a particular conflict but the uselessness of conflict in general. In short, it returned to the issue of "What makes news the 'news'?" To so many journalists, the only news worth reporting was bad news, and for that reason, the media thought Watergate was its salvation. Instead, it was the beginning of a quagmire.

THE CARTER MALAISE

Watergate accelerated the momentous changes in journalism after 1965; moreover, the media's sense of self-importance increased at the very time that the public's trust in journalism was decreasing. During this time, other changes were elevating the national news media to unparalleled levels of power in the political process, most notably changes in the rules of the political party process in which local machines and the state caucus lost influence, while political elites who had access to the national media benefited. In the Democratic Party, interest groups, particularly women, unions, and minorities, received guaranteed quotas at the national nominating convention, which, in turn, demanded that candidates for national office appease those groups. Whereas prior to 1970, local politicians who had built efficient machines and garnered local support could insist that the convention give the "favorite son" a speaking slot, and therefore free television exposure, now such slots were parceled out to the representatives of the interest groups, or, at least, those who purported to speak for them.

Political scientist Nelson Polsby astutely predicted that the rule changes would make the media the equal of the parties when it came to nominating presidents, and he said that show-business figures and rock stars would soon play a central role in presidential campaigning due to their public appeal and the demands for campaign cash.[40] Even before the curtains drew on Nixon's dark drama, an advisor to Georgia governor Jimmy Carter, Hamilton Jordan, recommended that Carter work immediately to generate "favorable stories in the national press."[41] National stories, he told Carter, "have to be carefully planned and planted," and he gave Carter a list of more than a dozen journalists whose favor he should curry, including Tom Wicker of the *New York Times* and Katherine Graham of the *Washington Post*.[42] Carter heeded Jordan's suggestion, inviting various journalists to his Georgia farm.

Although journalists would not admit their culpability in securing the nomination for McGovern in 1972, tacitly they took steps to ensure that any new Democratic candidate would not be as *overtly* liberal as the defeated South Dakotan. Consequently, a new feature of the 1976 campaign was a "media watch" section of reporters charged with keeping tabs on the performance of their colleagues: "We all did a little soul-searching after '72," noted Walter J. Pfister, Jr., of ABC, and "this year we wanted to make sure we didn't interfere with the process by our predictions."[43] We can speculate that what Pfister really means was "We wanted to make sure we didn't interfere with the process by our *biases*."

During the Democratic primary, journalists backed the icon of the Kennedy legacy, Ted Kennedy. Carter was too openly religious for their tastes, not liberal enough, and hardly in the style of JFK. But Kennedy had dug his own political grave with the Chappaquiddick incident, in which he plunged his car off a darkened bridge, resulting in the drowning death of a young campaign worker, Mary Jo Kopechne. Kennedy's actions immediately after the accident opened him to serious criticism. He apparently made no effort to rescue the woman, then he failed to notify police. Although Kennedy ran a brilliant campaign and came close, Chappaquiddick had done its damage.[44] Carter secured the nomination, followed by a narrow election victory over Gerald Ford, who had his own dull personality and the legacy of Nixon to overcome. But despite his sound policies of deregulating trucking, energy, and the airlines, Carter could not overcome the nation's high tax rates and increasing environmental and regulatory burdens on business, which by 1980 cost American enterprise $100 billion a year. Moreover, energy woes had returned, which further contributed to the business decline. Carter's response to these dismal signs was, in 1979, to blame the public in his "crisis of confidence" speech, better known as the "malaise" speech. This not only alienated the public, it soured what little of the press remained on his side, especially when he called for the resignations of all the major officials in his cabinet—the ultimate act of passing the buck.

After slashing spending on weapons and reducing readiness in the military, Carter had the bad luck of presiding when Muslim extremists overthrew the Shah of Iran and, viewing the United States as his ally, captured the U.S. Embassy there, holding 60 Americans hostage in Tehran. For the first time, television news linked a theme to near 24-hour-a-day programming. ABC news immediately sent a reporter from London to Tehran, who slipped inside the country just before the revolutionary forces shut down the airport. This provided ABC with regular late-night reports, which soon turned into *Nightline*, an hour-long news special every night hosted by Ted Koppel. Using the headline "The Crisis in Iran: America Held Hostage," the program attracted 12 million viewers at 11:30 at night and spiked up late-night average television viewing by about 4 million. Even Walter Cronkite adopted a new sign-off: "And that is how it was on [date], the [number] day of the hostages' captivity." By its daily presence, the hostage crisis reminded the public of the president's inability to find a solution. It "mushroomed, becoming a virtual fixation for the nation and its news organizations throughout much of the fourteen-month embassy siege."[45] Carter's efforts swung between futility and incompetence. Ironically, the hostage crisis deflected criticism from Carter's anemic record elsewhere and, temporarily, from the collapsing economy. As Robert Shogan, a reporter with *Newsweek* and the *Los Angeles Times*, pointed out, "The hostage crisis was the best campaign he [Carter] could devise" because it lowered expectations of Carter in the primaries.[46] After all, how could he campaign when he was absorbed with trying to release the hostages?

Carter's political team made a deliberate decision to move the president to the forefront of the hostage crisis. As one of his advisors, Hodding Carter, the assistant secretary of state for public affairs, noted, the image was "for there to be a very visibly concerned president who said in effect that the hostages' fate is a primary concern of the president of the United States."[47] President Carter later admitted, "It was an obsession with me," and he claimed that the publicity focused on the hostages made it more unlikely that any of them would be executed or tortured.[48] Such reasoning is, of course, absurd; for instance, despite great publicity, Daniel Pearl was murdered with great fanfare in 2001 by other Muslim radicals. Carter had personalized policy to the point that he became impotent. In essence, Carter was the exact opposite of Ronald Reagan, who was burdened by the plight of other hostages, but who publicly said little while covertly exploring alternatives for their release: Carter did little to actually effect their release, but publicly he spoke of them constantly. Thus the Iranians knew that by continuing to hold the hostages, they had the upper hand.

Carter's supporters blamed the media for goading him into military action, as if the mobs in front of Western cameramen outside the U.S. Embassy chanting, "Death to Carter," "Death to America" did not influence the public. Briefly, the old World War II patriotism returned. Robert Seigenthaler, an ABC vice president, snarled, "Here's [an American hostage] paraded in humiliating fashion. The hostage-takers were rubbing our noses in it—*and getting away with it!*"[49] And yet the American news media willingly stuck out their noses to be rubbed: The Iranian foreign minister Sadegh Gotzbadeh made the rounds of all the news talk shows, while behind the scenes he coached Iranian demonstrators on how to play to the cameras. Three reporters, including Mike Wallace, were granted interviews with the Ayatollah Khomeini, but whereas the Americans were accustomed to their game of "gotcha," they found the rules much different on foreign soil. Wallace's admission that the interview was "unsatisfactory" was an understatement: Khomeini used the presence of the three journalists to issue more demands.[50]

America Held Hostage was a watershed in media coverage of crises. Increasingly, journalists, stung by competition, found themselves turning a growing number of news events into "crises," and *America Held Hostage* provided a template for the media outlets to use when packaging and marketing a "crisis." Using a banner to lump together related, and even unrelated, stories to the hostage situation, ABC essentially waded into national security policy by pressing for negotiation over the release of hostages—a position that ran counter to the long-held American policy of refusing to deal with hijackers or other terrorists.

Although media coverage of the hostage crisis boosted Carter in the primaries, the issue doomed him in the national election, where voters perceived him as weak and unable to resolve the crisis. He experienced the single largest one-month drop in poll numbers since Gallup had begun polling. Worse, Carter drew as an opponent Ronald Reagan, a former actor and governor of California whose natural pleasantness insulated him from what would later be called "the politics of personal destruction." Pollster Pat Caddell later acknowledged the president's plight when he said, "The American people simply did not want Jimmy Carter to be their president if they could possibly avoid it. And so we had to find them a reason why they would be forced to keep him."[51] Carter's fate was sealed when a belated and bungled rescue attempt to free the hostages resulted in a desert disaster. Images of a burning helicopter and Iranians picking over the charred bodies of Americans flooded the airwaves. The commander-in-chief was seen as responsible—and worse, inept.

Meanwhile, Reagan was impossible to demonize in any serious way. He turned Carter's own 1976 campaign slogan, "Are you better off now than you were four years ago?" against him. The economy had gotten worse, with inflation rising at the same time that the nation plunged into a recession. Viewed by some as the perfect media candidate, Reagan's intellect and communication skills were vastly underestimated by his opponents. We know now that far from mumbling words penned by a speech writer, Reagan had developed a core conservatism largely on his own. He had used his time out of politics in the 1970s to refine it through hundreds of speeches and radio addresses he gave in several formats, collected in book form in *Reagan in His Own Hand*.[52] Instead of being a "script reader" as his critics charged, Reagan wrote the scripts! His ability to boil down complex issues to short statements, or sound bites, for television news baffled and irritated reporters, who felt they were being used, and his quips resonated with the public, thanks to his frequent direct appeals to common sense.

Despite press criticism of Carter, his advisors knew that journalists were comfortable with his liberalism. Reagan, on the other hand, posed a titanic threat, one far more serious than Nixon, who never embraced any coherent body of conservative thought. In many ways, Nixon was scarcely less liberal than Johnson, and it was under Nixon that the Great Society programs grew dramatically. Reagan, however, was a true believer in conservatism. He would not only work to implement his programs if elected, but he had the communication skills to explain to the American people why conservative solutions were the better choice. Carter's political troops launched into attack mode, trying to depict Reagan as "a saber rattling, inexperienced ideologue who lacks the judgment and compassion needed to be President."[53] Their rhetoric quickly deteriorated into venomous demagoguery, accusing Reagan of being responsible for the "stirrings of hate" between the races and of dividing "black from white, Jew from Christian, North from South."

Although the press printed such comments, the public did not buy them. But the handwriting was on the wall: anticipating a Reagan victory, the *Washington Post* pontificated, "There is no way, given the nature of the two prime contenders for the office, that the country is going to elect a President in November who is especially gifted or suited to the conduct of the office."[54] A nasty *New York Times* wrote, "Someone chases a voter down an alley, points a gun to his head, and demands an answer: 'Carter or Reagan?' After thinking for a moment the voter replies, 'Shoot.'"[55] Had Carter been the likely winner, would journalists have engaged in such a preempting of the results that they anticipated?

A retrospective on media performance in the 1980 election praised the efforts of the media, claiming that it made campaign information available to the public.[56] Yet Robert Shogan, in his review of journalists and elections, complained that the media needed to do more than "make information available—it had to organize the flood of events, place them in perspective, and help in the decision-making."[57] In other words, the news media needed to obtain the electoral result journalists wanted. Scurrying to cover themselves from other media criticism, Jack Germond and Jules Witcover rationalized that "if what the candidate says about 'substance' is covered too little, and the tone of his campaign or his personal foibles is covered too much, it's because what he says isn't newsworthy, and what he is doing really is trying to tell the voters more about himself."[58]

Merely covering the events accurately—let alone discussing issues thoroughly—seemed a daunting task to journalists at the Republican Convention. Cronkite, whose reporting became increasingly suspect over the years, went public with the story of a "definite plan" for Reagan to name Gerald Ford as his vice-presidential candidate. When informed by a junior reporter, Leslie Stahl, that Ford in fact had decided not to offer himself as a nominee, Cronkite muttered, "It's hard to believe."[59] Not only did the liberal media miss the "co-presidency" story of Ford, but it also wrongly emphasized the so-called gender gap, in which Carter and Reagan won about the same percentage of women, but Reagan beat Carter among men, 55 percent to 36 percent. Four years later, Reagan crushed Walter Mondale among men by 25 percent. In another example of how the conspiracy of shared values shapes the reportorial perspectives of journalists, the gender gap could *only* apply to Republican weaknesses among female voters—never to Democrat weaknesses with male voters.

Meanwhile, the hostages were released and arrived home almost simultaneously with Reagan's inaugural. Tom Sipos, working at liberal Channel L Working Group in New York, recalled the celebrations in New York City as the hostages were released. When he entered the studio, another journalist asked him what the hoopla was about. "The return of the American hostages, " Sipos replied. "You mean," said the other journalist in all seriousness, "the return of the American spies."[60]

RONALD REAGAN DEFIES THE MEDIA

Although the news media elites hated Nixon, some reporters did find it difficult to maintain the same level of personal animosity against Ronald Reagan, who seemed to genuinely like everyone. During the 1980 campaign, as was then common practice, the media blamed the public for electing Reagan. Democrats "came to believe that the public . . . did not seem to want to pay attention."[61] Reporters complained about lack of access to Reagan: "On Air Force One," Robert Shogan observed, "the eleven-member press pool was seated in the rear, well behind Reagan, and relied on briefings from press secretary [Larry] Speakes."[62] One anecdote on the objectivity of such journalists stands out.

During the 1981 assassination attempt on the president, who was shot through the lung, Secret Service agents whisked Reagan off to George Washington University Hospital, where he underwent surgery, but not before Nancy Reagan got to his bedside and a reporter heard him joke, "Honey, I forgot to duck." Just before the doctors put Reagan under anesthesia, he again quipped, "I hope you're all Republicans." Upon regaining consciousness, he wrote a light-hearted note to the doctors: "All in all, I'd rather be in Philadelphia." These comments leaked out to the public, engendering great affection for the stricken president. In direct contrast, Thomas Sipos, then an intern at CLWG television station at New York University, recalled that *the day Reagan was shot the newsroom erupted in cheers.* One staffer laughed about Reagan "wanting to keep his war wounds."[63] This is just another example of the divide between journalists and the public they pretend to serve.

Many in the administration thought the hostility of journalists was obvious. Secretary of State George Schultz noted that during the 1983 liberation of Grenada from Cuban invaders, "It seems as though the reporters were always against us. And so they're always seeking to report something that's going to screw things up."[64] When American troops drove the communists out, major media outlets were shocked to learn that despite their editorials against the invasion, and the journalists' claims to represent the view of most Americans, by their own admission the media's mail rooms were flooded with letters decrying their positions and expressing support for President Reagan. NBC, CBS, and ABC reported their mail running between five-to-one and nine-to-one in favor of Reagan's actions, despite their hostile coverage of the event.[65] Certainly in this case the public correctly perceived that the media had an agenda: editorial page editor Max Frankel of the *New York Times* glumly noted that some in the public assumed at the outset that "the press wanted to get in [to Grenada] not to witness the invasion on behalf of the people but to sabotage it."[66]

Reagan did not complain about press bias, but instead made an "end run" around the media. He went straight to the American public with speeches and public appearances. As he did, polls increasingly showed the press's credibility diminishing, while Reagan's popularity rose. This only infuriated journalists more. James Reston of the *New York Times* complained, "Not since the days of H. L. Mencken have so many reporters written so much or so well about the shortcomings of the President and influenced so few voters."[67] Note the implied *expectation* that the public would agree. Elizabeth Drew attempted to disparage and minimize Reagan's ability to connect with the public over the heads of the media by calling it "the Presidency as theater."[68] Politics, she said, was like show business: "You have a hell of an opening, coast for awhile, and then have a hell of a close."[69] In fact, the journalists' own myth now came back to haunt them. If Reagan was a B-movie actor, how did his "performance" suddenly soar to such new heights that the American public was constantly fooled? But if he wasn't acting, then it meant that the public actually agreed with his policies.

Without question, Reagan's team understood better than any previous president the importance of the camera. Since the press had to cover major presidential speeches, the location and setting of those speeches was critical, leading Joseph Angotti, a political director at NBC, to complain, "If Ronald Reagan makes a speech in front of the Statue of Liberty, and the speech has news in it, there is no way we can show Reagan the news, often forgetting that the slightest detail could result in death and carnage at the front. When the *New York Tribune* revealed where Gen. William Sherman's forces were rendezvousing with their supply vessels, a Confederate reader of the *Tribune*—Gen. William J. Hardee—learned of Sherman's location and attacked Union forces there. It wasn't the first time such a leak had occurred: Robert E. Lee learned of the movements of Gen. Ambrose Burnside from the pages of the *New York Daily News*, and on another occasion Lee withdrew from Richmond based on a *Philadelphia Inquirer* report about the location of McClellan's forces.[16]

The assassination of Lincoln proved the press event of the century. It arguably reached proportionally as many people as did Kennedy's assassination a hundred years later, with papers from Boston to San Francisco carrying the news in less than 12 hours.[17] Many assassination stories featured the inverted-pyramid style for the first time in at least four New York papers: the *Sun, Post, Times,* and *Tribune.* Lincoln's assassination increased the telegraph's influence as a tool of the news, further shaping conformity to the news.

The impact of the war and the influence of the wire services transformed journalistic styles and introduced a powerful emphasis on fact.[18] By 1866, Lawrence Gobright, the AP's Washington agent, concluded, "My business is merely to communicate facts. My instructions do not allow me to make any comments upon the facts which I communicate. . . . My dispatches are merely dry matters of facts and detail."[19] Nevertheless, the transition from a partisan press to an objective press was anything but complete: in the decade after the Civil War, objective stories still made up only about 40 percent of all news articles, with that share rising to more than 66 percent by 1900.[20]

THE ROLE OF INCREASED PROFIT SEEKING AND COMPETITION

As papers received less support from political parties, they had to earn their living in the marketplace; thus, a commercialized news business, oriented toward profit, sought to offend as few readers as possible. One editor likened a newspaper to a department store, which gave readers what they wanted, "just as the merchant gave his customers calico if they want[ed] it instead of silk."[21]

Major papers started to adopt these changes, but the new journalism was particularly noticeable in the penny presses, which emphasized business, replete with topics as varied as sports, local-interest issues, social news, and obituaries. Penny presses reduced space allocated to political news as publishers appealed to wider audiences. If there were editorials, they were separated from news, marking a sharp departure from antebellum journalism. "Pennys" virtually founded the working-class press, removing journalism from the hands of the elites by putting the cost of cal order, and that the "inverted-pyramid" style of presenting information, which began with a central fact (Union Army victory, for example) then moved to particulars (who, what, when, where, why), did not really emerge until after the war. However, developments in journalism on both sides of the conflict support the first interpretation. In the Confederacy, for example, John Thrasher, the superintendent of the Press Association of the Confederate States of America, instructed his association's reporters to submit clear and concisely written telegraphic stories, free of opinion or commentary. [10] Thrasher insisted correspondents eliminate extraneous words and "see where you can use one word to express what you have put in two or three." [11] He provided an example in which he italicized the words to be omitted:

> OKALONA, April 25—Our cavalry engaged *the* enemy yesterday at Birmingham. *The* fight lasted 2 1/2 hours. *The* enemy *were* completely routed, *with* 15 killed *and a* large number wounded. Col. Hatch *of the* 2d Iowa cavalry was seen *to* fall from his horse, which ran into *our* lines and was captured. Our loss *was* one killed and twenty wounded. *The* destruction of *the* bridge prevented pursuit. [12]

Lacking a press association, the Union government placed authority over battlefield reporting under the Department of War, which, in the East, was controlled almost exclusively by Gen. George B. McClellan. Soon after Edwin Stanton replaced Simon Cameron as war secretary in 1862, Stanton reviewed the flow of information and concluded that the Union cause was not aided by McClellan's control of most telegraphic dispatches from the front. Stanton received authorization from Lincoln to have total control of the telegraphs, and within two weeks, McClellan's personal telegraph office was dismantled and all lines routed through Stanton's office. [13] This not only removed a major anti-Lincoln editorial slant, but put Peter Watson, Stanton's close friend, in charge of press releases. Stanton reviewed daily reports, sending agents to sniff around telegraph bureaus, and ordering Charles Dana to spy on Gen. Ulysses Grant for signs of drunkenness or dereliction of duty. Lincoln, obsessed with the telegraphic reports from the front that rattled into Stanton's office, had his own chair there.

Stanton's dispatches, which papers disseminated as his "War Diary," often constituted the day's lead story. His terse, "facts-only" style, written in descending order of importance, helped establish the "inverted-pyramid" style and ran contrary to the chronological style still used by many reporters, which reserved the important facts for the end. [14] The lead, or the most important fact that the reader needed to know, always went in the headline, and from there "it was not a long distance to reserving the first paragraph of [the] stories . . . for the most newsworthy facts and then organizing supporting material in descending order of newsworthiness." [15] Journalists, however, did chafe at Stanton's control over

Control of the news was strict in the South, especially when it came to discussions of slavery. However, Lincoln's administration also censored a good deal of military news, especially troop dispositions, with War Secretary Edwin Stanton eventually taking control of the telegraphs and adeptly manipulating the war news. Most generals knew reporters could be dangerous foes (Napoleon, for instance, once said that one hostile editor was worth 1,000 men). Printed reports, however innocent appearing, might yield valuable gems to the enemy and result in battlefield deaths. Some journalists, however, did not aim even for accuracy: publisher Wilbur Storey told his reporters, "Telegraph fully all the news you can get and when there is no news send rumors."[3] Union General Henry Halleck denied reporters access to his camps, and his colleague, General Benjamin Butler, threatened to shoot one reporter. General George Meade, Union commander at Gettysburg, shipped a reporter out of his camp riding backward on a horse with a placard reading "Libeller of the Press."[4]

Although heavy handed with the press at first, Lincoln soon learned that unless papers were reporting specific military deployments, he was better off letting the journalists editorialize than fomenting the opposition that came from shutting a paper down. Papers should be left alone, he said, unless "they may be working *palpable* injury to the Military in your charge; and, in no other case will you interfere with the expression of opinion in any form, or allow it to be interfered with violently by others."[5]

THE TELEGRAPH AND "STRAIGHT NEWS"

Lincoln perceptively noticed that a shift toward straight news reporting gave the Associated Press (AP) out of New York a distinct advantage in giving the public what it wanted, as its writers already had pared their reports of excessive words and opinion. Better yet for Lincoln, without editorial comment, his actions received higher levels of public support. Thus, by its reporting style, the AP came as close to a White House press office as Lincoln could have hoped for.[6] It was not through administration pressure, though, that the AP had adopted its word economy, but rather, the AP had adapted to the technology of the telegraph, which "was superimposed on a news-gathering system that *already* placed a premium on apparent factual accuracy."[7] The telegraph replaced verbose writers, who embellished their stories, with "stringers" who submitted bare facts to minimize telegraph line charges.[8]

Some journalism historians claim that "the '*lead*' was war-born," meaning that the introduction, or news-lead, was introduced during the war and that this led to increased sales.[9] Others scholars maintain that well into the war, journalists still arranged their dispatches in chronologi-

TWO

Profits, Partisanship, and a War: The "Revolution in Journalism"

"Almost overnight," wrote L. Edward Carter of the Civil War, "it seemed that newspapers were quite different." The war contributed to the slow movement toward a more objective, fact-driven press—a "revolution in journalism."[1] War reporting occurred in relatively uncensored conditions, and the public's interest in combat actions required any profit-minded newspaper to drop partisan attacks and discuss actual events. Casualties, troop movements, and battlefield results became the most commonly written about subjects. Field reporters focused on the details of battle, the timing of events, and who was involved. Often newspapers' accuracy exceeded that of the scouts of both armies. Entire battle plans for Robert E. Lee's army and its movements were often published in Confederate papers, while Lee's spies learned from Northern papers who the new commanding general of the Union Army was at Gettysburg.

Whether reading of victory or defeat, the public gobbled up war news, paying good cash to satiate their hunger for hard news. Stories still featured an effusive 19th-century writing style, but the nature of the subject required writers to increasingly omit opinion. It did families little good to know how valiant each unit was; rather, they wanted to know was their son dead or alive? Did the 10th Indiana or Hampton's Legion see action? Readers craved accurate news, not sugar-coated fables: "The home front," noted Carter, "wanted unvarnished facts."[2] Certainly partisanship did not disappear, and at least one-third of the papers in New York—a hotbed of antiwar sentiment—were nevertheless viewed as pro-administration. Even those papers occasionally criticized Lincoln, though, and virtually every Northern city had an antiwar, or "Copperhead," paper.

without showing the statue behind him."[70] Moreover, the Reagan team anticipated, minimized, and circumvented journalistic framing by dictating coverage via the "line of the day," a concept developed by James Baker, the White House chief of staff. Baker reasoned that sound-bite-dependent media would be susceptible to well-designed phrases coming from the administration, and therefore he designed all speeches to contain lines that would get Reagan's position out. Reagan was the perfect president for this system. At home in front of crowds or cameras, the "Gipper" did not have to be "protected" from either venue.

Reporters were often only granted access to Reagan on the move, which was another masterful ploy by the president's team. On the one hand, it showed him constantly active and energetic, yet it limited follow-up questions from the press, allowing Reagan to good-naturedly grin, wave, and pretend not to hear. On the other hand, Reagan prepared for press conferences like few others. His staff would fire questions at him, try to trap him, and hand him small notes to remind him of answers they had discussed earlier. Mostly the notes consisted of mini-confidence boosters. Reagan rightly treated interaction with the press as combat, and he almost always came out on top.[71] He was so successful that House Speaker "Tip" O' Neill (D-MA) had the Congressional Research Service conduct a study of the fairness of Reagan's access to television, which concluded that coverage was not deliberately tilted toward the president, but that Reagan simply was a master.[72] On at least three occasions, the report found, Reagan's ability to appeal directly to the public shaped or changed policy, including a tax/budget vote and aid to El Salvador.

All this occurred even though mainstream press coverage still remained tilted against the president. Political scientist Doris Graber admitted that during the 1984 election the news media ran three "bad news" stories to every one "good news" story, and she puzzled over how Reagan remained in office under such a media storm. Graber concluded that the media could, after all, take credit: it had framed Reagan's re-election in terms of evaluating his performance in foreign policy and economic issues.[73] Perhaps it is difficult for Graber and other academics that the public, even faced with an unbalanced ration of bad news over good, *trusted* Reagan on both foreign and domestic policy because people saw the economic growth for themselves and knew intuitively that America was decisively winning the Cold War.

Most analysis of journalistic performance between 1980 and 1988 cleverly glosses over the press's role in attempting to discredit Reagan based on his age. Ann Coulter's *Slander* reviews the "coincidental" number of age-related articles that appeared when Reagan's election became a political possibility.[74] Consider that when liberals attacked Reagan's age in a number of editorials—for example, with one *Washington Post* writer saying Reagan was "not dumb but—well, 73 years old"—in the 10 months before the election, major articles on senility conveniently appeared in

Newsweek, Time, Ladies ' Home Journal, and *U.S. News & World Report.*[75] In one burst, opportunely arranged around the same time as the media's attack on Reagan's age, major magazines published more articles on senility than a LexisNexis search turned up during the entire last quarter of the 20th century in the same number of magazines.[76]

When age or competence did not stick as media criticisms, journalists appeared to be handed a loaded gun in the form of the Iran-Contra investigation. Reagan had unsuccessfully petitioned Congress for funds to support the Nicaraguan anticommunists fighting the communist Ortega government there. This policy intersected with ongoing negotiations to free hostages held by Iranian militants. Reagan took a personal interest in the hostages, and his subordinate, Adm. John Poindexter, approved a plan (which he kept from Reagan) to exchange arms for the hostages, in the process generating substantial money that would be funneled to the Contras, thus violating both the Boland Amendment, which limits a president's war-making powers, and the pledge not to negotiate with terrorists. When Democrats learned of the exchange, they held hearings, giving immunity to Marine Col. Oliver North, who had personally supervised the fund transfers, before learning what testimony he would give. North took full responsibility, refused to implicate Reagan, and made himself into a highly sympathetic public figure in the process, despite the print media's spin. The *Miami Herald* leaked government documents supposedly establishing a scheme for martial law—a story North called "not only wrong, but offensive." Press coverage of Iran-Contra, North concluded, was "bombastic and outrageous."[77]

Typically, subsequent journalism scholars blamed the public for failing to hold Reagan accountable. As Lois Liebovich wrote, "After several months, the public became bored with the story," and maintained, "Iran-Contra was complicated." Even "reporters who unflaggingly attempted to uncover the truth about Iran-Contra met with a bored or disinterested public response."[78] Lest anyone wonder about Liebovich's politics, she stated, "A careful examination of the Reagan legacy suggests that domestic policies were miserable failures and foreign policy had been largely driven by covert activities or unfolding events over which Reagan had no control."[79] The creation of 14 million net new jobs, the reduction of the unemployment rate by more than 3 percent, the explosion of new corporate start-ups, the reduction of double-digit inflation levels to near zero, the liberation of Grenada, and the quick response to Khaddafi's terrorism—these domestic and foreign policies were "miserable failures"? This is yet another example of how the conspiracy of shared values shapes the perceptions of reporters.

The anger over the public's unwillingness to dislike Reagan fueled an ongoing campaign to convince people that the economic growth they saw right in front of their eyes—14 million net new jobs; a rising standard of living; continued deregulation of airlines, trucking, and other services that lowered prices and increased access dramatically—was a mirage. This revisionist campaign, which began during the Reagan administration and accelerated in the Bush years, was exemplified by an excerpted series in the *Philadelphia Inquirer* of a book by Donald Bartlett and James Steele called *America: What Went Wrong?*[80] Bartlett and Steele complained that no one was "looking after" the middle class, and that the daily life of Americans was worse in areas such as health care, pensions, and foreign competition. Their "gloomster" premise, noted Jack Fuller, fit perfectly with the news-media template of the Reagan years, regardless of the facts, and did not "live up to the discipline of intellectual honesty" demanded of good reporting.[81] But the bias of the *Inquirer* was even more obviously evident than that: Can anyone imagine a major paper running a feature article during a Republican administration with the headline "America: What's Going Right?" an article that praises the administration's policies? The media's ongoing attempt to rewrite the history of the 1980s remains an enormous hurdle to understanding sound public policy.

ALL NEWS, ALL THE TIME

Just as Ronald Reagan was vanquishing Jimmy Carter, a revolution in television news quietly occurred when Atlanta radio station and Atlanta Braves baseball team owner Ted Turner founded the Cable News Network (CNN) as the nation's first 24-hour television news service. It "profoundly changed the character of American TV news," observed media critic Steve Barkin.[82] Major broadcast competitors' news divisions could not match CNN's instant coverage of breaking news stories. CNN's chief disadvantage was that when there was no breaking news, the network was saddled with a drone of old information, spiced up with a few "experts." Thus it had to increasingly "make news" out of criminal court cases, scandals, accidents, and polls.[83]

CNN attained a certain level of "journalistic maturity" in May 1989 when its cameras featured live coverage from Tiananmen Square in Beijing during a Sino-Soviet summit. Anchor Bernard Shaw and four correspondents covered a massive protest that erupted as mostly young Chinese demanded civil liberties. Protestors carried with them a paper-mache model of the Statue of Liberty, and they continued to march in defiance of martial law as tanks rolled into the streets. CNN managed to continue its live coverage until the Chinese pulled the plug, but the images brought the network a twentyfold increase in ratings.[84]

For all its innovation, CNN soon adopted the leftward bias of the established mainstream media. The network featured a lineup of liberal anchors such as Shaw, partisan poll-analysts like William Schneider, and the host of *Inside Politics*, Judy Woodruff, whose countenance instantly told the viewer on any election night whether Democrats were winning or losing. CNN went over the line with many viewers, however, with its coverage of the Gulf War in 1991, when its reporter, Peter Arnett, consistently delivered front-line reports that seemed designed to bolster Iraqi morale. The dilemma for an American citizen interested in the news was that CNN had the cameras, but to see the pictures, one had to suffer through Arnett or one of the other liberal anchors. Reagan escaped most of the bias at CNN through simple timing: the network had not grown sufficiently in his eight years to influence viewers. But CNN disliked his successor, George H. W. Bush, and the partisanship grew more obvious over time.

A more accurate "all news, all the time" station appeared in 1979, when the House began televising hearings. This was followed by the Senate in 1986, whereupon all House and Senate sessions were broadcast by C-SPAN (Cable Satellite Public Affairs Network). C-SPAN shaped politics every bit as much as the early partisan papers did, although in a different way. House "five-minute speeches," in which representatives received five minutes to speak on any topic every night, led to speeches made to virtually empty chambers. Since no one was listening except a few of the most die-hard constituents, C-SPAN encouraged some House members to say the most outrageous and sometimes false things, aware that no one was listening.

BRIEF CASE STUDY: CHRISTIAN BASHING

CNN extended another trend in American journalism, which was the ostracization of mainstream Christianity from the news. Reagan's election had boosted so-called fundamentalist Christians, and he had received the support of several conservative Christian groups. In that sense, Reagan threatened liberals (and, it turned out, journalists) by his conviction of the rightness of his cause, the same self-assuredness that Rush Limbaugh would soon demonstrate. In each case, though, there was more to it than merely confidence. Believing in the rightness of a cause implies there is a right side in which to believe and, by nature, a wrong to oppose. For Reagan to call the USSR the "evil empire," as he did in a March 1983 speech, not only clearly separated him from the "genteel" and "sophisticated" elites, but lent a certain religious component to his Cold War rhetoric.[85]

Journalists had become increasingly secular since the end of the Civil War, and while many influential Christian presses still published magazines, the number of daily or weekly newspapers with any denominational affiliation had dropped steadily. By the 1970s, religion was confined almost exclusively to the back pages of the local paper, usually just ahead of the obituaries or the want ads. At issue was the recurring problem for journalists: balance. Since they could not be fair and balanced by presenting all Protestant denominations' views, or even balance Jewish, Catholic, and Protestant coverage, reporters and editors simply abandoned religion as a topic. Coverage devolved to a certain logic: "Who is to say who is right or who is wrong?"

Had reporting merely stayed there, it would have been an injustice, but at least journalists would not have chosen sides. As it turned out, however, some denominations came under far more attack than others for their views on marriage, sin, homosexuality, evolution, and alcohol. Evangelicals, but especially fundamentalists (those who hold that the Bible is the revealed, inerrant word of God, and that it speaks clearly on these issues), proved easy targets for reporters, whose single-sentence quotation style made it impossible to present an answer to hostile questions that did not sound narrow-minded or unfeeling. The common approach was to ask a fundamentalist minister or layman a question based on the most extreme case, such as "Do you oppose abortion in the case of incest?" "What if a husband is unfaithful or abusive to his wife?" or "Is divorce always wrong?" Answers to such questions demand a context of the broader scope of Christian teachings and do not lend themselves to simple sound-bite answers for the six o'clock news. As they did with all other issues, journalists framed fundamentalist Christians by controlling the context.[86] Studies have shown that coverage of fundamentalist Christians was noticeably negative during the 1980s and 1990s, and these trends have only continued into the 21st century.[87]

WILLIE HORTON AND BEETLE BAILEY

Reagan's successor, George H. W. Bush, campaigned as a full-fledged "Reaganite," complete with promises to keep taxes low and national defense strong. Bush's opponent in the general election, the liberal governor of Massachusetts Michael Dukakis, provided all the ammunition Bush needed to win. Dukakis, trying to shore up his image as strong on national security, visited a tank factory and was photographed with his small head, ensconced in a giant tanker's helmet, peeping out of the hatch of the tank. He was promptly dubbed "Beetle Bailey." Then Bush, with the deft assistance of his strategist Lee Atwater, emphasized Dukakis's gubernatorial record of vetoing a law requiring teachers to lead their classes in the Pledge of Allegiance and his endorsement of a furlough system that released a convicted rapist named Willie Horton back into the community. While on release, Horton nearly killed one man and raped his former girlfriend before being captured. Horton, who was black, became Atwater's poster boy for the ills of the Dukakis campaign. Journalists took umbrage at Bush's use of the ad, yet those journalists covering the campaign routinely failed to notice that while the "Willie Horton ad" never used Willie Horton's name, someone else had: a Democratic candidate named Al Gore. Not only had Gore raised the furlough issue in April, but the largest-circulation magazine in the world, *Reader's Digest*, did its own Horton story in July. In fact, conservatives were distributing a Pulitzer-prize winning *Lawrence Eagle-Tribune* series on Horton all over the country.[88]

Whether the "Willie Horton ad" had the impact that either Bush supporters or critics claimed, Dukakis's personal appeal neared zero. His performance in the debate was abysmal, especially when Bernard Shaw asked him a hypothetical question: "Governor, if your wife were raped and murdered, would you favor an irrevocable death penalty for the killer?" Dukakis rambled about his opposition to capital punishment, when Americans were looking for the fire of a leader who would say, "I'd try to kill him myself." Yet rather than being upset at Dukakis's inane answer, the media was irate with Shaw. Walter Goodman called his question "repulsive."[89] In fact, Shaw had given Dukakis a magnificent hanging curve ball with which the candidate could demonstrate his emotions, his toughness, and his humanity. Instead, Dukakis's lame reply crushed his momentum.

The press also did its best to make the election about Iran-Contra, and a January 25, 1988, *CBS Evening News* interview with Dan Rather set the stage to drill the nominee about his part in the arms-for-hostages deal. Rather ended the interview with a string of accusations, but instead of intimidating Bush, Rather inadvertently shored up one of Bush's perceived weaknesses—the notion that he was a "wimp" and lacked fire. Bush's responses, even turning the tables on Rather by bringing up the reporter's recent seven-minute walkout of his news program (leaving the show with empty air), proved to many voters that Bush had fight in him. Afterward, writer Mary McGrory whined that Rather "has probably nominated the Republican candidate and may even have elected the next president."[90]

Even while grumbling about the inability of the press to "expose" Bush, journalists such as Richard Harwood, of the *Washington Post*, tried to dismiss notions that the press could influence the electorate by claiming that better coverage would only tell voters "what to think about," not how to vote.[91] Harwood insisted that "the press should set the agenda," a staggering statement if one subscribes to the view that the *people* should set the agenda. Repeatedly, consistently, and overwhelmingly, journalists missed the point by believing that if they merely framed the issues "the right way," the public would swallow their views. It simply never dawned on them that no matter how clearly reporters presented their own agenda, disguised by their framing of issues, voters usually had much different ideas about how the world worked and about how their political system should operate.

In 1992, the press had its chance at revenge on Bush. The nation had suffered a mild recession, yet had already started to rebound when the press began its drumbeat of negative news about jobs, layoffs, and — the new corporate word — "downsizing." Moreover, for the first time since Kennedy, the press had a young-appearing, young-acting Democratic candidate, Bill Clinton of Arkansas. Journalists would do their best to ensure his victory, forgetting the old adage about getting what you wish for.

Before looking more closely at the relationship between the press and the Clinton presidency (chapter 9), there are a few items that deserve our attention, notably, the role of polling (chapter 6), the role of the Internet and alternate reporting (chapter 7), and journalistic values and biases (chapter 8).

NOTES

1. Rick Stearns, a McGovern campaign official, quoted in Shogan, 66.
2. Frankel, quoted in Robert Shogan, *Bad News: Where the Press Goes Wrong in the Making of the President* (Chicago: Ivan R. Dee, Publisher, 2001), 66.
3. For material on conspiracies, see Mark Fenster, *Conspiracy Theories: Secrecy and Power in American Culture* (Minneapolis: University of Minnesota Press, 1999); Richard Hofstadter, *The Paranoid Style in American Politics* (Cambridge, MA: Harvard, 1965); Gordon S. Wood, "Conspiracy and the Paranoid Style: Causality and Deceit in the Eighteenth Century," *William and Mary Quarterly*, 39 (1982), 401–441; Richard O. Curry and Thomas M. Brown, eds., *Conspiracy: The Fear of Subversion in American History* (New York: Holt, Rinehart and Winston, 1972); and C. F. Graumann and Serge Moscovici, eds., *Changing Conception of Conspiracy Theory* (New York: Springer-Verlag, 1987).
4. Jonathan Vankin and John Whalen, *The 60 Greatest Conspiracies of All Time* (Seacacus, NJ: Carol Publishing, 1996); Jonathan Vankin, *Conspiracies, Coverups, and Crimes* (New York: Paragon House, 1991).
5. Jim A. Kuypers, "Framing Analysis," in Jim A. Kuypers, ed., *Rhetorical Criticism: Perspectives in Action* (Lanham, MD: Lexington Books, 2009), 182.
6. Peter A. Kerr and Patricia May, "Newspaper Coverage of Fundamentalist Christians, 1980–2000," *Journalism and Mass Communications Quarterly*, 79 (Spring 2002), 54–72.
7. Jim A. Kuypers, *Press Bias and Politics: How the Media Frame Controversial Issues* (Westport, CT: Praeger, 2002), 198.
8. Herbert J. Gans, *Deciding What's News: A Study of* CBS Evening News, NBC Nightly News, Newsweek *and* Time (New York: Pantheon Books, 1979), 16.
9. Gans, 147.
10. Noam Chomsky, "What Makes Mainstream Media Mainstream, from a Talk at Z Media Institute, June 1997, *Z Magazine*, June 1997, http://saturn.he.net/~danger/freepnet/scripts/shownote.php?LUkQyqri, 1879.
11. Chomsky.
12. Ann Coulter, *Slander* (New York: Crown, 2002), 166–167, conducted a LexisNexis search for these terms.
13. David S. Broder, "New Militants," *Washington Post*, April 5, 1981.
14. David M. Alpern, "The New Right: Betrayed?" *Newsweek*, February 7, 1983.
15. Charlotte Saikowski, "Religious Right Throws Its Weight Behind Reagan Reelection Effort," *Christian Science Monitor*, October 1984.
16. Gans, 155–156.

17. Jack Fuller, *News Values* (Chicago: University of Chicago Press, 1996), 34–35.

18. Matthew R. Kerbel, *If It Bleeds, It Leads: An Anatomy of Television News* (Boulder, CO: Westview, 2000).

19. Kerbel, 15–18.

20. Kerbel, 14.

21. Gans, 149.

22. Gans, 150.

23. Quoted in Gans, 149.

24. Gans, 151.

25. Joel Kotkin and David Friedman, "Clueless: Why the Elite Media Don't Understand America," *American Enterprise*, March/April 1998, 28–32, quotation on 29.

26. S. Rothman and S. R. Lichter, "Personality, Ideology, and Worldview: A Comparison of Media and Business Elites," *British Journal of Political Science* 15, no. 1 (1984), 43.

27. Reported by Brent Bozell III, "Media and Politics: Overcoming the Bias," Remarks given to the Union League Club (June 8, 2000). Figure on acceptance of homosexuality from "The People, the Press & Their Leaders," Pew Research Center for the People & the Press, May 1995.

28. Gans, 151. Emphasis mine.

29. CBS executive Ed Fouhy quoted in Steven Barkin, *American Television News* (Aramonk, NY: M.E. Sharpe, 2003), 81. See also Peter J. Boyer, *Who Killed CBS? The Undoing of America's Number One News Network* (New York: St. Martin's Press, 1988).

30. See "*Dateline NBC* Burns Media Credibility," *Washington Post*, February 23, 1993.

31. Barkin, 167.

32. Rothman and Lichter, 43.

33. Gans, 191.

34. Ron Powers, *The Newscasters: The News Business as Show Business* (New York: St. Martin's Press, 1977), 1.

35. Marc Gunther, *The House that Roone Built: The Inside Story of ABC News* (Boston: Little, Brown, 1994).

36. Geraldo Rivera with Daniel Paisner, *Exposing Myself* (New York: Bantam, 1991). Also see Neil Postman, *Amusing Ourselves to Death: Public Discourse in the Age of Show Business* (New York: Penguin, 1985).

37. Quoted in Barkin, 51.

38. Elsa Walsh, *Divided Lives: The Public and Private Struggles of Three Accomplished Women* (New York: Simon & Schuster, 1995), 67.

39. Vanocur quoted in Edward Jay Epstein, *News from Nowhere* (New York: Random House, 1973), 164–165.

40. Nelson Polsby, "The News Media as an Alternative to Party in the Presidential Election Process," in Robert A. Goodwin, ed., *Political Parties in the Eighties* (Washington, DC: American Enterprise Institute, 1980).

41. See Martin Schram, *Running for President 1976: The Carter Campaign* (New York: Stein and Day, 1977); and Jules Witcover, *Marathon: The Pursuit of the Presidency, 1972–1976* (New York: New American Library, 1977), 326.

42. Witcover, 326.

43. Shogan, 71.

44. Floyd Douglas Anderson, Andrew King, and Kevin McClure, "Kenneth Burke's Dramatic Form Criticism," in Jim A. Kuypers, ed., *Rhetorical Criticism: Perspectives in Action* (Lanham, MD; Lexington Books, 2009).

45. Robert J. Donovan and Raymond L. Scherer, *Unsilent Revolution: Television News and American Public Life, 1948–199* (Cambridge: Cambridge University Press, 1992), 142.

46. Shogan, 101.

47. Carter quoted in Hoard Husock and Pamela Varley, "Siege Mentality: ABC, the White House, and the Iran Hostage Crisis," Kennedy School of Government Case Program, Harvard University, 1988, 7.

48. Television interview with Carter, quoted in Donovan and Scherer, 145.

49. Quoted in Donovan and Scherer, 141.

50. Mike Wallace and Mary Paul Yates, *Close Encounters* (New York: William Morrow, 1984), 327.

51. Quoted in Shogan, 103.

52. Kiron K. Skinner, Annelise Anderson, and Martin Anderson, *Reagan in His Own Hand* (New York: Free Press, 2001).

53. Quoted in the *Los Angeles Times*, August 15, 1980.

54. Quoted in Shogan, 106; Anthony King, "How Not to Select Presidential Candidates," in Austin Ranney, ed., *The American Elections of 1980* (Washington, DC: American Enterprise Institute, 1980).

55. *New York Times*, October 26, 1980.

56. Jonathan Moore, ed., *The Campaign for President: 1980 in Retrospect* (Cambridge, MA: Ballinger, 1981).

57. Shogan, 107.

58. Jack W. Germond and Jules Witcover, *Blue Smoke and Mirrors: How Reagan Won and Why Carter Lost the Election of 1980* (New York: Viking, 1981), 264.

59. Jeff Greenfield, *The Real Campaign: How the Media Missed the Story of the 1980 Campaign* (New York: Summit, 1982), 63.

60. E-mail to Larry Schweikart from Thomas Sipos, September 16, 2003, used with permission.

61. Shogan, 125.

62. Shogan, 128.

63. E-mail to Larry Schweikart from Thomas M. Sipos, August 26, 2003; Thomas M. Sipos, "Media Cheered When Reagan Was Shot," www.freerepublic.com/focus/fr/594003/posts.

64. Quoted in Shogan, 127.

65. "Journalism Under Fire," *Time*, December 12, 1983.

66. Frankel quoted in Peter Stoler, *The War against the Press: Politics, Pressure and Intimidation in the 80s* (New York: Dodd, Mead and Company, 1986), 4. Apparently, the public was put off by the media's attacks on Reagan. NBC alone lost $50 million a year in a roaring economy, and from 1982 to 1987, the three networks saw their share of households that tuned in to watch their news drop from an 87 percent share to a 76 percent share. Worse, advertising revenues for all three networks dropped for the first time since the Nixon era. All of this occurred at a time when cable had only penetrated half of America's homes.

67. James Reston, "Reagan Beats the Press," *New York Times*, November 4, 1984.

68. Elizabeth Drew, "Letter from Washington," *New Yorker*, July 31, 1989.

69. James David Barber, "Reagan's Sheer Personal Likability Faces Its Sternest Test," *Washington Post*, January 20, 1981.

70. Quoted in Donovan and Scherer, 237.

71. See Donovan and Scherer, 190–194.

72. Denis Steven Rutkus, *President Reagan: The Opposition and Access to Network Airtime* (Washington, DC: Congressional Research Service, 1984).

73. Doris A. Graber, "Framing Election News Broadcasts: News Context and Its Impact on the 1984 Presidential Election," *Social Science Quarterly*, 68 (1987), 552–568.

74. Coulter, 127–132.

75. Coulter. 132.

76. Matt Clark, "The Doctors Examine Age," *Newsweek*, October 22, 1984; Evan Thomas, "Questions of Age and Competence; The President Seems Fit—But Is He Too Detached?" *Time*, October 22, 1984; Emma Elliot, "My Name Is Mrs. Simon," *Ladies Home Journal*, August 1984; "Today's Senior Citizens: 'Pioneers of New Golden Era,' Interview with Dr. Robert Butler, Geriatric Specialist," *U. S. News & World Report*, July

2, 1984 (compared to the only previous *U. S. News* article run eight years earlier, "How to Have a Longer Life and Enjoy It More, Interview with Dr. Robert N. Butler, Director, National Institute on Aging," *U. S. News & World Report*, July 12, 1976). See also the results of the LexisNexis searches cited in Coulter, notes 48–49.

77.   Alfonso Chardy, "Reagan Advisers Ran 'Secret Government,'" *Miami Herald*, July 5, 1987; Dave Lindorff, "Oliver's Martial Plan," *Village Voice*, July 21, 1987; Oliver L. North with William Novak, *Under Fire: An American Story* (New York: HarperCollins, 1991), 163–166.

78.   Louis W. Liebovich, *The Press and the Modern Presidency* (Westport, CT: Praeger, 1998), 140.

79.   Liebovich, 147.

80.   Donald L. Bartlett and James B. Steele, *America: What Went Wrong?* (Kansas City, MO: Andrews and McMeel, 1992).

81.   Fuller, 38.

82.   Barkin, 104.

83.   See Hank Whittemore, *CNN: The Inside Story* (Boston: Little, Brown, 1990); Porter Bibb, *It Aint' as Easy as It Looks: Ted Turner's Amazing Story* (New York: Crown, 1993); and Robert Goldberg and Gerald Jay Goldberg, *Citizen Turner: The Wild Rise of an American Tycoon* (New York: Harcourt Brace, 1995).

84.   Tom Rosenstiel, "How CNN Wrecked Television News," *New Republic*, August 22–29, 1994.

85.   See Thomas G. Goodnight, "Ronald Reagan's Re-formulation of the Rhetoric of War: Analysis of the 'Zero Option,' 'Evil Empire,' and 'Star Wars' Addresses,'" *Quarterly Journal of Speech* 72 (November 1986), 390–414.

86.   Peter A. Kerr and Patricia May, "Newspaper Coverage of Fundamentalist Christians, 1980–2000," *Journalism and Mass Communication Quarterly*, 79 (Spring 2002), 54–72.

87.   Kerr and May.

88.   See "Willie Horton Hilarity," Mediawatch, November 1992, http://secure. mediaresearch.org/news/mediawatch/1992/mw19921101jca.html.

89.   Walter Goodman, "Toward a Campaign of Substance in '92," *New York Times*, March 26, 1990.

90.   Mary McGrory, *Washington Post*, January 28, 1988.

91.   Richard Harwood, "The Press Should Set the Agenda," *Washington Post*, September 25, 1988.

SIX

Pushing Their Polls

Among the best illustrations of the media's template that there really *was* "no truth, only news" was its embrace of polling as news itself in the 1990s. On slow news days, a poll could stand alone as news. Polls only represent a snapshot of public opinion at any time: in the 1830s, Americans likely would have responded to a reasonably worded poll question on slavery by confirming that "while they personally disapproved of slavery, it should be legal." What polls do not represent is moral truth or fact at any time. The dictum "You can fool some of the people all of the time, and all of the people some of the time, but you can't fool all of the people all of the time" demonstrates well the danger of relying on the will of the majority at any given time. The concept that a fact is what a majority of people agree it is stands in sharp contrast to either scientific or moral constructs of fact. It embodies instead Emerson's comment that "the only good is what is after my own constitution."

Modern polls can be particularly destructive when commissioned by, or allied with, a media outlet that has an ideological agenda. In the 1980s, the *New York Times* began to poll with CBS, followed by the *Washington Post* with ABC. Even before, in 1976, CBS, NBC, and some newspapers began to use "precision journalism," in which they polled on issues and voter preferences so that, presumably, they would have a better idea as to what candidates and issues were "hot," and thus which ones to cover. Inevitably, the reporters' issues became the pollsters' issues, and framing became a polling tool just as it had become the tool of journalists. In polling, framing is even more important: everything depends on the wording of questions and the order in which questions are presented. For instance, a negative preamble such as "If x led to more children going hungry . . ." can provide the desired polling result. Introductory remarks can easily taint the polling results as well. For example, a question such as "The president's tax-cut proposal will add billions of dollars to the deficit. Do you favor or oppose this cut?" will certainly have a majority opposed to the tax cut. As with the framing of news stories, the wording of the polls often reveals clear methodological agendas, leading to the use of "hot-button" words or phrases that virtually ensure that whoever commissions the poll can claim they know what "the people want." Anytime a poll question includes a benefit without a cost, or a cost without a benefit, the findings are "predictable and almost meaningless," said Alice Rivlin, former Clinton budget director.[1] Polls commissioned by different sides of the voucher/school choice debate, for example, have arrived at diametrically opposite conclusions, and during the Clinton impeachment trial, polls showed that a majority of people thought perjury was an impeachable offense, and a majority thought the president had perjured himself—yet other polls showed that the public opposed impeachment.

During the 1980s, for the first time in history, polls themselves began to be treated as news items. This is partly attributable to the 24-hour-a-day news cycles that constantly needed new material to fill airtime. Whenever little genuine news existed, reporters could cover the latest poll that their news organization itself had commissioned. Perhaps more bluntly, when there was no news, they could make some up. To better stress the manipulated and manipulating nature of polls, I provide two somewhat extended examples: the Clinton administration, and the British manipulation of American polls circa World War II. Following this, we will look at some general examples of importance and examine some polling concerns from the 1990s through today.

TWO EXAMPLES: THE CLINTON PRESIDENCY AND THE BRITISH

By the 1990s and into the Clinton years, cooperation between news organizations and the polling industry raised suspicions that the media might be shaping polls to influence policy. Christopher Hitchens explained that the "polling business gives the patricians an idea of what the mob is thinking, and of how that thinking might be changed or, shall we say, 'shaped.'"[2] The conspiracy of shared values influenced the nature of what was reported. News polls tended to consistently favor progressive positions, often prompting an emotional rather than intellectual response; additionally, critics worried that polling led to an "obsession with salesmanship rather than governance."[3] They appeared to have a case when one considers the presidency of Bill Clinton.

Throughout the investigation of Clinton by Independent Counsel Kenneth Starr, and throughout the subsequent impeachment proceedings and Senate trial, the mainstream media ran weekly polls leading with the president's job-approval rating. Clinton's job approval consistently stayed above 65 percent, but the networks and major newspapers ignored or slighted other poll questions that showed Americans' positive personal opinion of the president as a role model, moral leader, or even potential business partner hovered at around 33 percent. The high job-approval poll numbers allowed Clinton apologists to saturate the airwaves with their reading of the data, namely, that the American people "do not what him removed from office over sex" as the Clinton team members nearly uniformly stated. CNN's political analyst and pollster, William Schneider, who had concocted many of the pro-Clinton polls, ran into the president at a White House reception in 1998. "I think I saved you," he informed Clinton.[4]

Dick Morris, Clinton's one-time personal political strategist, likely disagrees with Schneider, clearly thinking *he* saved Clinton. Clinton derived some of his obsession with polls from Morris, who was sensitive to criticism of this obsession and argued in his book *Behind the Oval Office* that Clinton did not use polling as a substitute for leadership but as "a tool for governing . . . to choose which of several of his current or contemplated positions were popular."[5] This is Morris-esque doublespeak, since he saw his use of polls as "a finely calibrated measurement of opinion."[6] At the height of the 1995 budget debate, for example, Clinton's pollsters surveyed every night, from seven in the evening until one the next morning. Even though polls showed strong dissatisfaction with entire segments of Clinton's budget, pollsters Mark Penn and Ed Schoen isolated a few specifics within the Republican budget that were unpopular, then launched a nationwide campaign based only on those issues.

Throughout this debate, the slanted polling using the Democrats' definitions to formulate questions provided the ammunition Clinton needed. For example, the Republican budget allowed Medicare, education, and other programs in question *to grow*, some at double the rate of inflation. Although they allowed the programs to grow, the Republicans had actually slowed their *rate of growth* and had not cut the actual program budgets. Even so, Clinton called this "cuts," and the journalists never questioned his use of the term (or anyone in the administration, who parroted it) for six full months, by which time the battle was over. Once Clinton got the press to accept the term "cuts," it was easy enough to get the *New York Times* to produce a slanted poll with the same terminology and, predictably, the desired results.

Another important but little-known example of polling manipulation shows that the historical record related to polling is not reassuring when it comes to instances of manipulation by interested parties. One of the most effective infiltrations of American polling organizations occurred just prior to World War II when British agents infiltrated most of the major polling firms.[7] Thomas Mahl's study of British covert operations produced some shocking revelations about the polling business, including a confession by a British agent, Hadley Cantril, who worked for Gallup, who admitted, "I have tried to influence poll results by suggesting issues and questions the vote on which I was fairly sure would be on the right side."[8]

British agents claimed they persuaded the Gallup organization to drop the results of polls that did not support aid to Britain, while analysis of 1939–1944 polls revealed that questions were routinely worded to yield results that supported Lend-Lease. British agents penetrated not only Gallup, but Roper, Market Analysts, and the National Opinion Research Center.[9] William Stephenson's famous book *A Man Called Intrepid* related a poll-rigging at a Moose Temple in Detroit in November 1941, wherein Stephenson commented that "great care was taken beforehand to make certain the poll results would turn out as desired."[10]

Another poll that should have alerted the media to the pollsters' bias involved Gallup's questioning of military-age men about whether they favored compulsory military service. An astonishing 81 percent said they did, at a time that congressional mail ran "overwhelmingly against conscription."[11] Another British agent, Francis Henson, bluntly stated that he helped write the polls.

As can be seen from these British examples and those from the Clinton years, polls are incredibly easy to manipulate to achieve desired ends. With this background, then, let us take a look at how the value of polls seeped into the awareness of politicians in America.

EXAMPLES OF IMPORTANCE: POLLS FOR THE PRESS AND POLITICIANS

By the 1960s, awareness of the power of polls had risen sharply among politicians. Good polling could save them from embarrassment and provide strategic information about which issues to emphasize. After Watergate, the link between polls and news became progressively clearer, and news organizations increasingly availed themselves of polling between 1973 and the 1990s. Magazines such as *Time*, *Newsweek*, and *U.S. News & World Report* utilized polling results as an integral part of their reporting in only 15–30 percent of their stories in 1973. By 1993, those percentages had leaped to 40–46 percent. Polling, in other words, accounted for almost half of the news.[12] Most major television news organizations allied with a major print and polling organization, leading to the NBC News/ *Wall Street Journal* poll, the ABC News/*Washington Post* poll, and the CBS News/*New York Times* poll.

This reality sharply contrasts with George Gallup's comment that "I've never seen one shred of evidence that polls affect voting behavior."[13] This is akin to large corporations saying that marketing does not affect purchasing behavior. Certainly Great Britain would not have devoted so many tight resources to American polls if she thought polls did not affect behavior. Ironically, Gallup's own poll played a critical role in solidifying the nomination of Richard Nixon over Nelson Rockefeller in 1968 after Rockefeller decided to focus all his campaign energy on persuading delegates to change their votes based on his ability to beat the Democrat Hubert Humphrey. Early polls had suggested Rockefeller could beat Humphrey but Nixon could not. But in the summer, a Gallup poll showed that Nixon and Rockefeller had switched positions, and that the former could beat Humphrey and Rockefeller could not. Having placed all his trust—and his ability to sway delegates—in the polls, Rockefeller died by them when they shifted.

By the 1980s, an irony presented itself. Although the public seemed infatuated with polls, most Americans also sensed that governing by polls stoked the coals of inherent dangers. An October 1988 poll (what else?) found that more than half of all Americans wanted a ban on the reporting of polls by news organizations in the last week of the presidential campaign. A similar NBC News/*Wall Street Journal* poll that year found that 63 percent thought that polls had too much influence on voters.[14] Reporter Robert Shogan, commenting on the abuse of polls showing that Democratic contender Michael Dukakis had substantial leads over Vice President George H. W. Bush, called this "one of the media's habitual failings—to report polls without explaining the limits on their significance."[15] It was not sufficient to merely state the margin of error of a poll; it was necessary to explain the overall "shallow and tenuous nature of voter attitudes."[16] One could almost say it was incumbent upon journalists to properly and accurately frame the poll numbers by providing meaningful context. In a sense, where George Gallup saw the political system as inherently elitist, stating that "polls constitute the most useful instrument of democracy ever devised," journalists increasingly fretted that polls might permit too much democracy unless the interpretation of polls by the press properly instructed public opinion.[17]

Even with these major reservations, the use (and abuse) of polling only grew: in the 1990s, polling on major issues occurred weekly, and during elections, the number of polls increased geometrically after 1980. Matthew Robinson notes that the Roper Center for Public Opinion Research counted 26 "horse race" polls in the 1980 election, 42 in 1988, 86 in 1992, and 136 by September 2000 with more than a month left in the election cycle.[18] Even before that, during the Clinton impeachment trials, poll results from one of the major news organizations appeared almost nightly. Between 1992 and 2008, the number of organizations conducting such polling tripled, and 491 polls were conducted during the 2008 election year.[19] Thus by the 2008 election, these numbers had grown at an amazing rate. Between January 2007 and the November election, the Project for Excellence in Journalism "examined 24,684 campaign stories. . . . In all, 58% of that coverage—the space studied in newspapers and online and time on television and radio—focused on the horse race, of which polling played a central role."[20]

A key difference between a biased news story and a biased poll is that the latter elicits an immediate response from the public, upon which people base political and marketing strategies. Getting the questions both accurate and reliable, therefore, becomes a central task for a pollster. It is essential to understand that the wording of any poll is critical, and completely objective wording is impossible. For example, in the debate over school vouchers, merely the use of the term "vouchers" biases the respondent negatively, while use of the term "parental choice" biases the respondent positively. Other "code phrases" easily bias the results. A CBS/*New York Times* poll asked the question about vouchers this way:

> Should parents get tax-funded vouchers they can use to help pay for tuition for their children to attend private or religious schools instead of public schools?

By including the term "tax-funded," the survey implied that tax dollars would go to help other peoples' children attend "private or religious" schools. The reality was that vouchers allowed people to use their own education tax dollars in a different way. Likewise, the phrase "instead of public schools" implied that such a plan would drain money from public schools—which was not necessarily the case if, in fact, competition forced the public schools to improve in quality.[21]

Pollsters well know that one way to achieve a positive result is to frame the question without any penalties, while including negative results automatically lowers the number of favorable responses. So with the same voucher question, another poll tried to bias the sample even more against school choice:

> Should parents get tax-funded vouchers even if that means public schools would receive less money?

Framing the question so that (1) vouchers were "tax-funded" and (2) public schools "would receive less money" was guaranteed to get an anti-voucher/anti-school choice response, which it did.[22] Similar wording regarding a missile defense system can be seen in the question, "Do you favor the United States *continuing to try to build* a missile defense system *in light of the fact* that $60 billion has already been spent on it?"[23] With this phrasing, the pollsters managed to rig the question three separate ways, in essence throwing in three conceptual zingers. First, the phrase "continuing to *try* to build" implies failure so far—rather than documented technical progress. As in all advanced systems, performance comes over time, and the more sophisticated the technology, the more gradual the improvement. Second, "in light of the fact," a qualifier, always elicits a higher negative response for a poll question. Third, the phrase "$60 billion has already been spent on it" again implies failure. Yet would anyone say, "Would you favor renewing your medical insurance next year in light of the fact that $75,000 has already been spent on it"? One phrase is irrelevant and unrelated to the other. In fact, with scientific research, the expenditure of $60 billion should be considered a positive, bringing the technology *closer* to fruition, but for a manipulative pollster, this phrase is a way to apply the kiss of death.[24]

Along these same lines, consider the wording of an ABC News/*Washington Post* poll of December 12–13, 1998, on the Clinton impeachment vote:

> The full House will vote on impeachment next week, and if the House impeaches Clinton, the Senate will decide whether he should be removed from office. Based on what you know, do you think Congress should or should not impeach Clinton and remove him from office?[25]

This poll stressed the worst possible outcome for Clinton—at the hands of the *Senate*—when purporting to ask a question about the actions of the *House.* If the person being polled missed it, the question used the phrase "removed [remove] . . . from office" not once, but twice. Naturally, many Americans view justice as a process rather than an immediate imposition of a sentence. An analogous question would be "Should O. J. Simpson be executed?" rather than "Do you think O. J. Simpson is guilty of murder?" Even Americans who thought O. J. Simpson was guilty would have been reluctant to leap to a sentence ahead of a verdict, yet that was exactly what the ABC poll asked of its respondents. When Zogby asked the question, he simply asked, "Should the House of Representatives vote 'yes' or 'no' to impeach the President and send him to trial in the Senate?" The phrase "and send him to trial," which accurately reflected the process of impeachment, implied a procedure of arriving at justice, reinforcing the image that Clinton would have his day in court. As might be expected, the wording made all the difference in the world. In the ABC poll, 61 percent opposed impeachment and removing Clinton from office, but in the Zogby poll, only 52 percent opposed impeachment.

However, there was yet another wording that produced a much different result. On December 10–11, *Newsweek* phrased the question this way:

> Which of the following do you think would be more damaging to our country and political system: having a trial in the U.S. Senate over the charges in the Lewinsky matter, OR, allowing President Clinton to finish his term with no official punishment for his behavior in the Lewinsky matter?

When phrased in this manner, a slight majority 41–39 percent, said that allowing Clinton to remain in office posed the greater harm. Moreover, while a majority disliked the option of forcing the president out, polls by Zogby began to peel away the veneer of public support for Clinton:

Now that the president has admitted to lying under oath in his testimony in the Paula Jones case, do you think he should consider leaving
office? [54–40 percent, yes]

If it turns out that the President encouraged anyone else to lie under
oath, do you think he should consider leaving office? [63–30 percent,
yes]

If it turns out that the President lied under oath in his testimony
before the grand jury, do you think he should consider leaving office?
[59–33 percent, yes].[26]

A CASE STUDY: USING COLUMBINE AND VIRGINIA TECH TO PROMOTE GUN CONTROL

Another flawed polling error is to conduct a survey immediately after a
major news event, which is precisely the scenario that emerged after the
Columbine shooting in 1999. Almost all major news stories carried a poll
about stricter gun-control measures, which were, of course, favored by
the media. Predictably, the "insta-poll" gave the journalists the answers
they sought. A *New York Times'* headline said, "The Politics of Guns:
Tilting Toward the Democrats," while the *Washington Post* chimed in,
"Littleton Alters the Landscape of Debate on Guns."[27] *Newsday* added,
"Gun Control Bolstered: Americans Want Tougher Laws, Poll Shows."[28]
The same occurred following the Virginia Tech massacre in April 2007.
Rasmussen found that "45% of American adults now say the country
needs stricter gun control laws while 37% disagree." Responsibly, Rasmussen also acknowledged the potentially tainted nature of the results:
"Rasmussen Reports will ask the same poll question again in a few weeks
to see whether the increased support for stricter laws is a temporary
reaction to the horrific news from Virginia or a lasting change."[29] Not all
polls were so conscientious. Trying to make hay out of the tragedy to
push their own antigun agenda, CBS and the *New York Times* released the
results of one of their insta-polls finding that 66 percent of Americans
thought that handgun sales should be more tightly controlled, although
noting that these "views are similar to those in the past."[30] The major
news outlets highlighted gun-control issues. For instance, CBS quipped,
"More Gun Control? Don't Hold Your Breath,"[31] and CNN opined, "Gun
control unlikely to get on agenda despite shootings."[32] Unfortunately,
this same pattern emerged after the 2011 Tucson shootings by Jared
Loughner and the 2012 murders at Sandy Hook Elementary School.

Here is a "double whammy" by the press: not only did journalists use
polls wrongly—immediately after an emotional event—they deliberately
misrepresented the results of the poll to give a boost to the policy solution they favored, namely, more gun control. Yet upon closer inspection,
we can see that what the media wanted was not what the polls showed at
all, particularly in the Columbine case. ICR Media, which did the polling

for the AP, tested the issue before Columbine and found that only 42 percent of Americans thought stricter gun laws would be "more effective" in reducing violence. In contrast, 47 percent favored more enforcement of laws already on the books. Immediately after the Columbine shooting, the number favoring more gun laws rose to 51 percent, while those who favored more enforcement of existing laws dropped to 39 percent.

However, when Gallup measured culpability for the shooting in a May 7–9, 1999, poll, asking, "What is the single most important thing that could be done to prevent another incidence of school shootings?" the pollsters were no doubt shocked to find that "Parental involvement/responsibility" was listed at a nearly 3-to-1 ratio over "Better gun control/laws/issues."[33] Then, a year after Columbine, NBC News and the *Wall Street Journal* asked what would be more effective in reducing gun violence, "passing new restrictions on the sale of handguns . . . ensuring stricter enforcement of existing laws on guns sales and ownership," or both measures. This time, by a more than three-to-one ratio, people supported "stricter enforcement." The option of "both measures," naturally, got the highest response (45 percent) because it (1) did not involve a choice and (2) did not posit a cost.[34] The refrain seems entrenched. A similar question was asked in a CNN/Opinion Research Corporation poll two years after the Virginia Tech massacre: "Would you like to see gun laws in this country made more strict, less strict, or remain as they are?" Of the respondents, 39 percent chose "more strict"; 15 percent chose "less strict," and a majority chose the answer that did not involve either a choice or a cost: "remain as they are" (46 percent).[35]

Of course, these types of responses left the press outraged at a public clearly out of step with journalistic views. Consider a column by Roger Rosenblatt in *Time*:

> As terrible as all the gun killings of the past few months have been, one has the almost satisfying feeling that the country is going through the literal death throes of a barbaric era. . . . My guess, in fact, is that the hour has come and gone—that the great majority of Americans are saying they favor gun control when they really mean gun banishment.[36]

Eight years later, Amanda Ripley, also writing in *Time*, used the Virginia Tech massacre to push the suggestion that more gun control is necessary:

> A year after the deadliest shooting in America, when a sad and angry English major killed 32 people and himself at the Blacksburg campus of Virginia Tech, only modest changes have been made to the country's gun control laws. These days it appears that the most lasting effect of mass-casualty shootings is to harden people's pre-existing opinions on emotionally loaded issues like gun control and privacy rights.[37]

Gun-control polling reflected the media's overwhelmingly biased and poor reporting on guns in general, whether it was the general support of the Brady Bill or refusal to cover or even report instances when guns were used by private citizens to save lives, as in the Pearl High School shooting case in Mississippi, where assistant principle Joel Myrick retrieved his .45 caliber semi-automatic pistol from his truck and kept the killer from doing even more damage. Accuracy in Media (http://www.aim.org/) has documented the profound antigun bias in the mainstream media, showing, for example, that during coverage of Brady Bill legislation, pro–gun-control guests/interviewees outnumbered anti-Brady guests by a margin of ten to one on some networks! The same type of reporting practices ensued following the Virginia Tech massacres. A study by the Culture and Media Institute found that the mainstream media completely ignored pro–gun rights examples. Instead, the "media had a field day during the week after the Virginia Tech campus shootings. . . . The major broadcast networks ran nearly 30 total stories promoting gun control, with another 24 from CNN, 9 in the *New York Times* and 20 in the *Washington Post*. The message was delivered with machine-gun regularity: lack of gun control led to the massacre, so more gun laws might prevent another massacre."[38]

ADDITIONAL POLLING CONCERNS: POLLSTERS AS POOR PROPHETS

The ability of pollsters to separate bias from their questions fundamentally relies on proper word choice in their polls; yet pollsters repeatedly fail to apply objective questions. Consider in more detail the congressional budget debate of 1995, where the newly elected Republican majority in the House sought to control the burgeoning federal deficits by *slowing the rate of growth* of many government programs. Nevertheless, some social programs would continue to grow rapidly, with Medicare increasing at twice the rate of inflation. House Democrats, in a strategy designed by Bill Clinton, labeled the slower growth of several programs "cuts," even though funding would actually increase. Pollsters uncritically accepted the Democrats' deceitful yet ingenious use of the term "cuts," asking questions such as this by a CBS/*New York Times* poll: "If you had to choose, would you prefer balancing the budget, or preventing Medicare from being significantly cut?"[39] Notice that the budget being balanced may not involve "cutting" Medicare any more than any other particular program—the two are not mutually exclusive. Rather, the faux poll question posed cutting Medicare as the *only* alternative involved in "balancing the budget." Moreover, there are smaller telltale signs of bias: the use of the word "prefer" vs. the harder "prevent," and the leading word "significantly." There was no indication in the poll that in reality, "significantly" amounted to $12 a month. Nevertheless, the poll achieved the objective of the *Times* with its results: 67 percent opposed a plan that would "significantly" cut Medicare. Having doctored the poll data, the *New York Times* then jimmied the reporting by relying on the polling data, with its headline "Americans Reject Big Medicare Cuts, New Poll Finds."[40] In this case the headline was somewhat accurate, because the poll did apparently have to search through several legitimately structured questions before "finding" the slanted question the pollsters employed. As expected, the paper's executive editor defended the poll as "straightforward honest journalism."[41] Apparently "straightforward honest journalism" at the *Times* did not require it to trumpet the fact that, according to its own poll, 82 percent of adults agreed that those with higher incomes should pay more for Medicare, or that less than a majority (49 percent) opposed having people pay a little more to retain Medicare services.

Questioning the accuracy of such flawed polls is even more prudent when one looks at the record of pollsters as prophets. Of course, there is the infamous "Dewey Beats Truman" poll of the presidential election of 1948, and since then not much has changed. The press uses polls to "prophesy" an ending coinciding with their wishes. For example, of five polls released on January 17, 2010, concerning the Massachusetts Senate race between Scott Brown and Martha Coakley, all but one showed Brown with a comfortable lead, with the odd man out showing a tie. The *Boston Globe* chose to ignore all the polls but one, using this headline to announce the results: "In a Dead Heat, Brown and Coakley Push toward Finish." The ignored polls had Brown up by 5, 7, 9, and 10 points.[42] Brown won by 52 to 47.

Of course, wishful thinking is not the only consideration for poor prophesying. All too often, pollsters forget (or ignore) the conditions under which a poll is conducted. When this comes to polls in foreign countries, the results are often meaningless. In Nicaragua, for example, during the 1990 election between the ruling communist Sandinista Party and the opposition party headed by Violeta Chamorro, North American pollsters routinely predicted a landslide Sandinista victory based on survey results, without ever questioning whether a poll taken in a quasi-dictatorship could produce meaningful results. Chamorro rode to a shocking victory—shocking, really, only to Western media elites who had believed their own flawed methodologies—and won the election with 55 percent of the popular vote.

The consistently poor showing of pollsters-as-prophets was reflected yet again in July 2000, when voters in Mexico, despite substantial polling data to the contrary, elected a new president and numerous members of his party to overthrow the more than 20-year reign of the ruling PRI Party. One analyst glumly noted, "People stepped into the voting booths on Sunday—especially the young voters who came put in [*sic*] big num-

bers, and the 15 percent who were undecided, and supported Fox . . .
They probably had already made up their minds for Fox and PAN legislators. They just did not tell us that."[43] One pollster who pegged the
Mexican election right, Maria de las Heras, "practically had to go into
hiding after publishing a poll showing . . . Fox 10 points ahead" prior to
the election.[44] As one analyst pointed out, government intimidation of
people in polls plays a role. Said Rob Allyn, who represented one of two
independent U.S. polling firms hired by Democracy Watch to conduct a
poll, "The reason most polls in Mexican media missed the mark is that
the government controls Mexican media and thus can manipulate and
control the polling."[45]

A similar situation surrounded reporting of the election in Iraq in
2002, in which President Saddam Hussein won nearly 100 percent of the
vote. Television journalists especially failed to mention that Iraqis did not
receive their food ration coupons until they had voted and, no doubt,
voted correctly. In Nicaragua and Iraq, the presumption by American
journalists of American concepts of electoral fairness and legality tainted
both the polling and the reporting of the process, which, in Iraq's case,
could hardly even be called an "election."

The poor predictions by pollsters are not restricted to foreign countries about which they know little, though. Sadly, many pollsters' prophecies involving American elections have been widely off the mark. In
what is sure to become as classic as the Dewey Beats Truman example, in
1994 no serious media analyst or pollster, except John Zogby, foresaw a
Republican House victory. When the Republicans won decisive control of
the House—always referred to as a "takeover" by broadcasters—it flew
in the face of virtually every major poll. Two days before the election, the
Washington Post published its "Crystal Ball" poll of fourteen prominent
journalists, pollsters, and political analysts. Only three of the fourteen
predicted that the Republicans would win the House and the Senate.
Even of those three, none came close to the final margin of victory in the
House (a 22-seat GOP gain, when the guesses were 3, 4, and 14).[46] Ever in
spin mode, the Democrats tried to put a happy face on their debacle, with
former Clinton advisor George Stephanopoulos, commenting that it
looked like a "pretty good night" so far![47]

Meanwhile, Zogby came under closer scrutiny, and was celebrated by
radio host Rush Limbaugh as his program's "official" pollster, even
though Zogby personally had registered as a Democrat. During the 1996
presidential election, Zogby had the final margins almost perfect, often
between 5 to 8 percent points closer to the election results than Gallup,
USA Today, Roper, and the network polling groups. Pressed to reveal his
secrets, Zogby explained that whereas most pollsters did surveys of
adults, his organization only polled likely voters based on previous voting participation. He also corrected for a built-in bias in polling in which
Democrats were much more likely to be polled, due to the fact that Re-

publicans were less willing to be polled. Nevertheless, several journalists ran hit pieces on Zogby because he was too accurate!

We saw a repetition of this in 2000. Except for Zogby and the usually reliable "Battleground Poll" which measures a wide range of voter attitudes and not just views of specific candidates, the political bias of pollsters themselves began to come through in comments made during the 2000 presidential elections. Republican George W. Bush consistently ran ahead of Democrat Al Gore even on issues that recently had begun to swing to the Democrats, especially gun control and Social Security. On national television, pollster William Schneider, after seeing results that showed Bush with a growing lead on gun control, blurted out that he couldn't believe the results and ordered his poll taken again.

A consistent problem with polling is simply the poor quality of the polls themselves. Looking for easy answers, scrambling to make news, and wishing to find evidence to support their own worldviews, the major polling institutions have demonstrated neither reliability or accuracy. For example, of eight major polling institutions (Portrait of America was not included) that surveyed during the 1996 presidential election, half exceeded the margin of error, two others were barely under the margin of error, and only two did not exceed the margin of error—Zogby and Battleground. Only one organization (Gallup) forecast Republican Bob Dole with a higher percentage than he actually got (0.3 percent), but still missed the spread between Dole and Democrat Bill Clinton by 11 percent overall, for an error of 2.5 percent over the final spread. CBS/*New York Times* was off by an eye-opening 18 percent from the final vote percentages.

One might dismiss such polling errors as merely that, errors, if the *direction* of the polls was not uniformly leftward. Gerald S. Wasserman, for instance, conducted an analysis of the polls in 1996 and concluded that pollsters virtually all overstated the margin of victory for Clinton over Dole. Everett Carl Ladd, director of the Roper Center for Public Opinion, stated, "Election polling had a terrible year in 1996 . . . [in that] most of the leading national polling organizations made pre-election estimates that diverged sharply from the actual vote."[48] Wasserman asked a different question: not whether the polls were "off," but what were the odds that they would *all be off in the same direction*? Analyzing the polls' margin of error and final difference, Wasserman computed the likelihood that chance would account for a "miss." When he factored in the pattern of results, again, in Clinton's favor, he concluded that the combined polling odds that would produce such flawed outcomes were 4,095 to one, or roughly the same odds as a non-golfer hitting a hole-in-one.[49]

Warren Mitofsky conducted an even more wide-ranging examination of polling in presidential elections, looking at the final polls in every election since 1956. His conclusions were chilling: "More than twice as many polls overstated the Democratic candidate's share of the vote than overstated the Republican's share."[50] Worse, the polls' margin of error for Democrats was higher than for polls that favored Republicans. In other words, a poll favoring a Republican had to have a much higher level of certainty before pollsters would report it.[51] For example, network news polls by CBS and ABC, plus Gallup and Harris—four of the five polls with the biggest impact on public perceptions about an election— universally overestimated the margin of Clinton's victory by 2 to 4 percent, while at the same time underestimating Bob Dole's percentages by about the same amount, for a net "impact swing" of 4 to 8 percent toward Clinton. Zogby and NBC/*Wall Street Journal* both predicted Clinton's final numbers with accuracy, but like the other pollsters under-predicted the vote for Bob Dole. The Battleground Poll had Clinton at 45 percent, but under-predicted Dole's turnout at 36 percent, or 14 percent less than what Dole actually received. We have already seen the Brown/Coakley poll interpretation by the *Globe*. This is all the more amazing because until 1960, some polls—especially Gallup—had a constant 2 to 3 percent bias in favor of Republicans! Something had changed after 1960, not only among journalists, but also among pollsters.

Do pollsters deliberately bias their work? One cannot rule it out, given our discussion of the British in World War II. Exactly how they bias their surveys, or in what ways they allow their biases to creep in, is worth examining. One common problem, largely addressed by Zogby, stems from those being surveyed. Until the 1990s, pollsters commonly used registered voters. These proved unreliable predictors, though, because registered voters did not always vote. In fact, many did not ever vote. Zogby, while not alone, was the best at establishing an archetype for a likely voter by asking a number of questions about previous voting habits. Essentially, he eliminated people who had not voted consistently in previous elections. Next, he observed that Gallup and Harris tended to over-sample Democrats by one to two points, in part because they often sampled over a weekend. After adjusting for likely voters and reducing the number of Democrats to a more accurate percentage of those who actually voted, Zogby achieved much higher accuracy than other pollsters, especially in 1996 and 1998. After that, other polling firms that had publicly criticized him changed quietly to his methodology.

In the 2000 presidential race, a mid-September *Newsweek* poll had Al Gore with a 14-point lead over George Bush, but only a week later, another *Newsweek* poll had the margin at only 2 points in Gore's favor. What could explain a 12-point shift in merely a week? Any number of things could account for the error, including a poor sample. In fact, pollsters' scientific terms, such as "margin of error" and "scientific sample," are buzz-words that mean very little. Harry O'Neill of Roper once quipped, "God forbid the public should ever find out that all sampling error and its 95 percent confidence interval really say is that if you conduct the same biased survey among the same unrepresentative sample 100 times, you will get the same meaningless results 95 times."[52]

Another problem cropped up as respondents saw that the media was using poll results to justify certain ideological positions. Some of those respondents being polled began to either lie or alter their answers to suit their own ideological purposes. For example, if a poll asked up front if someone was a registered Democrat or Republican, the responder might lie about his or her political affiliation. Such deliberate "jimmying" of poll results does not fit into the margin of error of most polls. While pollsters downplay such incidents, they undoubtedly happen more often than admitted. A 2008 study found that "nearly 11 percent of people who have reported being polled said they have lied to pollsters about their views on politics and public affairs."[53]

More difficult is arriving at objective wording and phrasing of poll questions. Some experts argue that polling almost never can reach a "true attitude" on an issue. University of California, Los Angeles, political scientist John Zaller contends that such pure positions do not exist.[54] Zaller has argued that all questions involve choices, and that the answer to any single question at any time requires that all choices facing an individual (in all their myriad manifestations) be asked, which, of course, is impossible. People can tell pollsters in all honesty one thing, then vote with equal honesty nearly the opposite way the next day. Votes require an assessment of all the variables—cost, time, danger, and so on. Poll questions exact no cost whatsoever, aside from a few moments' time.

These factors combine to cost pollsters some of their predictive power. In addition, it seems that the public increasingly realizes that those in the polling and media circles who administer, interpret, then report the polls do not share the views that are held by the majority of Americans. Many pollsters tend to ignore or downplay data that does not fit their templates, as in the case of Mexico or the 1994 elections. Not all pollsters are liberals, and conservatives use polls for their own purposes too. But seldom will conservatives assume that the media will either report, or, more important, report *accurately* the results of their surveys, whereas progressive polls almost exclusively obtain favorable coverage and well-chosen banner headlines such as "Support Drops for Bush Tax-Cut Proposal," or "Ashcroft Seen as Extreme in Social Views," or "Half 'Very Positive' about Obama Speech."

As noted, abuse of polls and statistics is exacerbated when polling occurs abroad, mainly due to cultural and language difficulties. Even if those problems are addressed, there still remains the bias involved in framing the poll's results. For example, a *USA Today* report of a Pew International Survey (June 5, 2003) of 20 nations about attitudes toward the United States led with the following paragraph:

As President Bush plunges into Middle East diplomacy, a survey of 20 nations and the Palestinian Authority shows widespread distrust of his leadership, skepticism in the region about his plan for peace and less regard for the United States around the world.[55]

That seems a pretty bleak assessment of U.S. leadership and "popularity"—if it is true. But what did the numbers inside the poll really say (see table 6.1).

In the responses from Israel to Brazil, positive attitudes toward America dropped slightly between 2000 and 2002 in most countries, then dropped sharply during the war in Iraq, then almost recovered to prewar levels; and in Nigeria, the image of the United States was even higher in 2003 than in 2000. The real decline in attitudes came in Muslim countries. However, in all the countries for which there was data from March to May 2003, attitudes actually improved. Would a reader have guessed that attitudes were improving based on the article?[56] Yet *USA Today* was not alone: in the *New York Times*, the headline was "World's View of U.S. Sours after Iraq War, Poll Finds." Although it might have been true to say that "since 2000 the world's view of the U.S. had soured," the *Times* headline was simply a misrepresentation. Likewise,

Table 6.1. International Favorable View of the U.S. (percent)

Nation	1999-2000	Summer 2002	March 2003	May 2003
Israel				79
Great Britain	83	75	48	70
Kuwait				63
Canada	71	72		63
Nigeria	46	77		61
Australia				60
Italy	76	70	34	60
South Korea	58	53		46
Germany	78	61	25	45
France	62	63	31	43
Spain	50		14	38
Russia	37	61	28	36
Brazil	56	52		34
Morocco	77			27
Lebanon		35		27
Indonesia	75	61		15
Turkey	52	30	12	15
Pakistan	23	10		13
Jordan		25		1
Palestinian Authority	14			1

the *Washington Post* echoed the anti-U.S. line with the headline "Arab Hostility toward U.S. Growing, Poll Finds," which was at least technically accurate, but generally misleading in terms of the trends in the poll.

Nor have news media pollsters in the United States corrected their progressive bias. Examples of this abound, and we will look now at three of the more common. In 2000, America saw an almost unprecedented presidential race ending with tight recounts in Florida. The news media may well have contributed to the post-election fight through its early calling of the election based on exit polls. Florida straddles two time zones, and the Voter News Service broke their own rules by calling the election for Gore prior to the closing of the polls in the western part of the state (a region with heavy Bush support). Voter turnout in the central time zone was thus suppressed. Thousands of Bush supporters simply went home after hearing the race called for Gore. Additionally, subsequent analysis of the polls found that the Voter News Service had somehow polled more Democrats than statistically necessary, thus biasing the results in favor of Gore.[57] Later congressional hearings on this matter eventually led to new broadcast guidelines starting in 2004. In a 2007 study, Uscinski examined the poll-based winner calls made by news organizations nationwide on election night 2000. He found that the states carried by Gore were called more quickly than states won by Bush.[58]

A second example involves a special October 2004 recall election that was held in California in which the Republican, actor Arnold Schwarzenegger, faced a sitting Democratic governor and the Lieutenant Governor in an idiosyncratic ballot that allowed voters to vote "No" (meaning for the sitting governor, Gray Davis) or "Yes," and if voting "Yes," voters could then vote for any of 123 candidates. An analysis of some 20 polls conducted over the month leading up to the election found that only one had the final numbers correct, and that the average of the polls put Schwarzenegger's percentage at 35 percent, when in fact he tallied 49 percent. Yet once again, pundits were more concerned with why Californians would elect "the Terminator" than with why their own projections were so inaccurate.

The presidential election of 2004 between Bush and Kerry provides yet another example of the press pushing certain polls that support their point of view. CNN in particular conducted polls that are becoming the stuff of legend. Steven Freeman, of the Center for Organizational Dynamics at the University of Pennsylvania, found that "in key state after key state, counts showed very different numbers than the polls predicted; and the differentials were all in the same direction." He found that in "ten of the eleven consensus battleground states, the tallied [vote percentages] differs from the predicted [vote percentages], and in every one, the shift favors Bush."[59] This simply means that somehow CNN had 10 of 11 polls skewed in Kerry's favor. This led CNN to predicting early the election for Kerry, as did other networks.[60] Of note is that once the actual voting numbers were returned, showing a Bush victory, the networks were reluctant to call many states, preferring to wait until the next day.

It seems reasonable to posit that polling and the liberal/progressive press achieve a mutually beneficial relationship, which flourishes well until someone exposes the flaws of polls or the bias of the press publicly. And when the polls do not support the press point of view, the press can simply twist the results to suit its need. For instance, in late 2008, MSNBC host Keith Olbermann deliberately ignored poll results that indicated how popular Gerald Ford was as a president (62 percent of Americans), and focused instead on the results indicating a negative view (26 percent of Americans). By ignoring the positive results, which actually made Ford around the fourth most popular president among the last ten presidents, Olbermann was somehow able to say that Ford was the twelfth most unpopular president in history.[61]

All this has been occurring against the backdrop of a continuing and growing reaction calling for more balanced journalism, partly in response to new media that bypasses the self-protection mechanism of the mainstream media. In this new media, the bias of the post-Kennedy media is increasingly exposed, and conservative positions are allowed to be presented. It is to these new voices we now turn.

NOTES

1. Rivlin quoted in Robert Shogan, *Bad News: Where the Press Goes Wrong in the Making of the President* (Chicago: Ivan R. Dee Publisher, 2001), 272.

2. Christopher Hitchens, *No One Left to Lie To: The Triangulations of William Jefferson Clinton* (New York: Verso, 1999), 35.

3. Herbert Asher, *Polling and the Public* (Washington, DC: Congressional Quarterly Press, 1992), 17.

4. Matthew Robinson, *Mobocracy: How the Media's Obsession with Polling Twists the News, Alters Elections, and Undermines Democracy* (Roseville, CA: Prima Publishing, 2002), 2.

5. Dick Morris, *Behind the Oval Office* (Los Angeles: Renaissance Books, 1999), 338.

6. Morris, 339. Morris was so enamored of polls, he referenced them more than 100 times in his book.

7. Thomas E. Mahl, *Desperate Deception: British Covert Operations in the United States, 1939–44* (Washington, DC: Brassey's, 1998).

8. Cantril quoted in Mahl, 74.

9. Michael Wheeler, *Lies, Damned Lies and Statistics* (New York: Liveright, 1976), 115–116.

10. William Stephenson, *A Man Called Intrepid: The Secret War* (New York: Ballantine, 1976), 324–325.

11. Mahl, 83; Garry J. Clifford and Samuel Spencer, *The First Peacetime Draft* (Lawrence, KS: University Press of Kansas, 1986), 139; and Garry J. Clifford, "Grenville Clark and the Origins of Selective Service," *Review of Politics*, 35 (January 1973), 17–40.

12. Herbert Asher, *Polling and the Public: What Every Citizen Should Know*, 3d ed. (Washington, DC: Congressional Quarterly, 1995), 3.

13. Gallup quoted in Wheeler, 104.

14. Asher, 17.

15. Shogan, 144.

16. Shogan,144.

17. Gallup quoted in Wheeler, 155.

18. Robinson, 23; Richard Benedetto and Jim Drinkard, "As Political Polls Grow, So Does Their Influence," *USA Today*, September 13, 2000.

19. Tom Rosenstiel and Bill Kovach, "Lessons of the Election," *The State of the News Media: 2009*, Pew Project for Excellence in Journalism, www.stateofthemedia.org/2009/narrative_special_lessonsoftheelection.php.

20. Rosenstiel and Kovach.

21. Examples quoted in Robinson, 19.

22. Robinson, 19.

23. Robinson, 18. Emphasis mine.

24. Robinson, 18. Emphasis mine.

25. Quoted in Robinson, 282.

26. 476. Quoted in Robinson, 290. Number rounded.

27. Alison Mitchell, "The Politics of Guns: Tilting Toward the Democrats," *New York Times*, May 14, 1999; Ceci Connolly, "Littleton Alters the Landscape of Debate on Guns," *Washington Post*, May 5, 1999.

28. "Gun Control Bolstered: Americans Want Tougher Laws, Poll Shows," *Newsday*, May 6, 1999.

29. "Following Virginia Tech Shooting, 45% Say U.S. Needs Stricter Gun Control Laws," Rasmussen Reports, April 20, 2007, http://beta.rasmussenreports.com/public_content/politics/current_events/gun_control/following_virginia_tech_shooting_45_say_u_s_needs_stricter_gun_control_laws.

30. "Guns and Violence," CBS News Poll, *New York Times*, April 20–22, 2007, www.cbsnews.com/htdocs/CBSNews_polls/aprbhandguns.pdf.

31. Scott Conroy, "More Gun Control? Don't Hold Your Breath: Stricter Gun Control Laws after Virginia Tech Shooting Would Be a Hard Sell," CBSNews.com, April 17, 2007, www.cbsnews.com/stories/2007/04/17/virginiatechshooting/main2695994.shtml.

32. Bill Schneider, "Gun Control Unlikely to Get on Agenda Despite Shootings," CNN.com, April 18, 2007, http://edition.cnn.com/2007/POLITICS/04/17/schneider.gun.control/index.html.

33. See the statistics in Robinson, 64–65.

34. These are discussed in Robinson, 66–67.

35. Bill Schnieder, "Schneider: Why the Public Opinion Shift on Gun Control?" politicalticker.blogs.cnn.com, April 8, 2009. See too CNN/Opinion Research Corporation Poll, April 3–5, 2009, http://politicalticker.blogs.cnn.com/2009/04/08/schneider-why-the-public-opinion-shift-on-gun-control/?fbid=2rNXeAE8U_L (Last accessed, April 21, 2010).

36. Roger Rosenblatt, "Get Rid of the Damned Things," *Time*, August 9, 1999.

37. Amanda Ripley, "Ignoring Virginia Tech," www.Time.com, April 15, 2008, www.time.com/time/nation/article/0,8599,1731195,00.html.

38. See David Niedrauer, "The Media Assault on the Second Amendment," *Eye on Culture* 1, no. 11 (2007). Quote by Kristen Fyle, "Knight Column: New Study Exposes Anti-gun Bias of Media," NewsBusters.org, August 29, 2007, http://newsbusters.org/blogs/kristen-fyfe/2007/08/29/knight-column-triggermen-aka-anti-gun-media.

39. *New York Times*, October 26, 1995.

40. Adam Clymer, "Americans Reject Big Medicare Cuts, New Poll Finds," *New York Times*, October 26, 1995.

41. Joseph Lelyveld quoted in Ian Fisher, "Battle over the Budget: The Polls," *New York Times*, October 27, 1995.

42. Tom Bevin, "The *Boston Globe* Puts Its Thumb on the Scale—Again," January 18, 2010, RealClearPolitics.com, http://realclearpolitics.blogs.time.com/2010/01/18/the-boston-globe-puts-its-thumb-on-the-scale-again/.

43. Ricardo Sandoval, "Fox May Have Pulled Sweep: Mexicans' Thorough Rejection of PRI Fooled the Experts," *Dallas Morning News*, July 4, 2000.

44. Lisa J. Adams, "Pollsters Get It Wrong in Mexican Election," July 9, 2000, www.freerepublic.com/forum/a3968d4727ae3.htm.

45. Allyn quoted in Adams.

46. James Fallows, *Breaking the News: How the Media Undermine American Democracy* (New York: Vintage Books, 1997 [1996]), 31–32.

47. Stephanopoulos quoted in Fallows, 63.

48. Carll Everett Ladd, "The Pollster's Waterloo," *Wall Street Journal*, November 19, 1996.

49. Gerald S. Wasserman, "Were the Polls Right? No. Only Once in 4,900 Elections Would Chance Alone Produce Such Failures," provided to the author. A summary of Wasserman's study appeared in R. Morin, "The Election Post-Mortem: The Experts Debate the Accuracy of Their Surveys," *Washington Post*, January 13, 1997. The article was posted on www.freerepublic.com/forum/a39c3ed7a475e.htm.

50. Warren J. Mitofsky, "Poll Review: Was 1996 Worse than 1948?" *Public Opinion Quarterly*, Spring 1998, 230–249, quotation on 245.

51. Mitofsky, 245. Although Mitofsky disputes pollster Everett Carl Ladd's claim that "election polling had a terrible year in 1996," citing a study done by the National Council on Public Polls.

52. Quoted in Shogan, 273.

53. "Lying Voters May Skew Poll Results," Zogby International, August 8, 2008, http://zogby.com/templates/printsb.cfm?id=18026.

54. John R. Zaller, *The Nature and Origins of Mass Opinion* (New York: Cambridge University Press, 1992), 95.

55. *USA Today*, June 5, 2003, www.usatoday.com/usatonline/20030604/5211095s.htm.

56. Thanks to Jim Miller for his column pointing this out, www.seanet.com/~jimxc/Politics/June2003_1.html.

57. Richard Morin and Claudia Deane, "Why the Fla. Exit Polls Were Wrong," *Washington Post*, November 8, 2000, www.washingtonpost.com/ac2/wp-dyn/A45950-2000Nov8?language=.

58. Joseph Uscinski, "Too Close Too Call? Uncertainty and Bias in Election Night Reporting," *Social Science Quarterly*, 88, no. 1 (2007).

59. Steven F. Freeman, "The Unexplained Exit Poll Discrepancy," Center for Organizational Dynamics at the University of Pennsylvania, December 29, 2004, p. 2.

60. Mark Jurkowitz, "Early Missteps, Late-Night Caution," November 4, 2004, Boston.com, www.boston.com/ae/media/articles/2004/11/04/early_missteps_late_night_caution_but_the_right_call/.

61. Brad Wilmouth, "Olbermann Distorts Poll to Discredit Cheney," December 19, 2008, Newsbusters.org, http://newsbusters.org/blogs/brad-wilmouth/2008/12/19/olbermann-disputes-cheney-gets-his-numbers-wrong.

SEVEN

The Rise of the Alternate News Media in Radio and Internet

For the media aristocracy, the 1970s and early 1980s only confirmed their view that Americans were intellectually incapable of sorting out complex issues. Journalists increasingly dismissed the citizenry as ill-informed and morally inferior. The reading and viewing public reacted by turning off the news and canceling their subscriptions in a "quiet consumers' boycott of the press."[1] Like steel and auto companies in the 1970s, the mainstream news media blamed its failures on outside forces, ignoring a very real reason for its decline: the one-sided slant of news. This was even true of media critics, such as James Fallows, who rationalized liberal press bias.[2]

In his defense of the press, Fallows cites a poll showing that a majority of reporters thought public officials *as a class* were more honest and more honorable than the general public, the opposite of what we have previously seen the general public thinks. This is not as surprising as it seems given news media distrust of the public, and its paternalistic attitude toward viewers and readers. Nor is it surprising that journalists see Washington, DC, as the main source of potential positive change, rather than people in their communities. In a recent study, 71 percent of media elites thought it was government's job to guarantee jobs, or more than double the percent of business elites who thought so. Whereas nine out of ten business leaders said that "people can be trusted," only seven of ten media elites thought people were trustworthy.[3]

With new competition from television, an opportunity appeared for a new class of journalists to develop different values and, hence, a slant on the news different from print journalists. Unfortunately, this did not happen. Instead, the "shared values" merely expanded from one group of journalists to another, with television even reinforcing certain liberal/

147

progressive tendencies in the news through its very technology and methodology. Images became supreme over content. Televised news, with its emphasis on sound bites and pictures, covered less content than even that found in print news. At the same time, newspapers, assuming that television news was actually covering the events of the day, increasingly drifted into "op-ed" descriptions weighed down by personal stories or human-interest angles. In either case, the media ignored deep questions of whether policies were right or wrong, beneficial or harmful, dwelling often instead on how the principals "would respond."[4]

By the 1980s, the liberal bias of virtually all major news organizations was so prevalent and obvious that consumers had grown frustrated and angry. Why was no one reflecting their point of view on the events? Where was their voice? The alternate to the slant in television and print news developed quickly, as only a market-based economy can allow, in two major markets: radio and the Internet. Although radio had been around as a commercial medium since the 1920s, its use as a news source had been eclipsed by both the mainstream papers and by the rise of the television age. All this changed when Rush Limbaugh emerged in 1984, bringing in his wake an army of conservative talk show hosts.[5]

The country was hungry for these alternate political voices, and by the mid-1990s, the nation's commercial (i.e., competitive) AM airwaves were dominated by conservative political talk. This momentous event was followed soon by another, this one based on a new, surprisingly innovative medium: the Internet. The Internet allowed political news to bypass large media gate-keepers and go directly to the public. In this chapter we will look at these alternate news trends, using as case studies the rise of Rush Limbaugh, Free Republic, the Drudge Report, and several A-list bloggers. The chapter ends by looking at failing liberal papers as a response to AM radio and the Internet.

RUSH AND THE RISE OF COMMERCIAL CONSERVATIVE RADIO

No person since Edward R. Murrow has changed journalism as much as Sacramento radio personality Rush H. Limbaugh, III. Born in 1951 into a political family in America's heartland at Cape Girardeau, Missouri, Limbaugh hardly seemed the kind of man to start a revolution: he was stocky and overweight, and he was a college dropout. Yet he loved radio, and unlike his attorney father and grandfather, Limbaugh eschewed a legal career and pursued his dream of being a "disc jockey."[6]

Limbaugh did not experience immediate success in radio. Several stations fired "Rusty" (the radio name he used). For a while he abandoned radio, working for the Kansas City Royals baseball team in public relations. Given a shot at a Kansas City radio station, Limbaugh revived his broadcast career, and was again fired. But his work came to the attention of Sacramento station KFBK, which empowered him to engage in all the on-air shenanigans he desired. "It was as if someone had told Pablo Picasso he could start coloring outside the lines," wrote Rodger Streitmatter.[7] Limbaugh's previous experience in rock 'n' roll broadcasting gave him insight into what was "hip" and trendy, which offset his political conservatism. Moreover, he employed humor—and not always subtly—to make his points. Limbaugh said what many thought, and he was not afraid to express his views publically in an era when speech was become increasingly "politically correct." Referring to the radical wing of the feminist movement as "feminazis," Limbaugh outraged mainstream reporters, who raised the point in every interview. It did not faze him: he called female reporters "anchor-babes" or "reporterettes." The National Organization for Women (NOW) became the "National Association of Gals" (NAGs). His theme song for every "feminist update" featured female vocalists disparaging men (singing, "You just can't shoot them . . . what are they good for?"), but with typical Limbaugh panache, the song had voices from a NOW meeting dubbed in at hyper-speed. As the NOW women screeched, "We're fierce, we're feminists, and we're in your faaaaaaacccceee," Limbaugh's raucous laughter rang out over the tape.

As the station's profits soared, allowing the company to raise advertising rates from $50 to $150 per minute, Limbaugh came to the attention of Edward McLaughlin, who created the Excellence in Broadcasting Network (EIB) as a vehicle to get Limbaugh's show into a national market. At the time, a daytime AM radio talk show that dealt with national politics simply did not exist. Virtually everyone told Limbaugh it would not work, and that talk radio was "local, local, local." Everyone warned him he could not do a three-hour political show by himself, and that he needed guests. Limbaugh felt in his bones, however, that American journalism had declined so much that it had left a massive void to be filled by anyone who could present a conservative analysis of the daily news in an entertaining way. Thus, during a typical show, Limbaugh would begin with a monologue about the day's top stories, interspersed with his own conservative analysis. Merely the selection of the stories Limbaugh covered, however, sharply distinguished him from the mainstream media. During the program, Limbaugh often introduced pieces of news that the mainstream media refused to cover, which he saw as important in the lives of average Americans.

He routinely contrasted the conservative position by playing sound bites from news conferences and television talk shows, following this up with commentary. On occasion, such as when the Chinese premier visited President Bill Clinton, Limbaugh gave a television-style "interpretation" of the premier's Chinese speech, as though he were a UN interpreter, only with what the premier "really said." Every major category of issues had an update theme, many provided by musician Paul Shanklin: news of sport utility vehicles (SUVs) was introduced by "In a Yugo" (from Elvis Presley's "In the Ghetto"), while homeless updates were introduced by "I Ain't Got No Home," by Clarence "Frogman" Henry. Individuals warranted their own theme songs: news about Soviet premier Michel Gorbachev was preceded by "Darth Vader's Theme" from *Star Wars*.

Although Limbaugh went over the edge at times (such as with his "caller abortions" in 1989, or when he declared that women got in auto accidents due to excessive farding [i.e., applying makeup in the car, but which people mistook for "farting"]), no one could deny that he stood for a clearly defined set of principles and that those were in most cases 180 degrees opposite the positions held by the mainstream news media.

Limbaugh debuted nationally in 1988 when he moved to New York City, and within five years he was the most listened-to radio personality in the country—arguably in history. He redefined AM radio, which, before Limbaugh, endlessly played Top 40 music hits, 24 hours a day. AM's one-time music dominance had started to weaken in the early 1970s with the advent of rebellious, underground FM radio stations. FM disc jockeys were unafraid to play songs lasting up to 20 minutes; or to play mood music carefully tailored to listeners high on drugs; or to premiere the most recent (but unknown) artists. Increasingly, AM became viewed as a "teeny bop" format—not for serious listeners or the truly hip.

Aside from a few public service shows on weekend mornings or in the wee hours of the night, there were virtually no talk-formatted shows. The dean of news/commentary was Paul Harvey, who seemed to have been born in a newsroom. After leaving the Army in World War II, Harvey got a job doing news reporting in Chicago, where he soon became a regional legend. Restrictions on broadcast signals and on licensing at that time prevented Harvey from even approximating Limbaugh's success (not to mention the "bombasticity" factor), but Limbaugh clearly loved Harvey and borrowed much from his news and analysis style. Still, Limbaugh greatly eclipsed Harvey when he arrived on the national scene. Nearly overnight, Limbaugh's popularity in New York spread to the rest of the nation, accelerated by a "Rush to Excellence" tour in which Limbaugh held political-style rallies with listeners in which he spoke from a stage. For the shy Limbaugh—who genuinely is ill at ease in crowds—the campaign paid off with unprecedented popularity.

Advertising rates on Limbaugh's show soared to $12,000 per minute in the early 1990s, and the value of a Limbaugh endorsement was seen in such products as Snapple, which skyrocketed after advertising on the show. Contrary to the views of many critics, who claimed Limbaugh was only successful when he had a Democrat in the White House to attack, the radio raconteur made his biggest gains during the presidency of George H. W. Bush, who invited him to spend a night in the Lincoln Bedroom.

Among the top factors contributing to Limbaugh's success was the phenomenal target presented by the national news media. He could take almost any subject and expose a liberal spin, and he often noted that he could do three hours a day just on media bias. From Limbaugh's point of view, the establishment press had so failed in reporting news objectively that it took 15 hours of solid conservative political commentary and news every week just to add balance. Actually, this became one of Limbaugh's many bylines: "I don't need balance on this program. I *am* balance." Even when some journalists took Limbaugh seriously, as did MSNBC's Brian Williams or NBC's Tim Russert, they often focused on his more traditional conservative themes rather than his astute inside-the-beltway political perceptions.

That is not to say Limbaugh has not been wrong. In 2000, he boldly predicted that Hillary Clinton would not run for the U.S. Senate seat from New York . . . right up until the moment she announced for the seat. Before the Iraq War, he confidently boasted that "before this is over," the French, Germans, and Russians would all be "on board" (in fact, none of them ever supported the war or the subsequent peace in any way). But such flawed predictions were less frequent than accurate observations. Limbaugh was one of the first—perhaps as early as 1997—to alert conservatives that Bill Clinton would not quietly leave the political stage as did his predecessors, but would comment on the policies of whoever won the presidency. "El Rushbo" was also prescient in predicting the next target of the "environmental whackos," as he labeled them, would be the SUV. One of the reasons he is so successful with predictions is that he makes so many of them. Once one turns out to be correct, he continually reiterates until another prediction comes true. Enough do come true that the odds are with him.

Perhaps part of his appeal is that in making predictions that most in his audience would want to come true, Limbaugh is able to keep his audience on the edge of their seats, as it were. However, the predictions themselves are only a small part of his appeal. For beneath Limbaugh's political predictions lies a consistent conservative view that categorizes people fairly accurately, if perhaps over-simplistically. The environmental movement, he claims, is the modern home of anti-capitalists (although Limbaugh is loath to use the term "communist" to describe any American, clearly by "anti-capitalists" he means communists). His view of the military ("The military exists to kill people and break things") has enabled him to accurately anticipate exactly how different administrations would conduct foreign conflicts based on their ideology and to correctly predict the outcome of the Gulf War in 1993 and the military aspects of the Iraq War of 2003. To critics, this makes his approach to issues "unsophisticated." Others can see that, like Reagan, Limbaugh realizes that most issues really are not that complicated, and that right and wrong answers do exist. In sharing his views, Limbaugh performs a teaching role, one in which he teaches conservatives how to counterargue with liberals. Although his critics make the claim that his discourse is radically right, Limbaugh's discourse is actually much more mainstream than his critics acknowledge. One extensive content analysis compared Rush's program content to public opinion data. In what must have shocked many on the left, Rush's ideas were pretty close to the mainstream.[8]

Limbaugh's ascent coincided with a vast revolution in the news. Even though in 1997 about 68 percent of Americans read a daily paper at least once a week, the nation's newspapers had seen their circulations fall, a trend continuing even today, with circulation down 10 percent since just 2003. Moreover, the number of competitors shrank continually between the 1980s and late 1990s.[9] Part of Limbaugh's appeal was that he read and analyzed news from hundreds of sources in the existing media, both print and televised, but presented it with his own point of view, often including new or unreported facts that completely changed the slant—if not the very core—of the story. In short, Limbaugh challenged both the gate-keeping and the framing of the mainstream media.

After the elections of 2002, in which the Republicans had historical gains for a party out of power, the Democrats mounted a new public-relations offensive against Limbaugh, beginning with the then new Minority Leader Tom Daschle singling out of Limbaugh in his post-mortems. Democrats complained they had no equivalent voice anywhere on talk radio, and numerous initiatives by liberals appeared in which a "liberal Rush Limbaugh" might be found. Yet no one surfaced. The liberal radio network Air America was launched in 2004 specifically to counter conservative talk radio. With commentators such as Al Franken and Randi Rhodes, it slid into bankruptcy in 2006, ultimately folding in 2010. Several liberal "Rush Limbaughs" repeatedly failed, the most prominent of whom was Jim Hightower, a Texas radio host whose Limbaugh-like show never took off; he now offers a two-minute daily commentary for syndication.

Why, then, could the liberals not find an answer to Limbaugh? Part of the answer may well lie in the duplication that liberal radio shows would have with the mainstream media; they simply do not offer alternate points of view. Another, more commercially important aspect should be considered, though. As Harry Shearer, a radio satirist, said, "Based on sheer radio professionalism, even a tribe of chimpanzees locked in a room would choose Rush Limbaugh over Jim Hightower." Hightower, Shearer noted, "has a voice like a cat being wrung through a dryer at slow speed. . . . Limbaugh didn't start in politics. . . . He learned the craft of broadcasting first."[10] Another reason no "liberal Rush Limbaugh" has captured the American listening public is the nature of radio, which demands active participation, as opposed to television, which is a passive medium oriented toward emotions. So-called liberal Rush Limbaughs always have faced a near-insurmountable problem in that much of the humor in Rush's program comes from the statements and sound bites of liberals themselves. Or, as Limbaugh notes, liberals are the entertainment.[11]

A few in the media "got it." In 2003, Dave Henry, writing in the *Amarillo Globe-News*, joked that the only worse investment than putting money into "liberal talk radio" was, perhaps, an "amusement/theme park in downtown Baghdad."[12] "Like most things," Henry pointed out, "it boils down to money [for advertisers], and lefty lightweights like Al Franken and Phil Donahue don't make enough of it." One program director Henry interviewed said, "Liberal radio has been tried and liberal radio fails because these guys can't get their advertising numbers."[13]

For the most part, liberals attempt to portray Limbaugh as merely an entertainer, yet such a characterization ignores his more important role. Limbaugh's greatest contribution is not in offering a *conservative* voice for a massive section of the American population, but in offering a *critical* analysis of the news that the mainstream networks and newspapers advance as objective. Countering Limbaugh's influence became something of an obsession with liberals. They focused on corporate control of media outlets, both print and broadcast, arguing that independent newspapers had been driven out of business and that most cities had a single corporate group owning most of the news outlets.[14] (Recall that some of this consolidation came from the newspapers themselves through the joint-operating agreements discussed in chapter 3.) When it came to daily newspapers, such criticisms missed the mark: in 1920, 31 groups owned 7.5 percent of the nations newspapers, but by 1986, there were 127 groups that owned 69.9 percent.[15] And in 2010, 119 groups owned about 82 percent, leaving the rest independently owned and operated.[16] It is hard to contend that a more than fourfold increase in the number of groups, with more than 119 competitors, is consolidation, regardless of the numbers of newspapers owned. And this does not account for "free papers," or "independent papers," many of which are weeklies, whose numbers have exploded since the early 1970s.

As far as radio consolidation is concerned, Limbaugh's show had already grown to its near-maximum size before Clear Channel Communications, Inc., owner of a nationwide network of radio stations, ever got involved; due to market forces and not regulation, his market could not grow a great deal further without impinging on contracts with existing stations. Limbaugh himself noted that it was the show's content that drew listeners, since Americans had found a show that presented news but which did not scorn their own values. And, of course, Limbaugh was entertaining.

He especially hammered the media's obsession with certain topics that tended to benefit . . . the media. For example, campaign finance reform (CFR), most recently before the Supreme Court as *Citizens United v. Federal Election Commission*, was a favorite of elite journalists because it tended to make them the gate-keepers of issues. CFR would limit "soft money" contributions, mostly by political action committees (PACs) that were concerned with specific issues, such as the environment or guns. Despite the fact that Americans spend more on chewing gum in an election cycle than they do on electing their officials (2008: $3.5 billion and $2.6 billion respectively),[17] the entire premise of CFR was an unconstitutional violation of freedom of speech (which the Supreme Court has defined as money, and subsequently in January 2010 struck down large portions of the bill).[18] The law benefited those who had good relations with the press and penalized those whom the press did not like, thus allowing journalists to give free advertising to those they favored under the guise of "news."

For example, take two imaginary candidates, Donny Dale, a Democrat whom the media favors, and Sarah Small, a Republican not in the good graces of the media. Despite protestations of fairness, the media will give Dale the better coverage, and if not more airtime, better sound bites, fewer hostile questions, and so on. Dale, realizing this, accuses his opponent of endorsing a plan to scale back government that will "poison our water and hurt our kids." What happens if the media either chooses not to run Small's responses, or worse, encourages further attacks? Small only had one recourse prior to the campaign finance reform law: she could use a PAC to place television or newspaper ads that carefully outlined the plan and countered her opponent, even though the ads might not mention her by name. In fact, similar industry-sponsored ads successfully defeated the 1993 Clinton health care plan through famous "Harry and Louise" ads that raised questions in the mind of the public. After initial passage of CFR, such ads were prohibited, and the public was at the mercy of the media. No candidate could run a fair race for office without the endorsement of the media at every level. Mainstream journalists loved CFR, and media elites championed it.

Limbaugh pummeled CFR, attacking it as a violation of the First Amendment, and he criticized Republican president George W. Bush for signing the legislation. Issues such as CFR put Limbaugh in his element. He easily captured the complexities of the legislation and boiled them down to their constitutional essentials. Limbaugh discussed court rulings, exposed back-room deals, and analyzed public statements for their propensity to grow government or violate the Constitution. Although the conspiracy of shared values still dominated the major networks and papers, they now had a heckler in the audience who had a national stage, three hours a day. And this heckler did his homework.

For example, Limbaugh alone publicized Elizabeth McGaughey's devastating critique of "Hillarycare" in 1995, dedicating hours to going over McGaughey's fine points for his audience. He even offered to give up his microphone to a debate over the measure between Hillary Clinton and McGaughey—an offer Clinton declined. During the 2000 election, Limbaugh provided much more accurate assessments of what the daily court rulings meant (thanks to Landmark Legal Foundation's Marc Levin's analysis) than did the major networks, who raced to get in front of the cameras with the news before they had even digested the major points of law.

More recently, Limbaugh hammered a theme that ran counter to the one pushed by the mainstream media. After the 2008 elections, which saw Republicans and conservatives reeling from electoral body blows, Limbaugh seemed almost alone in shouting out conservative ideals and the idea that victory would arise from the recent defeat. Just six weeks after Obama took office, Limbaugh gave a nationally televised speech at the annual meeting of the Conservative Political Action Conference. He boldly attacked Obama's plans, and urged conservatives to fight tooth and nail in defending the principles of Ronald Reagan. Democrats responded by attacking Rush, which only increased his popularity. Limbaugh responded by pushing the fight even further (and pushing his ratings up too). As pointed out by the *New York Times*, "Limbaugh saw that there was no way to stop the president's agenda. He dismissed the moderates' notion that compromising with the president would make Republicans look good to independents. Instead he decreed that the Republicans must become the party of no, and force Democratic candidates—especially centrists—to go into 2010 with sole responsibility for the Obama program and the state of the economy." [19] The plan appears to have worked, with Republicans making unprecedented gains in the House, wresting control from Democrats, while in the Senate the Republicans narrowed the gap, regaining the ability to filibuster.

THE INTERNET INFLUENCE

If Limbaugh was critical to the reestablishment of a competitive press, he was not alone in transforming journalism. Since Limbaugh, other radio personalities have emerged to help fill the airwaves with dialog running counter to that of the establishment media: Sean Hannity, Laura Ingraham, Armstrong Williams, Mark Levin, Glen Beck, Neal Boortz, G. Gordon Liddy, and many others. The Internet, though, provided an entirely new medium, one whose potential was even greater than radio for circumventing the establishment news media. The Internet was born without fanfare in the summer of 1969 when University of California, Los Angeles (UCLA) computer scientist Leonard Kleinrock and assistants hooked up two bulky computers with a 15-foot cable. [20] Kleinrock's exercise in linking computers stemmed from a 1968 Defense Advanced Research Projects Agency contract for a network of computers that would be decentralized enough that the failure of one would not cause the entire system to go down. This required a common language of data. By January 1970, UCLA was connected to Stanford Research Institute; the University of California, Santa Barbara; and the University of Utah. They were soon joined by six other institutions and began to exchange e-mail in 1972 under the network name ARPANET. The Internet would constitute the first major communications breakthrough since television, and it would accelerate the second transformation of journalism, opening reporters up to scrutiny and comment by their readers. By 2010, the International Telecommunication Union showed that almost 240 million Americans (around 77 percent) were accessing the Internet.[21]

However, it is a mistake to think that the news information aspect of the Internet succeeded because of the easy access to news the Internet offered, for the Internet did much more than provide rapid access to news (or even varied news sources). Part of its initial success was due to a simple function performed by some users: it exposed the media to an accountability it had not seen since the days of the Federalists. When the media policed itself and enforced objectivity, such a function was not in demand and could be provided by the occasional letter to the editor. But after the 1960s, a powerful demand was created for outlets to challenge news media bias. Limbaugh was the first outlet, and the Internet provided the second. In the pages that follow, I briefly look at some of the more important contributors to the Internet rebellion against the establishment media. Of the many examples of the new Internet journalism and how the Internet changed news, I feel that three deserve special attention: FreeRepublic.com, drudgereport.com, and several A-list blogs.

FREEREPUBLIC.COM—A "CONSERVATIVE NEWS FORUM"

In the 1980s, a computer programmer/analyst named Jim Robinson, who had developed several accounting programs for agribusiness companies, purchased software from his company, and along with two other employees, put up $9,000 to start his own corporation. After typical business ups and downs, Robinson was forced out of management due to his own physical limitations (muscular dystrophy) and his need to care for his stroke-ridden wife. He created another company, Electronic Orchard, to market accounting software for agribusiness.

During that time, Robinson followed the lurid exploits of Bill Clinton and started posting regular features on the Prodigy Whitewater website. Prodigy, however, stifled anti-Clinton discussion, controlling it through "a maze of politically correct 'chat rooms,' bulletin boards, and other features . . . [regulated by] omnipotent cyber-enforcers who could silence dissidents with the flick of a button."[22] Robinson thus created his own website, www.FreeRepublic.com, in 1996, convinced that if the public knew the truth about Clinton's "crooked financing," the "drug-running through Arkansas," and other evidence of corruption, "no way would he be reelected."[23]

Robinson vowed to see Clinton impeached, leading him to write the software and launch the FreeRepublic forum section in February 1997. He posted articles on the Clintons, taxes, and government corruption, and before long, other readers began posting articles of their own. As FreeRepublic's popularity soared, so did the hits on Robinson's website, to the point that his server could no longer handle the load. Nearly broke, Robinson took the advice of a poster who had Internet experience in providing free sites run by donations. Footing the cost of buying a new server in the hope that reader donations would reimburse him, Robinson was discovered by Matt Drudge (discussed later in this chapter), who linked to his site.

Shortly thereafter, with Robinson still struggling to avoid bankruptcy, James Golden—"Mr. Snerdly" of the *Rush Limbaugh Show*, he had left Limbaugh's program to start TalkSpot on the Web—provided FreeRepublic with access to his own site's larger server. Temporarily solvent, Robinson continued his quest to unseat Clinton by staging a March for Justice to Washington, DC, in 1998. The March for Justice attracted the attention of the Washington press, and one reporter astutely noted, "The success of the rally appears to have established the viability of the Internet as a grassroots political organizing tool for a disparate group of Clinton critics" including young, middle aged, and old.[24]

Suddenly FreeRepublic wielded considerable power in conservative circles, and its ability to unmask liberal intentions and to reveal facts not found in the mainstream press proved troublesome to the left. FreeRepublic's constant exposure of errors or biased interpretation in the *New York Times*, the *Washington Post*, and other liberal papers did, however, leave it open to attack. Those papers filed suit to stop reposting of their full articles on the site. Eventually the case was settled, with FreeRepublic able to post articles as long as it did not post the entire article and provided a link to the original article. Unable to shut down FreeRepublic, the mainstream press for the first time was open to near-instantaneous analysis and criticism, often by people with greater knowledge and more reliable information than the major media's own reporters. FreeRepublic had the ability to report breaking news not only from local news reports on-scene, but from "Freepers" (as members of FreeRepublic call themselves) who posted their own observations—often minutes before the national media had the story, as in the case of a New Jersey barge fire in 2003. (In March 2002, Internet journalists received further validation when U.S. District Court Judge Michael Posner ruled that amateur news gatherers on public access television had the same rights as "professionals.")[25]

By 2000, Brian Buckley, the president of Free Republic Institute and the operator of the site, estimated that official registrations had exceeded 60,000, with more than two million downloads a day occurring.[26] During the 2000 election, FreeRepublic was so loaded with people checking the news that its servers crashed (as did Drudge's site on election night 2000). These episodes shocked many into seeing that, for all its advantages, the Internet needed redundancies and backups for such situations if it was to stay competitive with the old, but reinforced, television networks.

The key to FreeRepublic's success was instant analysis. Each FreeRepublic post was followed by a threaded discussion, which often could veer off into any number of unrelated directions. Even among conservatives, the debate frequently got heated and people "flamed" each other routinely. Hot-button issues involved trade; religious battles between Catholics, Protestants, and nonbelievers; and foreign policy clashes between isolationists and interventionists. Although anyone could post anything, making perhaps most of what was written on any given subject suspect, professionals from all areas—lawyers, politicians, engineers, professors, doctors, military people—all joined in the discussions and added their expertise. When enough said similar things, a "public truth" soon emerged. But FreeRepublic had no monopoly over Internet political conversation, on either side of the spectrum, with www.capitolhillblue, www.democraticunderground.com, and countless other websites offering plenty of opportunity for discussion and analysis. The key was competition of ideas—something long missing from the mainstream press.

What went on at these Internet sites resembled the early period in American journalism when a newspaper was brought into a public place, read aloud, and people felt free to add their editorial comments or analysis as the news was read. For instance, The Laissez Faire City Times (once found at www.zolatimes.com) and frontpagemagazine.com invited not only original articles from writers on news and issues but contained an editorial box where readers could add to or challenge the articles as written. And the electronic age adds a dimension that could not have existed in early American times, namely, the permanence of archives, CD ROMs with information on disc, large storage servers, and most especially, printed threads from individual locations. Put another way, while 200 years ago, Americans' comments and analysis of the news vanished as soon as they were uttered, the newspapers remained, leaving the papers (and their errors of fact or analysis as "the final word"). But in the late 20th century, the *corrections* of fact and analysis remain the final word, even if often less-well-circulated or read than the original. This constitutes an important change, for it diminishes the power of journalists to escape their biases.

Limbaugh and the rise of the Internet crowned the second great transformation of the press since the days of Jacksonian partisanship. In a nutshell, the press had renounced, if unofficially, the attempt at value-free journalism of the early 1900s and landed squarely on the side of progressive, or ideological, reporting—news designed to shape present policies. Twenty years before Limbaugh, Drudge, or Fox News appeared, the shift back toward a biased, partisan press had begun, and objectivity was discarded.

THE INTERNET: MATT DRUDGE

In 1994 Matt Drudge established his website, www.drudgereport.com. Born in Maryland before moving to Los Angeles, Drudge held a number of minor jobs en route to his dream of becoming a journalist, including working a gift counter at CBS. Taking on the persona of "the Walter Winchell of the '90s" by sporting a floppy hat and, later, staging his television show in a darkened office befitting a private eye, Matt Drudge was, for all intents and purposes, the first "cyber reporter." Drudge certainly emerged as the most cited news-webmaster, gracing *People* magazine's "most intriguing" list. He became a household name after he exposed *Newsweek*'s spiking of the Clinton White House intern story. From his Hollywood apartment, Drudge worked his day gig at CBS studio, where he "discovered the trash cans in the Xerox room at Television City . . . stuffed to the brim each morning with Nielsen ratings—late century gold if I got in before the cleaning crew fed the shredders."[27] Given a computer by his father, Drudge collected e-mail addresses and sent out items related to Hollywood gossip, ratings, and political chatter picked up through contacts in Washington, DC, and New York.

Supported only by advertising from Radio Shack, Drudge turned his e-mail list from 5 addresses into 5,000 before creating a website in 1994, drudgereport.com, wherein he could break a story over the Internet before it hit the newsstands or the airwaves, preempting even hourly news reports on the radio. He especially relished deflating the networks or major studios with raw data from overnights and box office receipts—all before the *New York Times* or the *Washington Post* had their own websites. When they hustled to catch up, they found that Drudge could tap into their newsrooms and break stories "from their yet-to-be published goodies."[28] At night Drudge monitored news wires on an hourly basis, scouring the nation's papers and touching base with hundreds of insiders and reporters about breaking stories, earning him from *Slate* the sobriquet "the troll under the bridge of Internet journalism."[29] By preemptively reporting on the stories the major newspapers and television shows were about to run in their next-day editions, Drudge became the quintessential reporter who "scooped the scoopers," and the Drudge Report soon became one of the most visited sites on the Web by other reporters.

Limbaugh cited Drudge's posted articles frequently. Since they mostly came from the mainstream news organizations, it was hard to criticize the links. If Drudge's site had a weakness, though, it was that he relied on his sources' sources: he could only indirectly double-check details, although given the unwillingness of reporters to divulge their contacts, there was no way for mainstream journalists to confirm each others' reports either. Even with this limitation, though, Drudge's coverage (especially of the Lewinsky affair) proved remarkably accurate—in some cases defying specific denials by both the administration and other mainstream news sources.

Drudge's style and his instant popularity entertained and informed millions; others were frustrated and outraged, complaining that he did not act like a reporter in that he did not develop his own stories. For example, Frank Rich of the *New York Times* claimed in 1999, even before Drudge started his most rapid ascent, that Drudge "no longer has the power to terrorize the nation's news cycles . . . People turn to the Big Boys not amateur citizen-reporters for news."[30] On the day Rich published his column, there were more than 600 visits to drudgereport.com from . . . the *New York Times.*

Critics from the mainstream media overlooked the fact that Drudge actually did develop his own stories. His story was the next day's planned headlines—what was going to be reported—not so much the event itself. Moreover, his exposé of *Newsweek* spiking the Lewinsky story was itself a story, a story about bias in the press. As he told the National Press Club on June 2, 1998, "How did a story like Monica Lewinsky break out of a Hollywood apartment? What does that say about the Washington press corps?"[31] On top of this, however, Drudge also cultivated an extensive network of sources and informants in person in Hollywood, especially in the entertainment industry, providing him with the latest scoops on the movie industry. But his truly hot, and most important, tips came via e-mail from sources in Washington, DC, New York, and other locations. Using his computer, Drudge could gather and report information far faster than any of the traditional newspapers. Drudge knew that through the power of fiber and wire, computer reports could "scoop" even television, which, at best, could only report at specified intervals. Taking advantage of an unstated code of ethics in the world of television wherein one network was loathe to report scoops of rivals, Drudge availed himself of all the news "out there," not just stories developed "in house." This allowed him to offer much broader coverage than many news shows.

The tandem of a radio-empowered Limbaugh and an Internet-powered Drudge suddenly opened vistas many middle-of-the-road and conservative Americans had never seen or heard. Drudge posted *all* the interesting pieces, and linked to numerous major papers; then Limbaugh culled through Drudge and other links and read articles or parts of columns on the air. Within a few years, Drudge was seeing an estimated $800,000 per year profit, making him "pound for pound . . . the biggest, richest media mogul on the Web."[32] News junkies checked Drudge's site 10–20 times a day, and Drudge had a reputation of tripling another organization's website hits simply by linking to it on his page.

Drudge's contribution to the second transformation of journalism came in giving Web surfers the ability to search numerous papers and websites. Additionally, he sometimes "un-framed" the issues from the media frames. For example, whereas the *New York Times* might dedicate two or three front-page stories to a tax or budget bill—all with the same spin, but from different perspectives—Drudge might link the *Times* story next to a much different treatment offered by the *Washington Times* or *National Review Online*. While there was nothing he could do to change the intra-story framing through the use of code words or phrases, he could balance one story against another. Suddenly, through Rush Limbaugh and Drudge, Americans had an end-run around the mainstream news media—essentially with the fruits of its own reporters' work!

BLOGGING AGAINST THE MAINSTREAM

The Internet allowed for other challenges to the hegemony of the mainstream news media. Of particular note was the rise of blogging. According to the Pew Internet & American Life Project, by 2006, the "blog population has grown to about 12 million American adults, or about 8% of the adult internet users and . . . the number of blog readers has jumped to 57 million American adults, or 39% of the online population."[33] Blogging continues to grow. A blog is a single website on which an individual or group of individuals self-publishes material for the general public. These writings can take numerous forms, but for us, those writings that directly confront the establishment media are worthy of mention. Robert Mac-Dougall notes that at "their best, blogs represent a new form of open-sourced/open-access partisan press. . . . At their worst, blogs represent the latest form of mass-mediated triviality and celebrity spectacle, with the potential to create and sustain insulated enclaves of intolerance predicated on little more than personal illusion, rumor, and politically motivated innuendo."[34] What is of interest here are A-list blogs, which are extremely high readership blogs (some have hundreds of thousands of regular readers, many of whom have blogs of their own that link to the A-list blog). These blogs are listed on the Technorati Top 100 popular blogs list published by Technorati.com.[35]

Of particular note are those blogs that focus on political news and that link themselves to stories in the establishment media. News media researcher David Perlmutter argues that "bloggers help to compile information about political activity for the public; they also serve as correspondents who are able to access certain information and visit venues in a more feasible way than news journalists." He argues that "bloggers help to find and organize information for the public that would otherwise remain unreported. Furthermore, these bloggers serve as critics of the mainstream news media, its information, and the way it is presented."[36] Blogs are increasing the size of their audience, slowly eating into the mainstream news media's audience share: as of 2008, only 46 percent of Americans of all ages turned to newspaper articles or broadcast news for their information needs.[37] According to Pew, in 2012, "slightly more than one-in-ten (12%) of all Americans regularly read blogs about politics or current events and another 21% say they read them sometimes."[38]

As of 2006, approximately 11 percent of bloggers focused on politics and government.[39] Those directly taking on the establishment news media, really a "few dozen of them, known as the 'A-list' or 'political blogs,' [the top dozen or so with the most traffic] have been hailed as a new force in national politics."[40] Their accomplishments are noteworthy. They have

- debunked the forged documents about Bush's National Guard service touted by Dan Rather and CBS;
- debunked the news-media-supported story of Israel bombing a Palestinian ambulance in 2006;[41]
- debunked Maureen Dowd's misleading and inaccurate quotation of President Bush in May 2003, thereby coining the term, "dowdification";
- exposed misuse of fake anti-Israeli photographs by U.S. news media during the Lebanon War;[42]
- exposed the biases of the Lancet Study that overstated the death toll in Iraq; and
- exposed the almost total U.S. media blackout on showing the controversial prophet Muhammad cartoons.[43]

According to Michael Cornfield and colleagues,

> A-list bloggers occupy key positions in the mediascape. Journalists, activists, and political decision-makers have learned to consult political blogs as a guide to what is going on in the rest of the internet. The bloggers are fast to spot items of interest; they link to sources so that items may be verified and inspected at length; and they embroider items with witty captions and frequently passionate commentaries. Accordingly, when bloggers buzz, the big mouthpieces of society notice.[44]

Examples of these A-list blogs include instapundit.com, michellemalkin.com, littlegreenfootballs.com, mydd.com, newsbusters.com, and hotair.com.

In one sense, these blogs represent a type of citizen journalism that allows readers to skip mainstream media gate-keepers. These blogs "present a new context for understanding the role between journalists and their audiences in which the latter has the potential to become more involved, interactive, and a producer and not just a consumer of information."[45] They are not just one-way sources of information—blogger to passive readers. As Shayne Bowman and Chris Willis argue, what bloggers write "inevitably become[s] part of what is now called the 'blogosphere' . . . the linking to and discussion of what others have written or linked to, in essence a distributed discussion."[46]

Another growing function of blogs is discussed by Stephen Cooper in *Watching the Watchdog: Bloggers as the Fifth Estate.*[47] A central point made in this trenchant analysis is that "if the people need a watchdog to make sure the institution of government does not abuse the power they have granted it, would there not be a need for a comparable check on the press, as a social institution with power in its own right?"[48] In short, Cooper asks how bloggers function as news media critics, and he focuses specifically on political news commentary. At the heart of his analysis, Cooper suggests four genres of criticism functioning within this potential Fifth Estate.

First, political news blogs often challenge the accuracy of reports made by the mainstream news media. Within their blogs, bloggers check not only the factual accuracy of descriptions but check also the contextualization of quotations. They authenticate documents, reinterpret statistics, and check the trustworthiness of "memes," which is blog-talk for "'a discrete idea that replicates itself.'"[49] For example, bloggers caught *New York Times* columnist Maureen Dowd intentionally misquoting a statement by President Bush in such a way as to make it appear that he had declared victory in the war on terror. Cooper writes that in the "aftermath of this journalistic scandal, Dowd's name entered the lexicon of blogosphere jargon (Dowdification, n.d.). To dowdify, in blog-speak, is to selectively edit a quote in a way that distorts its meaning."[50] Perhaps the most infamous check of accuracy concerned the forged Bush National Guard memos highlighted on *60 Minutes.* The story, supported by the content of the memos, cast a negative light on President Bush's National Guard service. CBS posted copies of the memos on its website, and these copies quickly came under close scrutiny by political bloggers. According to Cooper, "In the end, the bloggers' doubts about the authenticity of the documents proved to be correct, and the mainstream outlet which had created the faulty report was forced to acknowledge this."[51]

Second, political news blogs act to dispute the mainstream news media frame, reframe an issue or event, or contextualize information when the news media fails to do so. As we've seen, framing is the process whereby communicators act—consciously or not—to construct a particular point of view that encourages the facts of a given situation to be viewed in a particular manner, with some facts made more or less noticeable than others. For example, when mainstream news outlets framed a firefight in Iraq to highlight the strength of the insurgents, political bloggers on rantingprofs.com demonstrated that the same set of facts provided in the paper could have been framed in such a way to demonstrate the overwhelming superiority of the responding American troops as they *crushed* the insurgents.[52]

Third, political news blogs act to dispute the mainstream news functions of agenda-setting and gate-keeping. Gate-keeping is about story selection: who decides what stories shall pass through the media gate. Agenda-setting goes a step beyond this; it shows that the amount of emphasis given to a particular event or issue raises awareness about that event or issue in the mind of the public. Because of this, the media sets an agenda of sorts concerning what is considered important to the public. Blogs challenge the mainstream news hegemony in this area by specifically raising awareness about events ignored by the mainstream news media. Blogs accomplish this through the questioning of the news judgment made by traditional journalists and editors, and also through the setting of alternate agendas.[53] For example, in America during the controversy over the publication of editorial cartoons depicting the Islamic prophet Muhammad, the mainstream news media effectively censored the images; only three newspapers and two broadcast outlets published the cartoons.[54] However, 146 bloggers published the images, thus effectively bypassing the mainstream media's gate-keeping function. Some blogs, such as michellemalkin.com, not only posted the cartoons but also closely scrutinized the role the mainstream media was playing in promoting acceptance of Muslim violence over depictions of the cartoons.[55] Another blog, zombietime.com, posted *Islamic* depictions of the prophet, again bypassing the American mainstream media's lock-out on this issue.[56]

Fourth, political news blogs act to critique the mainstream news general journalistic practices. This area concerns the actual reportorial practices of the reporters and editors. Specifically, blogs act to critique newsgathering practices, writing and editing practices, and error correction practices. For example, during the Iraq War, the U.S. military began the practice of embedding reporters in military units. This was a popular practice, but immediately following the fall of Hussein's regime, the practice fell off, not, as one might assume, because the military was phasing the program out, but rather because reporters discontinued their participation. Because of this, coverage of the aftermath of the war took the form of "hotel journalism," with Western journalists using local stringers instead of their own legs and eyes to generate stories. For example, Cori Dauber of rantingprofs.com wrote,

> As I've written repeatedly, I remain mystified by the argument that, although reporters feel they can't leave their hotels in many instances, but must rely on barely trained or untrained Iraqi stringers to do the actual reporting, embedding is not an alternative because it would provide access to only one side of the story. Sitting in the hotel provides access to *no* sides of the story—embedding would at least balance what the stringers are getting.
>
> Does embedding permit higher quality journalism? My argument there has been that the work produced by papers such as the *North County Times* and the *Richmond Dispatch* suggests that it certainly can.[57]

This is just one example of a critique of mainstream press reportorial practices, something in the past left only to an individual paper's ombudsman, and rarely creating national-level conversation.

One final note is in order. As blogs have cut into the market share of the mainstream news media, traditional journalists have begun to publish their own blogs. Definitely in the minority, many of these journalists, listed on cyberjournalist.net, often write as regular reporters for papers, and will later write on their blogs about what they have already published. Such journalists are sometimes called "j-bloggers." Jane B. Singer points out an interesting aspect of these j-bloggers that distinguishes them from political bloggers in general: "Although expressions of opinion are common, most journalists are seeking to remain gatekeepers even in this highly interactive and participatory format [the blogosphere]. Political j-bloggers use links extensively—but mostly to other mainstream media sites. At least in their early use [to 2005], journalists are 'normalizing' the blog as a component, and in some ways an enhancement, of traditional journalistic norms and practices."[58] We see, then, that journalists are embracing the new technology and forms, but with an end to maintaining their gate-keeping, interpretive functions, and market share. The latter is a very real concern, and one to which we now turn.

THE DEMISE OF THE LIBERAL NEWSPAPER

Undaunted and unconvinced by Limbaugh, Drudge, and the growing voice of independent political news blogs, defenders of the liberal media reacted by blaming news consumers for the ills of the establishment news media. According to this line of thinking, readers lacked the ability to distinguish fact from fiction, and thus were taken in by pseudo-journalists such as Drudge and Michelle Malkin. Yet no one could deny Drudge or Malkin's popularity. Jay Harris bemoaned the fact that the likes of "Matt Drudge and Don Imus have more influence than Bill Moyers and David Broder," and he complained that serious journalistic commentary was being replaced by "the shallow babble of the masses."[59] Democratic leader Lawrence O'Donnell admitted that Limbaugh had far more influence than the media realized.

Nevertheless, some executives recognized that the rise of Drudge, Limbaugh, Fox News, and the Internet bloggers reflected the serious credibility problems mainstream journalism faced. Stuart Garner, the president of Thomson Newspapers, acknowledged that his reporters took "ego trips" and complained that too many reporters "want to save the world, whether the world wants to be saved or not."[60] William Kovach, who had been an editor at the *Atlanta Constitution* and the *New York Times*, observed that after Watergate "a lot of people started showing up in newspaper offices because they saw journalism as *a route toward cele-*

brating themselves."[61] Kovach added that "kids come out of journalism schools wanting to be anchors. They are not that interested in the work of reporting or finding information. They want to be known."[62]

News, to these young journalists, was apparently not about facts. A bias against facts had permeated the deepest levels of the newsrooms of the nation's largest papers. For example, in October 2000, the *New York Times* metro editor Jonathan Landman issued a missive to his staffers, chiding them for "making too many mistakes."[63] During the first nine months of 2000, Landman discovered, the metro section ran 253 corrections—a 20 percent increase from the same period in 1999. Reporters had deliberately run facts that they had not checked, "hoping the [editor's] desk would catch it. . . . A copy editor let a mistake go by rather than persevering in an unpleasant fight with a reporter."[64] The paper went so far as to hire a "corrections commissioner." Yet the *Times* and other mainstream papers claimed Matt Drudge was not a "real reporter." If Drudge got his facts right and a *New York Times* reporter did not, who, then, was the more serious journalist?

As of 1998, the *New York Times, Dallas Morning News, Chicago Tribune, San Francisco Chronicle, Detroit Free Press, Arizona Republic, Boston Globe,* and even the *Wall Street Journal* had all seen circulation fall each year by about 0.02 to 1.3 percent since the early 1990s, despite an economic boom.[65] Trends did not improve in the new millennium, when the *New York Times* saw its six-month circulation plummet by 5.3 percent, with average circulation dropping by 60,000 copies.[66] A Pew Research Center survey in 2002 found that the number of people reading newspapers had fallen to 41 percent, down from 47 percent just two years earlier, and this thus could not be attributed to the 9/11 terror attacks that caused people to watch more television news than ever.[67] All this adds up simply: In real numbers, circulation continues a steady decline. This does not mean, though, that actual readership is down quite as much. In actuality, readership is not down so drastically when one takes into account online sources for news. As reported by Scarborough Research, "In more positive news for newspapers in the online space, a separate study from Nielsen Online for the Newspaper Association of America recently showed that, between 2005 and 2009, unique visitors to newspaper websites grew from a monthly average of 41.1 million to an average of 71.8 million. During the same period, print revenues plummeted from $22.2 billion in 2005 to $12.2 billion in the first half of this year, down 45%."[68] Unfortunately, much of the increase due to website readership results from searches that direct readers to a particular story, which after reading users leave the site. The manner in which traditional papers were read has simply changed for online viewers.

Part of journalism's unwillingness to confront reality lay in the fact that, like the behemoth railroads of the late 1800s, the papers managed to keep high economies of scale through consolidation, growing larger and larger while becoming more and more stultified. Gannett, for example, knocked out a 400 percent dividend rate increase in just four years: *USA Today* owner Al Neuharth boasted, "We like to make 15–20 percent a year. . . . If it looks like our profits might drop below 15 percent, we can just increase our advertising and circulation price."[69] A group of 167 community papers bought by Leonard Green and Partners in 1997 produced average profit margins of more than 30 percent, leading *Editor & Publisher* to claim that "despite the sad talk about declining newspaper circulation and the growth of interactive media, [a partner in Leonard Green] thinks papers are a tremendous investment."[70] Other chains showed similar profit margins, just as many railroads, in their semi-monopolistic states, reassured themselves that they had a continued stream of profits.

Typical of this attitude were the remarks of John Morton, writing in *Neiman Reports*, that the big papers were "turning their backs on news and comprehensive coverage—the very things that made them community institutions and valuable properties in the first place."[71] He failed to note that the very attraction of Neuharth's *USA Today* was that it *eschewed* local coverage for national news on all levels, correctly realizing that in fact Americans were mobile and transient.

Many papers assumed their problem lay in a failure to adopt the latest technology. As a result, online publishing became a vogue in the late 1990s. Websites freed papers from the dreaded deadline, and routinely a company's website might scoop its print edition. Yet Web papers consistently failed to show a profit. The *New York Times* online unit reported projected losses for 2000 would exceed $60 million, and in January 2001 the *Times* cut 17 percent of its online jobs. The *Los Angeles Times* anticipated net losses of $10–15 million. Even the *Wall Street Journal*, which charged a fee, claimed 375,000 online customers, yet barely inched toward profitability in 2000.[72] Reuters, the news and information provider, undertook a massive restructuring in 2000 by axing 1,700, after being "slow to react to the Internet."[73] John Kimball, the chief marketing officer for the Newspaper Association of America, admitted, "No one seems to have really figured out the revenue model here," and technology writer Jon Katz pointed out that merely having to register at a site—let alone pay a fee—leads readers to click "exit."[74] And an increasing number of net-oriented Americans read their news online for free: by 1999, some 10 percent had already canceled subscriptions to print newspapers because they received an online service.

Newspaper owners and editors remained optimistic. Only 6 percent of editors envisioned the end of print newspapers. Jay T. Harris, chairman and publisher of the *San Jose Mercury News*, told a dinner audience that he thought he would "be selling many tens of thousands more newspapers 10 years from now than I am today," and he added that "newspapers . . . will continue to flourish."[75] Harris's 2000 prediction for his own paper came true, but other mainstream papers simply contradict his projections. For example, between 2004 and 2010, most establishment press papers saw a large decline in circulation. Consider these leading mainstream newspapers:

- *USA Today*: 2004: 2,192,098; 2010: 1,826,622
- *New York Times*: 2004: 1,119,027; 2010: 951,063
- *Washington Post*: 2004: 760,034; 2010: 578,482
- *San Francisco Chronicle*: 2004: 499,008; 2010: 241,330[76]

Consequently, the Internet, which once seemed a savior of the print paper, merely caused more financial headaches. Some claimed "the Internet as media has failed," with "no future" for "content sites"[77] such as the left-wing site Salon, which "endured continued losses over its 15-year history" and almost collapsed in 2003.[78] In fact, as Rush Limbaugh said, "It's content, content, content." FreeRepublic.com and other political websites remained viable. Some, such as WorldNetDaily.com, not only linked to stories of the major papers but had their own stable of editorial writers who offered substantially different views than those typically found at the *Washington Post* or the *New York Times*.

One reason for the decline in mainstream print papers is that such cyberspace "papers" made it harder to hide bias, claims Paul Sperry of WorldNetDaily; providing the public with full-text versions of important documents, or entire transcripts of speeches, allowed them to form their own opinions.[79] And the Internet is only growing as a source of news— 48 percent of adults in 2001 would *occasionally* go online for news; as of 2008, almost 4 in 10 Americans of all ages *regularly* sought their news from Internet sources.[80] Viewed in this light, the Matt Drudges can only expect to see their influence increase.[81] After all, the Internet threatened to take control over the content of news shows away from editors and anchors and put it back in the hands of the people who read the news— exactly as it was when the broadside newspapers first appeared in America. Author and journalist Mitch Albom pointed out that on September 11, 2001, the first terrorist attacks came at 8:45 a.m. when many people had not read the morning papers (and, indeed, many morning papers on the West Coast had not even been delivered yet). As Albom noted, "With the first plane's fiery impact, all those newspapers were rendered obsolete."[82]

Yet Internet news was not without its critics. Some complained that a "digital divide" existed, thus stratifying Americans based on their access to a computer. The head of the NAACP, Kweisi Mfume, called it "technological segregation," and the ubiquitous Jesse Jackson termed the phenomena "classic apartheid."[83] There was only one problem: it was simply not true. By 2000, Americans of Hispanic descent were online at as high a percentage as whites, and Americans of Asian descent were the most "wired" group of all.[84] These figures were only growing: by 2005, 80 percent of black Americans had Internet access.[85] By 2008, 64 percent of American adults of Hispanic descent accessed the Internet regularly. Moreover, the number of households with computers exceeded 50 percent in 2000 and had risen to 80 percent by 2009.[86] Even then, as George Gilder pointed out, the "digital divide" involved the rich and middle classes paying the high costs of refining the technology so that virtually everyone could have access to the Internet for nothing.[87]

Of note is that the number of Americans online has risen so fast that surveys are having trouble staying abreast of the growth, and the fastest gains come among African Americans and Americans of Hispanic descent. One reason minorities "wired up" so quickly was that PC prices plunged, with base model PC prices falling from $1,747 in 1996 to $916 in 1999 to only $550 in 2008.[88] Increased computer possession and easier Internet connectivity both had their effects on new consumption. And when Americans went online for news, political news was the most sought after.[89]

A 1999 study showed that 67.5 million personal computers were connected to the Internet—an increase of 50 percent in just a year. More than half of all PCs in the United States were linked to the Internet, with the largest share of those being home PCs. Some 60 percent of all American households had logged on to the Internet at some time in 1998, a study from InfoBeads reported.[90] By June 2000, a majority of Americans had access to at least one computer—an 11 percent increase from 1997.[91] So widespread was Internet news that Columbia University's journalism school and the Online News Association announced a new set of international awards for excellence in Internet reporting. By 2009, these numbers had grown and only showed signs of increasing: 74 percent of Americans now used the Internet regularly, and many more had access through schools, public libraries, and friends.

In June 2000, a poll by the Pew Research Center confirmed the trends favoring Internet news when it found "key segments of the nation's news audience, particularly younger and better-educated Americans . . . are turning increasingly to the Internet."[92] With one-third of the public going online at least once a week in 2000 (compared to just 20 percent in 1998), and with 15 percent getting news from the Internet (a threefold increase over the same period), the trend was clear, and it has continued to the present day. With the exception of a few techno-Luddites, such as Langdon Winner and Chellis Glendinning, few argued that computers themselves posed a serious threat to values or progress.[93] Instead, news consumers celebrated emancipation from the 5:00 news tyranny: a UCLA study published in early 2003 showed that the Internet had cut into television time, and that time spent on the Net came directly out of television viewing time.[94] Recent surveys show similar growth. Internet-based news, both traditional and nontraditional, is encroaching on print and broadcast territories.[95]

As with almost every technological leap in American industrial history, the Internet-newspaper-cable fusion is met by a chorus of critics, ranging from intellectuals to journalists to small competitors fearing for their business survival. University of Chicago law professor Cass Sunstein called for censorship of free speech *only* on the Internet because the Internet allowed the public to have choices: "Consumers are able to see exactly what they want," he complained, warning of conservative websites and the public reading only conservative material.[96] This is a chilling threat posed by those championing the gate-keeping of the establishment press: if people can, and do, choose to read alternate viewpoints, they must be stopped, even by censorship. One tactic was to complain that Internet companies were being purchased by other media giants, and for this reason to call for more government control. Bill Kovach, curator of the Nieman Foundation for Journalism, complained, "You now have an Internet company that is merging with print, broadcast, and other forms of communication . . . which has no tradition, no history, no grasp of journalism and the principles that make journalism what it is."[97] Kovach seems unaware that the principles that made journalism what it was had been abandoned in the 1960s.

The news networks feel the pressure of Internet and cable: from 24 percent of the sets in use tuning in to CBS News in 1985, today it is less than half that. Likewise, ABC News, which had 21 percent of viewers in 1985, has less than 15 percent today, and NBC News has dropped to below 15 percent as well.[98] Executives do seem to agree that their market has been shrinking: ABC producer Phyllis McGrady said as early as 1997 that the numbers "were really dropping. . . . At first I thought it was just sort of a blip. Then I realized it was more than a blip."[99] Yet while the major news media executives recognized they had a problem, typically they failed to understand their all-permeating biases contributed to the problem, concluding instead that people were switching to Internet and cable because of slicker production, rather than searching for alternate points of view. Andrew Heyward, CBS News president, continuing to view the issue as "packaging," explained, "For us just to give headlines clearly isn't enough."[100]

Ironically, the print and television media saw the technology issues as a straw to which they clutched. After all, if technology explained their shrinking market share, it could be mastered easily enough, they reasoned. This excuse allowed them to ignore content and bias issues that accounted for much of their decline. Even more stunning, and something lost on the analysts, was the fact that Fox News—the only network without a distinct liberal bias—shot to the top of all cable ratings, burying CNBC, MSNBC, and CNN. In 2002, Fox gained 44 percent, averaging 667,000 total-day viewers, compared to CNN's 536,000 and MSNBC's 263,000 viewers.[101] In September 2003, Nielson reported that Fox News was the only cable news service to grow from a year earlier, gaining 20 percent, while rival CNN plunged another 9 percent and MSNBC lost 11 percent.[102] By mid 2010, Fox News dominated all other cable shows on a daily average: Fox News—1,400,000 viewers; CNN—493,000 viewers; MSNBC—432,000 viewers; CNBC—200,000 viewers. The numbers are even more dramatic when looking at prime time: Fox News—3,009,000 viewers; CNN—765,000 viewers; MSNBC—905,000 viewers; CNBC—201,000 viewers.[103]

What had gone virtually unnoticed by both national and local analysts of journalism was that the profession had become populated almost entirely by a group of reporters, editors, and anchors who were remarkably similar in not only their worldviews but their lifestyle choices. Their homogeneity contributed to a conspiracy of shared values, in which they *naturally* possessed similar biases. By the simple inclusion of alternate voices, Fox News, Rush, Drudge, and political news bloggers rocketed into importance, carving for themselves large portions of the traditional news media pie. In the next chapter, we'll look at establishment journalists: who they are, and how their collective identity contributes to their conspiracy of shared values.

NOTES

1. James Fallows, *Breaking the News: How the Media Undermine American Democracy* (New York: Vintage Books, 1997 [1996]), 3.
2. Fallows, 30–31.
3. Stanley Rothman and Amy E. Black, "Media and Business Elites: Still in Conflict?" *Public Interest*, Spring 2001, 72–86, esp. 83–84.
4. Fallows explains this phenomena as due to an affinity for "gamesmanship" among reporters, which insulates them from having to learn the particulars of difficult issues (146–147).
5. For a detailed investigation into the rise of political talk radio, see Randy Bobbit, *Us against Them: The Political Culture of Talk Radio* (Lanham, MD: Lexington Books, 2010).
6. There is no authorized biography of Limbaugh. Paul D. Colford, *The Rush Limbaugh Story: Talent on Loan from God, An Unauthorized Biography* (New York: St. Martin's Press, 1994), provides an unauthorized biography.
7. Rodger Streitmatter, *Mightier than the Sword* (Boulder, CO: Westview Press, 1997), 222.
8. Kathleen Hall Jamieson and Joseph N. Cappella, *Echo Chamber: Rush Limbaugh and the Conservative Media Establishment* (New York: Oxford University Press, 2010).
9. Ted J. Smith, III, S. Robert Licter, and Louis Harris and Associates, *What the People Want from the Press* (Washington, DC: Center for Media and Public Affairs, 1997), 16. See also www.stateofthemedia.org/2010/index.php.
10. Frank Rich, "Why Liberals Are No Fun" *New York Times*, July 20, 2003.
11. Rush Limbaugh, "Content, Not Consolidation, Saved Radio," www.rushlimbaugh.com, May 28, 2003.
12. Dave Henry, "'Vast Right-Wing Conspiracy' Is All Talk," *Amarillo Globe-News*, July 17, 2003.
13. Henry.

14. Interview with Chris Geovanis, stringer for Pacifica News, August 12, 2003, who contended that alternative sources for information had dried up, and that even local papers no longer were independent.

15. S. Lacy and T. F. Simon, *The Economics and Regulation of United States Newspapers* (Norwood, NJ: Ablex Publishing, 1993), 132–133.

16. www.stopbigmedia.com/chart.php?chart=pub.

17. http://nca.files.cms-plus.com/2009_Annual_Review.ppt and www.followthe money.org/database/nationalview.phtml?l=0&f=0&y=2004&abbr=0.

18. www.nytimes.com/2010/01/22/us/politics/22scotus.html?hp.

19. Zev Chafets, "The Limbaugh Victory," *New York Times*, May 19, 2010, www.nytimes.com/2010/05/20/opinion/20chafets.html.

20. Matthew Fordahl, "First Link of Future Internet Born Without Fanfare in Summer of '69," AP, August 30, 1999, www.freerepublic.com/forum/a37ca7b526ea.htm.

21. "United States of America," Internet World Stats, www.internetworldstats.com/am/us.htm.

22. Essay by poster named "Freedom Wins," "Corporate Liberals Target Conservative Web Site," http://bulldogbulletin.com/page1f.htm.

23. Jim Robinson, "History of FR," December 12, 2002, www.freerepublic.com/focus/news/805832/posts.

24. Robert Stowe, "The Freepers Go to Washington," *Washington Weekly*, November 2, 1998.

25. Justin Pope, "Judge Says Amateur News Gatherers on Public Access TV Have Same Rights as Professionals," March 7, 2002, http://ap.tbo.com/ap/breaking/MCA1LU5FHYC.html.

26. Buckley quoted in the transcript of NPR's *Talk of the Nation*, November 28, 2000.

27. Matt Drudge, with Julia Phillips, *Drudge Manifesto* (New York: New American Library, 2000), 27.

28. Drudge, 32.

29. Drudge, 33.

30. Rich quoted in Drudge, 99.

31. Drudge, 200.

32. Geoff Keighley, "The Secrets of Drudge Inc.," www.Business2.com via CNN Money, April 3, 2003. According to Keighley, Drudge and his assistant run the entire site from Miami.

33. "Blogging Is Bringing new Voices to the Online World," Pew/Internet & American Life Project, July 19, 2006, p. 1.

34. Robert MacDougall, "Identity, Electronic Ethos, and Blogs: A Technological Analysis of Symbolic Exchange on the New News Medium," *American Behavioral Scientist* 49, no. 4 (2005), 575.

35. Technorati, "Popular Blogs," www.technorati.com/pop/blogs.

36. Adria Y. Goldman and Jim A. Kuypers, "Contrasts in News Coverage: A Qualitative Framing Analysis of 'A' List Bloggers and Newspaper Articles Reporting on the Jena 6," *Relevant Rhetoric* 1, no. 1 (2010), www.relevantrhetoric.com. See also David Perlmutter, *Blogwars* (New York: Oxford University Press, 2008).

37. Pew Research Center for the People & the Press, "Key News Audiences Now Blend Online and Traditional Sources," August 17, 2008, http://people-press.org/report/444/news-media.

38. "In Changing News Landscape, Even Television Is Vulnerable: Trends in News Consumption: 1991–2012," Pew Research Center for the People & the Press, September 27, 2012, www.people-press.org/2012/09/27/section-2-online-and-digital-news-2/.

39. "Blogging Is Bringing New Voices to the Online World," Pew/Internet & American Life Project, July 19, 2006, 1.

40. Michael Cornfield, Jonathan Carson, Alison Kalis, and Emily Simon, "Buzz, Blogs, and Beyond: The Internet and the National Discourse in the Fall of 2004," Pew Internet & American Life Project, May 16, 2005, 3, www.pewinternet.org/ppt/BUZZ_BLOGS__BEYOND_Final05-16-05.pdf.

41. www.zombietime.com/fraud/ambulance/.

42. http://acjournal.org/holdings/vol9/summer/articles/fauxtography.html.

43. Michelle Malkin, "The Cartoons the Jihadists Don't Want You to See," michelle-malkin.com, October 22, 2005, http://michellemalkin.com/2005/10/22/the-cartoons-isla-mists-dont-want-you-to-see/.

44. Cornfield, Carson, Kalis, and Simon, 5.

45. Gracie Lawson-Borders and Rita Kirk, "Blogs in Campaign Communication," *American Behavioral Scientist* 49, no. 4 (2005), 556.

46. Shayne Bowman and Chris Willis, "We Media: How Audiences Are Shaping the Future of News and Information," The Media Center at the American Press Institute, www.hypergene.net/wemedia/weblog.php?id=P38.

47. The following six paragraphs were originally published in Robert E. Denton and Jim A. Kuypers, *Politics and Communication in America: Campaigns, Media, and Governing in the 21st Century* (Carbondale, IL: Waveland Press, 2008).

48. Stephen D. Cooper, *Watching the Watchdog: Bloggers as the Fifth Estate* (Spokane, WA: Marquette Books, 2006), 13.

49. Cooper, 97.

50. Cooper, 54. See specifically 47–54.

51. Cooper, 76–77. See especially 54–76.

52. Cooper, 106–108.

53. Cooper, 121–152.

54. This is our informal count.

55. See http://michellemalkin.com/archives/004413.htm.

56. See www.zombietime.com/mohammed_image_archive/.

57. Cori Dauber, "There Are Benefits to Embedding," April 21, 2005, www.rantingprofs.com/rantingprofs/2005/04/there_are_benef.html.

58. Jane B. Singer, "The Political J-Blogger: 'Normalizing' A New Media form to Fit Old Norms and Practices," *Journalism* 6.2 (2005), 173.

59. Harris quoted in "Publisher Sees Newspapers Flourishing in Internet Era."

60. Tim Jones, "A Simple Formula: Writing What People Will Read," *Chicago Tribune*, November 14, 1999.

61. Kovach quoted in Fallows, 160. Emphasis mine.

62. Kovach quoted in Fallows, 160.

63. "Awash in Errors, *Times* Metro Desk Recruits Corrections Czar," www.inside.com/Story, Cached/0,2770,10676_7_12_1,00.html.

64. "Awash in Errors."

65. "Circulation of 20 Biggest U.S. Papers," Washington Post.com, November 3, 1998.

66. "Ken Layne on Why the *New* [*York*] *Times* Circulation Has Plummeted 5.3% in the Last Six Months," May 6, 2003, www.kenlayne.com.

67. Will Lester, "More People Watching News, Fewer Reading It," June 10, 2002, www.boston.com.

68. "74% of Americans Still Read Newspapers," MC Marketing Charts, November 19, 2009, www.marketingcharts.com/print/74-of-americans-still-read-newspapers-11117/.

69. Neuharth quoted in Victor Jose, *The Free Paper in America: The Struggle for Survival* (Richmond, IN: Graphic Press, 2000), 68–69.

70. Jose, 78–79.

71. Roberts quoted in Jose, 84.

72. Tracy Robinson, "Print Discovers the Web, and in Doing So, It's Finding New Ways to Lose Money," *American Spectator*, May 2000, 58–59.

73. Clayton Hirst, "Reuters Will Axe 1,700 in Net Strategy," www.independent.co.uk/news/Business/Inside_Business/200-08/reuters130800.shtml.

74. Kimball quoted in Robinson, 59.

75. Harris quoted in Scott Sonner, "Publisher Sees Newspapers Flourishing in Internet Era," *Sacramento Bee*, April 1, 2000, online edition.

76. Figures from Burrelles Luce, "Top One Hundred Daily Newspapers in the US by Circulation," 2004 and 2010.

77. Michael Wolff interviewed by www.iwantmedia.com, February 1, 2001, www.iwantmedia.com/people1.html.

78. Dawn Kawamoto, "Is Salon.com Looking to Turn a Page with a Merger?" DailyFinance.com, www.dailyfinance.com/story/is-salon-com-looking-to-turn-a-page-with-a-merger/19736302/.

79. Paul Sperry, "Will Newspapers Go Extinct?" June 21, 2002, www.World NetDaily.com.

80. Pew Project for Excellence in Journalism, "State of the Media: 2009."

81. "Internet Grows as News Source," October 17, 2001, http://more.abcnews.go.com/sections/scitech/DailyNews/onlinenews_poll011017.html.

82. Albom quoted in Sperry.

83. Mfume quoted in "NAACP, AT&T Take on 'Digital Divide," Associated Press, July 13, 1999; Jackson quoted in "Wrassling Dinosaurs Scare Teleco Beasts," *Communication Today*, 6 (April 6, 2000).

84. James K. Glassman, "Digital Divide: The Search for Victims Continues," *Reason Magazine*, online edition, April 24, 2000.

85. "AOL: Some 80 Percent of African-Americans Online," VOX Marketing, October 17, 2005, www.marketingvox.com/aol_some_80_percent_of_africanamericans_online-020157/.

86. "An Overview of Home Internet Access in the U.S.," Nielsen Wire, December 2008, http://blog.nielsen.com/nielsenwire/wp-content/uploads/2009/03/overview-of-home-internet-access-in-the-us-jan-6.pdf.

87. George Gilder, *Telecosm: How Infinite Bandwidth Will Revolutionize Our World* (New York: Free Press, 2000).

88. Adam D. Thierer, "How Free Computers Are Filling the Digital Divide," *Heritage Foundation Backgrounder*, no. 1361, April 20, 2000, see chart "Average Price of 'Base Model' PCs Has Dropped Steadily," 4. See too "Average Mac Price Now 2X Windows PCs," *Electronista*, August 6, 2008, www.electronista.com/articles/08/08/06/mac.prices.2x.windows.pcs/.

89. "More than Half of Adults in U.S. Online, Study Says," Reuters, February 18, 2001, www.freerepublic.com/forum/a3a9073dc2bb7.htm.

90. Yahoo Business Wire, June 1, 1999, biz.yahoo.com.

91. Paul Recer, "Poll: Most of U.S. Has Computer Access," *Washington Post*, online edition, June 20, 2000.

92. Will Lester, "Web Attracts Younger News Audience," *Washington Post*, online edition, June 11, 2000.

93. Langdon Winner, *The Whale and the Reactor: A Search for Limits in an Age of High Tech* (Chicago: University of Chicago Press, 1986); Chellis Glendinning, *When Technology Wounds: The Human Consequences of Progress* (New York: Morrow, 1990).

94. Dawn C. Chmielewski, "UCLA Study Finds the Internet Poses a Major Threat to Television," *San Jose Mercury News*, January 30, 2003.

95. Pew Project for Excellence in Journalism, "State of the Media: 2009."

96. Ann Coulter, *Slander* (New York: Crown, 2002), 116.

97. Kovach quoted in *Editor & Publisher*, February 28, 2000. Similar views were expressed by Robert McChesney in *Rich Media, Poor Democracy: Communications Politics in Dubious Times* (Urbana: University of Illinois Press, 1999).

98. Peter Johnson, "Network News Feels the Heat: Big Three Shift Programming to Compete with Cable, Net," *USA Today*, August 7, 2000.

99. Johnson.

100. Johnson.

101. Craig Offman, "Bad Tiding for Cable News Pack," January 2, 2003, http://story.news.yahoo.com/news.

102. Andrew Grossman, "Fox News Gains, Other News Networks Fall," *Yahoo! News*, September 4, 2003.

103. "Cable News Ratings for Thursday, June 3, 2010," *TV by the Numbers*, June 3, 2010, http://tvbythenumbers.com/category/ratings/top-news/cable-news.

EIGHT

Journalistic Values and Biased Reporting

Throughout this book I have referred to "the press" or to the "news media." When I use these terms I am, of course, referring to the real persons who craft and report the news—to journalists. Yet who are these journalists? Insight into their personal politics, lifestyle choices, and even places of residence can shed light on their reporting practices. In a path-breaking 1986 study, Robert Lichter, Stanley Rothman, and Linda Lichter tracked the voting records and party affiliations of journalistic elites, finding that they have possessed evident liberal tendencies since at least 1966—or more than 40 years today.[1] Many of the revelations brought out in the Lichter, Rothman, and Lichter book and in their earlier study in *Public Opinion* magazine are often dismissed by left-wing groups, who claim that the entire media is conservative because it is capitalistic, but they have yet to produce counterevidence that would challenge the inescapable conclusion, namely, that the news media as a group is far to the left of the mainstream in America.

JOURNALISTS: A 40-YEAR SNAPSHOT

In this chapter I look closely at journalists as a group—their personal beliefs, political habits, and personal behaviors. I then look at how all of this influences their reporting on the issues of the day. Specifically, I provide a detailed demographic profile of contemporary journalists and then show how "who they are" influences the news. What I have found in my explorations gives not only pause, but cause for worry. And I am not alone in this concern. Without specifically addressing the bias issue, journalistic leaders were clearly worried when in April 2000 the

American Society of Newspaper Editors engaged in a long-term project called the "Journalism Credibility Project." Their purpose? To answer the question, "Why do so many Americans distrust what they read in newspapers?" Although panels met and "experts" debated various theories, few got to the essence of what I see as the problem. NBC News president Lawrence Grossman even insisted objectivity and credibility were overemphasized, and said, "We have to do things occasionally that people may not like, but are nonetheless important to do."[2]

WHO ARE CONTEMPORARY JOURNALISTS?

At almost the same time as the news industry began its self-assessment, Peter Brown, an editor at the *Orlando Sentinel*, conducted a survey using a professional pollster sent to reporters in five midsize cities in the United States, plus the large metro area of Dallas–Ft. Worth. Brown and pollster Bill Hamilton of Bethesda devised two separate surveys. One used 500 residents and 478 journalists in five cities: Dayton, Ohio; Tulsa, Oklahoma; Syracuse, New York; Roanoke, Virginia; and Chico/Redding, California. The other survey used a massive (by polling standards) database of 3,400 home addresses of journalists in 13 news organizations, including the *Minneapolis Star-Tribune*, the *Washington Post*, the *Denver Rocky Mountain News*, and many other large- to midsize city papers. In the first survey, the pollster phoned residents in those areas at random and asked the same questions posed to the reporters.

Responses to the Brown/Hamilton survey revealed a surprising disparity in lifestyles. Journalists were more likely to "have maids, own Mercedes and trade stocks, and less likely to go to church, do volunteer work or put down roots in a community."[3] They had few children, and tended to live in expensive urban neighborhoods. Taken together, their profiles revealed a class of people far outside the lifestyles of average Americans. With this patchwork of shared elite values, "advocacy of elite interests comes so easily that it scarcely seems like bias at all," said one media observer.[4]

Although most journalists ignore the disparity between the journalistic class and their audiences, there are a few exceptions. For example, Michael Kelly, a writer for the *Atlantic*, confirmed the cultural uniformity of journalists, especially those in Washington:

> They are parts of a product-based cultural whole, just like the citizens of Beverly Hills. . . . They go to the same parties, send their children to the same schools, live in the same neighborhoods. They interview each other, argue with each other, sleep with each other, marry each other, live and die by each other's judgment. . . . Not surprisingly, they tend to believe the same things at the same time . . . They believe that nothing a politician does in public can be taken at face value, but that

everything he does is a metaphor for something he is hiding. . . . Above all, they believe in the power of what they have created, in the subjectivity of reality and the reality of perceptions, in image.[5]

Joel Kotkin and David Friedman said, "The news media have come to resemble a modern-day caste, largely dominated by a relative handful of individuals sharing a common background and, in most cases, common real estate."[6] Despite hiring more minorities and women, "in their class and education . . . the media have become ever more rarified."[7] And more rarified they have become over time: in the 1970s, top editors and reporters in New York City and Washington were less likely than their elite counterparts in other professions to have attended Ivy League universities or been born into wealthy families, but by 1995, the media elites composed a higher proportion of Ivy League graduates than any other group in society except the highest-paid lawyers.[8] The trend continues to this day. Well-known reporters, such as Ted Koppel, can command $50,000 per speech at a university. Others plan their careers carefully to position themselves for better access to such speeches and for television—one reporter frequently reminded a news-talk host that he was only "right down the street," implying that the reporter could easily come in for an "expert" analyst position in the studio if the host needed one. This also tends to reinforce the "stay-around-Washington-and-New York" syndrome.

A certain amount of bias, as noted by economist Daniel Sutter, comes from self-selection: "the costs of membership in the [news] organization for individuals with dissenting [i.e., conservative] viewpoints can be extremely high."[9] Sutter noted that "people with the talent, temperament, and personality to be mainstream journalists might also be inclined toward liberal political causes."[10] Journalists appeared to agree with Sutter: a 1981 Brookings survey of journalists found that 51 percent said the Washington press corps had a political bias, and 96 percent of them perceived it was a liberal bias.[11]

AVERAGE AMERICAN AND AVERAGE JOURNALIST: A COMPARISON

The degree of separation between the average American and the average journalist is staggering. Although it is difficult to get a precise side-by-side snapshot for the press and the average American since the information being contrasted has been asked for at different times, some observations can be put forth. It is quite enlightening to look at the political self-descriptions of journalists, and then to compare that with the self-descriptions of Americans. Since tracking first began, the political self-descriptions of Americans have held amazingly constant, with approximately 20 percent considering themselves liberal (only in the run up to the 2008 election did that number break 20 percent, reaching a high of 22 percent), 40 percent considering themselves moderate, and 40 percent considering themselves conservative (see table 8.1[12]).

Table 8.1.   Political Self-Descriptions of Americans and American Journalists

Group	Americans	Press	Press	Press	Pressp>	D.C. Press	Press	Pressup >
Date	1980–2010	1981	1986	1992	1995	1996	2002	2004
Liberal	20%	54%	56%	47%	22%	61%	40%	34%
Moderate	40%			30%	64%	30%	33%	
Conservative	40%	19%	18%	25%	5%	9%	22%	7%

By any measure there exists a chasm between the political orientation of journalists and the Americans they pretend to represent. It is important to note that these are self-descriptions, thus based solely on what journalists say of themselves. Although it might appear that by 1995 the press was waking up to criticism of biased reporting and hiring more moderate reporters and editors, this is not the case. The 1995 results simply reflect the growing awareness of criticism of the press's political imbalance. Reporters were then, I am inclined to believe, simply describing themselves differently; in short, no matter what, call yourself a moderate and then do what you like. As will be shown later, reportorial *habits* continued unchanged. In any case, by 2004, the effect of negative criticism appeared to be wearing off. A Pew Research Center survey, asking the same questions as those in the 1995 survey above, found 34 percent of the press willing to again consider themselves liberal.[13]

Political orientation can also be linked to specific policies and beliefs. Let us turn for a moment to how Americans feel on certain issues, how they vote, and how they act, and contrast that with the feelings and actions of journalists. In terms of voting behavior, Lichter, Rothman, and Lichter found that at "least 81% of the news media had voted for the liberal Democrat for President in every election going back to 1964."[14] Since then, little has changed, as evidenced by the vote tallies for the winning candidate. Again, overwhelming support for the Democrat, minimal support for the Republican:

Voted for Reagan 1984
Press: 26%
Public: 59%

Voted for Bush 1988
Press: 19%[15]
Public: 53.4%

Voted for Clinton 1992
Press: 89%

Public: 43%

Voted for Clinton 1996
Press: not available
Public: 49.2%

Voted for Bush 2000
Press: not available
Public: 47.9%

Voted for Bush 2004[16]
Press: 19%
Public: 50.7%

Voted for Obama 2008
Press: not available
Public: 52.9%

Journalists don't just vote for liberal candidates and believe in liberal political positions. They also give to Democrats and liberal candidates overwhelmingly more than they give to conservatives or Republicans. For instance, "MSNBC.com identified 143 journalists who made political contributions from 2004 through the start of the 2008 campaign, according to the public records of the Federal Election Commission. An overwhelming majority of the newsroom checkbooks leaned to the left: 125 journalists gave to Democrats and liberal causes. Only 16 gave to Republicans. Two gave to both parties."[17] "Most" is a gross understatement: 87 percent gave exclusively to Democrats.

Social issues are another area in which journalists are clearly at odds with average Americans: Surveys conducted between 1995 and 2000 "found that 90% of the press favored abortion; 83% found nothing wrong with homosexuality; only 47% believed adultery to be wrong; 50% had no religious affiliation; and 85% seldom or never attended church or synagogue."[18] On the first issue mentioned above, 42 percent of Americans would favor a law that would restrict all abortion except to save the life of the mother.[19] Concerning homosexuality, 74 percent of Americans considered homosexual behavior unacceptable.[20] On the issue of adultery, 79 percent felt it always wrong (up to 90 percent if "almost always wrong").[21] On the religious front, 83 percent considered themselves Protestant or Catholic (2 percent Jewish), and 61 percent attended church or synagogue at least once a month.[22] Issues involving faith are particularly striking. The 2002 Pew Global Attitudes Project found that 58 percent of the general public thought that belief in God was necessary to be moral; only 6 percent of national journalists felt so, and that figure shrinks to a mere 3 percent when we are considering only self-described liberal journalists.[23]

In terms of political party identification, our national press in the 1990s was approximately 50 percent registered Democrat, 37 percent independent, and only 4 percent Republican, with 9 percent mentioning other parties.[24] During the same time period, the party affiliation of Americans was 31 percent Democrat, 39 percent independent, and 30 percent Republican.[25] In 2002, fewer reporters identified themselves as members of the Democratic party (37 percent) and more identified themselves as independent (34 percent).[26] All of these self-descriptions of journalists reveal a stunning difference between the social-political composition of Americans and the press that purports to provide them with news they can use. As summed up by Rich Noyes,

> Surveys over the past 25 years have consistently found journalists are much more liberal than the rest of America. Their voting habits are disproportionately Democratic, their views on issues such as abortion and gay rights are well to the left of most Americans and they are less likely to attend church or synagogue. When it comes to the free market, journalists have become increasingly pro-regulation over the past 20 years, with majorities endorsing activist government efforts to guarantee everyone a job and to reduce the income gap between rich and poor Americans.[27]

Americans are increasingly noticing this divide. *U.S. News & World Report* wrote,

> There is reason to worry that the cultural chasm between the majority of Americans and the Washington media is widening. A survey taken for *U.S. News* in the spring of 1995 found that 50 percent of voters thought the news media are strongly or somewhat in conflict with their goals, while only 40 percent thought the media are strongly or somewhat friendly to their goals. This was the worst approval rating of any group measured—even lower than the ratings for elected officials and lawyers.[28]

In the 21st century, the situation is clearly worse: 75 percent of Americans feel that the news media is more interested in "attracting the biggest" audience than in "keeping the public informed."[29] Americans are increasingly less likely to believe what they read in their daily papers as well. From 1984 to 2005, the percent of Americans finding news stories believable dropped from 84 percent to 54 percent, and during the same time period, those finding network news believable dropped from 87 percent to 64 percent.[30] We see also that Americans are increasingly rejecting the notion that the press is fair and accurate in its reportorial practices: from 1985 to 2009, belief in the accuracy of the press dropped from 55 percent to 29 percent of Americans; during the same time period, the number of Americans willing to say that the press "deals fairly with all sides" dropped from 34 percent to 18 percent.[31] Moreover, a whopping 70 percent of Americans feel that the press "tries to cover up its mistakes."[32] Additionally, the number of Americans believing the news media to be biased rose from 45 percent to 60 percent between 1985 and 2009.[33] Of those seeing biased political coverage, 45 percent saw it as liberal, and 15 percent saw it as conservative, with the rest either not knowing or feeling coverage was neither liberal or conservative.[34]

A 2009 study by Gallup found that party affiliation correlates to the amount of trust placed in the news media: 36 percent of Republicans, 39 percent of independents, and 58 percent of Democrats place a "great deal" to a "fair amount" of trust in the news media.[35] Of note as well is that as education level increases, trust in the news media decreases.[36] For instance, whereas 58 percent of Americans with a high-school-level education or less place a great deal to a fair amount of trust in the news media, only 39 percent of those with some college do so; college graduates and those with graduate degrees place roughly the same amount of trust in the news media, with 38 percent and 37 percent, respectively.

DO BELIEFS AND VALUES INFLUENCE REPORTING?

The real question, of course, is not so much what Americans perceive as what is actually in the reporting. Looking at reportorial practices, it is clearly one thing to self-describe as liberal, to vote consistently for Democrats and liberals, to donate to Democrats and liberals, and to believe in liberal policies and issues. It is another thing altogether to allow this to influence news reporting. Apologists say that news reporters are professionals, highly trained, and able to separate personal beliefs and political actions from their jobs. Jeffrey A. Dvorkin, writing for NPR about a recent Pew poll on journalist politics, issued this standard journalist apologia.

> The [Pew] poll never asks exactly how personal political attitudes impact on the ability of journalists to do their job. In that sense, I think the poll may be a disservice. It implies—but never explains how or if bias has an impact on journalism. The poll simply assumes . . . that bias makes its way into the journalism. More importantly in my opinion, the poll never asks about the political leanings of the media owners, publishers and upper management of news organizations. It is arguable that their politics are more influential than their employees in choosing the direction of a news organization.[37]

I debunk the myth of conservative ownership of news media in chapter 9. My main concern here is this question: Do the political proclivities of journalists influence their interpretation of the news? I answer that with a resounding yes. As part of my evidence, I consider testimony from journalists themselves. Based on what we have seen so far, and will see in the chapters that follow, *a solid majority of journalists do allow their political ideology to influence their reporting.* As I've mentioned in previous chapters, the move toward objective reporting was sideswiped by an interpretive impulse. This is a point noticed by others as well. Thomas Patterson, for instance, wrote that "facts and interpretation are freely intermixed in news reporting. Interpretation provides the theme, and the facts illuminate it. The theme is primary; the facts illustrative. As a result, events are compressed and joined together within a common theme. Reporters question politicians' motives and give them less of a chance to speak for themselves."[38]

There is even the growing admission from the press corps itself that partisan politics and political beliefs influence news reporting. A few examples below exemplify this growing trend.

- News media insider Bernard Goldberg wrote in the *Wall Street Journal*, "There are lots of reasons fewer people are watching network news, and one of them, I'm more convinced than ever, is that our viewers simply don't trust us. And for good reason. The old argument that the networks and other 'media elites' have a liberal bias is so blatantly true that it's hardly worth discussing anymore. No, we don't sit around in dark corners and plan strategies on how we're going to slant the news. We don't have to. It comes naturally to most reporters."[39]
- Experienced news commentator Robert Novack, in *USA Today* wrote that "members of the national media tend to share a uniformly liberal ideology. This does not mean they are meeting secretly every other week in someone's basement to get their marching orders. Rather, their ideology originates from a number of left-of-center experiences in their university education, tightly knit peer groups, and the milieu of popular culture since the 1960s."[40]
- Evan Thomas, *Newsweek* Washington bureau chief, wrote, "There is a liberal bias. It's demonstrable. You look at some statistics. About 85 percent of the reporters who cover the White House vote Democratic, they have for a long time. There is a, particularly at the networks, at the lower levels, among the editors and the so-called infrastructure, there is a liberal bias. There is a liberal bias at *Newsweek*, the magazine I work for."[41]
- Walter Cronkite, known and trusted by millions said, "Everybody knows that there's a liberal, that there's a heavy liberal persuasion among correspondents."[42]
- The *New York Times* recently admitted that it is "a liberal newspaper." Public Editor Daniel Okrent wrote, "Start with the editorial page, so thoroughly saturated in liberal theology that when it occasionally strays from that point of view the shocked yelps from the left overwhelm even the ceaseless rumble of disapproval from the right."[43] This is an important admission considering that the *New*

York Times is the paper most read by American journalists (38 percent).[44]

In 1998, *Editors & Publishers* asked news editors a pointed question: "How often do journalists' opinions influence coverage?" Of those questioned, 71 percent responded "often/sometimes," and only 26 percent answered "seldom." Only 1 percent answered "never."[45] The general public agrees: 89 percent feel that "the news media let their own political preferences influence the way they report the news," while only 8 percent said that this "seldom" happens.[46] Allowing some leeway for personal opinion is particularly dangerous and damaging to media credibility when viewed in light of these comments by Howard Kurtz of the *Washington Post*: "There is a diversity problem in the news business, and it's not just the kind of diversity we usually talk about, which is not getting enough minorities in the news business, but political diversity, as well, anybody who doesn't see that is just in denial."[47]

Another factor contributing in some degree to a liberal bias among self-selected liberal reporters is the screening function of the journalism schools. Increasingly, those schools have trained a larger part of the reporters, editors, and producers at leading news organizations. One study found that 40 percent of journalists with a college degree had majored in journalism.[48] Another study found that "about half of all U.S. journalists with college degrees have majored in journalism or [media] communication."[49] The products of these schools are overwhelmingly liberal. For example, in 1982, a survey found that 85 percent of the students of the Columbia Graduate School of Journalism identified themselves as liberal, while only 11 percent called themselves conservative—a virtual match for the voting data on journalists that other studies have revealed.[50] If the students were not already liberals when they entered graduate journalism schools, most of them had been sufficiently indoctrinated by the time they came out, and what few holdouts remained would find that dissenters were not rewarded in the workplace.

Apologists of the liberal slant in the media have attempted to minimize the results of such studies by claiming that most people do not get their news from the *New York Times* but from their local paper. That is indeed the case, and it is precisely why the liberal bias in journalism is so pervasive and is apparent in more than political positions. When it came to social views or lifestyle, Peter Brown's survey thoroughly reinforced previous Lichter-Rothman-Lichter polls, illustrating that even in midsize cities, journalists had a vastly different worldview and living standard than did those who read newspapers. As Brown concluded, "It doesn't make a difference if the guy who repairs your air conditioner lives the life you do. But journalists' view of the world determines not just how they cover a story, but what stories they cover."[51] The story of Brown's study was not carried by any of the major news networks or prominently reported—if reported at all—in the major newspapers. This is not surprising given that journalists admitted that four out of ten of them "have purposely avoided newsworthy stories or softened the tone of stories to benefit the interests of their own news organizations."[52]

The chasm between daily life in America and the views of journalists could not help but be shaped by these attitudes and experiences. The *Dayton Daily News* in Ohio, for example, brought in a consultant to rebuild circulation, and she observed that while Dayton is home to large numbers of blue-collar workers who "carried lunch buckets and ate Hamburger Helper . . . the paper's food editor insisted on articles on salmon, artichokes and asparagus."[53] Journalists are paid substantially more than the American average, with media elites living more like the rich than "average Americans." A study by Indiana University scholars found that median income among journalists has continued to increase, rising nearly 40 percent between 1992 and 1996.[54] Salaries of elite journalists take them even further from the field of the average American. In 2009, Katie Couric was paid approximately $15 million for one year;[55] Charlie Gibson, $8 million; Diane Sawyer, over $8 million; Dan Rather, over $6 million; Peter Jennings, an estimated $10 million.[56] The list continues: Brian Williams, $4–10 million, Charlie Gibson, $7 million, and so on.[57] Average journalists with over 20 years experience make between $45,000 and $100,000 annually.[58] Making more than $100,000 a year puts you in the top 15 percent of all income earners in America. Compare these figures with the average 2003 American *household* income of $43,318.[59] The average journalist's *individual* income as of 2001 was $43,588.[60]

Although by 1993 the percentage of Republicans had risen slightly (from 16.3 percent to 18.6 percent) and the percentage of Democrats had declined somewhat (37 percent, down from 38 percent in 1992), the typical paper still employs Democrats to Republicans at a minimum two-to-one ratio. Why so many Democrats? So many liberals? Barbara Oakley, writing for *Psychology Today*, provides an insightful answer:

> Unsurprisingly, self-selection plays an important role in choosing a job. People choosing to do work related to prisons, for example, commonly show quite different characteristics than those who volunteer for work in helping disadvantaged youths. Academicians have very different characteristics than CEOs—or politicians, for that matter.
>
> Harry Stein, former ethics editor of *Esquire*, once said: "Journalism, like social work, tends to attract individuals with a keen interest in bettering the world." In other words, journalists self-select based on a desire to help others. Socialism, with its "spread the wealth" mentality intended to help society's underdogs, sounds ideal.[61]

The upshot of this sameness among journalists is that the anchors of the major three broadcast news networks do not need to sit down to plan what to say or how to cover events—their very lifestyle and background infuses them with shared values.[62] Thus it seems reasonable to refer to a conspiracy of shared values that dominates the news. Speaking to the general differences between journalists and the public they purport to represent, the Pew Center quotes journalism researcher David Weaver: "While there are many theories for the discrepancy in the politics of journalists versus the public, Weaver believes it has a great deal to do with the kind of people attracted to the media profession. 'I think journalists in general tend to be social reformers,' he says, adding that he believes this reform impulse is 'basically liberal.'"[63]

HOW DOES THE LIBERAL BIAS WORK?

In the case of journalists, a conspiracy of shared values has fatal implications. It leads to templates of how one views the news, with the tendency to adopt such templates strengthened by the lack of competition among ideas within the mainstream news. It is encouraged and reinforced through a work environment accepting of particular templates and intolerant of others. These templates provide an easy mechanism for injecting bias into regular news offerings. There are five key ways in which the establishment media injects bias into its coverage.[64]

Sandwiching "refers to the placement of something between two other things of very different character. Generally speaking, the press places whatever side of the issue it does not support (layer 2) between complimentary points of view (layers 1 and 3), which invariably agree with the position espoused by the press."[65] Take for example, this story run in the *Daily News* (New York) in 1998 when Senator Trent Lott (R-MS) raised red flags concerning the appointment of an openly homosexual ambassador to a somewhat conservative Catholic country. You will see three distinct layers, the first, the press's point of view; the second, Lott's point of view; and the third, the press's point of view.

> (Layer 1) "Sen. Alfonse D'Amato . . . said Trent Lott . . . is blocking a vote on James Hormel's nomination as ambassador to Luxembourg simply because Hormel is gay. 'I fear Mr. Hormel's nomination is being obstructed . . . for one reason only: the fact that he is gay.'" Three more paragraphs support this point of view. Then Lott's side (layer 2) is presented: "Lott spokesman Susan Irby said Lott had received D'Amato's letter, but 'we have also heard from a number of people who don't share those views.'" The reporters then write (layer 3), "His [Hormel's] nomination was overwhelmingly approved by the Senate Foreign Relations Committee in the fall, but it has languished since then amid fierce opposition by social conservatives." The article ends with the reporters quoting D'Amato again: "D'Amato described Hormel as 'a highly qualified nominee' whose credentials 'are easily equal to or greater than those of most ambassadorial nominees.'" Thus the

story begins with a position opposed to Lott (layer 1), then an insertion from Lott's side is put in place (layer 2), and then the story ends with an insertion opposing Lott's point of view again (layer 3). Although Lott's side is grudgingly and tersely presented, by being sandwiched between two press-supporting points of view, its salience is minimized.[66]

Unbalanced use of sources refers to the press using outside sources to support its own point of view, but using the sources in such a manner as to make the majority or the conservative view look to be in the minority. Researchers have found that in terms of sheer numbers, more pro–press position sources are cited than anti–press position sources: "Whereas there are usually a wide variety of liberal sources, conservative sources are more often than not limited to a few national-level spokesmen."[67]

Take for instance the issue of gun control. Guests on morning and evening news shows are more likely to represent a pro-gun-control position by a ratio of 5-to-1 to 10-to-1 over Second Amendment supporters. For instance, during the debate over the Brady Bill, a gun registration bill, analysis of the networks' pro– and anti–Brady Bill coverage by the Media Research Institute found that 59 percent of the network reports were antigun, that only 4 percent could be considered pro-gun, and that spokesmen in favor of the Brady Bill outnumbered people opposing the bill on the four major news networks (ABC, CBS, NBC, CNN) by a ratio of 3 to 1.

In late 1999, another Media Research Center analysis of 653 morning and evening news programs found that the programs were more than twice as likely to feature guests and/or use sound bites from those advocating stricter gun control.[68] This is not limited to issues of gun control only, but rather spans all controversial issues: race, affirmative action, homosexual rights, etc. One study involving 116 mainstream newspapers found a minimum consistent two-to-one ratio of pro–press position to anti–press position sources used.[69] Simply put, the "press finds those who agree with its position much more readily than those who do not."[70]

Labeling involves the use of descriptive terms in such a way as to impart a positive resonance with pro-press positions and to impart a negative association with anti-press positions. These templates not only involve preconceived notions of how to frame questions—who are the "good guys" and "bad guys" on any given issue—but, more important, the very word use involved in shaping the bias of stories. The use of "loaded," or biased, terms has become so commonplace that reporters appear unaware of it. Eron Shosteck demonstrates well how this works in his April 27, 2000, column ("Pencil Necks") for the *National Journal*. Shosteck conducted an extensive LexisNexis database search to find out how balanced political terminology in journalism really was.[71]

The term "partisan Republican," for example, appeared 85 times in a 90-day period, whereas "partisan Democrat" only appeared 58 times in the same three-month span. The terms "hard right" (appearing 683 times) and "far right" (appearing 267 times) were used more than twice as often as "hard left" (appearing 312 times) and "far left" (appearing 130 times). Worse, when searching for references to "extreme right," the database search crashed because it exceeded 1,000 citations, whereas a search for "extreme left" only produced 58 citations. Labeling used by mainstream journalists was acceptable if Republicans were described as "far-right" or "ultra-conservative," but sometime in the 1980s, major news organizations ceased calling communist dictators "dictators," and instead referred to them as "leaders," even though some people winning elections in Third World countries were still referred to as "dictators" in their own countries. One sees this predictably with associations to Democrats (no label) and Republicans (labels). For instance, when John Roberts was nominated for the Supreme Court by George Bush, he was labeled by the AP and other news sources as a "conservative lawyer." Yet when Sonia Sotomayor was nominated by Barack Obama, she was not labeled as a "liberal lawyer," even when she was described as being able to "bring balance" to the court's so-called conservative agenda.[72]

For a more detailed example, consider the issue of gun control. A study by Brian Patrick focused on the use of language by "the elite press of the nation" (the *New York Times*, *Wall Street Journal*, *Washington Post*, *Christian Science Monitor*, *Los Angeles Times*, and *Washington Post*). Patrick covered 1,500 articles from January 1, 1990, to July 15, 1998, in which he contrasted coverage of the National Rifle Association with Handgun Control, the NAACP, the ACLU, and the American Association of Retired Persons (AARP).[73] Among the instances of media bias that Patrick documented were the subtle uses of pejorative labels for the NRA, such as "rich and paranoid"; loaded verbs of attribution ("claims" or "contends" rather than "said"); and loaded adjectives. He also found that NRA officials were quoted less often than officials in the other organizations in the study; that flattering feature stories appeared on Sarah Brady, but never on pro-gun advocates, such as then NRA president Charlton Heston; and that the press was more likely to write a story solely on a press release or press conference of the AARP, Handgun Control, or the NAACP than it was to write a story on a press release or press conference of the NRA. For example, after the shooting at Columbine High School, the entire press coverage about the NRA Convention to be held in Denver involved reports on the *controversy* generated by the convention being held at all. As Patrick concluded, the "data support a conclusion of systematic marginalization of the NRA in the elite newspaper coverage as compared with other interest groups."[74]

A fourth way in which the media opposes conservative tenets is by *showing "a distinct bias against conservative ideas."*[75] A simple experiment for anyone to try is to read (or listen to) any story involving conservatives or Republicans, and ask if they are portrayed in a positive light. Then do the same for a similar story involving liberals or Democrats. I think you will find that more often than not, conservatives and Republicans will not be positively portrayed, whereas liberal ideas and Democrats will be so portrayed. Tom Rosenstiel of the *Los Angeles Times* asked, "Was there bias in the press? Yes." He qualified it by saying that the "media's ideological slant is not a manifest conspiracy to harm Republicans, but a failure to understand some of their arguments."[76] Here is a journalist admitting to a conspiracy of shared values.

Fully in line with the above, and with the studies done by Brown and by the Lichters and Rothman, Patrick also found a conspiracy of shared values toward guns when it came to the press. He interviewed a small sample of ten reporters who had written on gun control, and he discovered that *all of them* had antigun views. One reporter anonymously said, "Elite reporters sympathize with gun-control positions." Another said, "NRA people are bloody-minded." One did not have to hear the reporters say such things to know their views: virtually none of the mainstream media covered the fact that federal gun prosecutions had plummeted in the Clinton administration (from 10,000 under George H. W. Bush to about 6,000 in 1997) despite the fact that Clinton continued to claim that gun violence was increasing faster than ever.[77]

Another sign of a reliable anti-conservatism is seen in the press bias against Christians. Pro-life marches in Washington, DC, regardless of size, are viewed as "off-limits" for reporters. A comparison of stories in 2003 on rallies in Washington offers an indication of the press's convictions. On January 18, opponents of the Iraq War held a protest at the National Mall, and four days later, thousands of pro-life marchers gathered for the annual March for Life. What was the coverage like? In a special article for worldmag.com, Tim Graham noted that the *"Washington Post* started promoting the antiwar rally five days before it occurred . . . [and had] three antiwar stories on the front page, and two broadsheet pages stuffed inside."[78] The antiwar marchers were still being featured in the paper several days after the rally, but the March for Life was not mentioned until the day of the rally, and then only on a single page emphasizing the concerns of abortion advocates. A photo of Planned Parenthood's 150 protestors graced the front page, but there was no photo of the tens of thousands of pro-life marchers who were the real story of the day. Moreover, as Graham noted, "many media outlets blurred the population of the abortion protests, so that the public couldn't tell which rally attracts tens of thousands, and which attracts tens."[79]

Or consider an astounding and telling comparison of front page *New York Times* coverage, placing copies of the front page of the *New York Times*'s coverage of the Los Angeles Jewish community center shooting on August 11, 1999, next to the *Times*'s front page coverage of the Texas church shooting on September 15, 1999, in which eight people died. The

Jewish community center received nearly three times the space as the Texas shooting (which by sheer numbers was a more serious crime), ostensibly because it was a "hate crime" and the church shooting was not. Even the wording of the headlines in each—"3 Small Boys Shot at California Day Camp," compared to "Gunman Opens Fire at a Texas Church"—makes the first crime seem more heinous than the second.

Exclusion of oppositional information is perhaps the most difficult type of bias to detect, or was at least prior to the growth of the Internet. The press frames information, and an important part of framing our understanding involves information that is left out so that it does not conflict with the dominate ideas being advanced. However, this "failure to report information that would contradict the press's own point of view or that would harm the standing of those with whom the press sympathizes is yet another way in which the press introduces its bias." [80] And we saw earlier how four in ten journalists willingly admitted to just such practices. Communication researchers know well the effect of the omission: the "media's inadvertent reinforcement of existing attitudes through omission is far from [a] trivial effect. . . . Holding support under adverse new conditions is a crucial goal in politics, not just winning over new supporters. So one way the media wield influence is by omitting or de-emphasizing information, by excluding data about an altered reality that might otherwise disrupt existing support." [81]

As one small example among tens of thousands, [82] consider President Clinton's comments at the 1997 Human Rights Campaign fund-raising dinner gala. This was an important and historic event, considering it was the first time a sitting president had spoken in such a pro–homosexual rights venue. The event was thick with media coverage. While speaking, the president was interrupted by homosexual activist hecklers in the crowd, who were yelling about AIDS. The president replied, "People with AIDS are dying. But since I've become President we're spending 10 times as much per fatality on people with AIDS as people with breast cancer or prostate cancer. And the drugs are being approved more quickly. And a lot of people are living normal lives. We just have to keep working on it." [83] This is, of course, a strikingly controversial statement concerning public policy and where public funds should go for the public health. This comment received little press attention, except for the press's observation that the president responded well to hecklers. As the following examples show, the press selectively quoted the president: "'People with AIDS are dying. But since I became president, we're spending 10 times as much' on research"; and "'People with AIDS are dying, but since I became President we're spending ten times as much' combating the disease. Mr. Clinton's words were drowned by applause that quickly turned into yet another standing ovation." What the press omits is that the standing applause was after the president had said he was spending 10 times as much on AIDS research per patient as he was for breast and prostate cancer research. Yet the press kept this information from the American public—not one paper provided the president's complete sentence. [84]

For years, pundits dismissed the notion that the media had a template, or "pack," mentality. Yet individual reporters confirm that such attitudes exist. Craig Cantoni, a columnist for the *Arizona Republic* who founded an environmental grass-roots group, recalled, "I could spoon feed the media anything. . . . I had the media eat out of our hand." [85] When he sent out press releases or submitted to interviews, reporters asked "all softball questions. There was no probing" into his data, he recalled. Moreover, Cantoni noted that if the press requested experts, he could "always find someone supporting our view." [86] Recent evidence seems to have proven beyond a shadow of a doubt that such templates or worldviews not only exist, but that they are so rigid that the use of wording in multiple stories is virtually identical. During the 2000 presidential campaign, for instance, the media latched onto the idea that Richard Cheney brought to the George W. Bush ticket gravitas—thus implying Bush was lacking in such a quality. Over the course of a single weekend, radio host Rush Limbaugh assembled recorded comments of nearly a dozen different reporters and pundits using the term "gravitas" to describe the Cheney selection. A LexisNexis search likewise turned up a multi-thousandfold increase in the use of the term "gravitas" over any previous month.

MEDIA FIASCOS

Producing biased stories was not the only change affecting the credibility of the mainstream media after the 1960s. Equally serious damage came from the adoption of reporting methodologies that downplayed the centrality of facts and simultaneously emphasized interpretation. This could have no other outcome but to result in a greater tendency by reporters to make up material. The instances of fictional reporting by journalists are too numerous to recount, but a few became public embarrassments and deserve mention here.

Among the most damaging episodes for the press came in September 1980 when a *Washington Post* reporter, Janet Cooke, published a story about an eight-year-old black heroin addict. A year later, it received a Pulitzer Prize, with the jury struck by the article's "quasi-realism, luminous detail, and implied sense of moral concern." [87] Only two days later, careful readers began to find problems in the Cooke story, whose "quasi-realism" turned out to be pure fabrication. The *Post* had to return the prize. Addressing the Cooke situation, *Washington Post* editor Ben Bradlee strenuously maintained that the "credibility of a newspaper is its most precious asset, and it depends almost entirely on the integrity of its reporters." [88] The Cooke story began to put a different slant on who was "crooked," though. Suddenly journalists, who had roamed virtually un-fettered in their use of anonymous sources and loose fact-checking, came under new scrutiny. New, but not sufficient. Far from reforming them-selves and spurring a new professionalism, journalists made excuses for Janet Cooke–type actions and, more important, did little to seriously change their reporting methods.

Far from it: the growth of "reality news" shows in the late 1980s pro-vided even greater incentives to make up news than ever before. In 1992, for instance, *Dateline NBC* was caught rigging a truck so it would ex-plode, then blaming the manufacturer. Shortly after that, a Portland, Maine, jury ordered NBC to pay more than half a million dollars to a trucker for damage to his reputation from a *Dateline* story about tired drivers. In June 1998, the *Boston Globe* had to fire columnist Patricia Smith after the paper found she had falsified quotations and sources in at least four columns; and the previous month the *New Republic* fired associate editor Stephen Glass for fabricating material in 27 out of 41 of his articles. Michael Lewis of the *New Republic* argued that a photographer should have the right to stage photographs on the grounds that journalism never delivers "an unadulterated slice of reality," and thus the photographers would be engaging in only a minor form of a common practice.[89] The *Cincinnati Enquirer* retracted a series about Chiquita, firing a lead report-er, issuing a page-one apology three days in a row, and paying a $10 million settlement—among the largest in journalistic history. But a most egregious error occurred at CNN, which on July 2, 1998, had to retract its June 7 story about the use of military nerve gas in Vietnam.

The story alleged that Green Berets deliberately used nerve gas on turncoats in Laos in 1970 in Operation Tailwind. But quickly it became apparent that (1) sarin gas was never even transported to Southeast Asia and (2) defectors were never targeted. Air Force Major Gen. (Ret.) Perry Smith, a former CNN consultant who quit in protest over the show, quickly scribbled a list of questions about what happened, then shipped the questions out over the Internet to some 300 of his best sources, whom he called "my e-mail brain trust." In a matter of days, Smith had not only identified the pilots of Laos but also located medics who testified that they had never seen any effects of gas exposure. Within two weeks of the show's airing, Smith and other veterans had provided conclusive proof that there was no use of gas in Operation Tailwind and, more important, that CNN had deliberately ignored or covered up evidence to that ef-fect.[90] Yet not only did CNN refuse to retract the story and issue an apology, but it ran a *second* show defending its initial report. Rick Kaplan, CNN's president, already had a track record of running such stories, having cooked up an infamous Food Lion story for ABC News/*Prime Time*. After CNN had to retract its story, reporter Peter Arnett backped-aled, claiming he was reading a script, that he did not have time to go through the materials, that the military hated him and thus would not conduct interviews with him, and that he did not know whether it was true or not—"A lot went on there [Laos] that we didn't know about."[91]

The establishment media is rife with invented stories, reported as being true and used to push a particular agenda: Jayson Blair, of the *New York Times*, fabricated stories about the Beltway sniper, and *Times* editor Howell Raines participated in the fabrication.[92] *USA Today* reporter Jack Kelley was found to have invented major portions of numerous stories over a ten-year period, including his alleged eye-witness account of a suicide bombing.[93] And hundreds of media outlets around the world, including the *New York Times*, the *Los Angeles Times*, the *Washington Post*, *Time*, the BBC, and others reported faithfully an apparent Hezbollah fabrication that on "the night of July 23, 2006, an Israeli aircraft intentionally fired missiles at and struck two Lebanese Red Cross ambulances performing rescue operations, causing huge explosions that injured everyone inside the vehicles."[94] These are but a few of a multitude of examples of mainstream media reporters creating stories or pushing fabricated stories.[95] If you want even more examples, Randall Hoven of *American Thinker* has compiled a list of 101 such instances. His list is instructive in that it covers "not just journalism, but any dishonesty as related to the public debate."[96] Tellingly, the majority of entries concern journalists.

SPEAKING FOR OTHERS: MORE ANALYSIS, LESS NEWS

A major result of the preponderance of shared values was the growing dominance of analysis over news. This was obvious in the steady decline in coverage of political candidates and their issues. In the 1992 presidential campaign, the Big Three network news shows covered policy positions of the candidates only 32 percent of the time, spending the remaining 68 percent of their coverage on the horse-race aspect of the election. Nowhere was this more apparent than in the sound-bite footage given to presidential candidates, which, from 1968 to 1988 fell from 42 seconds in a typical 30-minute broadcast to 9.8 seconds.[97] By 1992, the average candidate's sound bite was down to 8.4 seconds, while the amount of time taken up by correspondents' comments rose by 71 percent.[98] Average continuous quotations or phrases from a candidate in a front-page newspaper story dropped from fourteen lines to six.[99]

Some have argued that "the ideology of mainstream journalism is conflict."[100] Others, such as Jon Katz of *Rolling Stone*, identified the appearance of a "New News," which is "dazzling, adolescent, irresponsible, fearless, frightening and powerful . . . a heady concoction, part Hollywood film and TV movie, part pop music and pop art, mixed with popular culture and celebrity magazines."[101] This "New News," he predicted, would feature "singers, producers and filmmakers offering colorful, distinctive *often flawed* but frequently powerful visions of their truth."[102]

Media apologists, however, refuse to confront the demise of fact. Instead, they often project on the electorate as a whole their own agenda. Take, for example, the issue of campaign finance reform, which was pre-eminent in the minds of journalists, yet in poll after poll came in ninth or tenth as a priority in the minds of Americans, often garnishing less than 5 percent of the respondents. Whose issue *was* it? It was not the "voters' issue" but was, in fact, the "press's issue." On issues such as the death penalty, gun control, the environment, and campaign finance reform, the press repeatedly seeks to speak for others—to set an agenda with which the public does not necessarily agree. Nowhere is this better demonstrated than during wartime.

JOURNALISTS, BIAS, AND THE GULF WAR

Media biases surfaced in the Gulf War, which was the first fully covered "television war." Unlike Vietnam, where images had to be shipped home as camera film, CNN cameras in Baghdad dramatically reshaped how both the media and the military looked at the presence of journalists in wartime. Vietnam reporting had made the military skeptical of journalists' agendas. As Herbert Gans concluded, "The Pentagon ran so scared after the news coverage of Vietnam that it virtually took over the news coverage of the Grenada, Panama, and Gulf war."[103] Just four years earlier, Michael Deaver, one of Reagan's close advisors, wrote, "Television has absolutely changed our military strategy," but then wrongly predicted, "We will never again fight a major ground war."[104]

Reporters found themselves in new moral dilemmas. As Americans, they wanted a victory, but as journalists, they were disgusted by their own patriotism. A *New Yorker* writer confessed, "Sitting in my home by my TV set, I had felt not only horror at Saddam Hussein's deeds . . . but . . . an unfamiliar pride in our armed forces and their commanders. And the arguments against the war, which had been clear enough to me before it started, had begun to seem unreal."[105] But within days, the writer had come to his senses, and was "back on the side of the antiwar movement."[106] CNN's Bernard Shaw left Baghdad because he could no longer be "neutral." Peter Arnett, also of CNN, apparently did not even wish to be neutral, saying, "I am sick of wars, and I am here [in Baghdad] because maybe my contribution will somehow lessen the hostilities, if not this time, maybe next time."[107] Arnett proceeded to cover the bombing of two Baghdad power plants, where he reported "relentless attacks on civilian installations," without mentioning they were covered in camouflage.[108]

Wary of the bias present in the Vietnam coverage, the Pentagon attempted new directions in its handling of the press during the Gulf War. Although still committed to controlling information, Central Command developed a pool system, in which small groups of reporters were allowed to enter combat zones under strict control then return and share their observations with others. Gen. Colin Powell, then chairman of the Joint Chiefs of Staff, issued ground rules for military briefers to be "as truthful as possible within the necessary and reasonable constraints of the security."[109] He noted that what briefers said was being heard in Baghdad at the same time as it was in America. Reporters disliked the pool system and rebelled at the control of the Pentagon, but the American public supported the Defense Department's restrictions, with six out of ten Americans thinking that the military should exert "more control" over journalists.[110]

The pool system worked well precisely because it exposed journalists as "arrogant and anti-American." Daily press briefings that contrasted "well-groomed, neatly uniformed, confident, polite, and well-informed senior military officers [with an] often unkempt, rude, and absurdly ill-prepared press [were] devastating."[111] One columnist noted that the "adversarial antagonism toward just about everybody, self-satisfied arrogance in the face of authority, and . . . incredible ignorance about other cultures and war" told the public all it needed to know about the reporters.[112] Even the *Washington Post*'s senior editor Richard Harwood acknowledged, "Too many unprepared and dull-witted reporters demonstrated their incompetence day after day to television audiences throughout the world."[113]

On some occasions, journalists divulged tactical information to the enemy, as when CBS cameraman David Green told Dan Rather that he had just come through a point on the Kuwaiti border and that the Iraqis could "just walk in here." That same night, the networks announced the commencement of air operations against Iraq 15 minutes before many of the pilots had reached their targets, alerting the Iraqi anti-aircraft defenses.[114] When Gen. Norman Schwartzkopf learned that *Newsweek* had published a map showing a possible flanking attack through the western desert of Iraq—exactly Schwartzkopf's plan—Powell urged him not to react: "Other magazines are full of maps showing other battle plans. They're all just speculating."[115]

Powell and Schwartzkopf decided that rather than keeping information bottled up, they would use the reporters' lust for stories to their own advantage. They carefully manipulated the media to expect an amphibious invasion of Kuwait City by the Marines, and frequent images and reports of Marine activities in the Gulf tied down ten Iraqi divisions waiting for an attack that never came. The diversion also occupied 22 of 53 pool reporters who wanted the chance to storm ashore with the Marines.[116] Reporters probably would have been chagrined to know that they were little more than mud in the eyes of the troops: Chief Warrant Officer Eric Carlson said, "We regarded them as an environmental feature of the battlefield, kind of like the rain. If it rains, you operate wet."[117]

Journalists complained that the Pentagon defeated the press before it beat the Iraqis. The *Wall Street Journal* more aptly sized up the situation, noting that "the media is really a battlefield, and you have to win on it." [118]

Three factors counteracted the media's leftward and anti-military bias during the Gulf War. Ironically, the first was exposure. CNN's Peter Arnett, who provided pictures live from Baghdad, was so "unbiased" as to make clear his view that the Iraqis were victims of America. Arnett rushed to report stories of American bombs going astray, civilian deaths, and American aircraft shot down. Arnett's wartime reports bore the on-screen caution "Cleared by Iraqi Censors," essentially telling the viewer that what followed was propaganda. [119]

The second factor that took the war out of the journalists' hands was the high-tech nature of the war itself, which dictated the coverage in favor of American/coalition success. If reporters, driven by the ever-present deadline and imagery, were going to cover action, the only action they could cover was that of the American-led forces utterly destroying the enemy. In Vietnam this proved devastating for the military, whereas in Iraq, the opposite was true. Pictures of Tomahawk missile launches, aircraft leaving on missions or returning from sorties, and "gun camera" footage all dictated that reporters show American success. To produce "balance"—the "bad side" of the war—they either had to find coalition casualties (which, for the total war, were under 150) or evidence of American brutality. When a few reporters managed to find bombs that went off target, it only made the Pentagon's case more solid: Americans were going out of their way to limit civilian deaths. For the most part, reporters were overwhelmed by the hundreds of thousands of Iraqis surrendering, which itself made for tremendous television and which inspired public support even more. The journalists also missed the real story, which involved the wholesale destruction of Iraqi tanks that was actually occurring in the western deserts.

When the details of the western battles were learned, the evidence showed that small numbers of Americans repeatedly defeated a larger enemy who lacked sophisticated technology and, above all, skill and discipline. American forces easily defeated the Iraqis, which meant that Americans were safe and Iraqi soldiers were not. It was not a story the press could spin for ill.

A third factor involved the lack of service in the military by any of the journalists, especially Vietnam-era journalists. Those deficiencies were compounded by their unwillingness to obtain academic preparation in military affairs. In short, they simply had no real-world experience with things military, and it showed in the questions in their press briefings.

The closest the media came to influencing the war came at the end, when coalition forces had successfully encircled the retreating Iraqis and had started a systematic devastation of the withdrawing convoys on the "Highway of Death." Images at first seemed to confirm a massive slaughter was ensuing, but analysis showed that most of the vehicles were already abandoned when air strikes destroyed them. Most of the damage done on the Highway of Death was to abandoned Iraqi vehicles and tanks, but the pressure to refrain from obliterating the enemy grew strong. Schwartzkopf received calls from the White House expressing concern about public reaction. "I felt irritated," Schwartzkopf confessed. "Washington was ready to overreact, as usual, to the slightest ripple in public opinion [while I] would have been happy to keep on destroying the Iraqi military for the next six months."[120] Peter Baestrup observed that despite the successful handling of the press, this further separated the media and the military, noting, "Given the media's focus on conflict, deviance, and melodrama, most senior military men do not see the media as allies of civic peace and virtue. . . . There is no counterpart in journalism to 'duty, honor, country,' or to the military leader's ultimate responsibility for life and death and the nation's security."[121]

In retrospect, Schwartzkopf was right and President George H. W. Bush and Gen. Powell, wrong. Enough of the Iraqi military survived to put down rebellions from the Kurds and Shiites in subsequent years, and Saddam remained in power, for another Bush administration to deal with. Meanwhile, the military (and the country) learned yet another valuable lesson about journalists in wartime: if they are removed from the action, they certainly will write critical stories, if for no other reason than dissatisfaction with their situation. The next time America went to war, the Pentagon would adopt a much more successful strategy toward reporters.

THE COST TO JOURNALISM

The market has been making the press pay for these ethical lapses. We discussed the plummeting circulation of the dailies in chapter 7. Equally as telling were momentous shifts of news consumers that saw viewership of the nightly news programs drop by more than a third in ten years. In 1957, for example, CBS's nightly news reached 34 million people at least once a week, or roughly 20 percent of the adult population, and a much higher percentage of those with televisions in their houses.[122] By the peak of the Vietnam War, the Big Three television news shows on CBS, NBC, and ABC drew an audience of 35 million a night. Those numbers had plummeted by the 1990s, although some of the slack was picked up by the new cable network news programs, especially Ted Turner's CNN. Cable news struggled too. CNBC boasted only 376,000 homes by mid-1998, and CNBC and CNN put together barely had an audience equal to the population of Tucson, Arizona!

CNN plummeted 35 percent in prime-time household delivery in the second quarter of 2000, pushing CNN to its lowest marks since 1987.[123]

Both CNBC and MSNBC also suffered double-digit decreases in prime time. By January 2001, CNN announced huge layoffs, blaming its merger with America Online. CNN officials warned that up to one-fourth of its employees would be released.[124] Although the media elites tend to dismiss declines in viewership of mainstream media news as reactions against the scheduling of the news or as a result of the rise of the Internet, they have ceased to deny a collapse in news viewership. Instead, they have rationalized the decline by arguing that "appetite for news is slipping—from 53 percent in 1994 who closely followed the news to 45 percent."[125] Once again, the failure to understand these dynamics reflected a media template—a common misunderstanding of what the signals meant, much the way commanders in World War I continued to be baffled by the machine gun and the tank.

Attributing the decline in mainstream news viewership to poor time slots certainly does not explain the success of Fox News, which eclipsed more established and better-funded CNN in June 2000 across the board in what Matt Drudge called a "cable quake."[126] CNN's ratings had crashed, dropping 28 percent in daily viewership and 16 percent in prime time during the first three quarters of 2000, when Fox News witnessed a 42 percent prime-time increase.[127] After the 2000 presidential election, Fox News trounced all its cable competition for inauguration coverage, averaging a 2.5 rating to CNN's 2.0 and MSNBC's 1.6.[128] CNN barely beat Fox in total households—by fewer than 2 million homes, despite being available to 23 million more homes.

And it was not just CNN losing viewers. Mainstream local news telecasts at the traditional 5:00 hour had witnessed steady erosion, if not collapse, of their viewership. Insight Media Research in Malibu, California, found that television news watchers disliked local news so much that almost one-quarter of the viewers avoided the news altogether, "finding the stories repetitive and devoid of important information."[129]

Some in the media looked at the media's flagging influence as a sign that dark forces had declared a "war against the press."[130] However, the evidence thus far presented suggests strongly that persistent and increasingly one-sided partisan bias further chased off viewers and readers. In a sense, the press declared war against itself when it lost its credibility. In 1976, less than 30 percent of all Americans had a "great deal of confidence" in the press. By 1983, that number had dropped to an anemic 13 percent.[131] A Gallup poll in 2000 ranking the top ten confidence-inspiring institutions had "newspapers" and "TV news" coming in at ninth and tenth, respectively (the military was first and church was second).[132] Another survey reported that 53 percent of Americans thought the press had too much freedom, an increase of 15 percent in just two years. More startling to the news industry, 35 percent of those surveyed favored government regulation of the media, a jump from 15 percent two years before.[133] A similar disdain greeted television news. Almost half of the respondents to the Insight study mentioned above said it did not matter which station they watched because there was so little difference between stations.

Credibility as an issue presses on. According to a 2009 Gallup poll, only 45 percent of Americans have either a "great deal" or "a fair amount" of trust in the establishment news media.[134] Lifecom.com reported even lower numbers from the Sacred Heart University Polling Institute in 2008: "Just 19.6 percent of those surveyed could say they believe all or most news media reporting. This is down from 27.4 percent in 2003."[135] Any way one slices the numbers, the bottom line is that only a handful of Americans believe much, if any, of what the mainstream press says anymore.

NOTES

1. S. Robert Lichter, Stanley Rothman, and Linda S. Lichter, *The Media Elite: America's New Powerbrokers* (Bethesda, MD: Adler & Adler, 1986), 21, 28–30.

2. Kenneth E. John, "Grossman: News Yes, Polls No," *AAPOR News*, 13 (1986), 3.

3. John Leo, "Bad News," *New York Daily News*, April 15, 2000.

4. Jonathan Cohn, quoted in James Fallows, *Breaking the News: How the Media Undermine American Democracy* (New York: Vintage Books, 1997 [1996]), 79.

5. Michael Kelly, "The Game," *New York Times Magazine*, October 1993, 65.

6. Joel Kotkin and David Friedman, "Clueless: Why the Elite Media Don't Understand America," *American Enterprise*. November 1999, 29.

7. Kotkin and Friedman, 29.

8. Kotkin and Friedman, 29.

9. Daniel Sutter, "Can the Media Be So Liberal? The Economics of Media Bias," *CATO Journal*, 20 (Winter 2001), 440.

10. Sutter, 440.

11. Stephen Hess, *The Washington Reporters* (Washington, DC: Brookings Institution, 1981), 87.

12. The sources for table 8.1: Information for "Americans" from, Gallup Poll, "Conservatives Finish 2009 as No. 1 Ideological Group, (January 2010), http://www.gallup.com/poll/124958/Conservatives-Finish-2009-No-1-Ideological-Group.aspx. These figures have changed little over the past 25 years. For example, a 1988 USA Today poll (study number 3108) found a smaller number of liberals and conservatives: 32.7% conservative, 48.1% middle of the road, and 13.7% liberal. Gallup in 1992 found conservatives at 36%, moderates at 43%, and liberals at 17%. The Gallup survey cited above found 21% liberal, 36% moderate, and 40% conservative. Information for 1981 press from Brent Bozell III, "Media and Politics: Overcoming the Bias," Remarks given to The Union League Club (8 June 2000). Information for 1986 press from "The People, Press and Politics," Pew Research Center For The People & The Press, July 1985). Information for the 1992/1995 press from "The People, The Press & Their Leaders," Pew Research Center For The People & The Press, May 1995. Information for the 1996 press from Elaine S. Povich, Partners & Adversaries: The Contentious Connection Between Congress & the Media (Arlington Virginia: The Freedom Forum, Inc., 1996),170-180. A national sample of newspaper editors yielded similar results. 9% said they were liberal, 23% liberal to moderate, 35 % moderate, 19% moderate to conservative, and 6% conservative. Party affiliation corresponded to this: 31% Democrat, 39% independent, and 14% Republican, and 7% other parties. 60% voted for Bill Clinton in 1992. Information for the 2002/2004 press from http://www.mediaresearch.org/specialreports/2004/report063004_p2.asp.

13. www.mediaresearch.org/specialreports/2004/report063004_p2.asp.

14. Reported by Brent Bozell III, "Media and Politics: Overcoming the Bias," remarks given to the Union League Club, June 8, 2000.

15. Estimated.

16. www.mediaresearch.org/biasbasics/biasbasics3.asp.

17. Bill Dedman, "Journalists Dole Out Cash to Politicians," MSNBC, June 25, 2007, www.msnbc.msn.com/id/19113485/.

18. Bozell III. Figure on acceptance of homosexuality from "The People, the Press & Their Leaders," Pew Research Center for the People & the Press, May 1995.

19. Surveys by the Gallup Organization, April 1996. Reported in "Opinion Pulse: Issues," *American Enterprise*, September/October, 1996, 93.

20. Data provided by the Roper Center for Public Opinion Research, University of Connecticut. Survey was conducted by the Gallup Organization, May 2001, http://roperweb.ropercenter.uconn.edu/.

21. Lydia Saad, "Most Americans Would Soften U.S. Military's Rules against Adultery," Gallup News Service, June 13, 1998, www.gallup.com/poll/releses/pr970613.asp.

22. Gallup Poll Topic: Religion, www.gallup.com/poll/indicators/indreligion.asp.

23. *How Journalists See Journalists in 2004*, Pew Center for the People & the Press, 2005, 25–26.

24. This lopsided party affiliation continues when one moves beyond Washington: 44 percent of reporters polled nationwide considered themselves Democrats; 34 percent as independents; and only 16 percent identified themselves as Republicans. Freedom Forum–sponsored poll of 1,400 journalists across the country, 1992, http://www.freedomforum.org/. See too "Center Poll for the Freedom Forum: Survey of 139 Washington Bureau Chiefs and Congressional Correspondents," www.ropercenter.uconn.edu/.

25. Lydia Saad, "Independents Rank as Largest U.S. Political Group," Gallup News Service, April 9, 1999. The 1999 figures show 28 percent Republicans, 34 percent Democrats, and 38 percent independents, www.gallup.com/pool/releases/pr990409.asp.

26. "The American Journalist," Pew Research Center Project for Excellence in Journalism, www.journalism.org/node/2304.

27. Rich Noyes, "The Liberal Media: Every Poll Shows Journalists Are More Liberal Than the American Public—And the Public Knows It," Media Research Center, June 2004, www.mrc.org/SpecialReports/2004/report063004_p1.asp.

28. *U.S. News & World Report*, May 13, 1996, 40. The Times Mirror Center for the People & the Press recently changed its name to the Pew Center.

29. "Public More Critical of Press, But Goodwill Persists," Pew Research Center for the People & the Press, June 26, 2005, http://people-press.org/report/248/public-more-critical-of-press-but-goodwill-persists.

30. "Public More Critical of Press."

31. "Press Accuracy Rating Hits Two Decade Low," Pew Research Center for the People & the Press, September 13, 2009, http://people-press.org/report/543/.

32. "Press Accuracy Rating."

33. "Press Accuracy Rating."

34. "Many Americans Remain Distrusting of News Media," Gallup, October 1, 2009, www.gallup.com/poll/123365/americans-remain-distrusting-news-media.aspx.

35. "Many Americans Remain Distrusting."

36. "Many Americans Remain Distrusting."

37. Jeffrey A. Dvorkin, "Pew Study: Journalists and Liberals," NPR, June 2, 2004, www.npr.org/templates/story/story.php?storyId=1919999.

38. Thomas Patterson, "The News Media: An Effective Political Actor?" *Political Communication* 14 (4), 445–455.

39. Bernard Goldberg, "Networks Need a Reality Check," *Wall Street Journal*, February 13, 1996, A14.

40. Robert Novack, "Political Correctness Has No Place in the Newsroom," *USA Today*, March 1995, obtained from Proquest, http://proquest.umi.com/.

41. *Inside Washington*, May 12, 1996.

42. Walter Cronkite, Radio and TV Correspondents Association Dinner, March 21, 1996.

43. Daniel Okrent, "Is The *New York Times* a Liberal Newspaper?" *New York Times*, July 25, 2004), www.nytimes.com/2004/07/25/weekinreview/25bott.html?pagewanted=all&position.

44. David H. Weaver, Randal A. Beam, Paul S. Voakes, Cleveland G. Wilhoit, and Bonnie J. Brownlee, *The American Journalist in the 21st Century* (New York: Lawrence Erlbaum Associates, 2006), 24.

45. Reported in "Exhibit 1-11: Newspaper Editors," Media Research Center, www.mrc.org/static/biasbasics/Exhibit1-11NewspaperEditors.aspx.

46. "Media Seen As Fair, But Tilting to Gore," Pew Research Center for the People & the Press, October 15, 2000, http://people-press.org/report/29/media-seen-as-fair-but-tilting-to-gore.

47. "Our Delicately Balanced Media," *American Enterprise*, April/May 1996, 37.

48. David H. Weaver and G. Cleveland Wilhoit, *The American Journalist in the 1990s* (Mahwah, NJ: Lawrence Erlbaum, 1996), 35.

49. "Journalists Are More Likely to Be College Graduates," Poynter Online, April 10, 2003, www.poynter.org/content/content_view.asp?id=28790.

50. Lichter, Rothman, and Lichter, 48.

51. Julia Duin, "Editor's Study Finds Elitist 'Gap' between Journalists, Readers," *Washington Times*, March 29, 2000.

52. "Poll: Some Reporters Soften Stories," Newsday.com, April 30, 2000.

53. Duin.

54. Excerpts from Weaver et. al., 668,

55. www.cjr.org/behind_the_news/katie_and_diane_the_wrong_ques.php?page=all.

56. www.people.com/people/article/0,,624023,00.html.

57. http://nymag.com/guides/salary/14497/index1.html.

58. www.payscale.com/research/US/Job=Journalist,_Broadcast/Salary/by_Years_Experience.

59. www.census.gov/compendia/statab/2010/tables/10s0674.pdf.

60. The most current year for which these figures are available. From Weaver et. al.

61. Barbara Oakley, "Why Most Journalists Are Democrats: A View from the Soviet Socialist Trenches," *Psychology Today*, August 3, 2009, www.psychologytoday.com/blog/scalliwag/200908/why-most-journalists-are-democrats-view-the-soviet-socialist-trenches.

62. See Chomsky's comments in "What Makes the Mainstream Media Mainstream?" *Z Magazine*, June 1997, http://saturn.he.net/~danger/freepnet/scripts/shownote.php?LUkQyqri,1879.

63. Quoted in "The American Journalist," Pew Research Center Project for Excellence in Journalism, www.journalism.org/node/2304.

64. These are found in Jim A. Kuypers, *Press Bias and Politics: How the Media Frame Controversial Issues* (Westport, CT: Praeger, 2002), 210–235.

65. Kuypers, 210.

66. Kuypers, 210.

67. Kuypers, 212.

68. Ben Anderson, "Network Spinning Gun Control Debate," CNSNews.com, January 5, 2000, citing a study from the Media Research Institute authored by Geoffrey Dickens.

69. Kuypers, 212–213.

70. Kuypers, 212.

71. Shosteck's results are reported in Robert McFarland, "Conservatives Can Beat Liberal Media Bias," CNSNews.com, May 25, 2000.

72. Jesse J. Holland, "Roberts: Congress Can Trump Court Decision," Breibart.com, September 14, 2005; and Ben Feller, "Sotomayor Nominated to High Court: First Hispanic," Breibart.com, May 26, 2009.

73. K. Daniel Glover, "The NRA and the Press: A Case Study in Media Bias," IntellectualCapital.com, September 2, 1999.

74. Patrick quoted in Glover. See also Jeff Jacoby, "The Media's Anti-gun Bias," *Boston Globe*, January 17, 2000, A15.

75. Kuypers, 214. Emphasis mine.

76. Tom Rosenstiel, *Strange Bedfellows: How Television and the Presidential Candidates Changed American Politics, 1992* (New York: Hyperion, 1994), 333.

77. "BATF Referrals for Prosecution Peak in 1992," *American Guardian*, January 2000, 7.

78. Tim Graham, "Marching Orders," February 1, 2003, www.worldmag.com/world/issue/02-01-03/opening_2.asp.

79. Graham.

80. Kuypers, 215.

81. Robert M. Entman, "How the Media Affect What People Think: An Information Processing Approach," *Journal of Politics*, 51, no. 2 (May 1989), 367.

82. I am not engaging in hyperbole here. See Kuypers, 215–235, for an extended discussion of this.

83. Kuypers, 216.

84. Kuypers, 216.

85. Interview with Craig Cantoni, July 1, 2003.

86. Interview with Cantoni.

87. James Boylan, "Declarations of Independence," *Columbia Journalism Review*, November/December 1986, 43.

88. Bradlee quoted in David Mariness, "Post Reporter's Pulitzer Prize Is Withdrawn," *Washington Post*, April 18, 1981.

89. Michael Lewis, "Lights! Camera! News!" *New Republic*, February 28, 1994, 12.

90. Brigid McManamin, "Humbled by the Internet," *Forbes*, July 27, 1998.

91. Deborah Orin, "CNN Standing by Arnett . . . Barely," *New York Post*, July 9, 1998; Howard Kurtz, "Peter Arnett Spared More Punishment for CNN Story," *Washington Post*, July 9, 1998; and Howard Kurtz, "CNN Staffers Wait for the Other Shoe to Drop," *Washington Post*, July 7, 1998.

92. See G. Murphey Donvan, "The Internet and the Agora," *American Thinker*, February 27, 2010, www.americanthinker.com/2010/02/the_internet_and_the_agora.html.

93. Blake Morrison, "Ex-USA TODAY Reporter Faked Major Stories," USAToday.com, March 19, 2004, www.usatoday.com/news/2004-03-18-2004-03-18_kelley-main_x.htm.

94. This is an excellent example of how the alternative media is challenging the gate-keeping function of the establishment press. "The Red Cross Ambulance Incident: How the Media Legitimized an Anti-Israel Hoax and Changed the Course of a War," ZombieTime.com, August 23, 2006, www.zombietime.com/fraud/ambulance/.

95. For a longer, but by no means inclusive, list, see "The First Amendment Center: Ethics in Journalism," The Freedom Forum, May 24, 2007, http://catalog.freedomforum.org/FFLib/JournalistScandals.htm.

96. Randell Hoven, "Media Dishonesty Matters," *American Thinker*, October 8, 2007, www.americanthinker.com/2007/10/media_dishonesty_matters.html.

97. Lynne V. Cheney, *Telling the Truth: Why Our Culture and Our Country Have Stopped Making Sense—And What We Can Do About It* (New York: Simon & Schuster, 1995).

98. See Kiku Adatto, *Sound Bite Democracy: Network Evening News Presidential Campaign Coverage, 1968 and 1988* (Cambridge, MA: Harvard University Press, 1990), 23; S. Robert Lichter and Linda S. Lichter, eds., "Clinton's the One: TV News Coverage of the 1992 General Election," *Media Monitor*, November 1992, 2.

99. Thomas E. Patterson, *Out of Order* (New York: Vintage, 1994), 75.
100. Campbell cited in Fallows, 264.
101. Jon Katz, "Rock, Rap and Movies Bring You the News," *Rolling Stone*, March 5, 1992, 33, 40.
102. Katz, 40.
103. Herbert J. Gans, "Reopening the Black Box: Toward a Limited Effects Theory," in Mark Levy and Michael Gurevitch, eds., *Defining Media Studies: Reflections on the Future of the Field* (New York: Oxford University Press, 1994), 276.
104. Michael K. Deaver and Mickey Herkowitz, *Behind the Scenes* (New York: Morrow, 1987), 147.
105. "Talk of the Town," *New Yorker*, February 11, 1991, 25.
106. Robert J. Donovan and Raymond L. Scherer, *Unsilent Revolution: Television News and American Public Life, 1948–199* (Cambridge, MA: Cambridge University Press, 1992), 313.
107. Arnett quoted in Lee Edwards, *MediaPolitik* (Washington, DC: Catholic University Press, 2001), 80.
108. Quoted in Edwards, 80.
109. Powell quoted in Jeffery A. Smith, *War and Press Freedom: The Problem of Prerogative Power* (New York: Oxford University Press, 1999), 203.
110. Edwards, 77.
111. William V. Kennedy, *The Military and the Media* (Westport, CT: Praeger, 1993), 120.
112. "Editors Told War Coverage Was Thorough," *Portland* [Maine] *Press Herald*, October 18, 1991.
113. Georgie Anne Geyer, "Press Brought on Problems with Military, Public," *Harrisburg* [Pennsylvania] *Patriot-News*, March 6, 1991.
114. Richard Harwood, "The Press at War," *Washington Post*, March 10, 1991.
115. Powell quoted in Smith, 205.
116. Smith, 205.
117. Johanna Neuman, *Lights, Camera, War: Is Media Technology Driving International Politics?* (New York: St. Martin's Press, 1996), 10–11.
118. "U.S. Used Press as a Weapon," *Wall Street Journal*, February 28, 1991.
119. Walter Goodman, "CNN in Baghdad: Danger of Propaganda v. Virtue of Reporting," *New York Times*, January 29, 1991.
120. H. Norman Schwartzkopf, *It Doesn't Take a Hero* (New York: Bantam Books, 1992), 468–470.
121. Cited in Edwards, 87–88. See also Henry Allen, "The Gulf between Media and Military," *Washington Post*, February 21, 1991.
122. Peter Stoler, *The War against the Press* (New York: Dodd, Mead, 1986), 43.
123. Paula Bernstein, "Bad Ratings News at CNN," *Variety*, June 28, 2000, www.yahoo.com daily news.
124. "CNN Set for Large Number of Layoffs, Journal Says," CNN-Reuters, January 11, 2001.
125. Will Lester, "Web Attracts Younger News Audience," *Washington Post* online edition, June 11, 2000.
126. Matt Drudge, "Cable Quake: Fox News Beats CNN in Ratings; First Time During Breaking Event," www.drudgereport.com, June 27, 2000.
127. Paula Bernstein, "CNN Ratings Slip; Fox News Up 22% in 3Q!" Reuters, October 3, 2000.
128. Tom Bierbaum, "Fox News Trounces the Cable Competition on Inauguration Saturday," January 23, 2001, www.inside.com.
129. "Study: Viewers Disgusted with Local TV News," www.DrudgeReport.com, April 20, 2000, citing a forthcoming *Los Angeles Daily News* article.
130. Stoler.
131. "Journalism Under Fire," *Time*, December 12, 1983.

132. "Top Ten Confidence-Inspiring Institutions in 2000," *American Enterprise*, October/November 2000.

133. Similar numbers were reported in the "State of the First Amendment 2000," sponsored by the Freedom Forum's First Amendment Center, summarized in Joe Strupp, "Public: Press Has Too Much Freedom," *Editor & Publisher*, July 2000.

134. Lymari Morales, "Many Americans Remain Distrusting of News Media," Gallup, October 1, 2009, www.gallup.com/poll/123365/americans-remain-distrusting-news-media.aspx.

135. Steven Ertelt, "Another National Survey Finds Americans Believe National Media Biased," Lifenews.com, January 21, 2008, www.lifenews.com/nat3637.html.

NINE

The Clinton Manipulation and a Declining Press

Washington's 1998 winter was unusually warm. Visitors traipsed around the national monuments in short-sleeved shirts and sandals. Cold bursts occasionally swept in, only to yield to rising temperatures in a matter of days. Washington's political climate, though, was about to become even hotter than the weather. Weekends usually provided little by way of news, in part because the normal Washington rhythms stopped when the government shut down Friday afternoon, and in part because the weekly news cycle there gave way to a variety of news talk roundtables as DC elites scrambled for their Maryland estates and ocean-front resort homes. Little serious analysis occurred on the weekend talk shows because the format of a half-hour show, less advertising, allowed barely 17–19 minutes for actual content. Worse, to obtain "balance," producers always attempted to have at least one token spokesman for each side, with one or two hosts serving as little more than ringmasters. Without strict control, discussions devolved into a string of interruptions and clipped sentences. Seldom could a truly reasonable, or reasoned, thought be uttered.

Even to the politically astute, poring over transcripts after the fact, finding measured ideas and coherent sentences was a snipe hunt. More easily analyzed, however, were the political ebbs and flows, usually gleaned by eyeballing the guest roster, with the A-list names showing up when their positions were riding high in the polls and then replaced by no-name stand-ins when their political fortunes tumbled. It took only a glance to figure out who was winning the war of ideas, and who was the designated cannon fodder for the floundering opposition. Cable shows had drifted downward, spiraling into a genre in which virtually everyone talked at once; attacks were often personal (such as when Harvard professor Alan Dershowitz repeatedly shouted, "Shut him up, Chris," to

Chris Matthews when Republican Alan Keyes challenged the professor's views on the Constitution). Comical to the extreme, Democrat strategist James Carville put a trashcan over his head on *Crossfire* when the 2002 election returns showed his party had lost the House and Senate.

No political clique so thoroughly mastered the press—especially television's multi-guest programs—than the administration of William Jefferson "Bill" Clinton in the 1990s. Clinton "spinmeisters" (as they became known) proved so talented and skillful that their very techniques became the focus of news attention on many occasions, leading reporters to discuss the "spin" rather than the issue being "spun." Thus, rather than expressing shock at charges against the administration, pundits expressed admiration for how White House officials and spokesmen "responded" to "allegations."

The Clinton White House virtually pioneered a raft of new techniques for media control and for shaping public opinion. One trick involved releasing potentially damaging revelations in the form of public statements over a weekend, when most Americans do not pay attention to the news.[1] Another favorite tactic involved releasing small bits of damaging information in deliberate, sanctioned "leaks," diluting the impact of the harm, so that when the entire story came out in the mainstream press, the administration's spokesmen could say, "That's old news. Next question."[2] For instance, in the case of the transfers of critical technologies in the mid-1990s to the communist Chinese through Democratic National Committee surrogates such as Mochtar Riady, Maria Hsia, Johnny Chung, and John Huang, a series of *New York Times* stories dribbled out the information in such small amounts that it obscured the overall stunningly illegal behavior. (Many critics of the administration, including Limbaugh, maintained the administration carefully fed the *New York Times* specific details to minimize the effect of more damaging stories from rival *Washington Times*, whose own writer, Bill Gertz, had dug far more deeply than the *New York Times*'s Jeff Gerth.) This manipulation of the press was not happenstance; rather, it reflected a long-term and serious commitment to developing the necessary knowledge and skills for spin.

SPIN CYCLE

Bill and Hillary Clinton worked for years to perfect the control of the news media that would characterize their White House years; their dominance was so complete that most of the time journalists swore they were not being manipulated. The Clinton "spin cycle," as Howard Kurtz called it, began in earnest with the election of 1992, and the first crucial test came when the Clintons held a 1991 press conference in which Bill effectively shut off investigation into his past escapades with a short statement: "What you need to know is that we have been together for almost twenty years and have been married almost sixteen. . . . And we intend to be together thirty or forty years from now."[3] That press conference occurred on the very day new allegations from a nightclub singer in Little Rock, Arkansas, Gennifer Flowers, surfaced in the tabloid *Star*. Normally, it would have been easy enough for the Clintons to further bury the story, except Flowers had a tape recording with Clinton telling her to deny everything, and "as long as everyone hangs tough," there would be no story. Here was a situation far worse than the one that sank the campaign of Colorado senator Gary Hart just a few years earlier, yet the press all but ignored the story, asserting that it was "beneath them."[4] Al Hunt of the *Wall Street Journal* complained that the "shabby accusation . . . distorted and contaminated not only the political system but the judgment of some news media."[5] Jonathan Alter, a *Newsweek* columnist, argued that unlike Hart, Clinton had not lied about his past, when in fact, numerous women have come forth stating that he repeatedly lied about his past relationships with not only Flowers, but with Dolly Kyle Browning, Elizabeth Ward Gracen, Paula Jones, and Juanita Broaddrick.

What made the Clinton machine different? Rather than simply denying stories, it attacked those who questioned either Clinton or his wife, and did so with a ferocity rarely seen in high public office. Marlin Fitzwater, George H. W. Bush's press secretary, observed that he had never seen anything like the Clinton machine: "You see a White House that intimidates, that attacks the press, that threatens them with putting them out of business and never talking to them and never giving interviews and withholding stories. And you see the media reacting to it, allowing themselves in many cases to be intimidated in ways I never really thought was possible."[6]

Rather than alienating reporters, the attacks made them compliant. *Newsweek* reporter Robert Shogan recalled the turning point came when Mandy Grunwald, then candidate Clinton's media director, went on Ted Koppel's *Nightline* news show to "defend" Clinton from allegations concerning Gennifer Flowers. Koppel wanted to put the allegations in "perspective," to which Grunwald launched a scathing attack *on the host*, who immediately went on the defensive. Shogan noted that "Grunwald's attention-getting assault, followed by similar outbursts by other Clinton staffers, appeared to have a chilling effect on many in the media."[7] Fearful of new attacks, journalists only raised the Flowers allegations indirectly. Reporters used their by-now favorite tool, the poll, to refer to Clinton's sexual escapades, asking whether the allegations would change voters' support. Superficially, Clinton seemed undamaged by the *Star*/Flowers story, but focus groups showed that in fact their views were influenced by the assertions.[8]

Shogan was astounded at the pass Clinton got from the press. When Clinton said, "I got to live by the rules that work in America," Shogan noted, "No one in the media thought to question which rules it was that [he] lived by."[9] When Stan Greenberg, Clinton's pollster, told the candidate he was "damaged goods," Clinton staged a series of town meetings, where preselected audience members asked carefully defined questions that Clinton could hit out of the park. One of the weighty queries on an MTV "meeting" addressed the type of underwear he wore. At no time was he grilled about his draft record, Gennifer Flowers, or his Whitewater land dealings. Certainly this coverage was in part due to the hardball tactics used by the Clintons, but there was in part another explanation: the press wanted him to succeed in making political changes supported by the press. He would move the government to the left.

Contrast this to the coverage given to President George H. W. Bush (1988–1992). Plagued by a recession, he received a barrage of criticism from the media. When his campaign started to flounder, the media quickly made the campaign's "troubles," and not the issues, the story in itself. Dan Rather of CBS reported that Bush was putting down talk that "his reelection campaign is in retreat and in disarray."[10] How does a campaign prove that it is not "in disarray," when merely addressing such a story gives credence to it?

Clinton won a three-way election with only 43 percent of the vote—the lowest since Woodrow Wilson in 1912. Some journalists have tried to argue that the campaign "left a legacy of mutual suspicion between the new president and the media," but in reality, Clinton benefitted from perhaps the most docile press in the 20th century.[11] For example, the Clinton team had framed the economy of the 1980s as a "decade of greed," despite the fact that more people improved in income and wealth-holding than at any time in American history, and virtually every segment of the population witnessed economic improvement, most notably the black middle class.[12] Still, the strategy fit the press template: within a month of the release of Clinton's economic plan, the press fully embraced the frame. *Philadelphia Inquirer* reporter Alexis Moore referred to the nation's economic problems as being "the result of the past ten, twelve, fifteen years of . . . putting selfish[ness] and greed ahead of the needs of us all"; *Newsweek*'s Marc Levinson called the 1980s a "second Gilded Age—a time when, amid prosperity, many Americans became worse off"; and John Greenwald in *Time* called the Reagan years a time when "the rich got bigger yachts, the middle class foundered, and many of the poor went under."[13] Journalists also fawned over First Lady Hillary Clinton in ways that had not been exhibited since Jackie Kennedy and Camelot. Hillary Clinton was routinely portrayed as brilliant, and even as the "brains" behind Bill Clinton—whom the press touted as smart and a master of detail. We thus see reporting in a manner positive to the Clintons, a practice that certainly goes beyond team Clinton intimidation of the press.

Yet intimidation of the press was part of the "soft" coverage of the Clinton White House. When President George W. Bush fired only seven attorney generals in 2006, the press went on a witch hunt. Events such as Clinton's firing of *all* the U.S. attorneys or the allegations of drug use in the White House by former FBI agent Gary Aldrich scarcely drew a whisper from the mainstream news, in large part because Clinton's "war room" had perfected the counterstrike on anyone who dared raise substantive questions about a Clinton policy or about facts in either Clinton's past. With James Carville, Paul Begala, George Stephanopolous, and, later, Dick Morris generating faxes that would flood media coverage during the evening news shows, Clinton's war room intimidated many reporters. Others, who were already sympathetic to a liberal president, needed little encouragement to ignore elements of the Clintons that could damage his opportunities to foster change.

Journalists themselves have little doubt that they were biased toward the Clinton administration. Consider the following admissions:

- Evan Thomas of *Newsweek* said flatly, "The press is pro-Clinton."[14]
- Howard Kurtz of the *Washington Post* noted that "a favorable tone [about Clinton] sometimes creeps into daily coverage."[15]
- Joann Byrd, of the *Washington Post*, who once complained about a "bias police," gradually changed her point of view. She noted that many journalists who embraced "fairness," yet "dismissed objectivity as a pretentious fantasy that made stenographers of reporters and produced irresponsible journalism," were also those most likely to fall into biased reporting practices. Byrd examined pictures, headlines, and news stories in the *Post* during the 1992 election. She found that negative stories about Bush outnumbered negative stories about Clinton by a five-to-one margin, and she concluded, "Fairness—which was supposed to be a substitute for objectivity—is, it turns out, a very subjective successor."[16]
- Tim Graham asked of the pro-Clinton voting record of the press: "Did this preference for Clinton seep into media coverage? Reporters thought so. 'A substantial majority (55 percent) . . . believe that George Bush's [1992] candidacy was damaged by the way the press covered him. Only 11 percent feel that Gov. Clinton's campaign was harmed. . . . Interestingly, that didn't mean reporters believed coverage was unfair. 80 percent graded election coverage as good or excellent. . . . Damaging Bush and aiding Clinton weren't just politically satisfying, but journalistically virtuous."[17]

Be that as it may, even the generally favorable press coverage and the tightly scripted assaults by Carville's gang could not insulate Clinton from the fallout of his own policies. Public sentiment ran high against his attempt to remove a ban on homosexuals serving in the armed forces, reaching a high point when he installed Hillary as head of a commission to overhaul health care in America. The commission, meeting illegally in secret (as one court soon ruled), labored to install socialized medicine in the United States, and its 1,000+ page report, which was to be the basis for legislation, included laws that would imprison doctors who took cash for their services and regulated how many specialists in each field of medicine would be "allowed" by the federal government. Rush Limbaugh attacked the plan relentlessly on his radio show, and his deconstruction of "Hillarycare" sparked a national reaction. Congress subsequently voted it down overwhelmingly, and Bill Clinton's approval ratings dipped accordingly.

Bill Clinton found himself floundering, struggling in the polls and presiding over a huge electoral defeat in the 1994 House and state elections, putting Republicans in control of the House of Representatives for the first time in 40 years. Adhering to their "Contract with America," which listed ten items that would be merely brought up for a vote on the House floor, and which had been signed by every Republican House candidate, the GOP stunned both the Democrats and the press. Journalists and pollsters were blindsided by the Republican victory—only Robert Novak correctly predicted the GOP success before the election. It was perhaps the most stunning political revolution since the New Deal, especially when the GOP congressmen not only brought the items up for a vote, as they promised, but passed nine out of ten of the items in the House.

The success of the congressional Republicans made the president suddenly seem obsolete. Rather than leading change, he reacted to it. Clinton told a national news conference, "The president is relevant," but it seemed as if he needed to convince himself more than the viewers. In truth, Clinton was on the ropes, desperate for an event or issue he could use to turn the political tide. He soon got it. On April 19, 1995, an explosion decimated the Alfred P. Murrah Building in Oklahoma City, a traumatic event that gave Clinton the political miracle he needed. Before the FBI had any evidence on the case, Clinton blamed "right-wing extremist" organizations and even singled out "talk radio"—clearly an attack on Rush Limbaugh. (Initial indications pointed to Middle Eastern terrorists, and only later was it discovered that an unstable American named Timothy McVeigh, with the help of Terry Nichols, set the bomb, although tantalizing links to Iraq continued to materialize in subsequent years.)[18] McVeigh could be easily tied to "right-wing extremists" or "militia" groups, and thus the media never sought to investigate the matter further. He "fit the template" of a bomber, in their minds.[19]

Clinton nevertheless regained his relevance and surged back in the polls. That was the first of two counterpunches that would reestablish his influence in Washington. The second came during the budget battle of 1995 when the Republicans, seeking to distance themselves from criticism of law enforcement agencies, addressed the large federal budget deficits.

As mentioned in chapter 6, at almost no time did they actually cut a program's budget—rather, they reduced the *rate of growth* in the increase of new, anticipated expenditures. The Democrats labeled these increases "cuts," and the media willingly played along. No reporter challenged the Democrats' use of the term "cuts" (when they were really increases) for *six months*.

Ultimately, Clinton refused to sign the budget, and the Democrats in Congress assisted him in allowing the funding resolutions to expire, thus shutting down the government's nonessential services until a new bill could pass. What Speaker of the House Newt Gingrich and the House Republicans did not know was that Clinton had a back-room deal with the government employees union to blame the shut-down on the Republicans, even though the Democrats could have ended it instantly by passing the bill. In a coordinated and calculated media assault, the Democrats put "ordinary people" hurt by the shutdown on *Larry King Live* and other shows, reminding the public that the Republicans wanted to "cut" programs. Eventually, the GOP negotiated a deal to re-open the government, and while Clinton gave up as much as the Republicans did, the press portrayed the results as a Republican defeat.

Clinton's "victory," combined with the Washington media spin machine, had a chilling effect on the Republicans for the next three years. Many Republicans were convinced that Clinton had such mastery over the media that their message had no chance of reaching the voters. Others, traumatized by the charges of wanting to "poison" the water and air, became invisible. On the national stage, only Limbaugh and a handful of conservative writers insisted that Clinton was vulnerable and that the setbacks were not as serious as the Republicans thought. After all, the president was still in the midst of a potentially damaging investigation into both "Travelgate" and his Whitewater business dealings.

Travelgate occurred when Hillary Clinton fired the independent business running the White House travel office. This was a job that was contracted out to a bidder, but the same company, headed by Billy Dale, had handled travel for the press corps for years, through both Republican and Democrat administrations. However, it was within the purview of any administration to change firms. Mrs. Clinton did so, replacing Dale's group with one headed by her friends, Harry Thomason and Linda Bloodworth-Thomason and Susan Thomases (the producers of television shows such as *Designing Women*). Up to that point, nothing illegal had occurred. Part of the allegations involving Travelgate, however, were that Hillary, not wishing to be viewed as heartless, felt compelled to invent a reason for firing Dale, and thus he was investigated by the FBI for fraud and abuse. The investigation depleted his life savings and in the end found nothing. Starr's investigation could turn up no smoking-gun memo with Hillary's intentions on it, so she escaped further action. Although damaging, neither Whitewater nor Travelgate, nor even the mysterious appearance in Hillary Clinton's quarters of between 400 and 900 FBI files on individuals in government and the private sector (Filegate) seemed to affect Bill Clinton's popularity or job approval in the polls.

Mainstream journalists might not have asked tough questions, but the "new journalists"—the posters on websites and individual citizens who just liked to investigate things—assembled massively damning cases. One of the most thoroughly researched, and, eventually, most influential, was "The Downside Legacy of Bill Clinton," put together by a Texan named Sandi Venable who served as an unofficial secretary to FreeRepublic's website. In 1998, Venable, who went by her Freeper nickname "Alamo-girl," began assembling topics, names, and issues related to Clinton, then posting the information on the forum. Each category of Clinton's "crimes" was listed, with expected topics such as Whitewater and Fundraising accompanied by related sections such as Media Bias. The "Downside Legacy" grew so large (ultimately 10,000 pages), Venable had to remove it from FreeRepublic and get her own website, http://alamo-girl.com.

Clinton remained largely immune from these sorts of attacks for a number of reasons, one of which was certainly the fact that a rising employment rate and skyrocketing stock market left most voters unwilling to rock the boat. In the 1996 election, Clinton again faced no serious challenges on the "character" issue, in no small part because the Republican contender, Bob Dole, could not decide whether to run on the character issue or not. By the time he decided to make moral values and trustworthiness an issue, the campaign was over. Some of the worst press coverage, however, involved the campaign of conservative Republican challenger Patrick Buchanan, whose beliefs (unlike those of Dole and Clinton) gave the press an opportunity to denigrate conservative views. *Newsweek* featured on its cover a grim-faced Buchanan with the headline "Preaching Fear." *Time* gave its readers no interpretive options with its headline "The Case against Buchanan."[20] Ultimately, Buchanan proved little more than an irritant to Dole and did far less damage than did Perot—who stayed in the race long enough to siphon off 5 percent of the vote—but Clinton still could not win a majority of votes cast. For the second time, Clinton held office as the result of fewer than 50 percent of the American voters putting him there.

By that time, the Clinton team had its "talking points" strategy down pat. In the face of any character accusation, deny. Even if the accusation was true, and everyone knew it was true, deny it until the White House could come up with a strategy to explain it. Then Carville, Begala, pollster Mark Penn, Al Gore, Hillary, Donna Brazile, Lanny Davis, and other Democratic Party "talking heads" would respond to the criticism by attacking the critic. Using dirt from the critic's past (and, many suspected, gleaned from the FBI files in Hillary's quarters) or, in the case of a politician, using the person's own voting record to show inconsistencies, the administration team immediately made any Republican or journalist who challenged the administration line into a villain. A dual message emerged: to the critic, there was a threat of retaliation, and to the public, there was the notion that the attacks against Clinton were a coordinated effort by the right wing.

It certainly came as no surprise that journalists shied away from emerging stories that Clinton had had sex with a young White House intern. When the news leaked out, Clinton ordered pollster Stan Greenberg to conduct surveys, in which Greenberg found that Clinton only had two choices: resign, or deny the affair and find a way to survive. With help from the press, the full story did not come close to airing immediately. Instead, it was revealed over the course of several years, in numerous admissions and interviews, with the Clinton spinners counterattacking with their most vicious weapons. These weapons included impugning the character of the numerous women who came forth in the investigation, minimizing the facts of the stories through the "everyone-does-it" mantra (thus accusing living and dead presidents), and separating character from job performance by appealing to the private nature of sex between consenting adults.

Reporting the Clinton scandals accelerated the decline in the credibility of journalists by encouraging a decline in the most basic journalistic standards. A subsequent study on sourcing for the Lewinsky-related stories found that 13 of every 100 stories had two or more anonymous sources; only 25 of every 100 stories had one named source; only 1 of every 100 stories had two named sources. More disturbing, a quarter of all stories could be classified as "journalistic analysis."[21] Little of the Lewinsky story would have surfaced if not for a then little-known Hollywood Internet reporter, Matt Drudge. We turn now to an example of the old-guard news media hitting head-to-head with the new guard and how that impacted political news coverage—in this case, a scandal within the Clinton administration.

CASE STUDY: CLINTON, THE PRESS, AND NEW MEDIA INFLUENCES

On that particular January weekend in 1998, news magazines, as was routine, put their stories together for release the following week, with the two "majors," *Time* and *Newsweek*, in tight competition for readership, often mirroring each other to the extent that they not only ran the same lead stories but featured nearly identical covers. *U.S. News & World Report*, once a solid competitor, had fallen well behind the majors, followed by a string of more specialized and ideological magazines: *Atlantic Monthly*, *The Nation*, *National Review*, and *Harper's*. None of them came close to the circulation of the majors, with *Time* and *Newsweek* then boasting circulations of four million and three million, respectively. Even the nation's "newspaper of record," the *New York Times*, only had a subscription of 850,000, exceeded by both *USA Today* and the *Wall Street Journal*, each with 1.7 million. The *Washington Post* had barely grown, and other major papers, including the *Chicago Tribune*, the *Boston Globe*, and the *Houston Chronicle*, all had seen their circulation drop in 1999.

Naturally, when one of the majors had a scoop, it grabbed a momentary advantage over its rivals, and this would hold true with *Time* and *Newsweek* as well. Yet little in the way of significance emerged, and neither weekly claimed many true scoops. Additionally, both publications, we feel, relied on the *New York Times* to set the agenda. As media guru James Carey acknowledged in 1986, "The *New York Times* is important because it *establishes the salience of stories for the day.*"[22] Privately, almost any editor at any major national paper would admit that one of the first things he did in the 1990s each day was check the front page of the *New York Times*.

Given what we have covered thus far in this chapter, I am inclined to believe that part of the difficulty with the attainment of scoops was simply a willingness to overlook, or to only weakly pursue, stories that could harm the president, and thus his agenda. This predisposition to ignore or downplay potentially damaging information not only prejudiced how stories were covered, but which stories were covered. For example, when ostensibly one of the most important stories of the decade was breaking—the Chinese espionage/money-laundering scandals within the Clinton administration—there was virtually no television network prime-time news coverage of the revelations. Moreover, on the night the Cox Committee released its report on Chinese influence in the Clinton administration, two of the three major network news programs did not even lead their newscasts with the story. Certainly in a competitive market, one would expect differences of approach, style, and content in the news. Yet far too often, as this story illustrates, the modern media elite organizations will ignore major stories that simply do not fit their template.

However, sex, lies, and videotape did fit the template. So when *Newsweek* reporter Michael Isikoff, in January 1998, brought to his editors a story with both sex and political intrigue, it seemed exactly the kind of scoop that the news magazine would run on its front page. Isikoff had witnesses and other corroborating evidence for the sordid tale. Yet he hesitated, because the story involved the president of the United States and a sexual encounter with a 21-year-old White House intern, which could arguably be defended as a private or consensual affair. Nevertheless, pressured by breaking developments, Isikoff decided to write the story. Editors yanked it at the last minute after approving it earlier. This was all the more remarkable since they had brought Isikoff over from *Newsweek*'s corporate partner, the *Washington Post*, specifically to work on the numerous scandals spawned by the Clinton administration.

Isikoff had meticulous records, including White House WAVE logs that recorded who came and went at the White House; phone records confirming calls that his sources told him were of a sexual nature between the president and the young intern; and witnesses. There was no doubting his sources. But the editors wondered, "Is sex was worth reporting?" This seemingly simple, innocent question demonstrates the editorial framing of the future coverage of this story. It was to be about sex—ostensibly a *private* affair that could be defended as such by Clinton. It was not to be about perjury—ostensibly a *public* affair that could not be as easily defended.

Isikoff reminded them that a key aspect of the story was that the intern's role had arisen out of testimony taken in another court case, the civil case of *Paula Jones v. Clinton*, in which a woman from Arkansas had filed a civil suit against the president for sexual harassment during the time he was governor of Arkansas. Isikoff's witness said that she had been asked to lie about *another* woman supposedly assaulted by the president, who was being deposed by Jones's legal team.

Here was a story of titanic national import: Isikoff had evidence of perjury, subornation of perjury, and obstruction of justice that tracked to the Oval Office itself. Yet somehow the editors pulled the story; not, however, without a shouting match with Isikoff. One could possibly mark the tipping point of liberal journalism from that moment forward. The "story that wasn't" triggered a sea change in alternate media coverage. It constituted the first stage in the assault by alternate media on the bias malady of the Fourth Estate. And the person to ignite the firestorm that followed was a lone online computer news reporter from Hollywood named Matt Drudge.

Drudge had received invaluable advertising when nationally syndicated radio talk show host Rush Limbaugh in 1997 made several references to Drudge's website. In 1999, Agence France-Presse, one of the major news wire services (along with the AP, UPI, and Reuters) named Drudge's breaking of the Lewinsky story on the Internet one of the top ten news stories of the century. [23]

Drudge learned of the Isikoff story and reported it on January 17. [24] He subsequently discovered that the story had been killed, and he reported that fact less than two hours later. Drudge thus posted on his website the story that *Newsweek* refused to run *and* presented the details of the events behind the scenes at *Newsweek*. By emphasizing *Newsweek*'s role in killing the story, Drudge simultaneously raised two different critical issues. One issue, the president's perjury and obstruction of justice, constituted a constitutional violation similar to the crimes that forced Richard Nixon from office in 1974. The second issue—which the press either missed or deliberately ignored—was evidence of press bias: a major news magazine had refused to run a story critical of a president with whose views the editors and writers were sympathetic.

Drudge's report noted publicly that tapes of intimate phone conversations existed and that the woman had bragged about the affair to others.[25] Drudge had beaten the majors by 72 hours, and *Newsweek* "would remain paralyzed until Wednesday, when it finally published on America Online, itself an electronic news outlet."[26] The significance was not to be missed: for the first time since the sinking of the *Titanic*, the *way* news was transmitted radically changed the impact of the content. For the first time, the Internet had scooped print, radio, and televised news coverage.

Within a matter of weeks, the number of hits on Drudge's site soared from just over 50,000 to a quarter million, and by December 1998, Drudge had more than 1.1 million hits on a single day. Reeling from the negative exposure, establishment journalists lashed out. Some ascribed Drudge's rapid ascent to the fact that Washington insiders fed him stories and rumors so "caustic or so unimaginable every prudent journalist steps back."[27] Of course, this terrified mainstream journalists such as David Halberstam, who characterized the reporting of the Clinton scandals as "the worst year for American journalism [in 44 years]."[28] Halberstam blamed Drudge and other Internet journalists for "seriously trivializ[ing] the profession."[29] Members of the Washington–New York media axis wanted to deny or discredit Drudge, arguing that, lacking an editor, he could not be subject to a "gate-keeper"—some editorial Solomon who wisely divided the sheep from the goats of news. This criticism rings of irony given that the gate-keeper function was under attack because of much more substantial shifts in the biosphere of news reporting. This counterrevolution occurred because mainstream journalists had ceased reporting news and had sought to shape it, or even dictate it. As Bill Keller, managing editor of the *New York Times*, admitted, "Whether true objectivity is ever possible—I don't think that is what we're here for."[30]

Drudge's impact, and the impact of the Internet overall, reshaped the news business. Although it did not completely eliminate biases within stories, for the first time technology allowed interested citizens a variety of ways to acquire stories, so that sooner or later bias would be exposed. Many sites encouraged reader commentary that also could identify or expose biases of articles from mainstream journalists. Thus the existence of a truly democratic medium posed a gigantic threat to the establishment news media. The new media democratized news by providing the whole truth. Drudge, Limbaugh, and Fox News constituted obstacles to the old-boy network of establishment journalists telling the public what to think.

Drudge's and Limbaugh's spectacular rise also signaled broader and deeper trends in the ways Americans gathered information. This involved moving away from intermediaries—editors, news anchors, and so on—and changing the entire concept of news to a more democratized forum that allowed a radical type of free speech. Radio and Internet sources had ushered in this new era, and it was not long before broadcast news bias would have genuine competition in Fox News.

FAIR AND BALANCED

When conservative Australian media magnate Rupert Murdoch originated a 24-hour news channel in 1996 specifically to compete with CNN, he hired Roger Ailes, a former Republican political consultant to head the news division. Fox, whose slogan was "Fair & Balanced," stood in stark contrast to CNN and other mainstream news shows. Whereas CNN's news talk shows almost always featured two liberal guests, with a liberal host, and one conservative guest, Fox almost always kept the numbers equal, and usually had either a conservative host or a duo, like Sean Hannity and Alan Colmes, that represented both sides—an interesting approach that led Fox News to being labeled a "conservative" network by liberals. Although facing tremendous odds—the Fox News staff was 20 percent that of CNN's, its budget only 10 percent of its rival's, and it had to fight in the courts to open cable markets—Fox delivered not only new content but new packaging that featured "breaking news" headlines that interrupted normal news programming.

Fox's flagship program, *Special Report with Brit Hume* (a former ABC reporter) solidly defeated other cable news shows in its time slot, which by then included MSNBC (also formed in 1996). The stars of Fox were the commentary shows, such as *The O'Reilly Factor* with Bill O'Reilly, and *Hannity & Colmes*, but the actual news remained moderate in tone. Liberals, of course, did not see it that way. Ultra-liberal organizations such as FAIR charged that Fox was "the most biased name in news" because Fox did not slant the news toward the left. Robert MacNeil, former host of the *PBS MacNeil-Lehrer Report*, stated, "The Fox claim is a con on the public. . . . The network is blatantly unbalanced," which was a remarkable claim from a man whose network was itself under attack for bias and lack of balance.[31] Judy Woodruff, whose CNN show was hemorrhaging viewers, said, "Fox is concerned about its news reputation. At CNN, we don't need to use those terms."[32] Ailes responded to such complaints by pointing to Fox's ratings, and noted that "there are more conservatives on Fox [than on other networks], but we are not a conservative network. That disparity says far more about the competition."[33] Some liberal critics, such as Howard Kurtz of the *Washington Post*, admitted that "Fox's daily news, as opposed to their nighttime shouting-heads programming, is reasonably straight and balanced."[34] Ailes pointed out that "in most news, if you hear a conservative point of view, that's called bias. We believe if you eliminate such a viewpoint, *that's* bias. If we look conservative, it's because the other guys are so far to the left."[35]

The numbers tended to support Ailes. Fox's viewership among the 25–54 year-old demographic increased 430 percent from 1998 to 2001, while CNN's viewership declined by 28 percent. "Journalism became a mechanism of advocacy in the 60's," Ailes noted. Senior vice president John Moody provided a clear example of the difference Fox News offered: "Every time we do a story about someone being executed, it is *de rigueur* that we put in the lead why that person is being executed. Not a lead about a candlelight vigil. . . . We say up front, 'Joe Smith murdered his wife and three children.'"[36] Fox completed the counterattack on liberal dominance first started by the *Washington Times*, Limbaugh, and Drudge and other Internet journalists. Nevertheless, even with the appearance of those new sources, the establishment news media remained overwhelmingly saturated with liberal reporters, anchors, and producers who seemed bent on continuing down the same reportorial path.

Major newspapers and networks still sparingly hired conservatives, arguing that a conservative was an "ideologue," while a liberal was "open," and that conservative reporters could not keep their ideology in check, whereas it was asserted that liberal reporters could. In the 1960s, one senior editor said, "I wouldn't hire a Goldwaterite."[37] As an example, liberals protested loudly during the 2000 election when a cousin of George W. Bush, John Ellis, a Fox employee, allowed an unverified count of Florida votes that gave Bush a dominant lead to be included in Fox's totals. Although Fox quickly discovered the error, and corrected it, and although Fox, like every other network, had called Florida for Bush, liberals complained the Ellis had played a role in swinging the election. In short, conservatives or Republicans who sought jobs in journalism were suspect because they were "ideologues."

Yet there was no liberal opposition when ABC hired Clinton advisor George Stephanopoulos to head its Sunday morning news show; nor was there ever any mention in the press that PBS's Bill Moyers, who constantly produced left-wing documentaries, worked for Lyndon Johnson. Here is a partial list of former Democratic activists now working in mainstream media circles:

- NBC's Tim Russert worked for New York senator Pat Moynihan and former New York governor Mario Cuomo (both Democrats).
- CNN's Jeff Greenfield was a speechwriter for Massachusetts senator Ted Kennedy (a Democrat).
- CNBC's Chris Matthews was President Jimmy Carter's speechwriter and House Speaker Tip O'Neill's press secretary (both Democrats).
- NBC News political correspondent Ken Bode worked for Senator Morris Udall (an Arizona Democrat).
- NBC's Brian Williams worked under President Jimmy Carter.

- ABC News correspondent Rick Inderfurth worked for several Senate Democrats, worked in the Carter administration, then was Bill Clinton's assistant secretary of state for South Asian affairs.
- PBS's Elizabeth Brackett worked for the mayoral campaign of Chicago Democrat Bill Singer.
- NBC's Jane Pauley was an administrative assistant to the Indiana Democratic Central Committee.
- ABC reporter Pierre Salinger worked for President John Kennedy and briefly was an appointed Democratic U.S. Senator from California.
- *New York Times* editor/writer David Shipley was a speechwriter for the Clintons.
- *New Yorker* writer Ken Auletta worked for a half-dozen Democratic politicians.
- *New York Times* columnist Leslie Gelb served on the staff of two Democratic presidents, Jimmy Carter and Lyndon Johnson.
- Former *Los Angeles Times* publisher and former CNN CEO Tom Johnson was an aide to President Lyndon Johnson.
- *Washington Post* writer Walter Pincus worked for Senate Democrat J. W. Fulbright, and his wife was a Clinton appointee.
- *New Yorker* correspondent Sidney Blumenthal was a Clinton advisor.
- *Time* magazine's Washington bureau chief Strobe Talbott was a Clinton ambassador-at-large.
- *Nightline's* Tara Sonenshine worked for Clinton's National Security Council.
- *Nightline* producer Carolyn Curiel was a Democratic speechwriter.
- *New York Times* Washington correspondent Jack Rosenthal was an executive undersecretary of state in the Johnson administration.
- *E!'s* Eleanor Mondale is the daughter of former Democratic presidential candidate Walter Mondale.
- ABC's *This Week* cohost, Cokie Roberts, is the daughter of Democratic representatives.
- CNN's Christiane Amanpour is married to James P. Rubin, former Clinton State Department spokesman.
- The *Atlantic's* Linda Douglas is the former spokesperson for health care in the Obama administration.
- ABC correspondent Chris Cuomo is the son of former Democratic New York governor Mario Cuomo.[38]

With so many former Democrat activists now working in the mainstream media, it is difficult to comprehend the level of indignation when a Republican or conservative is hired. For example, no one expressed any outrage when George Stephanoupolos was hired, but in 1997, when CBS hired former Congresswoman Susan Molinari, a Republican from New

York, to co-anchor a Saturday morning show focusing on fitness, cooking, and movies, media pundits exploded: "CBS Adds Molinari, Loses Credibility"; "Hiring Susan Molinari, a Ratings-Hungry CBS Gave TV Journalism a Setback"; "Molinari Move to CBS Blurs Journalistic, Political Lines"; "Is It News, or Is It Propaganda?"[39] At the same time as CBS hired Molinari, it also hired former Democratic presidential candidate Bill Bradley to do "serious" news pieces, and nobody had any criticism.[40] How, one must wonder, is hiring a Republican news, whereas hiring a Democrat is not? This is yet another example of how the conspiracy of shared values works.

With such a proliferation of liberals and former Democrats in the editorial rooms and anchor desks of the mainstream media, I feel that a reasonable observer would find it difficult to think there would not be a leftward slant to the news, even if these correspondents worked diligently to keep their prejudices out. Instead, critics take refuge in the purported conservative ownership of media outlets. Tom Curley, CEO of the AP, observed without a hint of evidence that "most media are owned by Republican conservatives, so there is a healthy balance and tension" within the news organization.[41] Did Curley have in mind Ted Turner, Jeffrey Immelt, or Michael Eisner? Ownership, however, no more writes the stories than Virginia Tech president Charles Steger calls the plays for the Virginia Tech football team. Importantly, even if the majority of news media owners and CEOs were conservative (which they simply aren't), the managerial revolution had already separated management from ownership and left managers in the dominant position of setting corporate policy. And the "managers" in this case were the editors and producers.

The Clinton years show us the bias in the news media quite clearly. They also present us with a fascinating opportunity to see the crucial years during which the mainstream media was challenged by news media outsiders operating within the realms of radio, TV, and the Internet. In the next chapter, we will see the response of the establishment news media. Will it be a major change in response to hemorrhaging markets and lost credibility or will it be business as usual?

NOTES

1. Howard Kurtz, *Spin Cycle* (New York: Touchstone, 1998).
2. Kurtz, 166–183.
3. Robert Shogan, *Bad News: Where the Press Goes Wrong in the Making of the President* (Chicago: Ivan R. Dee Publishers, 2001), 155.
4. Shogan, 157.
5. Quoted in Ellen Ladowsky, "Bill Clinton Is No Victim of the Press," *New York Times*, March 24, 1992.
6. Fitzwater quoted in Bill Kovach and Tom Rosenstiel, *Warp Speed: America in the Age of Mixed Media* (New York: Century Foundation, 1999), 45–46.
7. Shogan, 158–159.

8. *Los Angeles Times*, February 2, 1992.

9. Shogan, 164.

10. Shogan, 171.

11. Shogan, 173.

12. Joseph Perkins, "The Good That Reagan Did for Black America," *San Diego Union-Tribune*, June 11, 2004, B-7. See also J. Daniel, "Tax Rates, Fairness, and Economic Growth: Lessons from the 1980s," Heritage Foundation, October 15, 1991. These assertions are not without their mainstream media detractors. For an example of the mainstream press framing of this issue, see "The Two Nations of Black America: An Analysis," PBS Frontline, February, 1998, www.pbs.org/wgbh/pages/frontline/shows/race/economics/analysis.html.

13. Moore on *Journalists' Roundtable,* C-SPAN, May 1, 1992; Marc Levinson, "The Fat and Happy '80s," *Newsweek*, May 4, 1992, 63; John Greenwald, "How I Won the War," *Time*, May 25, 1992, 67; and all can be found in Brent H. Baker and Time Graham, eds., *Notable Quotables*, May 1992. For the facts of the 1980s, see Larry Schweikart, *The Entrepreneurial Adventure: A History of American Business* (Ft. Worth, TX: Harcourt Brace, 2000), ch. 12–13; Isabel V. Sawhill and Mark Condon, "Is U.S. Income Inequality Really Growing?" *Policy Bites*, June 1992.

14. *Inside Washington,* WUSA radio, August 15, 1992, quoted in Cheney, 178.

15. Howard Kurtz, "Republicans and Some Journalists Say Media Trend to Boost Clinton, Bash, Bash," *Washington Post*, September 1, 1992.

16. Joann Byrd, "73 Days of Tilt," *Washington Post*, November 8, 1992.

17. Tim Graham and Jim Naureckas, "Q: Does Media Coverage of President Clinton Reveal a Liberal Bias?" *Insight*, July 22, 1996, 24.

18. See, for example, Micah Morrison, "Commentary," *Wall Street Journal*, September 22, 2002. Government information on the bombing appears in "Combating Domestic Terrorism: Hearing before the Subcommittee on Crime of the Committee on the Judiciary, House of Representatives, One Hundred Fourth Congress, First Session, May 3, 1995" (Washington, DC: Government Printing Office, 1995). David Hoffman and Charles Kay, in David Hoffman, *The Oklahoma City Bombing and the Politics of Terror* (Venice, CA: Feral House, 1998), present substantial evidence that McVeigh was in the company of more people than Nichols and that the truck bomb he used was not sufficient to cause the damage that the Murrah Building suffered.

19. Only later, on 9/11/01, would the significance of McVeigh's alleged contacts with Arabs become apparent, but by then the leads had dried up and the records effectively closed. By applying their "template" to Oklahoma City, journalists had closed off legitimate investigation. After Muslim terrorists attacked the World Trade Center in 2001, thought-provoking new evidence surfaced about McVeigh's contacts with Arabs prior to the Oklahoma City bombing, suggesting that perhaps the press "template" had stifled investigation down other, less obvious, avenues. See, for instance, "The Still-Ignored Evidence of Middle East Links to the Oklahoma City Bombing," WorldTribune.com, April 28, 2010, www.worldtribune.com/worldtribune/WTARC/2010/ss_terror0352_04_27.asp.

20. Shogan, 187.

21. Kovach and Rosenstiel, app. 1.

22. James Carey, "The Dark Continent of American Journalism," in Evea Stryker Munson and Catherine A. Warren, eds., *James Carey: A Critical Reader* (Minneapolis, MN: University of Minnesota Press, 1997), 160. Emphasis mine.

23. Agency France Press, May 4, 1999.

24. This material is now available in the Drudge archives, www.drudgereportarchives.com/data/2003/01/16/20030116_014732_ml.htm.

25. Website header titled "Drudge Lewinsky Flashback," www.drudgereport.com.

26. Dave Plotnikoff, "Online Gossip-Broker Becomes Source That the Media Can't Ignore," *San Jose Mercury News*, January 24, 1998.

27. Plotnikoff.

28. David Halberstam, "Preface," in Kovach and Rosenstiel, ix.

29. Halberstam, ix.

30. Bill Kovach and Tom Rosenstiel, *The Elements of Journalism: What Newspeople Should Know and the Public Should Expect* (New York: Crown, 2001), 42; David T. Z. Mindich, *Just the Facts* (New York: New York University Press, 1998), 115. By 1982, with the appearance of Curtis MacDougall's *Investigative Reporting*, 8th ed. (New York: Macmillan, 1982), the concept of objectivity was questioned outright.

31. Randy Dockendorf, "Neuharth Panel Asks: 'Is Media Fair?'" www.yankton. net/stories/092603/com_20030926028.shtml.

32. Quoted in Dockendorf.

33. Quoted in Marshall Sella, "The Red-State Network," *New York Times Magazine*, June 24, 2001, 26–33, 56, 62–63, quotation on 29.

34. Seth Ackerman, "The Most Biased Name in News," *Extra!* August 2001, 11, 56.

35. Sella, 28.

36. Sella.

37. Herbert J. Gans, *Deciding What's News: A Study of CBS Evening News, NBC Nightly News,* Newsweek *and* Time (New York: Pantheon Books, 1979), 191.

38. Ann Coulter, *Slander: Liberal Lies about the American Right* (New York: Three Rivers Press, 2003), 64–70.

39. Frazier Moore, "CBS Adds Molinari, Loses Credibility," *Chicago Tribune*, June 11, 1997; "Hiring Susan Molinari, a Ratings-Hungry CBS Gave TV Journalism a Setback," *Buffalo News*, June 9, 1997; and Sandy Grady, "Is It News, or Is It Propaganda?" *Buffalo News*, May 31, 1997.

40. Coulter, 70–71.

41. Dockendorf.

TEN

Bush and Election 2000: We Spin, You Figure It Out

During the 2000 presidential election, journalists faced a unique comparison between two men whose candidacies were a foregone conclusion (Al Gore for the Democrats and George W. Bush for the Republicans) and two "outsiders" or "mavericks" (Bill Bradley, Gore's challenger, and John McCain, Bush's challenger). Just how biased journalists had become showed itself in the treatment of these two outsiders. Bradley, admittedly a boring candidate, was ignored, while McCain became the darling of the media. In retrospect, the press coverage of McCain occurred mainly for two reasons: he was more liberal than Bush, and he had no chance of beating Gore. For either of those reasons, journalists latched onto McCain, whose tour bus, the "Straight Talk Express," offered them unlimited access to a candidate who shared many of their views.

Less-guarded comments by reporters showed why they favored McCain. Robert Shogan, who accompanied McCain on the Straight Talk Express, noted that "what caught the attention of reporters . . . was McCain's willingness to take these positions in defiance of almost everyone else of importance in his own party. Reporters saw this as a mark of courage and conviction."[1] Why, then, did the media not cover Democrats such as Georgia senator Zell Miller, who took "positions in defiance of almost everyone else in his own party?" Why was there no coverage of former Pennsylvania governor Robert Casey, whom the Democratic National Committee prohibited from speaking at the 1996 convention due to his pro-life views? The answer might be "Well, neither of those guys were presidential candidates." Why, then, did the press not fawn over Bill Bradley, who was far more liberal than Al Gore? The pattern was clear: Democrats bucking party bosses warranted no attention; Republicans bucking party bosses did warrant attention.

The media had its template with McCain and then had to explain its biased coverage. When Republican National Committee chairman Haley Barbour pointed out that the press was "slobbering" over McCain, *Washington Post* columnist Mary McGrory answered, "He is quite right. We are guilty as charged." The reason, she explained, for the media's adoration of McCain "is simple: he talks to us, returns our calls, says things he shouldn't, takes them back, and doesn't blame anybody else."[2] McGrory would not admit, however, a more important truth: had a candidate the media disagreed with, such as Bush or Steve Forbes, said "things he shouldn't," journalists would have crucified him as being incompetent and "lacking experience," and had he "taken them back," the attacks would have intensified, with the candidate accused of being guilty of "flip-flopping" and "distortions." Instead, the template said that if journalists could find a Republican who advanced their cause, he was worthy of coverage. McCain held out the hope of derailing Bush (who clearly was a threat to Gore) early in the campaign. It was clear to all, though, that McCain was unlikely to defeat Gore due to the Arizonan's inability to get out the Republican/conservative base. Thinking ahead, then, a McCain defeat could be blamed on a failure of conservative ideas, even though McCain never fully endorsed them in the first place.

The infatuation with McCain—which continued until he ran against Barack Obama—came down to a simple rule of Washington politics: If a Republican or conservative criticizes other Republicans or conservatives, that is newsworthy; but Democrats or liberals attacking other liberals is not. Hence, in the 2000 primaries, McCain was labeled a maverick by, among many others, Clarence Page.[3] Rush Limbaugh, disgusted with the lock-step nature of McCain's coverage, produced a montage of a dozen reporters, analysts, and other journalists using the term "maverick" to describe McCain within a span of a single week. Again, however, Democrat Zell Miller, who was highly critical of his own party's antiwar and anti-tax stances, was not labeled a maverick, and he received almost no coverage from the establishment press; only Republicans who attacked Republicans were deserving of the term "maverick."

In the 2000 primaries, the press continued to deceive the public about McCain, inaccurately covering the New Hampshire and Michigan open primaries, where voters who registered as independent could vote for any candidate, regardless of party. This led to orchestrated campaigns in which Democrats would reregister as independent to vote for McCain with the clear intention of reregistering again as Democrats once the primary was over. It was vote-tampering, pure and simple, with the objective of defeating Bush. Mainstream journalists ignored it, although later Robert Shogan admitted that "the handwriting was on the campaign wall, though few in the press bothered to read it or pass the word to their readers and viewers."[4] This had no basis in trying to gin up excitement to gain viewers, I believe, but rather derived from an ideologically driven desire to defeat Bush, the more formidable Republican candidate. Once the parties' national conventions met, the three major broadcast networks continued their trend of not allowing the candidates and parties to define themselves. The networks cut back coverage and featured almost no speeches from the convention floor, instead cutting away to commentators in the booth who gabbed about staging and images rather than content.

This was the message of the Clinton presidency—that how you spin is more important than the issues being spun. Given this, it is not so surprising then that Harvard's Shorenstein Center on the Press, in its Vanishing Voter Project, found that by a five-to-one margin, voters thought the coverage of the campaign was "uninformative."[5] This study also provides an example of how liberal beliefs find their way into interpretive reporting: press coverage of the two candidates was asserted to favor Bush. The Vanishing Voter Project claimed that Gore's coverage was slightly more negative than that given to Bush. Charles Peters, toward the end of the election, agreed: "If Bush wins, this could be the first election decided by the press."[6] Robert Shogan chimed in, saying "The press's coverage hurt Gore's cause more than it did Bush's."[7] The irony, though, as Peters admitted, was that "most reporters will finally cast their own votes for Gore."[8] Even if a majority of stories and editorials were classified as negative toward Gore (something to be viewed with skepticism), the report did not consider *how* reporters often support liberal candidates and policies by using *negative* assessments. For instance, by stating that liberal politicians *don't go far enough* in a certain policy direction, reporters can provide a *negative* assessment that actually *promotes* the liberal policy or encourages the liberal politician to go even further.[9]

Be that as it may, the claim that the press favored Bush in the 2000 election is simply specious. A simple counting of positive and negative stories, without the context in which they occur, is misleading. It does not account for when a preponderance of stories appears, or which subjects they touch on, or even total word count. Bush's policies received overwhelmingly negative coverage, with almost two-thirds of the stories critical of Bush's positions on education, taxes, or the economy. But by far the most damaging story of the campaign came four days before the election, when a Democrat activist released information that in 1976 Bush had been convicted of driving under the influence of alcohol. There was more coverage of the Bush DUI story than of all the foreign policy issues put together. This 24-year-old charge slammed Bush's image of honesty and threw just enough dirt on his campaign to cost him substantially—by the account of Bob Beckel, a Democratic strategist, a million votes nationally. After the election, journalists lamented their inability to elect Gore. Shogan grumbled, "Here was the governor of Texas, possessed of slim credentials, a nondescript intellect, and an underwhelming persona running a nose ahead of the incumbent vice president of an administration that had presided over a time of unparalleled prosperity."[10]

As striking as these considerations may be, they pale when juxtaposed with the press's failure to let the candidates speak for themselves.[11] According to a study of the election by the Center for Media and Public Affairs, broadcast news coverage of the election showed an increase in airtime over the 1996 election, but a reduction from the 1992 election.[12] Continuing a trend, journalists gave candidates less time to speak than ever before. Reporters' chatter consumed 72 percent of news time, as contrasted with only 12 percent from the candidates themselves. The average length of candidate sound bites also continued to plummet, from 43.1 seconds in 1968 to a scant 7.8 seconds by 2004.[13] Tellingly, the longest, unbroken appearance by George W. Bush was a 13-minute visit on *The David Letterman Show* on October 19, 2000, which exceeded his speaking time on all three network news shows combined. Gore's Letterman appearance exceeded all his other television appearances for the entire month of September 2000. Media coverage also continued to perpetuate a horse-race image, with 71 percent of the stories emphasizing the horse race; only around 40 percent of all stories engaged in some type of policy discussion (although this percentage was up slightly since 1988).[14] Coverage continued a trend in which reporters and anchors hogged increasing amounts of the camera time; analysts told the public what the candidates said, rather than allowing the candidates to speak directly to the public; and critical coverage of all positions (especially of conservatives) grew.

CASE STUDY: VOTER NEWS SERVICE

Unfortunately, biased coverage of the campaign itself was only the beginning of election coverage in the 2000 election, as the news media made a blatant effort to swing the results to Gore through abuse of Voter News Service (VNS) data that the networks used to call a state for a particular candidate. What appeared at one point to be a Bush electoral landslide became the tightest race in American history. Even before election night, the networks admitted they had massive problems with VNS. Many had simply abandoned the VNS projections; others attempted to shore up VNS exit-pollers with additional personnel.

VNS operates using part-time workers, including scores of college students, the unemployed, and stay-at-home-mothers—all paid $175 a day—to approach voters at specifically targeted bellwether precincts that have over time provided indicators of the voting behavior of a state as a whole. These precincts are often in swing areas, where the Democrat-Republican mix is in proportion to the national percentages, and which have previously sided with winning candidates. However, every voter leaving the poll is not interviewed—only a fixed percentage—and increasingly voters in these areas have become skittish about giving interviews to VNS personnel. Further, some states do not permit pollsters to stand within 75 feet of polling places, thus excluding many voters who drive into a parking lot.

In addition to those constraints, during this election VNS had exit pollsters in only 1 percent of the nation's precincts. In Florida, VNS only obtained responses from 0.07 percent of the six million voters who cast votes in the 2000 presidential race. Privately VNS found that it was having to interview considerably larger numbers of exiting voters to obtain the same raw numbers that it did in the early 1990s. And VNS did not even attempt to deal with Florida's 600,000 absentee ballots—10 percent of the state's entire vote. (VNS editorial director Murray Edelman, in a staggering understatement, later said, "We did not correctly anticipate the impact of the absentee vote.")[15] Even more awkward, a severe problem of Democratic bias afflicted the VNS numbers, and VNS was aware of it. One insider said of the VNS people, "They've been fairly candid about it in meetings over the years. . . . They are aware there's been a Democratic bias in the survey."[16] For instance, this VNS bias had Democrat Dick Swett beating Republican Bob Smith for the New Hampshire Senate seat in 1996 by a 52–47 percent margin. After the votes were counted, the margin was right—but Smith was the winner.

The networks knew of these problems as well, and at first appeared to exercise due caution. At 7:08 p.m. eastern time, CBS news anchor Dan Rather said, "We would rather be last in reporting a return than to be wrong. . . . Because if we say somebody's carried a state, you can pretty much take it to the bank. Book it. That's true."[17] This from a network that called Kentucky and Indiana at 6:00 p.m. when there remained hundreds of thousands of voters west of the time zone line who still had another hour to vote. CBS also called Vermont and South Carolina precisely at 7:00 p.m., before a single vote had been tallied. As election night wore on, however, the indications were unavoidable that the media had a vested interest in helping to elect Gore. Attempting to sway people who had not yet cast their ballots by preventing a Bush "wave," the major networks all withheld calling states for Bush based on VNS exit polling data. Their actions were different when calling for Gore, however.

In those states where Bush led by significant margins, the networks labeled the race "too close to call," whereas in states where Gore led, the networks tabbed him as the winner on the basis of far smaller percentages. Sometimes the differential between Bush and Gore calls was hours, despite the vastly larger advantages in the Bush states over those called for Gore (see table 10.1).

Normally such calls might not matter, but in an election this close— and with the bias of *all* the calls leaning left—the media/polling apparatus actually took on the role of vote tampering. Note that even though in Arizona Bush won by seven points, the call took over an hour longer than

Table 10.1.   CNN's 'Calls' for Bush and Gore, 2000"

Gore/Bush State Won	"Spread" (%)	Time Before "Call" Was Made
MAINE (Gore)	5	10 minutes
ALABAMA (Bush)	15	25 minutes
NORTH CAROLINA (Bush)	13	39 minutes
GEORGIA (Bush)	12	59 minutes
WASHINGTON (Gore)	5	1 hr., 08 minutes
PENNSYLVANIA (Gore)	4	1 hr., 24 minutes
MINNESOTA (Gore)	2	1 hr., 25 minutes
COLORADO (Bush)	9	2 hrs., 41 minutes
ARIZONA (Bush)	7	2 hrs., 51 minutes
TENNESSEE (Bush)	3	3 hrs., 03 minutes
WEST VIRGINIA (Bush)	6	3 hrs., 16 minutes
ARKANSAS (Bush)	6	3 hrs., 42 minutes

Source: Ann Coulter, *Slander: Liberal Lies about the American Right* (New York: Three Rivers Press, 2003), 87.

Minnesota, which Gore won by only two points; or that in Arkansas, which Bush carried by a safe six points, it took CNN almost four hours to call the state for Bush, whereas it gave Gore Pennsylvania after only an hour with a much smaller lead. Bush's lead in Alabama, North Carolina, and Georgia was two to three times greater than Gore's lead in Maine, yet CNN took up to six times longer to call those states for Bush. "Look at this! Look at the war in Georgia!" said Bernard Shaw. "Too close to call!"[18] Jeff Greenfield echoed this line: "This has got to be a shocker in Austin. They had this one put away in their pocket for weeks, if not months."[19] These pundits had not seen a single actual vote count, but rather eagerly rushed to offer opinions based on unverified, unvalidated data, even if it completely contradicted all recent history and their own experience. The conspiracy of shared values provides a reason: it gave the liberal Democrat an advantage.

The apparent attempt by CNN and other networks to delay calling states that Bush won and to get Gore victories "on the table early" smacked of manipulation of the election. A subsequent independent report commissioned by CNN itself, submitted by a panel of independent journalists, hedged, but grudgingly agreed, calling the network's vote coverage "a debacle," and called the actions of the major networks an "abuse of power."[20] In a post-mortem, CBS conducted a probe into its news-gathering on election day. Although the network accepted responsibility for inaccurately calling Florida and New Mexico (despite Rather's promise that you could "take it to the bank"), its 87-page report did not admit to any underlying bias and continued to implicate Voter News Service.[21] Nevertheless, the conclusion of CBS's probe—"CBS News blew it"—spoke far louder than its denial of any bias and could have been the byline of the previous 30 years of journalism: "The Journalists Blew It."

Actual vote counts, as opposed to VNS projections, showed that Bush swept the South, and most of the Midwest to the Far West, with a few exceptions. He also carried the crucial swing state of Ohio. Gore notched California, the upper tier of the Midwest, and the Northeast. Then, in a shocker, the establishment news media announced that Gore had won Florida—before the polls closed in the western part of the state. By all accounts this caused numerous Bush voters on highways en route to vote to abandon their intention to vote.[22] After all, Gore had won the state. Or had he? After a few hours, the networks backtracked, saying Florida was "too close to call."[23] In fact, Bush led in every tallied count in the state at the time, although he watched a large lead of more than 10,000 votes shrink in the final minutes of counting to 537 votes. By that time, every other state had been called (except Alaska and Hawaii, whose three electoral votes each canceled each other out). With Florida's 25 electoral votes, Bush had 271 and the election. Without them, Gore would take the electoral college. At 3:00 in the morning, after the final votes in Florida had certified Bush the winner by 537 votes, Gore telephoned Bush with his concession. Under Florida's laws, however, the closeness of the vote triggered an automatic recount, and Gore, sensing he still had a chance, called Bush back an hour later to retract the concession. The recount cost Bush votes, but he still emerged with a 327-vote lead.

What followed was an infamous series of protests, contests, and court challenges to the election in Florida by Gore, all of which produced no "new" votes. Quite the contrary, the more the Florida election officials recounted, the larger Bush's margin grew. Nevertheless, a recurring theme on news shows was that "if every vote was counted," Gore would win Florida and the election. The United States Supreme Court, acting under a constitutional deadline for certifying the electors in a national election, voted seven to two against allowing further recounts of selected precincts as a violation of the civil rights of other citizens in precincts not under challenge.

A frenzy of media-sponsored recounts ensued, with journalists convinced they could prove that Gore won Florida. The recounts continued until well into May 2001. Most of the recounts found that Bush would have won under most standards: a *USA Today/Miami Herald* survey of 61,000 ballots, followed by a broader review of 111,000 overvotes (where voters marked more than one candidate's name, and which were thus disallowed), found that if Gore had received the manual recounts he requested in four counties, Bush would have gained yet another 152 votes, and if the Supreme Court had not stopped the hand counting of the undervotes (ballots where a hole had not been punched cleanly through), Bush would have won under three of four standards for determining voter intent.[24] Apparently desperate for any standard that might have given Gore the victory, *USA Today* noted that Gore won most of the overvotes. Yet by any sane standard, marking multiple names for the same position invalidates a ballot.

As disturbing as this may seem, a ray of hope emerged throughout it all. The 2000 election ended all pretense of an objective news media. In its place, however, emerged perhaps something more powerful—a *competitive* media in which consumers could double-check the facts from each side, and in which alternative voices could challenge the spin coming from mainstream sources. Unlike the Jacksonian partisan presses, though, the new competitive press was not beholden directly to the parties. Instead, its bosses were the consumers of news. Drudge, the Internet bloggers, Limbaugh, the *Washington Times*, and Fox News provided sufficient counterbalance that the mainstream media could no longer completely control the news. If the newly elected Bush team needed to get out important stories or scoops not covered by the liberal press, now (unlike in the past) there were alternatives.

NEW MILLENNIUM, OLD PRESS

George W. Bush had scarcely settled into the White House before the mainstream press pounced again. The major papers, especially the *New York Times*, launched an offensive against Vice President Richard Cheney's connections with "big oil," hammered at the president's tax-cut proposals, and pushed the theme that Bush had not won a majority of the popular vote.[25] Journalists were emboldened further by the summer defection from the single-vote Republican majority in the Senate (courtesy of Cheney's tie-breaking vote) of Vermont Republican senator Jim Jeffords, who changed his affiliation to Independent and caucused with the Democrats to give them a one-vote majority in the Senate. Reporters peppered the White House with questions about whether or not Bush was alienating so-called moderate senators, and whether he should "reach out" to the Democrats more.

During the summer of 2001, the country was rocked by corporate scandals at Global Crossing, Enron, and WorldCom, in which executives had fraudulently posted profits from sham companies, cashed out, and left the stockholders and employees to deal with the resulting bankruptcies. Although the press went out of its way to try to connect those scandals to the Bush administration—Enron, after all, was in Houston—it made almost no mention of massive stock profits made at Global Crossing by the head of the Democratic National Committee (and Clinton friend) Terry McAuliffe. Stocks prior to 9/11 were at historic highs, and the unemployment rate was a low 4.2 percent, yet the news media hammered Bush on the economy.

Coverage of the economic news from 1998 to 2002 revealed a continuation of media negativism. One study found that journalists framed news as negative more often than positive (42 percent of the stories versus 30 percent), and that this emphasis on "bad news" may have had "serious consequences for both expectations and performance of the economy."[26] Historically, both the print and television media have distorted economic news for the worst, as several studies have confirmed.[27] One key study of *New York Times* coverage between 1981 and 1992 found that the newspaper followed negative economic conditions more closely than positive economic conditions, and that the negative coverage did "exert significant influence on public opinion," even after controlling for other effects.[28] Looking at framing of economic issues, in which facts ("the Dow was up 30 points today") were slanted either as positive ("good news for the stock market today") or negative ("more bad news for Wall Street today"), the authors found a relationship between unfavorable reporting and lagging public attitudes about the economy. As the authors concluded, although the news media does not change people's views about their current economic condition, it does influence strongly their view of the future.[29] During the Clinton recession from 1999 to 2002, the press virtually ignored any evidence linking the downturn to the Clinton years and instead focused on the recession's timing under President George H. W. Bush.

Yet as the major networks' news programs continued to lose viewers, and as the major papers hemorrhaged circulation, they paid little attention to content. Instead, they turned yet again to "packaging" to solve their problems. CNN especially had continued to lose viewers, but executives rationalized the losses as related to production techniques and the use of "dramatic footage." But even some of CNN's competitors started to acknowledge that the major news networks had lost credibility. ABC's executive producer of *Nightline*, Tom Bettag, admitted that "distrust of the media in this country is well-founded, and we bring it on ourselves by not making clear what's real and what's not real."[30] Even so, Bettag's solutions consisted of clarifying what scenes were dramatizations rather than addressing the news media's leftward slant.

This led the networks down blind alleys of trying to find the right anchor, or "face," that would attract viewers, oblivious that any "face" that delivered accurate and balanced news would have an audience. First, CBS tried to promote Connie Chung, which proved a failure. CNN touted its rising star, Aaron Brown, who once asserted that he "was the face of CNN," then the network hired Fox's Paula Zahn. None of these moves had any positive impact on CNN's drooping ratings, nor did it bode well for television journalism when its commitment to its stars superseded its commitment to accurate news. CNN was not alone in using personalities to try to bolster its ratings. ABC threw former Clinton aide George Stephanopoulos into its regular Sunday morning news show. The networks, however, were about to be handed a second chance to recapture their audience—one that no one expected.

9/11: AMERICA'S WAKE-UP CALL

Reading news stories from September 10, 2001, in retrospect, is a surreal experience. Unlike December 6, 1941, when tensions with Japan were obvious (and a conflict all but eminent), the threat to America's home-land from Muslim terrorists prior to 9/11 did not register even a blip on the public's radar screen. Even the 1993 bombing of the World Trade Center and the overseas attacks on American embassies, housing com-plexes, and the *U.S.S. Cole* all seemed too irrational to ascribe to a malev-olent, well-financed, and determined group. America's print and televi-sion journalists thus busied themselves with dissecting President Bush's recent statement on stem-cell research, or continued to dwell on corpo-rate scandals that absorbed Wall Street.

Then, on a sunny, still, Tuesday morning in September, two airliners were flown into the twin towers of the World Trade Center as a third plane plunged into the Pentagon and heroic passengers prevented a fourth plane from hitting its intended target, either the White House or the Capitol. A new day of infamy was instantly etched into the minds of Americans: 9/11. For a few brief days, the press, both print and electronic, suddenly did its job again. Reporting seemed more responsible, and even overtly liberal outlets such a CNN provided solid news with a high de-gree of accuracy. Although at first the networks nearly overwhelmed the public with continual, repetitious images of the airplanes and collapsing towers—"probably the most powerful image of our time," observed ABC News head David Westin—after a week they refrained from showing the airplane impact and collapsing towers.[31]

Polls reflected the public's appraisal of the media, with public approv-al rising in almost all polls from September to November. Naturally— and rightly so—journalists praised each other's coverage. Gloria Cooper, of the *Columbia Journalism Review*, intoned, "The nation's news media conducted themselves with the courage, honesty, grace, and dedication a free society deserves."[32] The *Baltimore Sun* chimed in, noting, "Most news organizations rose to the challenge, providing an enormous amount of coverage of Afghanistan and post-Sept. 11 events."[33] Even conservative pundits, such as Peggy Noonan, lauded the news media's work in the first weeks after 9/11.[34]

Then, virtually overnight, the media reverted to form, printing Demo-crat accusations that the president had information about the possibility of the attacks and failed to act. This was captured on the front page of the *New York Post* in block letters: "BUSH KNEW." Obscure FBI agents, who had written memos that disappeared into the system, were featured in countless stories implying that the administration failed. Likewise, after a period of relatively little observable action in Afghanistan, the media started to repeat Democratic criticisms of administration "inaction" — in a case of superb bad timing, when, almost as soon as Democrat leaders issued their public statements, bombing in Afghanistan began. Nevertheless, pundits dourly warned of the freezing Afghan winter and of the difficulties of a guerilla war. One academic study of the establishment news media reporting of 9/11 and the war on terror found

> the press actively contested the framing of the War on Terror as early as eight weeks following 9/11. . . . When taking into consideration how themes are framed, we found that the news media framed its response in such a way that it could be viewed as supporting the idea of some action against terrorism, while concomitantly opposing the initiatives of the President. . . . Shortly after 9/11 the news media was beginning to actively counter the Bush administration and beginning to leave out information important to understanding the Bush Administration's conception of the War on Terror.[35]

By November 2001, the mainstream press had squandered the good will it earned in the immediate aftermath of 9/11. A Gallup poll released that month found that whereas President Bush had an 89 percent approval rating with the public, the news media came in dead last in the survey, behind the Post Office, vilified attorney general John Ashcroft, and the Centers for Disease Control. Respondents disapproved of the news media by a 54 to 43 percent margin.[36]

Given their predictions, journalists were flummoxed by the quick success in Afghanistan, eagerly uttering the scare-term "quagmire" when the Taliban government did not instantaneously dissolve at the start of military action. Yet after only a few weeks, the U.S.-supported Northern Alliance had routed the Taliban and al-Quaeda, killing or chasing most of them into the hills, and it did so with only a handful of casualties. Over the subsequent year, culminating in an unprecedented midterm out-of-power success for the Republicans, the press consistently failed to understand either Bush's personal appeal or the popularity of programs of tax cuts and stronger national defense backed by the Republicans.

In political reporting, the press was similarly unable to grasp the possibility that the public understood, yet *still* rejected the Democrats' positions; instead, they pushed the frame that the Democrats "did not get their message out." Well into 2003, the Democrats' "inability to get their message out" continued to dominate political reporting, even to the point of convincing the Democrats to oppose the war and to oust House Minority Leader Richard Gephardt and replace him with Nancy Pelosi of California.

Bush had begun laying out his case for a pre-emptive war with Iraq not long after the Taliban was routed in Afghanistan. Concerned that al-Quaeda might obtain weapons of mass destruction—especially chemical or biological weapons—from Iraq, Bush prepared America for toppling the totalitarian government of Saddam Hussein. His "axis of evil" phrase in his 2002 State of the Union speech specifically identified Iraq, Iran, and North Korea as patrons of terrorism. Then, in a bluntly critical speech before the United Nations, Bush detailed every UN resolution Saddam had violated. Congress quickly gave him a resolution (H.J. Res. 114) authorizing a war with Iraq: The House passed the resolution on October 10, 2002, by a vote of 296 to 133, and the Senate passed the resolution on October 11, 2002, by a vote of 77 to 23.

GETTING "EMBEDDED" WITH THE PRESS

Anyone who thought the news media might have become more responsible in the post-9/11 era, even with new competition, was in for a surprise. Prime-time pundits and newspaper editorialists leaped at the opportunity to predict disaster before and after American troops were committed in Iraq. A litany of their prophecies, or "analysis," includes

- Chris Matthews, in the *San Francisco Chronicle*, August 25, 2002 ("To Iraq and Ruin"): "This invasion of Iraq, if it goes off, will join the Bay of Pigs, Vietnam, Desert One, Beruit and Somalia in the history of military catastrophe."
- Former CBS News anchor Walter Cronkite issued a similar gloomy prediction, fearing "the military is always more confident than circumstances show they should be," and said when he looked at America's future that it was "very, very dark."
- R. W. "Johnny" Apple, in the *New York Times*, March 30, 2003 ("Bush Peril: Shifting Sand and Fickle Opinion"): "With every passing day, it is more evident that the allies made two gross military misjudgments in concluding that coalition forces could safely bypass Basra and Nasiriya and that Shiite Muslims in southern Iraq would rise up against Saddam Hussein . . . 'Shock and awe' neither shocked nor awed."
- The *Washington Post* ran a front-page story on April 14, 2003, in which it said that the U.S. invasion force was "not large enough or powerful enough to take Baghdad by force."
- The *Washington Post* just three days earlier had published a story in which it claimed officers were comparing Secretary of Defense

Donald Rumsfeld to Vietnam-era Secretary of Defense Robert McNamara.

- Ted Koppel, traveling with the troops on March 25, 2003, warned that Americans should "forget the easy victories of the last 20 years. This war is more like the ones we knew before." (Quite the contrary, "this war" proved to be shorter than *any* in the nation's history, and quite unlike the "ones we knew before.")
- CNN's Wolf Blitzer, on February 25, 2003, had a graphic at the bottom of the screen: "If War Happens, Another Quagmire?"
- John McWethy, an ABC news correspondent, reported to Peter Jennings that "this could be a long war." Jennings answered, "As many people had anticipated." (Again, what is remarkable is that this was the shortest war in American history.)
- CBS News anchor Dan Rather, on January 24, 2003, intoned that "to win this time," U.S. forces would have to "wage a perilous battle in the streets of Baghdad" and warned that "civilians will fight, too." (Apparently these were not the same massive crowds that pulled down the statues of Saddam. At any rate, U.S. troops took Baghdad in less than 48 hours to minor resistance. [37]

This list of stunningly wrong predictions under the guise of analysis represents only a tiny fraction of the torrential outpouring of bad news that descended from the press on a daily basis.

Fortunately, the American public could see the truth, due to a remarkable Pentagon plan for dealing with wartime news. Even ABC News reporter Sam Donaldson called the program a "stroke of genius." What evened out the playing field for news coverage of the war? It was a strategy called "embedding," which was the brainchild of Victoria "Torrie" Clarke, a former press secretary for John McCain and the Pentagon's assistant secretary for public affairs. Clarke had conceived the strategy in the fall of 2002, as the Bush administration made its case to the United Nations. Her idea involved staging an "end run" around the bias of the editors and newsrooms, taking the story of combat straight to the American public.

Clarke persuaded her boss, Secretary of Defense Donald Rumsfeld, who told the National Security Council in a memo, "We need to tell the factual story—good and bad—before others seed the media with disinformation and distortions, as they most certainly will continue to do. . . . Our commanders can ensure the media get to the story alongside the troops." They concluded that to facilitate access to the forces, "we will embed media with our units [who] will live, work, and travel as part of the units." [38] Although the embedded journalists could expect the same protection as any other member of the U.S. military—that is, they could rely on their embedding units to assist them—media members had to carry and load their own equipment, could not carry firearms, and had to pay for their own smallpox and anthrax vaccinations. Further, they had to sign an agreement not to sue the U.S. government for injury or death. They were allowed to show all the war footage they wanted, but they could not reveal the exact locations of their units without prior approval of the commanders, and were prohibited from photographing or otherwise showing the faces of POWs or detainees. In February, news organizations were given a set number of slots, which they were able to barter with each other, subject to Clarke's approval. More than 500 reporters, producers, and cameramen (90 percent of them American) were embedded.

Pentagon planners candidly admitted they wanted to "counter the historical lies and disinformation of the Iraqi regime" and (though they did not openly say so) America's own biased news media. Rumsfeld approved a new standard for releasing of information, having those in charge ask, "Why not release?" rather than "Why release?" The Pentagon made much information available that in previous wars would have been censored, including the size of the friendly force in approximate terms, a description of the type of action (i.e., "land-based" or "air-based"), types of ordinance expended, types of forces involved, and operation code names. Troop strength, specific aircraft or ships, and the rules of engagement remained restricted.

As surprising as it may seem, liberals complained about *too much* unfiltered coverage of the war—too much information that reached the public without going through processing by journalists such as Jonathan Alter, Peter Jennings, or Katie Couric. Neal Gabler of *Salon* insultingly wrote that the embedded reporters were "patsies" and "P.R. flacks" because they bonded with the troops. More importantly, he said, "We need the 'larger picture,'" and he urged more "context," meaning more of a slant on the images and stories that the public saw. I am inclined to believe that what really bothered Gabler was that a group of liberal journalists did not control the flow of images and information or their subsequent interpretation.[39] The *Los Angeles Times* jumped on board, lamenting that the journalists were too close to the facts: "These policies raise questions about the balance and sensitivity of wartime media coverage."[40]

Yet the reporters in the field had a much different sense of how the war was going than the editors' desks and news studios back home. A BBC reporter blasted his own organization for blatantly distorting reports from the field to give the war a negative slant. Paul Adams, in a memo to his superiors, denounced the BBC's coverage: "Who dreamed up the line that the coalition are achieving 'small victories at a very high price?' The truth is exactly the opposite . . . [as] the gains are huge and the costs relatively low."[41] Adams admitted that he was "gobsmacked to hear, in a set of headlines today, that the coalition was suffering 'significant casualties.' This is simply NOT TRUE."[42] Another correspondent, Martin Walker of UPI, admitted that "something fundamental has happened to the

British and U.S. media during this war. Those who have spent time on the front lines with coalition troops . . . have learned to love the military."[43] Martin found a "very different view" among the journalists in the field from the "large and skeptical media corps" back at the headquarters briefings.[44] One academic study, examining 66 stories from the war—26 from embedded reporters and 40 from non-embedded reporters—found a significant difference in the reports. Non-embedded reporters were "less able to separate preconceptions" and more often than not based their reports on domestic fears of potential resistance rather than actual instances of resistance.[45] The study's researchers found that the pre-existing templates (news frames) held by the reporters were a determining factor in the differences between behind-the-line and embedded reporting practices.

> Embedded reporters, observing direct contradictions of their previously established frames, were in a better position to report on what they actually witnessed. In some sense, then, this presented audiences with a choice on how to view the war. Embedded reporters presented a much more positive view of US military actions and possibilities than did their behind-the-lines counterparts. Once the practice of embedded reporting diminished, readers increasingly lost this choice, because the previously established and dominate framing of the mainstream press returned.[46]

This study showed the power of the journalist preconceptions by detailing how journalists based in Baghdad during the war (yes, prior to its capture by U.S. troops) would uncritically accept, and with little or no comment pass along as verified news, the "statements of the Iraqi minister of information, Muhammed Saeed al-Sahaf. Only when the combat reached Baghdad itself did some journalists began to question the veracity of al-Sahaf's statements, particularly when al-Sahaf denied the presence of Allied forces which were visible from the hotel in which the reporters were staying."[47]

Perhaps the most significant journalism story to emerge from the war was the admission of CNN chief news executive Eason Jordan in the *New York Times* that CNN had deliberately buried negative stories about Saddam and his thuggish sons to stay in the good graces of the regime.[48] Jordan justified lying to the American public, saying that it would have "jeopardized the lives of Iraqis, particularly those on our Baghdad staff," although it seems to me that CNN never dutifully applied such concerns to American soldiers in harm's way. Later, *New York Times* writer John Burns would recount how journalists took the Iraqi information minister (known as "Baghdad Bob" by Americans watching the war) "out for long candlelit dinners, plying him with sweet cakes, plying him with mobile phones at $600 each for members of his family, and giving him bribes of thousands of dollars."[49] Burns admitted that Western reporters were accompanied by "handlers" at all times. Nevertheless, he argued, it was "not impossible to tell the truth," even in Iraq, but rather his colleagues "rationalized [evil] away." Referring to journalists' unwillingness to confront the evil of Saddam Hussein, Burns concluded, "There was a gross abdication of responsibility."[50]

The slanted war coverage caused the public to steadily lose confidence in the rest of the media. On May 28, 2003, *USA Today*'s headline blared, "Trust in Media Keeps on Slipping."[51] Columbia University sociology and journalism professor Todd Gitlin tried to explain the decline as common to all institutions, but in fact, it was not: confidence in the military, churches, and the office of the president had increased.[52] A Pew Research Center poll in July 2003, in fact, found that Americans expected their journalists to show patriotism, with 76 percent saying news organizations should embrace a "decidedly 'pro-American' viewpoint." Nearly 60 percent said that news organizations "do not pay attention" to complaints about inaccuracy, and 53 percent still thought that the media was biased. Just under half thought that the press was too critical of the United States.[53] Gallup found that by September 2003, 82 percent of the respondents had confidence in the military, and 55 percent in the presidency, but only 35 percent had confidence in television news, and only 33 percent in newspapers.[54] Of course, newsrooms continued to act in the same predictable manner. For instance, the MSNBC newsroom actually *booed* President Bush during his 2003 State of the Union speech.[55]

Fox News, uniquely, continued to gain viewers, seeing its viewership rise 133 percent from January 2000 to February 2001, rapidly catching up with CNN in total households (342,000 for CNN; 258,000 for Fox).[56] The differences in numbers were almost entirely explained by the cable companies that did not carry Fox but which had begun to at a rapid rate by late 2001. A full 20 percent of Americans turned to Fox News for their news coverage—an astounding number considering that Fox, a cable outlet, was available in only a fraction of the homes in which NBC, CBS, or ABC could be received. On cable, it was not even close: by July 2003, Fox's share of the five-network cable-news audience surpassed 50 percent in prime time for the quarter, improving its standings during the war by an incredible 95 percent. CNN, on the other hand, lost another 12 percent of its audience.[57]

Coverage of the war through the reports of the "embeds" had proven that when journalists report the facts about the armed forces, the public decides for itself how to interpret those facts—and the public's esteem for both the military and journalists rises. But when journalists engage in critical reporting designed to undermine the effort of the armed forces, both the military and journalists suffer.

BUSH COVERAGE: THE REMAINING YEARS

The negative coverage of the war and the Bush administration continued throughout Bush's time in office. Consider, for instance, the immediate aftermath of the first stage of the Gulf War. U.S. troops had been overwhelmingly successful; in but six short weeks, the coalition forces had overthrown Hussein. Returning from a tour in the Gulf, the USS *Abraham Lincoln* cruised toward California and a rendezvous with President Bush who was to arrive by military jet on the carrier and deliver a speech. The crew of the *Lincoln* proudly displayed a banner announcing the success of their own ship: "Mission Accomplished." The president spoke of the end to the first phase of the war, his pride in American troops, and of the ongoing war on terror: "The war on terror is not over; yet it is not endless. We do not know the day of final victory, but we have seen the turning of the tide. No act of the terrorists will change our purpose, or weaken our resolve, or alter their fate. Their cause is lost. Free nations will press on to victory." [58]

Bush did link the Iraq War to the larger concern of the war on terror, stating clearly that the war on terror was not ended. The news media did relay this message. At the same time, instead of discussing the president's message, or the nature of the conflict, the establishment news media used this event as an opportunity to pounce. For example,

> *Nightline* used this as an opportunity to reframe the president's message about the war to one about the economy. As part of its news segment on the president's speech, it presented a compilation of interviews among "average" Americans:
>
> ABC News reporter Chris Bury: "And here in the US?"
>
> Male, Number One: "Time to do something about the economy."
>
> Male, Number Two: "*The economy sucks right now.*"
>
> Female, Number One: "You know, just the economy, *getting that back on board right now*, you know, really being focused on the American public."
>
> Bury later states, "In his speech tonight, the President wrapped his remarks on Iraq in the popular cloak of the war on terrorism. Certainly the public gives him high marks for that . . . But [our survey] also suggests some *danger signs for the President on economic issues.*"
>
> To which ABC News reporter Michel Martin replies, "And when Americans are asked about the most pressing concerns, as we did today in several cities, it is *the economy that emerges as the clear and present*

danger. Even with many voters, like the woman in Atlanta, who supported the war."

Female, Number Three: "There's so many older people that *don ' t have
very much of an income*. And I know that the drugs, medicine and things
are *so expensive* that a lot of them have to make choices. You know, *am I
going to take my medicine or am I gonna eat today or pay my bills?*"

Female, Number Four: "I think *our attention needs to be focused on the
economy*. And President Bush needs to help us come up with a plan."

Summing all of this up, Betsy Stark, of ABC News stated, "So, you put
it all together and . . . *I think there ' s plenty of reason for people to feel
anxious*, even though the numbers say *the economy continues to limp
along*."

Reporter Michel Martin diminishes even this small bit of praise: "In an
ABC News poll released this evening, *nearly half of those surveyed said
most people have lost ground financially since the President took office*. Just
10 percent said most are better off. And *there is real doubt* about the
President's plan for the economy."

Male, Number Two was then shown saying: "Over two million
Americans have lost their job since Bush took office. *The economy sucks
right now*. Not, not solely because of him. But if he was a good president, he would be *trying to fix that instead of manufacturing a war* that
everyone can rally behind him so he can get re-elected."[59]

And so it was for the other major networks and for the major papers
covering this event. Give lip service to the troops, then hammer Bush on
the economy. Although there was a minor recession caused by the combination of the dotcom bubble bursting and the 9/11 attacks, by all credible
accounts the country was already on its way to recovery by the time of
Bush's speech. Recall that at this point—May 1, 2003—the Dow had already climbed from a low of 7,673 in March 2003 to 8,454 on May 1, 2003.
Unemployment was at 6 percent.

Of note about this speech was the means by which President Bush
arrived on the carrier: jet plane. CBS said, "The president's made-for-TV
arrival on the . . . Lincoln signals the opening of his 2004 campaign and
his expected focus on national security. And with polls showing the
struggling economy is by far the biggest concern of most Americans, Mr.
Bush is also determined not to repeat his father's mistake of appearing
unconcerned."[60]

Forty-seven of ninety-one broadcasts mentioning the president's address made mention of the arrival.[61] Certainly the means of arrival was
news. It is not, after all, usual for a president to land on a carrier, much
less in a jet. The usual means would be by helicopter. The original plan

was for the president to arrive by jet because the carrier would be too far out to sea for the trip to be made by helicopter. The president was a former jet pilot, and he relished this opportunity for a combat-jet trip. However, between the time of the announcement and set plans for the jet trip, the weather changed, and the carrier had to speed up, thus arriving closer to shore sooner than expected. Instead of simply docking a day early, however, the carrier instead followed standard Navy procedure and cruised in circles offshore so as to dock as scheduled because families, friends, all maintenance personnel, and onshore preparations were all scheduled for the carrier's arrival at the prearranged time the next day. The president made the decision to stick with the original plan and arrive by jet, which from the Navy's point of view was actually a safer alternative than to taxi out by helicopter. The press had a different story—a different frame—one which showed either intentional ill will or a stunning ignorance of Navy protocol. Take these for example:

- Political commentator Chris Matthews asked, "Can top gun Bush now score a victory for our economy? Lights, camera, action. The president bonds with troops in a war-ending spectacle. Was this a Reaganesque moment or what?" Matthews's guest Lou Dobbs (CNN) simply said it was "a stunt."[62]
- The *Washington Post* wrote, "For Bush . . . the whole day was devoted to linking his presidency to the aura of the U.S. Military. When the . . . S-3B carrying Bush made its tailhook landing on the aircraft carrier . . . Bush emerged from the cockpit in full olive flight suit and combat boots, his helmet tucked jauntily under his left arm. As he exchanged salutes with the sailors, his ejection harness, hugging him tightly between the legs, gave him the swagger of a top gun."[63]
- The *New York Times*, was rather uncomplimentary, as were others: "Mr. Bush emerged for the kind of photographs that other politicians can only dream about. He hopped out of the plane with a helmet tucked under his arm and walked across the flight deck with a swagger that seemed to suggest that he had seen 'Top Gun.'"[64]
- Maureen Dowd (of "dowdification" fame) wrote, "Out bounded the cocky, rule-breaking, daredevil flyboy, a man navigating the Highway to the Danger Zone, out along the edges where he was born to be, the further on the edge, the hotter the intensity. He flashed that famous all-American grin as he swaggered around the deck . . . Compared to Karl Rove's . . . myth-making cinematic style, Jerry Bruckheimer's movies look like 'Lizzie McGuire.' This time Maverick [President Bush] didn't just nail a few bogeys. . . . this time the Top Gun [President Bush] wasted a couple of nasty regimes . . . He swaggered across the deck to high-five his old gang."

Speaking for the president, she had him say, "That's right . . . I am dangerous."[65]

- Paul Krugman linked President Bush to Georges Boulanger, a "French General, minister of war, and political figure who led a brief but influential authoritarian movement that threatened to topple [France's] Third Republic in the 1880s."[66] Krugman juxtaposed "that history" with "George Bush's 'Top Gun' act . . . c'mon, guys, it wasn't about honoring the troops, it was about showing the president in a flight suit—[it] was as scary as it was funny. A U.S.-based British journalist told me that he and his colleagues had laughed through the whole scene. And nobody seemed bothered that Mr. Bush, who appears to have skipped more than a year of the National Guard service that kept him out of Vietnam, is now emphasizing his flying experience."[67]

- *World News Tonight* trumpeted this opening story line: "Bush Exploits War for Photo Op." Peter Jennings cast the landing as a "powerful photo opportunity" and then paraphrased Democrat attacks as "asking government auditors to figure out how much the trip cost the taxpayers" and claiming that it was "an affront to the Americans killed or injured in Iraq for the President to exploit the trappings of war for the momentary spectacle of a speech."[68]

The message was clear: Bush was *Top Gun* role-playing. Almost exclusively ignored were the reasons for the jet landing: the weather, the families on shore arriving a day later, and the Navy preference for safety. Willful disregard for the facts was evidenced, as this excerpt from *Bush's War* describes:

> Frank Rich, ignoring utterly Navy protocol and weather reports, wrote: "The White House has absorbed the [Jerry] Bruckheimer aesthetic so fully that its 'Top Gun' was better, not to mention briefer, than the original [movie *Top Gun*]. [The] return of the Lincoln and its eagerly homeward bound troops was delayed by a day to accommodate the pageantry of Mr. Bush's tailhook landing." E. J. Dionne Jr. also disregarded information contrary to his beliefs when he wrote: "Bush and his White House say whatever is necessary, even if they have to admit later that what they said the first time wasn't exactly true. Consider this paragraph from the New York Times . . . about [the] Bush-in-a-flight-suit moment. 'The White House said today that President Bush traveled to the carrier . . . on a small plane because he wanted to experience a landing the way carrier pilots do, not because the ship would be too far out to sea . . . to arrive by helicopter. . . .' Now that's very interesting. You can be absolutely sure that if an Al Gore White House had . . . misled citizens about the reason . . . Gore would have been pilloried. . . . Yet Bush's defenders have done a good job selling the idea that it's churlish to raise questions . . . even if the White House was not exactly honest about the circumstances of the flight."[69]

The pattern for Bush reporting was clear. Whenever Bush gave a speech about the war on terror or national security, the press would reframe the occasion to highlight *what it considered* a stagnant economy or economic recession. Although the recession was considered officially over by the last quarter of 2003, the press nevertheless continued to insist that the recession was only deepening.

That is, one would assume, until evidence was overwhelming that the economy was steaming along. By November 2003, unemployment was a low 5 percent, and the Dow was around 10,000. Yet criticism of the economy continued throughout the president's tenure in office, until 2006 when the Dow was over 11,000 and unemployment was under 5 percent. Whereas in the past the press would interject the economy as part of the media frame, now the press would pointedly ignore it.

Another way that the press ignored information that ran counter to its template can be see in coverage of the president's November 2005 Veteran's Day speech. In this speech the president not only commemorated veterans, he used the opportunity to lay out in quite some detail the general strategy in Iraq and in the larger war on terror. The press response to this major policy speech is instructive. Instead of relaying to the American people the strategy for winning the war presented by President Bush (the major reason for the speech in the first place), they instead insisted that the president *had yet* to detail such a strategy.

For example, *NBC Nightly News* highlighted this statement by former Clinton press secretary Joe Lockhart: "They [think they] have a PR problem; they don't. They have a policy problem. He's got to come clean, talk about how difficult this issue is and lay out some sort of strategy that the American public can get behind for success in bringing the troops home."[70] *USA Today* wrote, "The best chance of salvaging an acceptable outcome is for the United States to stay long enough to see a stable government and strong Iraqi military force in place. There's no guarantee this will happen. For Bush, the challenge is not so much to stay the course as to define it—with the candor the American people deserve and the complexity this mission demands."[71]

Eugene Robinson of the *Washington Post* bluntly wrote, "'Stay the course' doesn't play as a strategy when the course seems to lead nowhere. What is victory in Iraq? When will we know we've won? When the simmering, low-level civil war we've ignited sparks into full flame and somebody takes over the country? The mess that George Bush and Co. have created . . . doesn't have an unmessy solution. [Congressman John] Murtha's plan—just get out—isn't really attractive, but at least it's a plan. The saying goes that when you're in a hole, the first thing to do is to stop digging. But the president . . . just keeps burrowing deeper into that pile of manure."[72] Of note is that the president had just laid out a comprehensive, *five-part* strategy for Iraq and the war on terror. If, however, you were to have missed the president's speech, having only establishment media for news, you would have no idea that such a strategy existed.

The intense negative coverage of the Bush tenure in office has been well documented by many others. Take for an example the observations published in *Media Matters*; these offer an instructive insight into how the networks covered Bush while in office. Taking a snapshot, for instance, of two months of coverage in 2006, *Media Matters* found that the top focus of evening news was overwhelmingly Iraq, followed by Katrina, terrorism, and immigration. All, of course, are important issues, however, the *tone* of the coverage was anything but even-handed. Overall, the three major networks provided an amazing 74 percent negative coverage. Specifically on foreign policy concerns, Bush was given a jaw-dropping 94 percent negative coverage. In matters of domestic policy things were a bit better with merely a 74 percent negative coverage.[73] This is actually slightly better than the previous year, which saw 79 percent negative coverage. This type of negative reporting existed throughout Bush's tenure in office. Unlike negative commentary concerning liberal politicians, where the press criticizes them for not going far enough to the left, this negative coverage was constructed to contradict and condemn.

COLORING THE NEWS

The coloring of the news by the establishment press was perhaps most apparent when instances of abuse were so considerable and public that the press was forced to act. For example, the leader of the antiwar news, the *New York Times*, whose editorials had universally predicted doom and gloom, remained unrepentant until a war-related story brought a major scandal to the paper and shook its foundations. In May 2003, Jayson Blair, a reporter who was not embedded, but who had covered war-related "human interest" stories stateside, resigned amidst a tumult over his sources.[74] According to the *Times* own report, Blair "misled readers and *Times* colleagues with dispatches that purported to be from Maryland, Texas and other states, when often he was far away, in New York." Further, he "fabricated comments . . . concocted scenes . . . lifted material from other newspaper and wire services. . . . And he used these techniques to write falsely and emotionally about . . . the anguish of families grieving for loved ones killed in Iraq."[75]

The *Times* knew Blair was lying in his articles for nearly a year before his resignation. In April 2002, the metropolitan editor warned in an e-mail to administrators, "We have to stop Jayson from writing for the *Times*. Right now."[76] Despite the fact that by November 2002 Blair's reporting was known to be false and his sources fabricated and plagiarized, he remained on the job. In one article, Blair "incorporated at least a half-dozen passages lifted nearly verbatim from other news sources."[77] The treatment of Blair, who is black, raised suspicions of affirmative action run amok: the *New York Times* promoted Blair ahead of many more qualified reporters to an intermediate reporter, just one step away from a full-time reporter, despite a stunning lack of experience.

By late 2001, the paper knew Blair was a journalistic disaster waiting to happen, but dared not remove him for what some consider to be racial reasons. The extent of internal awareness of Blair's falsifications and errors was revealed in a series of letters passed among the top administrators of the paper in January 2002.[78] After a short hiatus Blair took for "personal reasons," the editors astonishingly assigned him to the DC sniper case. Blair promptly shook his onsite supervisors and delivered a scoop on one of the snipers, attributed entirely to unidentified law enforcement sources, claiming that the authorities were feuding with federal officials over custody of the suspects. Everyone involved quickly disputed the report and produced proof that Blair had again made up material. Despite knowing that Blair had a "pathological pattern of misrepresentation," managing editor Howell Raines rewarded Blair with the lead in the sniper coverage.[79] While Blair supposedly was in Maryland covering the sniper case, he was actually in New York finishing a book proposal *about* the sniper case.

When the Iraq War broke out, the *Times* continued to assign Blair to important stories, such as Pfc. Jessica Lynch's reunion with her family, for which Blair fabricated details and conversations. Although the paper fired Blair at that point, reporters and editors thought the paper had not gone far enough to restore its credibility. Matt Drudge's May 13, 2003, headline, "NY Times Newsroom in Crisis," summed it up.[80] One unidentified employee called the editors' memo a "whitewash," and another said, "Heads should roll."[81] Pressure built on Raines and publisher Arthur Sulzberger, Jr., who had emphasized "liberalism and diversity over honest journalism."[82] Immediately, other plagiarism or source-related problems arose with other writers, including Pulitzer-prize-winning journalist Rick Bragg.[83] The pattern was, apparently, enough for Sulzberger, who forced the resignation of Howell Raines and Gerald Boyd, the paper's managing editor.[84]

Neither the *Times*, nor CNN, nor the rest of the journalistic establishment seemed to have learned anything from their scandals or their plummeting ratings. The decline of the *Times* continued well into 2003, when its editor claimed that the nation's television audience was "burned out" on serious news.[85] Attempting to blame falling ratings on the Iraq War or on summer doldrums, the *Times* struggled to explain why Fox was not affected by the same problems. In fact, by June and July 2003, about 24.1 million people watched the three main evening newscasts, compared to 24.3 million in 2001. Fox's audience continued to grow, from 612,000 to 735,000 in one year, while CNN, MSNBC, CBS, and ABC all saw audience size fall.[86] The slide continued into September 2003, when the first weeks of ratings fell again from the previous year.[87] The continued negative, anti-conservative aspect of the mainstream press only exacerbated a problem involving the rise of Internet-based alternative news. Americans were not going online to look exclusively at broadcast or traditional paper websites, but to *alternate* news sites as well. Additionally, "the time people spent on each site fell at many papers, suggesting much of that traffic comes from searches with users lingering only briefly rather than reading the news as they would in a print paper."[88] They were, of course, seeking out *additional* information to balance what they perceived as bias in establishment news.

By mid-2010, during prime time Fox was outperforming the other major 24-hour news networks *combined*:

Fox—2,284,000 viewers
MSNBC—857,000 viewers
CNN—454,000 viewers
CNBC—174,000 viewers

Broadcast news has seen a sharp decline in viewership as well. In 1980 approximately 53 million viewers tuned in; by 2008, only 23 million tuned in.[89] The printed press has also continued its slip, losing between 2 and 4.5 percent circulation every six months between 2003 and 2008.[90] The print circulation slide from 2001 to 2008 equals roughly 13.5 percent for the daily and 17.3 percent for the Sunday editions.[91]

Increasingly, the mainstream media is a creature on the path to extinction—at least as a dominant, gate-keeping, agenda-setting form. The decline in objective news had sparked a revolution that resulted in competitors such as Limbaugh, Fox, Drudge, and Internet news sites. Although novelist Michael Crichton would call the mainstream news outlets the "Mediasaurus," it was their dominance, not the organizations themselves, that was becoming extinct when faced with new competition. And as we will see in the next chapter, just like dinosaurs of all eras, the Mediasaurus was also showing a continued inability to adapt to a new environment.

NOTES

1. Robert Shogan, *Bad News: Where the Press Goes Wrong in the Making of the President* (Chicago: Ivan R. Dee Publisher, 2001), 211.

2. Mary McGrory, "Anatomy of a Swoon," *Washington Post*, February 10, 2000.

3. Clarence Page, "New Hampshire and the Making of a Media Darling," *Chicago Tribune*, February 6, 2000.

4. Shogan, 223.

5. Shorenstein Center on the Press, Politics, and Public Policy, "Vanishing Voter Project," press release, June 1, 2000, quoted in Shogan, 218.

6. Charles Peters, "Tilting at Windmills," *Washington Monthly*, October 2000, quoted in Shogan, 245.

7. Shogan, 245.

8. Peters.

9. See Jim A. Kuypers, *Press Bias and Politics: How the Media Frame Controversial Issues*. (Westport, CT: Praeger, 2002).

10. Shogan, 243.

11. Michael Massing, "CBS: Sauterizing the News," *Columbia Journalism Review*, March/April 1986, 27–37.

12. "Media Study Group: CMPA's Media Monitor Reports on How TV News Covered the General Election Campaign," January 15, 2001, www.freerepublic.com/forum/a3a62cc63220b.htm.

13. George C. Edwards, Martin P. Wattenberg, and Robert L. Lineberry, *Government in America: People, Politics, and Policy*, 9th ed. (Longman, 2007). "Campaign 2004," *Media Monitor* 18, no. 6 (2004), www.cmpa.com/files/media_monitor/04novdec.pdf.

14. See "Media Study Group" report.

15. Bill Sammon, *At Any Cost* (Washington: Regnery, 2001), 26.

16. Sammon, 26.

17. Sammon, 23.

18. Sammon, 35.

19. Sammon, 35.

20. David Bauder, "CNN Vote Coverage Called 'Debacle,'" Associated Press, Yahoonews.com, February 2, 2001.

21. "Election Night: What Went Wrong?" http://cbsnewyork.com/main/topstories/story_004130232_html.

22. The Western part of the state is a traditionally Republican-leaning portion of the state.

23. "Five Weeks of History," *USA Today*, December 14, 2000.

24. "Florida Voter Errors Cost Gore the Election," *USA Today*, May 11–13, 2001.

25. There remain over 1.5 million uncounted absentee ballots. Until they are counted, we will never know for certain who "won" the popular vote.

26. Joe Bob Hester and Rhonda Gibson, "The Economy and Second-Level Agenda Setting: A Time-Series Analysis of Economic News and Public Opinion about the Economy," *Journalism and Mass Communication Quarterly*, 80 (2003), 73–90.

27. David E. Harrington, "Economic News on Television: The Determinants of Coverage," *Public Opinion Quarterly*, 53 (Spring 1989), 17–40; Institute for Applied Economics, *Network Television Coverage of Economic News* (New York: Institute for Applied Economics, 1984); Herbert Stein, "Media Distortions: A Former Official's View," *Columbia Journalism Review*, 13 (March-April 1975), 37–41; and Ben Wattenberg, *The Good News Is the Bad News Is Wrong* (New York: Simon & Schuster, 1984).

28. Robert K. Goidel and Ronald E. Langley, "Media Coverage of the Economy and Aggregate Economic Evaluations: Uncovering Evidence of Indirect Media Effects," *Political Research Quarterly*, 48 (June 1995), 313–328.

29. Hester and Gibson.

30. Quoted in Steve M. Barkin, *American Television News* (London: M.E. Sharpe, 2003), 13.

31. Quoted in Howard Kurtz, "ABC Stops Replay of Endless Tragedy," *Washington Post*, September 19, 2001. The impact footage on a major television news cast was essentially removed from any broadcasts after 2001, although a few specials have run on cable channels, such as the Discovery Channel; and on September 11, 2003, ABC carried a "live" tape reliving the *Good Morning America* show from 9/11.

32. Gloria Cooper, "For the Record," *Columbia Journalism Review*, March/April 2002, 7.

33. "Serious Agenda, Serious Interest," *Baltimore Sun*, December 24, 2001.

34. Peggy Noonan, "What I Saw at the Devastation," *Wall Street Journal*, September 13, 2001.

35. Jim A. Kuypers, Stephen Cooper, and Matthew Althouse, "George W. Bush, the American Press, and the Initial Framing of the War on Terror after 9/11," in Robert E.

Denton, ed., *The George W. Bush Presidency: A Rhetorical Perspective* (Lanham, MD: Lexington Books, 2012), 89–112.

36. Brent Baker, "Public Disapproval for Media Coverage," Media Research Center, November 15, 2001, www.pollinreport.com/terror.htm.

37. The Media Research Center has compiled most of these excerpts: "*Washington Times* Documents Media's Doomsaying Predictions," April 15, 2002, www.mediaresearchcenter.com/cyberalerts/2003/cyb20030414.asp. Comments from Chris Matthews and Johnny Apple are found in "Hall of Shame," *National Review Online*, April 10, 2003, http://nationalreview.com/nr_comment/nr_comment041003.asp; Cronkite's comments appear in Rob Jennings, "Former CBS Anchor Cronkite Voices Disappointment in Move to War," March 19, 2003, www.dailyrecord.com/news/03/03/19/news6-cronkite.htm.

38. Joel Rosenberg, "Rumsfeld Memo to National Security Council: How to Win the Spin War," *World Magazine*, March 27, 2003, www.worldmag.com. Segments were excerpted on www.freerepublic.com/focus/f-news/877282/posts.

39. Gabler quoted in George Neumayr, "Embedded Patsies," *American Prowler*, March 27, 2003, www.spectator.org/article.asp?art_id-2003_3_26_23_14_27.

40. Quoted in Neumayr.

41. Adams quoted in Brent Baker, "BBC Reporter 'Gobsmacked' by BBC's Distorted War Reporting," Media Research Center, March 27, 2003, www.freerepublic.com/focus/f-news/876963/posts.

42. Baker.

43. Martin Walker, "Commentary: How the Media Changed," www.upi.com/view/cfm?StoryID=20030408-071952-7876r.

44. Walker.

45. Jim A. Kuypers and Stephen Cooper, "A Comparative Framing Analysis of Embedded and Behind-the-Lines Reporting on the 2003 Iraq War," *Qualitative Research Reports in Communication* 6, no. 1 (2005), 8.

46. Kuypers and Cooper, 8.

47. Stephen Cooper and Jim A. Kuypers, "Embedded versus Behind-the-Lines Reporting on the Second Gulf War," in Ralph D. Berenger, ed., *The Global Media Goes to War* (Spokane, WA: Marquette Books, 2004), 161–172.

48. Eason Jordan, "The News We Kept to Ourselves," *New York Times*, April 11, 2003.

49. John Burns, "There Is Corruption in Our Business," *Editor & Publisher*, September 15, 2003.

50. Burns. Coverage of the war and related issues brought out the "yellow journalism" in some of the more biased British and American journalists, so much so that the UK *Guardian* found itself having to retract two separate stories related to its antiwar stance.

51. Peter Johnson, "Trust in Media Keeps on Slipping," *USA Today*, May 28, 2003.

52. James L. Gattuso, "Who to Watch? The Iraqi War and the Myth of Media Concentration," March 26, 2003, Competitive Enterprise Network, www.cei.org/utils/printer.cfm?AID=3423.

53. Jennifer Harper, "Public Wants Patriotic But Unbiased Reporters," *Washington Times*, July 14, 2003.

54. http://pollingreport.com, poll of September 17, 2003.

55. Mark Finklstein, "MSNBC Newsroom Booed Bush State of the Union," newsbusters.org, August 16, 2007, http://media.newsbusters.org/stories/msnbc-newsroom-booed-bushs-state-union.html?q=blogs/mark-finkelstein/2007/08/16/msnbc-newsroom-booed-bushs-state-union.

56. Howard Kurtz, "Doing Something Right: Fox News Sees Ratings Soar, Critics Sore," *Washington Post*, February 5, 2001, http://wasingtonpost.com/wp-dyn/articles/A26378-2001Feb4.html.

57. Andrew Grossman, "Fox News Triumphs Over Rivals," Reuters, July 2, 2003, www.freerepublic.com/focus/f-news/939217/posts.

58. George W. Bush, "President Says Saddam Hussein Must Leave Iraq Within 48 Hours: Remarks by the President in Address to the Nation," *Office of the Press Secretary,* 17 March 2003, www.whitehouse.gov/news/releases/2003/03/20030317-7.html.

59. "Nightline Unfinished Business," *Nightline,* ABC News Transcripts, American Broadcasting Companies, May 1, 2003. Emphasis mine.

60. "President Bush Out Pushing His Tax Cut Plan and Campaigning for Re-election," *CBS Evening News,* CBS Evening News Transcripts, CBS Worldwide, May 2, 2003.

61. Jim A. Kuypers, *Bush's War: Media Bias and Justifications for War in a Terrorist Age* (Lanham, MD: Rowman & Littlefield, 2006), 86.

62. "The Chris Matthews Show," *The Chris Matthews Show,* NBC News Transcripts, National Broadcasting Company, May 4, 2003.

63. Dana Milbank, "For Bush, the Military Is the Message for '04," *Washington Post,* May 2, 2003, A1.

64. David E. Sanger, "Aftereffects: President Bush Declares 'One Victory in a War on Terror,'" *New York Times,* May 2, 2003, A1.

65. Maureen Dowd, "The Iceman Cometh," *New York Times,* May 4, 2003, D13.

66. "Georges Boulanger," *Encyclopedia Britannica,* http://search.eb.com.

67. Paul Krugman, "Man on Horseback," *New York Times,* May 6, 2003, A31.

68. "USS Abraham Lincoln Sailors Back Home, Bush Exploits War for Photo Op," *World News Tonight with Peter Jennings,* ABC News Transcripts, American Broadcasting Companies, May 6, 2003.

69. Kuyper, 91–92.

70. "Ongoing Debate over Iraq between Republicans and Democrats Getting Very Partisan and Nasty," *NBC Nightly News,* NBC News Transcripts, National Broadcasting Company, November 19, 2005.

71. Editorial, "Congress Finally Debates War But Finds No Easy Solution," *USA Today,* November 21, 2005, A145.

72. Eugene Robinson, "No Way Out for Bush and Co.," *Washington Post,* November 22, 2005, A29.

73. "Covering Bush—The Same Old Story: How the TV Networks Have Portrayed President Bush," *Media Monitor* 20, no. 2 (2006), 4.

74. "*Times* Reporter Who Resigned Leaves Long Trail of Deception," *New York Times,* May 11, 2003, www.nytimes.com/2003/05/11/national/11PAPE.html?ei=5062& en=09f4da45425ca9b.

75. "*Times* Reporter Who Resigned."

76. "*Times* Reporter Who Resigned."

77. "*Times* Reporter Who Resigned."

78. "*Times* Reporter Who Resigned."

79. "Times Reporter Who Resigned."

80. "Emergency Meeting Called at Old Gray Lady; *NY Times* Newsroom in Crisis," www.drudgereport.com, May 13, 2003.

81. Keither Kelly and Dan Mangan, "*Times* in Mutiny over Bosses' 'Whitewash,'" *New York Post,* May 13, 2003.

82. George Neumayr, "The Howell Problem," *American Prowler,* May 13, 2003, www.spectator.org/article.asp?art_id=2003_5_12_23_52_53.

83. Keith J. Kelly and Lauren Barack, "Top Writer on Ice in *New Times Scandal,*" *New York Post,* May 24, 2003.

84. Jacques Steinberg, "Executive Editor of the *Times* and Top Deputy Step Down," *New York Times,* June 5, 2003.

85. Jim Rutenberg, "Suffering News Burnout? The Rest of America Is, Too," *New York Times,* August 11, 2003.

86. John Dempsey and Paula Bernstein, "Top Exec Out As CNN Seeks Clues to Blues," Reuters, August 30, 2000.

87. Caroline Wilbert, "CNN's Prime-time Ratings Still Down Despite Overhaul," *Atlanta Journal-Constitution,* September 23, 2003, online edition.

88. "Audience," *State of the News Media: 2009*, Pew Project for Excellence in Journalism, www.stateofthemedia.org/2009/narrative_newspapers_audience.php?media=4&cat=2.

89. "Audience," www.stateofthemedia.org/2009/narrative_networktv_audience.php?cat=2&media=6.

90. "Audience," www.stateofthemedia.org/2009/narrative_newspapers_audience.php?media=4&cat=2.

91. "Audience," www.stateofthemedia.org/2009/narrative_newspapers_audience.php?media=4&cat=2.

ELEVEN

Obama 2008 and the Contemporary Establishment News Media

We have already seen the political leaning of the press: liberal/progressive. We have already answered the question of whether or not this political leaning asserts itself in news coverage: it does. We have also seen how the press shows a tendency to favor Democrats over Republicans and liberals over conservatives. Yet with the rise of alternative news sources, with the increase in criticism directed at the political bias of the establishment press, and with the resulting decline in circulation and viewership, will we see a change in mainstream press reportorial practices? To answer this concisely, let us now look at an area of politics rich with reportorial possibilities and excitement: presidential politics. In this chapter I present three broad considerations: a collection of general observations; the presidential election of 2008; and President Obama's first two years in office. In the final chapter I'll offer several observations about the 2010 and 2012 elections and the partisan press today.

GENERAL OBSERVATIONS

Thus far we have covered journalistic practices up to around 2007. In the years leading up to 2013 there was only a continuation of the press practices we have already covered in the previous chapters. What I share here are a few of what I consider to be the more interesting and important mainstream news media reporting events.

Certainly one can still say that the news media engages in selective reporting, and a few incidents will exemplify this practice. Consider the 2005 State of the Union speech. During this speech the Democrats in the chamber broke decorum rules by openly and verbally contradicting and booing the president on several occasions.[1] No mention of this was made by the major networks, CNN, or MSNBC. No major paper reported the incident. However, when a lone Republican, Joe Wilson (R-SC), said, "You lie" when Obama said in a speech to a joint session of Congress in 2009 that illegal immigrants would not be covered under the proposed health care overhaul bill, the press plastered it all over the news. American papers mentioned the incident 1,960 times, and broadcast and cable pressed the issue as well: CNN 377 times, MSNBC 239 times, Fox News, 134 times. The major networks pushed the story in their evening news shows for several days, with NBC presenting 47 stories, ABC, 27, and CBS, 22. The reportorial partisanship is simply stunning.

Here are some other quick examples.

- President Obama's inaugural address was certainly a newsworthy item, one that was duly covered by the press. President Bush's farewell speech given in Midland, Texas, was shown live only by Fox News; CNN made only passing reference to it the following day. Few American papers reported it.
- During the hotly contested 2008 Senate race in Massachusetts between Martha Coakley and Scott Brown, CNN aired live the concession speech of Democrat Coakley but did not air the victory speech of Tea Party–supported Republican Brown.[2]
- During the 2008 presidential campaign, the *New York Times* saw fit to publish candidate Obama's letter concerning his policy positions on the Iraq War, but when candidate McCain submitted his own letter on that topic, the *Times* saw fit to reject it because, in the opinion of the *Times*, it criticized Obama while not focusing enough on what McCain would do.[3]

These are not, unfortunately, isolated examples. They represent the mainstream media engaging in selective reporting, a practice that usually acts to help liberal causes and hinder conservative causes; or, one that shows Democrats in a positive light and Republicans in a negative light. A few more examples should clearly demonstrate this trend.

One example I consider most telling is the 2010 renewal of the Patriot Act. As political blogger Ed Morrissey pointed out, "During George Bush's term in office, every renewal of the Patriot Act became grand theater, with newspapers inveighing against the overreach of Bush and the danger to American liberty in the bill, which wasn't an *entirely* vacuous argument. Protesters would fill streets, and reporters would demand positions from various members of Congress. So what happened this year?"[4] A LexisNexis search of the week following the vote found only 44 mentions of the Patriot Act renewal among wire services; only 5 mentions among major U.S. papers; and only 15 mentions in news transcripts. Most of these mentions were along the lines of this announcement on CNN: "The Senate is voting to extend the Patriot Act for another year.

Key provisions are scheduled to expire Sunday and that includes court-approved wiretaps on multiple phones. Now supporters say extending the law enables authorities to keep important tools in the fight against terrorism. It now heads to the House."[5] Contrast this with the 2005 renewal. During the week following the vote there were 175 mentions of the Patriot Act renewal among wire services; 42 mentions among major U.S. papers; and 434 mentions in news transcripts. The *New York Times* offers examples of typical comments from the establishment press: "The law has become a lightning rod for critics who say it invites abuses and Big Brother-like tactics by the government"; "Critics of the Patriot Act called the amendments to the House bill cosmetic and far short of what they said was needed to ease growing public concerns about the government's powers to fight terrorism"; "'We think the House of Representatives missed an opportunity to enact real improvements to the Patriot Act, to enact real amendments that would protect our civil liberties and restore appropriate checks and balances.'"[6]

Ed Morrissey points out that this difference in reporting "brings us to the main point. Republicans have mostly supported this bill because they believe it a necessary tool for counterintelligence and counterterrorism. Democrats mainly opposed it as a way to rally political opposition to Bush and the Republicans. Now that they're in charge and responsible for preventing attacks, that Patriot Act looks pretty darned good to most of them."[7]

Other examples include the lack of media coverage during the 2008 presidential primaries (and after) of Democrat John Edwards's affair with Reille Hunter. It took the *National Enquirer* and later *New York Magazine* to put this information on the radar screen of politically interested Americans.[8] It again took the *National Enquirer* to alert the establishment media to allegations of Democrat and anthropogenic-global-warming-champion Al Gore sexually assaulting a masseuse, a story the news media generally ignored, even after allegations from other masseuses surfaced.[9] The establishment press also ignored "Climategate" until *Comedy Central* made it an issue, and even then it downplayed the significance of the event.[10] It also ignored or downplayed the significant public admission of NASA administrator Charles Bolden "that the 'foremost' mission of the space agency is to improve relations with the Muslim world."[11]

On top of this, the media continues to admit to a liberal/progressive bias and to engage in biased behavior. The Media Research Center, a right-leaning organization dedicated to "bringing balance" to the news media, has catalogued thousands of direct quotes from establishment news reporters.[12] There are simply too many to list, but a few telling examples include *New York Times* public editor Daniel Okrent responding to the question "Is the *New York Times* a liberal paper with "Of course it is. . . . These are the social issues: gay rights, gun control, abortion and environmental regulation, among others. And if you think the *Times* plays it down the middle on any of them, you've been reading the paper with your eyes closed."[13] ABC *20/20* coanchor John Stossel said to cnsnews.com reporter Robert Bluey, "At ABC, people say 'conservative' the way people say 'child molester.'"[14] *Newsweek*'s Evan Thomas had this to say: "There is a liberal bias. It's demonstrable."[15] And here is *Washington Post* political reporter Thomas Edsall:

> The mainstream press is liberal. . . . Since the civil rights and women's movements, the culture wars and Watergate, the press corps at such institutions as the *Washington Post*, ABC-NBC-CBS News, the *NYT*, the *Wall Street Journal*, *Time*, *Newsweek*, the *Los Angeles Times*, the *Boston Globe*, etc. is composed in large part of "new" or "creative" class members of the liberal elite—well-educated men and women who tend to favor abortion rights, women's rights, civil rights, and gay rights. In the main, they find such figures as Bill O'Reilly, Glenn Beck, Sean Hannity, Pat Robertson, or Jerry Falwell beneath contempt.[16]

The exposé of Journolist, or the "J-list," a listserve on Google of over 400 liberal journalists started by *Washington Post* blogger and *Newsweek* columnist Ezra Klein, furthered the charge of liberal bias in the establishment press. More to the point, it showed journalists at the highest levels of national reporting actively colluding to slant stories to help Obama and to hurt conservatives. Although first mentioned in July 2007 by Mickey Kaus in *Slate*,[17] it was not until the story broke in *Politico*—an online alternative news site, by the way—that the true nature of the list emerged and the story caught on.[18] Examples of what members of the list wrote include bald instances of hatred and overt planning to kill stories unfavorable to Democrats.

For example, Jonathan Strong of the *Daily Caller* reported that killing the Jeremiah Wright story because it would negatively impact Barack Obama was discussed on the list.[19] Spencer Ackerman of the *Washington Independent*, wrote, "If the right forces us all to either defend Wright or tear him down, no matter what we choose, we lose the game they've put upon us. Instead, take one of them—Fred Barnes, Karl Rove, who cares—and call them racists."[20] The hatred of conservatives ran strong on this list. Jonathan Strong reported comments posted by Sarah Spitz, an NPR affiliate producer, over what she would do if she were to witness Rush Limbaugh having a heart attack. She "wrote that she would 'laugh loudly like a maniac and watch his eyes bug out' as Limbaugh writhed in torment. In boasting that she would gleefully watch a man die in front of her eyes, Spitz seemed to shock even herself. 'I never knew I had this much hate in me,' she wrote. 'But he deserves it.'"[21] The same article also reports *Bloomberg News* reporter Ryan Donmoyer comparing members of the Tea Party movement to Nazis.

A most telling charge was leveled by Tucker Carlson, who edited several of Strong's articles about Journolist. Carlson wrote in a July 22, 2010, article,

> Again and again, we discovered members of Journolist working to coordinate talking points on behalf of Democratic politicians, principally Barack Obama. That is not journalism, and those who engage in it are not journalists. They should stop pretending to be. The news organizations they work for should stop pretending, too. I've been in journalism my entire adult life, and have often defended it against fellow conservatives who claim the news business is fundamentally corrupt. It's harder to make that defense now. It will be easier when honest (and, yes, liberal) journalists denounce what happened on Journolist as wrong.[22]

Journolist was shut down shortly after its inner workings were exposed to fresh air. Not long after, though, it secretly resurrected itself as the Cabalist. Initial reports indicate that groupthink is alive and well in reconstituted form. Jeffrey Goldberg of the *Atlantic* reported that in a July 2010 exchange on this list, members discussed how to respond to the *Daily Caller* news articles about Journolist:

> The members of Cabalist . . . spent much of yesterday debating whether to respond collectively or individually to the Daily Caller series, or to ignore it. This prompted one participant . . . to note, with unusual self-awareness for this group, that "it's pretty ironic that people seem to have made a collective decision not to write about this story because of the way that doing so might influence the media narrative." In other words, members of Journolist 2.0 were debating whether to collectively respond to a Daily Caller story alleging—inaccurately, in their minds— that members of Journolist 1.0 (the same people, of course) made collective decisions about what to write.[23]

OBAMA AND THE 2008 ELECTION

The growing and rampant abdication of journalistic responsibility is evidenced further by looking at the manner in which the mainstream press covered the presidential election of 2008 between Democrat Barack Obama and Republican John McCain. Example after example demonstrates a continuing decline of nonpartisan coverage and objective reporting.

The Center for Media and Public Affairs conducted a content analysis of almost 500 election news stories aired on the main evening news shows on ABC, CBS, NBC and Fox during the primaries. It found that "on-air evaluations of Hillary Clinton were nearly 3 to 2 negative (42% positive vs. 58% negative comments), while evaluations of her closest competitor Barack Obama was better than 3 to 2 positive (61% positive vs. 39% negative)." As bad as it was for Clinton, Republicans had it worse: Mitt Romney with only 40 percent positive, Rudy Giuliani with 39 percent positive, and John McCain with 33 percent positive. Of note is that on Fox News, "evaluations of all Democratic candidates combined were split almost evenly—51% positive vs. 49% negative, as well as all evaluations of GOP candidates—49% positive vs. 51% negative. On the three broadcast networks, opinion on the Democratic candidates split 47% positive vs. 53% negative, while evaluations of Republicans were more negative—40% positive vs. 60% negative."[24] Interestingly, the public seemed aware of this tilt:

> [Only] days after a Rasmussen Reports survey was released showing more than three times as many likely voters "believe most reporters will try to help Obama with their coverage" than help John McCain, a Fox News/Opinion Dynamics poll taken July 22–23 of 900 registered voters discovered six times as many think "most members of the media" want Obama to win than wish for a McCain victory. On Thursday's Special Report, FNC's Brit Hume relayed: "67 percent of the respondents think most media members want Obama to win. Just 11 percent think most in the media are for McCain."[25]

The *Washington Post* provides an excellent example of why voters felt this way. Devoting an entire article to candidate Obama's daily exercise regimen, the paper highlighted how "during his Hawaii vacation . . . he was photographed looking like the paradigm of a new kind of presidential fitness, one geared less toward preventing heart attacks than winning swimsuit competitions. The sun glinted off chiseled pectorals sculpted during four weightlifting sessions each week, and a body toned by regular treadmill runs and basketball games."[26]

Most definitely the public noticed such instances of obvious praise and adulation. For instance, a July 2008 Rasmussen poll "found that 49 percent of voters believe most reporters will try to help Obama with their coverage . . . [whereas]14 percent . . . believe most reporters will try to help John McCain win."[27] *Time* magazine ran an exposé of sorts titled "Crushing on Obama," in which the writer plainly admitted to both Obama bias and liberal bias: "Why are the media so smitten with Obama? Journalists have an affinity for the Democratic nominee in part because he is a wordsmith and they make a living manipulating words and symbols, so they have a special appreciation for his gifts. But another part of the reason is, yes, plain old liberal bias."[28] Note that not only a liberal bias is admitted, but a *deliberate manipulation* of words and symbols as a job criterion. A September 2008 Rasmussen poll found even more striking results: "Seven out of 10 voters (69%) remain convinced that reporters try to help the candidate they want to win, and this year by a nearly five-to-one margin voters believe they are trying to help Barack Obama."[29] By the time of the election, Pew Research Center found that by "a margin of 70%–9%, Americans say most journalists want to see Obama, not John

McCain, win on Nov. 4." Amazingly, this belief crossed party lines: "90% of GOP voters say most journalists are pulling for Obama. More than six-in-ten Democratic and independent voters (62% each) say the same."[30] *Washington Post* ombudsman Debra Howell wrote, "The Post provided a lot of good campaign coverage, but readers have been consistently critical of the lack of probing issues coverage and what they saw as a tilt toward Democrat Barack Obama. My surveys, which ended on Election Day, show that they are right on both counts."[31]

These latest findings unfortunately only solidify the trend seen during presidential elections since 1992. When asked who the media favors, the American public overwhelmingly sees Democrat favoritism:

1992: 52 percent Democrat; 17 percent Republican
1996: 59 percent Democrat; 17 percent Republican
2000: 47 percent Democrat; 23 percent Republican
2004: 50 percent Democrat; 22 percent Republican
2008: 70 percent Democrat; 9 percent Republican[32]

With this type of open bias operating, is it any wonder that 89 percent of Americans believe that reporters "often" or "sometimes" let their political partisanship influence their news reporting?[33] Or that every "year from 2001 through 2009, Gallup found roughly three times more Americans said the media are too liberal vs. those who claimed a pro-conservative bias"?[34] Zogby found similar results, with the "vast majority [83%] of American voters believ[ing] media bias is alive and well," and of those, "nearly two-thirds (64%) . . . said the media leans left" while only "slightly more than a quarter of respondents (28%) said they see a conservative bias."[35]

As was demonstrated in previous chapters, the personal actions of journalists demonstrate their predilections. In July 2007, MSNBC published a list of top journalists who made political campaign contributions. Of the 143 reported, 125 gave to Democrats, 16 to Republicans, and 2 to both parties. Of note is that of the Fox News journalists who made contributions, 2 gave to Republicans and 9 gave to Democrats.[36] William Tate found that this trend continued with the 2008 election:

> An analysis of federal election records shows that the amount of money journalists contributed so far this election cycle favors Democrats by a 15:1 margin over Republicans, with $225,563 going to Democrats, only $16,298 to Republicans. 235 journalists donated to Democrats, just 20 gave to Republicans—a margin greater than 10:1. An even greater disparity, 20:1, exists between the number of journalists who donated to Barack Obama and John McCain.
>
> Searches for other newsroom categories (reporters, correspondents, news editors, anchors, newspaper editors and publishers) produces 311 donors to Democrats to 30 donors to Republicans, a ratio of just over

10:1. In terms of money, $279,266 went to Democrats, $20,709 to Republicans, a 14:1 ratio.[37]

Tate went on to look at specific news organizations such as NBC, CBS, Fox News, MSNBC, CNN, the AP, Reuters, the *Washington Post*, the *New York Times*, and *USA Today*. He found a giving ratio of 100 to 1 in favor of Democrat candidates.[38]

Not only do journalists give financial support to Democrats, they overwhelmingly vote Democrat as we saw in previous chapters. *Washington Post* Ombudsman Deborah Howell wrote, "I'll bet that most Post journalists voted for Obama. I did. There are centrists at The Post as well. But the conservatives I know here feel so outnumbered that they don't even want to be quoted by name in a memo."[39] We don't yet know how much journalists donated specifically to the Obama campaign, although one study did conclude that employees of ABC, CBS, and NBC news were lopsided in their donations: "Obama received 710 contributions from the employees for $461,898. On the other hand, John McCain . . . received only 39 contributions totaling $26,926 from the media employees."[40] We also do not know yet what percentage of journalists voted for Obama. Although such information would supplement our examples of bias, it is unnecessary in making the case; instead, we can look at an entire host of questionable reportorial practices during the 2008 presidential campaign to better understand the nature of bias operating within the establishment press. The below examples represent only a short list of some of the more memorable.[41]

Regarding the education level of the two political newcomers, Obama and Republican vice-presidential candidate Sarah Palin: Obama went to Occidental College and then transferred to Columbia. The media certainly pushed hard the idea that Barack Obama is "intelligent," "smart," and "probably the smartest guy ever to become president."[42] Yet collectively the press never investigated his reputed IQ scores, college test results, his transcripts, and so on.[43] However, Palin's college transfers culminating with a degree from the University of Idaho were somehow linked to a diminutive intelligence, evidence that she is "just a hockey mom." Obama's experience as a community organizer, six years as a state senator, and four years as a U.S. senator made him experienced enough to be president, but Palin's four years as city council member, six years as mayor, and two years as governor, somehow left her unqualified for the role of vice president.

Obama writes two books, both praised and held out as "literary masterpieces" despite large errors concerning "such elemental matters of grammar as the necessary agreement of verbs and nouns in a sentence,"[44] and despite having passages that contradict his campaign rhetoric or passages that suggest a different attitude toward whites than his post-racial politics suggest. In contrast, the AP sends not one, but eleven reporters to Alaska to fact-check Sarah Palin's book.

Both Tom Brokaw and Charlie Rose stated that they (and the media and public) do not really know who Obama is.[45] And that's it. No investigation to find out. However, the media investigates every small detail of the Republican ticket, publishing first and fact-finding second, even to the point of printing unsubstantiated insinuations, not even an accusation, that McCain had an extramarital affair.[46]

Palin's statement about seeing Russia from Alaska (which one actually can)[47] was presented as clear evidence of her naiveté; McCain's statement that he did not know how many houses he owns (through his wife) was derided. However, Obama's saying that he had visited 57 states during the campaign, with one left to go, was generally excused as coming from a tired campaigner, and then dropped. Biden's numerous gaffes during the campaign, including his line "a three-letter word—Jobs: J . . . O . . . B . . . S," were, if even reported, excused and then dropped.[48]

At the end of the 2008 campaign, the Center for Media and Public Affairs (CMPA) conducted content analysis of campaign coverage. Their findings show even more of an Obama frenzy than the examples above: Barack Obama received "the best press CMPA has ever measured for a presidential nominee" with 68 percent of his stories rated as positive. Democrats in general had 66 percent positive stories, whereas John McCain had only 33 percent of his stories rated as positive, and Republicans in general had only 34 percent positive. Thus "Obama's press was 2 to 1 positive; John McCain's was 2 to 1 negative."[49] Additionally, "Obama's policies also got better press than McCain's did" with twice as many positive stories running for Democratic policies than for Republican policies. In terms of stories framed as a horse race, the numbers were even more skewed: "Evaluations of the horse race were nearly three times as positive toward the Democratic ticket (91%) as they were toward the Republican ticket (31%)."[50] The vice-president nominees just followed the trend: "Sarah Palin's coverage was 2 to 1 negative; Joe Biden's was light but balanced."[51]

The Center for Media and Public Affairs was not the only group to notice that the establishment press was overwhelmingly in favor of Obama and the Democrats:

> A joint survey by the Project for Excellence in Journalism and Harvard's Joan Shorenstein Center on the Press, Politics and Public Policy . . . found that in covering the current presidential race, the media are sympathetic to Democrats and hostile to Republicans.
>
> Democrats are not only favored in the tone of the coverage. They get more coverage period. This is particularly evident on morning news shows, which "produced almost twice as many stories (51% to 27%) focused on Democratic candidates than on Republicans."

The most flagrant bias, however, was found in newspapers. In reviewing front page coverage in 11 newspapers, the study found the
tone positive in nearly six times as many stories about Democrats as it
was negative.[52]

Of particular note is that in the category of front-page coverage, the study
found that Obama's coverage was an eye-popping 70 percent positive.

OBAMA IN OFFICE: THE PRESS CONTINUES THE CAMPAIGN

During the election the establishment news media literally campaigned
for Obama. Chris Matthews, who had shed tears of joy over an Obama
speech, and compared Obama to Jesus, also provided perhaps the best-
known establishment press salivation moment when he stated on air, "I
have to tell you, you know, it's part of reporting this case, this election,
the feeling most people get when they hear Barack Obama's speech. My, I
felt this thrill going up my leg. I mean, I don't have that too often."[53]

Shortly after the election, Howard Kurtz, writing for the *Washington
Post*, explained the "giddy sense of boosterism" from the establishment
media:

> Perhaps it was the announcement that NBC News is coming out with a
> DVD titled "Yes We Can: The Barack Obama Story." Or that ABC and
> USA Today are rushing out a book on the election. Or that HBO has
> snapped up a documentary on Obama's campaign.
>
> Perhaps it was the Newsweek commemorative issue—"Obama's
> American Dream"—filled with so many iconic images and such stir-
> ring prose that it could have been campaign literature. Or the Time
> cover depicting Obama as FDR, complete with jaunty cigarette holder.
>
> Are the media capable of merchandizing the moment, packaging a
> president-elect for profit? Yes, they are.[54]

The Pew Research Center's Project for Excellence in Journalism found
that Obama "has enjoyed substantially more positive media coverage
than either Bill Clinton or George Bush during their first months in the
White House. Overall, roughly four out of ten stories, editorials and op-
ed columns about Obama have been clearly positive in tone, compared
with 22% for Bush and 27% for Clinton in the same mix of seven national
media outlets during the same first two months in office. . . . The study
found positive stories about Obama have outweighed negative by two-
to-one (42% vs. 20%) while 38% of stories have been neutral or mixed."[55]

Of particular note is that Pew found that "the topics covered have also
been different for Obama versus his predecessors. Roughly twice as
much of the coverage of Obama (44%) has concerned his personal and
leadership qualities than was the case for Bush (22%) or Clinton (26%).
Less of the coverage, meanwhile, has focused on his policy agenda."[56]

Of course, all of these generalizations are derived from numerous specific instances. In what follows I offer what I believe to be a few of the more interesting examples of how the media continued to campaign for President Obama after he was elected.

When one delves more deeply into the content of the coverage, one finds a disturbing trend. Far from unifying the country, Obama has changed from a rhetoric of hope during his campaign to a rhetoric of division since he took office. In his first inaugural address Obama stressed, "We have chosen hope over fear," yet a mere two weeks later he was pushing a rhetoric of "crisis" and "catastrophe" in order to drum up support for his economic stimulus bill.[57] The press has ignored, and in some cases, encouraged this change in tone.

Anyone who offers criticism of President Obama faces a serious charge, especially in light of what the press calls the first post-racial presidency: they face being called racist. For instance, MSNBC's Keith Olbermann spoke of the state that gave Obama a whopping 26-point win over McCain and was about to hand Republican Scott Brown a win in the special Senate election in 2010. Instead of heralding this for what it was, a repudiation of *Obama's policies*, Olbermann, stated, "Is this vote to any degree just a euphemism the way 'state's rights' was in the 60s?"[58] That is, racism. This was not the only time Olbermann has explained criticism as motivated by racial hatred. After the 2010 State of the Union address, Olbermann did not even use subtlety, but rather simply called Obama's critics "racist white guys."[59] Sarah Palin's use of the phrase "a professor of law standing at the lectern" to describe Obama's delivery of a particular speech, was quickly described by an Obama supporter as racist, and that characterization was passed along by the mainstream media.[60] Paul Krugman called those opposing Obama's health care reform racists.[61] Former president Jimmy Carter, in an interview on NBC news, said that "'an overwhelming portion' of those opposing President Obama's policies are racist."[62] This hypocrisy is not lost on those who keep an eye on politics in this country. Daniel T. Zanoza of Republicans for Fair Media points out that

> during U.S. Supreme Court Clarence Thomas' contentious confirmation process he was called everything from an unqualified jurist to a sexual predator. Yet the left faced no charges regarding racist motivations concerning their verbal assaults on Thomas. Other victims of vicious attacks from liberals include Former Secretary of State Condoleezza Rice and current Republican Party Chairman Michael Steele. In Rice's case, political cartoons often portrayed her as an Aunt Jemima-type character. The depictions were clearly racist and over the top. Steele is called an Uncle Tom by those on the left and the media give his attackers a pass as well.[63]

On these points David Brooks commented that "we live in a nation in which some people see every conflict through the prism of race. So over the past few days, many people, from Jimmy Carter on down, have argued that the hostility to President Obama is driven by racism. Some have argued that tea party slogans like "I Want My Country Back" are code words for white supremacy. Others say incivility on Capitol Hill is magnified by Obama's dark skin." Brooks instead suggests the dislike for Obama's policies comes from tension between traditional working-class values clashing with those of the urban elite.[64] In other words, the journalistic conspiracy of shared values makes it easy for the press to push the urban elite racism frame while ignoring working-class understanding of political issues.

As Obama's approval numbers began to drop, the press, instead of looking at the policies under attack, instead actively encouraged the president to take a more aggressive posture against opponents, and it applauded him when he did so. More aggressive partisanship was explained this way: "President Barack Obama, after a year of fitfully searching for compromise, is taking a more aggressive tack with his Republican adversaries, hoping to energize Democratic voters and possibly muscle in some Republican support in Congress."[65] Of only two Obama supporters quoted, both blamed Republicans for the tone and encouraged the president. This is by no means an isolated example; establishment journalists numerous times encouraged the president to take a more aggressive stance against political rivals and also on policy issues.

- "If Obama Is Serious He Should Get Tough with Israel."[66]
- "At some point, he [Obama] needs to—metaphorically, of course—actually slug somebody."[67]
- CNN stated that it was "time for Obama to go 'gangsta' on GOP."[68]
- NBC News stated, "The President is gonna decide where he is still gonna call Republicans out on where they're gonna make the tough choices and the tough votes. Because that's where he's gonna get his groove back."[69]
- Former CBS news anchor Dan Rather on MCNBC stated that President Obama "has to realize that Mitch McConnell has virtually said so that politically he wants to cut out his heart and throw his liver to the dogs. He has to be a fighter."[70]
- ABC News put it in this perspective: "Is Obama 'Too Nice' to Make Tough Decisions? The White House Pushes Back against Claims the President Is Not Tough Enough."[71]
- In instances where a positive spin was more easily put in place, the press was quick to praise: Boyce Watkins of *Black Voices* wrote, "Barack Obama Got Gangsta with His Critics: Good for Him."[72]

Perhaps all the talk about being more forceful in pushing his agenda had an effect. During his 2010 State of the Union address, Obama pointedly attacked the Supreme Court of the United States for a decision they made that ran counter to a Democrat-favored program. The situational dynamics were unprecedented: the justices were in attendance, and a sitting president openly denounced their court decision, egging on fellow Democrats to jeer them and overturn the decision. Georgetown University law Professor Randy Barnett pointed out that "this was a truly shocking lack of decorum and disrespect towards the Supreme Court for which an apology is in order."[73] Establishment press reports on this amazing incident minimized the president's culpability and instead shifted the attention to Justice Alito, who "appeared" to silently mouth the words "not true" in response to the president's attack.

Another sign that the press was giving early free passes to the Obama administration can by seen when one looks at any number of seemingly random activities. Taken together, however, they add up to a consistent pattern of pro-Obama slant. For instance, the establishment press allowed the White House to preselect those reporters who would be allowed to ask the president a question at press conferences.[74] Polls purporting to show public opinion supporting Obama or his agenda were weighted heavier with Democrats than actually represented in the general population. One example of this is a CNN/Opinion Research Corporation poll on President Obama's 2009 health care speech to Congress: the poll surveyed only 18 percent Republicans but 45 percent Democrats.[75] Other examples included several CBS election polls that were skewed more heavily for Democrats than for Republicans.[76] Even the AP is in this group: A March 2010 AP popularity poll showed Obama at 53 percent, yet reports of this poll failed to note that the sample was skewed to favor Democrats by an 11-point advantage (Democrats at 45 percent and Republicans at 34 percent).[77]

These are not, unfortunately, isolated examples traced to prove favoritism toward Obama, but rather a continuation of a trend of misrepresentation of polling results skewed to favor the Democratic agenda.[78] The president's health care plan, for instance, received amazing support from the mainstream press. According to Rich Noyes, "At the outset, the networks permitted little conservative dissent. The Media Research Center's Business and Media Institute calculated that during the first six months of 2009, 70 percent of soundbites supported Obama's liberal health care ideas and gave short shrift to complaints about the hefty price tag."[79] During the year prior to the health care act vote, members of the press proactively supported the legislation and compared opponents to terrorists (MSNBC's Keith Olbermann), called them immoral (ABC News/*Time*'s Mark Halperin), and accused them of anti-Obama sentiment that would kill half the country (MSNBC's Dylan Ratigan).[80]

Unfortunately for Americans, the list of press Obama partisanship examples goes on and on.

- Whereas President Bush was severely castigated for the federal government response to Katrina, the slow and inept federal response and mismanagement of the Gulf BP oil spill was explained away.[81]
- Related to the above, during the height of the spill's coverage, BP CEO Tony Hayward was soundly criticized for yachting on his first day off in almost eight weeks, but President Obama was given a free pass for what would turn out to be his 32nd time golfing since assuming office.[82]
- Whereas President Bush was given consistent negative press coverage during the Iraq War, President Obama received limited coverage concerning the war, often going months without even a reporter's question, even though he ran on the promise of bringing the troops home, and in his first year of office the death toll was the third highest during the entire ten years of the war.[83]
- When the death toll in Iraq under Bush stood at 1,000, the press ran hundreds of stories; when the death toll under Obama in Afghanistan stood at 1,000, *following his combat surge*, the press provided only minimal and perfunctory coverage.[84]
- The press downplayed allegations that Barack Obama knew of former Illinois governor Blagojevich's plan to obtain a presidential cabinet post in exchange for appointing Valerie Jarrett to the U.S. Senate.[85]

Other notable omissions in news coverage for 2009 included

- Obama's green jobs czar Van Jones, one-time Marxist and recently on *Time*'s Environment Heroes list, made numerous controversial statements about Republicans and also signed a document alleging U.S. government collusion in 9/11. It was only *after* his resignation that many establishment press venues, such as ABC, NBC, and the *Los Angeles Times*, even mentioned the story.[86] None mentioned his self-avowed communism.[87]
- It was only after the story had run on Fox extensively for six days that the other major networks and papers reported on the infamous ACORN sting: "While the video aired heavily on Fox News, the networks evening news shows stayed silent for six days, until after both houses of Congress moved to deny the group's millions of dollars in federal funding. Eventually, ABC and CBS aired only one full story. NBC aired three."[88] As Stanley Kurtz wrote, "Obama has had an intimate and long-term association with the Association of Community Organizations for Reform Now (ACORN), the largest radical group in America."[89] The press minimized this link and minimally reported the story.[90]
- White House communications director Anita Dunn was exposed telling the graduating class of St. Andrew's Episcopal School that

communist mass-murderer Mao Tse-tung was one of her "favorite philosophers." As reported by the Media Research Center, "this speech clip was completely ignored by ABC, CBS, NBC, NPR, *Time*, *Newsweek*, *USA Today*, and the *New York Times*." The networks instead focused on Dunn attacking Fox News. To put this omission into perspective, imagine if Bush's communications director Dan Bartlett had said that Benito Mussolini was one of his favorite philosophers.[91]

Some might suggest that beginning in late summer 2010, there appeared press reports that seemed to be responding to the president's low poll numbers and to be taking him to task for his policy stances and his political associations. Headlines such as "How Barack Obama Became Mr. Unpopular,"[92] "Disappointed Supporters Question Obama,"[93] and "The Sweep: How Did Obama Lose His Mojo?"[94] began to appear. Seemingly going negative against their former hero, these articles and others like them actually represent journalists *justifying* the president's unpopular policies and *supporting the president* by downplaying criticism against him. Just as seen in chapter 10, the press is actually using a negative tone to *support* a favored politician.

When looking closely at the press reports, one actually finds that it is frustration over changes not going fast enough and far enough, and even some soul searching about expecting too much from any one person. For example, CNN's Jon Stewart as quoted on CNN's *Political Ticker*: "'I think people feel a disappointment in that there was a sense that Jesus will walk on water and now you are looking at it like, "Oh look at that, he's just treading water". . . . I thought he'd do a better job' said Stewart. Stewart, who maintains he ultimately does not regret his vote for Obama, said he is 'saddened' the president hasn't done more to change the structure of Washington."[95] Yes, Stewart actually refers to Obama as the Messiah.

CNN ticker producer Alexander Mooney, who wrote the above referenced article, simply did what other journalists were doing at this time: place Stewart in the category of "the legion of frustrated supporters of President Obama" who were saddened that the president had not been able to go farther with his changes. So not his policies, not his ideology, but rather what the president had accomplished had fallen short of expectations. Thus Mooney was showing support for Obama's agenda, while at the same time reporting on negative feelings associated with the president.

Writing of the perception that the president had moved from "Obama as political savior to Obama as creature of Washington," *Time's* Michael Sherer explained, "Obama has been unexpectedly passive at moments as President," and "Obama's personal and financial appeals have been swamped by the depth of the recession and have had little visible effect."

He concluded the story with this explanation and a quote from an Obama supporter: "The disappointment is matched by a real yearning for a leader who can make a difference. 'I think he's trying,' says Griffin, the laid-off payroll administrator who said she didn't know what Obama had done for her. 'Nobody can turn it around overnight.'"[96] The *New York Times* explained the frustration and concern as Obama not going far enough and fast enough, with the president's own words at a town hall meeting: "'My goal here is not to convince you that everything is where it needs to be,' the president said, 'but what I am saying is that we are moving in the right direction.'"[97] Seemingly these articles critique the president, yet closer inspection reveals that they actually explain away the criticism and offer support. As Stanley Crouch writes, "He's President, not a superhero."[98]

As can be seen, the press overwhelmingly supported Barack Obama during and after the election. How this support and the conspiracy of shared values played out in the 2010 midterms and 2012 presidential elections is discussed in the next chapter.

NOTES

1. www.realclearpolitics.com/video/2009/09/10/flashback_democrats_boo_bush_at_2005_state_of_the_union.html.

2. "Republican Wins Senatorial Election in Massachusetts; Alive after Seven Days," CNN Larry King Live, January 19, 2010.

3. "*New York Times* Rejects McCain Essay," CNN, July 21, 2008, www.cnn.com/2008/POLITICS/07/21/mccain.nyt/index.html.

4. Ed Morrissey, "Patriot Act Renewal Passes House," hotair.com, February 26, 2010, http://hotair.com/archives/2010/02/26/patriot-act-renewal-passes-house/.

5. "Health Care Fight in Plain Sight: Obama to Host Televised Summit." CNN, February 25, 2010. The LexisNexis search used the terms "patriot act" and "vote."

6. Eric Lichtblau, "House Votes for a Permanent Patriot Act," *New York Times*, July 22, 2005, A11. Quote by ACLU.

7. Morrissey.

8. P. J. Gladnick, "*New York Magazine* Illustrates Edwards Scandal Story with Hilarious Art," newsbusters.org, January 12, 2010, http://newsbusters.org/blogs/p-j-gladnick/2010/01/12/new-york-magazine-illustrates-edwards-scandal-story-hilarious-art#ixzz0cSMGlgsO.

9. Ben Smith, "The Gore Complaint," *Politico*, June 23, 2010, www.politico.com/blogs/bensmith/0610/The_Gore_complaint.html.

10. "Comedy Central Scoops Network News on Climate-Gate Scandal," Fox News, December 3, 2009, www.foxnews.com/scitech/2009/12/03/comedy-central-scoops-network-news-climate-gate-scandal/.

11. Chad Groening, "Muslim Pandering 'Not Good for the Country,'" *One News Now*, July 8, 2010, www.onenewsnow.com/Culture/Default.aspx?id=1080246.

12. See "Journalists Admitting Liberal Bias, Part One," Media Research Center, www.mrc.org/static/biasbasics/JournalistsAdmittingLiberalBiasPartOne.aspx; and "Journalists Admitting Liberal Bias, Part Two," Media Research Center, www.mrc.org/static/biasbasics/JournalistsAdmittingLiberalBiasPartTwo.aspx. In a special 20th-anniversary edition of its "Notable Quotables," the MRC published a select list of what the organization considers the "most notable" of 20 years worth of quotes dem-

onstrating an overt liberal bias in the establishment media. See "MRC's 20th Anniversary Edition," Media Research Center, October 22, 2007, www.mrc.org/notablequotables/bestof/20thnq/anniversaryedition.asp.

13. "Journalists Admitting Liberal Bias, Part Two"

14. "Journalists Admitting Liberal Bias, Part Two."

15. "Journalists Admitting Liberal Bias, Part Two."

16. "Journalists Admitting Liberal Bias, Part One."

17. Mickey Kaus, "Educating Ezra Klein," *Slate*, July 27, 2007, www.slate.com/id/2171362/- kleinklub.

18. Michael Calderone, "JournoList: Inside the Echo Chamber," March 17, 2009, www.politico.com/news/stories/0309/20086.html.

19. Jonathan Strong, "Documents Show Media Plotting to Kill Stories about Rev. Jeremiah Wright," *Daily Caller*, July 20, 2010, http://dailycaller.com/2010/07/20/documents-show-media-plotting-to-kill-stories-about-rev-jeremiah-wright/.

20. James Taranto, "Call Them Racists: How Journolist Tried to Suppress the News," *Wall Street Journal*, July 20, 2010, http://online.wsj.com/article/SB10001424052748703724104575379200412040286.html.

21. Jonathan Strong, "Liberal Journalists Suggest Government Censor Fox News," *Daily Caller*, July 21, 2010, http://dailycaller.com/2010/07/21/liberal-journalists-suggest-government-shut-down-fox-news/.

22. Tucker Carlson, "Letter from Editor-in-Chief Tucker Carlson on *The Daily Caller*'s Journolist Coverage," *Daily Caller*, July 22, 2010, http://dailycaller.com/2010/07/22/letter-from-editor-in-chief-tucker-carlson-on-the-daily-callers-journolist-coverage/.

23. Jeffrey Goldberg, "Meet the New Journolist, Smaller Than the Old Journolist," *Atlantic*, July 21, 2010, www.theatlantic.com/national/archive/2010/07/meet-the-new-journolist-smaller-than-the-old-journolist/60159/.

24. "Election Watch '08: Early Returns," *Media Monitor*, 21, no. 2 (November/December 2007).

25. Brent Baker, "Fox Poll: Two-Thirds Recognize Journalists Want Obama to Win," newsbusters.org, July 29, 2008, http://newsbusters.org/blogs/brent-baker/2008/07/25/fox-poll-two-thirds-recognize-journalists-want-obama-win.

26. Eli Saslow, "As Duties Weigh Obama Down, His Faith in Fitness Only Increases," *Washington Post*, December 25, 2008, www.washingtonpost.com/wp-dyn/content/article/2008/12/24/AR2008122402590.html.

27. "Belief Growing That Reporters are Trying to Help Obama Win," Rasmussen Reports, July 21, 2008, www.rasmussenreports.com/public_content/politics/elections/election_2008/2008_presidential_election/belief_growing_that_reporters_are_trying_to_help_obama_win.

28. Ramesh Ponnuru, "Crushing on Obama," *Time*, July 31, 2008, www.time.com/time/magazine/article/0,9171,1828309,00.html.

29. "69% Say Reporters Try to Help the Candidate They Want to Win," Rasmussen Reports, September 10, 2008, www.rasmussenreports.com/public_content/politics/elections/election_2008/2008_presidential_election/69_say_reporters_try_to_help_the_candidate_they_want_to_win.

30. "Most Voters Say News Media Wants Obama to Win," Pew Research Center for the People & the Press, October 22, 2008, http://people-press.org/report/463/media-wants-obama.

31. Debra Howell, "Remedying the Bias Perception," *Washington Post*, November 16, 2008, www.washingtonpost.com/wp-dyn/content/article/2008/11/14/AR2008111403057.html.

32. "Most Voters Say News Media Wants Obama to Win."

33. "Media Seen as Fair, But Tilting to Gore," Pew Research Center for the People & the Press, October 15, 2000.

34. "Documenting the Media's Lopsided Liberal Slant," Media Research Center, February 18, 2010, www.mrc.org/realitycheck/realitycheck/2010/20100217054609.aspx. See Gallup summation at www.pollingreport.com/media.htm.

35. "Zogby Poll: Voters Believe Media Bias Is Very Real," *Student News Daily*, March 21, 2007, www.studentnewsdaily.com/biased-item/zogby_poll_voters_believe_media_bias_is_very_real/.

36. Bill Dedman, "The List: Journalists Who Wrote Political Checks," MSNBC, July 15, 2007, www.msnbc.msn.com/id/19113455/.

37. William Tate, "Big Media Puts Its Money Where Its Mouth Is," *American Thinker*, September 7, 2008, www.americanthinker.com/2008/07/big_media_puts_its_money_where.html.

38. Tate.

39. Debra Howell, "Remedying the Bias Perception," *Washington Post*, November 16, 2008, www.washingtonpost.com/wp-dyn/content/article/2008/11/14/AR2008111403057.html.

40. Steven Ertelt, "Pro-Abortion Obama, Democrats Got 88 Percent of Media Donations in 2008," Lifenews.com, September 15, 2010, www.lifenews.com/2010/09/15/nat-6663/; See also http://washingtonexaminer.com/blogs/beltway-confidential/obama-democrats-got-88-percent-2008-contributions-tv-network-execs-writers.

41. My thanks to communication professor Terrence Warburton of Edinboro University for suggesting this list.

42. Clarice Feldman, "Just How Smart Is Obama?" *American Thinker*, July 27, 2009, www.americanthinker.com/2009/07/just_how_smart_is_obama.html.

43. This fell to the nontraditional media, such as the blog Atlas Shrugs. See "Obama's Mythical Intelligence," Atlas Shrugs, May 31, 2008, http://atlasshrugs2000.typepad.com/atlas_shrugs/2008/05/obama-mythical.html.

44. Feldman. See too, Dean Barnett, "How Smart Is Obama?" *Weekly Standard*, May 29, 2008, www.weeklystandard.com/Content/Public/Articles/000/000/015/150jyxzw.asp.

45. Charlie Rose, "A Conversation with Tom Brokaw," October 30, 2008, www.charlierose.com/view/interview/9330.

46. Jim Rutenberg, Marilyn W. Thompson, David D. Kirkpatrick, and Stephen Labaton, "For McCain, Self-Confidence on Ethics Poses Its Own Risk," *New York Times*, February 21, 2008, A1. See too Thomas M. Defrank and Leo Standora, "John McCain Affair Rumor Swirls," *New York Daily News*, February 21, 2008, www.nydailynews.com/news/politics/2008/02/21/2008-02-21_john_mccain_affair_rumor_swirls.html.

47. Nina Shen Rastogi, "Can You Really See Russia from Alaska?" *Slate*, September 15, 2008, www.slate.com/id/2200155/.

48. "Biden's List of Political Blunders," foxnews.com, July 28, 2009, www.foxnews.com/politics/2009/07/28/bidens-list-political-blunders/.

49. "Election Watch: Campaign 2008 Final," *Media Monitor* 23, no. 1 (Winter 2009).

50. "Election Watch: Campaign 2008 Final."

51. "Election Watch: Campaign 2008 Final."

52. Editorial, "Even Harvard Finds the Media Biased," *Investors Business Daily*, November 1, 2007, www.ibdeditorials.com/IBDArticles.aspx?id=278808786575124.

53. "Chris Matthews: 'I Felt This Thrill Going Up My Leg' As Obama Spoke," Huffington Post (March 28, 2008), www.huffingtonpost.com/2008/02/13/chris-matthews-i-felt-thi_n_86449.html.

54. Howard Kurtz, "A Giddy Sense of Boosterism," *Washington Post*, November 17, 2008, C1.

55. "Obama's First 100 Days," The Pew Research Center's Project for Excellence in Journalism, April 28, 2009, www.journalism.org/analysis_report/obamas_first_100_days.

56. "Obama's First 100 Days."

57. Charles Krauthammer, "The Fierce Urgency of Pork," *Washington Post*, February 6, 2009, www.washingtonpost.com/wp-dyn/content/article/2009/02/05/AR2009020502766_pf.html.

58. Ed Morrissey, "Olby: Massachusetts Suddenly Turned Racist!" hotair.com, January 20, 2010, http://hotair.com/archives/2010/01/20/olby-massachusetts-suddenly-turned-racist/.

59. "MSNBC Calls Obama Critics Racist," *Daily Caller*, January 29, 2010, http://dailycaller.com/2010/01/29/msnbc-calls-obama-critics-racist/.

60. Jane Yager, "Calling Obama 'Professor' Is Palin Code for 'Uppity' Prof," Newser, February 11, 2010.

61. Amy Ridenour, "Black Group Condemns Krugman Race Comments," newsbusters.org, August 7, 2009, http://newsbusters.org/blogs/amy-ridenour/2009/08/07/black-group-condemns-krugman-race-comments.

62. "Are Obama's Critics Racist? Jimmy Carter Thinks So," *Los Angeles Times*, September 16, 2009, http://latimesblogs.latimes.com/washington/2009/09/are-obamas-critics-racist-jimmy-carter-thinks-so.html.

63. Daniel T. Zanoza, "Obama Used Race to Get Elected: Critics Racist? I Don't Think So," rffm.org, September 21, 2009, http://rffm.typepad.com/republicans_for_fair_medi/2009/09/obama-used-race-to-get-elected-critics-racist-i-dont-think-so.html.

64. David Brooks, "No, It's Not about Race," *New York Times*, September 17, 2009, www.nytimes.com/2009/09/18/opinion/18brooks.html?_r=1&ref=davidbrooks.

65. Jonathan Weisman, "Obama Steps Up Confrontation," *Wall Street Journal*, March 30, 2010, http://www.newser.com/story/80621/calling-obama-professor-is-palin-code-for-uppity-prof.html.

66. Aron David Miller, "If Obama Is Serious He Should Get Tough with Israel," *Veterans Today*, February 4, 2009, www.veteranstoday.com/2009/02/04/if-obama-is-serious-he-should-get-tough-with-israel/comment-page-1/.

67. Eugene Robinson, "Obama Can't Create Change with Words Alone," *Washington Post*, January 26, 2010, www.washingtonpost.com/wp-dyn/content/article/2010/01/25/AR2010012502832.html.

68. Roland S. Martin, "Time for Obama to Go 'gangsta' on GOP," CNN, February 9, 2010, http://articles.cnn.com/2010-02-09/opinion/martin.obama.republicans_1_recess-appointments-tired-president-obama?_s=PM:OPINION.

69. David Gregory, quoted in www.mrc.org/notablequotables/nq/2010/201011 14022552.aspx.

70. Dan Rather, quoted in www.mrc.org/notablequotables/nq/2010/2010111 4022552.aspx.

71. David Kerley, "Is Obama 'Too Nice' to Make Tough Decisions? The White House Pushes Back against Claims the President Is Not Tough Enough," ABC News, October 18, 2009, http://abcnews.go.com/Politics/president-obama-tough-make-important-decisions-health-care/story?id=8858172.

72. Boyce Watkins, "Barack Obama Got Gangsta with His Critics: Good for Him," *Black Voices*, September 10, 2009, http://insurance.blackvoices.com/2009/09/10/barack-obama-speech-before-congress/.

73. Randy Barnett, "State of the Union: How Did He Do? SCOTUS v POTUS," Politico, January 27, 2010, www.politico.com/arena/perm/Randy_Barnett_79413362-DD20-46A2-A092-D0579CC7D13F.html.

74. Editorial, "Obama's Press List: Membership Shall Have Its Privileges, *The Wall Street Journal*, February 11, 2009.

75. Matthew Balan, "CNN's Polling Before and After Obama Speech Skewed Democratic," newsbusters.org, September 10, 2009, www.newsbusters.org/blogs/matthew-balan/2009/09/10/cnns-polling-after-obama-speech-skewed-democratic.

76. CBS News Poll, "The Primaries Over . . . The General Election Looms," June 4, 2008, www.cbsnews.com/htdocs/pdf/may08b-GENERALELECTION.pdf . See too Ed Morrissey, "CBS Poll: Still Skewed, Still Unreliable," hotair.com, June 5, 2008, http://hotair.com/archives/2008/06/05/cbs-poll-still-skewed-still-unreliable/.

77. Ed Morrissey, "AP poll has Obama at 53%, but . . ." hotair.com, March 10, 2010.

78. See, for example, Noel Sheppard, *"Washington Post*/ABC News Poll Tremendously Skews Democrat Respondents," newsbusters.org, October 10, 2006, http://newsbusters.org/node/8221.

79. Rich Noyes, "ObamaCare Aided by Big Doses of Media Spin," Media Research Center, March 15, 2010, www.mrc.org/realitycheck/realitycheck/2010/20100314053918.aspx.

80. "ObamaCare Aided," www.mrc.org/realitycheck/uploads/20100315.pdf.

81. Rich Noyes and Kyle Drennen, "Media Double Standard on Gulf Coast Disasters," *Wall Street Journal,* May 29, 2010, http://online.wsj.com/article/SB10001424052748704596504575272980707029378.html.

82. "Canceled Poland Trip Frees Obama for Golf," *Washington Times* (April 19, 2010, www.washingtontimes.com/news/2010/apr/19/canceled-poland-trip-frees-time-for-obama-to-play-/. See also Scott Whitlock, "Network Morning Shows Rage against BP CEO's Yachting Trip, Ignore Obama's Golf Outing," Media Research Center, June 21, 2010, www.mrc.org/biasalert/2010/20100621024727.aspx.

83. "New Issues Push Iraq Off Radar for Obama, Press," *Washington Times*, March 4, 2010, www.washingtontimes.com/news/2010/mar/04/for-obama-and-press-iraq-falls-off-radar/.

84. Robert H. Reid, "Afghanistan War Death Toll: 1,000 U.S. Military Dead," Huffington Post, May 28, 2010, www.huffingtonpost.com/2010/05/28/afghanistan-death-toll-100_n_593087.html.

85. Natasha Korecki and Sarah Ostman, "Harris: Obama Knew of Blagojevich Plot," *Chicago Sun-Times*, June 24, 2010, www.suntimes.com/news/metro/blagojevich/2427402,CST-NWS-BLAGO24.article.

86. "Omitting for Obama: How the Old Media Deliberately Censored New Media Scoops in 2009," Media Research Center, 2010, www.mediaresearch.org/SpecialReports/2010/OmittingforObama/fullStudy.aspx.

87. "Obama's Green Jobs Czar Van Jones Quits Under Fire," *Los Angeles Times*, September 5, 2009, http://latimesblogs.latimes.com/washington/2009/09/obama-adviser-van-jones.html.

88. "Omitting for Obama."

89. Stanley Kurtz, "Inside Obama's ACORN," *National Review*, May 29, 2008, www.nationalreview.com/articles/224610/inside-obamas-acorn/stanley-kurtz.

90. Dan Gainor, "ACORN Story Grows But Mainstream Media Refuse to Cover It," Fox News, September 14, 2009, www.foxnews.com/opinion/2009/09/14/dan-gainor-acorn-media-ignore/.

91. "Omitting for Obama."

92. Michael Sherer, "How Barack Obama Became Mr. Unpopular," *Time*, September 2, 2010, www.time.com/time/nation/article/0,8599,2015629,00.html.

93. Sheryl Gay Stolberg, "Disappointed Supporters Question Obama," *New York Times*, September 20, 2010, www.nytimes.com/2010/09/21/us/politics/21obama.html?_r=3&hp.

94. Ed Henry, "The Sweep: How Did Obama Lose His Mojo?" CNN, September 22, 2010, www.cnn.com/2010/POLITICS/09/22/obama.mojo/index.html?hpt=C1.

95. Alexander Mooney, "Stewart 'saddened' by Obama," CNN, September 23, 2010, http://politicalticker.blogs.cnn.com/2010/09/23/stewart-saddened-by-obama/?hpt=T2.

96. Sherer.

97. Sheryl Gay Stolberg, "Disappointed Supporters Question Obama," *New York Times*, September 20, 2010, www.nytimes.com/2010/09/21/us/politics/21obama.html?_r=3&hp.

98. Stanley Crouch, "He's President, Not a Superhero," *New York Daily News*, September 27, 2010, www.nydailynews.com/opinions/2010/09/27/2010-09-27_hes_president_not_a_superhero.html.

TWELVE

The 2010 and 2012 Elections

CNN's Mark Preston summed up the news media framing of the upcoming midterm elections: "With only 15 days remaining before Election Day 2010 and early voting already happening in several states, the midterm marathon is now a sprint as Democrats work frantically to establish a beachhead to protect their congressional majorities while Republicans hope voter anger over the economy propels them into power." Viewed in terms of framing, the Republicans are just sitting around, allowing anger about the economy (not cap and trade, not health care legislation) to spring them into power, whereas Democrats are "working" actively to stay in power.[1] This type of framing concerning Democrats and Republicans, liberals and conservatives, and President Obama and his critics, continued into election 2010 and beyond. This final chapter covers areas of mainstream press reporting that most clearly demonstrate the continuing and in some cases growing partisanship, with attention to the following subjects and events: Tea Party election coverage; post-election coverage; Ft. Hood, the Tucson shooting, and hate speech; and the Wisconsin Public Unions budget battle of February and March 2011. This is followed by a brief overview of the 2012 election coverage and then a final summary of our history.

TEA PARTY ELECTION COVERAGE

Undoubtedly the Tea Party is among the biggest political stories in the past ten years. A grassroots movement, it swelled in political influence in the span of a short year to completely reshape the political landscape. Such a momentous event should have occasioned press coverage, and it did. Unfortunately, once again, the coverage of the Tea Party Movement is another example of our partisan mainstream press. In a lengthy and thorough study, Rich Noyes of the Media Research Center found that broadcast coverage concerning the Tea Party Movement broke into two broad phases. First, from the Tea Party's inception in early 2009, the press simply acted to dismiss the movement.

- "ABC, CBS and NBC aired a mere 61 stories or segments over a twelve-month period [February 2009 through March 2010], while another 141 items included brief references to the movement. [The] networks virtually refused to recognize the Tea Party in 2009 (just 19 stories), with the level of coverage increasing only after Scott Brown's election in Massachusetts."[2]
- "Most of the networks' 2009 coverage was limited to individual Tea Party rallies: six reports on the April 15, 2009 "tax day" protests, along with five other brief mentions; just one report on the July 4 rallies; and six full reports on the September 12 rally on Capitol Hill, plus eight brief mentions."[3]
- "Such coverage is piddling compared to that lavished on protests serving liberal objectives. The Nation of Islam's "Million Man March" in 1995, for example, was featured in 21 evening news stories on just the night of that march—more than the Tea Party received in all of 2009. The anti-gun "Million Mom March" in 2000 was preceded by 41 broadcast network reports . . . heralding its message, including a dozen positive pre-march interviews with organizers and participants, a favor the networks never granted the Tea Party."[4]

However, after Scott Brown announced his Senate bid in September 2009, the networks began a shift in coverage, and one that disparaged the Tea Party.

- "After the September 12, 2009 rallies, the networks suggested the Tea Party was an extreme or racist movement. On CBS . . . Bob Schieffer decried the 'angry' and 'nasty' Capitol Hill rally, while ABC's Dan Harris scorned protesters who "waved signs likening President Obama to Hitler and the devil . . . Some prominent Obama supporters are now saying that it paints a picture of an opposition driven, in part, by a refusal to accept a black President.'"[5]
- "44 percent of network stories on the Tea Party . . . suggested the movement reflected a fringe or dangerous quality. ABC's John Berman was distressed by 'a tone of anger and confrontation' he claimed to find at [a] Tea Party convention . . . NBC's Brian Williams trumpeted Jimmy Carter's charge that the Tea Party was motivated by race: 'Signs and images at last weekend's big Tea Party march in Washington and at other recent events have featured racial and other violent themes, and President Carter today said he is extremely worried by it.'"[6]

Noyes points out that although "network reporters have strained to protect left-wing causes (such as the antiwar movement) [from] the outrageous acts of individual protesters, they were quick to smear the entire Tea Party based on isolated reports of poor behavior."[7] As an example he points out that on the "night of the final vote on ObamaCare in March . . . ABC's Diane Sawyer cast Tea Partiers as out-of-control marauders, 'roaming Washington, some of them increasingly emotional, yelling slurs and epithets.' CBS's Bob Schieffer also cast a wide net, accusing 'demonstrators' of hurling 'racial epithets' and 'sexual slurs,' and even conjured images of civil-rights era brutality: 'One lawmaker said it was like a page out of a time machine.'"[8]

Ultimately, Noyes suggests a conclusion not at all at odds with what we have seen thus far in our history of the partisan press:

> While the broadcast networks seldom devolved into the juvenile name-calling and open hostility evident at the liberal cable news networks, their coverage of the Tea Party's first year reflected a similar mindset of elitist condescension and dismissiveness. Given how the networks have provided fawning coverage and helpful publicity to far-less consequential liberal protest movements, their negative treatment of the Tea Party is a glaring example of a media double standard. Rather than objectively document the rise and impact of this important grassroots movement, the "news" networks instead chose to first ignore, and then deplore, the citizen army mobilizing against the unpopular policies of a liberal President and Congress.[9]

Noyes is not alone in finding this coverage slanted. The Pew Research Center's Project for Excellence in Journalism found that in the later stages of the 2010 election, Tea Party candidate Christine O'Donnell received more press coverage than any other political figure except president Obama. Almost all of her coverage, and of other Tea Party candidates, was negative.

> A significant portion of the coverage of [Tea Party] candidates like O'Donnell and Paladino had a gawking, quasi-voyeuristic component, with the media drawn to controversy and color. That didn't necessarily add much depth to the public understanding of the tea party phenomenon. And a qualitative evaluation of election coverage finds that in much of the media, there was more of a fierce partisan argument about what the tea party was than a journalistic exploration of that subject.[10]

The Media Research Center found that Tea Party candidates Joe Miller and Christine O'Donnell were labeled by the press as "ultra-conservatives," yet *no* Democrats were labeled as ultra-liberal. In Pennsylvania, Pat Toomey was labeled "conservative," yet Joe Sestak was not labeled "liberal." Ultimately the study found that "the evening news at ABC, CBS, and NBC, between Sept. 1 and Oct. 25, repeatedly smeared conservative and Tea Party candidates as 'extreme,' 'fringe,' or 'out of the mainstream.' Yet in those broadcasts, not one left-wing candidate from the party of Obama/Reid/Pelosi was labeled in the same way. Not one."[11]

POST-ELECTION COVERAGE

In 1994 the establishment press credited the Republican sweep to irrational, angry voters. Peter Jennings, during one of his radio commentaries, represented well the overall theme then portrayed by the press:

> Some thoughts on those angry voters. Ask parents of any two-year-old and they can tell you about those temper tantrums: the stomping feet, the rolling eyes, the screaming. It's clear that the anger controls the child and not the other way around. It's the job of the parent to teach the child to control the anger and channel it in a positive way. Imagine a nation full of uncontrolled two-year-old rage. The voters had a temper tantrum last week. . . . Parenting and governing don't have to be dirty words: the nation can't be run by an angry two-year-old.[12]

As the *Washington Times* reported, "Newsweek Senior Writer Joe Klein wholly agreed with Mr. Jennings, and took the argument to a new level: 'The public seemed more intolerant than involved, uninterested in what the candidates have had to say, blindly voting. . . . The president might argue, with some justification, that it's the media's fault: We're allergic to good news.'"[13] Cal Thomas asked a good question concerning the news media's response to the 1994 election, one which could also be asked of the 2010 election: "Why do liberals such as Jennings refuse to believe it was their failed ideas—not voter anger—that did them in?"[14]

The Republican sweep of the 2010 election was momentous. In the House the Democrats began with 256 seats over the Republicans' 179; after the election, the Republicans had 239 seats and the Democrats 187. Republicans picked up five seats in the Senate. Republicans won ten new governor seats. Twenty state legislative chambers switched from Democrat to Republican. No matter how you looked at it, the Democrats took a pounding beyond any election since 1938. There was no getting around this fact. Newspaper headlines did reflect the trouncing. In a review of 100 mainstream news headlines concerning the election, the Pew Research Center's Project for Excellence in Journalism found that

> the headlines overwhelmingly hammered home a simple, unadulterated point—a Republican romp. In a format that is designed to distill things into their barest essentials, and to some extent is harder for the partisans to spin, the message was clear.
> Colorful headlines, so to speak, abounded. "Red Wave," declared the Indianapolis Star in a headline that was close kin to "Voters See Red" in the Quad City Times of Iowa and "Crimson Tide" in the Patriot-News of Harrisburg Pennsylvania. Several papers, including the Arizona Republic and Miami Herald, went with the phrase "Power Shift,"

a sentiment closely related to the Memphis Commercial Appeal headline, "Right Turn" and "Making a Right Turn" in the Omaha World-
Herald.[15]

Another study by the center found that "newspapers, particularly on
their front pages, offered synthesis and unified verdicts (GOP triumph).
Television leaned more toward speculation and differing narratives
(coming from talking heads)."[16]

Yet headlines are followed by a story or commentary, and television
news moves directly into a story. How would the press *explain* or *describe*
the historic election? *Time* explained it away this way—as predictable:
"The Republicans did win a grand victory in the midterms this year. But
that was historically inevitable given the stalled economy, unemployment of 9.8 percent and the President's questionable decision to spend an
inordinate amount of time and political capital enacting health care reform."[17] Others *explained it away* in a number of similar ways.

- E. J. Dionne simply parroted a report from the liberal Center for
  American Progress: "The most 'parsimonious' explanation of the
  results rests on 'a few fundamental factors.' These include 'the poor
  state of the economy; the abnormally conservative composition of
  the midterm electorate; and the large number of vulnerable seats in
  conservative-leaning areas. These trends cost the Democrats their
  House majority but were not strong enough to sweep them out in
  the Senate.'"[18]
- *New York Times* columnist Frank Rich wrote, "You can't win an
  election without a coherent message. Obama, despite his administration's genuine achievements, didn't have one. The good news—
  for him, if not necessarily a straitened country—is that the G.O.P.
  doesn't have one either."[19]
- Maureen Dowd, also of the *New York Times*, wrote, "Even though it
  was predicted, it was still a shock to see voters humiliate a brilliant
  and spellbinding young president, who'd had such a Kennedy-like
  beginning, while electing a lot of conservative nuts. . . . Republicans
  outcommunicated a silver-tongued president who was supposed to
  be Ronald Reagan's heir in the communications department."[20]
- David Broder, of the *Washington Times*, explained it all away with
  this opening: "The message to President Obama from Tuesday's
  election could not have been plainer: Don't abandon your goals.
  Change your way of operating. There will be a temptation to interpret the Democrats' loss of their House majority and of at least six
  Senate seats as a rejection of Obama's first-term agenda, the one on
  which he was elected in 2008. American voters are not that flighty
  or unsettled. What happened was that Obama ran into several crises that he and others had not anticipated, and the cumulative
  weight of those problems ended up frustrating him."[21]

- Bill Press, in an article titled "The American People Don't Get It," wrote, "Clearly, the Obama White House didn't do a good enough job selling their product," and "American voters are also fickle and dumb."[22]
- Stanley Crouch, writing in the *Daily News* (New York) blamed the losses on the public being "misled" and "manipulated": "Last week, big lies and big money spoke so loudly and with such influence that our political system was dramatically changed for the time being."[23]

There were of course other reasons given; for instance, columnist Michael Silverstein blamed the loss on the Democrats doing nothing about the greed of Wall Street.[24] That the Democrats did not do enough for the economy was also often suggested. The idea behind all of these comments, and one reflected in hard-news stories, was the Democrats simply did not do enough to get their message out and that voters were too stupid to understand all the good that had happened to them.

FT. HOOD, THE TUCSON SHOOTING, AND HATE SPEECH

On November 5, 2009, at Fort Hood, Army Major Nidal Malik Hasan, an American-born Muslim of Palestinian descent, shot 42 persons, killing 13, all while shouting, "Allahu Akbar!" President Obama responded to this attack, and one aspect of his remarks was widely parroted by the establishment press: "We don't know all the answers yet. And I would caution against jumping to conclusions until we have all the facts."[25] ABC, CBS, NBC, MSNBC, CNN, and Fox News all reported on this, and major papers followed through as well, with hard-news stories also echoing the calls of various liberal opinion writers to avoid jumping to conclusions. These calls for civility and patience came to an abrupt halt a little over a year later after another terrible shooting.

On January 8, 2011, Jared Lee Loughner was arrested near Tucson, Arizona, for shooting 19 people, 6 of whom died from the wounds. Democrat U.S. Representative Gabrielle Giffords was among those shot. News reports immediately identified Giffords as the target of the attack, and the news media immediately speculated that Loughner was a right-wing nut egged on by venomous right-wing political talk. It took a blog post from the *Phoenix News Times* to publicize that former classmates of Loughner called him a "left-wing Pothead."[26] These facts that ran contrary to establishment news media framing about Loughner went largely unreported; as we will see, they did not fit in with how the media wanted to interpret the event.

The Pew Research Center found that only 12 percent of all published stories about the shooting between January 10 and January 16 were straight news stories. A total of 20 percent profiled the shooter, and 27 percent, the single largest category of coverage, were devoted to exploring the role of political rhetoric in the shooting. Looking specifically at political blogs, Twitter and social media, Pew also examined the tone of the conversation about political rhetoric. The study found that "considerably more of the discussion about political rhetoric featured the left blaming the right rather than the other way around. According to the analysis from January 8–16, a full 59% of the commentary in blogs, Twitter and social media involved liberals blaming conservatives for their tone. That was more than twice the amount of the discussion (28%) that involved conservatives criticizing the left or defending themselves." [27]

It was not just blogs and so forth linking conservative politics to the shooting. The *Wall Street Journal* reported that broadcast news stories about the shooting specifically linked conservative speech to Loughner's actions. Specifically, the *Wall Street Journal* looked at

> all 55 broadcast network stories or segments discussing the discourse from just after the shooting (January 8) through the evening of the national memorial service on January 12, reviewing the ABC, CBS and NBC morning, evening and Sunday talk shows.
>
> While many of those stories offered general comments about "harsh rhetoric," about three-fifths (31) contained specific references to instances of supposedly intemperate speech. Of those specific examples elevated by the media, more than eight out of ten (82%) were about the conduct of conservatives or Republicans, compared with just 11% which talked about liberals or Democrats. [28]

The Media Research Center published a study in which they highlighted the mainstream press's attack on conservatives, Sarah Palin, and conservative talk radio following the shootings. Here are a few examples they provide:

- Luke Russert of NBC/MSNBC: "Remember, this is the deepest fear that was in the back of everybody's mind going through the health care debate. A lot of members were threatened. Congresswoman Giffords' windows at her district office were broken. . . . There is [*sic*] a lot of fringe groups that were very upset with the health care law, felt that the federal government was overstepping its bounds, and that was in—within everyone's mind. It looks sadly like it's come to fruition today."
- Paul Krugman of the *New York Times*: "We don't have proof yet that this was political, but the odds are that it was. She's been the target of violence before. . . . Her father says that 'the whole Tea Party' was her enemy. And yes, she was on Sarah Palin's infamous 'crosshairs' list. Just yesterday, Ezra Klein remarked that opposition to health reform was getting scary. Actually, it's been scary for quite a while, in a way that already reminded many of us of the climate that preceded the Oklahoma City bombing. . . .Violent acts are what

happen when you create a climate of hate. And it's long past time for the GOP's leaders to take a stand against the hate-mongers."

- Nancy Cordes of CBS News: "Giffords was one of 20 Democrats whose districts were lit up in crosshairs on a Sarah Palin campaign Web site last spring. Giffords and many others complained that someone unstable might act on that imagery."
- Jessica Yellin of CNN: "On Twitter and Facebook, there is a lot of talk, in particular, about Sarah Palin. As you might recall, back in March of last year, when the health care vote was coming to the floor of the House and this was all heating up, Palin tweeted out a message on Twitter saying 'common sense conservatives, don't retreat—instead reload.' And she referred folks to her Facebook page. On that Facebook page was a list of Democratic members she was putting in crosshairs, and Gabrielle Giffords was one of those in the crosshairs."
- Bob Schieffer on *Face the Nation*: "You know, Congresswoman Giffords had received threats before. That's something that we might have overlooked here. Her office was trashed during the health care debate. When she showed up on Sarah Palin's political action committee Web site as one of those who had been targeted for defeat, it shows her in the crosshairs there. She warned herself that this kind of thing could have serious repercussions."
- Chris Matthews of MSNBC: "What's been the role of talk radio in fueling the heated language? . . . People like Mark Levin, Michael Savage, for example who every time you listen to them are furious, furious at the Left with anger that just builds and builds in their voice, and by the time they go to commercial, they're just in some rage, every night, with ugly talk. Ugly sounding talk. And it never changes. It never modulates. . . . They do see the other end of the field as evil, as awful. Not just disagreeable but evil. And they use that language, when they talk about the other side, isn't that part of the problem? And my question is doesn't that give the moral license to people who have crazy minds to start with?"[29]

Fox News was the only major media outlet to point out the numerous instances of hatred coming from the left, both in print and broadcast:

Montel Williams, host, *Montel Across America*: So Michele [Bachmann], slit your wrists. Go ahead. Why not? And if you don't want to, I mean, or—or you know, do—do us all a better thing, move that knife up about two feet. Start right at the collarbone.

Mike Malloy, host, *The Mike Malloy Show*: I'm waiting for the day when I pick it up—and pick up a newspaper or click on the Internet and found out he's choked to death on his own throat fat or a great blob of saliva or something. You know, whatever. Go away Rush [Limbaugh]. You make me sick.

Ed Schultz, host, *The Ed Schultz Show*: He is an enemy of the country, in my opinion, Dick Cheney is. He is an enemy of the country. Lord, take him to the Promised Land, will you? See, I don't even wish the guy goes to hell; I just want him to get the hell out of here.[30]

Yet these and other examples, such as death threats against conservative Supreme Court Justice Antonin Scalia and Justice Clarence Thomas (and his wife),[31] or Democratic Representative Michael Capuano's public statements to Wisconsin union supporters that "every once in awhile you need to get out on the streets and get a little bloody when necessary,"[32] go largely ignored by the mainstream press. There were calls for patience, for not jumping to conclusions, after the Ft. Hood shootings, but impatience, jumping to conclusions, and outright speculation after the Tucson shootings. Yet this is the same news media.

WISCONSIN PUBLIC UNIONS BUDGET BATTLE OF FEBRUARY AND MARCH 2011

The protests over Wisconsin governor Scott Walker's plan to scale back public employee benefits and collective bargaining ability is an ongoing story. However, enough is out that one can discern the general thrust of press coverage. Given our journalistic history so far, the routine is clear: the press will side with union/liberal protestors and Democrats, and it will be alternative and conservative media that publishes information that the mainstream press leaves out. The images of the union protests provides us with a fine example of how this process works.

For example, on February 16, 2011, the *New York Times* published a slide-show of eight images. Those pictures that included protesters showed them smiling, waiving innocuous signs, and mostly gathered in large crowds—all peaceful. Governor Walker was shown sitting alone, hunched over his desk. The one negative sign shown was at the end of the show. It was an image predominantly of the sign, comparing Walker to former Egyptian president Hosni Mubarak, with the background showing the protestor as being alone.[33] CNN had similar images, showing bright, cheery protestors waving signs reading, "Solidarity!" and "Care about educators like they care for your child."[34]

CBS News offered more of the same, smiling protestors, en mass, with supporting signs: "Don't Balance the Budget on the Backs of Our Teachers."[35] And so it continued for the establishment press.

There were, however, many other signs available to show, and other types of protestors in the crowd. Hotair.com, a news media watchdog site, published numerous images of protestors with signs and attitudes very different than those shown by the mainstream press. Here are some examples of the signs the press ignored: a sign comparing Governor Walker to a terrorist; a sign calling him "Al-Qaeda Scott"; a sign reading,

"Stop the Dictator" and another sign asking, "Which side are you on?" with images of Ike and Hitler; a sign showing Walker made to look like Hitler, with the caption "Heil Walker"; a Walker/Hitler Photoshopped image, with the caption "Exterminating Union Workers"; a sign reading, "Walker Blows Koch"; a sign saying, "Scott Walker: The Reason We Need Planned Parenthood"; a sign suggesting, "Socialism and Liberation"; and a sign saying, "FUCK [a synonym here for Fascist Union Community Killer] Scott Walker."[36]

On this issue of visual imagery, one study of the news media coverage found that

> none of these signs in the hands of liberal protesters have drawn the slightest complaint from network journalists. MRC [Media Research Center] analysts examined all 53 ABC, CBS and NBC morning and evening news stories, segments and anchor briefs on the Wisconsin protests from Thursday, February 17 (when they first drew major national coverage) through Monday, February 21. While eight of the 53 stories (15%) visually displayed one or more of the signs described above, none elicited a single remark from the network correspondents.[37]

Part of this can be explained by the conspiracy of shared values. Reporters simply cannot keep themselves from being sympathetic to the protestors. However, this can also lead to double standards, and CBS's Bob Schieffer provides a classic example of this in practice. During a Tea Party (conservative) protest in March 2010 he declared, "A year-long debate that's been rancorous and mean from the start turned even nastier yesterday. Demonstrators protesting the bill poured into the halls of Congress shouting 'kill the bill' and 'made in the USSR.'" Yet a year later, when Wisconsin protestors (liberal) were chanting, "Kill the bill," and showing images of Scott Walker in crosshairs and comparing him to Hitler and Egyptian president Hosni Mubarak, Schieffer had no such criticism: "Thousands of demonstrators took to the streets again in Madison, Wisconsin as they marched to protest major cuts in state spending. The question is, will the protests spread to other states where similar proposals to cut spending are also being contemplated?"[38]

Some news commentators actually supported the Mubarak comparison, pushing the theme that a democratically elected governor following through on a campaign promise was equivalent to a Middle East totalitarian. For example,

- NBC's Brain Williams: "From the Mideast to the American Midwest tonight, people are rising up. Citizens' uprisings are changing the world."
- ABC's Christiane Amanpour: "This week: people power making history. A revolt in the Midwest and a revolution sweeping across the Middle East. . . . Populist frustration is boiling over this week—

as we've said, not just in the Middle East, but in the middle of this country as well."

- The *New York Times*: "The images from Wisconsin—with its protests, shutdown of some public services and missing Democratic senators, who fled the state to block a vote—evoked the Middle East more than the Midwest. The parallels raise the inevitable question: Is Wisconsin the Tunisia of collective bargaining rights?"[39]

Other important items necessary for full contextualization of the protests were ignored.

- It took a local radio news station to break the story of Republican lawmakers receiving death threats. The mainstream press largely ignored this.[40]
- The press overlooked the fact that the protestors actually overran the police in order to occupy the state capital building. The *New York Times* made it look as if the police were able to maintain control.[41]
- Wisconsin has the highest per-pupil spending in the Midwest. Despite this, 33 percent of Wisconsin's 4th graders and 22 percent of 8th graders read below basic level. The press failed to bring up this type of contextual information.[42]
- Polls (particularly a *New York Times*/CBS poll) were shown demonstrating public support solidly backing the protestors.[43] *USA Today* ran this headline: "Poll: Americans Favor Union Bargaining Rights."[44] An exposure of the loaded questions used to produce those results, as well as other polls that showed support for Walker, were ignored.[45]

OTHER ITEMS OF NOTE

In so many instances we see the news media collectively leaning toward an interpretation of a particular event, and in such cases the lean is to the left. In quick succession, let us go through several examples that have occurred since 2010.

- When the Patriot Act was extended in 2009, liberal activists and the press, both of whom protested extensions under Bush, remained calm and silent. The 2010 extension, already mentioned, saw a similar response. Those papers that covered the extension used only the most perfunctory descriptions.[46]
- In February 2011, President Obama decided that the Defense of Marriage Act was unconstitutional, so he directed the Justice Department to discontinue its defense. A sitting president, constitutionally bound to uphold the laws of the land, is now actively ignoring that law. How did the press respond? The *Washington Post*

editorially supported the president when it wrote, "Attorney General Eric H. Holder Jr. declared . . . that the Justice Department would no longer be an advocate for the indefensible—a law that relegates the nation's gay and lesbian citizens to second-class status. It was a decision as bold as it was risky." Calling the Defense of Marriage Act both "unwise" and "distasteful," the paper says nothing about the president circumventing both Congress and the Supreme Court in determining the constitutionality of the law.[47] In short, the paper ignored a very different storyline, one exploring the president's dereliction of duty. NPR approvingly mentioned the refusal in the context of admonishing the administration for continuing to deny health care benefits to the partners of homosexuals.[48] One blogger at bigthink.com wrote, "Good news," and then unknowingly summed up the position of the mainstream press: "The Justice Department is not flouting the rule of law, as some critics have suggested. It is merely declining to dig itself a deeper hole in defense of an unconstitutional and discriminatory law."[49] Other establishment press outlets such as the *New York Times,* ABC News, CBS News, and CNN reported in similar fashion.[50] *USA Today* mentioned the decision as well, only to state that the "anti-gay marriage law [was] dealt a setback" and that it was a "major legal reversal," even though no court had ruled on the matter. Note that the paper could easily have written *the defense of marriage law was dealt a setback,* but instead the reporters inserted their own opinion in the flow of a hard-news story. Nothing was mentioned about dereliction of duty.[51] Of note is that it was conservative publications such as *National Review*[52] and conservative news sites and bloggers such as wnd.com, newsbusters.com, and hotair.com that pointed out the concern about upholding the Constitution.[53]

- There remained a general positive note of reporting for President Obama moving into 2011. Politico.com reported that "Time's Mark Halperin has hailed Obama as 'magnetic,' 'distinguished' and 'inspiring'—in one story. ABC's Christiane Amanpour saw 'Reaganesque' optimism and 'Kennedyesque' encouragement—all in one speech. Howard Fineman, the former Newsweek columnist who now writes for the Huffington Post, said conductor Obama was now leading a 'love train' through D.C."[54]
- One month before Obama won the 2008 presidential election, gas prices were averaging an eye-popping $3.61 per gallon. The recession quickly caused these prices to plummet to an average of around $1.75 per gallon by the time Obama took office. From that point on, a slow and steady rise occurred, with prices averaging $2.70 in January 2010, a 65 percent increase. By April 2011, the average price per gallon was $3.79.[55] A similar explosion of gas prices occurred during the final years of the Bush presidency. The

coverage of these two events is instructive: "As gas prices rose in 2008, network reporters mentioned President Bush in 15 times as many stories, than they brought up President Obama in a similar period in 2011. Comparing a 20 day span of rising gas prices in 2008 to 24 days of rising prices in February 2011, the Business and Media Institute found the networks did more than 2 1/2 times as many stories during the Bush years versus Obama." [56] Of note is that the press kept the attention on this difficult area and often blamed Bush administration policies for the rise in prices. [57] However, in 2010 and 2011, the press blamed, well, not Obama. [58] MSNBC actually stated that Obama was not to blame, but that Bush should be blamed. [59] As gas prices rose, the fact that Obama's secretary of the interior Ken Salazar, as a Democrat and a U.S. senator, was on record for supporting $10.00 a gallon gas received little attention. [60] Columnist Larry Elder highlighted the dearth of press attacks on Obama about rising gas prices when he wrote, "$5 Gas Predicted under Obama—What, No Pitchforks?" [61]

* The Guantanamo Bay terrorist detention center was a constant source of press pressure against the Bush administration. Presidential candidate Obama declared that he would close the center. In February 2009, President Obama said he had ordered the closing of the center. By February 2011, Obama reversed that order. The action was received with virtual silence from the press. [62]

Of course, the mainstream news media, both print and broadcast, continue to lose viewers and circulation. Average "daily circulation fell 5 percent in the six months that ended Sept. 30, [2010,] compared with the same period a year earlier." [63] Tom Blumer of newsbusters.com noted that "the Big Three Networks' evening news shows came in with audiences almost 20 percent lower during the week before and the week of the 2010 midterm elections compared to the same two weeks in 2006." [64] Meanwhile Fox News continues to pull in new viewers as CNN and the major broadcast news shows stay in decline. [65] As for the talking-head cable war, again, we see that shows that avoid pushing a liberal/progressive point of view simply outpace those that do. Total viewers as of mid-March 2011:

Fox News, O'Reilly—3,271,000
Fox News, Hannity—2,432,000
Fox News, Beck—2,334,000
Fox News, Baier—2,301,000
Fox News, Shep—2,039,000
Fox News, Greta—1,691,000
CNN, Cooper—1,170,000
CNN, Blitzer—1,028,000
CNN, Piers—958,000

MSNBC, Maddow—933,000
CNN, King—927,000
MSNBC, O'Donnell—817,000
MSNBC, Shults—810,000
MSNBC, *Hardball with Chris Matthews*—784,000

How do the mainstream press explain their continued decline? Dan Radmacher, an editor of the *Roanoke Times*, sums it up well:

> Attacks on the credibility of the press—the mainstream media now juvenilely derided as the "lamestream media" by the likes of Sarah Palin—have been going on for decades, even after then-Republican Party chairman Rich Bond admitted back in 1992 that GOP complaints about a biased media were part of a strategy designed to "work the ref." "If you watch any great coach, what they try to do is 'work the refs,'" Bond said in a 1992 Washington Post article. "Maybe the ref will cut you a little slack next time." Twenty years later, much of the public assumes without thought that the mainstream media have a liberal bias—Fox News aside, naturally. Sadly enough, some networks like MSNBC, trying to outfox Fox, live up to those expectations. Most networks, however, do not. Partisans have done a good job of tearing down the credibility of the media, with the occasional unfortunate assist by some journalists. [66]

That's it . . . conservatives such as Sarah Palin have attacked the integrity of the press, and an overwhelming majority of "thoughtless" Americans simply agreed, thus leading to the breath-arresting decline in press circulation, viewership, and credibility. Perhaps if Radmacher and others would turn the pointed finger 180 degrees they might then be closer to the truth. The press has nobody to blame for its predicament other than itself. Until that reality hits, journalists and editors such as Radmacher will continue on the same path, much like an alcoholic who says, "I don't have a drinking problem."

How is it that the press simply refuses to see its own biases in operation? Perhaps the conspiracy of shared values offers one explanation. Journalists do not actually need to meet in back rooms (or online, as Journolist and Cabalist demonstrate) in order to plot outcomes of bias. By simply being part of such a homogenous group, they enact a type of groupthink, perpetuating liberal beliefs and attitudes that find their way into news. Social psychologist Jonathan Haidt calls such a grouping of like-minded others a "tribal-moral community," and he suggests that members are "united by 'sacred values' that hinder research and damage their credibility—and blind them to the hostile climate they've created for non-liberals." [67]

A FEW WORDS ON ELECTION 2012 COVERAGE

The trends we discussed above unfortunately continued into election 2012. As of this writing the election is just barely over, so detailed studies have yet to emerge. There are, however, some analyses that suggest the mainstream press essentially repeated its 2008 performance in helping the Democratic candidate and hurting the Republican. Taken together, these observations and analyses indicate strongly that the press aided Barack Obama in six ways.

First, the overall tone of election coverage favored President Obama. As pointed out on Investors.com, "The media lauded Obama no matter how horrendous his record, and they savaged Obama's Republican contenders as ridiculous pretenders."[68] For example, Romney was particularly singled out for any gaffes and also for partisan fact-checking.[69] Along these lines, Pew conducted a major study of the 2012 campaign coverage and found that throughout most of the general campaign, President Obama received "slightly better coverage in the mainstream press than Governor Romney did"; however, during the final week of coverage before the election, "Obama's coverage improved dramatically while Romney's coverage stayed about the same but shrank in volume."[70]

Putting this into perspective, "fully 29% of the Obama stories were positive compared to 19% which were negative. . . . Romney's coverage in that final week slipped slightly [with] 16% of his stories . . . positive compared to 33% that were negative."[71] In terms of coverage, from "October 1 to 28, Romney and Obama were both covered at roughly the same amount. Obama was a significant presence (meaning he was in 25% of the story or more) in 75% of the campaign-related coverage compared to 71% for Romney. But in the final week, a bigger discrepancy was seen as Obama was a significant presence in 80% of the coverage, and Romney was a significant presence in 62%."[72] In practical terms, the above figures mean that Obama simply received more and better press than did Romney.

Second, the Bengazhi, Libya, consulate attack was not aggressively investigated.[73] Initially the press seemed to suggest that this would be an opportunity for President Obama to show his leadership abilities. However, as evidence surfaced to show instead a botched response, misrepresentation of motives, and miscommunication between different departments within the executive branch, the networks and major papers engaged in delaying reporting and in ignoring pertinent facts. Throughout October, breaking "developments exposing the administration's failure to provide adequate security, or contradictions in their public statements, were either given stingy coverage or buried completely."[74] To put this in perspective, contrast the Benghazi coverage with the coverage given to the Iran-Contra scandal detailed in chapter 5.

Third, debates and press interviews were biased in President Obama's favor.[75] For example, whereas the first of the three presidential debates (and one vice-presidential debate) had Jim Lehrer allowing the candidates to generally speak without interruption and to direct the flow of the debate, those moderators that followed took a different tack. Lehrer was roundly castigated by the mainstream press for failing to dominate the debate, and this "criticism may have encouraged the activist approach taken by ABC's Martha Raddatz in the October 11 vice-presidential debate and by CNN's Candy Crowley in the October 16 town-hall debate, as both of those journalists repeatedly interrupted the Republican candidate and larded the discussion with a predominantly liberal agenda."[76]

Fourth, Attorney General Eric Holder and the Obama administration's role in the gun-running program Fast and Furious was minimized.[77] Instead of aggressively pursuing leads and reporting facts, the major networks simply downplayed the significance of the program. As one example of this, consider that "none of the three broadcast networks—ABC, CBS, or NBC—devoted a single second of coverage to [Mexican] Univision's politically devastating investigative report about the Obama Administration's . . . Fast and Furious." As one news critic stated, "The deaths of 14 more Mexican youths and the discovery of 57 more guns because of this deadly Fast and Furious scandal is news any way you look at it, and the networks completely ignored it."[78]

Fifth, the press offered only minimal reporting on the poor state of the economy and a looming major debt and entitlement crisis.[79] *Investors Business Daily* noted, "The press studiously ignored the ongoing economic catastrophe under Obama, while parading any 'green shoot' they could find that suggested growth was around the corner."[80] For instance, gas prices nearly doubled during President Obama's first term in office, but the press virtually ignored this; when gas prices spiked under President Bush the press raised it as an ongoing issue.[81] The overall state of the economy in 2004 "was far better than it is today—higher growth, lower unemployment, smaller deficits and cheaper gasoline—yet network coverage that year was twice as hostile to Bush than it was towards Obama" in 2012. Of note is that one summary study found that when "Republican Presidents have faced reelection, network reporters made sure to spotlight economic 'victims'—the homeless man, the woman without health insurance, the unemployed worker, the senior citizen who had to choose between medicine and food. But this year, with an economy as bad as any since the Great Depression, those sympathetic anecdotes have vanished from the airwaves—a huge favor to Obama and the Democrats."[82]

Sixth, military deaths in Iraq and Afghanistan were minimally reported.[83] As pointed out by gestetnerupdates.com, "You sure know that we lost 4,000 troops in Iraq, but do you know that since the OBL [Osama bin Laden] Mission the U.S. lost more than 600 troops in Afghanistan? Do you know that we lost more troops in Afghanistan under Obama who 'is ending the war' than during eight years of Bush? Do you know that in the six months leading up to the 2008 elections we lost less troops in Iraq (where we were 'stuck') than the number we lost in recent months in Afghanistan (where things are 'ending')?"[84]

Additionally, when the death toll in Iraq under President Bush hit 2,000 in October 2005, all major networks ran multiple stories on their morning and evening news shows. Yet when the death toll in Afghanistan hit 2,000, well into President Obama's first term, only CBS even mentioned it.

THE DEATH OF A MYTH: THE PARTISAN PRESS TODAY

It saddens me to write that Joseph Pulitzer's motto, "Accuracy! Accuracy! Accuracy!" has ceased to be the guiding principle of most modern mainstream news sources.[85] As Jack Fuller, president of the Tribune Publishing Company, observed, "Journalism's unacknowledged shame is how often it fails to live up to Pulitzer's standard even with respect to the most commonplace details."[86] I believe that the press should be fair in its treatment of all sides of an issue, a position well within the mainstream of journalism ethics researchers. For example, Louis A. Day suggested that reporters must "clearly distinguish between fact and opinion."[87] Reporters have an obligation to the general public, and this involves placing "news stories into 'perspective' by providing 'relevant background.'" To do this well necessitates being objective, fair, and truthful. According to Mitchell Stephens, objectivity involves both impartiality and the reflection of the "world as it is, without bias or distortion of any sort."[88] This is, of course, an idealistic goal, but one for which journalists ought to strive.

In chapter 3 we covered the Commission on Freedom of the Press and its report titled *A Free and Responsible Press*. Summing up the idea of the report, Theodore Peterson wrote, "Freedom carries concomitant obligations; and the press, which enjoys a privileged position under our government, is obliged to be responsible to society for carrying out certain essential functions of mass communication in contemporary society"[89] Four of the essential functions bear mentioning here.

1. The press must provide "a truthful, comprehensive, and intelligent account of the day's events in a context which gives them meaning."[90]
2. The press must serve as a "forum for the exchange of comment and criticism."[91]
3. The press must project "a representative picture of the constituent groups in society."[92]
4. The press must provide "full access to the day's intelligence."[93]

Of course, if you were to ask random journalists if they follow these guidelines, most would answer yes. It is certainly true that the majority of the mainstream press do profess to follow, and most likely to incorporate into their reporting, the ideas expressed by the Commission on Freedom of the Press. One can see this expressed in many news organizations' codes of ethical conduct. As I noted earlier, the statement of principles of the American Society of Newspaper Editors has numerous articles, of which articles 1 and 4 are worth repeating.

> ARTICLE I: The primary purpose of gathering and distributing news and opinion is to serve the general welfare by informing the people and enabling them to make judgments on the issues of the time.
> ARTICLE IV: Every effort must be made to assure that the news content is accurate, free from bias and in context, and that all sides are presented fairly. Editorials, analytical articles and commentary should be held to the same standards of accuracy with respect to facts as news reports. Significant errors of fact, as well as errors of omission, should be corrected promptly and prominently. [94]

The Society of Professional Journalists also professes such values: "Members of the Society of Professional Journalists believe that public enlightenment is the forerunner of justice and the foundation of democracy. The duty of the journalist is to further those ends by seeking truth and providing a fair and comprehensive account of events and issues. [Journalists must be aware of] their own cultural values and avoid imposing those values on others." [95]

Although these codes express clear ideals, I feel that the mainstream press today has abandoned their ideals, leaving them as relics of a bygone day. Not only has the media increasingly abandoned objectivity, it has, in the minds of a large portion of the news-consuming audience, become associated with negativity about American society and pessimism in general. This tendency colors its phrases and frames every report. Not surprisingly, successful news outlets, including Fox News and Rush Limbaugh, have approached the world from a more positive perspective—not that all news is good, but that good news, funny stories, and uplifting reports constitute as much of what makes news as disasters, debauchery, and decline. Michael Crichton predicted as much in 1996 when he argued that the new technology would increase a reader's choices, and in turn the reader's selectivity. Increasingly, "people understand that they pay for information. On-line databases charge by the minute. As the link between payment and information becomes more explicit, consumers will naturally want better information. They'll demand it, and they'll be willing to pay for it. There is going to be—I would argue there already is—a market for extremely high-quality information." [96]

Yet consistently journalists shrink from objective or neutral models with the excuse that such reporting would be too dry. Fuller, for example, contends, "People don't usually find perfectly neutral accounts interesting, because bare recitation of fact can be tedious and leaves too much unresolved."[97] Yet individuals do not leave such things "unresolved" for long if there is genuine competition in the coverage of news. If balance is no longer a workable model within individual news organizations, it certainly can be attained through competition between news outlets. In our case today, we see this with the growing influence of the alternative media.

Fuller's claim that "good news . . . will get out" is true only if there is a diversity of views to ensure that it gets out.[98] Although it is true to an extent that "bad news sells," the *interpretation* of that news has been one-sided for nearly 50 years. It is repeatedly confirmed in poll after poll that large percentages of Americans think the news media is too liberal, while only a small percentage (fewer than 15 percent) think it is too conservative.[99] Over more than a century, journalism worked to establish a reputation for objectivity and fairness—and was somewhat successful for much of that time. But at the same time, journalism wrapped itself in attitudes and methodologies that tended to make it hostile to all authority, suspicious of all good news, and, after the 1950s, increasingly angry at the status quo. Eventually, the objective side of news gave way to a reformist/antagonistic journalism that was overwhelmingly slanted to the left. Americans did not mind the slant. What they disliked was slant in the guise of objectivity, and a domination of the views from one side. Americans, after all, embrace competition, and it is no different with news.

Our second great transformation of American journalism, then, did not reinstate objective journalism, but rather began the revival of *competitive* journalism, where people could discern for themselves that which was true. It began with the *Washington Times*, Rush Limbaugh, the Internet, and Fox News; it included news watchdog sites such as hotair.com and mrc.org; and significantly, because the transformation posed hurdles to the continued monopoly of the mainstream press, the established liberal media did not take it lying down. In 2003, having failed to find the "liberal Rush Limbaugh," liberal/progressives turned to government to revive the "fairness doctrine," a 1950s-era concept abolished in 1987 that treated television and radio broadcasters as public services and required them to provide fairness in their broadcasting practices. Although this may sound reasonable, in practice it meant that journalists got to judge what would be considered fair, and, more important, that station owners and managers were under tremendous pressure from vocal special-interest groups to avoid offending any of them, regardless of the profitability of the programming. The result was not competition of ideas, but a stale sameness that reflected, in general, the liberal views of the large news organizations.

So far fallen is the mainstream press today that in 2009 its Democratic allies in Congress were calling again for a fairness doctrine, called by some the Hush Rush [Limbaugh] Bill. More disturbing, when considered against a backdrop of press freedom, were congressional calls for bailing out or subsidizing the mainstream news establishment to the tune of some 30 billion dollars per year over a three-year period.[100] As of this writing, these initiatives have fallen flat.

As noted, liberals failed in their quest to find any liberal Rush Limbaughs, provoking a series of initiatives, including one by a wealthy Chicago couple to fund a network of liberal radio stations. Many liberals admitted that the left failed at talk radio: "Liberal hosts, such as Mario Cuomo, have flopped. Liberals mostly think that's because their arguments are too nuanced for the black-and-white talk culture."[101]

Aside from the fleeting flirtation with objectivity in the weeks following 9/11, the American mainstream press in the early 21st century has increasingly embraced its 1830s partisan roots—and this is not all bad. For the first time in 50 years, there is a growing and genuine competition of *ideas* between journalists, albeit between mainstream journalists and alternative journalists. Although the liberal template still exists, it no longer goes unchallenged. Patently untrue statements, convenient omissions of fact, and obvious slanting, or framing, today meet with rapid counterarguments and sound-bite examples from alternate news sources that reach audiences of tens-of-millions, although still smaller than that reached by the mainstream press. It is a growing influence and competition, not true competition as yet.

Perhaps more important, after 1960 journalism became much like the rust-belt smokestack industries. It drifted into a lethargy of uncompetitive practices, eschewing innovation and abandoning the methodology that had made it dominant. In the process, liberal journalists lost their ability to debate issues with conservatives who had struggled for decades in minority status, honing their skills at debating and analysis. When the few conservative journalists finally applied those finely sharpened tools to news coverage, the result was so "old" that it was considered novel. Suddenly a network used "Fair & Balanced" as its trademark, and meant it, offering ideas on both sides that would never be broached on NBC, CBS, or ABC. Suddenly AM radio completely revitalized itself around conservative political analysis, thriving commercially by offering alternate interpretations to that published by the mainstream press. It was certainly not just Limbaugh, as he was joined by Neal Boortz, G. Gordon Liddy, Sean Hannity, Larry Elder, Armstrong Williams (the latter two being black conservatives), Michael Savage, and many others. One could hear conservative ideas from coast to coast. Although some hosts were argumentative and bombastic, many had sharp intellects and keen debating skills. At the same time, the Internet offered news that had been blacked out by the mainstream press and provided instant analysis and counterarguments to liberal/progressive journalism. Sites such as hotair.com, michellemalkin.com, and newsbusters.com immediately linked articles, charts, data, facts, and any information needed to confront poor or left-leaning reporting. While some may disagree with the ideas and interpretations, one must acknowledge that the very fact of disagreement confirms that there is now competition among ideas, something lacking in the mainstream press prior to the second great transformation.

The conservative journalists emerged from decades of abuse, attacks, and hostility as they stood firm in their beliefs. Only the strongest, best-prepared, and shrewdest survived, but when they did, they resembled Toyota and Honda assaulting a fat, uncompetitive, and listless Detroit in the 1970s, with much the same result. As the new conservative wave swept through, liberal politicians, long used to a pliant press to peddle their ideas, found their positions genuinely examined and usually criticized. Consider that when George Gilder and Charles Murray wrote their scathing critiques of the welfare state in the early 1980s, it took almost a decade for those arguments to filter into the Republican Party until they were passed as part of welfare reform in the mid-1990s.[102] During that interim, conservative journalists digested their arguments on social policy and economics, debating with colleagues raised on Keynes, Galbraith, and Harrington, and developing coherent and formidable intellectual positions in the process.

I feel that much of the wailing and gnashing of teeth in the mainstream press today stems from its own sloth. Its once-unassailable position has been wrested away by hungry new journalists (not all of whom are conservative) who are not afraid to ask, "What's your source?" or "Where did you get that data?" These alternative journalists—again, still a tiny minority to the old mainstream press—have had ripple effects. Mainstream press journalists as well as liberal politicians now must contend with oppositional points of view in print, on the airwaves, and online. Whereas I would like to have seen a response to this challenge in the form of a return to more objective reporting, the response to this new challenge to the authority of the mainstream press has been anger and, as shown in the previous pages, hostility.

Consequently, three cheers for the new competitive and increasingly partisan press. It beats the old "nonpartisan" but liberal/progressive press; for if we cannot have objectivity, let us have a competition of ideas. James Madison would have been quite comfortable with that situation, seeing factions as a sure guarantor of American democracy. A one-sided press is in no one's interest unless it is a press focused on both neutrality and the truth, values which journalism began to suppress in the late 1950s. In its place, we will be fortunate to have an adversarial press—not as adversaries with the president or Congress, but with each other, because the First Amendment is far too powerful a protection to shield only part of the political spectrum. Conservatives *are* confident because they think their ideas are right and only need to be heard. As our history of the news media shows, for too long media liberals—whether they thought they were right or not—squelched opposing views, much the way Martin van Buren attempted to silence all critics of slavery over a century and a half ago. Journalism today has many outlets, and the competition for a share of the news-hungry audience is fierce. This competition promotes the clash of ideas, something ultimately beneficial to our republic.

NOTES

1. Mark Preston, "Preston on Politics: Election Marathon Is Now a Sprint," CNN, October 18, 2010, http://www.cnn.com/2010/POLITICS/10/18/preston.on.politics/index.html?hpt=T1.

2. Rich Noyes, "TV's Tea Party Travesty: How ABC, CBS, and NBC Dismissed and Disparaged the Tea Party Movement," Media Research Center, 2010.

3. Noyes.

4. Noyes.

5. Noyes.

6. Noyes.

7. Noyes.

8. Noyes.

9. Noyes.

10. "The Year in News: The 2010 Midterms: A Tea Party Tale," Pew Research Center's Project for Excellence in Journalism, January 11, 2011, www.journalism.org/analysis_report/2010_midterms_tea_party_tale.

11. "Liberal Media Biggest Loser in Midterm Elections," *Watchdog* 17, no. 12, December 2010, 1, http://mrc.org/flash/2010/Watchdog-dec2010.pdf.

12. Peter Jennings, ABC Radio News Commentary, November 14, 1994.

13. L. Brent Bozell III, "Pooh-Poohing Election Results," *Washington Times*, November 26, 1994, D1.

14. Cal Thomas, "The Big News Media's Temper Tantrum," *Orlando Sentinel*, November 27, 1994, http://articles.orlandosentinel.com/1994-11-27/news/9411280209_1_voting-republican-temper-tantrum-anger.

15. "Parsing Election Day Media—How the Midterms Message Varied by Platform: Newspaper Headlines—A Republican Romp," journalism.org, November 5, 2010, http://www.journalism.org/2010/11/05/newspaper-headlines-republican-romp/.

16. "Parsing Election Day Media," www.journalism.org/analysis_report/parsing_election_day_media_how_midterms_message_varied_platform.

17. Joe Klein, "Media Noise: The Year of Living Predictably," *Time*, December 29, 2010, www.time.com/time/politics/article/0,8599,2039920,00.html.

18. E. J. Dionne, "What Really Happened in the 2010 Election," *Washington Post*, November 8, 2010, http://voices.washingtonpost.com/postpartisan/2010/11/what_really_happened_in_the_20.html?hpid=opinionsbox1.

19. Frank Rich, "Barack Obama: Phone Home," *New York Times*, November 7, 2010, WK8.

20. Maureen Dowd, "Republican Party Time," *New York Times*, November 3, 2010, A27.

21. David Broder, "Obama Deferred to Congress. Wrong Model," *St. Paul Pioneer Press*, November 3, 2010.

22. Bill Press, "The American People Don't Get It," *Orlando Sentinel*, November 4, 2010, http://articles.orlandosentinel.com/2010-11-04/news/os-ed-bill-press-110410-2010

1104_1_big-change-election-outcome-voters.

23. Stanley Crouch, "For Love of Money and Fear of Truth," *Daily News*, November 8, 2010, A24.

24. Michael Silverstein, "Why the Republicans Triumphed, in Two Words," *Moderate Voice*, November 3, 2010.

25. "Obama: Don't Jump to Conclusions," CBS News, November 6, 2009, www.cbsnews.com/stories/2009/11/06/national/main5551286.shtml.

26. James King, "Jared Loughner, Alleged Shooter in Gabrielle Giffords Attack, Described by Classmate as 'Left-Wing Pothead,'" *Phoenix News Times*, January 8, 2011, http://blogs.phoenixnewtimes.com/valleyfever/2011/01/jared_loughner_alleged_shooter.php.

27. Mark Jurkowitz, "Media Analysis: How the Press Covered the Tragedy in Tucson," Pew Research Center Publications, January 19, 2011, http://pewresearch.org/pubs/1863/media-analysis-giffords-shooting-political-rhetoric.

28. Rich Noyes, "MRC Study: By 8-to-1 Margin, Media Target Conservative Speech after Tucson Shooting," *Wall Street Journal*, January 20, 2011, http://online.wsj.com/article/SB10001424052748704590704576092450900271660.html.

29. "Special Edition: Conservatives in the Crosshairs," Media Research Center, January 24, 2011, www.mrc.org/notablequotables/nq/2011/20110123025557.aspx.

30. "The O'Reilly Factor, "President Obama and the Smear Merchants," foxnews.com, January 13, 2011, www.foxnews.com/on-air/oreilly/transcript/president-obama-and-smear-merchants.

31. GOP Lawmakers Call for Probe into Possible 'Threats' against Thomas, Scalia," foxnews.com, March 3, 2011, www.foxnews.com/politics/2011/03/03/gop-lawmakers-probe-alleged-threats-thomas-scalia/?test=latestnews.

32. Capuano Backs Off from Controversial Comment," whdh.com, February 24, 2011.

33. "Marching on the Capital: Slideshow," *New York Times*, February 16, 2011, www.nytimes.com/slideshow/2011/02/16/us/WISCONSIN.html.

34. Michael Martinez, "Education Funding Crisis Expected to Grow Beyond Wisconsin," CNN, February 18, 2011, http://edition.cnn.com/2011/US/02/17/education.funding.crisis/index.html?eref=edition_us.

35. Stephanie Condon, "Wisconsin Battle Over State Workers Turns Into National Debate," CBS News, February 18, 2011, www.cbsnews.com/8301-503544_162-20033383-503544.html.

36. Ed Morrissey, "Pictorial: Protest Saturday in Wisconsin," hotair.com, February 20, 2011, http://hotair.com/archives/2011/02/20/pictorial-protest-saturday-in-wisconsin/. See too http://hotair.com/archives/2011/02/17/the-historical-illiteracy-of-wisconsin-teachers/.

37. Rich Noyes and Scott Whitlock, "Wisconsin Unions vs. the Tea Party: A Classic Double Standard," Media Research Center, February 22, 2011, www.mediaresearch.org/realitycheck/realitycheck/2011/20110222015522.aspx.

38. Noyes and Whitlock.

39. "Bemoaning an 'Assault' on Unions, Have the Governors Gone Too Far?" *Notable Quotables*, 24, no. 5 (March 7, 2011), www.mrc.org/notablequotables/nq/2011/20110306094724.aspx.

40. Jon Byman, "Capital Chaos: Lawmakers Get Death Threats," 620 WTMJ News Radio, March 10, 2011, www.620wtmj.com/news/local/117732923.html.

41. http://graphics8.nytimes.com/images/2011/03/10/us/10wisconsin_337_span/10wisconsin_337-popup.jpg.

42. "Revenues and Expenditures for Public Elementary and Secondary Education: School Year 2007–08," National Center for Education Statistics, http://nces.ed.gov/pubs2010/expenditures/tables/table_03.asp; "The Nation's Report Card: Reading 2009," National Center for Education Statistics, http://nces.ed.gov/nationsreportcard/pdf/main2009/2010458.pdf; Terrence P. Jeffrey, "Two-Thirds of Wisconsin Public-

School 8th Graders Can't Read Proficiently," cnsnews.com, February 22, 2011, http://cnsnews.com/news/article/two-thirds-wisconsin-public-school-8th-g.

43. Ed O'Keef, "Poll: Majority Backs Government Workers in Unions," *Washington Post*, March 1, 2001, http://voices.washingtonpost.com/federal-eye/2011/03/poll_majority_back_public-sect.html?sid=ST2011022503108.

44. Dennis Cauchon, "Poll: Americans Favor Union Bargaining Rights," *USA Today*, February 23, 2011, www.usatoday.com/news/nation/2011-02-22-poll-public-unions-wisconsin_N.htm.

45. www.reuters.com/article/2011/02/24/us-wisconsin-protests-poll-idUSTRE71N73M20110224; see also Joseph Klein, "Phony *New York Times*/CBS News Poll on Public Union Collective Bargaining Rights," News Real Blog, March 1, 2011, www.newsrealblog.com/2011/03/01/phony-new-york-timescbs-news-poll-on-public-union-collective-bargaining-rights/.

46. Associated Press, "Obama Signs Temporary Extension of Patriot Act," *Washington Post*, January 25, 2011, www.washingtonpost.com/wp-dyn/content/article/2011/02/25/AR2011022505562.html.

47. Editorial, "A Stand for Equality," *Washington Post*, February 24, 2011, A18.

48. "U.S. Sends Conflicting Signals on Gay Marriage Law," *Morning Edition*, NPR, March 1, 2011.

49. Lindsay Beyerstein, "Obama Admin. Declines to Defend Entire 'Defense of Marriage Act,'" bigthink.com, February 28, 2011, http://bigthink.com/ideas/31383.

50. http://abcnews.go.com/Politics/obama-administration-drops-legal-defense-marriage-act/story?id=12981242; http://articles.cnn.com/2011-02-23/politics/obama.gay.marriage_1_jay-carney-obama-administration-justice-department?_s=PM:POLITICS; www.nytimes.com/2011/02/24/us/24marriage.html; www.cbsnews.com/8301-503544_162-20035398-503544.html.

51. Kevin Johnson and Joan Biskupic, "Anti-Gay Marriage Law Dealt a Setback; Obama Team Says It Won't Defend DOMA," *USA Today*, February 24, 2011, 4A.

52. Robert H. Bork, "Offense to the Constitution Act—Such Is the Obama Administration's Refusal to Defend DOMA," *National Review*, March 21, 2011.

53. Bob Unruh, "Obama, Holder Contend Homosexuality 'Immutable,'" wnd.com, February 23, 2011, www.wnd.com/2011/02/267385/.

54. John F. Harris and Jim Vandehei, "How President Obama Plays the Media Like a Fiddle," Politico, February 7, 2011, www.politico.com/news/stories/0211/48940.html.

55. Frank Ahrens and Mike Musgrove, "Rising Gas Prices Could Be a Drag on Economic Recovery," *Washington Post*, January 8, 2010, www.washingtonpost.com/wp-dyn/content/article/2010/01/07/AR2010010704255.html; see also "Gasoline and Diesel Fuel Update," U.S. Energy Information Administration, January 22, 2013, www.eia.doe.gov/oil_gas/petroleum/data_publications/wrgp/mogas_home_page.html.

56. Julia A. Seymour, "Networks Link Bush to 'Skyrocketing' Gas Prices 15 Times More Than Obama," Business and Media Institute, March 1, 2011, www.mrc.org/bmi/articles/2011/Networks_Link_Bush_to_Skyrocketing_Gas_Prices__Times_More_Than_Obama.html.

57. See, for instance, Jim Efstathiou, Jr., "Gas Price Surge under Bush Follows Unchecked Refinery Mergers," Bloomberg, May 17, 2004, www.bloomberg.com/apps/news?pid=newsarchive&sid=aI43GNSYkDDQ&refer=news_index ; www.democrats.com/gas; Don Gonyea and Alex Chadwick, "Bush Touts Solutions to Rising Gas Prices," NPR News, April 26, 2006, www.npr.org/templates/story/story.php?storyId=5361835; "Bush: No Quick Fix for Gas Prices," MSNBC, May 5, 2008, www.msnbc.msn.com/id/24465000/; Betsy Stark, "Bush Calls Rising Gas Prices 'Major Problem,'" ABC News, April 18, 2006, http://abcnews.go.com/WNT/story?id=1857043&page=1.

58. See, for instance, Tom Doggett, "Gasoline Cost to Jump $700 for Average Household," Reuters, March 9, 2011, www.reuters.com/article/2011/03/09/us-usa-gasoline-price-idUSTRE7286IO20110309; Rory Cooper, "In Pictures: Bush Vs. Obama On Gas Prices," The Foundry, March 4, 2011, http://blog.heritage.org/2011/03/04/in-pictures-bush-vs-obama-on-gas-prices/.

59. "'You Should Be Blaming George W. Bush!': MSNBC's Cenk On Rising Gas Prices," www.youtube.com/watch?v=__a8mfDZuQM&feature=player_embedded.

60. Mark Tapscott, "Would Salazar Support $10-Per-Gallon Gas Today, as He Did in 2008?" *Washington Examiner*, March 8, 2011, http://washingtonexaminer.com/blogs/beltway-confidential/2011/03/would-salazar-support-10-gallon-gas-today-he-did-200 8.

61. Larry Elder, "$5 Gas Predicted under Obama—What, No Pitchforks?" *Jewish World Review*, December 30, 2010, www.jewishworldreview.com/cols/elder1230 10.php3.

62. Fox News was the only major press organ to devote a real analysis to this. "Why Is Left Silent on Obama's Gitmo Reversal?" Fox News, March 8, 2011, www. foxnews.com/on-air/oreilly/transcript/why-left-silent-obamas-gitmo-reversal.

63. Andrew Vanacore, "US Newspaper Circulation Down, Decline Rate Slows," Boston.com, October 25, 2010, www.boston.com/business/technology/articles/2010/10/25/us_newspaper_circulation_down_5_percent/.

64. Tom Blumer, "Big 3 Nets' Evening News Election and Pre-Election Week Audiences Down Nearly 20% from 2006," newsbusters.org, November 12, 2010, http://newsbusters.org/blogs/tom-blumer/2010/11/12/big-3-nets-evening-news-election-and-pre-election-week-audiences-down-ne.

65. Gillian Reagan, "ABC, CBS Evening News Continue to Hemorrhage Viewers," Business Insider, April 2, 2010, www.businessinsider.com/nbc-abc-cbs-evening-news-continue-to-lose-viewers-2010-4.

66. Dan Radmacher, "The Institutions of Liberty Are in Grave Peril," *Roanoke Times*, February 12, 2011, H1.

67. John Tierney, "Social Scientist Sees Bias Within," *New York Times*, February 8, 2011, A1.

68. L. Brent Bozell, "Media Stayed in the Bag for Obama during 2012 Election," Investors.com, November 7, 2012, http://news.investors.com/ibd-editorials-on-the-right/110712-632612-media-bias-showed-in-uncritical-coverage-of-obama.htm?p=full.

69. Rich Noyes, "Five Ways Media Bias Tipped the Scales in Favor of Obama," Media Research Center, November 9, 2012, www.mrc.org/media-reality-check/five-ways-media-bias-tipped-scales-favor-obama.

70. "The Final Days of the Media Campaign 2012: Final Weeks in the Mainstream Press," Pew Research Center's Project for Excellence in Journalism, November 19, 2012, www.journalism.org/analysis_report/final_weeks_mainstream_press.

71. "The Final Days of the Media Campaign 2012"

72. "The Final Days of the Media Campaign 2012."

73. Bozell; "Five Big Stories the Media Will 'Discover' after the Election," Investors.com, November 7, 2012, http://news.investors.com/ibd-editorials/110712-632397-five-stories-the-media-have-buried-.htm#ixzz2IpIWQWNz; Yossi Gestetner, "If You Doubt Media Bias Helped Obama Win, Answer Those Questions," Gestetner Updates: Jewish Political News Updates, November 9, 2012, http://gestetnerupdates.com/2012/11/09/if-you-doubt-media-bias-helped-obama-win-answer-those-questions/; Matthew Clark, "Mainstream Media Helps Obama Hide Truth on Terrorist Attack," *ACLJ*, November 6, 2012, http://aclj.org/war-on-terror/mainstream-media-helps-obama-hide-truth-terrorist-attack; Noyes.

74. Noyes.

75. Bozell; Noyes.

76. Noyes.

77. Gestetner.

78. "Bozell on Spiked Fast and Furious News: 'Another Example of the Media Deliberately Rigging This Election,'" newsbusters.org, October 2, 2012, http://newsbusters.org/blogs/tim-graham/2012/10/02/bozell-spiked-fast-and-furious-news-another-example-media-deliberately-r.

79. Noyes.

80. "Five Big Stories."

81. Doug Powers, "Dana Perino: Media Blamed Bush for High Gas Prices But Gives Obama a Pass," michellemalkin.com, February 20, 2012, http://michellemalkin.com/2012/02/20/perino-media-bush-gas-prices/; Gestetner.

82. Noyes.

83. Gestetner.

84. Gestetner.

85. Quoted in Edwin Emery, *The Press in America*, 2nd ed. (Englewood Cliffs, NJ: Prentice-Hall, 1962), 374.

86. Jack Fuller, *News Values* (Chicago: University of Chicago Press, 1996), 11.

87. Louis A. Day, *Ethics in Media Communication* (Belmont, CA: Wadsworth Publishing Company, 1991), 35.

88. Mitchell Stephens, *A History of News: From the Drum to the Satellite* (New York: Viking Penguin, 1988), 264.

89. Fred S. Siebert, Theodore Peterson, and Wilbur Schramm, *Four Theories of the Press* (Urbana, IL: University of Illinois Press, 1956), 74.

90. Siebert, Peterson, and Schramm, 87.

91. Siebert, Peterson, and Schramm, 89.

92. Siebert, Peterson, and Schramm, 91.

93. Siebert, Peterson, and Schramm, 91.

94. American Society of Newspaper Editors Statement of Principles. "ASNE's Statement of Principles was originally adopted in 1922 as the 'Canons of Journalism.' The document was revised and renamed 'Statement of Principles' in 1975." The full document can be obtained at www.asne.org/kiosk/archive/principl.htm.

95. Code of Ethics, Society of Professional Journalists, http://spj.org/ethics_code.asp.

96. Michael Crichton, "The Mediasaurus: Today's Mass Media is Tomorrow's Fossil Fuel," *Wired*, September/October 1993, 57–58.

97. Fuller, 30.

98. Fuller admits that reporters should not report every view, only those of "informed, reasonable people," and then agrees that a "journalist's bias may unduly restrict what he considers the range of reasonable, informed opinion" (32).

99. See, for instance, Frank Newport and Joseph Carroll, "Are the News Media Too Liberal?" October 8, 2003, www.gallup.com. This contradicts a study by Brian Goff and Robert D. Tollison, "Why Is the Media So Liberal?" *Journal of Public Finance and Public Choice*, 8 (1990), 13–21.

100. Dan Gainor, "Print Media: Next Government Bailout," *Human Events*, March 18, 2010, www.humanevents.com/article.php?id=36075.

101. Ronald Brownstein, "With Click of a Mouse, Liberals Find Answer to Limbaugh," *Los Angeles Times*, July 7, 2003, http://articles.latimes.com/2003/jul/07/nation/na-outlook7.

102. George Gilder, *Wealth and Poverty* (New York: Basic Books, 1981); Charles Murray, *Losing Ground: American Social Policy, 1950–1980* (New York: Basic Books, 1984).

Index

About the Author

Jim A. Kuypers is associate professor of communication at Virginia Tech. He is the author or editor of nine books and a former editor for the *American Communication Journal*. He is the recipient of the American Communication Association's Outstanding Contribution to Communication Scholarship Award, the Southern States Communication Association's Early Career Research Award, and Dartmouth College's Distinguished Lecturer Award. His research interests include meta-criticism, the moral/poetic use of language, and political communication, particularly ways in which the news media influence political understanding.

A DOCUMENTARY HISTORY OF
CONSERVATION IN AMERICA

A
DOCUMENTARY
HISTORY
OF
CONSERVATION
IN AMERICA

EDITED BY ROBERT McHENRY
WITH CHARLES VAN DOREN

Introduction by
Lorus and Margery Milne

PRAEGER PUBLISHERS
New York · Washington · London

S
930
.M18

PRAEGER PUBLISHERS

111 Fourth Avenue, New York, N.Y. 10003, U.S.A.
5, Cromwell Place, London SW7 2JL, England

Published in the United States of America in 1972
by Praeger Publishers, Inc.

© 1972 by Praeger Publishers, Inc.

All rights reserved

Library of Congress Catalog Card Number: 72–168342

Printed in the United States of America

CONTENTS

FOREWORD

Conjure up an image of a desolate wasteland, a trackless desert, a blasted heath, a lifeless mountain top; next to it place the beaming, benevolent figure of Mother Nature, proffering a cornucopia of delights, while at her feet lie the lion and the lamb: two views, metaphorically poles apart but equally vivid and true, that man at various times and places has taken of the natural world that is his home. Nor are these by any means the only alternatives, for the range of attitudes that have been held toward nature is vast and encompasses an almost infinite variety of shadings and combinations. It seems no surprise, after all, that, in his hundreds of thousands of years on earth, man has changed his outlook on nature, while it is perhaps strange that, in all that time, he has not attained anything like a stable consensus. Although all have been invoked, neither religion, art, nor science has been equal to the task of devising a frame of relationship with nature within which all men could comfortably place themselves.

Primitive man, had he reflected upon it—of course, we do not know that he did not—would doubtless have found within himself a severely ambiguous attitude. On the one hand, nature was the source of his food and shelter and other necessities; on the other hand, it was the source of all that was mysterious and terrifying, from wild predators to thunderstorms to volcanoes. Improvements in hunting and fishing skills and tools and the invention of agriculture increased his control over his food supply and made possible a certain sense of security. All that remained for untamed nature then was the terrible, and cultures the world over peopled the wilderness beyond the fence with demons, demigods, and all manner of evil spirits. Even the Greeks, who in their high civilization could rhapsodize on the beauty of the cultivated countryside, at the same time avoided the woods and mountains for fear of Pan and his satyrs.

Judaeo-Christian religious thought introduced another emotional strain in the man-nature relationship, one that reveals itself from the first chapter of Genesis down through the history of the Church. From the beginning, God's creation is divided into two antithetical parts: There is the Garden of Eden, but east of Eden is the wilderness. The former is a place of ease and freedom from care; the latter, one of toil and danger. Furthermore, God's first command to Adam and Eve is to "be fruitful, and multiply, and replenish the earth, and subdue it, and have dominion over . . . every living thing." The Garden is good; the wilderness is bad and to be conquered.

As theology evolved into the Middle Ages, nature ceased to be thought of as God's creation and became, instead, the sign and even the substance of evil, of sin. Satan was often said to abide outside the pale, and even those who were prone to see a certain beauty in wild nature fought the tendency as still another worldly snare turning the mind from its sole legitimate concern, the soul's salvation. In the seventeenth century, and perhaps earlier, some went so far as to posit that the Garden of Eden had once spread over the entire earth and that the wilderness had appeared at the moment, and as a result, of man's fall. That primordial act of disobedience had caused the creation of mountains and deserts and other "ugly" terrestrial features as visible signs of the rifts in God's originally smooth and lovely plan. Such views added force to the injunction to "subdue the earth" by turning man's conquest of "raw" nature into an analogue of redemption.

"God almighty first planted a garden," declared Francis Bacon, and with the essential import of that sentiment Western culture was in general agreement from the Greeks to the Enlightenment. Nature attained its highest state—and thereby became beautiful—only when transformed by the hand of man into a garden (it might be an actual garden, or a park, or even a farm). For the fundamental characteristics of a garden are manifest order and harmony, precisely the qualities that form the classical definition of beauty. There, in the garden, the mind as well as the body finds its own repose. As Marvell wrote:

> Meanwhile the mind, from pleasure less,
> Withdraws into its happiness;—
> The mind, that ocean where each kind
> Does straight its own resemblance find;
> Yet it creates, transcending these,
> Far other worlds, and other seas,
> Annihilating all that's made
> To a green thought in a green shade.

The romantic movement, beginning in the eighteenth century and continuing on into the nineteenth, was revolutionary in many respects, not the least of which was the change it brought about in the man-nature relationship. For the mechanical deism of an earlier age, romanticism substituted organicism and sundry forms of pantheism: God was seen as immanent in nature—all nature and particularly wild nature unspoiled by man. Suddenly the Alps, for instance, were looked upon no longer as blemishes on the face of the earth, much less as subtle reproaches to man's moral and physical weakness, but, rather, as awe-inspiring monuments to the sweeping grandeur of nature and of nature's God. Yet, so ingrained was the classical definition of beauty that the word could not be used even by the most effusive early romantics to describe the aesthetic appeal of such grand scenes. Instead, the Alps were said to be *sublime;* only in a later day of more liberal usage did they become beautiful.

Romanticism bloomed late in America, but by the 1830's it was in full cry in the work of the Hudson River School of painters, led by Thomas Cole, who instituted a small revolution of his own by picturing lovely Catskill landscapes with no human figures in them at all. American romanticism reached its peak with the Transcendentalists of New England, and it was one of them, Thoreau, who pushed the wilderness cult to its farthest bound by declaring baldly that "in wildness is the preservation of the world." That mysterious statement is endlessly thrilling to many moderns; it would have appeared merely captious and wrong to almost any reader a hundred years before it was written.

Not at all coincidentally, the rise and flowering of romanticism were contemporary with the first great surge of the Industrial Revolution, which saw Blake's "dark Satanic mills" (note the relocation of the spirit of evil) begin the heavy assault on nature that has grown ever heavier in the nearly two centuries since. No such thing as an assault was planned or even foreseen, of course. The men who built the industries—like the industries, which, once built, became no longer identifiable with any particular man—did not intend to plunder limited resources, ravage landscapes, or pollute air and water. Captivated by the new material power and economic wealth unleashed by technology, they simply did so by the way, in pursuit of the goddess Progress. They were joined in the chase by almost everyone else, from poets to divines. There was little time to spare to think about unfortunate side effects—and, for decades, little apparent reason. Only toward the end of the nineteenth century, and then to but a few men, came the realization that perhaps such effects were rather more central than "side."

Isolated voices had 'ong warned against unwise agricultural practices and the wholesale felling of forests, but not until the first years of the twentieth century did such ideas dawn on the public consciousness. By such men as Gifford Pinchot, America was introduced to the concept of "conservation," by which was meant at the time little more than greater efficiency in the use of resources. The early conservationists tended to see themselves as a conscientious adjunct to business; far from denigrating progress, they hoped to promote it by adding a limited amount of forethought to the list of business virtues. Thus, in the larger context of the evolution of man's conscious relationship with nature, the conservation movement of the first part of this century was a sort of interlude, more of an epilogue to the last than a prologue to the next stage.

What will that next stage be? Do we know? Can we know yet? Probably not—despite the widespread interest in the question at the present time. We have no picture of the future that is certain and sure; all we have, perhaps, is an image of a door just barely opened, through which we can peek but not see clearly. What we see is a pair of alternatives. Whether either will be realized, or neither, cannot be known.

One alternative image, sad as it may seem to those who retain *nostalgie pour la boue*, is that of a mechanized garden that extends over the entire earth, with nature neatly ordered and controlled, all remaining wilderness turned into "recreational areas," and man at peace with himself and with his servant technology. The other alternative is desolation, period. It could be caused by atomic bombs or by the slower "population bomb" that such prophets as Paul Ehrlich have begun to warn us about, but the result would be the same in either case. The earth would be empty of life and human warmth—a new sort of wilderness, but brought about by man's moral and physical and mental weakness, as predicted of old.

*   *   *

The first settlers in North America were faced by a virgin wilderness that consisted, beyond the seacoast, almost entirely (as far as they knew) of deep forest. Because the Indians who inhabited it were, however justifiably, increasingly hostile and reminiscent of old European myths of the wild man, the prospect of the New World to early colonists—as distinct from explorers who did not have to live there—was often bleak and frightening. Though they were, of course, a great deal more sophisticated than primitive men had been, their outlook was sometimes strikingly similar. In less than four centuries, however, Americans have transformed that wilderness into the most advanced industrial and urbanized state in the world. Thus it is possible to trace, within a relatively short time span, the record of man's changing ideas about himself in relation to nature by viewing the American experience. This book is an attempt to do that.

What follows is a collection of carefully selected and edited passages drawn from hundreds of authors and sources on the subject of man and his world. Most are of American origin, but there are also numerous selections from works written elsewhere, enough to indicate that the ideas and problems treated are of more than American relevance—Western, if not worldwide. Most of the passages are short in order to allow for the greatest possible variety and comprehensiveness.

The basic organization of the book is topical, as a glance at the table of contents will show. Because the relationship of man and nature has changed through time, selections within a topic and the topics themselves are ordered in something like an evolutionary sequence.

Part I, entitled "In the Beginning," consists essentially of celebrations of nature, but from two points of view. One regards nature as good and beautiful; the other, as providing, particularly in America, all the necessities of man in unending abundance. The emphasis in these pieces is often on the endless resources of the newly discovered continent. No more than a hint is given in any of the selections of the coming realization that those resources are not, and could not be, infinite.

Part II, entitled "Man's Dominion," touches on two main themes, which together reflect a single fundamental activity of man. It contains celebrations of progress—success stories, as it were, in man's never-ending battle with nature to perpetuate himself on earth. But it also contains numerous "horror stories"—accounts of how things went wrong. Sometimes the authors of these were not aware of the horror they were describing when they wrote, but we can see it, all too clearly, now.

Part III, entitled "The Flaming Sword," deals with three closely connected subjects. One is the conservation movement of the end of the nineteenth century and the beginning of the twentieth. The heroes and the villains of this movement are alike represented. (Who is a hero and who is a villain will have to depend, one supposes, on the reader's point of view.) Next is that complex of facts and attitudes that goes under the modern name "ecology." The book contains little technical ecology, strictly speaking, but the more popular writings of noted ecologists are represented. Finally, the part deals with the somewhat more abstract ideas of such men as Aldo Leopold. Seeing with greater clarity than most the problems that we now face or are about to face, Leopold proposed that nothing less than a new moral attitude toward nature, perhaps an almost religious one, was needed to protect us from what he considered to be imminent disaster.

The last part, entitled "Paradise and Apocalypse," is divided into two sections. Each is concerned with the future, but two quite different visions are represented. The first section contains passages from the works of authors who feel that the future can, or will, be almost a new paradise. In the second appear selections by authors who fear that, instead of a paradise, the future will be a kind of hell.

We hesitated for some time before deciding to place paradise first and apocalypse second. We could have done it the other way around; our order does not reflect any settled convictions on our part. Perhaps, in the end, the decision was aesthetic, or perhaps it reflects a basically didactic attitude on our part. Even if the future need not be terrible, it surely cannot hurt to remind ourselves that it could be—if.

*   *   *

Editorial notes appear in many places throughout the text. Sometimes these deal with general ideas and introduce a number of selections; sometimes they concern individual selections and are in the nature of headnotes for them. In any event, an indication of author and source precedes each selection, but, because these are often very brief, author and selection indexes appear at the back of the book to make possible the location of particular selections and to provide full bibliographical information.

It is not pretended that this book is a definitive treatment of the subject; if such a thing is possible at all, it is not within the scope of any single volume. Rather, the purpose here is to be as wide-ranging, as interesting, and as stimulating as possible. The ideas are general, and the emphasis is usually on approaches and viewpoints, rather than on facts and specific programs; concerning pollution, for example, the discussion centers on the feasibility and implications of control rather than on technical proposals about how to achieve it. It is our hope, in short, that the book will construct a background and a context against and within which readers may view their world.

*   *   *

The editors received much help in the preparation of this book and owe thanks to many people—notably, to Wayne Moquin, who suggested and located many of the selections included; to Carolee Morrison, who assisted in many phases of the project; and to Helen Hanson, who obtained permissions to reprint certain copyrighted materials. Acknowledgments for such permissions appear in the customary place in the volume.

ROBERT MCHENRY
CHARLES VAN DOREN

Chicago, Illinois
January, 1972

ACKNOWLEDGMENTS

The editors wish to express their gratitude for permission to reprint material from the following sources:

Ballantine Books, Inc., for portions of *The Population Bomb*, by Dr. Paul R. Ehrlich, copyright © 1968 by Paul R. Ehrlich. All rights reserved.

Cambridge University Press for portions of Chapter 7 of *The Universe Around Us*, by Sir James Jeans.

The Center for the Study of Democratic Institutions for portions of "The Wild Places," by Thomas Merton, "All About Ecology," by William Murdoch, and "Everyone Wants to Save the Environment but No One Knows Quite What to Do," by Frank M. Potter, Jr., reprinted, respectively, from the July, 1968, January, 1970, and March, 1970, issues of *The Center Magazine*, a publication of the Center for the Study of Democratic Institutions in Santa Barbara, California. Also for portions of "The Politics of Ecology," by Aldous Huxley, an Occasional Paper, © 1963 by The Fund for the Republic, Inc.

Collins-Knowlton-Wing, Inc., for portions of "Spring, and a Time to Listen," and "Summer, a Time for Perspective," by Hal Borland, from *The Progressive*, April and July, 1970, copyright © 1970 by Hal Borland. Collins-Knowlton-Wing and the executors for the Estate of H. G. Wells for portions of "The Time Machine" from *Twenty-Eight Science Fiction Novels*, copyright © 1960. All rights reserved.

The Columbia Forum for portions of "Toward a Non-Malthusian Population Policy," by Jean Mayer, from *The Columbia Forum* (Summer, 1969), Vol. XII, No. 2, copyright 1969 by the Trustees of Columbia University in the City of New York. Cowles Book Company, Inc., for portions of *The Conservation Fraud*, by Charles Zurhorst.

Mrs. Bernard DeVoto for portions of "The West: A Plundered Province," by Bernard DeVoto, © 1934 by Minneapolis Star Tribune Co., Inc., reprinted from the August, 1934, issue of *Harper's Magazine*.

Doubleday & Company, Inc., for "what the ants are saying," copyright 1935 by Doubleday & Company, Inc., from the book *The Lives and Times of Archy & Mehitabel* by Don Marquis. Also for portions of "The Artifact as a Cultural Cipher," by Richard S. Latham, from *Who Designs America?* ed. by Laurence B. Holland, © 1966 by the

Trustees of Princeton University for the Program in American Civilization at Princeton University. Doubleday & Company, Inc., and Granada Publishing Limited for portions of "The History," from *The Next Million Years*, by Charles Galton Darwin, copyright 1952 by Charles Galton Darwin.

Dover Publications, Inc., for portions of *Peter Kalm's Travels in North America*, ed. by Adolph B. Benson.

E. P. Dutton & Co., Inc., for portions of "Record Seventeen," from the book *We* by Eugene Zamiatin, tr. by Gregory Zilboorg, copyright 1924 by E. P. Dutton & Co., Inc., renewed 1952 by Gregory Zilboorg, published by E. P. Dutton & Co., Inc., in a paperback edition.

Paul R. Ehrlich for portions of "Eco-Catastrophe!" from *Ramparts*, September, 1969, copyright 1969 by Paul R. Ehrlich.

Fortune for portions of "The Half-Finished Society," by Edmund K. Faltermayer, from the March, 1965, issue of *Fortune Magazine*, by special permission, © 1965 Time Inc.

W. H. Freeman and Company for portions of "The Human Ecosystem," by Marston Bates, from *Resources and Man: A Study and Recommendations*, by the Committee on Resources and Man of the Division of Earth Sciences, National Academy of Sciences–National Research Council, with cooperation of the Division of Biology and Agriculture, copyright © 1969.

Frances Howard Goldwyn for portions of *The Winning of Barbara Worth*, by Harold Bell Wright.

Harcourt Brace Jovanovich, Inc., for "pity this busy monster, manunkind," by E. E. Cummings, from his volume *Poems 1923–1954*, copyright 1944 by E. E. Cummings. Also for portions of *The City in History: Its Origins, Its Transformations, and Its Prospects*, by Lewis Mumford, © 1961 by Lewis Mumford.

Harper & Row, Publishers, Inc., for portions of "A Day at Niagara," from *Sketches New and Old*, by Mark Twain. Harper & Row, Publishers, Inc., and Victor Gollancz Ltd. for portions of "Ages of Plenty," from *Profiles of the Future*, by Arthur C. Clarke, copyright © 1962 by Arthur C. Clarke.

Harvard University Press for portions of *From Scotland to Silverado*, ed. by James D. Hart, Cambridge, Mass.: The Belknap Press of Harvard University Press, copyright 1966 by the President and Fellows of Harvard College. Also for portions of *The Life and Works of Thomas Cole*, by Louis LeGrand Noble, ed. by Elliot S. Vessell, Cambridge, Mass.: The Belknap Press of Harvard University Press, copyright 1964 by the President and Fellows of Harvard College.

Hill and Wang, Inc., and Nannine Joseph for "So Fair a World It Was" and "Indian Hunter," from *That Shining Place: New Poems by Mark Van Doren*, copyright © 1969 by Mark Van Doren.

Holt, Rinehart and Winston, Inc., and the Estate of Robert Frost for "The Vantage Point" and "A Brook in the City," from *The Poetry of Robert Frost,* ed. by Edward Connery Lathem, copyright 1923, 1934, © 1969 by Holt, Rinehart and Winston, Inc., copyright 1951, © 1962 by Robert Frost.

The Johns Hopkins Press for portions of "The Economics of the Coming Spaceship Earth," from *Beyond Economics: Essays on Society, Religion and Ethics,* by Kenneth E. Boulding.

Houghton Mifflin Company for portions of *The Works of Thoreau,* ed. by Henry Seidel Canby. Also for portions of *The Human Use of Human Beings,* by Norbert Wiener, copyright 1950, 1954 by Norbert Wiener. Also for portions of *The Life and Letters of John Muir,* by William Frederic Bade, copyright 1924 by Houghton Mifflin Company. Also for portions of *Silent Spring,* by Rachel Carson, copyright 1962 by Rachel L. Carson.

International Famous Agency, Inc., for portions of "Nor Any Drop to Drink," by James Dugan, from *Playboy,* September, 1966, copyright © 1966 by HMH Publishing Co.

International Institute for Environmental Affairs for portions of "The Shape of the Predicament: A Shorthand Note," a paper prepared for use in the Executive Seminar Program of The Aspen Institute for Humanistic Studies, 1970, by Thomas W. Wilson, Jr., of the International Institute for Environmental Affairs.

The Kiplinger Washington Editors, Inc., for portions of "America the Beautiful: Heritage or Honky-Tonk," from *Changing Times,* the Kiplinger Magazine, (November, 1962, issue), copyright 1962 by The Kiplinger Washington Editors, Inc., 1729 H. Street, N.W., Washington, D.C. 20006.

Alfred A. Knopf, Inc., for portions of *Science in the Cause of Man,* by Gerard Piel, copyright © 1961, 1962 by Gerard Piel. Alfred A. Knopf, Inc., and Faber and Faber Limited for "Anecdote of the Jar," from *The Collected Poems of Wallace Stevens,* copyright 1923, 1951, by Wallace Stevens.

Robert Lantz-Candida Donadio Literary Agency, Inc., for portions of "Wind River Mountains," from *My Wilderness: East to Katahdin,* by William O. Douglas, copyright © 1961 by William O. Douglas.

J. B. Lippincott Company for portions of "The Asphalt Shroud," from *Road to Ruin,* by A. Q. Mowbray, copyright © 1969, 1968 by A. Q. Mowbray.

Little, Brown and Company and Robert Lantz-Candida Donadio Literary Agency, Inc., for portions of *A Wilderness Bill of Rights* by William O. Douglas, © 1965 by William O. Douglas. Little, Brown and Company and Fairfield Osborn for portions of *Our Plundered Planet,* by Fairfield Osborn, copyright 1948 by Fairfield Osborn.

Look for portions of "America the Beautiful?" by David Perlman from the November 4, 1969, issue of *Look Magazine*, copyright 1969 by Cowles Communications, Inc.

McGraw-Hill Book Company for portions of Chapter 3 of *Rich Land Poor Land: A Study of Waste in the Natural Resources of America*, by Stuart Chase, copyright 1936 by Stuart Chase.

The Macmillan Company for portions of "How to Found a Settlement," from *American History Told by Contemporaries*, ed. by Albert Bushnell.

Dr. Lorus J. Milne and Dr. Margery Milne for portions from *The Valley: Meadow, Grove and Stream*, copyright © 1959, 1963 by Lorus J. Milne and Margery Milne.

William Morrow & Company, Inc., for portions of "Why I Came," from *The Best Nature Writing of Joseph Wood Krutch*, copyright 1952 by Joseph Wood Krutch.

The Nation for portions of "Outrage on Bodega Head," by Gene Marine, from the June 23, 1963, issue of *The Nation*.

National Parks Association for portions of "The Nation as a Park," by Gerald M. Weinberg, from *National Parks & Conservation Magazine*, 44 (272), May, 1970.

National Wildlife for portions of "After Earth Day," by Gladwin Hill, from the August–September, 1970, issue of *National Wildlife Magazine*, copyright 1970 by the National Wildlife Federation.

Natural History for portions of "An Environmental Lawyer Urges: Plead the Ninth Amendment!" by E. F. Roberts, from *Natural History*, August–September, 1970, copyright Natural History Magazine, 1970.

New Directions Publishing Corporation and Laurence Pollinger Limited for "Classic Scene," by William Carlos Williams, from *Collected Earlier Poems*, copyright 1938 by William Carlos Williams.

The New York Times Company for portions of "Smog Linked to 18 Deaths in a Day," "20 Dead in Smog: Rain Clearing Air," and "Denies Smog Zinc Blame," © 1948 by The New York Times Company. Also for "Observer," by Russell Baker, © 1963 by The New York Times Company. Also for portions of "Paradise Is Stripped," by Harry M. Caudill, © 1966 by The New York Times Company. Also for "Death Comes to the Peregrine Falcon," by David R. Zimmerman, "Dumping of Gas Not Final Answer," by Tom Wicker, and "Deaths from Parathion, DDT Successor, Stir Concern," by John Noble Wilford, © 1970 by The New York Times Company.

Oxford University Press for a portion of *A Sand County Almanac with Other Essays on Conservation from Round River*, by Aldo Leopold, © 1949, 1953, 1966 by Oxford University Press, Inc.

Gifford B. Pinchot for portions of Chapter 7 of *The Fight for Conservation*, by Gifford Pinchot, copyright 1910 by Doubleday, Page & Company, renewed 1937 by G. Pinchot.

Pitman Publishing for portions of *Man Makes Himself*, by V. Gordon Childe.

Playboy and Robert Lantz-Candida Donadio Literary Agency, Inc., for portions of "The Public Be Damned," by William O. Douglas, from *Playboy*, July, 1969, copyright © 1969 by *Playboy*.

Frederik Pohl for portions of *The Space Merchants*, by Frederik Pohl and C. M. Kornbluth, copyright 1952, by Rediffusion Television, Ltd.

The Progressive for portions of "A Not So Silent Spring," by Gladwin Hill, from *The Progressive*, April, 1970.

Random House, Inc., for portions of *Democracy in America*, by Alexis de Tocqueville, ed. by Phillips Bradley, copyright 1945 by Alfred A. Knopf, Inc. Also for "Science," from *Selected Poetry of Robinson Jeffers*, copyright 1925 and renewed 1953 by Robinson Jeffers. Also for portions of "Erie: Life on a Dying Lake," from *Out of Place in America*, by Peter Schrag, copyright © 1969 by Peter Schrag.

Henry Regnery Company for portions of "The Pillage of the Earth," from *The Failure of Technology*, by Friedrich Georg Juenger, copyright 1949 by Henry Regnery Company.

The Saturday Evening Post for portions of "Our Dying Waters," by John Bird, from *The Saturday Evening Post*, April 23, 1966, © 1966 The Curtis Publishing Company. The Saturday Evening Post and Robert Wernick for portions of "Let's Spoil the Wilderness," by Robert Wernick, from *The Saturday Evening Post*, November 6, 1965, © 1965 The Curtis Publishing Company.

Saturday Review and Isaac Asimov for portions of "The Fourth Revolution," by Isaac Asimov, from *Saturday Review*, October 24, 1970, copyright 1970 Saturday Review, Inc. Saturday Review and Frank K. Kelly for portions of "The Possibilities of Transformation: A Report on the State of Mankind: 1970," March 7, 1970, *Saturday Review*, copyright 1970 Saturday Review, Inc. Saturday Review and C. W. Griffin, Jr., for portions of "America's Airborne Garbage," by C. W. Griffin, Jr., from May 22, 1965, *Saturday Review*, copyright 1965 Saturday Review, Inc.

The Scarecrow Press and Philip Marsh for portions of "The Philosopher of the Forest," from *The Prose of Philip Freneau*, copyright 1955 by Philip M. Marsh.

The Sierra Club for portions of "Wilderness and Man in 2065," from *Wilderness in a Changing World*, ed. by Bruce Kilgore, copyright 1966 by The Sierra Club. Also for "Telling It Like It Isn't," from the *Sierra Club Bulletin*, March, 1970, copyright 1970 by The Sierra Club. The Sierra Club and Paul Lambert for portions of "Crisis," by Paul Lambert, from the *Sierra Club Bulletin*. April, 1971, copyright 1971 by The Sierra Club.

Time for portions of "Pesticides: The Price for Progress," from *Time, The Weekly Newsmagazine*, copyright Time Inc., 1962. Also for portions of "The Age of Effluence," from *Time, The Weekly Newsmagazine*, copyright Time Inc., 1968.

The University of Chicago Press and Leonard Hall for portions of *Stars Upstream: Life Along an Ozark River*, copyright 1958 by The University of Chicago.

University of Nebraska Press for portions of *Black Elk Speaks: Being the Life Story of a Holy Man of the Oglala Sioux*, © 1961 by the University of Nebraska Press.

University of North Carolina Press and the Institute of Early American History and Culture for portions of *The History and Present State of Virginia*, by Robert Beverley, copyright 1947 by The University of North Carolina Press.

University of Oklahoma Press for portions of *A Tour on the Prairies*, by Washington Irving, copyright 1956 by the University of Oklahoma Press. Also for portions of *The Journals of Zebulon Montgomery Pike*, ed. by Donald Jackson, copyright 1966 by the University of Oklahoma Press.

University of Pittsburgh Press for portions of *A Topographical Description of the Dominions of the United States of America*, by T. Pownall, © 1949 by the University of Pittsburgh Press.

Vanguard Press, Inc., for portions of *100,000,000 Guinea Pigs*, by Arthur Kallet and F. J. Schlink.

The Viking Press and McIntosh and Otis, Inc., for portions of *The Grapes of Wrath*, by John Steinbeck, copyright 1939, © renewed 1967 by John Steinbeck. Also for portions of *The Challenge of Man's Future*, by Harrison Brown, copyright 1954 by Harrison Brown.

Vineyard Gazette, for portions of "Of Time and the Economy," by Henry Beetle Hough, from *Vineyard Gazette*, March 25, 1960.

The World Publishing Company and Harold Matson Company, Inc., for portions of "The Threat to Life in the Sea," by Gordon Rattray Taylor, from *The Doomsday Book*, copyright © 1970 by Gordon Rattray Taylor.

Yale University Press for portions of *The Travels of William Bartram*, ed. by Francis Harper.

A DOCUMENTARY HISTORY OF
CONSERVATION IN AMERICA

INTRODUCTION: AWARENESS OF THE LIVING WORLD

Lorus and Margery Milne

On the wall above a doorway in the old laboratory building where we two met as students, an exhortation by Louis Agassiz still hangs where he had tacked it. In large Spencerian script, he had admonished, "Study NATURE, not Books." That doorway formerly led to the library of the marine science center he founded.

Another Louis—the French Pasteur—around a century ago advised, "Chance favors the mind that is prepared." Yet, as we think about it, we feel sure that each of these great men would have conceded merit in the other's dictum. Agassiz wanted his students close to the tide pools while they were summering and studying on Cape Cod; he had no objection to their being well informed from books before they came. Pasteur's focus was on chancy experimental work, based upon sound information and careful consideration of how the outcome could be most informative.

Today, the Marine Biological Laboratory on Cape Cod and the Pasteur Institute in Paris are both centers in which graduate students and Nobel laureates explore questions that Agassiz and Pasteur might have called "secrets of nature." Generally, the modern approach to the living world in these laboratories is deliberately aimed at minutiae. The small details prove to be pieces in a single jigsaw puzzle, each new discovery a part of the larger picture.

The number of specialists and the refinement of their goals have increased in the past century at a pace that corresponds to the population growth in the Western world. New frontiers of understanding extend around fresh fringes of the known, on a total perimeter that enlarges rapidly and irregularly. The situation can be likened to a little mountain of verifiable information from the peak of which greater perspective can be gained in looking toward the vast wilderness of ignorance that surrounds all human endeavors.

The Expansion of Mankind

The number of knowledgeable people in the world and the heritage they share have increased more in this century than during all previous history. Recent discoveries greatly improve the reliability with which we can reconstruct the various phases of human progress. Even if specific events do not repeat themselves, the over-all trends continue in a way deserving careful analysis.

We can feel confident that, from among dozens of different primates in Africa two or three million years ago, a few evolved in human directions. The members of at least two species learned to use fire as a tool. The two now known as *Homo erectus* and *Homo sapiens* expanded their territories for gathering food, first in Africa, then in warmer parts of Eurasia. About a million years ago, one species vanished while the other prevailed. The latter diversified into Bushmen in South Africa, Negroes in equatorial Africa, forest-dwelling Pygmies in the Congo Basin and in Southeast Asia, Caucasoid people of many skin colors across southern Europe and North Africa to the Indian subcontinent, and Mongoloid people north of the Himalayas.

With only the dog as a domesticated companion and no tradition of husbanding animals or plants, some of these early people spread to Australia by way of the East Indian islands. Primitive Mongoloids ranged northeast to Alaska and used a land bridge into the Americas, later becoming Amerindians. For thousands of years, they lived as opportunists, hunting and fishing and gathering wild foods. In the old world, meanwhile, some Caucasoid and Mongoloid peoples learned the advantages of domesticating animals and plants. This cultural change, which occurred approximately 12,000 years ago in Asia Minor and 8,000 years ago in China, increased spectacularly the supply of food and fiber. Peoples who adopted the new ways were able to displace those who clung to the old traditions of food-gathering. The Caucasoids spread to the wilds of northwestern Europe, across Asia as far as northern Japan, and south to northern Africa. They displaced some of the Negroid people, who adopted only portions of the new culture and who in turn began moving south, displacing the Bushmen and most of the Pygmies. In Southeast Asia, in an area of competition between Caucasoid and Mongoloid colonists, the Asiatic Pygmies vanished altogether.

With the domestication of plants and animals, fewer people than before were needed to provide food and fiber. Yet the supply of these became so reliable that the rest of each human population could live in growing communities, specializing in urban occupations. From a world population of less than 10 million people 12,000 years ago, the total for mankind doubled and redoubled. It reached about 545 million in A.D. 1650.

We think of the 1600's as the period when Caucasoid colonists with firearms and traditions of agriculture and industry began significantly to displace Amerindians in the new world. In South Africa, Caucasoid settlements and farms around Cape Town expanded northward, only to encounter Negroid peoples spreading south through the Transvaal. Explorers to even more remote regions laid the basis for Caucasoid displacement of indigenous peoples in Australia and, to a lesser extent, in New Zealand, which Polynesian Maoris had reached around A.D. 900. To the extent that native people declined to adopt the new ways of raising crops and building industrial cities, they lost out in the competition for land.

The seventeenth century also witnessed the Great Fire of London and the Great Plague that affected much of Europe. Not until recently did anyone notice that, when London was rebuilt, construction was with brick, stone, tile, and slate because wood and thatch had become too scarce. The wood supply had been exhausted in providing fuel for the iron industry, for no one then had learned to use coal or petroleum or to tap wells of natural gas. Bubonic plague did not recur with comparable severity because the source of infection in roof rats diminished along with the thatch. Rat fleas were no longer in such close proximity to people that the disease could be so easily transmitted to man in crowded cities. Similarly, even without new knowledge, malaria disappeared from cities like London and Moscow at a rate directly related to the elimination of the mosquito's marshy breeding place.

Not enough attention was paid, perhaps, to the change in human environmental conditions when, after about 1750, technology found ways to subsidize human enterprises with energy from fuels other than wood. The change meant releasing solar energy captured by green plants millions of years ago. From coal to petroleum to natural gas to thermonuclear reactions, engineering techniques have vastly augmented man's power. This made possible the improvements in use of resources, and enabled the total human population to reach 1 billion in 1840, 2 billion in 1927, 3 billion in 1959 —heading for 7 billion by the year 2000.

More than half of these people, however, are malnourished, easy victims of local famine or a sudden outbreak of communicable disease. Most are so preoccupied with survival that they are unaware of the unpaid costs of technological advance—the soot, other industrial and agricultural wastes, and discarded products that become junk or garbage, further polluting the environment.

Awareness of the Environment

Today's population grew up in an era in which large portions of habitable land already had been converted from farms into housing developments, industrial sites, roadways, parking lots, and garbage dumps. It saw these uses of land, which produce neither food nor fiber, supplemented by airports, vast lakes behind man-made dams, and corridors beneath power transmission lines where no bush or tree was allowed to grow. Progress seemed served while increasing numbers of people lost direct contact with the world that fed them, replenished their oxygen, renewed the waters, and sustained animal life in precarious balance. Not only had the world never before supported so many people, but never had so many of them been so out of touch with nature. Yet scientific knowledge grew rapidly, communications continued to improve, and affluence spread ever more widely in the industrialized countries.

As we think about this gradual change during the last few decades and a while before, we realize that even a well informed person tended to substitute musty research for fresh observation. Certainly, the perusal of Western literature turns up many a person who rebelled for a time against this trend. The seventeenth-century poet George Herbert wrote, "More servants wait on man / Than he'll take note of. In every path / He treads down that which doth befriend him." Gilbert White, an eighteenth-century preacher in Selborne, was fascinated by all the lesser kinds of life he found while taking his daily walks, and concluded that "all nature is so full, that that district produces the greatest variety, which is the most examined."

Yet literary men with a sympathy, even a deep admiration, for nature often seem to shut out the fresh air for fear of catching cold from the world beyond the study door. How great was the contrast between John Muir, the champion of wilderness, and Ralph Waldo Emerson, when Emerson came all the way from Boston to visit the new Yosemite National Park but neglected to experience with Muir the unique redwood groves in darkness.

To some extent, literary men can be found expressing in poetry and prose their love of the natural world, imagining its delights as an exquisite pastiche from their readings and boyhood recollections. Frequently these outpourings share an appreciation for a world that has largely passed away without the writers' knowing it. The outdoors continues to change faster than the most alert scientists can measure or predict.

Our own explorations of distant continents have shocked us into realizing that people, roads, and the pollution of technology are everywhere. Any place on earth is within less than four days' travel of any other. It is easier to find a place unvisited by man for weeks at a time at the center of a thousand-acre farm in the United States than in any habitable area of Africa or tropical America. Since 1950, when the United Nations made the first reliable estimate of the earth's human population, even the most dedicated ecologists have admitted that they can no longer find a place to study nature where man's influence can be ignored. Radioactive fallout from thermonuclear explosions has settled everywhere. Toxic dusts such as DDT have invaded every land from pole to pole, every river, every ocean. Only time can diminish the unprecedented accumulation of these molecules. A continued increase in their concentration in soils and seas is guaranteed at least to 1985. Yet scientists who have no financial stake in the use of the pollutants have found a widespread effect on life far more disastrous than any local hurricane, volcanic eruption, sheep-made desert, or plow-made dust bowl.

None of our natural senses directly informs us about radio-activity in our environment or about toxic molecules such as DDT that are dangerous at extremely low concentrations. These hazards, which have become universal, can be detected only with special instruments and a high competence in using them. Nor is there yet comforting agreement concerning the maximum "safe, permissible" dose in a day, a year, or a lifetime.

Our eyes do tell us when they sting with smog from automobile exhaust in Denver, Johannesburg, or Rome. Eyes see the pall of contaminated air over the major cities and many minor ones; they notice gray dust billowing upward from cement-factory chimneys and black soot from industrial stacks of a thousand kinds. Noses need time to become accustomed to the sulfurous fumes from a paper mill, the hydrocarbons leaking from an oil refinery, the stench of dead fish along the shore of a polluted lake. Ears lose their sensitivity, often permanently, when continually overstimulated by the staccato din of a pneumatic drill or the roar of jet aircraft close by. Taste, which is limited to salty, sour, sweet, and bitter, is less often affronted—and often fooled deliberately—by manu-facturers of packaged foods. Touch we simply try to avoid, whether of oily masses and jetsam along a shore or of people in a crowded place.

The Rules of Nature

Refined to an ultimate simplicity, our conclusion that the world is now seriously polluted rests on the realization that the natural processes of decay and dissolution cannot recycle the chemical substances added to the environment as fast as human activities are scattering them. All life makes use of the same raw materials. They accumulate in vast reservoirs—the oceans, the atmosphere, and the earth itself. From these, life takes what it needs and can absorb. One kind of life may get many substances from another kind. Ultimately, the bacteria and other decomposers release the materials into the reservoirs again.

All of these natural processes make use of energy that came originally from the sun. Captured by green plants, energy is stored in organic compounds for minutes, hours, days, years, or millennia. Ecologists study the flow of energy from green plants to plant-eating animals, then to animal-eating animals, and finally to the decomposers. At every transfer, and in life processes such as respiration, some of the energy is lost as heat. Sir Isaac Newton based his second law of thermodynamics on this natural loss of heat. Eventually, all of the energy captured by green plants is released as heat radiating away from the earth, thus balancing the heat budget of our planet.

Living things have evolved distinctive ways of benefiting from the recycling of chemical elements while growing and reproducing with energy acquired directly from the sun, or indirectly through food. Now mankind is endangering this balance by overloading the natural patterns of recycling—by releasing in a few decades the energy that has long been in storage (as in coal) or that had no solar energy to "repay" (as in thermonuclear reactions). For the last two centuries, these practices have multiplied with scant regard for possible consequences. Today, at last, scientists are trying to measure the rate of change in our environment due to human activities, on the one hand, and to the nonhuman kinds of life plus geological forces, on the other. In one instance after another, mankind seems to be fighting against time—acting in such haste that disasters multiply.

"Give Earth a Chance"

In the affluent nations, we try to refresh our senses and renew our awareness of the world by using vacation time to visit places where nature retains some wildness. The recreational value of open country has increased in proportion to the number of people who can afford to enjoy it. We approve of programs to conserve green belts around our cities and public lands within easy reach. Yet many successful efforts have been nullified by federal or state planners who chose to transform a sanctuary by running a superhighway through it, or inundating it with water behind a new dam. Even without these conflicts in value, Wisconsin's leading wildlife manager, Aldo Leopold, pointed out: "All conservation of wildlife is self-defeating, for to cherish we must touch and fondle. And when enough have touched and fondled, there is no wildlife left to cherish."

Frequently, haste makes waste in ways that later require for correction more expenditure than can be allocated. We encountered an example of this recently when we visited Newfoundland, where natives and visitors alike enjoy the unpolluted streams and forests and breathe some of the cleanest air in North America. We came because of publicity linked to a celebration shared by all of Canada, for which the Newfoundland administration decided to have their principal road paved from east to west. They imported the necessary equipment and greatly improved the twisting road that had served for years. Paving operations held up traffic but caused little change in the handsome landscape.

The publicity release we read before our visit did not mention that as soon as construction had ended, drivers found that curves (rather than a rough surface) slowed their travel. Almost immediately, the roadmakers were recalled and commissioned to provide an almost straight route across Newfoundland. The newest paved road would be wider and make obsolete the previous one, which was merely a series of U-shaped byways where visitors might park. We arrived when neither road could be traveled easily, while bulldozers were rolling up the muskeg like a thick carpet. Masses the width of a bulldozer blade and six feet high were heaped in unsightly spirals on either side of the road, each one a layer of black acid soil in which the roots of bushes and trees provided some reinforcement. The soil itself was the product of thousands of years of natural processes that began when the Ice Age glaciers melted away, allowing colonists to move in on a mineral wasteland. The bushes and trees appeared more recently. Yet in so northern a part of America, these masses will not decompose readily because of the short summers. Without a major investment in restoration, the edges of the "improved" road will be scarred for decades or centuries to come.

Limited planning can also be seen operating in technological solutions to a variety of recognized needs. The full cost of accomplishing the desired end is seldom included, because the predicted price makes no provision for restoring the scene as nearly as possible to the condition in which man found it. On the smallest scale, this is the economy of the company that sells candy and beverages in containers that do not decompose promptly after use; and the unconcern of the consumer of the candy and beverage who neglects to dispose of the package properly. As the number of people on earth increases, there is more rather than less need for the mutual courtesy of obliterating all traces of man's presence at a picnic site or in a public part of a housing area. On a far larger scale, concern for the environment extends to expensive recycling of the wash water from an industrial plant or bringing back from an adventure on the moon every bit of man-made solids. It is painful to look at the moon as the newest international trash pile. If people cannot afford to clean up after themselves, they may soon find that human life is more expensive than the universe can sustain.

Modern civilization is well supplied with information and critiques that point out bias or deficiencies. A skeptic can easily crosscheck most statements that seem suspicious before considering the implications. Comparison is of the essence. For example, statistics may be grouped to show that an affluent American uses ten times as much energy in a lifetime as a poor American, and a hundred times as much as a poor inhabitant of India. Along with this expenditure of energy goes the use of nonrenewable raw materials and the production of waste products that have a negligible salvage value at present. The impact of Americans on the world environment is out of all proportion to that of people in less industrialized nations. Thus, environmental deterioration is *our* responsibility. We also produce half of the man-made dust on earth, and this now equals in amount all of the natural dust raised by tornadoes and discharged from erupting volcanoes.

In regard to our role in the world, an even more shocking calculation can be offered: the species *Homo sapiens*, which is just one among more than 1.5 million kinds of life on earth, has managed to acquire and employ 1 per cent of the world's resources, both renewable (fresh water and timber) and nonrenewable (ores and petroleum). Here, perhaps, is the modern measure of our success in following the biblical injunction to "take dominion over all the world and subdue it."

Dominance by mankind increases as the human population rises, if only through progressively depriving other kinds of life of a place to live. The ecologist calls this "competitive exclusion" and says that the other species lose out by "loss of habitat." On the Great Plains of North America, the pampas of Argentina, and the semiarid areas of Australia, grain fields and domestic cattle for human benefit now displace the native wildlife. We have almost lost our buffalo grass and bison, prairie dogs and wolves. In the Southern Hemisphere, the excluded ones include less familiar plants and animals such as vizcachas and kangaroos.

In a way, it is surprising that only a few hundred kinds of prominent mammals and birds have become extinct, while many thousands have diminished in extent of range to mere remnants of their former territories. The world has no more dodos—those huge flightless pigeons of Mauritius and adjacent islands in the Indian Ocean. Passenger pigeons, which may have been the most abundant birds on earth when the Pilgrim fathers landed on the shores of New England, could withstand neither the destruction of their habitat nor the massive campaigns to convert them into food for colonial families. From both the old world and the new, wild bison are gone, although captive herds can still be seen in parks. These are conspicuous losses, but there are many lesser ones as well. Endangered species are now being studied with a view to saving them, if possible, particularly by scientists connected with the International Union for the Conservation of Nature and the World Wildlife Fund, both headquartered in Morges, near Lausanne, Switzerland.

Certainly, many people from all walks of life react strongly to news of an endangered species or a threatened habitat, but to the extent that their reactions subside quickly, they have little effect. The people who really influence the actual trends are the ones who keep abreast of the changing scene and exert resistance, individually and in groups, against whatever technological programs fail to provide adequately for environmental care. Progress must not be halted, but technological restraint has become imperative; so, for at least a while, has a slower rate of increase in the world's population. Otherwise, ecological disaster is inevitable. The chief question is which, among many possible calamities, will be the first to strike a devastating blow.

The Perils of Simplicity

Our greatest fear is that those people the world over who have the power to formulate policy will continue to think in narrowly nationalistic terms on an array of distracting trivia and to succumb to the all-too-human tendency to confuse the oversimplification of problems with their solution. Our optimism-pessimism quotient varies from moment to moment with our changing estimates of what influential people will do. Today, only a few show any awareness of the real alternatives facing them, or recognize how soon the opportunity to choose may disappear forever. If men continue to value quantity more highly than quality, the living world is in real trouble. The nonhuman world lacks the ability to unite in order to correct the course mankind has traveled during the last few thousand years.

Among distracting trivia, we would include the nationality of the first man on Mars and the name of the country with the most survivors after a nuclear holocaust. While the space program and the equipment developed and stockpiled for military preparedness receive much attention and public money, very little goes toward protecting the environment during man's constant search for nourishment and living space.

There is a great and pressing need to learn how many people the world can reasonably be expected to support with modern technology and resources, while protecting nonhuman species from loss of habitat and extermination. Some contend, with supporting statistics, that if democratic availability of high-quality living is contemplated, the maximum number of people consistent with minimal deterioration of the environment is not over 500 million —the total passed around A.D. 1600, when technology was relatively primitive. Other demographers, who would settle for a simplified world, mention numbers between the 7 billion anticipated in the year 2000 and something less than the 42 billion that will be on hand in 2100 if the current excess of births over deaths is sustained.

Simplification has long been a technique that man has turned to good advantage. Divide and conquer. Make an outline and fill it in. Or, in raising food for ever more people, limit the agricultural undertaking in a particular area to one or two crop plants whose genetic constitution fits almost perfectly the local climate, the kinds of fungus diseases and insect pests, the soil type, the program of application of fertilizer and pesticides, and whatever other factors can be predicted in advance. The yield from this deliberate monoculture is high, its efficiency impressive—unless a new disease or pest gets in and spreads quickly, unimpeded, from one uniform plant to the next, until the whole crop is doomed. Mass production can turn to mass destruction, for in a simplified system the vulnerability of the enterprise is high.

Today geneticists, who are expected to continually improve the hereditary lines of crop plants to match the special techniques in monoculture, can be heard complaining that their resource of inheritable features is drying up. All over the world, agriculturalists are turning to the new high-yield strains, expanding their fields, and achieving clean cultivation. This eliminates the ancestral and related plants from which the features that make the new strains so productive are derived. If the only crop plants left are the artificially tailored ones, this man-guided evolution will end, with the diseases and pests winning out after all.

The natural complexity of the nonhuman world baffled scientists until the present century, when ecological studies began to clarify the interrelationships and make them meaningful. Living things do not fall into neat categories. Just because a fox is an expert catcher of rabbits and a carnivore does not mean that it goes hungry if rabbits are scarce. A fox is an opportunist with a preference for rabbits, but a liking for mice, insects, and a surprising assortment of plants. It can manage on almost any combination of these and changes its diet according to season, weather, and the shifts in food supply. The fox is just one member of a web of food relations that link the members of every wild community. The more complex the system, the less it changes from year to year. Its stability is the exact opposite of man's monoculture, evolving as it does without guidance of any kind.

Simpler systems are now being examined in which some stress restricts the number of kinds of life in a region. In the arctic and antarctic tundras and high on mountains, close to the snow line, cold weather kills off all but the most hardy species. In deserts, drought is fatal to a majority of living things. In these places, a few species may be abundant but the variety of life is small. The plants and animals present show their adaptive features in coping with the particular stress that gives them privacy. Generally, they cannot cope with additional stresses, such as fires, spilled oil, bulldozers, and well-drilling machinery.

One way of observing the effects of oversimplification is by deliberately setting up a microcosm in a closed jar. Our first attempt at this was during our days in graduate school. Into a gallon container with clear glass walls and tight screw cap we introduced some soil, fresh water, water plants, a small fish, aquatic snails and insects, and then sealed the top. The fish soon died of starvation, without having eaten all of the snails, insects, or vegetation; it decomposed and left no trace. The insects disappeared after two generations. The snails lasted longer, but also vanished. That left the plants, which gradually adjusted until they were in balance with the light they received from the window, the heat that escaped from the jar, and the rate at which bacteria in the water decomposed dead fragments and renewed the supply of dissolved nourishment. Sixteen years later, we returned to the professor's office, where his secretary still kept her eye on the sealed jar. We opened it and found the air inside fresh as a mountain breeze. But, short of investigating with a microscope, we could find no trace of animal life of any kind and not much variety in the surviving vegetation.

It is not farfetched to imagine the world of the not-too-distant future as lacking in animals as our gallon microcosm was after sixteen years. Some purists already have urged replacing all wild areas with a planned combination of farm land and urban centers. They would limit the world deliberately to mankind and his favored kinds of plants and animals as a support system—one that some-day might be replaced with suitable machines. We see very little to look forward to in realizing such a scheme, for no system of man's devising has yet proved completely foolproof and immune to accidents. How vulnerable is man willing to be? Can it be determined beforehand that no planner will ruin the enterprise through a miscalculation, that the power will never go off, that every possible geological force will be provided for? What pleasures could the individual find in such a highly organized existence, for surely the planners would also try to regulate personal life from beginning to end.

The alternative is still open: to conserve complexity by finding a new ethic, a fresh set of values in which no monopoly is claimed over the earth's resources. To do so will not be easy, for the cost will be borne by people, many of whom are poor, are city-dwellers living in cramped quarters far removed from the plants and animals that renew their oxygen supply, provide their food, and recycle their wastes. To help convince all people that conservation of these unseen resources is essential, we feel a special, pressing need to share as widely as possible an awareness of the living world. This anthology will, hopefully, help to reach those for whom the jargon and statistics of the scientists are unpalatable fare. We would like to have more who endorse this belief of Henry David Thoreau's: "This curious world which we inhabit is more wonderful than it is convenient; more beautiful than it is useful; it is more to be admired than to be used."

Part One

IN THE BEGINNING

In the beginning
God created the heaven and the earth. . . . And God saw every thing
that he had made, and, behold, it was very good.

Celebrations of nature
abound in all literatures and may be found as far back as one
wishes to look. For the Romans, as for the Greeks before them,
pastoral poetry was an established genre, and the works of even
earlier cultures were similar in outlook, if less formal. It is safe to
assume that the same was true of oral literature before the invention of writing. The pervasiveness of nature themes in early literature is hardly surprising, of course, for what more potent inspiration
to poetry could be imagined than nature in all its splendor and
mystery? But, though it is impossible to date the origins of nature
literature, we may assume an evolutionary point of view for a
moment and consider the fact that, to celebrate or even to form a
conception of nature, man had first to attain a marked degree of
self-consciousness and thereby to hold himself, in some sense,
apart from the world. We may even risk the speculation that this
very step might well serve to identify the onset of civilization.

Given so venerable a tradition, then, any examination of man's
complex relationship to nature does well to begin with it. This is
all the more so because nature writing itself reflects the range and
complexity of the subject; it can comprise anything from the most
superficial effusions on a bit of scenery to the most profound
ruminations on the meaning of life.

*   *   *

Part I is a collection of what may be called nature writing, miscellaneous (but not random) choices out of a vast field. The first selection, comprising five separate pieces, and the second are English and French and account between them for a relatively long time span. They appear at the beginning mainly in order to avoid the danger of developing a parochial attitude from the heavy emphasis in this book on American materials. Each part, indeed, contains such gentle reminders that, while most of the specific problems and responses discussed are American, they are at the same time a part of general human experience.

Selection 3 introduces the New World through the eyes, appropriately, of Christopher Columbus. The next several selections are principally descriptions by early explorers and settlers of the scenes they encountered in the new land, but in Selection 8 Philip Freneau presents an early example of what, in the hands of Emerson (Selection 17), Thoreau (Selection 19), Muir (Selection 25), Krutch (Selection 31), and others was to become the distinctive style of American nature philosophy. This growth complemented the new discoveries of the period of westward expansion, and through much of Part I reflective passages from nature poetry and philosophy alternate with descriptive writings by explorers who published to the world the wonders of the American land.

The last six selections (34–39) form a separate subsection of their own, one in which, by way of prelude to Part II, some of the same ground and time are covered—in two cases by the same authors—from a slightly different point of view. The difference is rather like that between first impressions and second thoughts and can perhaps be best expressed by the shift in outlook implied by the phrases "nature the beautiful" and "nature the bountiful."

THE UNPLANTED GARDEN

[The five poems that follow span some six centuries of English literature. Each celebrates nature in a somewhat different fashion, but it is not hard to detect the growth of a mood that emerges finally as anguish over the ever increasing distance between civilized man and the world around him.]

I.

SUMER IS ICUMEN IN
[Thirteenth century]

Sumer is icumen in,
　　Lhudè sing cuccu;
Groweth sed and bloweth med
　　And springth the wudè nu.
　　　　Sing cuccu!
Awè bleteth after lomb,
　　Lhouth after calvè cu;
Bulluc sterteth, buckè verteth;
　　Murie sing cuccu.
　　　　Cuccu, cuccu,
　　Wel singès thu, cuccu,
　　Ne swik thu naver nu.
Sing cuccu nu! Sing cuccu!
Sing cuccu! Sing cuccu nu!

Icumen, *come.* Lhudè, *loud.* Sed, *seed.* Med, *mead.* Nu, *now.* Awe, *ewe.* Lhouth, *lows.* Cu, *cow.* Sterteth, *leaps.* Verteth, *breaks wind* (?). Murie, *merry.* Swik, *stop.*

William Shakespeare

UNDER THE GREENWOOD TREE [1600]

Under the greenwood tree
Who loves to lie with me,
And turn his merry note
Unto the sweet bird's throat,
Come hither, come hither, come hither:
Here shall he see
No enemy
But winter and rough weather.

Who doth ambition shun,
And loves to live i' the sun,
Seeking the food he eats,
And pleased with what he gets,
Come hither, come hither, come hither:
Here shall he see
No enemy
But winter and rough weather.

Andrew Marvell

THE GARDEN [ca. 1650]

How vainly men themselves amaze,
To win the palm, the oak, or bays,
And their incessant labors see
Crowned from some single herb or tree
Whose short and narrow-vergèd shade
Does prudently their toils upbraid,
While all the flowers and trees do close
To weave the garlands of repose!

Fair Quiet, have I found thee here,
And Innocence, thy sister dear?
Mistaken long, I sought you then
In busy companies of men.

Your sacred plants, if here below,
Only among the plants will grow;
Society is all but rude
To this delicious solitude.

No white nor red was ever seen
So amorous as this lovely green.
Fond lovers, cruel as their flame,
Cut in these trees their mistress' name.
Little, alas! they know or heed,
How far these beauties hers exceed!
Fair trees! wheres'e'er your bark I wound,
No name shall but your own be found.

When we have run our passion's heat,
Love hither makes his best retreat.
The gods, that mortal beauty chase,
Still in a tree did end their race;
Apollo hunted Daphne so,
Only that she might laurel grow;
And Pan did after Syrinx speed,
Not as a nymph, but for a reed.

What wondrous life is this I lead!
Ripe apples drop about my head;
The luscious clusters of the vine
Upon my mouth do crush their wine;
The nectarine, and curious peach,
Into my hands themselves do reach;
Stumbling on melons, as I pass,
Ensnared with flowers, I fall on grass.

Meanwhile the mind, from pleasure less,
Withdraws into its happiness;—
The mind, that ocean where each kind
Does straight its own resemblance find;
Yet it creates, transcending these,
Far other worlds, and other seas,
Annihilating all that's made
To a green thought in a green shade.

Here at the fountain's sliding foot,
Or at some fruit-tree's mossy root,
Casting the body's vest aside,
My soul into the boughs does glide:
There, like a bird, it sits and sings,
Then whets and combs its silver wings,
And, till prepared for longer flight,
Waves in its plumes the various light.

Such was that happy garden-state,
While man there walked without a mate:
After a place so pure and sweet,
What other help could yet be meet!
But 'twas beyond a mortal's share
To wander solitary there:
Two paradises 'twere in one,
To live in paradise alone.

How well the skillful gardener drew
Of flowers, and herbs, this dial new;
Where, from above, the milder sun
Does through a fragrant zodiac run,
And, as it works, the industrious bee
Computes its time as well as we!
How could such sweet and wholesome hours
Be reckoned but with herbs and flowers?

Alexander Pope

ODE ON SOLITUDE [ca. 1700]

Happy the man whose wish and care
    A few paternal acres bound,
Content to breathe his native air
    In his own ground.

Whose herds with milk, whose fields with bread,
    Whose flocks supply him with attire,
Whose trees in summer yield him shade,
    In winter fire.

Bless'd who can unconcern'dly find
    Hours, days, and years slide soft away,
In health of body, peace of mind,
    Quiet by day;

Sound sleep by night: study and ease
    Together mix'd; sweet recreation;
And innocence, which most does please,
    With Meditation.

Thus let me live, unseen, unknown,
   Thus unlamented let me die;
Steal from the world, and not a stone
   Tell where I lie.

William Wordsworth

THE WORLD IS TOO MUCH WITH US [1806]

The world is too much with us: late and soon,
Getting and spending, we lay waste our powers:
Little we see in Nature that is ours;
We have given our hearts away, a sordid boon!
This Sea that bares her bosom to the moon;
The winds that will be howling at all hours,
And are up-gathered now like sleeping flowers;
For this, for everything, we are out of tune;
It moves us not.—Great God! I'd rather be
A Pagan suckled in a creed outworn;
So might I, standing on this pleasant lea,
Have glimpses that would make me less forlorn;
Have sight of Proteus rising from the sea;
Or hear old Triton blow his wreathèd horn.

2.

Jean Jacques Rousseau

THE FALL FROM NATURE [1755]

[The nature celebrated
in pastoral poetry is that of the countryside rather than the wilderness. Benign and domesticated, it is a place of deep, quiet joy for
those who dwell there and a place of escape and refreshment for
those who do not. The idea of escaping or returning to nature was
one of the dominant themes of the period of the romantic movement in the arts, a period whose rapid growth of commerce and
urbanism repelled many. A closely allied theme was the revival of

the notion of a "Golden Age" in history, when there was as yet no gulf between man and nature.]

So long as men remained content with their rustic huts, so long as they were satisfied with clothes made of the skins of animals and sewn together with thorns and fish-bones, adorned themselves only with feathers and shells, and continued to paint their bodies different colours, to improve and beautify their bows and arrows and to make with sharp-edged stones fishing boats or clumsy musical instruments; in a word, so long as they undertook only what a single person could accomplish, and confined themselves to such arts as did not require the joint labour of several hands, they lived free, healthy, honest and happy lives, so long as their nature allowed, and as they continued to enjoy the pleasures of mutual and independent intercourse. But from the moment one man began to stand in need of the help of another; from the moment it appeared advantageous to any one man to have enough provisions for two, equality disappeared, property was introduced, work became indispensable, and vast forests became smiling fields, which man had to water with the sweat of his brow, and where slavery and misery were soon seen to germinate and grow up with the crops.

Metallurgy and agriculture were the two arts which produced this great revolution. The poets tell us it was gold and silver, but, for the philosophers, it was iron and corn, which first civilised men, and ruined humanity.

3.

Christopher Columbus

LETTER TO LORD RAPHAEL SANCHEZ [1493]

[Columbus's discovery of America was a consequence of both the renewal of intellectual vitality and daring of the Renaissance and the parallel growth of world commerce. Seeking a trade route to an established market, he never quite reconciled himself to having found instead a New World that seemed to him rather less useful. He was, nonetheless, sensitive to the natural beauty of the islands he visited. The explorers and finally settlers who followed him during the next several centuries were similarly struck by the bounty of nature in the new land and particularly by its untamed and unspoiled aspect.]

This said island of Juana is exceedingly fertile, as indeed are all the others; it is surrounded with many bays, spacious, very secure, and surpassing any that I have ever seen; numerous large and healthful rivers intersect it, and it also contains many very lofty mountains. All these islands are very beautiful, and distinguished by a diversity of scenery; they are filled with a great variety of trees of immense height, and which I believe to retain their foliage in all seasons; for when I saw them they were as verdant and luxuriant as they usually are in Spain in the month of May, some of them were blossoming, some bearing fruit, and all flourishing in the greatest perfection, according to their respective stages of growth, and the nature and quality of each: yet the islands are not so thickly wooded as to be impassable. The nightingale and various birds were singing in countless numbers, and that in November, the month in which I arrived there. There are besides, in the same island of Juana, seven or eight kinds of palm trees, which, like all the other trees, herbs, and fruits, considerably surpass ours in height and beauty. The pines also are very handsome, and there are very extensive fields and meadows, a variety of birds, different kinds of honey, and many sorts of metals, but no iron. In that island also which I have before said we named Española, there are mountains of very great size and beauty, vast plains, groves, and very fruitful fields, admirably adapted for tillage, pasture, and habitation. The convenience and excellence of the harbours in this island, and the abundance of the rivers, so indispensable to the health of man, surpass anything that would be believed by one who had not seen it.

4.

John Sparke

THE SECOND VOYAGE OF JOHN HAWKINS [1565]

[Late in 1564, the great English admiral John Hawkins sailed from Plymouth for the West Indies on a trading and exploring expedition. The summer of the following year found him in Florida, which he mistook for an island. Among the men accompanying Hawkins was John Sparke, who wrote the following account of the voyage. Although the commercial opportunities presented by the New World were never far from his mind, Sparke's imagination was clearly stirred by the land itself, and his description of the wildlife of Florida sometimes strayed to the fanciful.]

The commodities of this land are more then are yet knowne to any man: for besides the land itselfe, whereof there is more then any king Christian is able to inhabit, it flourisheth with medow, pasture ground, with woods of cedar and cypres, and other sorts, as better cannot be in the world, they have for apothicary herbes, trees, roots and gumme great store, as Storax liquide, Turpintine, Gumme, Myrre and Frankinsense, with many others, whereof I know not the names. Coulers both red, black, yellow, and russet, very perfect, wherewith they [the Indians] paint their bodies, and deere skinnes which they weare about them, that with water it neither fadeth away, nor altereth couler.

.   .   .   .

Of beastes in this country, besides Deere, Foxes, Hares, Pollcats, Cunnies, Ownces, Leopards, I am not able certainely to say: but it is thought that there are Lions and Tygers as well as Unicornes, Lions especially, if it bee true that it is said of the enmity betweene them and the Unicornes. For there is no beast but hath his enemy, as the Cunny the Polcat, a Sheepe the Wolfe, the Elephant the Rinoceros, and so of other beasts the like: insomuch, that whereas the one is the other can not be missing. And seeing I haue made mention of the beastes of this Countrey, it shal not be from my purpose to speak also of the venomous beastes, as Crocodiles, whereof there is a great abundance, Adders of great bignesse, wherrof our men killed some of a yard and a halfe longe. Also I heard a miracle of one of these adders, vpon which a Faulcon seazing, the saide adder did clasp her taile about her, which the French Captaine seeing, came to the rescue of the faulcon, and tooke her slaying the adder, and this faulcon being wilde hee did reclaime her, and kept her for the space of 2. months, at which time for very want of meat he was faine to cast her off. On these adders the Frenchmen did feede to no litle admiration of vs, and affirmed the same to be a delicate meate. And the Captaine of the Frenchmen saw also a Serpent with 3. heads and 4. feete, of the bignesse of a great Spaniell, which for want of a harquebusse he durst not attempt to slay. Of the fishe also they haue in the riuer, pike, roche, salmon, troute, and diuers other small fishes, and of a great fish, some of the length of a man and longer, being of bignesse accordingly, hauing a snoute much like a sworde of a yard long. There be also of sea fishes which wee sawe comming along the coast flying, which are of the bignesse of a smelt, the biggest sorte whereof haue four winges, but the other haue but two. Of these we sawe comming out of Guinea, a hundreth in a companie, which being chased by the Gilt heads, otherwise called the Bonitoes, doe to auoide them the better take their flight out of the water, but yet are they not able to flie farre, because of the drying of their winges, which serue them not to flye but when they are moyste, and therefore when they can flye no further fall into the water, and hauing wette their winges take a newe flight againe. These Bonitoes be of bignesse like a carpe, and in colour like a mackarell, but it is the swiftest fish in swimming that is, and followeth her praye very fiercely not onely in the water, but also out of the water: for as the flying fish taketh her flight, so doeth this Bonitoe leape after them, and taketh them sometime aboue the water. They were some of those Bonitoes, which being galled by a fisgig did follow our ship comming out of Guinea 500. leagues.

There is a sea foule also that chaseth this flying fish as wel as the Bonito: for as the flying fish taketh her flight, so doth this foule pursue to take her, which to beholde is a greater pleasure then hauking, for both the flights are as pleasant, and also more often then 100. times: for the foule can flie no way but one or other lighteth in her pawes, the nomber of them are so abundant. There is an innumerable yonge frie of these flying fishes which commonly keepe about the shippe, and are not so big as butterflies, and yet by flying doe auoyde the vnsatiablenesse of the Bonito. Of the bigger sort of these fishes, we tooke many, which both night and day flew into the sailes of our shippe, and there was not one of them which was not worth a Bonito: for being put vpon a hooke drabling in the water, the Bonito would leape thereat, and so was taken. Also; we tooke many with a white clothe made fast to a hooke, which being tied so short in the water, that it might leape out, and in, the greedie Bonito thinking it to be a flying fish leapeth thereat, and is deceiued. Wee tooke also Dolphins, which are of very goodly colour and proportion to beholde, and no lesse delicate in taste. Foules also there be many, both vpon lande and vpon sea. But concerning them on the land I am not able to name them, because my abode was there so short. But for the foule of the fresh riuers, these two I noted to be the chiefe, whereof the Flemengo is one, hauing all redde fethers, and long redde legs like a Herne, a necke according to the bill redde, whereof the vpper nebbe hangeth an inche ouer the nether. And an Egripte which is all white as the swanne, with legges like to an hearneshewe, and of bignesse accordingly, but it hath in her taile feathers of so fine a plume, that it passeth the Estridge his feather. Of sea foule aboue all other not common in Englande, I noted the Pellicane, which is faigned to be the louingest birds that is:

which rather then her yong shoulde want, will spare her heart
bloud out of her bellie, but for all this louingness she is very deformed to beholde, for shee is of colour russet, notwithstanding in
Guinea I have seene of them as white as a swanne, hauing legges
like the same, and a body like the Herne, with a long necke, and
a thicke long beake, from the nether iawe whereof downe to the
breast passeth a skinne of such a bignesse, asisable to receive a
fishe as bigge as ones thigh, and this her bigge throat and long bill
doeth make her seeme so ougly.

Here I haue declared the estate of Florida, and the commodoties
therein to this day knowen, which although it may seeme vnto
some, by the meanes that the plentie of Golde and Siluer is not
so abundant, as in other places, that the cost bestowed vpon the
same, will not bee able to quite the charges: yet am I of the
opinion that by that which I haue seene in other Islandes of the
Indians, where such increase of cattell hath been that of twelue
head of beasts in 25. yeeres, did in the hides of them raise 1000.
pound profite yeerely, that the increase of cattell onely would raise
profite sufficient for the same. For wee may consider, if so small
a portion did raise so much gaines in such a short time, what
would a greater doe in many yeeres. And surely I may this affirme,
that the ground of the Indians for the breed of cattell, is not in
any point to be compared to this of Florida, which all the yeere
long is so greene, as any time in the Sommer with vs: which surely
is not to be marueiled at, seeing the Countrey standeth in so watrie
a climate: for once a day withoute faile, they haue a showre of
raine. Which by meanes of the Countrey it selfe, which is drie, and
more feruent hot then ours, doeth make all things to flourish
therein, and because there is not the thing wee all seeke for, being
rather desirous of present gaines, I do therefore affirme the attempt thereof to be more requisite for a prince, who is of power
able to goe thorow with the same, rather than for any subject.

5.

Edward Williams

VIRGINIA [1650]

[By 1650, several
colonies were firmly established along the North American coast
and enthusiastic colonists were eager for more settlers to join them.

The book from which the following selection originates was published in London as an advertisement of the attractions of Virginia.]

The scituation and Climate of *Virginia* is the Subject of every Map, to which I shall refer the curiosity of those who desire more particular information.

Yet to shew that Nature regards this Ornament of the new world with a more indulgent eye then she hath cast upon many other Countreys, whatever *China, Persia, Japan, Cyprus, Candy, Sicily, Greece,* the South of *Italy, Spaine,* and the opposite parts of *Africa,* to all which she is parallel, may boast of, will be produced in this happy Country. The same bounty of Summer, the same milde remission of Winter, with a more virgin and unexhausted soyle being materiall arguments to shew that modesty and truth receive no diminution by the comparison.

Nor is the present wildnesse of it without a particular beauty, being all over a naturall Grove of Oakes, Pines, Cedars, Cipresse, Mulberry, Chestnut, Laurell, Sassafras, Cherry, Plumtrees, and Vines, all of so delectable an aspect, that the melanchollyest eye in the World cannot look upon it without contentment, nor content himselfe without admiration. No shrubs or underwoods choake up your passage, and in its season your foot can hardly direct it selfe where it will not be died in the bloud of large and delicious Strawberries: The Rivers which every way glide in deepe and Navigable Channels, betwixt the brests of this uberous Countrey, and contribute to its conveniency beauty and fertility, labour with the multitude of their fishy inhabitants in greater variety of species, and of a more incomparable delicacy in tast and sweetnesse then whatever the European Sea can boast of: Sturgeon of ten feet, Drummes of sixe in length; Conger, Eeles, Trout, Salmon, Bret, Mullet, Cod, Herings, Perch, Lampreyes, and what ever else can be desired to the satisfaction of the most voluptuous wishes.

Nor is the Land any lesse provided of native Flesh, Elkes bigger then Oxen, whose hide is admirable Buffe, flesh excellent, and may be made, if kept domesticke, as usefull for draught and carriage, as Oxen. Deere in a numerous abundance, and delicate Venison, Racoones, Hares, Conyes, Bevers, Squirrell, Beares, all of a delightfull nourishment for food, and their Furres rich, warme, and convenient for clothing and Merchandise.

That no part of this happy Country may bee ungratefull to the Industrious, The ayre it selfe is often clouded with flights of Pigeons, Partriges, Blackbirds, Thrushes, Dottrels, Cranes, Hernes, Swans, Geese, Brants, Duckes, Widgeons, Oxeyes, infinites of wilde Turkeyes, which have been knowne to weigh fifty pound weight, ordinarily forty.

. . . .

Those who have travelled and viewed *Persia*, unanimously relate wonders of her admirable fertility in all sorts of Graine and Fruits, with an unexpressible abundance of Silke and Wines: In which this her rich-bosomed Sister claimes an equality in her plenty of Mulberries, Silke, and Gums, Vines, Maiz, Rice, and all sorts of Graine: onely as a fuller-dowryed Sister she merits a priority in fertility, pleasure, health, and temperature, a Virgin Countrey, so preserved by Nature out of a desire to show mankinde fallen into the Old age of the Creation, what a brow of fertility and beauty she was adorned with when the World was vigorous and youthfull, and she her selfe was unwounded with the Plough-shares, and unweakened by her numerous future teemings.

6.

Thomas Pownall

BLUE RIDGE [1784]

The individual Trees of those Woods grow up, have their Youth, their old Age, and a Period to their Life, and die as we Men do: You will see many a Sapling growing up, many an old Tree tottering to its Fall, and many fallen and rotting away, while they are succeeded by others of their Kind, just as the Race of Man is: By this Succession of Vegetation this Wilderness is kept cloathed with Woods just as the human Species keeps the Earth peopled by its continuing Succession of Generations. As it happens to Man in the Course of Fate that sometimes epidemic Distempers, Deluges, or Famine have swept whole Nations off at once, so here, by a like Fate, Epidemic Distempers, to which even the Forests are liable, have destroyed whole Tracts of Woods at once. Deluges in the Vallies, Fire & Hurricanes on the mountains have also in their course often done the same. Wherever this at any Time hath happened, one sees a new Generation bearing all the Appearance of an European new Plantation growing up. If the Soil has suffered no great Change, Woods of the same Genus arise; if it hath undergone any Change, either for the better or for the worse, then, as from a Nidus prepared for a new Brood, we see Woods of a different Species, which before appeared rarely, and as Aliens in the Place, now from a new power of Vegetation, springing up and possessing the Land as the predominant Wood.

If here I should attempt to describe the Colouring of these Woods, I should be at a Loss what Season of the Year to choose, whether the sober Harmony of Greens that the Woods in all their various Tints give in Summer; or whether the flaunting Blush of Spring, when the Woods glow with a thousand Tints that the flowering Trees and Shrubs throw out. If I should persuade the Painter to attempt the giving a real and strict Portrait of these Woods in Autumn, he must mix in upon his Canvass all the Colours of the Rainbow, in order to copy the various and varied Dyes which the Leaves at the Fall assume: The Red, the Scarlet, the bright and the deep Yellow, the warm Brown, the White which he must use, would give a prismatic motley Patch-work that the Eye would turn away from, and that the Judgement would not bear; and yet the Woods in this embroidered Garb have in real Nature a Richness of Appearance beyond Conception. But this is not the only Instance, there are many which I, who have used myself to draw from Nature, have observed, wherein Nature will not bear a Portrait, and wherein she is never less imitated than when she is attempted to be literally copied.

. . . .

The Vales between the Ridges of these Mountains have all one and the same general Appearance, that of an Amphitheatre enclosing, as it were, an Ocean of Woods swelled and depressed with a waving Surface like that of the great Ocean itself: Though the Ridges of the Mountains run, as I have said, in nearly parallel Lines, yet at Times, by the Means of Branchings and Spurs of Mountains, they every here and there seem to close, and where they do so, the Land of the Vale also rises in irregular hilly Land, which is the Circumstance that gives this general Appearance of an Amphitheatre to these Vales, when from any of the Mountains above one looks down into them. If the Spectator hath gotten a Stand on some high Mountain so as to look across any Number of the Ridges which may be less high than that he stands on, he then sees a repeated Succession of Blue and Purple parallel waving Lines behind each other, with here and there a Breaking-off or Gap in them; here and there sudden Endings of them in perpendicular bluff Points and Knobs, as they are by the People called; and here and there high elevated Peaks; all which, together with the general Direction of the Ridges, are Points which mark the Geography of the Country to the Indians, and even in a very sufficient practical Way the general Bearings to the Geographical Surveyor.

. . . .

As the general, and I had almost said, the only Way of travelling this Country in its natural State is by the Rivers and Lakes, the Portages or Carrying-places from one Water to another, or along the Shores where the Navigation is obstructed by Rifts or Falls in the same River, are particularly and pretty exactly marked and set down. The general Face of the Country, when one travels it along the Rivers through Parts not yet settled, exhibits the most picturesque Landscapes that Imagination can conceive, in a Variety of the noblest, richest Groupes of Wood, Water, and Mountains. As the Eye is lead on from Reach to Reach, at each Turning of the Courses, the Imagination is in a perpetual Alternative of curious Suspense and new Delight, not knowing at any Point, and not being able to discover where the Way is to open next, until it does open and captivates like Enchantment.

      Ignotas tentare Vias, atque inter opacum
        Allabi nemus——
      Olli Remigio Noctemque Diemque fatigant,
        Et longos superant Flexus, variisque teguntur,
      Arboribus, viridasque secant placido Æquore Sylvas.

But while the Eye is thus catching new Pleasures from the Landscape, with what an overflowing Joy does the Heart melt while one views the Banks where rising Farms, new Fields, or flowering Orchards begin to illuminate this Face of Nature; nothing can be more delightful to the Eye, nothing go with more penetrating Sensation to the Heart. To any one that has the Habit of Drawing from Nature, the making Sketches of these picturesque Scenes would be ample Employment: Some are so astonishingly great, that none but those who have made the Trial know how difficult it is to bring up the Scale of the ordinary Objects to this, which is (as it were) beyond the Garb of Nature.

7.

Thomas Jefferson

THE POTOMAC AND NATURAL BRIDGE [1781]

                          The passage of the Potomac through the Blue Ridge is, perhaps, one of the most stupendous scenes in nature. You stand on a very high point of land. On your right comes up the Shenandoah, having ranged along the foot of the mountain an hundred miles to seek a vent. On your left approaches the Potomac, in quest of a passage also. In the moment of their junction, they rush together against the mountain, rend it asunder, and pass off to the sea. The first glance of this scene hurries our senses into the opinion, that this earth has been

created in time, that the mountains were formed first, that the
rivers began to flow afterwards, that in this place, particularly,
they have been dammed up by the Blue Ridge of mountains, and
have formed an ocean which filled the whole valley; that continuing to rise they have at length broken over this spot, and have
torn the mountain down from its summit to its base. The piles of
rock on each hand, but particularly on the Shenandoah, the evident
marks of their disrupture and avulsion from their beds by the
most powerful agents of nature, corroborate the impression. But
the distant finishing which nature has given to the picture, is of
a very different character. It is a true contrast to the foreground.
It is as placid and delightful as that is wild and tremendous. For
the mountain being cloven asunder, she presents to your eye,
through the cleft, a small catch of smooth blue horizon, at an infinite distance in the plain country, inviting you, as it were, from
the riot and tumult roaring around, to pass through the breach
and participate of the calm below. Here the eye ultimately com-
poses itself; and that way, too, the road happens actually to lead.
You cross the Potomac above the junction, pass along its side
through the base of the mountain for three miles, its terrible
precipices hanging in fragments over you, and within about twenty
miles reach Fredericktown, and the fine country round that. This
scene is worth a voyage across the Atlantic.

. . . .

The *Natural Bridge*, the most sublime of nature's works, though
not comprehended under the present head, must not be pretermit-
ted. It is on the ascent of a hill, which seems to have been cloven
through its length by some great convulsion. The fissure, just at
the bridge, is, by some admeasurements, two hundred and seventy
feet deep, by others only two hundred and five. It is about forty-
five feet wide at the bottom and ninety feet at the top; this of
course determines the length of the bridge, and its height from the
water. Its breadth in the middle is about sixty feet, but more at
the ends, and the thickness of the mass, at the summit of the arch,
about forty feet. A part of this thickness is constituted by a coat
of earth, which gives growth to many large trees, The residue, with
the hill on both sides, is one solid rock of lime-stone. The arch approaches the semi-elliptical form; but the larger axis of the ellipsis,
which would be the cord of the arch, is many times longer than
the transverse. Though the sides of this bridge are provided in
some parts with a parapet of fixed rocks, yet few men have resolution to walk to them, and look over into the abyss. You involun-
tarily fall on your hands and feet, creep to the parapet, and peep
over it. Looking down from this height about a minute, gave me a
violent head-ache. If the view from the top be painful and intolerable, that from below is delightful in an equal extreme. It is impossible for the emotions arising from the sublime to be felt beyond what they are here; so beautiful an arch, so elevated, so light,

and springing as it were up to heaven! the rapture of the spectator is really indescribable!

[After the first flush of excitement over the prospect of a new and inviting land died down, the American colonists set about the hard work of gaining a livelihood. Unspoiled nature was all very well, but, Golden Age myths notwithstanding, transplanted Europeans were determined to re-create the patterns and amenities of life as they had known it. Not until a certain degree of stability and civility had been achieved did the Americans have leisure to contemplate their surroundings. The gradual evolution of specifically American institutions, capped by the Revolutionary War, gave a marked nationalistic tone to their reflections on nature.]

8.

Philip Freneau

THE PHILOSOPHER OF THE FOREST [1781–82]

[Poet, essayist, and editor, Philip Freneau was an intensely patriotic man whose early writings won him the title of "poet of the Revolution." The selections below are from *The Philosopher of the Forest*, a series of essays originally published in the *Philadelphia Freemen's Journal;* the autobiographical material in the first is fictional.]

I drew my first breath upon the borders of Switzerland, on the south side, and within view of that stupendous range of mountains known by the name of *Jura*. Here, in a solitary valley, my ancestors had for many ages taken up their abode, having, as I have been told, ever supported the character of plain, industrious people, who were acquainted with no other than the rural life; perhaps

nearly resembling that so much celebrated in the early ages of innocence and rustic simplicity.

. . . .

A beautiful grove of ancient oaks had grown and flourished for
many centuries adjoining my before mentioned progenitor's little
estate, which he held in fee simple. His farm-house was situated almost under the shade of these oaks, but, unfortunately, the soil they
grew upon belonged to another person, residing in a neighbouring
canton, who now took it into his head to have the whole forest cut
down, and the land cleared for the purposes of agriculture.—From
the earliest days of my childhood I had experienced the most lively
emotions of pleasure in rambling uncontrouled and at full liberty,
among these venerable shades; I had therefore conceived an unspeakable affection for this tall and delightful grove, and heard the
sound of the fatal ax with the most painful sensations of grief; and
had a favourite nymph or hamadryad of the forest (according to the
opinion of the ancients) resided in every tree, I could not have
been more sensibly afflicted.—All my endeavours to dissuade the
proprietor of these trees from his fatal resolution, proved vain. He
obstinately persisted therein, calling me, at the same time, fool
and madman for repining *at the advantages of so enlarged a prospect*. The days of my felicity were, therefore, now at an end. Gloomy
thoughts took possession of my soul, and I soon formed a design
of quitting my native land forever, and retiring to some other part
of the world.

WHAT soon after confirmed me in my purpose, was the additional mortifying circumstance of his erecting a large stone building within two hundred paces of our old and venerable habitation,
which he peopled with a set of animals, whose humour, sentiments
and conversation were, in every respect, diametrically opposite to,
and engaged upon different objects from my own.

LABOURING under such accumulated misfortunes, which I con-
fess, notwithstanding, will appear to most men to be little better
than imaginary, I soon disposed of my paternal inheritance, and
with a dejected heart and a tearful eye, took my leave of it forever.
—The charming solitude and privacy that was wont to reign
through this delightful haunt, was now lost and vanished. It was
no longer sheltered from the bleak north-east wind. It was laid
open to the view of the adjacent country, and crowds of travellers
—a misfortune indeed; as rural quiet and unobserved retirement
were ever the darling objects of my soul. There is something in
woods and solitudes congenial with my nature—it was in these the
VISIBLE DEITY took leave of man when he left him to the mercy
of the elements, and to the vanity of his own inventions; and it is
in these that I conceive the mind still finds itself in the best humour to contemplate, in silent admiration, the great and inexhaustible source of all things. Towns and palaces are my abhorrence, and
if at any time I have found it necessary to reside in great cities

(as I once did in Moscow in Russia, for more than six months)
still, by intervals I retired to the forests, and conversed with the
simple genius of the wilderness—a conversation I infinitely prefer
to that of heroes, kings, statesmen, or philosophers themselves.

. . . .

When nature first brought forth her infant, the American world,
to enjoy the blessings and vivifying influences of the new created
sun, as if conscious of the injuries this part of her creation was to
suffer in future ages, she seemed particularly industrious, she took
especial care to plant it in such a situation that many hundreds
of centuries, an immense number of years must elapse, before it
could possibly be discovered by the greedy natives of the eastern
continent.

"Till more than five thousand years have passed away (said
she) it shall be inaccessible to all, except a few tribes of wandering
Tartars, who from time to time may find their way thither by
accident; literally *the children of nature,* wild as the wind and
waves, and free as the animals that wander in the woody or the
watry waste. The magnet alone, continued she, shall enable the
polished people of the eastern regions to discover and ravage the
delectable lands I have formed in the opposite hemisphere; but
that fossil, the invaluable loadstone, I will bury deep in the earth,
unobserved its wonderful properties, till destiny and over-ruling
fate, whose decrees no one can obviate, to my extremest grief,
shall disclose it to the eye of avarice, ambition, and scrutinizing
curiosity, and prompt a bold and daring *Columbus* to go in quest
of those shores which it will not be in my power any longer to
conceal."

So spoke NATURE, the mother of all men, and all things. In the
mean time ages rolled away: the old world was peopled, un-
peopled, and peopled again. Nations grew and flourished: they
quarrelled, they fought, and made peace: the *four great mon-
archies* succeeded each other, and fell again into decay, with their
emperors, kings and heroes, by far less durable than the lifeless
marble columns which to this day mark the spot where their
proudest capitals stood, or where their most famous battles were
fought. These nations had their ages of politeness and barbarism,
ignorance and science, misery and felicity: the follies of one age
were acted over again by another, and each retired in its turn to
the receptacles of silence, solitude and darkness, to make room for
succeeding generations.

But still America lay unknown and undiscovered, with all her
islands, lakes, mountains, woods, plains, capacious harbours and
extended shores. Here the fish sported in the waters, undisturbed
by hooks or acts, and the beasts of the forest enjoyed a secure
repose. The poets of the eastern world were in the mean time
amusing their iron hearted contemporaries with the fictions of a
golden age; their fabulous Arcadias and Saturnian kingdoms; the

ideas and actions of which must have owed their existence to the
magic power of fancy alone, as they were wholly ignorant that
the happy scenes, the innocent people and pastoral ages, of which
they sang, were at that moment realizing in another quarter of
the globe, as yet unexplored and unknown.

. . . .

My friend, the clergyman, informs me, that after passing a ridge
of lofty mountains extending on the western frontiers of these re-
publics, a new and most enchanting region opens, of inexpressible
beauty and fertility. The lands are *there* of a quality far superior
to those situated in the neighbourhood of the sea coast: the trees
of the forest are stately and tall, the meadows and pastures spacious, supporting vast herds of the native animals of the country;
which own no master, nor expect their sustenance from the hands
of men. The climate, he says, is moderate and agreeable; there the
rivers no longer bend their courses eastward to the Atlantic, but
inclining to the west and south, and moving with a gentle current
through the channels that Nature has opened, fall at length into
that grand repository of a thousand streams, *Mississippi*, who collecting his waters, derived from a source remote and unknown, rolls
onward through the frozen regions of the north, and stretching
his prodigiously extended arms to the east and west, embraces
those savage groves and dreary solitudes, as yet uninvestigated by
the traveller, unsang by the poet, and unmeasured by the chain of
the geometrician; till uniting with the *Ohio* and turning due south,
receiving afterwards the *Missouri* and a hundred others, this prince
of rivers, in comparison of whom the *Nile* is but a small rivulet,
and the *Danube* a ditch, hurries with his immense flood of waters
into the Mexican sea, laving the shores of many fertile countries
in his passage, inhabited by savage nations to this day almost unknown and without a name.

9.

Philip Freneau

THE INDIAN STUDENT [1788]

[A corollary to the
myth of the Golden Age was the idea of the Noble Savage who lived
in close and constant communion with nature and was thereby

morally superior to, and philosophically wiser than, the man cor-
rupted by civilization. Rousseau and others of his turn of mind
delightedly seized upon the American Indian as the epitome of the
Noble Savage.]

From Susquehanna's farthest springs
Where savage tribes pursue their game,
(His blanket tied with yellow strings,)
A shepherd of the forest came.

Not long before, a wandering priest
Expressed his wish, with visage sad—
'Ah, why (he cried) in Satan's waste,
'Ah, why detain so fine a lad?

'In white-man's land there stands a town
'Where learning may be purchased low—
'Exchange his blanket for a gown,
'And let the lad to college go.'—

From long debate the council rose,
And viewing Shalum's tricks with joy
To Cambridge Hall, o'er wastes of snows,
They sent the copper-coloured boy.

One generous chief a bow supplied,
This gave a shaft, and that a skin;
The feathers, in vermillion dyed,
Himself did from a turkey win:

Thus dressed so gay, he took his way
O'er barren hills, alone, alone!
His guide a star, he wandered far,
His pillow every night a stone.

At last he came, with foot so lame,
Where learned men talk heathen Greek,
And Hebrew lore is gabbled o'er,
To please the Muses,—twice a week.

Awhile he writ, awhile he read,
Awhile he conned their grammar rules—
(An Indian savage so well bred
Great credit promised to the schools.)

Some thought he would in law excel,

Some said in physic he would shine;
And one that knew him, passing well,
Beheld, in him, a sound Divine.

But those of more discerning eye
Even then could other prospects show,
And saw him lay his Virgil by
To wander with his dearer bow.

The tedious hours of study spent,
The heavy-moulded lecture done,
He to the woods a hunting went,
Through lonely wastes he walked, he run.

No mystic wonders fired his mind;
He sought to gain no learned degree,
But only sense enough to find
The squirrel in the hollow tree.

The shady bank, the purling stream,
The woody wild his heart possessed,
The dewy lawn, his morning dream
In fancy's gayest colours dressed.

'And why (he cried) did I forsake
'My native wood for gloomy walls;
'The silver stream, the limpid lake
'For musty books and college halls.

'A little could my wants supply—
'Can wealth and honour give me more;
'Or, will the sylvan god deny
'The humble treat he gave before?

'Let seraphs gain the bright abode,
'And heaven's sublimest mansions see—
'I only bow to Nature's God—
'The land of shades will do for me.

'These dreadful secrets of the sky
'Alarm my soul with chilling fear—
'Do planets in their orbits fly,
'And is the earth, indeed, a sphere?

'Let planets still their course pursue,
'And comets to the centre run—
'In Him my faithful friend I view,
'The image of my God—the Sun.

'Where Nature's ancient forests grow,
'And mingled laurel never fades,
'My heart is fixed;—and I must go
'To die among my native shades.'

He spoke, and to the western springs,
(His gown discharged, his money spent,
His blanket tied with yellow strings,)
The shepherd of the forest went.

10.

William Bartram [1791]

[One of the foremost botanists of his time, William Bartram spent the years 1773–77 exploring the wilderness of Georgia, Florida and the Carolinas. His elaborated field notes, published in 1791, won the admiration of scientists throughout the world, and his felicitous literary style received favorable attention from Wordsworth and Coleridge.]

The Indian not returning this morning, I set sail alone. The coasts on each side had much the same appearance as already described. The Palm trees here seem to be of a different species from the Cabbage tree; their strait trunks are sixty, eighty or ninety feet high, with a beautiful taper of a bright ash colour, until within six or seven feet of the top, where it is a fine green colour, crowned with an orb of rich green plumed leaves: I have measured the stem of these plumes fifteen feet in length, besides the plume, which is nearly of the same length.

The little lake, which is an expansion of the river, now appeared in view; on the East side are extensive marshes, and on the other high forests and Orange groves, and then a bay, lined with vast Cypress swamps, both coasts gradually approaching each other, to the opening of the river again, which is in this place about three hundred yards wide; evening now drawing on, I was anxious to reach some high bank of the river, where I intended to lodge, and agreeably to my wishes, I soon after discovered on the West shore, a little promontory, at the turning of the river, contracting it here to about one hundred and fifty yards in width. This promontory is a peninsula, containing about three acres of high ground, and is one entire Orange grove, with a few Live Oaks, Magnolias and

Palms. Upon doubling the point, I arrived at the landing, which is a circular harbour, at the foot of the bluff, the top of which is about twelve feet high; and back of it is a large Cypress swamp, that spreads each way, the right wing forming the West coast of the little lake, and the left stretching up the river many miles, and encompassing a vast space of low grassy marshes. From this promontory, looking Eastward across the river, we behold a landscape of low country, unparalleled as I think; on the left is the East coast of the little lake, which I had just passed, and from the Orange bluff at the lower end, the high forests begin, and increase in breadth from the shore of the lake, making a circular sweep to the right, and contain many hundred thousand acres of meadow, and this grand sweep of high forests encircles, as I apprehend, at least twenty miles of these green fields, interspersed with hommocks or islets of evergreen trees, where the sovereign Magnolia and lordly Palm stand conspicuous. The islets are high shelly knolls, on the sides of creeks or branches of the river, which wind about and drain off the super-abundant waters that cover these meadows, during the winter season.

. . . .

How harmonious and soothing is this native sylvan music now at still evening! inexpressibly tender are the responsive cooings of the innocent dove, in the fragrant Zanthoxilon groves, and the variable and tuneful warblings of the nonparel; with the more sprightly and elevated strains of the blue linnet and golden icterus; this is indeed harmony even amidst the incessant croaking of the frogs; the shades of silent night are made more chearful, with the shrill voice of the whip-poor-will and active mock-bird.

My situation high and airy, a brisk and cool breeze steadily and incessantly passing over the clear waters of the lake, and fluttering over me through the surrounding groves, wings its way to the moonlight savannas, while I repose on my sweet and healthy couch of the soft Tillandsi ulnea-adscites, and the latter gloomy and still hours of night passed rapidly away as it were in a moment; I arose, strengthened and chearful, in the morning. Having some repairs to make in the tackle of my vessel, I paid my first attention to them; which being accomplished, my curiosity prompted me to penetrate the grove and view the illumined plains.

What a beautiful display of vegetation is here before me! seemingly unlimited in extent and variety; how the dew-drops twinkle and play upon the sight, trembling on the tips of the lucid, green savanna, sparkling as the gem that flames on the turban of the Eastern prince; see the pearly tears rolling off the buds of the expanding Granadilla; behold the azure fields of cerulean Ixea! what can equal the rich golden flowers of the Cana lutea, which ornament the banks of yon serpentine rivulet, meandering over the meadows; the almost endless varieties of the gay Phlox, that enamel the swelling green banks, associated with the purple Verbena corymbosa, Viola, pearly Gnaphalium, and silvery Perdicium; how fantastical looks the libertine Clitoria, mantling the shrubs, on the vistas skirting the groves. My morning excursion finished, I returned to the camp, breakfasted, then went on board my boat, and gently descended the noble river and passed by several openings of extensive plains and meadows, environing the East Lake, charming beyond compare; at evening I came to at a good harbour, under the high banks of the river, and rested during the night, amidst the fragrant groves, exposed to the constant breezes from the river: here I made ample collections of specimens and growing roots of curious vegetables, which kept me fully employed the greatest part of the day, and in the evening arrived at a charming spot on the East bank, which I had marked on my ascent up the river, where I made some addition to my collections, and the next day I employed myself in the same manner, putting into shore frequently, at convenient places, which I had noticed; and in the evening arrived again at the upper store, where I had the pleasure of finding my old friend, the trader, in good health and chearful, and his affairs in a prosperous way. There were also a small party of Indians here, who had lately arrived with their hunts to purchase goods. I continued a few days at this post, searching its environs for curious vegetable productions, collecting seeds and planting growing roots in boxes, to be transported to the lower trading house.

. . . .

How glorious the powerful sun, minister of the Most High, in the rule and government of this earth, leaves our hemisphere, retiring from our sight beyond the western forests! I behold with gratitude his departing smiles, tinging the fleecy roseate clouds, now riding far away on the Eastern horizon; behold they vanish from sight in the azure skies!

All now silent and peaceable, I suddenly fell asleep. At midnight I awake; when raising my head erect, I find myself alone in the wilderness of Florida, on the shores of Lake George. Alone indeed, but under the care of the Almighty, and protected by the invisible hand of my guardian angel.

II.

James Smith [1797]

[In 1797, the Reverend James Smith of Virginia traveled to the Northwest Territory and set down these reflections about the region that is now Ohio and Indiana. The journal entry is dated October 21, 1797.]

Having now travelled between 3 and 400 miles thro this country, I think I can form a tolerable judgment of the same and will as concisely as possible, give a general description of the same before I leave it. The land naturally claims the first place. Bordering on the rivers, the land exceeds description. Suffice it to say that the soil is amazing rich, not subject to overflow, unbroken with gulches and gutters, as level as a bowling plain and vastly extensive. Leaving the rivers a high hill skirts the low ground. Here the land is still amazing fertile, covered with a heavy growth of timber, such as white and red oak, hickory, ash, beech, sugar tree, walnut, buckeye &c. Here a number of small streams take their rise; then gently creep along thro the winding valleys, and in their course these winding streams, form a great quantity of excellent meadow land. These streams uniting increase their consequence; the meadows enlarge and extend themselves, till they discharge their crystal streams into the rivers.

As to mountains, there are properly speaking none; there are however high hills from which a beautiful view of the adjoining country presents itself. There is generally but little stone. Quarries of free-stone are plenty on the Scioto and limestone in many places. The land is generally very light, soft and easy to cultivate. Indian corn grows to great perfection; wheat, oats, rye &c thrive amazing well. All kinds of roots, such as potatoes, turnips, and the like grow extremely well. Cotton also grows very well and hemp and flax come to great perfection.

Grass of the meadow kind grows all over this country and white clover and blue grass grow spontaneously wherever the land is cleared. A country so famous for grass must of course be excellent for all kinds of stock. Here I saw the finest beef and mutton, that I ever saw fed on grass. Hogs also increase and fatten in the woods in a most surprizing manner. Exclusive of tame cattle, great numbers of wild beasts as bears, buffalo, deer, elk &c shelter in these immense woods. The rivers produce an infinite number of fish; besides geese, ducks and the like, turkies, pheasants, partridges &c are produced in great plenty and get exceeding fat on the produce of the forest. Honey itself is not wanting to make up the rich variety. Incredible numbers of bees have found their way to this delightful region and in vast quantities deposit their honey in the trees of the woods, so that it is not an uncommon thing for the people to take their wagon and team and return loaded with honey.

The water of this country is generally very good. The rivers are clear as crystal and the springs are bold, good and in considerable plenty.

The air appears clear and serene not subject to dampness and vapors, which render a country unwholesome. Neither does it appear subject to those sudden changes and alterations which are so pernicious to health and prejudicial to fruits and vegetables. When these things are duly considered the country which possesses these natural advantages surely merits notice.

12.

Zebulon M. Pike [1806]

[Zeb Pike, best known for discovering Pike's Peak, was a lieutenant when he commanded a small army detachment sent to explore the Upper Mississippi River. While negotiating with Indians and establishing U.S. government authority in the area, he made detailed observations of the country. In this passage he describes the region north of La Crosse, Wisconsin.]

In this division of the Mississippi the shores are more than three-fourths prairie on both sides, or, more properly speaking, bald hills, which, instead of running parallel with the river, form a continual succession of high perpendicular cliffs and low vallies: they appear to head on the river, and to traverse the country in an angular direction. Those hills and vallies give rise to some of the most sublime and romantic views I ever saw. But this irregular scenery is sometimes interrupted by a wide extended plain, which brings to mind the verdant lawn of civilized life, and would almost induce the traveller to imagine himself in the centre of a highly cultivated plantation. The timber of this division is generally birch, elm and cottonwood, all the cliffs being bordered by cedar.

The navigation unto the [Upper] Iowa river is good; but from thence to the Sauteaux river is very much obstructed by islands; and in some places the Mississippi is uncommonly wide, and divided into many small channels, which from the cliffs appear like so many distinct rivers, winding in a parallel course through the same immense valley. But there are few sand-bars in those narrow channels: the soil being rich, the water cuts through it with facility.

La Montaigne qui Trompe dans l'Eau stands in the Mississippi near the E. shore, about 50 miles below the Sauteaux river, and is about two miles in circumference, with an elevation of two hundred feet, covered with timber. There is a small river which empties into the Mississippi, in the rear of the mountain, which, I conceive, once bounded the mountain on the lower side, and the Mississippi on the upper, when the mountain was joined to the main by a neck of prairie low ground, which in time was worn away by the spring freshes of the Mississippi; and thus formed an island of this celebrated mountain. Lake Pepin (so called by the French) appears to be only an expansion of the Mississippi. It commences at the entrance of the Sauteaux river, and bears N. 55 W. to Point de Sable 12 miles, which is a neck of land making out about one mile into the lake from the W. shore, and is the narrowest part of the lake. From here to the upper end the course is nearly due W. about 10 miles, making its whole length 22 miles, and from four to one and a half miles in width, the broadest part being in the bay below Point de Sable. This is a beautiful place; the contrast of the Mississippi full of islands, and the lake with not one in its whole extent, gives more force to the grandeur of the scene. The French, under the government of M. Frontenac, drove the Reynards (or Ottaquamies) from the Ouiscousing, and pursued them up the Mississippi, and, as a barrier, built a stockade on Lake Pepin, on the W. shore, just below Point de Sable; and, as was generally the case with that nation, blended the military and mercantile professions, by making their fort a factory for the Sioux. The lake, at the upper end, is three fathoms deep; but this, I am informed, is its shoalest part. From the Iowa river to the head of Lake Pepin, the elk are the prevailing species of wild game, with some deer, and a few bear.

From the head of Lake Pepin about 12 miles to the Cannon river, the Mississippi is branched out into many channels, and its bosom covered with numerous islands. There is a hill on the W. shore, about six miles above the lake called the Grange, from the summit of which you have one of the most delightful prospects in nature. When turning your face to the E. you have the river winding in three channels at your feet; on your right the extensive bosom of the lake, bounded by its chain of hills, in front over the Mississippi, a wide extended prairie; on the left the valley of the Mississippi, open to view quite to the St. Croix, and partly in your rear, the valley through which passes the Riviere *au Canon*; and when I viewed it, on one of the islands below, appeared the spotted lodges of the Red Wing's band of Sioux. The white tents of the traders and my soldiers, and three flags of the United States waving on the water, which gave a contrast to the still and lifeless wilderness around, and increased the pleasure of the prospect.

13.

William Cullen Bryant

INSCRIPTION FOR THE ENTRANCE TO A WOOD [1821]

Stranger, if thou hast learned a truth which needs
No school of long experience, that the world
Is full of guilt and misery, and hast seen

Enough of all its sorrows, crimes, and cares,
To tire thee of it, enter this wild wood
And view the haunts of Nature. The calm shade
Shall bring a kindred calm, and the sweet breeze
That makes the green leaves dance, shall waft a balm
To thy sick heart. Thou wilt find nothing here
Of all that pained thee in the haunts of men,
And made thee loathe thy life. The primal curse
Fell, it is true, upon the unsinning earth,
But not in vengeance. God hath yoked to guilt
Her pale tormentor, misery. Hence, these shades
Are still the abodes of gladness; the thick roof
Of green and stirring branches is alive
And musical with birds, that sing and sport
In wantonness of spirit; while below
The squirrel, with raised paws and form erect,
Chirps merrily. Throngs of insects in the shade
Try their thin wings and dance in the warm beam
That waked them into life. Even the green trees
Partake the deep contentment; as they bend
To the soft winds, the sun from the blue sky
Looks in and sheds a blessing on the scene.
Scarce less the cleft-born wild-flower seems to enjoy
Existence, than the wingèd plunderer
That sucks its sweets. The mossy rocks themselves,
And the old and ponderous trunks of prostrate trees
That lead from knoll to knoll a causey rude
Or bridge the sunken brook, and their dark roots,
With all their earth upon them, twisting high,
Breathe fixed tranquillity. The rivulet
Sends forth glad sounds, and tripping o'er its bed
Of pebbly sands, or leaping down the rocks,
Seems, with continuous laughter, to rejoice
In its own being. Softly tread the marge,
Lest from her midway perch thou scare the wren
That dips her bill in water. The cool wind,
That stirs the stream in play, shall come to thee,
Like one that loves thee nor will let thee pass
Ungreeted, and shall give its light embrace.

thoroughly delighted him, and the book that resulted—*A Tour on the Prairies*—has delighted readers ever since.]

Our march this day was animating and delightful. We were in a region of adventure; breaking our way through a country hitherto untrodden by white men, except perchance by some solitary trapper. The weather was in its perfection, temperate, genial and enlivening; a deep blue sky with a few light feathery clouds, an atmosphere of perfect transparency, an air pure and bland, and a glorious country spreading out far and wide in the golden sunshine of an autumnal day; but all silent, lifeless, without a human habitation, and apparently without a human inhabitant! It was as if a ban hung over this fair but fated region. The very Indians dared not abide here, but made it a mere scene of perilous enterprise, to hunt for a few days, and then away.

After a march of about fifteen miles west we encamped in a beautiful peninsula, made by the windings and doublings of a deep, clear, and almost motionless brook, and covered by an open grove of lofty and magnificent trees. Several hunters immediately started forth in quest of game before the noise of the camp should frighten it from the vicinity. Our man, Beatte, also took his rifle and went forth alone, in a different course from the rest.

For my own part, I lay on the grass under the trees, and built castles in the clouds, and indulged in the very luxury of rural repose. Indeed I can scarcely conceive a kind of life more calculated to put both mind and body in a healthful tone. A morning's ride of several hours diversified by hunting incidents; an encampment in the afternoon under some noble grove on the borders of a stream; an evening banquet of venison, fresh killed, roasted, or broiled, on the coals; turkeys just from the thickets and wild honey from the trees; and all relished with an appetite unknown to the gourmets of the cities. And at night—such sweet sleeping in the open air, or waking and gazing at the moon and stars, shining between the trees!

. . . .

After a toilsome march of some distance through a country cut up by ravines and brooks, and entangled by thickets, we emerged upon a grand prairie. Here one of the characteristic scenes of the Far West broke upon us. An immense extent of grassy, undulating, or, as it is termed, rolling country, with here and there a clump of trees, dimly seen in the distance like a ship at sea; the landscape deriving sublimity from its vastness and simplicity. To the southwest, on the summit of a hill, was a singular crest of broken rocks, resembling a ruined fortress. It reminded me of the ruin of some

Moorish castle, crowning a height in the midst of a lonely Spanish landscape. To this hill we gave the name of Cliff Castle.

The prairies of these great hunting regions differed in the character of their vegetation from those through which I had hitherto passed. Instead of a profusion of tall flowering plants and long flaunting grasses, they were covered with a shorter growth of herbage called buffalo grass, somewhat coarse, but, at the proper seasons, affording excellent and abundant pasturage. At present it was growing wiry, and in many places was too much parched for grazing.

The weather was verging into that serene but somewhat arid season called the Indian Summer. There was a smoky haze in the atmosphere that tempered the brightness of the sunshine into a golden tint, softening the features of the landscape, and giving a vagueness to the outlines of distant objects. This haziness was daily increasing, and was attributed to the burning of distant prairies by the Indian hunting parties.

We now came once more in sight of the Red Fork, winding its turbid course between well-wooded hills, and through a vast and magnificent landscape. The prairies bordering on the rivers are always varied in this way with woodland, so beautifully interspersed as to appear to have been laid out by the hand of taste; and they only want here and there a village spire, the battlements of a castle, or the turrets of an old family mansion rising from among the trees, to rival the most ornamented scenery of Europe.

16.

Thomas Cole [1835]

[One of the foremost American artists of the nineteenth century, Thomas Cole was a founder of the Hudson River School of landscape painting. His deep love of nature focused particularly on the Catskill Mountains, among which he had his studio. The following selection is from his journal entry for July 6, 1835.]

We did not rise remarkably early, but were ready for breakfast. . . . We strolled down to the small lake which lies a few hundred yards from the house. It is diminutive, but has beautiful, as well as grand features—rich forests and mountains. . . . We pursued our way to the lower one, which is much larger and more beautiful. I pointed out a view that I once painted; which picture, I believe, was the first ever painted of the lake that will be hereafter the subject of a thousand pencils. . . . Several years ago I explored its shores for some distance; but thick woods and swampy grounds impeded me in those attempts. I enriched my sketchbook with studies of the fine dead trees, which stand like spectres on the shores. . . . As we made our way to an opening through the woods, which disclosed the lake in a charming manner, we perceived a rude boat among the bushes: this was exactly what we wanted. We pushed it off, and leaped into it, as if the genius of the deep had placed it there for our special purpose. . . . Before us spread the virgin waters which the prow of the sketcher had never yet curled, enfolded by the green woods, whose venerable masses had never figured in annuals, and overlooked by the stern mountain peaks, never beheld by Claude or Salvator, nor subjected to the canvass by the innumerable dabblers in paint of all past time. The painter of American scenery has, indeed, privileges superior to any other. All nature here is new to art. No Tivolis, Ternis, Mont Blancs, Plinlimmons, hackneyed and worn by the daily pencils of hundreds; but primeval forests, virgin lakes and waterfalls, feasting his eye with new delights, and filling his portfolio with their features of beauty and magnificence, hallowed to his soul by their freshness from the creation, for his own favoured pencil.

17.

Ralph Waldo Emerson [1836]

[Emerson was the intellectual and spiritual leader of the New England Transcendentalists, who derived their inspiration from three principal sources: the romantic movement in the arts, German idealistic philosophy, and the immediate natural world. He first outlined his thoughts on man and nature in a slim volume entitled simply *Nature* in 1836.]

To go into solitude, a man needs to retire as much from his chamber as from society. I am not solitary whilst I read and write, though nobody is with me. But if a man would be alone, let him look at the stars. The rays that come from those heavenly worlds will separate between him and what he touches. One might think the atmosphere was

made transparent with this design, to give man, in the heavenly
bodies, the perpetual presence of the sublime. Seen in the streets
of cities, how great they are! If the stars should appear one night in
a thousand years, how would men believe and adore; and preserve
for many generations the remembrance of the city of God which
had been shown! But every night come out these envoys of beauty,
and light the universe with their admonishing smile.

The stars awaken a certain reverence, because though always
present, they are inaccessible; but all natural objects make a kindred impression, when the mind is open to their influence. Nature
never wears a mean appearance. Neither does the wisest man ex-
tort her secret, and lose his curiosity by finding out all her perfection. Nature never became a toy to a wise spirit. The flowers, the
animals, the mountains, reflected the wisdom of his best hour, as
much as they had delighted the simplicity of his childhood.

When we speak of nature in this manner, we have a distinct but
most poetical sense in the mind. We mean the integrity of impression made by manifold natural objects. It is this which distinguishes the stick of timber of the wood-cutter from the tree of
the poet. The charming landscape which I saw this morning is
indubitably made up of some twenty or thirty farms. Miller owns
this field, Locke that, and Manning the woodland beyond. But none
of them owns the landscape. There is a property in the horizon
which no man has but he whose eye can integrate all the parts, that
is, the poet. This is the best part of these men's farms, yet to this
their warranty-deeds give no title.

To speak truly, few adult persons can see nature. Most persons
do not see the sun. At least they have a very superficial seeing. The
sun illuminates only the eye of the man, but shines into the eye
and the heart of the child. The lover of nature is he whose inward
and outward senses are still truly adjusted to each other; who has
retained the spirit of infancy even into the era of manhood. His
intercourse with heaven and earth becomes part of his daily food.
In the presence of nature a wild delight runs through the man, in
spite of real sorrows. Nature says—he is my creature, and maugre
all his impertinent griefs, he shall be glad with me. Not the sun or
the summer alone, but every hour and season yields its tribute of
delight; for every hour and change corresponds to and authorizes
a different state of the mind, from breathless noon to grimmest
midnight. Nature is a setting that fits equally well a comic or a
mourning piece. In good health, the air is a cordial of incredible
virtue. Crossing a bare common, in snow puddles, at twilight, under
a clouded sky, without having in my thoughts any occurrence of
special good fortune, I have enjoyed a perfect exhilaration. I am
glad to the brink of fear. In the woods, too, a man casts off his
years, as the snake his slough, and at what period soever of life is
always a child. In the woods is perpetual youth. Within these
plantations of God, a decorum and sanctity reign, a perennial festival is dressed, and the guest sees not how he should tire of them

in a thousand years. In the woods, we return to reason and faith. There I feel that nothing can befall me in life—no disgrace, no calamity (leaving me my eyes), which nature cannot repair. Standing on the bare ground—my head bathed by the blithe air and uplifted into infinite space—all mean egotism vanishes. I become a transparent eyeball; I am nothing; I see all; the currents of the Universal Being circulate through me; I am part or parcel of God. The name of the nearest friend sounds then foreign and accidental: to be brothers, to be acquaintances, master or servant, is then a trifle and a disturbance. I am the lover of uncontained and immortal beauty. In the wilderness I find something more dear and connate than in streets or villages. In the tranquil landscape, and especially in the distant line of the horizon, man beholds somewhat as beautiful as his own nature.

The greatest delight which the fields and woods minister is the suggestion of an occult relation between man and the vegetable. I am not alone and unacknowledged. They nod to me, and I to them. The waving of the boughs in the storm is new to me and old. It takes me by surprise, and yet is not unknown. Its effect is like that of a higher thought or a better emotion coming over me, when I deemed I was thinking justly or doing right.

. . . .

Nature satisfies by its loveliness, and without any mixture of corporeal benefit. I see the spectacle of morning from the hilltop over against my house, from daybreak to sunrise, with emotions which an angel might share. The long slender bars of cloud float like fishes in the sea of crimson light. From the earth, as a shore, I look out into that silent sea. I seem to partake its rapid transformations; the active enchantment reaches my dust, and I dilate and conspire with the morning wind. How does Nature deify us with a few and cheap elements! Give me health and a day, and I will make the pomp of emperors ridiculous. The dawn is my Assyria; the sunset and moonrise my Paphos, and unimaginable realms of faerie; broad noon shall be my England of the senses and the understanding; the night shall be my Germany of mystic philosophy and dreams.

Not less excellent, except for our less susceptibility in the afternoon, was the charm, last evening, of a January sunset. The western clouds divided and subdivided themselves into pink flakes modulated with tints of unspeakable softness, and the air had so much life and sweetness that it was a pain to come within doors. What was it that nature would say? Was there no meaning in the live repose of the valley behind the mill, and which Homer or Shakspeare could not re-form for me in words? The leafless trees become spires of flame in the sunset, with the blue east for their background, and the stars of the dead calices of flowers, and every withered stem and stubble rimed with frost, contribute something to the mute music.

The inhabitants of cities suppose that the country landscape is pleasant only half the year. I please myself with the graces of the winter scenery, and believe that we are as much touched by it as by the genial influences of summer. To the attentive eye, each moment of the year has its own beauty, and in the same field, it beholds, every hour, a picture which was never seen before and which shall never be seen again. The heavens change every moment, and reflect their glory or gloom on the plains beneath. The state of the crop in the surrounding farms alters the expression of the earth from week to week. The succession of native plants in the pastures and roadsides, which make the silent clock by which time tells the summer hours, will make even the divisions of the day sensible to a keen observer. The tribes of birds and insects, like the plants punctual to their time, follow each other, and the year has room for all. By watercourses, the variety is greater. In July, the blue pontederia or pickerel-weed blooms in large beds in the shallow parts of our pleasant river, and swarms with yellow butterflies in continual motion. Art cannot rival this pomp of purple and gold. Indeed the river is a perpetual gala, and boasts each month a new ornament.

18.

Charles Lanman [1846]

[Charles Lanman was an avid fisherman and amateur explorer, as well as a writer and newspaperman of some note. In this selection, from *Summer in the Wilderness*, he describes a portion of a trip into the Great Lakes region.]

At one time I gazed upon a noontide panorama. Not a breath of air was stirring, and the atmosphere was hot and sultry. The leaves and the green waves of the distant prairie were motionless. The birds were tired of singing, and had sought the shadowy recesses of the wood. The deer was quenching his thirst in some nameless stream, or panting with heat in some secluded dell. On an old dry tree, whose giant arms stretched upward as if to grasp the clouds, a solitary bald eagle had perched himself. It was too hot even for him to enjoy a bath in the upper air; but presently, as if smitten with a new thought, he spread out his broad pinions, and slowly ascended to the zenith,—whence I fancied that the glance of his keen eyes could rest upon the Atlantic and Pacific. The butterfly and wild bee were resting on the full-blown flowers; and perfect silence was in the Indian village. The children, exhausted with heat and play, had gone to lie down, some in their cabins, and some in the cool shadow of the trees. Earth and air were so tranquil, that it seemed as if nature was offering up a prayer. Winding far away to the south was the Mississippi, fading away to the bending sky.

In a few moments a little cloud had obscured the sky. The wind was rising, and was followed by a roaring sound,—and now the storm was spending its fury upon forest and prairie. The dreadful thunder echoed through the chambers of the firmament, and the fiercest lightnings flashed forth their fire. The forests were bending as if every tree would break. An old oak, which stood in its grandeur upon the plain, now lay prostrate,—even as God will sometimes dash to the earth some proud and insolent man. The parched soil was deluged with rain. But finally the storm had spent its fury, and the clouds, like a routed army, were passing away in dire confusion. A rainbow then arched the heavens, and a fresh but gentle breeze was fanning my cheek, and thrilling my whole being with rapture.

I also looked upon this wilderness landscape at the evening hour. As the sun descended, the clouds came out to meet him, decked in their most gorgeous robes, while the evening star smiled at his approach. He had left the valleys in twilight, and I knew that his last beams were gilding with gold the Rocky Mountains. The moon ascended to her throne; and the whippoorwill had commenced her evening hymn. On heavy wings a swan flew past me; she was going perhaps to her home on the margin of Hudson's Bay. A stir was in the Indian village, for they had returned with their canoes loaded with game. The customary festival had commenced, and most strangely did their wild music sound, as it broke on the surrounding solitude. The doe had gone to her grassy couch, the feathered multitudes were sleeping, and the mantle of perfect silence had fallen upon the world.

It was now midnight, and I stood in the centre of an apparently boundless wilderness of forests and prairies;—while far away to the northwest reposed a range of hills, which seemed to me like a vast caravan of the antediluvian Mound Builders. The moon had compassed the heavens, and was near her setting. A thousand stars were by her side. She flooded with her silver beams the leaves, the waves, and distant hills. Every voice within the Indian village was hushed. The warrior, asleep upon his mat, was dreaming of a new victory lost or won; the youth was dreaming of the dark-eyed maiden whom he loved; and the child was dreaming of the toys of yesterday. The pale face had not yet trespassed upon their rights; and as they were at peace with the Great Spirit, they were contented and happy. Holy and impressive was the hour. The wind was up, and wailed an awful anthem as it swept through the dark pines. It came to my ear like the death-wailings of a world. The owl was noiselessly flying from tree to tree, and the beautiful whippoorwill was sleeping. The splash of a leaping trout, or the howl of a wolf, were the only sounds which fell upon my ear. I looked, and looked,—wondering, wondering. And when I retraced my journey from the summit of the Elk Hills and the margin of Elk Lake, few and brief were the words that escaped my lips, for my heart was oppressed with the majesty of God.

. . . .

No one, who has never witnessed them, can form any idea of the exquisite beauty of the thousand lakes which gem the western part of Michigan. They are the brightest and purest mirrors the virgin sky has ever used to adorn herself. Their banks are frequently dotted by human dwellings, the humble though comfortable abodes of a sturdy yeomanry. That one which takes its name from an Indian called Baubeese, and which is the outlet of the St. Joseph river, I will match against any other of its size in the world.

Notwithstanding what has been so often said by the artificial inhabitants of cities, concerning the hardships and ignorance of the backwoodsman's life, there is many a stout heart, exalted mind, and noble soul, whose dwelling-place has been for years on the borders of these very lakes. I know this to be true, for I have slept beneath their roofs, and often partaken of their johnny-cake and fat quails. No,—no. I love these men as brothers, and shall always frown upon that cit or dandy who sets down aught against them,— in malice or in ignorance.

19.

Henry David Thoreau [1854]

[In some ways a disciple of Emerson and in many other ways a unique and independent thinker, Henry David Thoreau pursued his famous experiment in deliberate living on Emerson's land at Walden Pond. His relationship with nature was a complex one of many levels and moods, as these passages from *Walden* illustrate.]

I did not read books the first summer; I hoed beans. Nay, I often did better than this. There were times when I could not afford to sacrifice the bloom of the present moment to any work, whether of the head or hands. I love a broad margin to my life. Sometimes, in a summer morning, having taken my accustomed bath, I sat in my sunny doorway from sunrise till noon, rapt in a revery, amidst the pines and hickories and sumachs, in undisturbed solitude and stillness, while the birds sang around or flitted noiseless through the house, until by the sun falling in at my west window, or the noise of some traveller's wagon on the distant highway, I was reminded of the lapse of time. I grew in those seasons like corn in the night, and they were far better than any work of the hands would have been. They were not time subtracted from my life, but so much over and above my usual allowance. I realized what the Orientals mean by contemplation and the forsaking of works. For the most part, I minded not how the hours went. The day advanced as if to light some work of mine; it was morning, and lo, now it is evening, and nothing memorable is accomplished. Instead of singing like the birds, I silently smiled at my incessant good fortune. As the sparrow had its trill, sitting on the hickory before my door, so had I my chuckle or suppressed warble which he might hear out of my nest. My days were not days of the week, bearing the stamp of any heathen deity, nor were they minced into hours and fretted by the ticking of a clock; for I lived like the Puri Indians, of whom it is said that 'for yesterday, today, and tomorrow they have only one word, and they express the variety of meaning by pointing backward for yesterday, forward for tomorrow, and overhead for the passing day.' This was sheer idleness to my fellow-townsmen, no doubt; but if the birds and flowers had tried me by their standard, I should not have been found wanting. A man must find his occasions in himself, it is true. The natural day is very calm, and will hardly reprove his indolence.

. . . .

For what reason have I this vast range and circuit, some square miles of unfrequented forest, for my privacy, abandoned to me by men? My nearest neighbor is a mile distant, and no house is visible from any place but the hill-tops within half a mile of my own. I have my horizon bounded by woods all to myself; a distant view of the railroad where it touches the pond on the one hand, and of the fence which skirts the woodland road on the other. But for the most part it is as solitary where I live as on the prairies. It is as much Asia or Africa as New England. I have, as it were, my own sun and moon and stars, and a little world all to myself. At night there was never a traveller passed my house, or knocked at my door, more than if I were the first or last man; unless it were in the spring, when at long intervals some came from the village to fish for pouts—they plainly fished much more in the Walden Pond of their own natures, and baited their hooks with darkness—but they soon retreated, usually with light baskets, and left 'the world to darkness and to me,' and the black kernel of the night was never profaned by any human neighborhood. I believe that men are generally still a little afraid of the dark, though the witches are all hung, and Christianity and candles have been introduced.

Yet I experienced sometimes that the most sweet and tender, the most innocent and encouraging society may be found in any natural object, even for the poor misanthrope and most melancholy man. There can be no very black melancholy to him who lives in the midst of nature and has his senses still. There was never yet such a storm but it was Æolian music to a healthy and innocent ear. Nothing can rightly compel a simple and brave man to a vulgar sadness. While I enjoy the friendship of the seasons I trust that nothing can make life a burden to me. The gentle rain which waters my beans and keeps me in the house today is not drear and melancholy, but good for me too. Though it prevents my hoeing them, it is of far more worth than my hoeing. If it should continue so long as to cause the seeds to rot in the ground and destroy the potatoes in the low lands, it would still be good for the grass on the uplands, and, being good for the grass, it would be good for me. Sometimes, when I compare myself with other men, it seems as if I were more favored by the gods than they, beyond any deserts that I am conscious of; as if I had a warrant and surety at their hands which my fellows have not, and were especially guided and guarded. I do not flatter myself, but if it be possible they flatter me. I have never felt lonesome, or in the least oppressed by a sense of solitude, but once, and that was a few weeks after I came to the woods, when, for an hour, I doubted if the near neighborhood of man was not essential to a serene and healthy life. To be alone was something unpleasant. But I was at the same time conscious of a slight insanity in my mood, and seemed to foresee my recovery. In the midst of a gentle rain while these thoughts prevailed, I was suddenly sensible of such sweet and beneficent society in Nature, in the very pattering of the drops, and in every sound and sight around my house, an infinite and unaccountable friendliness all at once like an atmosphere sustaining me, as made the fancied advantages of human neighborhood insignificant, and I have never thought of them since. Every little pine needle expanded and swelled with sympathy and befriended me. I was so distinctly made aware of the presence of something kindred to me, even in scenes which we are accustomed to call wild and dreary, and also that the nearest of blood to me and humanest was not a person nor a villager, that I thought no place could ever be strange to me again.

. . . .

Sometimes, having had a surfeit of human society and gossip, and worn out all my village friends, I rambled still farther westward than I habitually dwell, into yet more unfrequented parts of the town, 'to fresh woods and pastures new,' or, while the sun was setting, made my supper of huckleberries and blueberries on Fair

Haven Hill, and laid up a store for several days. The fruits do not
yield their true flavor to the purchaser of them, nor to him who
raises them for the market. There is but one way to obtain it, yet
few take that way. If you would know the flavor of huckleberries,
ask the cow-boy or the partridge. It is a vulgar error to suppose
that you have tasted huckleberries who never plucked them. A
huckleberry never reaches Boston; they have not been known
there since they grew on her three hills. The ambrosial and essential part of the fruit is lost with the bloom which is rubbed off in
the market cart, and they become mere provender. As long as
Eternal Justice reigns, not one innocent huckleberry can be transported thither from the country's hills.

20.

Walt Whitman

From SONG OF MYSELF [1855]

A child said *What is the grass?* fetching it to me with full
  hands,
How could I answer the child? I do not know what it is
  any more than he.

I guess it must be the flag of my disposition, out of hopeful
  green stuff woven.

Or I guess it is the handkerchief of the Lord,
A scented gift and remembrancer designedly dropt,
Bearing the owner's name someway in the corners, that we
  may see and remark, and say *Whose?*

Or I guess the grass is itself a child, the produced babe of
  the vegetation.

Or I guess it is a uniform hieroglyphic,
And it means, Sprouting alike in broad zones and narrow
  zones,
Growing among black folks as among white,

Kanuck, Tuckahoe, Congressman, Cuff, I give them the
  same, I receive them the same.

And now it seems to me the beautiful uncut hair of graves.

. . . .

I believe a leaf of grass is no less than the journey-work
  of the stars,
And the pismire is equally perfect, and a grain of sand,
  and the egg of the wren,
And the tree-toad is a chef-d'œuvre for the highest,
And the running blackberry would adorn the parlors of
  heaven,
And the narrowest hinge in my hand puts to scorn all
  machinery,
And the cow crunching with depress'd head surpasses any
  statue,
And a mouse is miracle enough to stagger sextillions of
  infidels.

. . . .

I think I could turn and live with animals, they're so
  placid and self-contain'd,
I stand and look at them long and long.

They do not sweat and whine about their condition,
They do not lie awake in the dark and weep for their sins,
They do not make me sick discussing their duty to God,
Not one is dissatisfied, not one is demented with the mania
  of owning things,
Not one kneels to another, nor to his kind that lived thou-
  sands of years ago,
Not one is respectable or unhappy over the whole earth.
So they show their relations to me and I accept them,
They bring me tokens of myself, they evince them plainly
  in their possession.

I wonder where they get those tokens,
Did I pass that way huge times ago and negligently drop
  them?

21.

Walt Whitman

WHEN I HEARD THE LEARN'D ASTRONOMER [ca. 1864]

When I heard the learn'd astronomer,
When the proofs, the figures, were ranged in columns be-
    fore me,
When I was shown the charts and diagrams, to add, divide,
    and measure them,
When I sitting heard the astronomer where he lectured
    with much applause in the lecture-room,
How soon unaccountable I became tired and sick,
Till rising and gliding out I wander'd off by myself,
In the mystical moist night-air, and from time to time,
Look'd up in perfect silence at the stars.

22.

John Greenleaf Whittier

From SNOWBOUND [1866]

Unwarmed by any sunset light
The gray day darkened into night,
A night made hoary with the swarm
And whirl-dance of the blinding storm,
As zigzag, wavering to and fro,
Crossed and recrossed the wingèd snow:
And ere the early bedtime came

The white drift piled the window-frame,
And through the glass the clothes-line posts
Looked in like tall and sheeted ghosts.

So all night long the storm roared on:
The morning broke without a sun;
In tiny spherule traced with lines
Of Nature's geometric signs,
In starry flake, and pellicle,
All day the hoary meteor fell;
And, when the second morning shone,
We looked upon a world unknown,
On nothing we could call our own.
Around the glistening wonder bent
The blue walls of the firmament,
No cloud above, no earth below,—
A universe of sky and snow!
The old familiar sights of ours
Took marvellous shapes; strange domes and towers
Rose up where sty or corn-crib stood,
Or garden-wall, or belt of wood;
A smooth white mound the brush-pile showed,
A fenceless drift what once was road;
The bridle-post an old man sat
With loose-flung coat and high cocked hat;
The well-curb had a Chinese roof;
And even the long sweep, high aloof,
In its slant splendor, seemed to tell
Of Pisa's leaning miracle.

. . . .

All day the gusty north-wind bore
The loosening drift its breath before;
Low circling round its southern zone,
The sun through dazzling snow-mist shone.
No church-bell lent its Christian tone
To the savage air, no social smoke
Curled over woods of snow-hung oak.
A solitude made more intense
By dreary-voicëd elements,
The shrieking of the mindless wind,
The moaning tree-boughs swaying blind,
And on the glass the unmeaning beat
Of ghostly finger-tips of sleet.
Beyond the circle of our hearth
No welcome sound of toil or mirth
Unbound the spell, and testified
Of human life and thought outside.
We minded that the sharpest ear

The buried brooklet could not hear,
The music of whose liquid lip
Had been to us companionship,
And, in our lonely life, had grown
To have an almost human tone.

. . . .

The moon above the eastern wood
Shone at its full; the hill-range stood
Transfigured in the silver flood,
Its blown snows flashing cold and keen,
Dead white, save where some sharp ravine
Took shadow, or the sombre green
Of hemlocks turned to pitchy black
Against the whiteness at their back.
For such a world and such a night
Most fitting that unwarming light,
Which only seemed where'er it fell
To make the coldness visible.

. . . .

Our uncle, innocent of books,
Was rich in lore of fields and brooks,
The ancient teachers never dumb
Of Nature's unhoused lyceum.
In moons and tides and weather wise,
He read the clouds as prophecies,
And foul or fair could well divine,
By many an occult hint and sign,
Holding the cunning-warded keys
To all the woodcraft mysteries;
Himself to Nature's heart so near
That all her voices in his ear
Of beast or bird had meanings clear,
Like Apollonius of old,
Who knew the tales the sparrows told,
Or Hermes, who interpreted
What the sage cranes of Nilus said;
A simple, guileless, childlike man,
Content to live where life began;
Strong only on his native grounds,
The little world of sights and sounds
Whose girdle was the parish bounds,
Whereof his fondly partial pride
The common features magnified,
As Surrey hills to mountains grew
In White of Selborne's loving view,—
He told how teal and loon he shot,
And how the eagle's eggs he got,

The feats on pond and river done,
The prodigies of rod and gun;
Till, warming with the tales he told,
Forgotten was the outside cold,
The bitter wind unheeded blew,
From ripening corn the pigeons flew,
The partridge drummed i' the wood, the mink
Went fishing down the river-brink.
In fields with bean or clover gay,
The woodchuck, like a hermit gray,
   Peered from the doorway of his cell;
The muskrat plied the mason's trade,
And tier by tier his mud-walls laid;
And from the shagbark overhead
   The grizzled squirrel dropped his shell.

23.

Gustavus C. Doane [1870]

[Under the command of General H. D. Washburn, a federally sponsored scientific expedition was undertaken in 1870 to explore and report on the Yellowstone Valley. Until that time, the seemingly fabulous tales of mountain men had been all that was known of one of the most spectacular of nature's works. This selection is from the official report of the expedition.]

Fifth day—August 26.

—We left camp at 11 o'clock a.m., and crossed Gardiner's River, which at this point is a mountain torrent about twenty yards wide and three feet in depth. We kept the Yellowstone to our left, and finding the cañon impassable passed over several high spurs coming down from the mountains, over which the way was much obstructed by falling timber, and reached, at an elevation of 7,331 feet, an immense rolling plateau extending as far as the eye could reach. This elevated scope of country is about thirty miles in extent, with a general declivity to the northward. Its surface is an undulated prairie dotted with groves of pine and aspen. Numerous lakes are scattered throughout its whole extent, and great numbers of springs, which flow down the slopes and are lost in the volume of the Yellowstone. The river breaks through this plateau in a winding and im-

passable cañon of trachyte lava over 2,000 feet in depth; the middle
cañon of the Yellowstone, rolling over volcanic boulders in some
places, and in others forming still pools of seemingly fathomless
depth. At one point it dashes here and there, lashed to a white
foam, upon its rocky bed; at another it subsides into a crystal
mirror wherever a deep basin occurs in the channel. Numerous
small cascades are seen tumbling from the rocky walls at different
points, and the river appears from the lofty summits a mere ribbon
of foam in the immeasurable distance below. This huge abyss,
through walls of flinty lava, has not been worn away by the waters,
for no trace of fluvial agency is left upon the rocks; it is a cleft
in the strata brought about by volcanic action, plainly shown by
that irregular structure which gives such a ragged appearance
to all such igneous formations. Standing on the brink of the chasm
the heavy roaring of the imprisoned river comes to the ear only in
a sort of hollow, hungry growl, scarcely audible from the depths,
and strongly suggestive of demons in torment below. Lofty pines
on the bank of the stream "dwindle to shrubs in dizziness of distance." Everything beneath has a weird and deceptive appearance.
The water does not look like water, but like oil. Numerous fish-
hawks are seen busily plying their vocation, sailing high above the
waters, and yet a thousand feet below the spectator. In the clefts
of the rocks down, hundreds of feet down, bald eagles have their
eyries, from which we can see them swooping still further into
the depths to rob the ospreys of their hard-earned trout. It is
grand, gloomy, and terrible: a solitude peopled with fantastic
ideas; an empire of shadows and of turmoil.

.   .   .   .

Sixth day—August 27.—Barometer, 23.70; thermometer, morning,
46°; elevation, 6,546 feet. We remained in camp at Hot Springs
Creek awaiting the arrival of the rest of the party. In the morning
I rode down to the confluence of the two rivers and found the
East Fork to be a smaller stream than Gardiner's River. . . . Standing on the margin of the stream, a few hundred yards further down,
is Column Rock, a huge pile of alternate layers of basalt and
amygdaloid cement, several hundred feet in height, surmounted by
a pinnacle of trap, the columns of which are exactly perpendicular,
and of a perfect outline. The great curiosity of the locality, however,
is the Tower Fall of Hot Spring Creek, where that stream is
precipitated, in one unbroken body, from an amygdaloid ledge, a
sheer descent of 115 feet, into a deep gorge, joining the Yellowstone
a few hundred yards below. At the crest of the fall the stream has
cut its way through amygdaloid masses, leaving tall spires of rock
from 50 to 100 feet in height, and worn in every conceivable shape.
These are very friable, crumbling under slight pressure; several of
them stand like sentinels on the very brink of the fall. A view from
the summit of one of these spires is exceedingly beautiful; the clear
icy stream plunges from a brink 100 feet beneath to the bottom of

the chasm, over 200 feet below, and thence rushes through the narrow gorge, tumbling over boulders and tree trunks fallen in the channel. The sides of the chasm are worn away into caverns lined with variously-tinted mosses, nourished by clouds of spray which rise from the cataract; while above, and to the left, a spur from the great plateau rises above all, with a perpendicular front of 400 feet. The fall is accessible either at the brink or foot, and fine views can be obtained from either side of the cañon. In appearance, they strongly resemble those of the Minnehaha, but are several times as high, and run at least eight times the volume of water. In the basin we found a large petrified log imbedded in the débris. Nothing can be more chastely beautiful than this lovely cascade, hidden away in the dim light of overshadowing rocks and woods, its very voice hushed to a low murmur, unheard at the distance of a few hundred yards. Thousands might pass by within a half mile and not dream of its existence; but once seen, it passes to the list of most pleasant memories. In the afternoon the remainder of the party arrived, having lost the trail on the previous day.

.   .   .   .

Twenty-eighth day—September 18.—We broke camp at 9 o'clock, traveling along the slopes of the ridges, skirting the ravines through falling timber, and passing in many places over swampy terraces, for a distance of three miles, when we suddenly came upon a mountain torrent, 40 feet wide, and running through a gorge of trachyte lava 200 feet in depth. This was the Firehole River, heading in a lake a few miles to the south. Following down the course of this stream we presently passed two fine roaring cascades, where the water tumbled over rocks to the depth of 20 and 50 feet successively. These pretty little falls, if located on an eastern stream, would be celebrated in history and song; here, amid objects so grand as to strain conception and stagger belief, they were passed without a halt.

Shortly after the cañon widened a little, and on descending to a level with the stream we found ourselves once more in the dominions of the Fire King. Scattered along both banks of the infant river were boiling springs, depositing calcareous craters. These varied from 2 to 12 feet across, and were all in active eruption, the cones deposited varying from 3 to 40 feet in height, and sometimes covering a space of one-fourth of an acre. A feature of these craters is, that they gradually seal themselves up and stop the flow of their water, by depositing around the interior edges a deep fringe of rock, the points of which finally meet across the openings of the craters, forming a sort of sieve, which finally closes entirely, forcing the waters to break out in some other place. Numbers of these self-extinguished craters are seen scattered along both banks of the stream, having now become cones of solid rock. Most of the waters are clear, and the deposits are usually calcareous, but we found a few springs of water resembling ink, from which the deposit was a black hard rock, composed largely of silica, and extremely flinty, shattering the blades of our hatchets, and giving forth showers of sparks when struck by them. The valley here descended rapidly, and we soon saw in front dense columns of steam rising above the hills. After traveling two miles among these springs of various kinds, and through several bogs on the slopes, we came suddenly upon an open rolling valley of irregular shape, about two miles in width and three in length. This valley is known in the wretched nomenclature of this region as the Firehold, and contains phe-nomena of thermal springs unparalleled upon the surface of the globe. Crossing the river we moved down to a central point of the valley, and camped in a little grove of pine timber near the margin of a small marshy lake, around which were to be seen numerous fresh signs of buffalo, driven out by the noise of our hasty intru-sion. Distance 6 miles.

Barometer, 22.70; thermometer, 40°; elevation, 6,626 feet.

The valley is of triangular shape, with an obtuse angle on the south side of the river, which runs parallel with its longer side, and about three hundred yards from the foot of the range. At the apex of the obtuse angle a stream 50 feet wide comes in from the south, joining the main river in the midst of the valley, below its central point. The mountain ridges on all sides are 1,500 feet in height, composed of dark lava, in solid ledges, are heavily wooded, and very steep. Small groves of timber also cover the highest points of the valley, which is a succession of ridges, and of rounded knolls capped by springs, the intervening depressions being rendered marshy by the overflow of their waters. The whole surface of the basin, to an unknown depth, is a calcareous bed, deposited from the springs. Near the head of the valley, immediately after crossing to the south side of the river, we came to one of the geysers, which was at the time throwing water, with a loud hissing sound, to the height of 125 feet. In a few minutes the eruption ceased, and we were enabled to approach the crater. This had originally been a crack or fissure in the calcareous ledge, the seam of which could be traced by minute vents a distance of 60 feet, but was now closed up by deposits from the water to an opening 7 feet long by 3 feet wide in the center, from which the steam escaped with a loud, rushing sound. The hillock formed by the spring is 40 feet in height, and its base covers about four acres. Near the crater, and as far as its irruptive waters reach, the character of the deposit is very peculiar. Close around the opening are built up walls, 8 feet in height, of spherical nodules, from 6 inches to 3 feet in diameter. These, in turn, are covered on the surface with minute globules of calcareous stalagmite, incrusted with a thin glazing of silica. The rock, at a distance, appears the color of ashes of roses, but near at hand shows a metallic gray, with pink and yellow margins of the utmost delicacy. Being constantly wet, the colors are brilliant beyond description. Sloping gently from this rim of the crater, in every direction, the rocks are full of cavities, in successive terraces, forming little pools, with margins of silica the color of silver, the cavities being of irregular shape, constantly full of hot water, and precipitating delicate coral-like beads of a bright saffron. These cavities are also fringed with rock around the edges, in meshes as delicate as the finest lace. Diminutive yellow columns rise from their depths, capped with small tablets of rock, and resembling flowers growing in the water. Some of them are filled with oval pebbles of a brilliant white color, and others with a yellow frost-work which builds up gradually in solid stalagmites. Receding still further from the crater, the cavities become gradually larger, and the water cooler, causing changes in the brilliant colorings, and also in the formations of the deposits. These become calcareous spar, of a white or slate color, and occasionally variegated. The water of the geyser is colorless, tasteless, and without odor. The deposits are apparently as delicate as the down on the butterfly's wing, both in texture and coloring, yet are firm and solid beneath the tread. Those who have seen stage representations of "Alladin's Cave," and the "Home of the Dragon Fly," as produced in a first-class theater, can form an idea of the wonderful coloring, but not of the intricate frost-work, of this fairy-like, yet solid mound of rock, growing up amid clouds of steam and showers of boiling water. One instinctively touches the hot ledges with his hands, and sounds with a stick the depths of the cavities in the slope, in utter doubt in the evidence of his own eyes. The beauty of the scene takes away one's breath. It is overpowering, transcending the visions of the Moslem's Paradise. The earth affords not its equal. It is the most lovely inanimate object in existence.

.   .   .   .

Opposite camp, on the other side of the river, is a high ledge of stalagmite, sloping from the base of the mountain down to the river; numerous small knolls are scattered over its surface. The craters of boiling springs from 15 to 25 feet in diameter; some of these throw water the height of 3 and 4 feet. In the summit of this bank of rock is the grand geyser of the world, a well in the strata 20 by 25 feet in diametric measurements, the perceptible elevation of the rim being but a few inches and when quiet having a visible depth of 100 feet. The edge of the basin is bounded by a heavy fringe of rock, and stalagmite in solid layers is deposited by the overflowing waters. When an eruption is about to occur the basin gradually fills with boiling water to within a few feet of the surface, then suddenly, with heavy concussions, immense clouds of steam rise to the height of 500 feet. The whole great body of water, 20 by 25 feet, ascends in one gigantic column to the height of 90 feet, and from its apex 5 great jets shoot up, radiating slightly from each other, to the unparalleled altitude of 250 feet from the ground. The earth trembles under the descending deluge from this vast fountain, a thousand hissing sounds are heard in the air; rainbows encircle the summits of the jets with a halo of celestial glory. The falling water plows up and bears away the shelly strata, a seething flood pours down the slope and into the river. It is the grandest, the most majestic, and most terrible fountain in the world. After playing thus for twenty minutes it gradually subsides, the water lowering into the crater out of sight, the steam ceases to escape and all is quiet. This grand geyser played three times in the afternoon, but appears to be irregular in its periods, as we did not see it in eruption again while in the valley. Its waters are of a deep ultramarine color, clear and beautiful. The waving to and fro of the gigantic fountain, when its jets are at their highest, and in a bright sunlight, affords a spectacle of wonder of which any description can give but a feeble idea. Our whole party were wild with enthusiasm.

24.

Nathaniel Pitt Langford [1871]

[The published report on the Yellowstone expedition was followed by a campaign on the part of naturalists and publicists that resulted in the establishment of the Yellowstone Valley as the first national park in 1872. The article in which these passages appear was written by a member of the expedition.]

Early the next morning our commander and several others left camp in search of a ford, while the writer and Lieutenant Doane started in the direction of a lofty mountain, from the summit of which we expected to obtain a satisfactory observation of the southern shore of the lake. At the expiration of two hours we reached a point in the ascent too precipitous for further equestrian travel. Dismounting, we led our horses for an hour longer up the steep side of the mountain, pausing every few moments to take breath, until we arrived at the line of perpetual snow. Here we unsaddled and hitched our horses, and climbed the apex to its summit, passing over a mass of congealed snow more than thirty feet in thickness. The ascent occupied four hours. We were more than 600 feet above the snow line, and by barometric calculation 11,350 feet above the ocean level.

The grandeur and vast extent of the view from this elevation beggar description. The lake and valley surrounding it lay seemingly at our feet within jumping distance. Beyond them we saw with great distinctness the jets of the mud volcano and geyser. But beyond all these, stretching away into a horizon of cloud-defined mountains, was the entire Wind River range, revealing in the sunlight the dark recesses, gloomy cañons, stupendous precipices, and glancing pinnacles; which everywhere dotted its jagged slopes. Lofty peaks shot up in gigantic spires from the main body of the range, glittering in the sunbeams like solid crystal. The mountain on which we stood was the most westerly peak of a range which, in long-extended volume, swept to the southeastern horizon, exhibiting a continuous elevation more than thirty miles in width; its central line broken into countless points, knobs, glens, and defiles, all on the most colossal scale of grandeur and magnificence. Outside of these, on either border, along the entire range, lofty peaks rose at intervals, seemingly vying with each other in the varied splendors they presented to the beholder. The scene was full of majesty. The valley at the base of this range was dotted with small lakes and cloven centrally by the river, which, in the far distance, we could see emerging from a cañon of immense dimensions, within the shade of which two enormous jets of steam shot to an incredible height into the atmosphere.

This range of mountains has a marvelous history. As it is the loftiest, so it is the most remarkable lateral ridge of the Rocky Range. The Indians regard it as the "crest of the world," and among the Blackfeet there is a fable that he who attains its summit catches a view of the land of souls, and beholds the happy hunting-grounds spread out below him, brightening with the abodes of the free and generous spirits.

. . . .

We bade adieu to Yellowstone Lake, surfeited with the wonders we had seen, and in the belief that the interesting portion of our journey was over. The desire for home had superseded all thought of further exploration. We had seen the greatest wonders on the continent, and were convinced that there was not on the globe another region where, within the same limits, nature had crowded so much of grandeur and majesty, with so much of novelty and wonder. Our only care was to return home as rapidly as possible. Three days of active travel from the head-waters of the Madison, would find us among the settlers in the beautiful lower valley of that picturesque river, and within twelve miles of Virginia City, where we hoped to meet with Mr. Everts, and realize afresh that "all is well that ends well."

Judge, then, what must have been our astonishment, as we entered the basin at mid-afternoon of our second day's travel, to see in the clear sunlight, at no great distance, an immense volume of clear, sparkling water projected into the air to the height of one hundred and twenty-five feet. "Geysers! geysers!" exclaimed one of our company, and, spurring our jaded horses, we soon gathered around this wonderful phenomenon. It was indeed a perfect geyser. The aperture through which the jet was projected was an irregular oval, three feet by seven in diameter. The margin of sinter was curiously piled up, and the exterior crust was filled with little hollows full of water, in which were small globules of sediment, some having gathered around bits of wood and other nuclei. This geyser is elevated thirty feet above the level of the surrounding plain, and the crater rises five or six feet above the mound. It spouted at regular intervals nine times during our stay, the columns of boiling water being thrown from ninety to one hundred and twenty-five feet at each discharge, which lasted from fifteen to twenty minutes. We gave it the name of "Old Faithful."

25.

John Muir [1871]

[John Muir, perhaps the greatest American naturalist, devoted most of his life to studying the Yosemite Valley of California and fighting for its preservation. In 1871, the valley was visited by Ralph Waldo Emerson, whom he regarded as a disciple does his master; thirty years later, Muir wrote this account of the occasion.]

Early in the afternoon, when we reached Clark's Station, I was surprised to see the party dismount. And when I asked if we were not going up into the grove to camp they said: "No; it would never do to lie out in the night air. Mr. Emerson might take cold; and you know, Mr. Muir, that would be a dreadful thing." In vain I urged, that only in homes and hotels were colds caught, that nobody ever was known to take cold camping in these woods, that there was not a single cough or sneeze in all the Sierra. Then I pictured the big climate-changing, inspiring fire I would make, praised the beauty and fragrance of sequoia flame, told how the great trees would stand about us transfigured in the purple light, while the stars looked down between the great domes; ending by urging them to come on and make an immortal Emerson night of it. But the house habit was not to be overcome nor the strange dread of pure night air, though it is only cooled day air with a little dew in it. So the carpet dust and unknowable reeks were preferred. And to think of this being a Boston choice! Sad commentary on culture and the glorious transcendentalism.

Accustomed to reach whatever place I started for, I was going up the mountain alone to camp, and wait the coming of the party next day. But since Emerson was so soon to vanish, I concluded to stop with him. He hardly spoke a word all the evening, yet it was a great pleasure simply to be near him, warming in the light of his face as at a fire. In the morning we rode up the trail through a noble forest of pine and fir into the famous Mariposa Grove, and stayed an hour or two, mostly in ordinary tourist fashion,—looking at the biggest giants, measuring them with a tape line, riding through prostrate fire-bored trunks, etc., though Mr. Emerson was alone occasionally, sauntering about as if under a spell. As we walked through a fine group, he quoted, "There were giants in those days," recognizing the antiquity of the race. To commemorate his visit, Mr. Galen Clark, the guardian of the grove, selected the finest of the unnamed trees and requested him to give it a name. He named it Samoset, after the New England sachem, as the best that occurred to him.

The poor bit of measured time was soon spent, and while the saddles were being adjusted I again urged Emerson to stay. "You are yourself a sequoia," I said. "Stop and get acquainted with your big brethren." But he was past his prime, and was now as a child in the hands of his affectionate but sadly civilized friends, who seemed as full of old-fashioned conformity as of bold intellectual independence. It was the afternoon of the day and the afternoon of his life, and his course was now westward down all the mountains into the sunset. The party mounted and rode away in wondrous contentment, apparently, tracing the trail through ceanothus and dogwood bushes, around the bases of the big trees, up the slope of the sequoia basin, and over the divide. I followed to the edge of the grove. Emerson lingered in the rear of the train, and when he reached the top of the ridge, after all the rest of the party were over and out of sight, he turned his horse, took off his hat and waved me a last good-by. I felt lonely, so sure had I been that Emerson of all men would be the quickest to see the mountains and sing them. Gazing awhile on the spot where he vanished, I sauntered back into the heart of the grove, made a bed of sequoia plumes and ferns by the side of a stream, gathered a store of firewood, and then walked about until sundown. The birds, robins, thrushes, warblers, etc., that had kept out of sight, came about me, now that all was quiet, and made cheer. After sundown I built a great fire, and as usual had it all to myself. And though lonesome for the first time in these forests, I quickly took heart again,—the trees had not gone to Boston, nor the birds; and as I sat by the fire, Emerson was still with me in spirit, though I never again saw him in the flesh.

26.

Robert Louis Stevenson [1879]

[During 1879–80 the great Scottish author visited California. This account of his crossing of the Sierra Nevada was first published in 1892 and later formed part of *The Amateur Emigrant*.]

Of all the next day I will tell you nothing, for the best of all reasons, that I remember no more than that we continued through desolate and desert scenes, fiery hot and deadly weary. But some time after I had fallen asleep that night, I was awakened by one of my companions. It was in vain that I resisted. A fire of enthusiasm and whisky burned in his eyes; and he declared we were in a new country, and I must come forth upon the platform and see with my own eyes. The train was then, in its patient way, standing halted in a by-track. It was a clear, moonlit night; but the valley was too narrow to admit the moonshine direct, and only a diffused glimmer whitened the tall rocks and relieved the blackness of the pines. A hoarse clamour filled the air; it was the continuous plunge of a cascade somewhere near at hand among the mountains. The air struck chill, but tasted good and vigorous in the nostrils—a fine, dry, old mountain atmosphere. I was dead sleepy, but I returned to roost with a grateful mountain feeling at my heart.

When I awoke next morning, I was puzzled for a while to know if it were day or night, for the illumination was unusual. I sat up at last, and found we were grading slowly downward through a long snowshed; and suddenly we shot into an open; and before we were swallowed into the next length of wooden tunnel, I had one glimpse of a huge pine-forested ravine upon my left, a foaming river, and a sky already coloured with the fires of dawn. I am usually very calm over the displays of nature; but you will scarce believe how my heart leaped at this. It was like meeting one's wife. I had come home again—home from unsightly deserts to the green and habitable corners of the earth. Every spire of pine along the hill-top, every trouty pool along that mountain river, was more dear to me than a blood-relation. Few people have praised God more happily than I did. And thenceforward, down by Blue Cañon, Alta, Dutch Flat, and all the old mining camps, through a sea of mountain forests, dropping thousands of feet toward the far sea-level as we went, not I only, but all the passengers on board, threw off their sense of dirt and heat and weariness, and bawled like schoolboys, and thronged with shining eyes upon the platform, and became new creatures within and without. The sun no longer oppressed us with heat, it only shone laughingly along the mountain-side, until we were fain to laugh ourselves for glee. At every turn we could see farther into the land and our own happy futures. At every town the cocks were tossing their clear notes into the golden air, and crowing for the new day and the new country. For this was indeed our destination; this was "the good country" we had been going to so long.

By afternoon we were at Sacramento, the city of gardens in a plain of corn; and the next day before the dawn we were lying-to upon the Oakland side of San Francisco Bay.

[By the beginning of the twentieth century, the frontier had vanished and little remained in the way of undiscovered territory. The pressures of a rapidly expanding civilization beat against nature and man alike and instilled a note of urgency and even desperation in the writings of those who delighted in the feeling of closeness to the unspoiled land.]

27.

George S. Evans

THE WILDERNESS [1904]

The wilderness hath charms. To go to it is to return to the primitive, the elemental. It is reached by the trail, the oldest thoroughfare of man. The trail breathes out the spirit of romance.

It may date back to the days when the aborigines gave chase to the deer and the elk beneath the branches of the leafy forest. In pioneer days, the trail may have had its sanctity invaded by a white-skinned cavalcade, intent on finding gold. It has probably felt the hoofs of a steed carrying a fugitive from justice into a wild fastness. Over it have passed the strongest, bound to the hunting grounds to kill them venison. Over it passes in procession horses and men, carrying supplies to the cattle station, or the sheep-herder.

The trail winds around and up mountains, whose heads touch

heaven. It makes its way down leafy forest aisles; it leads past trickling springs, surrounded by moss-covered bowlders; it penetrates Nature's Titanic quarries; it crosses the range where cloud and wind, frost and snow, contend with bowlder and dwarf timber.

The question of transportation of supplies over the trail is solved by the bronco, the pack-saddle and the diamond hitch, by men of the horse and saddle.

The wilderness still exists. Man has ravaged and plundered the earth in large measure, but there are still great tracts of wilderness where bear and deer and cougar wander as in the days of old. From the southern line of Mendocino County in California, bounded on the west by the sea, and on the east by the eastern wall of the Coast Range, running north for league after league lies a great tract of comparatively untamed wilderness. Here and there on the edge of this land is a settler's clearing marred by burnt, gnarled stumps. A few winding roads connect scattered villages. But go far enough, even these disappear. Press on, and you come to the true wilderness. Mountains clad in cloaks of forest verdure, rise like giants. Rough peaks flout high their banners of snow. Scarred and furrowed canyon sides are covered with an almost impenetrable thicket of brush. Little streams trickle down over rocks, through grassy glades to join the mad foam creek at the bottom of the gorge. Mountain lakes and pools glimmer. Forest oceans mingle with the sky.

Away off, far from the haunts of man, you pitch your camp by some cool spring. Your horse has brought you over the trail safely. The supplies have arrived without accident. The air is bracing. Mountain piled on mountain, vast wastes of forest verdure, bowlders heaped on bowlders, tracts of brush and leafy glades mark this primeval waste—a workshop of the gods.

Dull business routine, the fierce passions of the market place, the perils of envious cities become but a memory. At first you are apalled by the immensity of the wilderness. You do not seem to be a part of the waste. You do not seem to fit into the landscape. The rocks have equanimity, the mountains ruggedness, the trees sturdiness, the wind savagery. You have none of these attributes. You are awe stricken, meek, filled with wonder. Your guide has lived in the wilderness for years. He is not awed by it, but seems to blend into it, to be a part and parcel of it. He has taken on the attributes of the wild and rugged land.

Almost imperceptibly a sensation of serenity begins to take possession of you. You explore deep canyons, climb vast mountains, penetrate shaggy forests, follow the meanderings of wild, turbid streams. You begin to take on some of the characteristics of the denizens of the woods. Your step becomes lighter, your eyesight keener, your hearing more acute. You think of the civilization you have left behind. Seen through the eyes of the wilderness, how stupid and inane it all seems. The mad eagerness of money-seeking men, the sham pleasures of conventional society, the insistence upon

the importance of being in earnest over trifles, pall on you when
you think of them.

28.

Robert Frost

THE VANTAGE POINT [1913]

If tired of trees I seek again mankind,
  Well I know where to hie me—in the dawn,
  To a slope where the cattle keep the lawn.
There amid lolling juniper reclined,
Myself unseen, I see in white defined
  Far off the homes of men, and farther still,
  The graves of men on an opposing hill,
Living or dead, whichever are to mind.

And if by noon I have too much of these,
  I have but to turn on my arm, and lo,
  The sunburned hillside sets my face aglow,
My breathing shakes the bluet like a breeze,
  I smell the earth, I smell the bruisèd plant,
  I look into the crater of the ant.

29.

"David Grayson" (Ray Stannard Baker)

THIS WONDERFUL, BEAUTIFUL AND INCALCULABLY INTERESTING EARTH! [1917]

It is astonishing
how many people there are in cities and towns who have a secret
longing to get back into quiet country places, to own a bit of the

soil of the earth, and to cultivate it. To some it appears as a trouble-some malady only in spring, and will be relieved a whirl or two in country roads, by a glimpse of the hills, or a day by the sea; but to others the homesickness is deeper seated and will be quieted by no hasty visits. These must actually go home.

I have had, in recent years, many letters from friends asking about life in the country; but the longer I remain here, the more I know about it, the less able I am to answer them—at least briefly. It is as though one should come and ask: "Is love worth trying?" or, "How about religion?" For country life is to each human being a fresh, strange, original adventure. We enjoy it, or we do not enjoy it, or more probably, we do both. It is packed and crowded with the zest of adventure, or it is dull and miserable. We may, if we are skilled enough, make our whole living from the land, or only a part of it, or we may find in a few cherished acres the inspiration and power for other work, whatever it may be. There is many a man whose strength is renewed like that of the wrestler of Irassa, every time his feet touch the earth.

Of all places in the world where life can be lived to the fullest and freest, where it can be met in its greatest variety and beauty, I am convinced that there is none to equal the open country, or the country town. For all country people in these days may have the city, some city or town not too far away; but there are millions of men and women in America who have no country and no sense of the country. What do they not lose out of life!

I know well the disadvantages charged against country life at its worst. At its worst there are long hours and much lonely labor and an income pitifully small. Drudgery, yes, especially for the women, and loneliness. Where is there not drudgery when men are poor, where life is at its worst? But I have never seen drudgery in the country comparable for a moment to the dreary and lonely drudgery of city tenements, city mills, factories and sweat shops. And in recent years both the drudgery and loneliness of country life have been disappearing before the motor and trolley car, the telephone, the rural post, the gasolene engine. I have seen a machine plant as many potatoes in one day as a man, at hand work, could have planted in a week.

There are indeed a thousand nuisances and annoyances that men must meet who come face to face with nature herself. You have set out your upper acres to peach trees; and the deer come down from the hills at night to strip the young foliage; or the field mice in winter, working under the snow, girdle and kill them. The season brings too much rain, and the potatoes rot in the ground; the crows steal the corn, the bees swarm when no one is watching, the cow smothers her calf, the hens' eggs prove infertile, and a storm in a day ravages a crop that has been growing all summer. A constant warfare with insects and blights and fungi, a real, bitter warfare, which can cease neither summer nor winter.

It is something to meet, year after year, the quiet implacability of the land. While it is patient, it never waits long for you. There is a chosen time for planning, a time for cultivating, a time for harvesting. You accept the gage thrown down well and good—you shall have a chance to fight. You do not accept it? There is no complaint. The land cheerfully springs up to wild yellow mustard and dandelion and pigweed, and will be productive and beautiful in spite of you.

Nor can you enter upon the full satisfaction of cultivating even a small piece of land at second hand. To be accepted as One Who Belongs, there must be sweat and weariness.

If one has drained his land, and plowed it, and fertilized it, and planted it and harvested it—even though it be only a few acres— how he comes to know and to love every rod of it. He knows the wet spots, and the stony spots, and the warmest and most fertile spots, until his acres have all the qualities of a personality, whose every characteristic he knows. It is so also that he comes to know his horses and cattle and pigs and hens. It is a fine thing, on a warm day in early spring to bring out the beehives and let the bees have their first flight in the sunshine. What cleanly folk they are! And later to see them coming in yellow all over with pollen from the willows!

It is a fine thing to watch the cherries and plum trees come into blossom, with us about the first of May, while all the remainder of the orchard seems still sleeping. It is a fine thing to see the cattle turned for the first time in spring into the green meadows. It is a fine thing, one of the finest of all, to see and smell the rain in a corn field after weeks of drought. How it comes softly out of gray skies, the first drops throwing up spatters of dust and losing themselves in the dry soil. Then the clouds sweep forward up the valley, darkening the meadows and blotting out the hills, and then there is the whispering of the rain as it first sweeps across the corn field. At once what a stir of life! What rustling of the long green leaves. What joyful shaking and swaying of the tassels! And have you watched how eagerly the grooved leaves catch each early drop and, lest there be too little rain after all, conduct it jealously down the stalk where it will soonest reach the thirsty roots? What a fine thing is this to see!

One who thus takes part in the whole process of the year comes soon to have an indescribable affection for his land, his garden, his animals. There are thoughts of his in every tree, memories in every fence corner. Just now, the fourth of June, I walked down past my blackberry patch, now come gorgeously into full white bloom, and heavy with fragrance. I set out these plants with my own hands. I have fed them, cultivated them, mulched them, pruned them, staked them, and helped every year to pick the berries. How could they be otherwise than full of associations. They bear a fruit more beautiful than can be found in any catalogue, and stranger and wilder than in any learned botany book.

Why, one who comes thus to love a bit of countryside may enjoy it all the year round. When he awakens in the middle of a long winter night he may send his mind out to the snowy fields—I've done it a thousand times—and visit each part in turn, stroll through the orchard and pay his respects to each tree (in a small orchard one comes to know familiarly every tree as he knows his friends), stop at the strawberry bed, consider the grape trellises, feel himself opening the door of the warm, dark stable and listening to the welcoming whicker of his horses, or visiting his cows, his pigs, his sheep, his hens, or so many of them as he may have.

So much of the best in the world seems to have come fragrant out of fields, gardens and hillsides. So many truths spoken by the Master Poet come to us exhaling the odors of the open country. His stories were so often of sowers, husbandmen, herdsmen; his similies and illustrations so often dealt with the common and familiar beauty of the fields. "Consider the lilies how they grow." It was on a hillside that he preached his greatest sermon, and when in the last agony he sought a place to meet his God, where did he go but to a garden? A carpenter, you say? Yes, but of this one may be sure: there were gardens and fields all about; he knew gardens, and cattle, and the simple processes of the land; he must have worked in a garden and loved it well.

A country life rather spoils one for the so-called luxuries. A farmer may, indeed, have a small cash income, but at least he eats at the first table. He may have the sweetest of the milk—there are thousands, perhaps millions, of men and women in America who have never in their lives tasted really sweet milk—and the freshest of eggs, and the ripest of fruit. One does not know how good strawberries or raspberries are when picked before breakfast and eaten with the dew still on them. And while he must work and sweat for what he gets, he may have all these things in almost unmeasured abundance, and without a thought of what they cost.

A man from the country is often made uncomfortable, upon visiting the city, to find two ears of sweet corn served for twenty or thirty cents, or a dish of raspberries at twenty-five or forty, and neither, even at their best, equal in quality to those he may have fresh from the garden every day. One need say this in no boastful spirit, but as a simple statement of the fact; for fruits sent to the city are nearly always picked before they are fully ripe, and lose that last perfection of flavor which the sun and the open air impart; and both fruits and vegetables, as well as milk and eggs, suffer more than most people think from handling and shipment. These things can be set down as one of the make-weights against the familiar presentation of the farmer's life as a hard one.

One of the greatest curses of mill or factory work, and with much city work of all kinds, is its interminable monotony; the same process repeated hour after hour and day after day. In the country there is, indeed, monotonous work, but rarely monotony. No task continues very long; everything changes infinitely with the seasons. Processes are not repetitive but creative. Nature hates monotony, is ever changing and restless, brings up a storm to drive the hay-makers from their hurried work in the fields, sends rain to stop the plowing, or a frost to hurry the apple harvest. Everything is full of adventure and vicissitude! A man who has been a farmer for two hours at the mowing, must suddenly turn blacksmith when his machine breaks down, and tinker with wrench and hammer; and later in the day he becomes dairyman, farrier, harness-maker, merchant. No kind of wheat but is grist to his mill, no knowledge that he cannot use! And who is freer to be a citizen than he? Freer to take his part in town meeting and serve his state in some one of the innumerable small offices which form the solid blocks of organization beneath our commonwealth.

What makes any work interesting is the fact that one can make experiments, try new things, develop specialties, and *grow*. And where can he do this with such success as on the land—and in direct contact with nature.

30.

Robert Marshall

WILDERNESS ESTHETICS [1930]

In examining the esthetic importance of the wilderness I will not engage in the un-profitable task of evaluating the preciousness of different sorts of beauty, as, for instance, whether an acronical view over the Grand Canyon is worth more than the Apollo of Praxiteles. For such a rating would always have to be based on a subjective standard, whereas the essential for any measure is impersonality. Instead of such useless metaphysics I shall call attention to several respects in which the undisputed beauty of the primeval, whatever its relative merit, is distinctly unique.

Of the myriad manifestations of beauty, only natural phenomena like the wilderness are detached from all temporal relationship. All the beauties in the creation or alteration of which man has played even the slightest rôle are firmly anchored in the historic stream. They are temples of Egypt, oratory of Rome, painting of the Renaissance or music of the Classicists. But in the wild places nothing is moored more closely than to geologic ages. The silent wanderer crawling up the rocky shore of the turbulent river could be a savage from some prehistoric epoch or a fugitive from twentieth century mechanization.

The sheer stupendousness of the wilderness gives it a quality of intangibility which is unknown in ordinary manifestations of ocular beauty. These are always very definite two or three dimensional objects which can be physically grasped and circumscribed in a few moments. But "the beauty that shimmers in the yellow afternoons of October, who ever could clutch it." * Any one who has looked across a ghostly valley at midnight, when moonlight makes a formless silver unity out of the drifting fog, knows how impossible it often is in nature to distinguish mass from hallucination. Any one who has stood upon a lofty summit and gazed over an inchoate tangle of deep canyons and cragged mountains, of sunlit lakelets and black expanses of forest, has become aware of a certain giddy sensation that there are no distances, no measures, simply unrelated matter rising and falling without any analogy to the banal geometry of breadth, thickness and height. A fourth dimension of immensity is added which makes the location of some dim elevation outlined against the sunset as incommensurable to the figures of the topographer as life itself is to the quantitative table of elements which the analytic chemist proclaims to constitute vitality.

Because of its size the wilderness also has a physical ambiency about it which most forms of beauty lack. One looks from outside at works of art and architecture, listens from outside to music or poetry. But when one looks at and listens to the wilderness he is encompassed by his experience of beauty, lives in the midst of his esthetic universe.

A fourth peculiarity about the wilderness is that it exhibits a dynamic beauty. A Beethoven symphony or a Shakespearean drama, a landscape by Corot or a Gothic cathedral, once they are finished become virtually static. But the wilderness is in constant flux. A seed germinates, and a stunted seedling battles for decades against the dense shade of the virgin forest. Then some ancient tree blows down and the long-suppressed plant suddenly enters into the full vigor of delayed youth, grows rapidly from sapling to maturity, declines into the conky senility of many centuries, dropping millions of seeds to start a new forest upon the rotting débris of its own ancestors, and eventually topples over to admit the sunlight which ripens another woodland generation.

Another singular aspect of the wilderness is that it gratifies every one of the senses. There is unanimity in venerating the sights and sounds of the forest. But what are generally esteemed to be the minor senses should not be slighted. No one who has ever strolled in springtime through seas of blooming violets, or lain at night on boughs of fresh balsam, or walked across dank holms in early

* Ralph Waldo Emerson, *Nature.*

morning can omit odor from the joys of the primordial environment. No one who has felt the stiff wind of mountaintops or the softness of untrodden sphagnum will forget the exhilaration experienced through touch. "Nothing ever tastes as good as when it's cooked in the woods" is a trite tribute to another sense. Even equilibrium causes a blithe exultation during many a river crossing on tenuous foot log and many a perilous conquest of precipice.

Finally, it is well to reflect that the wilderness furnishes perhaps the best opportunity for pure esthetic enjoyment. This requires that beauty be observed as a unity, and that for the brief duration of any pure esthetic experience the cognition of the observed object must completely fill the spectator's cosmos. There can be no extraneous thoughts—no question about the creator of the phenomenon, its structure, what it resembles or what vanity in the beholder it gratifies. "The purely esthetic observer has for the moment forgotten his own soul"; * he has only one sensation left and that is exquisiteness. In the wilderness, with its entire freedom from the manifestations of human will, that perfect objectivity which is essential for pure esthetic rapture can probably be achieved more readily than among any other forms of beauty.

31.

Joseph Wood Krutch [1952]

[Author, educator, and critic Joseph Wood Krutch published in 1948 a superb biography of Thoreau; four years later, somewhat in emulation of his subject, he left New York for the Arizona desert. In the essay from which this selection is taken, he explained some of his reasons for making such a radical move.]

A dozen years ago, on a trip undertaken without much enthusiasm, I got off the train at Lamy, New Mexico, and started in an automobile across the rolling semidesert toward Albuquerque. Suddenly a new, undreamed-of world was revealed. There was something so unexpected in the combination of brilliant sun and high, thin, dry air with a seemingly limitless expanse of sky and earth that my first reaction was delighted amusement. How far the ribbon of road beckoned ahead! How endlessly much there seemed to be of the majestically

* Irwin Edman, *The World, the Arts and the Artist.*

rolling expanse of bare earth dotted with sagebrush! How monotonously repetitious in the small details, how varied in shifting panorama! Unlike either the Walrus or the Carpenter, I laughed to see such quantities of sand.

Great passions, they say, are not always immediately recognized as such by their predestined victims. The great love which turns out to be only a passing fancy is no doubt commoner than the passing fancy which turns out to be a great love, but one phenomenon is not for that reason any less significant than the other. And when I try to remember my first delighted response to the charms of this great, proud, dry, and open land I think not so much of Juliet recognizing her fate the first time she laid eyes upon him but of a young cat I once introduced to the joys of catnip.

He took only the preoccupied, casual, dutiful sniff which was the routine response to any new object presented to his attention before he started to walk away. Then he did what is called in the slang of the theater "a double take." He stopped dead in his tracks; he turned incredulously back and inhaled a good noseful. Incredulity was swallowed up in delight. Can such things be? Indubitably they can. He flung himself down and he wallowed.

For three successive years following my first experience I returned with the companion of my Connecticut winters to the same general region, pulled irresistibly across the twenty-five hundred miles between my own home and this world which would have been alien had it not almost seemed that I had known and loved it in some previous existence. From all directions we crisscrossed New Mexico, Arizona, and southern Utah, pushing as far south as the Mexican border, as far west as the Mojave Desert in California. Guides led us into the unfrequented parts of Monument Valley and to unexplored cliff dwellings in a mesa canyon the very existence of which was nowhere officially recorded at the time. We climbed the ten-thousand-foot peak of Navajo Mountain to look from its summit across the vast unexplored land of rocks which supported, they said, not one inhabitant, white or Indian. Then one day we were lost from early morning to sunset when the tracks we were following in the sand petered out to leave us alone in the desert between Kayenta and the Canyon de Chelly.

To such jaunts the war put an end. For seven years I saw no more of sand and sunshine and towering butte. Meanwhile I lived as happily as one could expect to live in such years. The beautiful world of New England became again my only world. I was not sure that I should ever return to the new one I had discovered. Indeed it receded until I was uncertain whether I had ever seen it at all except in that previous existence some memory of which seemed to linger when, for the first time in this one, I met it face to face. Now and then, on some snowy night when the moon gleamed coldly on the snow, I woke from a dream of sun and sand, and when I looked from my window moon and snow were like the pale ghosts of sand and sun.

At last, for the fifth time, I came again, verifying the fact that remembered things did really exist. But I was still only a traveler or even only the traveler's vulgar brother, the tourist. No matter how often I looked at something I did no more than look. It was only a view or a sight. It threatened to become familiar without being really known and I realized that what I wanted was not to look at but to live with this thing whose fascination I did not understand. And so, a dozen years after I first looked, I have come for the sixth time; but on this occasion to live for fifteen months in a world which will, I hope, lose the charm of the strange only to take on the more powerful charm of the familiar.

Certainly I do not know yet what it is that this land, together with the plants and animals who find its strangeness normal, has been trying to say to me for twelve years, what kinship with me it is that they all so insistently claim. I know that many besides myself have felt its charm, but I know also that not all who visit it do, that there are, indeed, some in whom it inspires at first sight not love but fear, or even hatred. Its appeal is not the appeal of things universally attractive, like smiling fields, bubbling springs, and murmuring brooks. To some it seems merely stricken, and even those of us who love it recognize that its beauty is no easy one. It suggests patience and struggle and endurance. It is courageous and happy, not easy or luxurious. In the brightest colors of its sandstone canyons, even in the brightest colors of its brief spring flowers, there is something austere.

.   .   .   .

But what, I ask myself again, is the true nature, the real secret of that charm? I am no simple stoic. Hardship and austerity do not in themselves make an inevitable appeal to me and they are not only, not even principally, what I seek here. Everywhere there is also some kind of gladness.

Perhaps some of this glad charm is physical. To many people at least, dry warmth gives a sense of well-being and is in its own way as stimulating to them as the frosty air of the north is to others, caressing rather than whipping them into joyous activity. Some more of the charm is, I am sure, aesthetic. The way in which both desert and plateau use form and color is as different from the way in which more conventionally picturesque regions use them, as the way of the modern painter is different from that of the academician. But there is also, I am sure, a spiritual element. Nature's way here, her process and her moods, corresponds to some mood which I find in myself. Or, if that sounds too mystical for some tastes, we can, perhaps, compromise on a different formulation. Something in myself can be projected upon the visible forms which nature assumes here. She permits me to suppose that she is expressing something which another much-loved countryside left, for all the richness of the things it did express, unsaid, even unsuggested. To try to find out what that may be is the reason I have come once more to look at, to listen to, and, this time if possible, to be more intimately a part of, something whose meaning I have sensed but not understood.

32.

Mark Van Doren

INDIAN HUNTER [1969]

Forgivé me, little antelope,
I kill you so that I may live;
Also my son; also his starving
Mother, whom I still can save
If only I can bring you down—
There—that arrow was my own—
Forgive me, little twitching thing
Of whom tonight we all will sing:

One for three,
And nothing wasted;
On your smallest
Bones we feasted.

May you not be
Too much missed,
Youngest one
That trotted last.

33.

Hal Borland

SUMMER: A TIME FOR PERSPECTIVE [1970]

The rootless discontents have since time immemorial scorned the ones who put down roots and live close to the land. They have called such people backward and conservative and behind the times. But if there is such a thing as true radicalism—and the radical is the one who gets down to the root of the matter, right out of old Latin—it is the man on the soil. He is there at the source, and that is where he gets his meanings, not from airy speculation but from experience and first-hand observation. Not all the landsmen, to be sure; I have said before and say again that the rural lunkhead is as witless as the city dolt. But the chances of finding fundamental truth, the probability of reaching some point of perspective, are better away from the crowds.

I defy anyone to live intimately with spring, to be witness at the rebirth of the green world, and still think that man owns the earth. It isn't so much a matter of humility as of plain common sense. We keep forgetting that the rivers weren't all made by the Army's Corps of Engineers and that the hills weren't piled up by a fleet of bulldozers. And this lack of memory, or whatever you wish to call it, is responsible for a great many problems that some people insist must be solved by noon tomorrow and some other people insist cannot ever be solved because we have to spend so much in Vietnam and on the space program.

Out here we know who didn't make the hills, even if we aren't altogether positive who did. And we know that trees grow, grass spreads over the bare places, daisies and buttercups bloom, and maple leaves turn yellow and red in the autumn without one bit of human help. We aren't exactly humble about it, but we do smile when we hear talk about man's obligation to run the world. We have found that life proceeds on a fairly even keel as long as you respect the land, abide by the seasons, and don't try to tell your neighbor how to run his household.

And here it is summer again, and despite all the uproar by human beings the season follows its own pattern. We are trying to keep up with it, but not to outrace it or in any way supervise it. Hot afternoons and long moonlit nights and fireflies in the grass; aphids in the garden, green beans by the peck, an oriole in the maple across the road, and a brown thrasher singing like mad every evening. Summer. Why can't we all take the time to sit in the shade, now and then, and think how lucky we are to be human and to have this earth to live on?

VISIONS OF HARVEST

[The colonization of the New World was not, of course, undertaken for the benefit of nature-lovers, nor were the nearly three centuries of westward expansion primarily a search for scenery. Gold was uppermost in the minds of the Spanish conquerors; the French sought the Indian fur trade; and the English settled on and farmed the rich soils of the Atlantic seaboard. Early descriptions of America noted the beauty of the land, as we have seen, but were even more effusive about its bounty. As exploration became more intense, and as new technologies required new raw materials, attention shifted from the soil and the plentiful game to the lumber in the forests, the minerals in the ground, the power in the streams. Americans gradually came to see their country as an inexhaustible storehouse of wealth that, though locked up in a multitude of forms, was accessible through determination, ingenuity, and—increasingly—use of the machine.

A few selections will suffice to indicate the growing wonderment and often childlike delight felt by Americans as they discovered how rich was the land to which they had come.]

34.

Francis Higginson

NEW-ENGLAND'S PLANTATION [1629]

It is a land of divers and sundry sorts all about Masathulets Bay, and at Charles river is as fat black earth as can be seen anywhere; and in other places you have a clay soil, in other gravel, in other sandy, as it is all about our Plantation at Salem, for so our town is now named.

The form of the earth here, in the superficies of it, is neither too flat in the plainness, nor too high in hills, but partakes of both in a mediocrity, and fit for pasture or for plough or meadow ground, as men please to employ it. Though all the country be, as it were, a thick wood for the general, yet in divers places there is much ground cleared by the Indians, and especially about the Plantation; and I am told that about three miles from us a man may stand on a little hilly place and see divers thousands of acres of ground as good as need to be, and not a tree in the same. It is thought here is good clay to make brick and tiles and earthen pots, as need to be. At this instant we are setting a brick-kiln on work, to make bricks and tiles for the building of our houses. For stone, here is plenty of slates at the Isle of Slate in Masathulets Bay, and limestone, freestone, and smooth-stone, and iron-stone, and marble-stone also in such store, that we have great rocks of it, and a harbour hard by. Our Plantation is from thence called Marble-harbour.

Of minerals there hath yet been but little trial made, yet we are not without great hope of being furnished in that soil.

The fertility of the soil is to be admired at, as appeareth in the abundance of grass that groweth every where, both very thick, very long, and very high in divers places. But it groweth very wildly, with a great stalk, and a broad and ranker blade, because it never had been eaten with cattle, nor mowed with a scythe, and seldom trampled on by foot. It is scarce to be believed how our kine and goats, horses and hogs do thrive and prosper here, and like well of this country.

. . . .

This country aboundeth naturally with store of roots of great variety and good to eat. Our turnips, parsnips and carrots are here both bigger and sweeter than is ordinarily to be found in England. Here are also store of pumpions, cowcumbers, and other things of that nature which I know not. Also, divers excellent pot-herbs grow abundantly among the grass, as strawberry leaves in all places of the country, and plenty of strawberries in their time, and penny-royal, winter-savory, sorrel, brooklime, liverwort, carvel, and watercresses; also leeks and onions are ordinary, and divers physical herbs. Here are also abundance of other sweet herbs, delightful to the smell, whose names we know not, and plenty of single damask roses, very sweet; and two kinds of herbs that bear two kinds of flowers very sweet, which they say are as good to make cordage or cloth as any hemp or flax we have.

Excellent vines are here up and down in the woods. Our Governor hath already planted a vineyard, with great hope of increase.

Also, mulberries, plums, raspberries, currants, chestnuts, filberts, walnuts, small-nuts, hurtleberries, and haws of white-thorn, near as good as our cherries in England, they grow in plenty here.

For wood, there is no better in the world, I think, here being four sorts of oak, differing both in the leaf, timber, and color, all excellent good. There is also good ash, elm, willow, birch, beech, sassafras, juniper, cypress, cedar, spruce, pines and fir, that will yield abundance of turpentine, pitch, tar, masts, and other materials for building both of ships and houses. Also here are store of sumach trees, that are good for dyeing and tanning of leather; likewise such trees yield a precious gum, called white benjamin, that they say is excellent for perfumes. Also here be divers roots and berries, wherewith the Indians die excellent holding colors, that no rain nor washing can alter. Also we have materials to make soap ashes and saltpetre in abundance.

. . . .

New-England hath water enough, both salt and fresh. The greatest sea in the world, the Atlantic Sea, runs all along the coast thereof. There are abundance of islands along the shore, some full of wood and mast to feed swine, and others clear of wood, and fruitful to bear corn. Also we have store of excellent harbours for ships, as at Cape Anne, and at Masathulets Bay, and at Salem, and at many other places; and they are the better, because for strangers there is a very difficult and dangerous passage into them, but unto such as are well acquainted with them they are easy and safe enough.

The abundance of sea-fish are almost beyond believing; and sure I should scarce have believed it except I had seen it with mine own eyes. I saw great store of whales, and grampuses, and such abundance of mackerels that it would astonish one to behold; likewise codfish, abundance on the coast, and in their season are plentifully taken. There is a fish called a bass, a most sweet and wholesome fish as ever I did eat; it is altogether as good as our fresh salmon; and the season of their coming was begun when we came first to New-England in June, and so continued about three months' space. Of this fish our fishers take many hundreds together, which I have seen lying on the shore, to my admiration. Yea, their nets ordinarily take more than they are able to haul to land, and for want of boats and men they are constrained to let a many go after they have taken them; and yet sometimes they fill two boats at a time with them. And besides bass, we take plenty of scate and thornback, and abundance of lobsters, and the least boy in the Plantation may both catch and eat what he will of them. For my own part, I was soon cloyed with them, they were so great, and fat, and luscious. I have seen some myself that have weighed sixteen pound; but others have had divers times so great lobsters as have weighed twenty-five pounds, as they assured me.

Also, here is abundance of herring, turbot, sturgeon, cusks, haddocks, mullets, eels, crabs, muscles, and oysters. Besides, there is probability that the country is of an excellent temper for the making of salt; for, since our coming, our fishermen have brought home very good salt which they found candied by the standing of the sea-water and the heat of the sun upon a rock by the sea-shore; and in divers salt marshes that some have gone through, they have found some salt in some places crushing under their feet, and cleaving to their shoes.

And as for fresh water, the country is full of dainty springs, and some great rivers, and some lesser brooks; and at Masathulets Bay they digged wells and found water at three foot deep in most places; and near Salem they have as fine clear water as we can desire, and we may dig wells and find water where we list.

. . . .

The temper of the air of New-England is one special thing that commends this place. Experience doth manifest that there is hardly a more healthful place to be found in the world that agreeth better with our English bodies. Many that have been weak and sickly in Old England, by coming hither have been thoroughly healed, and grown healthful and strong. For here is an extraordinary clear and dry air, that is of a most healing nature to all such as are of a cold, melancholy, phlegmatic, rheumatic temper of body. None can more truly speak hereof by their own experience than myself. My friends that knew me can well tell how very sickly I have been, and continually in physic, being much troubled with a tormenting pain through an extraordinary weakness of my stomach, and abundance of melancholic humors. But since I came hither on this voyage, I thank God I have had perfect health.

35.

Edward Williams [1650]

[In the lengthy dedication of his pamphlet on the attractions of Virginia, Edward Williams addressed Parliament directly and outlined several reasons for encouraging the establishment of colonies.]

To the end you may in all things either parallel or transcend that Romane greatnesse, of which you are the inimitable exemplary, who inriched the heart and strengthened the armes of their Dominions by dispersing Colonies in all Angles of their Empire, Your pious care hath already layed a most signall foundation by inviting incouragements to undertakers of that nature: In the pursuit whereof let me beg the liberty in this paper, under your Honours Patronage to publish the many pressing and convincing reasons which have and may induce you to prosecute a designe of such universall concernment.

· ·

All Materialls for shipping, as Timber, Cordage, Sailes, Iron, Brasse, Ordnance of both mettals, and what ever else we are necessitated to supply our wants with out of the Easterne Countries, who make it not unusuall to take advantages of their neighbours necessity, and often times upon a pretence of difference or mis-intelligence betwixt us, embrace an occasion to over-rate or over-custome their commodities, or (a reall quarrell widening) sell it to other Nations from whence we are forced to supply our selves at a second or third market.

It will give us the liberty of storing a great part of Europe with a larger plenty of incomparable better fish, then the Hollander hath found meanes to furnish it withall, and will make us in no long tract of time, if industriously prosecuted, equall, if not transcend him in that his most beneficial staple.

It will be to this Common wealth a standing and plentifull magazine of Wheat, Rice, Coleseed, Rapeseed, Flax, Cotton, Salt, Potashes, Sope-ashes, Sugars, Wines, Silke, Olives, and what ever single is the staple of other Nations, shall be found in this joyntly collected.

It will furnish us with rich Furrs, Buffs, Hides, Tallow, Biefe, Park, &c. the growth and increase of Cattell in this Nation, receiving a grand interuption and stop, by killing commonly very hopefull yong breed to furnish our markets, or store our shipping, meerly occasioned by want of ground to feed them, whereas those Provinces afford such a large proportion of rich ground, that neither the increase of this or the succeeding age can in any reasonable probability overfeed the Moiety.

· ·

That all these, and many inestimable benefits may have their rise, increase, and perfection from the South parts of Virginia, a country unquestionably our own, devolved to us by a just title, and discovered by John Cabot *at the English expences, who found out and tooke seisure, together with the voluntary submission of the Natives to the English obedience of all that Continent from* Cape Florida *Northward, the excellent temper of the air, the large proportion of ground, the incredible richnesse of soile, the admirable abundance of Minerals, vegetables, medicinall drugs, timber, scituation, no less proper for all European commodities, then all those Staples which entitle* Chine, Persia, *and other the more opulent Provinces of the East to their wealth, reputation, and greatness (besides the most Christian of all improvements, the converting many thousands of the Natives) is agreed upon by all who have ever viewed the Country.*

36.

Robert Beverley

THE PRESENT STATE OF VIRGINIA [1722]

There is likewise found great Variety of Earths for Physick, Cleansing, Scouring, and making all Sorts of Potters-Ware; such as Antimony, Talk, yellow and red Oker, Fullers-Earth, Pipe-Clay, and other fat and fine Clays, Marle, &c. In a Word, there are all kinds of Earth fit for Use.

They have besides in those upper Parts, Coal for Firring, Slate for Covering, and Stones for Building, and Flat-Paving in vast Quantities, as likewise Pibble-Stones. Nevertheless, it has been confidently affirm'd by many, who have been there, that there is not a stone in all the Country. If such Travellers knew no better than they said, my Judgment of them is, that either they were People of extream short Memories, or else of very narrow Observation. For tho' generally the lower Parts are flat, and so free from Stones, that People seldom Shoe their Horses; yet in many Places, and particularly near the Falls of the Rivers, are found vast Quantities of Stone, fit for all kind of Uses. However, as yet there is seldom any Use made of them, because commonly Wood is to be had at much less Trouble. And as for Coals, it is not likely they should ever be used there in any thing, but Forges and great Towns, if ever they happen to have any; for, in their Country Plantations, the Wood grows at every Man's Door so fast, that after it has been cut down, it will in Seven Years time, grow up again from Seed, to substantial Fire-Wood; and in Eighteen or Twenty Years 'twill come to be very good Board-Timber.

For Mineral Earths, 'tis believ'd, they have great Plenty and Variety, that Country being in a good Latitude, and having great Appearances of them. It has been proved too, that they have both Iron and Lead, as appears by what was said before, concerning the Iron-Work, set up at *Falling-Creek*, in *James* River, where the Iron proved reasonably good: But before they got into the Body of the Mine, the People were cut off in that fatal Massacre; and the Project has never been set on Foot since. However, Col. *Byrd*, who is Proprietor of that Land, is at this Time boring, and searching after the richest Veins, near the Place of the former Work;

which is very commodious for such an Undertaking, by reason of the Neighbourhood of abundance of Wood, running Water, Fire-Stone, and other Necessaries for that Purpose.

It is also said, that there is found good Iron Ore at *Corotoman*, and in several other Parts of the Country.

The Gold-Mine, of which there was lately so much Noise, may, perhaps, be found hereafter to be some good Metal, when it comes to be fully examined. But, be that as it will, the Stones, that are found near it in great Plenty, are valuable; their Lustre approaching nearer to that of the Diamond, than those of *Bristol* or *Kerry*. There is no other Fault in them, but their Softness, which the Weather hardens, when they have been some time exposed to it, they being found under the Surface of the Earth. This Place is about a Day's Journey from the Frontier Inhabitants of *James River*.

. . . .

Besides all these, our Natives had originally amongst them, *Indian* Corn, Peas, Beans, Potatoes, and Tobacco.

This *Indian* Corn was the Staff of Food, upon which the *Indians* did ever depend; for when Sickness, bad Weather, War, or any other ill Accident kept them from Hunting, Fishing and Fowling; this, with the Addition of some Peas, Beans, and such other Fruits of the Earth, as were then in Season, was the Families Dependance, and the Support of their Women and Children.

There are Four Sorts of *Indian* Corn, Two of which are early ripe, and Two, late ripe; all growing in the same manner; every single Grain of this when planted, produces a tall upright Stalk, which has several Ears hanging on the Sides of it, from Six to Ten Inches long. Each Ear is wrapt up in a Cover of many Folds, to protect it from the Injuries of the Weather. In every one of these Ears, are several Rows of Grain, set close to one another, with no other Partition, but of a very thin Husk. So that oftentimes the Increase of this Grain amounts to above a Thousand for one.

. . . .

How the *Indians* order'd their Tobacco, I am not certain, they now depending chiefly upon the *English*, for what they smoak: But I am inform'd, they used to let it all run to Seed, only succouring the Leaves, to keep the Sprouts from growing upon, and starving them; and when it was ripe, they pull'd off the Leaves, cured them in the Sun, and laid them up for Use. But the Planters make a heavy Bustle with it now, and can't please the Market neither.

37.

Ferdinand V. Hayden

MINERALS IN NEBRASKA [1867]

The bluffs along the Missouri seemed to be formed of irregular beds of soft sandstone and liminated arenaceous clays. High up in the hills at some distance from the river there is a bed of limestone twelve to eighteen inches in thickness, which is quarried extensively and profitably. On the Missouri bottom, about on a level with high-water mark, a well was dug sixteen feet in depth; a seam of coal was penetrated, which is represented as four inches thick on one side of the well, and about ten on the other. These beds in the vicinity change rapidly, both in thickness and texture, within very short distances. Again, at Brownsville there is a seam of coal accompanied by many of the plants which are peculiar to the carboniferous rocks in other States. There is from four to six inches of good coal—the whole bed of black shale and coal is about twelve inches in thickness. There is a fine quarry of limestone at this point, which is of very superior quality for building purposes, but there is too much sand and clay in it to be converted into a good quality of lime. The bed is about three feet in thickness near the water's edge, concealed by high water at this time. There is a bed of micaceous, fine-grained sandstone which cleaves naturally into most excellent flagstones, which are much used here. These rock quarries are of great value to the people of Nemaha county. The materials for making brick abound everywhere in this region—clays, marl, and sands are abundant and of excellent quality.

Should the future prosperity of the country demand it, there are abundant materials for the manufacture of what is called in England, and recently brought into use in this country, "patent concrete stone." It is composed of small fragments of stone or sand reduced to a paste by a fluid silicate, then moulding the material into any required form and dipping into the chloride of calcium. The little particles of sand are thus cemented together, and it is wonderful how rapidly this rock can be formed and how durable it becomes. This is a matter which seems to me worthy of notice in the final report.

38.

[*General Land Office Report*]

OUR MINERAL FUTURE [1870]

The extent of our mineral resources is in general but imperfectly apprehended, notwithstanding the continual accumulation of knowledge on this subject. Even our splendid agricultural capacities, with advantages of soil, climate, and geographical position, will probably be surpassed by the majestic results of our mineral industry when once a scientific system shall control our enterprise.

. . . .

Our mineral treasures are gathered in a mighty elliptical bowl, the outer rim of which skirts the Atlantic coast to the Gulf of Mexico, and thence, crossing the Mississippi Valley, runs northward with the plains lying at the eastern base of the Rocky Mountains, and round by the great lakes to the place of beginning. The rim of this basin is filled with exhaustless stores of iron ore of every variety and of the best quality. In the midst of this great basin the carboniferous ores are fully as abundant as they are in England, but have hither to been left unwrought in consequence of the cheaper rate of producing the richer ores from the rim of the basin along the Atlantic slope of the great Appallachian Chain of mountains. From the Hudson River to the heart of Georgia, the outcrop of magnetic ore extends 1,000 miles in length, traversing seven States in its course. Parallel to this is the great limestone valley, which lies along the margin of the great Appallachian coal field, in which lie buried masses of brown hematite, the abundance of which, especially in Virginia, Tennessee, and Alabama, staggers the imagination. Again, within the coal basin itself is a stratum of red fossiliferous iron ore, beginning in a thin seam in New York, and expanding in Alabama to a breadth of 100 miles, with beds often 15 feet in thickness. Beneath this bed, but still above water level, are thick coal seams exposed in mountain sides, which are covered with timber available for mining or for the manufacture of charcoal iron. West of the Mississippi is traced, through Arkansas and Missouri, a wonderful range of red oxide iron, outcropping often in mountains of almost solid ore, rising hundreds of feet above the surface, with deep and broad foundations, extending an undetermined distance downward into the earth. This range, crossing the Mississippi, culminates in ore beds which have excited the wonder of the world. Along the Adirondacks are beds of iron of the same character, completing the metallic circle to the magnetics of the Atlantic slope. Within this circle, and intermingled with the coal beds, are various local deposits of fossiliferous and hematite ores, the proximity of which to the coal beds has aroused the iron industry of the nation. On the Pacific slope, amid its glittering golden and silver deposits, iron has, as yet, been found in but limited quantities; yet, it is thought that a more careful survey of the mineral deposits of the Sierra Nevada will develop a respectable amount of iron ores, though probably not to be compared with the enormous resources of the eastern and middle slopes of our continent.

This rapid summary of our iron resources exhibits a latent industrial power, the results of which we can scarce conceive. We have, as yet, begun only to chip the rim of our great iron basin in a few places.

39.

Ralph Waldo Emerson

DIVINITY SCHOOL ADDRESS [1838]

In this refulgent summer, it has been a luxury to draw the breath of life. The grass grows, the buds burst, the meadow is spotted with fire and gold in the tint of flowers. The air is full of birds, and sweet with the breath of the pine, the balm-of-Gilead, and the new hay. Night brings no gloom to the heart with its welcome shade. Through the transparent darkness the stars pour their almost spiritual rays. Man under them seems a young child, and his huge globe a toy. The cool night bathes the world as with a river, and prepares his eyes again for the crimson dawn. The mystery of nature was never displayed more happily. The corn and the wine have been freely dealt to all creatures, and the never-broken silence with which the old bounty goes forward has not yielded yet one word of explanation.

One is constrained to respect the perfection of this world in which our senses converse. How wide; how rich; what invitation from every property it gives to every faculty of man! In its fruitful soils; in its navigable sea; in its mountains of metal and stone; in its forests of all woods; in its animals; in its chemical ingredients; in the powers and path of light, heat, attraction and life, it is well worth the pith and heart of great men to subdue and enjoy it. The planters, the mechanics, the inventors, the astronomers, the builders of cities, and the captains, history delights to honor.

Part Two

MAN'S DOMINION

And God said, Let us make man in our image, after our likeness: and let them have dominion over the fish of the sea, and over the fowl of the air, and over the cattle, and over all the earth, and over every creeping thing that creepeth upon the earth.

Civilization has meant, for nature, not only celebration by man but also interference, domination, and even destruction. Judaeo-Christian tradition, amplified by Greek rationalism and sealed by the astonishing success of the scientific revolution, has given us a world picture with man in the foreground: man, pre-eminent among the creatures, into whose hands the world is given; man, by turns the subjugator and the steward of nature.

The tool by which man has gained and extended his power over the rest of nature is his technology. Beginning with the invention of weapons with which to hunt game, through the development of agriculture with which to regulate nature's food-producing processes, to the huge dams, atomic bombs, airplanes, pesticides, cities, and other means by which nature is assaulted, tamed, and turned to man's purposes, technology has brought forth a world both magnificent and terrible. For, while brain and hand have risen nimbly to every challenge, wisdom and foresight have often limped behind.

We have surmised that celebrations of nature marked the onset of civilization; civilization, however, is powered by technology and embodied in its multifarious products. Thus increasingly immersed in his own works, man has come to celebrate himself at the expense of nature.

*   *   *

Part II begins with nine background selections drawn from other places and times, all but one of which contribute to the notion of man's dominion over nature. The first (Selection 40) indicates the deep, perhaps essential character of this notion, for in it God deeds the world for a second time to man. Noah is given temporal dominion in even stronger terms than was Adam, despite the fact that the Fall and the Flood have intervened. The readings that follow amplify the idea through various means, the most powerful being, of course, science. In Selection 46, included as much for spice as for balance, Jonathan Swift casts his jaundiced eye on the excesses and absurdities into which man's pride in his scientific ingenuity can lead him.

Selections 49 through 69 follow America westward and through time as it grows from a patchwork of insecure settlements into a mighty nation, gathering confidence and pride along the way. The readings range from thoughtful appraisals of the job and means at hand, through self-congratulations on conquests won, to stirring calls to ever more ambitious action. Mark Twain's wry comments (Selection 59) are, like Swift's, introduced for their bracing effect. Selections 70 through 78 continue along the same line, but with a significant difference in tone. The nineteenth century's infant industrialism, with its tunnel vision and cocksureness, gives way to the twentieth century's doubts and worries, voiced or unvoiced, of adolescence. Selection 78, also from Mark Twain, breaks the chronological sequence but not the train of thought in expressing in a beautiful metaphor the conflict of knowledge and innocence that confronts modern man no less than it did Adam.

The second section of Part II, comprising Selections 79 through 131, recounts the same story of a growing and industrializing America but as if the coin had been flipped or, as the introduction to the section suggests, from the backside. It is an account of things gone wrong—mistakes, failures, disasters. From Peter Kalm's description of ruinous agricultural practices in Selection 83 to Selection 130's revelation of human tragedy brought by powerful pesticides, it is a rear-view history of technological progress. Selection 131 ends the section and Part II with the suitably pessimistic observation that, with regard to industrial growth and is concomitant pollution of the environment, we are doomed to success.

CONQUERING
THE WILDERNESS

40.

THE STEWARDSHIP OF MAN—GENESIS 9:1-3

And God blessed
Noah and his sons, and said unto them, Be fruitful, and multiply,
and replenish the earth.

And the fear of you and the dread of you shall be upon every
beast of the earth, and upon every fowl of the air, upon all that
moveth upon the earth, and upon all the fishes of the sea; into your
hand are they delivered.

Every moving thing that liveth shall be meat for you; even as the
green herb have I given you all things.

41.

Aeschylus

From PROMETHEUS BOUND [ca. 460 B.C.]

Listen to the tale
Of human sufferings, and how at first
Senseless as beasts I gave men sense, possessed them
Of mind. I speak not in contempt of man;

I do but tell of good gifts I conferred.
In the beginning, seeing they saw amiss,
And hearing heard not, but, like phantoms huddled
In dreams, the perplexed story of their days
Confounded; knowing neither timber-work
Nor brick-built dwellings basking in the light,
But dug for themselves holes, wherein like ants,
That hardly may contend against a breath,
They dwelt in burrows of their unsunned caves.
Neither of winter's cold had they fixed sign,
Nor of the spring when she comes decked with flowers,
Nor yet of summer's heat with melting fruits
Sure token: but utterly without knowledge
Moiled, until I the rising of the stars
Showed them, and when they set, though much obscure.
Moreover, number, the most excellent
Of all inventions, I for them devised,
And gave them writing that retaineth all,
The serviceable mother of the Muse.
I was the first that yoked unmanaged beasts,
To serve as slaves with collar and with pack,
And take upon themselves, to man's relief,
The heaviest labour of his hand: and I
Tamed to the rein and drove in wheeléd cars
The horse, of sumptuous pride the ornament.
And those sea-wanderers with the wings of cloth,
The shipman's waggons, none but I contrived.
These manifold inventions for mankind
I perfected,

. . . .

But hear the sequel and the more admire
What arts, what aids I cleverly evolved.
The chiefest that, if any man fell sick,
There was no help for him, comestible,
Lotion or potion; but for lack of drugs
They dwindled quite away; until I taught them
To compound draughts and mixtures sanative,
Wherewith they now are armed against disease.
I staked the winding path of divination
And was the first distinguisher of dreams,
The true from false; and voices ominous
Of meaning dark interpreted; and tokens
Seen when men take the road; and augury
By flight of all the greater crook-clawed birds
With nice discrimination I defined;
These by their nature fair and favourable,
Those, flattered with fair name. And of each sort
The habits I described; their mutual feuds

And friendships and the assemblages they hold.
And of the plumpness of the inward parts
What colour is acceptable to the Gods,
The well-streaked liver-lobe and gall-bladder.
Also by roasting limbs well wrapped in fat
And the long chine, I led men on the road
Of dark and riddling knowledge; and I purged
The glancing eye of fire, dim before,
And made its meaning plain. These are my works.
Then, things beneath the earth, aids hid from man,
Brass, iron, silver, gold, who dares to say
He was before me in discovering?
None, I wot well, unless he loves to babble.
And in a single word to sum the whole—
All manner of arts men from Prometheus learned.

42.

Plato

From PHAEDRUS [ca. 380 B.C.]

Socrates: But let me ask you, friend: have we not reached the plane-tree to which you were conducting us?

Phaedrus: Yes, this is the tree.

Socrates: By Herè, a fair resting-place, full of summer sounds and scents. Here is this lofty and spreading plane-tree, and the agnus castus high and clustering, in the fullest blossom and the greatest fragrance; and the stream which flows beneath the plane-tree is deliciously cold to the feet. Judging from the ornaments and images, this must be a spot sacred to Achelous and the Nymphs. How delightful is the breeze:—so very sweet; and there is a sound in the air shrill and summerlike which makes answer to the chorus of the cicadae. But the greatest charm of all is the grass, like a pillow gently sloping to the head. My dear Phaedrus, you have been an admirable guide.

Phaedrus: What an incomprehensible being you are, Socrates:

when you are in the country, as you say, you really are like some stranger who is led about by a guide. Do you ever cross the border? I rather think that you never venture even outside the gates.

Socrates: Very true, my good friend; and I hope that you will excuse me when you hear the reason, which is, that I am a lover of knowledge, and the men who dwell in the city are my teachers, and not the trees or the country. Though I do indeed believe that you have found a spell with which to draw me out of the city into the country, like a hungry cow before whom a bough or a bunch of fruit is waved. For only hold up before me in like manner a book, and you may lead me all round Attica, and over the wide world.

43.

Francis Bacon

THE SPHINX [1608]

Sphinx, says the story, was a monster combining many shapes in one. She had the face and voice of a virgin, the wings of a bird, the claws of a griffin. She dwelt on the ridge of a mountain near Thebes and infested the roads, lying in ambush for travellers, whom she would suddenly attack and lay hold of; and when she had mastered them, she propounded to them certain dark and perplexing riddles, which she was thought to have obtained from the Muses. And if the wretched captives could not at once solve and interpret the same, as they stood hesitating and confused she cruelly tore them to pieces. Time bringing no abatement of the calamity, the Thebans offered to any man who should expound the Sphinx's riddles (for this was the only way to subdue her) the sovereignty of Thebes as his reward. The greatness of the prize induced Oedipus, a man of wisdom and penetration, but lame from wounds in his feet, to accept the condition and make the trial: who presenting himself full of confidence and alacrity before the Sphinx, and being asked what kind of animal it was which was born four-footed, afterwards became two-footed, then three-footed, and at last four-footed again, answered readily that it was man; who at his birth and during his infancy sprawls on all fours, hardly attempting to creep; in a little while walks upright on two feet; in later years leans on a walking-stick and so goes as it were on three; and at last in extreme age and decrepitude, his sinews all failing, sinks into a quadruped again, and keeps his bed. This was the right answer and gave him the victory; whereupon he slew the Sphinx; whose body was put on the back of an ass and carried about in triumph; while himself was made according to compact king of Thebes.

The fable is an elegant and a wise one, invented apparently in allusion to Science; especially in its application to practical life. Science, being the wonder of the ignorant and unskilful, may be not absurdly called a monster. In figure and aspect it is represented as many-shaped, in allusion to the immense variety of matter with which it deals. It is said to have the face and voice of a woman, in respect of its beauty and facility of utterance. Wings are added because the sciences and the discoveries of science spread and fly abroad in an instant; the communication of knowledge being like that of one candle with another, which lights up at once. Claws, sharp and hooked, are ascribed to it with great elegance, because the axioms and arguments of science penetrate and hold fast the mind, so that it has no means of evasion or escape; a point which the sacred philosopher also noted: *The words of the wise are as goads, and as nails driven deep in*. Again, all knowledge may be regarded as having its station on the heights of mountains; for it is deservedly esteemed a thing sublime and lofty, which looks down upon ignorance as from an eminence, and has moreover a spacious prospect on every side, such as we find on hill-tops. It is described as infesting the roads, because at every turn in the journey or pilgrimage of human life, matter and occasion for study assails and encounters us. Again Sphinx proposes to men a variety of hard questions and riddles which she received from the Muses. In these, while they remain with the Muses, there is probably no cruelty; for so long as the object of meditation and inquiry is merely to know, the understanding is not oppressed or straitened by it, but is free to wander and expatiate, and finds in the very uncertainty of conclusion and variety of choice a certain pleasure and delight; but when they pass from the Muses to Sphinx, that is from contemplation to practice, whereby there is necessity for present action, choice, and decision, then they begin to be painful and cruel; and unless they be solved and disposed of they strangely torment and worry the mind, pulling it first this way and then that, and fairly tearing it to pieces. Moreover the riddles of the Sphinx have always a twofold condition attached to them; distraction and laceration of mind, if you fail to solve them; if you succeed, a kingdom. For he who understands his subject is master of his end; and every workman is king over his work.

44.

Francis Bacon

THE GOAL OF SCIENCE [1620]

The real and legitimate goal of the sciences, is the endowment of human life with new inventions and riches.

. . . .

It remains for us to say a few words on the excellence of our proposed end. If we had done so before, we might have appeared merely to express our wishes, but now that we have excited hope and removed prejudices, it will perhaps have greater weight. Had we performed and completely accomplished the whole, without frequently calling in others to assist in our labors, we should then have refrained from saying any more, lest we should be thought to extol our own deserts. Since, however, the industry of others must be quickened, and their courage roused and inflamed, it is right to recall some points to their memory.

First, then, the introduction of great inventions appears one of the most distinguished of human actions, and the ancients so considered it; for they assigned divine honors to the authors of inventions, but only heroic honors to those who displayed civil merit (such as the founders of cities and empires, legislators, the deliverers of their country from lasting misfortunes, the quellers of tyrants, and the like). And if anyone rightly compare them, he will find the judgment of antiquity to be correct; for the benefits derived from inventions may extend to mankind in general, but civil benefits to particular spots alone; the latter, moreover, last but for a time, the former forever. Civil reformation seldom is carried on without violence and confusion, whilst inventions are a blessing and a benefit without injuring or afflicting any.

. . . .

Again, let anyone but consider the immense difference between men's lives in the most polished countries of Europe, and in any wild and barbarous region of the new Indies, he will think it so great, that man may be said to be a god unto man, not only on account of mutual aid and benefits, but from their comparative states —the result of the arts, and not of the soil or climate.

45.

René Descartes

THE USE OF SCIENCE [1637]

So soon as I had acquired some general notions concerning Physics, and as, beginning to make use of them in various special difficulties, I observed to what point they might lead us, and how much they differ from the principles of which we have made use up to the present time, I believed that I could not keep them concealed without greatly sinning against the law which obliges us to procure, as much as in us lies, the general good of all mankind. For they caused me to see that it is possible to attain knowledge which is very useful in life, and that, instead of that speculative philosophy which is taught in the Schools, we may find a practical philosophy by means of which, knowing the force and the action of fire, water, air, the stars, heavens and all other bodies that environ us, as distinctly as we know the different crafts of our artisans, we can in the same way employ them in all those uses to which they are adapted, and thus render ourselves the masters and possessors of nature.

46.

Jonathan Swift [1725]

[Not everyone was dazzled by the great strides being made in the sciences, of course. In this selection, the great English satirist, in the character of the peripatetic Lemuel Gulliver, describes a visit to a scientific academy in the land of Lagado.]

The first man I saw, was of a meagre aspect, with sooty hands and face; his hair and beard long, ragged and singed in several places. His cloaths, shirt, and skin, were all of the same colour: he had been eight years upon a project for extracting sun-beams out of cucumbers; which were to be put into vials, hermetically sealed, and let out to warm the air, in raw inclement summers. He told me, he did not doubt, in eight years more, that he should be able to supply the governor's gardens with sun-shine at a reasonable rate; but, he complained that his stock was low, and intreated me to give him something as an encouragement to ingenuity, especially since this had been a very dear season for cucumbers: I made him a small present, for my lord had furnished me with money on purpose, because he knew their practice of begging from all who go to see them.

I went into another chamber, but was ready to hasten back, being almost overcome with a horrible stink: my conductor pressed me forward, conjuring me in a whisper to give no offence, which would be highly resented; and therefore, I durst not so much as stop my nose. The projector of this cell, was the most ancient student of the academy: his face and beard were of a pale yellow; his hands and cloaths dawbed over with filth. When I was presented to him, he gave me a very close embrace, (a compliment I could well have excused:) his employment from his first coming into the academy was an operation to reduce human excrement to its original food by separating the several parts, removing the tincture which it receives from the gall, making the odour exhale, and scumming off the saliva. He had a weekly allowance from the society, of a vessel filled with human ordure, about the bigness of a Bristol barrel.

I saw another at work to calcine ice into gun-powder, who likewise shewed me a treatise he had written, concerning the malleability of fire, which he intended to publish.

. . . .

In another apartment, I was highly pleased with a projector, who had found a device of plowing the ground with hogs, to save the charges of plows, cattle, and labour. The method is this: In an acre of ground you bury at six inches distance, and eight deep, a quantity of acorns, dates, chestnuts, and other maste or vegetables, whereof these animals are fondest; then you drive six hundred or more of them into the field, where in a few days they will root up the whole ground in search of their food, and make it fit for sowing, at the same time manuring it with their dung. It is true, upon experiment, they found the charge and trouble very great, and they had little or no crop. However, it is not doubted that this invention may be capable of great improvement.

. . . .

There was an astronomer who had undertaken to place a sundial upon the great weather-cock on the town-house, by adjusting the annual and diurnal motions of the earth and sun, so as to answer and coincide with all accidental turnings of the wind.

. . . .

I visited many other apartments, but shall not trouble my reader with all the curiosities I observed, being studious of brevity.

I had hitherto seen only one side of the academy, the other being appropriated to the advancers of speculative learning; of whom I shall say something when I have mentioned one illustrious person more, who is called among them, 'The universal artist.' He told us, he had been thirty years employing his thoughts for the improvement of human life. He had two large rooms full of wonderful curiosities, and fifty men at work: some were condensing air into a dry tangible substance, by extracting the nitre, and letting the aqueous or fluid particles percolate: others softening marble for pillows and pincushions; others petrifying the hoofs of a living horse, to preserve them from foundering. The artist himself was at that time busy upon two great designs: the first, to sow land with chaff, wherein he affirmed the true seminal virtue to be contained, as he demonstrated by several experiments which I was not skilful enough to comprehend. The other was, by a certain composition of gums, minerals, and vegetables outwardly applied, to prevent the growth of wool upon two young lambs; and he hoped in a reasonable time to propagate the breed of naked sheep all over the kingdom.

47.

Voltaire [1752]

[In this fantasy, Micromégas, a giant from the star Sirius, and his companion, a lesser giant from the academy of the planet Saturn, visit the earth and, with the aid of a powerful magnifying glass, discover human beings, who to their surprise seem to exhibit some evidences of intelligence.]

"But," said the dwarf, "this globe is so badly constructed and so irregular; it is of a form which to me seems ridiculous! Everything here is in chaos, apparently. Do you see how none of those little brooks run straight? And those ponds which are neither round, square, oval, nor of any regular form? Look at all those little pointed things with which this world is studded; they have taken the skin off my feet! (He referred to the mountains.) Do you not observe the shape of the globe, how flat it is at the poles, and how clumsily it turns round the sun, with result that the polar regions are waste places? What really makes me think there is no one on the earth is that I cannot imagine any sensible people wanting to live here."

"Well, well!" said Micromégas, "perhaps the people who live here are not sensible after all. But anyway there is an indication that the place was not made for nothing. You say that everything here looks irregular, because in Jupiter and Saturn everything is arranged in straight lines. Perhaps it is for that very reason there is something of a jumble here. Have I not told you that in my travels I have always observed variety?"

. . . .

Mr. Micromégas then asked another of the wise men he held on his thumb what his soul was, and what it did.

"Nothing at all," replied the disciple of Malebranche. "God does everything for me. I see everything in Him, I do everything in Him. It is He who does everything without my interfering."

"It would be as well worth while not to exist," said the sage from Sirius. "And you, my friend," he continued to a Leibnitzian who was there, "what is your soul?"

"My soul," answered the Leibnitzian, "is a hand which points the hours while my body ticks: or, if you prefer it, it is my soul which ticks while my body points the hour: or again, my soul is the mirror of the universe, and my body is the frame of the mirror. That is quite clear."

A humble partisan of Locke stood nearby, and when he was spoken to at last, replied: "I do not know how I think, but I do know that I have never thought save by virtue of my senses. That there are immaterial and intelligent beings I do not doubt: but that it is impossible for God to endow matter with mind I doubt very much. I hold the power of God in veneration: I am not free to set bounds to it: I predicate nothing: I am content to believe that more things are possible than we think."

The animal from Sirius smiled. He did not think the last speaker the least wise. The dwarf from Saturn would have embraced the follower of Locke had it not been for the difference in their proportions.

But, unluckily, there was present a minute animalcule in a clerical hat who interrupted the other animalcule philosophers. He said he understood the whole mystery; that the explanation was to be found in the *Summa* of St. Thomas. He looked the two celestial inhabitants up and down, and asserted that their persons, worlds, suns, and stars were created solely for man.

At this speech the two travelers fell on top of each other, suffocating with that inextinguishable laughter which, according to Homer, is the lot of the gods. Their shoulders and stomachs heaved, and amid these convulsions the ship which the Sirian held on his thumb fell into one of the Saturnian's trousers pockets. These two good people tried to find it for a long time and, having recovered it at last, set everything very nicely in order. The Sirian picked the maggots up again and spoke to them once more with much kindness, although at the bottom of his heart he was rather angry that such infinitely small creatures should be possessed of an arrogance almost infinitely great. He promised to prepare for them a fine volume of philosophy, written very small so that they might be able to read it, and that in the volume they would find an explanation for everything. And to be sure, he did give them this book before he left them. They took it to Paris to the Academy of Science: but when the aged secretary opened it he found nothing but blank pages. "Ah!" said he. "I thought as much."

48.

William Wordsworth

COMPOSED UPON WESTMINSTER BRIDGE [1802]

[Even though primarily a poet of nature, Wordsworth could be moved by the splendor and charm of a man-made environment—provided, however, that he caught it, as here, yet asleep, while the air was still smokeless.]

Earth has not anything to show more fair:
Dull would he be of soul who could pass by
A sight so touching in its majesty:
This city now doth like a garment wear
The beauty of the morning; silent, bare,
Ships, towers, domes, theaters, and temples lie
Open unto the fields, and to the sky;
All bright and glittering in the smokeless air.
Never did sun more beautifully steep
In his first splendor valley, rock, or hill;
Ne'er saw I, never felt, a calm so deep!
The river glideth at his own sweet will:
Dear God! the very houses seem asleep;
And all that mighty heart is lying still!

[America's value, in the eyes of most explorers and settlers, lay not in the actuality of wilderness and natural beauty but in the potential for economic development. Whether they saw the American future in terms of agriculture, commerce, or manufacturing, they agreed that here was an opportunity to create a new and great civilization. All the necessary material resources lay ready at hand; man's energy and ingenuity had only to be applied to bring forth a nation that would dazzle the world.]

49.

M. G. Jean de Crevecoeur

THE MAKING OF AMERICANS [1782]

[Jean de Crèvecoeur, a French immigrant farmer, took a hardheaded view of the needs of the new nation and, as this selection makes quite clear, had little time for effusions on nature or on the mythical Noble Savage.]

But to return to our backsettlers. I must tell you that there is something in the proximity of the woods which is very singular. It is with men as it is with the plants and animals that grow and live in the forests; they are entirely different from those that live in the plains. I will candidly tell you all my thoughts, but you are not to expect that I shall advance any reasons. By living in or near the woods, their actions are regulated by the wildness of the neighborhood. The deer often come to eat their grain, the wolves to destroy their sheep, the bears to kill their hogs, the foxes to catch their poultry. This surrounding hostility immediately puts the gun into their hands; they watch these animals, they kill some; and thus by defending their property, they soon become professed hunters; this is the progress; once hunters, farewell to the plow. The chase renders them ferocious, gloomy, and unsociable: a hunter wants no neighbor; he rather hates them, because he dreads the competition. In a little time their success in the woods makes them neglect their tillage. They trust to the natural fecundity of the earth, and therefore do little; carelessness in fencing often exposes what little they sow to destruction; they are not at home to watch; in order therefore to make up the deficiency, they go oftener to the woods. That new mode of life brings along with it a new set of manners, which I cannot easily describe. These new manners, being grafted on the old stock, produce a strange sort of lawless profligacy, the impressions of which are indelible. The manners of the Indian natives are respectable, compared with this European medley. Their wives and children live in sloth and inactivity; and having no proper pursuits, you may judge what education the latter receive. Their tender minds have nothing else to contemplate but the example of their parents; like them they grow up a mongrel breed, half civilized, half savage, except nature stamps on them some constitutional propensities. That rich, that voluptuous sentiment is gone that struck them so forcibly; the possession of their freeholds no longer conveys to their minds the same pleasure and pride. To all these reasons you must add their lonely situation, and you cannot imagine what an effect on manners the great distances they live from each other has! Consider one of the last settlements in its first view; of what is it composed? Europeans who have not that sufficient share of knowledge they ought to have in order to prosper; people who have suddenly passed from oppression, dread of government, and fear of laws into the unlimited freedom of the woods. This sudden change must have a very great effect on most men, and on that class particularly. Eating of wild meat, whatever you may think, tends to alter their temper, though all the proof I can adduce is that I have seen it; and having no place of worship to resort to, what little society this might afford is denied them. The Sunday meetings, exclusive of religious benefits, were the only social bonds that might have inspired them with some degree of emulation in neatness. Is it then surprising to see men thus situated, immersed in great and heavy labors, degenerate a little? It is rather a wonder the effect is not more diffusive. The Moravians and the Quakers are the only instances in exception to what I have advanced. The first never settle singly, it is a colony of the society which emigrates; they carry with them their forms, worship, rules, and decency: the others never begin so hard, they are always able to buy improvements, in which there is a great advantage, for by that time the country is recovered from its first barbarity. Thus our bad people are those who are half cultivators and half hunters; and the worst of them are those who have degenerated altogether into the hunting state. As old plowmen and new men of the woods, as Europeans and new made Indians, they contract the vices of both; they adopt the moroseness and ferocity of a native, without his mildness, or even his industry at home. If manners are not refined, at least they are rendered simple and inoffensive by tilling the earth; all our wants are supplied by it, our time is divided between labor and rest, and leaves none for the commission of great misdeeds. As hunters it is divided between the toil of the chase, the idleness of repose, or the indulgence of inebriation. Hunting is but a licentious idle life, and if it does not always pervert good dispositions, yet, when it is united with bad luck, it leads to want: want stimulates that propensity to rapacity and injustice, too natural to needy men, which is the fatal gradation. After this explanation of the effects which follow by living in the woods, shall we yet vainly flatter ourselves with the hope of converting the Indians? We should rather begin with converting our backsettlers; and now if I dare mention the name of religion, its sweet accents would be lost in the immensity of these woods. Men thus placed are not fit either to receive or remember its mild instructions; they want temples and ministers, but as soon as men cease to remain at home, and begin to lead an erratic life, let them be either tawny or white, they cease to be its disciples.

50.

William Cooper [ca. 1806]

[William Cooper, father of James Fenimore Cooper, was the founder and principal citizen of Cooperstown, New York. Here, he describes his venture as an entrepreneur in the woods.]

In 1785 I visited the rough and hilly country of Otsego, where there existed not an inhabitant, nor any trace of a road; I was alone three hundred miles from home, without bread, meat, or food of any kind; fire and fishing tackle were my only means of subsistence. I caught trout in the brook, and roasted them on the ashes. My horse fed on the grass that grew by the edge of the waters. I laid me down to sleep in my watch-coat, nothing but the melancholy Wilderness around me. In this way I explored the country, formed my plans of future settlement, and meditated upon the spot where a place of trade or a village should afterwards be established.

In May 1786 I opened the sales of 40,000 acres, which, in sixteen days, were all taken up by the poorest order of men. I soon after established a store, and went to live among them, and continued so to do till 1790, when I brought on my family. For the ensuing four years the scarcity of provisions was a serious calamity; the country was mountainous, there were neither roads nor bridges.

. . . .

I had not funds of my own sufficient for the opening of new roads, but I collected the people at convenient seasons, and by joint efforts we were able to throw bridges over the deep streams, and to make, in the cheapest manner, such roads as suited our then humble purposes.

. . . .

This was the first settlement I made, and the first attempted after the revolution; it was, of course, attended with the greatest difficulties; nevertheless, to its success many others have owed their origin. It was besides the roughest land in all the state, and the most difficult of cultivation of all that has been settled; but for many years past it has produced every thing necessary to the support and comfort of man. It maintains at present eight thousand souls, with schools, academies, churches, meeting-houses, turnpike roads, and a market town. It annually yields to commerce large droves of fine oxen, great quantities of wheat and other grain, abundance of pork, pot ash in barrels, and other provisions; merchants with large capitals, and all kinds of useful mechanics reside upon it; the waters are stocked with fish, the air is salubrious, and the country thriving and happy. When I contemplate all this, and above all, when I see these good old settlers meet together, and hear them talk of past hardships, of which I bore my share, and compare the misery they then endured with the comforts they now enjoy, my emotions border upon weakness, which manhood can scarcely avow.

. . . .

You have now before you, as well as I can explain, the advantages and the difficulties which belong to an enterprize in new lands. But let me be clearly understood in this, that no man who does not possess a steady mind, a sober judgment, fortitude, perseverance, and above all, common sense, can expect to reap the reward, which to him who possesses those qualifications, is almost certain.

51.

Thomas Jefferson [1785, 1816]

[In his *Notes on the State of Virginia*, Jefferson outlined succinctly and poetically the classic agrarian argument against industrialization; in a letter to Benjamin Austin thirty-one years later, he described the change of mind that alterations in world politics had forced upon him. What had not changed, however, was his firm conviction that America was to be possessed and developed by man for the good of man.]

The political economists of Europe have established it as a principle, that every State should endeavor to manufacture for itself; and this principle, like many others, we transfer to America, without calculating the difference of circumstance which should often produce a difference of result. In Europe the lands are either cultivated, or locked up against the cultivator. Manufacture must therefore be resorted to of necessity not of choice, to support the surplus of their people. But we have an immensity of land courting the industry of the husbandman. Is it best then that all our citizens should be employed in its improvement, or that one half should be called off from that to exercise manufactures and handicraft arts for the other? Those who labor in the earth are the chosen people of God, if ever He had a chosen people, whose breasts He has made His peculiar deposit for substantial and genuine virtue. It is the focus in which he keeps alive that sacred fire, which otherwise might escape from the face of the earth. Corruption of morals in the mass of cultivators is a phenomenon of which no age nor nation has furnished an example. It is the mark set on those, who, not looking up to heaven, to their own soil and industry, as does the husbandman, for their subsistence, depend for it on casualties and caprice of customers. Dependence begets subservience and venality, suffocates the germ of virtue, and prepares fit tools for the designs of ambition. This, the natural progress and consequence of the arts, has sometimes perhaps been retarded by accidental circumstances; but, generally speaking, the proportion which the aggregate of the other classes of citizens bears in any State to that of its husbandmen, is the proportion of its unsound to its healthy parts, and is a good enough barometer whereby to measure its degree of corruption. While we have land to labor then, let us never wish to see our citizens occupied at a workbench, or twirling a distaff. Carpenters, masons, smiths, are wanting in husbandry; but, for the general operations of manufacture, let our workshops remain in Europe. It is better to carry provisions and materials to workmen there, than bring them to the provisions and materials, and with them their manners and principles. The loss by the transportation of commodities across the Atlantic will be made up in happiness and permanence of government. The mobs of great cities add just so much to the support of pure government, as sores do to the strength of the human body. It is the manners and spirit of a people which preserve a republic in vigor. A degeneracy in these is a canker which soon eats to the heart of its laws and constitution.

* * *

You tell me I am quoted by those who wish to continue our dependence on England for manufactures. There was a time when I might have been so quoted with more candour. But within the thirty years which have since elapsed, how are circumstances changed! We were then in peace; our independent place among nations was acknowledged. A commerce which offered the raw material, in exchange for the same material after receiving the last touch of industry, was worthy of welcome to all nations. It was expected, that those especially to whom manufacturing industry was important, would cherish the friendship of such customers by every favour, and particularly cultivate their peace by every act of justice and friendship. Under this prospect, the question seemed legitimate, whether, with such an immensity of unimproved land, courting the hand of husbandry, the industry of agriculture, or that of manufactures, would add most to the national wealth? And the doubt on the utility of the American manufactures was entertained on this consideration, chiefly, that to the labour of the husbandman a vast addition is made by the spontaneous energies of the earth on which it is employed. For one grain of wheat committed to the earth, she renders twenty, thirty, and even fifty fold; whereas to the labour of the manufacturer nothing is added. Pounds of flax, in his hands, on the contrary, yield but pennyweights of lace. This exchange too, laborious as it might seem, what a field did it promise for the occupation of the ocean; what a nursery for that class of citizens who were to exercise and maintain our equal rights on that element? This was the state of things in 1785, when the Notes on Virginia were first published.

. . . .

We must now place the manufacturer by the side of the agriculturalist. The former question is suppressed, or rather assumes a new form. The grand inquiry now is, shall we make our own comforts, or go without them at the will of a foreign nation? He, therefore, who is now against domestic manufacture, must be for reducing us either to dependence on that foreign nation, or to be clothed in skins, and to live like wild beasts in dens and caverns. I am not one of these. Experience has taught me that manufactures are now as necessary to our independence as to our comfort.

52.

[From the *Tennessee Herald*]

ADVERTISING A TOWN [1818]

On the 16th. day of
March 1818 (being the next Monday after the close of the Public
Land Sales at Huntsville) will be offered for sale to the highest
bidder on the premises; A part of the lots laid out for the new
town of Cotton Port.

The Town is laid out on the West Bank of Limestone river; one
mile above its junction with the Tennessee and a little below the
south Beaver Dam and the Piney Fork.

The situation is high and dry, promises to be as healthy as any
other place in the Alabama Territory, as near the Tennessee, is
sufficiently level, and elevated above the reach of the highest floods
of the Tennessee.

Within the limits of the Town are two never failing springs of
good water. The appearance of the Land and the success of similar
experiments in the country adjacent, justify a belief that on almost
every lot a well of good water may be had at a moderate depth
without blowing rock.

Limestone River from the Tennessee to this place is navigable at
all seasons of the year by the largest Keel and flat Bottom'd boats
used in the Navigation of the Tennessee. Limestone here affords a
safe harbor of deep still water, in which the greatest floods, boats
will be entirely free from the dangers to be at such times apprehended from the strong and rapid current and sudden risings and
fallings of the Tennessee. The situation at which Cotton Port is laid
out, has in fact long since been proved by the observation and experienced of the planters of the western and the north-western
parts of Madison county, to be the place which Nature has distinctly marked out for the commercial centre of the very fertile
country adjacent.

. . . .

Men of Industry, Enterprize & Judgement in almost every walk
of life, who seek to better their condition, in a new and unoccupied
field of action, will not be slow in forming their conclusions if they
can rely upon these statements.

. . . .

Trade cannot stagnate here. Industrious and ingenious mechanics must see that the inhabitants of such a country will want houses, furniture, farming utensils, leather, saddles, boots, shoes, &c. and will be able to pay good prices for them. The upper country on the Tennessee and Holston rivers and their branches will afford, at a very trifling expence for water carriage down the river, abundant supplies of provisions, iron, lumber and other raw materials.

A good dry road can be had from Cotton-Port, north to Elk river. The proprietors of the land laid out for the town intend to build a bridge across Limestone; and to make a good road for several miles towards the rich country about the Big Prairie.

From Cotton-Port to Falls of the Black Warrior, as good a road can probably be had as from any place on Tennessee river. The distance is about 100 miles.

The Trustees of the town, will reserve for public benefit, two lots including the two springs, two or more lots for a place of public worship, a school house, and such other public buildings as the prospects of the place may seem to require.

In the plan of the town the Trustees have endeavored to avoid every thing which will tend to bring all its population and business into one span, and leave the rest of the lots unoccupied. They have endeavored so to arrange the streets, lots, &c. as to secure to the future inhabitants as far as practicable, the benefits of shade and a free circulation of air, and to every family a piece of garden ground.

53.

Alexis de Tocqueville

THE AMERICAN SELF-IMAGE [1832]

In Europe people talk a great deal of the wilds of America, but the Americans themselves never think about them; they are insensible to the wonders of inanimate nature and they may be said not to perceive the mighty forests that surround them till they fall beneath the hatchet. Their eyes are fixed upon another sight: the American people views its own march across these wilds, draining swamps, turning the course of rivers, peopling solitudes, and subduing nature. This magnificent image of themselves does not meet the gaze of the Americans at intervals only; it may be said to haunt every one of them in his least as well as in his most important actions and to be always flitting before his mind.

54.

C. Fenno Hoffman

THE UNFINISHED ADIRONDACKS [1839]

Admitting the existence of occasional slight earthquakes in this region, I am not enough of a naturalist to surmise what may be their effect upon the geological features of the country. They seem, however, among other things, to indicate the *unfinished state of the country*, if I may so express myself.

They are among the agents of nature, still at work in completing a portion of the world hardly yet ready to pass from her hands into those of man. The separation of the water from the land, which classic cosmogonists tell us followed the birth of light, in evolving the earth from chaos, is not here completed yet. There are lakes on the tops of mountains, and swamps among wildernesses of rocks, which are yet to be drained by other means than the thick exhalations which carry them into the atmosphere, or the dripping mosses through which they ooze into the valleys, where day by day the new soil for future use accumulates.

Had our New York Indians, who now find it so difficult to hold on to their level and fertile lands in the western part of the state, but "located" their reservations among these mountains, they might have escaped the cupidity of the whites for centuries yet to come, and have hunted the deer, the moose, and the bear, or trapped for the martin, the sable, and the ermine, all of which still abound here, without molestation, save from the occasional white hunter that might intrude upon their grounds when chasing the wolf or panther from the settled regions, to the east and west of them. There are settlements upon some of these lakes, which were commenced more than thirty years since, and which can now boast of but two or three families as residents, and these are isolated from the rest of the world, with twenty miles of unbroken forest between them and more prosperous hamlets. But the immense beds of iron-ore and other minerals recently discovered, with the increased demand for timber in our Atlantic cities, and of charcoal to work the mines here, must now bring the country into general notice, and hasten its settlement. The demolition of the pine forests, and the conversion of less valuable wood into charcoal, will rapidly clear the country, and convert the lumber-men and charcoal-burners into farmers; while the old race of hunters already begin to find a new employment in acting as guides to the owners of lands, and projecting roads for them through districts where an ordinary surveyor could hardly be paid for the exercise of his profession.

55.

Ralph Waldo Emerson [1844]

[Though often thought of as a philosopher of the "return-to-nature" school, Emerson was wise enough to see the other side of the coin. In an essay entitled "Nature" in his *Essays: Second Series*, he pointed out that, as man is a part of nature, so too, in a very real sense, are his works.]

Things are so strictly related, that according to the skill of the eye, from any one object the parts and properties of any other may be predicted. If we had eyes to see it, a bit of stone from the city wall would certify us of the necessity that man must exist, as readily as the city. That identity makes us all one, and reduces to nothing great intervals on our customary scale. We talk of deviations from natural life, as if artificial life were not also natural. The smoothest curled courtier in the boudoirs of a palace has an animal nature, rude and aboriginal as a white bear, omnipotent to its own ends, and is directly related, there amid essences and billets-doux, to Himmaleh mountain-chains and the axis of the globe. If we consider how much we are nature's, we need not be superstitious about towns, as if that terrific or benefic force did not find us there also, and fashion cities. Nature, who made the mason, made the house. We may easily hear too much of rural influences. The cool disengaged air of natural objects makes them enviable to us, chafed and irritable creatures with red faces, and we think we shall be as grand as they if we camp out and eat roots; but let us be men instead of woodchucks and the oak and the elm shall gladly serve us, though we sit in chairs of ivory on carpets of silk.

This guiding identity runs through all the surprises and contrasts of the piece, and characterizes every law. Man carries the world in his head, the whole astronomy and chemistry suspended in a thought. Because the history of nature is charactered in his brain, therefore is he the prophet and discoverer of her secrets. Every known fact in natural science was divined by the presentiment of somebody, before it was actually verified. A man does not tie his shoe without recognizing laws which bind the farthest regions of nature: moon, plant, gas, crystal, are concrete geometry and numbers. Common sense knows it own, and recognizes the fact at first sight in chemical experiment. The common sense of Franklin, Dalton, Davy and Black is the same common sense which made the arrangements which now it discovers.

56.

Jesup W. Scott

THE GREAT WEST [1853]

The west is no longer the west; nor even the *great* west. It is the great centre. It is the body of the American eagle whose wings are on the two oceans. The centre of population seeking the centre of territorial productiveness, long since, in its movement westward, passed the Alleghenies, and is now making its way in a north-westerly direction through Ohio. Our people, after nearly two centuries spent in multiplying their numbers, and gathering their strength on the Atlantic border, broke over the mountain barriers, and spread themselves, scatteringly, over the vast interior plain. Persons are living who saw this plain one vast desert of forest and prairie; it now contains, within our national boundary, fourteen millions of people; including the Canadas, it numbers sixteen millions. Every year is adding, by natural increase and immigration, materially to this number. From the old States and from Europe, an annual tide pours into it, rich with the youth and vigor inherited from generations inured to think and to labor; this tide, increasing from year to year, promises to swell from hundreds of thousands to millions, and, so far is this influx from lessening the inducements to future immigration, that every million of new comers creates new comforts for the common use of the millions who follow.

The central plain, including Texas and Canada, contains not less than sixteen hundred thousand square miles, equal to one thousand million acres of land, fit for cultivation. Divided equally among the sixteen millions now living on it, every man, woman and child, would have sixty-four acres, and the population average ten to the square mile; with fifty to the square mile, like Ohio, it would contain eighty millions; or, like Massachusetts, 132 to the square mile, it would number two hundred and twelve millions; or if, like England, it had 327 to the square mile, it would have five hundred and twenty three millions. All these millions and more, will, one day, find here an ample and happy home. They will have descended from an ancestry formed of the strongest spirits of the old world and the new; men seeking difficulties for the enjoyment of overcoming them. It may require a period of two hundred years fully to people the North American plain; but, within the present century, before the year 1900, within the lifetime of persons now living, it will contain seventy-five millions, being nearly three times the present number of the whole nation. In its vast extent it has a marked unity of character. From the Gulf of Mexico to Hudson's Bay and the Polar Sea, from the Appalachian mountains on the east to the Rocky mountains bounding it on the west, its surface is nearly unbroken. The lakes of the north spread out their wide waters almost on the general level of the plain, while the rivers, which pour their accumulated waters into the gulf, have excavated their own channels, deep but narrow, towards their sources, gradually approximating their waters to the general surface, until they elevate their beds above the general plain at their mouths. For commercial and social purposes, it is the more one whole because of its lakes and rivers. By these channels are its people bound together. Even if steam had not begun its race on the land, its triumph on our interior waters, in cementing the bonds of union among its various parts, would have been complete. From the remotest regions, men and the products of their labor are transported by steam to the central marts of trade. In short, steam, working on our waters, has made our commerce one and our people a brotherhood. Diversity of climate, employment, and mineral products, tend only to strengthen this unity. Steam, working on rail-roads, will soon give great intensity to the forces now operating to bring the remotest parts of the plain into intimate relations of friendship and trade. The change is coming upon us so rapidly, that only the young can fully comprehend it. Like a splendid dream will it appear to people of mature age. Before the census of 1860 shall be printed, the whistle of the locomotive and the roar of the rolling train will be heard at nearly every house and hamlet of the wide central plain, and no one but a hermit will be willing to live beyond the cheering sound these will give forth.

All the changes in business and social relations which will grow directly out of the general extension of rail-roads, it is not given to anyone to foresee. That it will promote the growth of leading centres of commerce and manufacture, is already made manifest by the experience of the old States and England. Indeed no one could, with reason, expect any other result. Whether this will be permanent or not, may admit of a doubt. The rail-road has the power to spread out the city as well as to bring within its borders the various people needful to furnish it with the many wants of a high civilization. Our leading cities will be very populous, and spread over a wide surface. In our central plain will, probably, grow up the hugest aggregations of people in the world. Before it reaches the density of England, it will contain one or more cities numbering ten millions. Long before that period elapses, improvements in cultivation will so reduce the number needed to grow the food and raw materials of manufacture, that one-fourth of the population will be ample to effect that result; leaving three-fourths to be engaged in pursuits more profitably carried on in cities, where the greatest variety of employments furnishes the needed materials for the most effective co-operative industry.

The most fertile imagination, furnished with all the facts, would be at fault in predicting the condition of the community who will dwell on the central plain twenty years in the future. What development of commercial intercourse; what diversification of agricultural and mechanical operations, invited and rewarded by quick and cheap channels of transport; what development of architectural beauty, in rail-road stations, private residences, villages and cities; what public adornment of grounds, where learning, religion and gratitude erect their spacious halls, beautiful temples, and lofty monuments! The earth has no other such theatre for the growth of a rich and virtuous community. Nowhere else can so great a plain, of such fertility, in a climate so temperate, provided with so many natural channels of intercourse, and inviting so strongly such as man can make, inhabited by so energetic and intelligent a people, be pointed out on the face of our globe. Hither are hastening, as if conscious that a new Eden of happiness is about to be opened, hopeful and strong men, from all the nations and regions which breed reading, thinking, and promptly acting people. The history of mankind furnishes no parallel to the rapid colonization in progress here. From all the enlightened nations of the old world and from all the old States of our Union, multitudes are pouring in, which swell, in magnitude, with every revolving year. The imagination can conceive nothing more imposingly grand than this march of humanity westward, to enter into possession of "time's noblest Empire." No logical induction, no mathematical demonstration can be clearer to our mind, than that here will come together the greatest aggregations of men in cities,—outrivalling in splendor as in magnitude, all which past ages have produced.

57.

[From *Harper's New Monthly Magazine*]

AMONG THE WHEAT-FIELDS OF MINNESOTA [1868]

Wheat is planted in Minnesota as early as the weather and ground will permit. In April the plow is put to the soil and the seed sown, or earlier if possible; they plow deep, and allow one and a half to two bushels of seed to the acre. Wheat requires a dry soil and cool temperature. A good average yield is sixteen or twenty bushels to the acre, although many acres yield twenty-five or thirty bushels. By sowing early the grain has full opportunity to ripen slowly and surely; by sowing late the berry is "in the milk" when the hot, scorching days of August come, and the excessive heat blights it, drying and withering it up. In the best quality the berries are large, plump, and full.

As one goes over the country in the fall of the year he sees vast tracts of "new breaking," where the virgin soil, black as ink, and rich almost to glutinousness, has been broken by the plow, and the soil turned bottom upward in long, dark bands or layers as far as the eye can reach. Here it is exposed for months to the wind and weather till it decomposes and becomes fit for agricultural purposes. Every year vast tracts of prairie are thus turned over, or "broken," and with the next the loam is leveled and the seed is cast in; and thus large additions are annually made to the aggregate amount of acres of wheat.

Take your stand on one of these "new breaking-pieces," and look perhaps in any direction, and you will find yourself inclosed by its dreary strips of black loam; not a blade of grass nor a single leaf will appear. It is a picture of desolation and vacancy; nature and life are in their embryo; not a glimpse can be seen of their future creations. Nothing can exceed the contrast between this and what these same fields will present a year or two afterward, when they stand yellow with the harvest, an emblem of cheerfulness and prosperity.

. . . .

Wheat matures from about the beginning to the middle of August. The whole country then awakens from its long slothfulness.

Business revives. Interest, energy, and happiness every where appear. No one who has ever witnessed the dullness pervading all departments of business during the winter and spring can comprehend the great and sudden transformation which the incoming crop produces. Mechanics, tradesmen, wheat-buyers, railroads, steamboats—all seem to be indued with new life and vigor: every where is activity, bustle, and confusion. Wheat, owing to the prolonged rains, was planted quite late this year, and consequently was not so soon in getting to market as usual.

In the beginning of August the writer was stopping at St. Charles, a brisk little town on the Winona and St. Peter Railroad, 28 miles from the Mississippi River. All these railroad stations are "wheat outlets," whither the grain flows in steady streams from the outlying country. And so, too, are the different towns and steamboat landings on the Mississippi. Often the visitor sailing up the river is astonished to see the boat stop at some bluff so precipitous that it seems fool-hardy to attempt to ascend it; on the slope of which, however, he discovers one or two stores and saloons, and towering far above them the tall form of the inevitable "grain-elevator," with its brownish red front and vans for catching the wind. This certainly can not be a city, even in infancy, for there is no chance on these steep hill-sides for the most modest town to grow. But the traveler sees the propriety of it all when he is informed that this apparently impracticable and insignificant spot is an outlet for immense quantities of wheat, which is received in the tall elevator, and delivered below into barges to be carried to the markets of the East. Wheat thus delivered in "bulk" occupies many hours in loading, and often the down steamboat is delayed all this time, much to the yawning weariness of the impatient passengers.

58.

John H. Henry

INTERNAL IMPROVEMENTS [1868]

The rapid and vast increase of the internal commerce of the United States, with its stimulating effect on our increasing agricultural resources of our country, must arouse the commercial energy to keep pace with its vast developments. Our large rivers and navigable streams, canals, railroads, the great highways of internal commerce, are now taxed far beyond their capacity to accommodate the wants of an industrial and commercial people, while our government and people are busy extending her railroads in the frozen and bleak parts of our country, almost unfit for the abode of man. The most beautiful and salubrious portion of the continent is almost neglected.

Trade and communication is the life of the nation. We must grasp the rich commerce of China and Asia, by a grand system of railroads to the Pacific coast. The Southern Pacific railroad through Texas will prove the only practical line, while the extreme Northern lines will become a burden on account of the extreme ice and snow. God grant they may all be a success. Let our people and government be up and doing. Our internal commerce demands our best energies. When all our vast railroads, canals, and telegraph lines are completed, and rivers improved, with our thousands of steam horses, steam and canal boats, moving every second in the day, who can calculate the immense extension which our internal trade will assume, and what will be the result in regard to the price of all the comforts of life. Railroads, canals, and steam navigation has already done wonders in reducing the price of breadstuffs in our country, and it will undergo greater changes when we shall complete our vast system of internal improvements.

The distant States of California and Oregon have become the greatest wheat growing States, according to population, in the Union. Commerce is not prepared to transport her surplus of wheat. The great State of Texas, in the north-western part, on Red River, is the greatest wheat and grain growing country in the south-west. Commerce is not prepared to render her any assistance in bringing her products to market. The great Sabine and Neosho canal will be to her what the Mississippi river is to Illinois and Missouri, her great centre of trade. West of this great canal, is the greatest wheat and grain growing country in the United States, and it will produce the most powerful influence upon the price of provisions in America.

The time is near at hand when Ohio, Indiana, and Illinois will hardly be able to produce bread for their own people.

In improving rivers, canals, and building railroads, we have already surpassed all the nations of the earth; creating a system of internal improvements which facilitates the transportation of mineral and agricultural products at extremely low rates. With all our great progress in internal improvements, we have a vast and important work before us when we look over our country and see the millions and millions of acres of fertile lands that are far away from any of the highways of trade. We feel it is the duty of the government, and the people, that are so blessed with these channels of commerce, to extend their railroads and canals to those needy fertile regions.

. . . .

The internal trade of the United States at this time stands preëminently conspicuous, and overshadows all others. Although the export and import trade of our country is largely beyond our comprehension in our infancy as a nation, it is nothing in comparison with our great internal trade. Our country, from its extent of territory, must increase in proportion to the increase of population, which will soon have attained to over a hundred millions or more, developing the resources of a continent—the extent and national wealth of which will vastly exceed those of other nations. Our country, in its extent of domain, has diversity of production. The products of the South being cotton, rice, sugar and tobacco, must be exchanged for the products of the North, creating internal trade of the most gigantic character. As the tide of emigration flows into the new and enticing West, commerce must flow to the East and South, to the great cities of New York and Baltimore, on the Atlantic coast, and New Orleans and Galveston, on the Gulf coast. The cotton, sugar, corn, wheat and bacon of the South and West must be conveyed to these centres of internal trade. At the rate which our wealth and population are increasing, in 1920 our population will be a hundred millions, our wealth will be counted by billions of dollars, our science of government, under no slave institutions, but all free, will be brought to such perfection that the vast wealth produced by our unlimited internal resources will open all the arteries of trade in our common country, moving with beautiful harmony with all the departments of government. Our nation is vast—her bounds are oceans. She must absorb all the continent of North America, which embraces the best part of the world, giving us the means of internal navigation and trade which, if rightly used, must rule the world.

·Although our country, vast in extent, is capable of supporting as dense a population as any other nation to the square mile, it is not probable it will be greater than seventy-five to the square mile. Leaving out 2,500,000 square miles for the deserts and cold, inhospitable regions of the extreme north, leaving a balance of eight millions of square miles, we will then have a population of seven hundred millions of inhabitants, speaking the same tongue, and living under one federal government, with internal trade in proportion to the wants of the people, presenting the grandest spectacle of national power and prosperity.

.   .   .   .

Our inheritance is beyond our comprehension, our climate superior, our country bounded by oceans and traversed by noble rivers and lakes. In my humble opinion, all that is needed to make us the most prosperous and strongest nation of the globe, is to develop the intercommunication of our country, and place strong bridles on our wild water-horses which eat so much of our wealth, annually swallowing millions of acres of our choicest land as their food.

When all these improvements are made, and the iron horse breathes the Atlantic and Pacific air, we can then be called the first nation of the earth, for extent and density of soil and climate, and internal communication, and the variety and inexhaustible successes with labor, capital and enterprise, will entitle our country to the first rank.

Our country—the great nation—we boast of our greatness—she is emphatically the great nation. Where can we find our country's equal in geographical and natural advantages, in material progress or in general prosperity? As a united and a free people, the United States presents to the nations of the world a spectacle that must excite the grandest wonder and admiration.

59.

Mark Twain [1869]

[Mark Twain, an acute observer and tireless satirist of the foibles of men, reserved his sharpest wit for examples of self-importance. In this brief passage, he demolishes the average tourist encountering one of nature's grandest works.]

On the Canada side you drive along the chasm between long ranks of photographers standing guard behind their cameras, ready to make an ostentatious frontispiece of you and your decaying ambulance, and your solemn crate with a hide on it, which you are expected to regard in the light of a horse, and a diminished and unimportant background of sublime Niagara; and a great many people *have* the incredible effrontery or the native depravity to aid and abet this sort of crime.

Any day, in the hands of these photographers, you may see stately pictures of papa and mamma, Johnny and Bub and Sis, or a couple of country cousins, all smiling vacantly, and all disposed in studied and uncomfortable attitudes in their carriage, and all looming up in their awe-inspiring imbecility before the snubbed and diminished presentment of that majestic presence whose ministering spirits are the rainbows, whose voice is the thunder, whose awful front is veiled in clouds, who was monarch here dead and forgotten ages before this hackful of small reptiles was deemed temporarily necessary to fill a crack in the world's unnoted myriads, and will still be monarch here ages and decades of ages after they shall have gathered themselves to their blood-relations, the other worms, and been mingled with the unremembering dust.

There is no actual harm in making Niagara a background whereon to display one's marvelous insignificance in a good strong light, but it requires a sort of superhuman self-complacency to enable one to do it.

When you have examined the stupendous Horseshoe Fall till you are satisfied you cannot improve on it, you return to America by the new Suspension Bridge, and follow up the bank to where they exhibit the Cave of the Winds.

60.

John Stuart Mill [1874]

[In one of his *Three Essays on Religion,* John Stuart Mill summarized briefly his view of nature as no more than a field of possibility, a neutral background against which man himself creates the good.]

The word nature has two principal meanings: it either denotes the entire system of things, with the aggregate of all their properties, or it denotes things as they would be, apart from human intervention.

In the first of these senses, the doctrine that man ought to follow nature is unmeaning, since man has no power to do anything else than follow nature; all his actions are done through and in obedience to some one or many of nature's physical or mental laws.

In the other sense of the term, the doctrine that men ought to follow nature or, in other words, ought to make the spontaneous course of things the model of his voluntary actions is equally irrational and immoral: irrational, because all human action whatever consists in altering, and all useful action in improving, the spontaneous course of nature; immoral, because the course of natural phenomena being replete with everything which when committed by human beings is most worthy of abhorrence, any one who endeavoured in his actions to imitate the natural course of things would be universally seen and acknowledged to be the wickedest of men.

The scheme of nature regarded in its whole extent cannot have had, for its sole or even principal object, the good of human or other sentient beings. What good it brings to them is mostly the result of their own exertions. Whatsoever in nature gives indication of beneficent design proves this beneficence to be armed only with limited powers; and the duty of man is to co-operate with the beneficent powers, not by imitating but by perpetually striving to amend the course of nature—and bringing that part of it over which we can exercise control more nearly into conformity with a high standard of justice and goodness.

61.

[From *Scribner's Monthly*]

THE GROWTH OF CITIES IN THE UNITED STATES [1878]

[Principal among the works of man is, of course, the city, which, in a remarkable insight, is recognized in this article as being not merely a collection of buildings or a concentration of people but a cultural and techno-logical artifact—a machine.]

With a constantly augmenting percentage of the increase of population becoming dwellers in cities, the ratio of town to rural population will not be long in reaching a much higher standard than one-fifth, which it was in 1870; the more especially, as that percentage was then three times as great as it was in 1840. This proportion of 38 per cent includes not only those states, as Illinois and Missouri, where the urban population is small as compared with that of New York or Massachusetts; but it also includes such territory as Kansas, Arkansas and Mississippi, where there is no city population at all to speak of. In New York, during the last decade, the number of inhabitants in the rural districts actually decreased; the gain in the total population of that state being 502,000, and in the city population, 505,000. In England or France this would not be an extraordinary fact, for both have a very dense population; but occurring in this country, and in a state where there are not a hundred inhabitants to the square mile, it exhibits, with great force, the tendency toward concentration in cities.

. . . .

It remains to consider the agencies which are at work changing the proportion of the number of persons engaged in agriculture to the extent of the soil which they till, and the cause which creates the agents. Of these instrumentalities, we have space to notice only those two whose effects are most marked.

The first is agricultural machinery. A writer in a recent number of "Harper's Magazine" states facts from which we collect, that the number of persons required to produce a given amount of grain from a given tract of land and deliver it ready for use to the consumer, in 1840 and 1870, is about as eight to one. The introduction of machinery covers the handling and production of the raw materials alone, but embraces nearly every stage through which the grain passes, from its first planting until it is about to be converted into a manufactured article. It includes the harrow, the drill, the reaper, and thrasher and mower, the railroad, the steamship, the plow, and most especially the elevator.

On this calculation alone it would seem that the proportion of city population to rural may be seven times as great now as it was thirty years ago.

The second of these agencies is the railroad, or more properly the application of steam to dynamics, and chiefly in the way of transportation. The immense city population of the United States is made possible only by this discovery. A few great metropolises might exist at different intervals, without the facilities for intercourse which steam has given; but a considerable urban population, outside of the capitals, would be out of the question in a territory not three or four times more densely inhabited than Ohio (66 to the square mile).

But in considering these two factors as agents of the law of the growth of cities, they must not be confused with its cause. The reason of the increase of towns does not lie in any of the modern inventions, but is coincident with the influence that produced the inventions themselves. It has been frequently noticed that the most marked feature of social progress in recent times has been the extent to which automatic machines have taken the place of human hands, and the general prevalence of the principle of association in labor. It is believed that the tendency of civilization is toward the increase of intellectual, and the decrease of manual, activity; that in accordance therewith, society endeavors to produce the works necessary for its subsistence and convenience in shorter period, and with less bodily exertion, to the end of obtaining leisure for other pursuits. The impulse is universal. It affects every business and every circumstance of life. In obedience to its influence, each occupation of life, from the sawing of logs, to communicating with persons on the opposite side of the world, has attracted the attention of inventors, whose one problem is to multiply the working powers of mankind; to accomplish a given result by the substitution of the forces of nature where the forces of the human body were before used.

But among all the contrivances for effecting a saving of time and labor the city is scarcely second even to the steam-engine. In connection with the latter, it becomes the chief instrumentality in the promotion of civilization—at least in the movement which we call social progress. It is the principle of association carried out to its fullest extent. Agricultural pursuits necessitate a very considerable diffusion of population, while nearly every other employment is benefited by concentration.

62.

Walt Whitman

THE MISSISSIPPI VALLEY [1879]

Grand . . . is the thought that doubtless the child is already born who will see a hundred millions of people, the most prosperous and advanc'd of the world, inhabiting these Prairies, the great Plains, and the valley of the Mississippi.

. . . .

Speaking generally as to the capacity and sure future destiny of that plain and prairie area (larger than any European kingdom) it is the inexhaustible land of wheat, maize, wool, flax, coal, iron, beef and pork, butter and cheese, apples and grapes—land of ten million virgin farms—to the eye at present wild and unproductive—yet experts say that upon it when irrigated may easily be grown enough wheat to feed the world.

. . . .

The valley of the Mississippi river and its tributaries, (this stream and its adjuncts involve a big part of the question,) comprehends more than twelve hundred thousand square miles, the greater part prairies. It is by far the most important stream on the globe, and would seem to have been marked out by design, slow-flowing from north to south, through a dozen climates, all fitted for man's healthy occupancy, its outlet unfrozen all the year, and its line forming a safe, cheap continental avenue for commerce and passage from the north temperate to the torrid zone. Not even the mighty Amazon (though larger in volume) on its line of east and west—not the Nile in Africa, nor the Danube in Europe, nor the three great rivers of China, compare with it. Only the Mediterranean sea has play'd some such part in history, and all through the past, as the Mississippi is destined to play in the future. By its demesnes, water'd and welded by its branches, the Missouri, the Ohio, the Arkansas, the Red, the Yazoo, the St. Francis and others, it already compacts twenty-five millions of people, not merely the most peaceful and money-making, but the most restless and warlike on earth.

. . . .

To-day one of the newspapers of St. Louis prints the following informal remarks of mine on American, especially Western literature: "We called on Mr. Whitman yesterday and after a somewhat desultory conversation abruptly asked him: 'Do you think we are to have a distinctively American literature?' 'It seems to me,' said he, 'that our work at present is to lay the foundations of a great nation in products, in agriculture, in commerce, in networks of intercommunication, and in all that relates to the comforts of vast masses of men and families, with freedom of speech, ecclesiasticism, &c. These we have founded and are carrying out on a grander scale than ever hitherto, and Ohio, Illinois, Indiana, Missouri, Kansas and Colorado, seem to me to be the seat and field of these very facts and ideas.' "

63.

Robert Louis Stevenson

AMERICAN ENERGY [1879]

But let him imagine a young man who shall have grown up in an old and rigid circle, following bygone fashions and taught to distrust his own fresh instincts, and who now suddenly hears of a family of cousins, all about his own age, who keep house together by themselves and live far from restraint and tradition; let him imagine this, and he will have some imperfect notion of the sentiment with which spirited

English youths turn to the thought of the American Republic. It seems to them as if, out west, the war of life was still conducted in the open air, and on free barbaric terms; as if it had not yet been narrowed into parlours, nor begun to be conducted, like some unjust and dreary arbitration, by compromise, costume, forms of procedure, and sad, senseless self-denial. Which of these two he prefers, a man with any youth still left in him will decide rightly for himself. He would rather be houseless than denied a pass-key; rather go without food than partake of a stalled ox in stiff, respectable society; rather be shot out of hand than direct his life according to the dictates of the world.

He knows or thinks nothing of the Maine Laws, the Puritan sourness, the fierce, sordid appetite for dollars, or the dreary existence of country towns. A few wild story-books which delighted his childhood form the imaginative basis of his picture of America. In course of time, there is added to this a great crowd of stimulating details—vast cities that grow up as by enchantment; the birds, that have gone south in autumn, returning with the spring to find thousands camped upon their marshes, and the lamps burning far and near along populous streets; forests that disappear like snow; countries larger than Britain that are cleared and settled, one man running forth with his household gods before another, while the bear and the Indian are yet scarce aware of their approach; oil that gushes from the earth; gold that is washed or quarried in the brooks or glens of the Sierras; and all that bustle, courage, action, and constant kaleidoscopic change that Walt Whitman has seized and set forth in his vigorous, cheerful, and loquacious verses. Even the shot-gun, the navy revolver and the bowie knife, seem more connected with courage than with cruelty. I remember a while ago when Chicago was burned, hearing how a man, ere he began to rebuild his house, put up a board with some such inscription as the following: "All lost. Have a wife and three children. Have the world to begin again;" and then in large capitals the word: "*Energy.*" The pluck and the expansion are alike youthful, and go straight to a young heart. Yes, it seemed to me, here was the country after all; here the undaunted stock of mankind, worthy to earn a new world.

[Once the myth of the Great American Desert was dispelled by a number of well-planned scientific expeditions into the Western interior, the prospect of agriculture on the plains was immediately raised. Lack of water was recognized as the main problem; one theory, later proved disastrously mistaken, was that the gradual establishment of cropland in the rather dry region would, by increasing the rainfall, set up a progressive cycle of agricultural development.]

64.

William A. Bell

FARMING THE PLAINS [1867]

I think, most assuredly, if we consider even what I have said, there cannot be a doubt that all this region, extending beyond the 99th meridian, and almost to the 100th in Kansas, is susceptible of cultivation throughout without irrigation, and is likely to yield abundant crops and large profits to the farmer.

Not many miles west of Fort Hayes, vegetation begins to suffer from the diminution in the rain-fall, and the general fertility which I have been describing gradually disappears. Streams become less frequent, and dry arroyos take their place. Scrub bushes even are hard to find, and the only fuel to be had during marches of twenty miles or more, is the dry chips of the buffalo dung. Both to the north and south, this line of demarcation exists between the well-watered plains to the eastward, and the more arid regions separating them from the Rocky Mountains. To the north, the line deflects eastward, and to the south it diverges to the west, so that a greater portion of Nebraska is dry and unproductive than of Kansas; while Kansas, taken as a whole, is less fertile throughout than the Indian territory south of it.

There are places where this dry belt is very narrow, and were it absolutely desirable for a trans-continental railroad to avoid it altogether, and to pass all the way to the Rocky Mountains through land capable of continuous cultivation, either with or without irrigation, this might easily be accomplished by leaving the present road at Salina, or Fort Harker, crossing direct to the Arkansas River, following it to New Fort Lyon, and then continuing up the Purgatoire into New Mexico. It is, however, often considered better to make short cuts, than to keep too persistently to the fertile valleys.

Some dozen miles from Fort Hayes, as I have said, we began to enter this impoverished country, and as we advanced day by day, the marks of less frequent rains left their impress on the mineral, as well as on the vegetable kingdom. The country was not so well rounded off into rolling prairie; the bluffs stood out more sharp and bold; and the effects of floods and freshets were more distinctly visible. These are appearances which always increase with the dryness of the region. In a great many instances, the soft, dry land had, in process of time, been washed away from the harder foundations, leaving the latter standing on the open plain as grotesque masses of sandstones, marls, &c.

.   .   .   .

The worst part of the route was from Donner Station, twenty miles west of Hayes, to within twenty miles of Fort Wallace, a district of about sixty miles across, and even over this sixty miles there was no lack of forage; and in many places very fair grazing could be had, suitable either for sheep or for horned cattle. On nearing the Rocky Mountains the rain-fall gradually increases. Along its eastern spurs it is pretty abundant, producing a good growth of hardy and nutritious grasses, amongst which may be noticed the mountain bunch-grass, as well as the grama (*Boutelorea oligastuchya*), both most excellent for cattle.

Early in March I found the cattle actually fat; they had been out all winter, without shelter or hay, and the frost was still in the ground. I am now speaking of the country between Fort Wallace and Denver, and north of Denver, towards the Black Hills. I may add, however, that the entire belt of country along the spurs of the mountains, especially to the southward, cannot, except in New Mexico, be surpassed by any other region for purposes of sheep farming.

Almost due west of Fort Wallace, a considerable spur from the mountains juts out into the plains. This spur is thickly covered with fine pine timber—a treasure almost beyond price in such a region; and, curious enough, while the timber grows above, a fine bed of coal lies below the surface. This forest is entered about one hundred and eighty miles from Fort Wallace, and extends for at least forty miles up into the mountains.

Whether it is that the timber attracts an additional quantity of moisture, or prevents it from evaporating when deposited, or whether the soil is unusually rich, I know not; but I can say of my own knowledge, that in this district vegetation is very luxuriant, and the country very beautiful. Along the streams flowing from the mountains around Denver and south of it, fine crops and vegetables can be raised by irrigation; but as the altitude of these regions is very great (about 6,000 feet), crops do not flourish much farther north at that elevation. As only a small proportion of these streams on leaving the mountains succeed in crossing the comparatively dry part of the plains, and as the few which do not sink flow for one or two hundred miles with much-diminished volume, I fear that but little irrigation can be obtained from them, and I am decidedly of opinion that, without irrigation, crops cannot at present be raised.

This leads naturally to a very important question. As settlers advance from the East; as they sow corn, plant trees, and open up the soil, will the rain-fall increase to any considerable extent? The knowledge gained from many places in the Western country, where farming on a large scale has already existed for years, leaves no doubt now, that this question can safely be answered in the affirmative. The district around Salt Lake is the most striking example I have met with; here, since cultivation has extensively been carried on, the rain-fall has been nearly doubled, and during months which used always to pass by with cloudless skies, reviving showers are of frequent occurrence, and heavy dews refresh the ground. We may confidently expect, therefore, that the area of arable land on these vast plains will gradually increase, and that the dry belt of country will become narrowed indefinitely, by the skill and industry of the husbandman.

65.

James Realf, Jr.

IRRIGATION IN DAKOTA [1891]

Shall we make it "rain from the earth, when the sky fails"? is now, thanks to an editor, the great Dakotan question. It is a question of many facets. What does it cost, will it pay, is it safe, or must it ultimately poison the ground by sowing the land with salt like a vandal conqueror, and creating a Sahara for immediate posterity? . . . There has certainly been a great change in the climate of Utah since irrigation was begun there, and an appreciable change in some parts of Southern California, though not in Colorado, as far as can be learned. It is a well-known fact that rain storms follow the course of streams, and as a system of irrigation multiplies universally the evaporation of a region, besides multiplying small streams and enlarging others, and as hollows would often be ponded by the waste water, an increase in the area watered by local showers is naturally to be expected. Moreover, the burning winds that so often scorch the crops will be somewhat softened by traversing so much moist ground and so many streams. Trees, too, grow more readily in the moistened land, and in turn protect the land from the hot winds. Given a proper system of irrigation in operation for twenty-five years, and the epithet, treeless, need not be applied to Dakota.

. . . .

No division of the United States has a better credit in commercial circles than Utah, and this is not due to the peculiar institution of polygamy, but to the perfect system of irrigation. The careful husbanding of the waters that come down the Wahsatch Range on mountains, has transmuted a dreary desert of sand and sage brush into what most travellers regard as a garden, and what possibly to the faithful appears symbolically a Paradise.

.   .   .   .

The next and really the most important question—for man should not work for the present and immediate future without the keenest regard to the rights of posterity—is whether, under Dakotan conditions, artesian irrigation is safe; whether there is not danger of its poisoning the ground. Professor Upham unhesitatingly declares that on account of the alkaline and saline properties in these artesian waters a continued use of them for many years would render the land worthless. The assertion is a rounder one than scientific men generally make, and must be received with caution, though emanating from so high a source, for many samples of South Dakotan waters, tested at Brookings, have shown no alkaline reaction at all, and the professor's reasoning seems to rest chiefly upon the North Dakotan waters, which for some reason show larger saline percentages than the South. Then, too, he proceeds on the theory that a yearly supply of one foot of water is necessary, whereas half that amount during the dryest year, supplied through the five growing months, would insure good crops. Four inches last July would have saved the harvest. But anyway the entire amount of saline matter in South Dakotan waters, according to Prof. Lewis McLouth, does not, on the average, exceed one fifth of one per cent after subtracting all inert substances, such as sand, clay, limestone, and iron ores; so that, if six inches of water were applied to the lands, and all evaporated on the surface, the salty crust would be one 1-160 of an inch thick. But as a part of the water would run off into the streams, and much of it, diluted with rain-water, would soak into the ground, the salty ingredients would be mixed at once with at least a foot of the surface earth, and would form less than one fifteenth of one per cent of the weight of that soil. These ingredients are salts of lime, magnesia, potash, and soda. Now Dr. Bruckner, in an analysis of some soil in Holland, which he pronounces remarkably rich, says that it contains over fifteen per cent of these same ingredients, or two hundred and twenty-five times as much as six inches of artesian water would give to a foot of Dakotan soil within a year. So it would take two hundred and twenty-five years for this soil to acquire as much of these saline ingredients as the rich soil of Holland already possesses.

We might go further into this subject and show that every ingredient of these artesian well salts is a necessary food for many plant tissues; but even if the accumulation of salty substances were thought dangerous, it is to be remembered that during five of the ten years since the settlement of the Jim Valley, the rainfall has been ample, and if this average should continue, the land could be allowed to rest from irrigation for one half of the time so that the floods of rain-water would wash away the surplus saline matter.

Enough has now been said to show that in South Dakota, at least, no harm is likely to accrue to the soil under five hundred years, if South Dakota chemists are to be trusted. By that time chemistry will have advanced from an analytic to a creative science, and if what was once ignorantly termed "The Great American Desert" should suddenly lapse into a saline state, a speedy cure for that condition may be counted on with confidence.

66.

James A. Waymire

IRRIGATION IN CALIFORNIA [1898]

The cultivation of the soil under irrigation may be properly termed intensive cultivation. It requires thoughtful consideration as to the amount of water suitable to the different soils and to the growth of different plants. Careful experiments must be made year after year. The effect of water upon different kinds of fruit, grains and grasses; the best means of applying the water, and the best time to apply it; all demand a degree of attention and skill which call upon the farmer for the exercise of his highest intellectual powers. Indeed, irrigation will afford a field for the most highly educated men and women. It will become a profession as learned as the law or medicine, and far more useful. Our common schools, high schools, and even the University, cannot perform greater service to the State than to lead the people, by competent and practical instruction, into a successful practise of this ancient art.

. . . .

It is said by good authority that one half the population of the world is supported from irrigated lands. The Anglo-Saxon has not been accustomed to irrigation. Occupying a region where there is a copious rainfall, he has not found it necessary to resort to the artificial application of water. In the United States the acquisition of California and the territory west of the Mississippi has brought this subject to his attention, and he is now rapidly mastering it, as he does all other difficult problems. In California we have an area of about one hundred million acres, of which about 40 per cent is said to be arable land. The other 60 per cent constitutes a great chain of mountains, which runs from north to south nearly seven hundred miles and in the northern parts sweep westward and follow the coast the full length of the State. Much of this mountainous region will be utilized for the production of grasses and fruits; but its principal service will be as an inexhaustible storehouse of minerals and an unfailing reservoir for the irrigation of the valleys below. Of the arable lands of the State, three fourths are arid, and all of it will be benefited by irrigation. In France and other European countries great expense has been profitably incurred in the irrigation of land where the rainfall is greater than in any portion of California. In the Sacramento and San Joaquin valleys lies one of the greatest bodies of arable land, free from waste, in the world. It is perhaps equal to the inhabited portion of the valley of the Nile, and its climate is much more salubrious. In Southern California there are numerous small but exceedingly fertile valleys absolutely dependent upon irrigation. In that section of the State more attention has been given to the subject than in the northern portion. Yet when we come to figure up the amount of money expended in the irrigation of our lands it is surprising to find how little has been invested and how much has been accomplished. All the enterprises under control of private corporations have not employed more than twenty millions of dollars in the aggregate. The irrigation districts, good, bad, and indifferent, have expended less than eight millions. Altogether the expenditures do not exceed the amount of capital invested in the street railroads of San Francisco. The capital of one water company—that which supplies our largest city—is almost equal to the capital invested in irrigation enterprises throughout the State. Nearly ten times as much has been levied in assessments for the Comstock lode in the State of Nevada. Yet without irrigation California cannot progress. Her cities are absolutely dependent upon the products of the soil. It is to state a well known fact to say that all wealth must come from the soil—the farm, the mine, or the forest. Most people would say that the most important industry of California is that of mining, because it has attracted most attention. Judged by the value of product, the agricultural interest is far more important. Statistics will show that our agricultural product always exceeds one hundred million dollars per annum, and some years amounts to half as much again. Our mines of gold, silver, quicksilver, copper, lead, and all other metals do not exceed thirty millions a year. The manufactured products of the State sometimes exceed one hundred millions, but they include many things which, properly speaking, should be classed as agricultural products, such as flour, canned fruits, and lumber.

67.

Albert Bushnell Hart

THE FUTURE OF THE MISSISSIPPI VALLEY [1900]

What is the likelihood
that the population of the Mississippi Valley will continue to increase? Nowhere in the world are the conditions of subsistence
more favorable, for the fertility of the soil and the variety of climate
make possible an unequalled food-supply, which so far has sufficed
not only for the people of the valley, but for their brethren on the
sea-coast and for millions of Europeans. For many years to come
this food-supply can be steadily increased, both by opening up
hitherto untilled lands and by more intensive culture. In the similar
Yang-tse-kiang and Hoang-ho valleys in China about three hundred
millions of people live from an area about as large as the Mississippi
Valley. When we compare means of transportation in China with
those in the Mississippi Valley, when we see how easy it is in
America to send a surplus from one district to supply a deficiency
in another, when we consider the enormous credit facilities which
enable the community to endure one or two, or even three, years
of bad crops without starvation anywhere, there seems to be no
reason why the Mississippi Valley may not some time contain a
population of 350,000,000 comfortable people, or ten times its
present number. The difficult problem is not to raise sufficient crops,
but to keep upon the land a sufficient number of persons to till
it; but the Mississippi Valley is the home of a most skilful system of
machinery, which amplifies the labor of the farmer twentyfold.

. . . .

The greatest checks to the rapid increase of national population
in the history of the world have been famine, disease, and war. The
days have passed when a Texan could curiously inquire: "What
do these people in New York mean by talking about people starving to death? Doesn't any darned fool know enough to take his
rifle and shoot a beef critter when he's hungry?" Yet, so far as we
can look into the future, there will be bread and to spare for the
children of this great household. Epidemics and disease may sweep
through the country; since the days of La Salle fever and ague has
been the bane of every community in the Mississippi Valley, except
the one in which you happen to be living at the moment; but there

has been no wide-sweeping epidemic in the West since the cholera
year of 1832. The advance of medical science makes the Mississippi
Valley reasonably safe from devastation by pestilence. As for war,
the Mississippi Valley has now no enemies within the Union, and
from invasion St. Louis is as safe as Nijni-Novgorod or Stanley
Pool.

Hence the only probable check upon the rapid increase of
population is one which has already made itself felt throughout
the Union—the increasing difficulty of giving children a good start,
and the consequent diminution of the size of families. Seventy years
ago plenty of people in Ohio had twenty adult uncles and aunts,
many of them married; and some young people could boast of
a hundred first cousins. Today, except among foreigners, a family
of six is remarkable. This means a lower rate of increase. The
Mississippi Valley has more than doubled its population in every
twenty-five years during the last century. At that rate it would have
560,000,000 in the year 2000. But he would be a bold man who
would predict a population of 200,000,000 in that year, for it would
be almost as dense as Belgium or Holland.

If the present average scale of living continues, every doubling
of the population will mean a doubling of available capital and
wealth. But who can say whether the mechanical discoveries of the
next century may not vastly increase the average wealth? and, on
the other hand, who can say how far property may be concentrated
in a few hands or combined in some kind of national socialism?
The wealth of the Mississippi Valley in arable land already lies
beneath the feet of the people, but the upper slopes on the Appalachian rim of the valley are still very little cultivated, though
the Tennessee, Kentucky, and Georgia mountains are probably
capable of supporting as abundant and as thriving a population as
that of the Black Forest or the ranges of the Jura Mountains. In
the lowlands exhausted soils, formerly allowed to go to ruin, are
now restored by the wide-spreading use of fertilizers; and as population grows and land becomes more valuable, a stop will be put
to the annihilation of soil through cutting off the timber and the
consequent waste of the steep slopes thus exposed to running
water. Everywhere a more intensive cultivation must come in.

68.

Harold Bell Wright [1911]

[In *The Winning of
Barbara Worth*, a novel of what he called the "ministry of Capital,"
Harold Bell Wright wrote in glowing and sometimes almost martial

tones of the men who advanced civilization by bringing water to the arid lands of the Southwest. The book appeared less than a decade after the passage of the 1902 Newlands Act, which had put the federal government into the business of reclamation.]

Somewhere in the eternity that lies back of all the yesterdays, the great river found the salt waves of the ocean fathoms deep in what is now The King's Basin and extending a hundred and seventy miles north of the shore that takes their wash to-day. Slowly, through the centuries of that age of all beginnings, the river, cutting canyons and valleys in the north and carrying southward its load of silt, built from the east across the gulf to Lone Mountain a mighty delta dam.

South of this new land the ocean still received the river; to the north the gulf became an inland sea. The upper edge of this new-born sea beat helpless against a line of low, barren hills beyond which lay many miles of a rainless land. Eastward lay yet more miles of desolate waste. And between this sea and the parent ocean on the west, extending southward past the delta dam, the mountains of the Coast Range shut out every moisture-laden cloud and turned back every life-bearing stream. Thus trapped and helpless, the bright waters, with all their life, fell under the constant, fierce, beating rays of the semitropical sun and shrank from the wearing sweep of the dry, tireless winds. Uncounted still, the centuries of that age also passed and the bottom of that sea lay bare, dry and lifeless under the burning sky, still beaten by the pitiless sun, still swept by the scorching winds. The place that had held the glad waters with their teeming life came to be an empty basin of blinding sand, of quivering heat, of dreadful death. Unheeding the ruin it had wrought, the river swept on its way.

And so—hemmed in by mountain wall, barren hills and rainless plains; forgotten by the ocean; deserted by the river, that thirsty land lay, the loneliest, most desolate bit of this great Western Continent.

But the river could not work this ruin without contributing to the desert the rich strength it had gathered from its tributary lands. Mingled with the sand of the ancient sea-bed was the silt from faraway mountain and hill and plain. That basin of Death was more than a dusty tomb of a life that had been; it was a sepulchre that held the vast treasure of a life that would be—would be when the ages should have made also the master men, who would dare say to the river: "Make restitution!"—men who could, with power, command the rich life within the tomb to come forth.

But master men are not the product of years—scarcely, indeed, of centuries. The people of my story have also their true beginnings in ages too remote to be reckoned. The master passions, the govern-

ing instincts, the leading desires and the driving fears that hew
and carve and form and fashion the race are as reckless of the years
as are wave and river and sun and wind. Therefore the forgotten
land held its wealth until Time should make the giants that could
take it.

. . . .

On the high ground near the foot of the hill at the canyon's
mouth she asked him to turn around and stop. Willard Holmes
had been too much occupied with the team and the girl to notice
the landscape; and now that wonderful view of the Mesa, The
King's Basin and the mountains burst upon him without warning.
No sane man could be insensible of the grandeur of that scene. The
man, whose eyes had looked only upon eastern landscapes that
bore in every square foot of their limited range the evidence of
man's presence, was silent—awe-stricken before the mighty expanse of desert that lay as it was fashioned by the creative forces
that formed the world. Turning at last from the glorious, ever-
changing scenes, wrought in colors of gold and rose and lilac and
purple and blue, to the girl whose eyes were fixed questioningly
upon him, he said in a low voice: "Is it always like this?"

Barbara nodded. "Always like that, but always changing. It is
never the same, but always the same. Like—like life itself. Do you
understand?"

He turned again to the scene in silent wonder.

"Do you like my Desert?" she asked, after a little time had
passed.

His mind caught at the expression. "Do you mean to say that
that is The King's Basin—that we are going *there* to work?"

"Why, of course." She laughed uneasily. "Don't you like it?"

"Like it?" he repeated. "But is there anyone living out there?"

She was amazed at his words. "Living there? Of course not. But
you are going to make it so that thousands and thousands can
live there—you and the others. Don't you understand?" Her voice
expressed a shade of impatience.

"I'm afraid I did not realize," he answered slowly.

"That's just it!" she cried, thoroughly aroused now and speaking
passionately. "That's just the trouble with you eastern men; you
don't realize. For years the dear old Seer and a few others have
been trying to make you see what a work there is to do out here,
and you won't even look up from your little old truck patches to
give them intelligent attention. You think this King's Basin is
big? Why, the Seer says that if every foot of that land was under
cultivation it wouldn't be a posy bed beside what there is to do
in the West. I suppose you must have done some great things in
your profession, Mr. Holmes, or those capitalists wouldn't have
sent you out here; but you can't have done anything that will mean
to the world what the reclamation of The King's Basin Desert will

mean one hundred years from now, because this work is going to *make* the people realize, don't you see?"

. . . .

As Jefferson Worth gazed at the wonderful scene, a vision of the changes that were to come to that land passed before him. He saw first, following the nearly finished work of the engineers, an army of men beginning at the river and pushing out into the desert with their canals, bringing with them the life-giving water. Soon, with the coming of the water, would begin the coming of the settlers. Hummocks would be leveled, washes and arroyos filled, ditches would be made to the company canals, and in place of the thin growth of gray-green desert vegetation with the ragged patches of dun earth would come great fields of luxuriant alfalfa, billowing acres of grain, with miles upon miles of orchards, vineyards and groves. The fierce desert life would give way to the herds and flocks and the home life of the farmer. The railroad would stretch its steel strength into this new world; towns and cities would come to be where now was only solitude and desolation; and out from this world-old treasure house vast wealth would pour to enrich the peoples of the earth.

69.

Sir James Jeans [1929]

[The eminent mathematician and physicist Sir James Jeans published in 1929 *The Universe Around Us*, a popular survey of the current state of astronomy. In one rather gloomy chapter, he discusses the cosmic implications of the second law of thermodynamics (which states that the universe must eventually "run down") and then narrows his view slightly to consider the prospects of mankind. The shadow of the ultimate tragedy in the background serves only to intensify his highly optimistic feelings about man's future progress.]

Apart from improbable accidents, it seems that if the solar system is left to the natural course of evolution, the earth is likely to remain a possible abode of life for thousands of millions of years to come.

If so, we may perhaps be glad that our lives have fallen in the beginning, rather than at the end, of this great stretch of time. We may well imagine that if man survives to the end of it, he will have infinitely more knowledge than now, but one thing he will no longer know—the thrill of pleasure of the pioneer who opens up new realms of knowledge. Disease, perhaps even death, will have been conquered, and life will doubtless be safer and incomparably better-ordered than now. It will seem incredible that a time could have existed when men risked, and lost, their lives in traversing unexplored country, in climbing hitherto unclimbed peaks, in fighting wild beasts for the fun of it. Life will be more of a routine and less of an adventure than now; it will also be more purposeless when the human race knows that within a measurable space of time it must face extinction and the eternal destruction of all its hopes, endeavours, and achievements.

The 10,000 million years which seems a possible future for the existence of life on earth is more than three times the past age of the earth, and more than 10,000 times the period through which humanity has so far existed on earth. Let us try to set these times in their proper proportion by the help of yet another simple model. Take a postage stamp, and stick it on to a penny. Now climb Cleopatra's needle and lay the penny flat, postage stamp uppermost, on top of the obelisk. The height of the whole structure may be taken to represent the time that has elapsed since the earth was born. On this scale, the thickness of the penny and postage stamp together represents the time that man has lived on earth. The thickness of the postage stamp represents the time he has been civilized, the thickness of the penny representing the time he lived in an uncivilized state. Now stick another postage stamp on top of the first to represent the next 10,000 years of civilization, and keep sticking on postage stamps until you have a pile as high as the towers of Westminster Abbey. Such a pile still provides an inadequate representation of the length of the future which, so far as astronomy can see, probably stretches before civilized humanity, unless an accident cuts it short. The first postage stamp was the past of civilization; a column higher than the abbey is its future. Or, to look at it another way, the first postage stamp represents what man has already achieved; a pile which out-tops Westminster Abbey represents what he may achieve, if his achievement is proportional simply to his time on earth.

Up to now, we know that his achievement has not been simply proportional to his time. In some respects at least—the mechanical arts, for instance—we advance at an ever increasing tempo. The contributions of successive generations are not equal, but continually increase in geometrical progression, so that material civilization advances more in a generation now than it did in a millennium when it was at its commencement. If this continual speeding-up were to persist throughout the whole astronomical future of the earth, it is impossible to imagine what the rate of advance would become before life disappeared from earth. But we can think of only too many factors which are likely to compel a slowing-down before long.

We must remember too that we cannot count on such a length of future with any certainty. Accidents may happen to the race as to the individual. Celestial collisions may occur; shrinking into a white dwarf, the sun may freeze terrestrial life out of existence; bursting out as a nova it may scorch our race to death. Accident may replace our tower of postage stamps by a truncated column of only a fraction of the height of which we have spoken. Even so, our race has an "expectation of life" which must be measured in terms of thousands of millions of years. It is a period which the human mind, as apart from the mind of the mathematician, can hardly conceive with any clearness. For all practical purposes the only statement that conveys any real meaning is that our race may look forward to occupying the earth for a time longer than any we can think of, and achieving incomparably more than anything we can possibly imagine.

Looked at in terms of space, the message of astronomy is at best one of melancholy grandeur and oppressive vastness. Looked at in terms of time, it becomes one of almost endless possibility and hope. As inhabitants of a civilized earth, we are living at the very beginning of time. We have come into being in the fresh glory of the dawn, and a day of almost unthinkable length stretches before us with unimaginable opportunities for accomplishment. Our descendants of far-off ages, looking down this long vista of time from the other end, will see our present age as the misty morning of the world's history; they will see our contemporaries of to-day as dim heroic figures who fought their way through jungles of ignorance, error and superstition to discover truth, to learn how to harness the forces of nature, and to make a world worthy for mankind to live in. We are still too much engulfed in the greyness of the morning mists to be able to imagine, even vaguely, how this world of ours will appear to those who will come after us and see it in the full light of day. But by what light we have, we seem to discern that the main message of astronomy is one of hope to the race and of responsibility to the individual—of responsibility because we are drawing plans and laying foundations for a longer future than we can well imagine.

[By the middle of the twentieth century, America had long since ceased to expand geographically, but the civilization it had created continued to intensify at a dizzying pace. Paeans to progress gradually gave way to more sober analyses as it came to be realized that technological development was not the simple upward path it had been thought to be. The core of the old faith remained essentially unchanged—man could, indeed, better his life on earth—but the wisdom of pursuing the goal solely by means of a blind and single-valued science was called increasingly into question. The change, a subtle one of mood, was expressed among the more reflective as caution and among the diminishing numbers of traditional celebrants as defensiveness.]

70.

V. Gordon Childe

PROGRESS AS A POINT OF VIEW [1936]

As scientists we cannot ask History: "Have we progressed? Does the multiplication of mechanical devices represented by airplanes, hydroelectric stations, poison gas, and submarines constitute progress?" A question so formulated can have no scientific meaning. There is no hope of any agreement upon its answer. That would depend entirely upon the caprice of the inquirer, his economic situation at the time, and even on the state of his health. Very few people will come to the same conclusion.

If you like rapid movement and the freedom from limitations on time and space provided by modern facilities for locomotion and illumination, you may answer in the affirmative. But not unless you are in an economic position to enjoy such facilities, not if your lungs have been filled with mustard gas, or your son has just been blown to pieces with a shell. If you have a romantic affection for the "unspoiled countryside" and no passion for roaming far abroad or turning night into day for study, you will query the reality of a progress thus attested, and look back regretfully upon the "more peaceful" days of a century or two ago. You will conveniently forget the drawbacks to the simple life—the vermin in the picturesque thatch, the disease-germs swarming in contaminated wells and open middens, the bandits and the press-gangs lurking in the woods and alleys. Dumped down in a village in Turkestan, you might revise your opinion. A pickpocket must regard from his professional standpoint electric light, the telephone, and automobiles (if used by the police) as signs of regression. He will sigh for the dark and narrow alleys of a previous century. Persons devoted to the grosser forms of cruelty will not accept the suppression of legal torture and the elimination of public executions as signs of progress, but of the reverse.

71.

Norbert Wiener

THE SHORT HISTORY OF PROGRESS [1950]

Our worship of progress may be discussed from two points of view: a factual one and an ethical one—that is, one which furnishes standards for approval and disapproval. Factually, it asserts that the earlier advance of geographical discovery, whose inception corresponds to the beginning of modern times, is to be continued into an indefinite period of invention, of the discovery of new techniques for controlling the human environment. This, the believers in progress say, will go on and on without any visible termination in a future not too remote for human contemplation. Those who uphold the idea of progress as an ethical principle regard this unlimited and quasi-spontaneous process of change as a *Good Thing*, and as the basis on which they guarantee to future generations a Heaven on Earth. It is possible to believe in progress as a fact without believing in progress as an ethical principle; but in the catechism of many Americans, the one goes with the other.

. . . .

Besides the comfortable passive belief in progress, which many Americans shared at the end of the nineteenth century, there is another one which seems to have a more masculine, vigorous connotation. To the average American, progress means the winning of the West. It means the economic anarchy of the frontier, and the vigorous prose of Owen Wister and Theodore Roosevelt. Historically the frontier is, of course, a perfectly genuine phenomenon. For many years, the development of the United States took place against the background of the empty land that always lay farther to the West. Nevertheless, many of those who have waxed poetic concerning this frontier have been praisers of the past. Already in 1890, the census takes cognizance of the end of the true frontier conditions. The geographical limits of the great backlog of un-consumed and unbespoken resources of the country had clearly been set.

It is difficult for the average person to achieve an historical per-spective in which progress shall have been reduced to its proper dimensions. The musket with which most of the Civil War was fought was only a slight improvement over that carried at Water-loo, and that in turn was nearly interchangeable with the Brown Bess of Marlborough's army in the Low Countries. Nevertheless, hand firearms had existed since the fifteenth century or earlier, and cannon more than a hundred years earlier still. It is doubtful whether the smoothbore musket ever much exceeded in range the best of the longbows, and it is certain that it never equaled them in accuracy nor in speed of fire; yet the longbow is the almost unimproved invention of the Stone Age.

Again, while the art of shipbuilding had by no means been completely stagnant, the wooden man-of-war, just before it left the seas, was of a pattern which had been fairly unchanged in its essentials since the early seventeenth century, and which even then displayed an ancestry going back many centuries more. One of Columbus' sailors would have been a valuable able seaman aboard Farragut's ships. Even a sailor from the ship that took Saint Paul to Malta would have been quite reasonably at home as a fore-castle hand on one of Joseph Conrad's barks. A Roman cattleman from the Dacian frontier would have made quite a competent *vaquero* to drive longhorn steers from the plains of Texas to the terminus of the railroad, although he would have been struck with astonishment with what he found when he got there. A Babylonian administrator of a temple estate would have needed no training either in bookkeeping or in the handling of slaves to run an early Southern plantation. In short, the period during which the main conditions of life for the vast majority of men have been subject to repeated and revolutionary changes had not even begun until the Renaissance and the great voyages, and did not assume any-thing like the accelerated pace which we now take for granted until well into the nineteenth century.

Under these circumstances, there is no use in looking anywhere in earlier history for parallels to the successful inventions of the steam engine, the steamboat, the locomotive, the modern smelting of metals, the telegraph, the transoceanic cable, the introduction of electric power, dynamite and the modern high explosive missile, the airplane, the electric valve, and the atomic bomb. The inven-tions in metallurgy which heralded the origin of the Bronze Age are neither so concentrated in time nor so manifold as to offer a good counter-example. It is very well for the classical economist to assure us suavely that these changes are purely changes in de-gree, and that changes in degree do not vitiate historic parallels. The difference between a medicinal dose of strychnine and a fatal one is also only one of degree.

72.

Gerard Piel [1955]

[The publisher of *Scientific American*, Gerard Piel delivered in 1955 the Walgreen Lectures at the University of Chicago, from the first of which the following selection is taken.]

As the richest and most powerful of all nations, America represents science and democracy in their hour of triumph. Its wealth and abundance are the standard to which other peoples aspire. It is the example of America that today moves the colonial regions to disturb the world with unrest and revolution.

Sometimes the dimensions of America can amaze even us. They are a measure of the enormously fruitful power of science applied to the exploitation of a continent. Each year the American people produce and consume more than half of the world's output of energy. We use more than a third of the world's energy merely to heat the indoor spaces in which we live and work. We constitute a scant one fifteenth, 6 per cent, of the world's population, but we produce and consume more than half of its steel and a corresponding percentage of just about all the other products of technology. We work at tasks that few other people in the world would recognize as work, and we spend fewer hours of the day and fewer years of our lives engaged in work. We consume the fruit of our labors in an abundance and variety of goods that are unknown to the daily existence of most of the rest of mankind. By comparison with other peoples, the well-to-do members of our society make up more than two thirds of our families. Though the poor are still with us, they and their needs have ceased to provide the typical issues of our domestic politics.

This popularization of the abundance that flows from the application of science has been accompanied by the equal popularization of an enthusiastically utilitarian faith in science. There is no problem, in the American view, that science cannot solve, from the control of weather to the cure of cancer. As in the historic case of the atomic bomb, we need only invest a sufficient number of billions of dollars and we shall have the answer. This applies even to our economic problems. Americans expect that the continued advance of science will maintain their industrial system in the state of perpetual flux and expansion that is needed to sustain full employment.

The welfare of science in America would seem to be secured as well by the degree to which its outlook is imbued in our folk culture. We may have occasion to deplore the ignorance of science among a people who are so dependent upon science. But the truth is that dryads, leprechauns, and trolls have long since fled a culture that prizes oil burners, television sets, internal combustion engines, deep freezers, and all the other devices that ease and complicate our existence. These inanimate gadgets, animated only by the mechanic's tools, have generated a powerful antidote to the pathetic fallacy that once populated the universe with the creatures of man's fear and imagination. Almost everybody now has acquiesced in the Copernican revolution and the displacement of our earth and us from the center of the universe. There is general recognition of the idea that the cosmos is a vast impersonal system, ordered by laws of mechanics. The germ theory of disease brings people to their doctors, not to their knees. In our law there is increasing acceptance of the idea of the criminal as a victim of psychological and sociological handicaps, an object for treatment, not for vengeance. In the relationships of man to man, our fellow citizens are agreed that all men are members of the human race, and they expect that we will eventually learn to act like members of the same human family.

It is doubtful that such a universal acceptance of the rational and scientific view can be found among the people of any other nation. Future historians may well conclude that it was in the inculcation of the rational outlook on the world among our citizens in all occupations and professions that science had its greatest impact in our time upon the life of mankind.

73,

PESTICIDES FOR PLENTY [1962]

[Shortly after the publication of *Silent Spring*, Rachel Carson's terrifying indictment of the wholesale use of pesticides in America, *Time* magazine printed a review taking the opposite view.]

Lovers of wildlife often rhapsodize about the "balance of nature that keeps all living creatures in harmony," but scientists realistically point out that the

balance was upset thousands of years ago when man's invention of
weapons made him the king of beasts. The balance has never
recovered its equilibrium; man is the dominant species on his
planet, and as his fields, pastures and cities spread across the land,
lesser species are extirpated, pushed into refuge areas, or domesticated.

Some species, most of them insects, benefit increasingly from
man's activities. Their attacks on his toothsome crops are as old
as recorded history—the Bible often refers to plagues of locusts,
cankerworms, lice and flies—but their damage was only sporadi-
cally serious when population was small and scattered. Modern,
large-scale agriculture offers a paradise for plant-eating insects.
Crops are grown year after year in the same or nearby fields, helping insect populations to build up. Many of the worst pests are
insect invaders from foreign countries that have left their natural
enemies behind and so are as free as man himself from the check
of nature's balance.

Agricultural scientists try hard to find ways to check insect pests
by tricks of cultivation. They import the ancient enemies of invading foreign insects and foster the resident enemies of native pests.
They are developing bacterial diseases to spread pestilence among
insect populations. Because these tactics alone are seldom enough
to protect the tender plants of modern, high-yield farms, the use
of insecticides is economically necessary. Tests run by the Department of Agriculture show that failure to use pesticides would
cost a major part of many crops; a 20-year study proved that
cotton yields would be cut by 40%. Production of many kinds of
fruit and vegetables would be impossible; unsprayed apple trees,
for instance, no longer yield fruit that is sound enough to be
marketed. Potato fields swept by the Colorado beetle or late blight
(the fungus that caused the great Irish potato famine of 1846)
yield hardly any crop.

Chemical insecticides are now a necessary part of modern U.S.
agriculture, whose near-miraculous efficiency has turned the ancient tragedy of recurrent famine into the biologically happy problem of what to do with food surpluses. Says Entomologist George
C. Decker of the Illinois Agricultural Experiment Station: "If we
in North America were to adopt a policy of 'Let nature take its
course,' as some individuals thoughtlessly advocate, it is possible
that these would-be experts would find disposing of the 200 million
surplus human beings even more perplexing than the disposition
of America's current corn, cotton, and wheat surpluses."

74.

Robert Wernick

LET'S SPOIL THE WILDERNESS [1965]

The trumpeting voice of the wilderness lover is heard at great distances these days. He is apt to be a perfectly decent person, if hysterical. And the causes which excite him so are generally worthy. Who can really find a harsh word for him as he strives to save Lake Erie from the sewers of Cleveland, save the redwoods from the California highway engineers, save the giant rhinoceros from the Somali tribesmen who kill those noble beasts to powder their horns into what they fondly imagine is a wonder-working aphrodisiac?

Worthy causes, indeed, but why do those who espouse them have to be so shrill and intolerant and sanctimonious? What right do they have to insinuate that anyone who does not share their passion for the whooping crane is a Philistine and a slob? From the gibberish they talk, you would think the only way to save the bald eagle is to dethrone human reason.

I would like to ask what seems to me an eminently reasonable question: *Why shouldn't we spoil the wilderness?*

Have these people ever stopped to think what the wilderness is? It is precisely what man has been fighting against since he began his painful, awkward climb to civilization. It is the dark, the formless, the terrible, the old chaos which our fathers pushed back, which surrounds us yet, which will engulf us all in the end. It is held at bay by constant vigilance, and when the vigilance slackens it swoops down for a melodramatic revenge, as when the jungle took over Chichen Itza in Yucatán or lizards took over Jamshid's courtyard in Persia. It lurks in our own hearts, where it breeds wars and oppressions and crimes. Spoil it! Don't you wish we could?

Of course, when the propagandists talk about unspoiled wilderness, they don't mean anything of that sort. What they mean by wilderness is a kind of grandiose picnic ground, in the Temperate Zone, where the going is rough enough to be challenging but not literally murderous, where hearty folk like Supreme Court Justice Douglas and Interior Secretary Udall can hike and hobble through spectacular scenery, with a helicopter hovering in the dirty old civilized background in case a real emergency comes up.

Well, the judge and the Secretary and their compeers are all estimable people, and there is no reason why they should not be able to satisfy their urge for primitive living. We ought to recognize, however, that other people have equally strong and often equally legitimate urges to build roads, dig mines, plow up virgin land, erect cities. Such people used to be called pioneers; now they are apt to be called louts. At all events, we are faced with sets of conflicting drives, and it is up to us to make a rational choice among them.

The trouble is, it is difficult to make a rational choice when one of the parties insists on wrapping all its discourse in a vile metaphysical fog.

.   .   .   .

No one who reads it can forget the passage in which John Muir, the great American naturalist, describes how, at the height of a tempest in the high Sierras, he lashed himself to the trunk of a giant pine and for hours heaved and swung with the great tree, while the wind howled and whole forested mountainsides quivered to its blasts. The scene has a splendid absurdity about it.

I am reliably informed that it is impossible to duplicate Muir's experience in present-day California. There is not a high tree left in the state from which you can't see the lights of cars stabbing through the night on some freeway or other. And of course that spoils everything. For the particular sensation, the *frisson*, that John Muir was after, was not simply a physical one—you could get the same by lashing yourself to the mast on the Empire State Building. It was the exultant triumphant feeling of riding the blasts, of soaring over a vast stretch of pure convulsed nature, and doing it alone, without another human soul in reach of sight or sound.

I am sure that in losing opportunities for this sensation, Californians have suffered a great loss. It is, however, a loss which I am afraid we will have to put up with.

75.

John F. Buchanan

PROTECTING NATURE FROM NATURE [1966]

Over the centuries, the true cyclical pattern of our forests has been growth, disease, decay, death, followed by the cleansing purge of natural wildfire with resulting re-birth and new growth. Man has, and rightly so, subverted this natural cycle. We can no longer tolerate unchecked wildfire as a balancing agent.

What, then, must we do to correct the imbalance in the ecological cycle created by our suppression of fire? Man must substitute man's management instead of nature's age-old management to maintain balance in our forest. What are the tools of scientific forest management? They are access, harvest, insect control, fire prevention and suppression, and tree planting—Access, above all, as it is the key to sound, many-use, resource management—Harvest, to remove diseased and decadent trees, to increase water production, to improve game habitat—Insect and fire control, to prevent catastrophic destruction—Tree planting, to hasten the renewal of our forest wealth.

The miners, stockmen, water users, the vast majority of our recreationists, timber harvesters, and public land managers ask only that resource facts prevail over resource folly. A forest, like a city, is an ever-changing, living organism. Lock up the Western Forests in barren, single-use preservation, neglect them, subject them to non-management, look the other way when they are ravaged by uncontrolled fire, disease and insects, and as surely as God made them, they will suffer the blight and devastation of our cities.

76.

William J. Moshofsky [1970]

[This selection is drawn from a speech delivered at Pendleton, Oregon, on January 19, 1970, by an executive of the Georgia-Pacific Corporation and reprinted in part in the *Sierra Club Bulletin*.]

I strongly believe there is real need for reinforcing this basic idea—making the most of your talents and abilities—because it is under attack from many quarters. In almost every magazine, every newspaper, it seems, there is far too much ridicule of the achievements and accomplishments of the past, far too much emphasis on leisure as an end goal —along with a sickening pessimism and fear about the future of life in general.

Take the currently hot political issue—environment. There's no question that all of us should be deeply concerned about our environment. But haven't we always, really? To be sure I had the right understanding of environment, I checked my Funk & Wagnall. Environment is defined to be *"One's surroundings or external circumstances collectively."* That covers just about everything, doesn't it?—food, shelter, security from harm, transportation, as well as air, water and aesthetics. It also has to include "other people."

The brave pioneers who settled this land faced Indians, harsh winters and a vast unconquered forbidding wilderness. That was their environment. Thanks to their courage, energy, skill and tenacity, the way was cleared for development of one of the most dynamic, productive, affluent regions in the history of Man.

Here in the Northwest in about one hundred years (really a short period in man's history) we've built large cities and healthy communities, developed outstanding highways, railroads, telephone, TV and radio communications systems, huge electric power systems, highly productive farms and forests, and great industrial complexes. And all this has been done while increasing our standard of living, educating our youth, carrying an increasing welfare roll for the less fortunate, helping the nation fight four very costly wars, and providing huge chunks of our earned wealth for foreign aid. And it was all done under a free, Democratic society. It's truly a fantastic story of man conquering and coming to terms with his environment.

But what do we hear these days—

—Prophets of gloom and doom are everywhere.
—One of the most popular conference themes is "can Man survive?"
—Ban DDT and other pesticides.
—Don't build any more dams, or nuclear power plants.
—Ban the Pill.
—Let's stop growth.

I think this last one is the topper. Just last week I read an article in the Wall Street Journal about a "non-conference" scheduled last weekend by the ecology center in Berkeley. Where? At your home. The whole idea was that they wanted people to stay home. "Don't write papers or read papers. Don't consume jet fuel or rent cars." A Sierra Club member went further saying "imagine what would happen if no one consumed anything for two days." Another so-called conservation group said "the non-conference will bring into focus the concept of a no-growth economy, which is likely to become the rallying cry of the conservation movement."

Such unreasoning, fear-ridden, emotional over-reaction! We'd certainly never have won the West with people like this. Man must progress and grow—we can't stand still!

Don't get me wrong, I'm all for a livable environment, and for the most part I don't question the honest concerns of all these people. We are all interested in having the cleanest, prettiest, healthiest and most livable environment.

But for heaven's sake, let's not over-react. If we develop a hang-nail, we don't cut off our arm.

We must use our scientific skills, knowhow and resources to tackle the real problems whe have in an orderly and reasonable way.

And it has to be a balanced approach—we've got to provide jobs, food, shelter, transportation, electric power, taxes for government services and national defense and for all the rest of our basic needs. They are all pretty fundamental aspects of our environment.

77.

Charles Zurhorst

A MISLEADING MYTH [1970]

During the past two decades the field of conservation has become dominated by various conservation organizations. And, if they have one thing in common other than political power, it is the use of an emotional appeal in their crusades.

This is particularly true in the case of those groups that rely heavily on contributions from the general public to support their operations. However, in their attempts to impress and motivate the public they often carry their emotional appeal to a point of misleading exaggeration and gross distortion of facts.

Take, for instance, one of their favorite themes: "the good old days," which they use in criticism of America's pioneers. To these conservationists, "the good old days" were wonderful days of home-baked bread, majestic forests, and expansive wide-open spaces.

They never mention that these were also the days of epidemics of typhoid fever, scarlet fever, and smallpox and that there were many deaths from an illness called acute indigestion, which is known today as appendicitis and rarely kills anyone. They also ignore the fact that, in these "good old days," sixty was a very old age, and the mother who made the home-baked bread was an old woman at thirty-five, and looked it.

They do, however, emphasize that America was—not is, but was —a wonderful country, until the pioneers ruined it.

A booklet titled *Would You Like to Have Lived When?* speaks dramatically of the days when "the trees were very tall, and there were no streets at all." Published by the National Wildlife Federation as "a conservation education publication," it is distributed for the use of teachers in third, fourth, and fifth grades.

Referring to America's pioneers, the booklet tells its young readers, in all uppercase letters:

"THEY CUT DOWN TOO MANY TREES"
"THEY KILLED TOO MANY BIRDS"
"THEY KILLED TOO MANY BUFFALOES"
"THEY PLOWED TOO MUCH LAND"

It then asks, "Why did people waste these treasures?" And, although the question is not answered in the booklet, it does deserve an answer in order to set the record straight.

The early American pioneers did not consider their actions as wasteful. They did not see, and could not possibly have seen, this country as it exists today. And when "the good old days" are viewed as the pioneers saw them, it is obvious that no "treasures" were "wasted." They were traded for safety and progress.

These pioneers had no corner supermarket; they had no knowledge of scientific farming. The "too much land" they plowed was their assurance that they would have ample food for their families during the coming year.

To the early Americans, buffaloes were a vile, filthy menace. They would attack humans. They would stampede a herd of cattle. And the "too many buffaloes" that were killed provided food for the thousands of workmen who built the Union Pacific and Northern Pacific railroads across the nation's frontier.

The "too many birds" the pioneers killed were birds that were eating their grain.

And the "too many trees" they cut down were forests where danger constantly lurked in the form of wild animals or bands of marauding Indians. What is more, these "too many trees" that they cut down may well have stood where Minneapolis, or Seattle, or some other major city stands today.

[Science as an intellectual pursuit has given man knowledge about nature; made concrete through technology, it has given him a lever with which to exercise great effect on nature. In both respects it has profoundly altered his relationship with the world around him. Man has, as we have seen, benefited from his science, but he has also, as we shall see, been victimized by it. Regardless of practical outcomes, however, the central fact is that he has placed the tools of his own devising between himself and his world: Power has been gained at the expense of intimacy.]

78.

Mark Twain

LOSING THE RIVER [1883]

The face of the water, in time, became a wonderful book—a book that was a dead language to the uneducated passenger, but which told its mind to me without reserve, delivering its most cherished secrets as if it uttered them with a voice. And it was not a book to be read once and thrown aside, for it had a new story to tell every day. Throughout the long twelve hundred miles there was never a page that was void of interest, never one that you could leave unread without loss, never one that you would want to skip, thinking you could find higher enjoyment in some other thing. There never was so wonderful a book written by man; never one whose interest was so absorbing, so unflagging, so sparklingly renewed with every reperusal. The passenger who could not read it was charmed with a peculiar sort of faint dimple on its surface (on the rare occasions when he did not overlook it altogether); but to the pilot that was an *italicized* passage; indeed, it was more than that, it was a legend of the largest capitals, with a string of shouting exclamation points at the end of it, for it meant that a wreck or a rock was buried there that could tear the life out of the strongest vessel that ever floated. It is the faintest and simplest expression the water ever makes, and the most hideous to a pilot's eye. In truth, the passenger who could not read this book saw nothing but all manner of pretty pictures in it, painted by the sun and shaded by the clouds, whereas to the trained eye these were not pictures at all, but the grimmest and most dead-earnest of reading matter.

Now when I had mastered the language of this water, and had come to know every trifling feature that bordered the great river as familiarly as I knew the letters of the alphabet, I had made a valuable acquisition. But I had lost something, too. I had lost something which could never be restored to me while I lived. All the grace, the beauty, the poetry, had gone out of the majestic river! I still kept in mind a certain wonderful sunset which I witnessed when steamboating was new to me. A broad expanse of the river was turned to blood; in the middle distance the red hue brightened into gold, through which a solitary log came floating, black and conspicuous; in one place a long, slanting mark lay sparkling upon the water; in another the surface was broken by boiling, tumbling rings, that were as many-tinted as an opal; where the ruddy flush was faintest, was a smooth spot that was covered with graceful circles and radiating lines, ever so delicately traced; the shore on our left was densely wooded, and the somber shadow that fell from this forest was broken in one place by a long, ruffled trail that shone like silver; and high above the forest wall a clean-stemmed dead tree waved a single leafy bough that glowed like a flame in the unobstructed splendor that was flowing from the sun. There were graceful curves, reflecting images, woody heights, soft distances; and over the whole scene, far and near, the dissolving lights drifted steadily, enriching its every passing moment with new marvels of coloring.

I stood like one bewitched. I drank it in, in a speechless rapture. The world was new to me, and I had never seen anything like this at home. But as I have said, a day came when I began to cease from noting the glories and the charms which the moon and the sun and the twilight wrought upon the river's face; another day came when I ceased altogether to note them. Then, if that sunset scene had been repeated, I should have looked upon it without rapture, and should have commented upon it, inwardly, after this fashion: "This sun means that we are going to have wind tomorrow; that floating log means that the river is rising, small thanks to it; that slanting mark on the water refers to a bluff reef which is going to kill somebody's steamboat one of these nights if it keeps on stretching out like that; those tumbling 'boils' show a dissolving bar and a changing channel there; the lines and circles in the slick water over yonder are a warning that that troublesome place is shoaling up dangerously; that silver streak in the shadow of the forest is the 'break' from a new snag, and he has located himself in the very best place he could have found to fish for steamboats; that tall dead tree, with a single living branch, is not going to last long, and then how is a body ever going to get through this blind place at night without the friendly old landmark?"

No, the romance and beauty were all gone from the river. All the value any feature of it had for me now was the amount of usefulness it could furnish toward compassing the safe piloting of a steamboat. Since those days, I have pitied doctors from my heart. What does the lovely flush in a beauty's cheek mean to a doctor but a "break" that ripples above some deadly disease? Are not all her visible charms sown thick with what are to him the signs and symbols of hidden decay? Does he ever see her beauty at all, or doesn't he simply view her professionally, and comment upon her unwholesome condition all to himself? And doesn't he sometimes wonder whether he has gained most or lost most by learning his trade?

WASTING THE LAND

[By its more fervent partisans, technology has often been portrayed as a miraculous cornucopia, pouring forth riches without end and promising the coming of Utopia. But, just as it is generally forgotten that "Utopia" translates literally as "no (such) place," so is it sometimes ignored that the cornucopia has a back portion into which, rather less miraculously, the raw material of riches is put. It also has, to stretch the image a bit farther, a sewer and a smokestack.

In its earliest and simplest forms, technology was little more than an easier and more efficient way of doing things that would happen in any case. Primitive agriculture was merely a slight reorganization in time and space of the natural pattern of growth; chipped-flint weapons were superior to rocks for bringing down game, but, whatever was used, the game would come down; the wheel made it easier to move an object that had to be moved in some fashion. Even industrial technology had, in the beginning, a relatively innocuous effect on the natural world. Two developments, widely separated in time but very similar in essence and effect, radically altered this simple order: The concentration of population in cities vastly increased the pressure of cultivation on available arable land, and, much later, the explosion of industrialization from the late eighteenth century on made rapidly multiplying demands on natural resources. Both processes created huge problems of waste disposal.]

79.

Tobias George Smollett [1771]

[In this passage from an epistolary novel, *The Expedition of Humphrey Clinker*, the author has Matthew Bramble describe life in London to his friend Dr. Lewis. The picture of urban civilization in the eighteenth century painted here is not exaggerated and can be found in numerous other works of the time.]

What temptation can a man of my turn and temperament have, to live in a place where every corner teems with fresh objects of detestation and disgust? What kind of taste and organs must those people have, who really prefer the adulterate enjoyments of the town to the genuine pleasures of a country retreat? Most people, I know, are originally seduced by vanity, ambition, and childish curiosity; which cannot be gratified, but in the *busy haunts of men:* but, in the course of this gratification, their very organs of sense are perverted, and they become habitually lost to every relish of what is genuine and excellent in its own nature.

.   .   .   .

I am pent up in frowzy lodgings, where there is not room enough to swing a cat; and I breathe the streams of endless putrefaction; and these would, undoubtedly, produce a pestilence, if they were not qualified by the gross acid of sea-coal, which is itself a pernicious nuisance to lungs of any delicacy of texture: but even this boasted corrector cannot prevent those languid, sallow looks, that distinguish the inhabitants of London from those ruddy swains that lead a country-life—I go to bed after midnight, jaded and restless from the dissipations of the day—I start every hour from my sleep, at the horrid noise of the watchmen bawling the hour through every street, and thundering at every door; a set of useless fellows, who serve no other purpose but that of disturbing the repose of the inhabitants; and by five o'clock I start out of bed, in consequence of the still more dreadful alarm made by the country carts, and noisy rustics bellowing green pease under my window. If I would drink water, I must quaff the maukish contents of an open aqueduct, exposed to all manner of defilement; or swallow that which comes from the river Thames, impregnated with all the filth of London and Westminster——Human excrement is the least offensive part of the concrete, which is composed of all the drugs, minerals, and poisons, used in mechanics and manufacture, enriched with the putrefying carcasses of beasts and men; and mixed with the scourings of all the wash-tubs, kennels, and common sewers, within the bills of mortality.

This is the agreeable potation, extolled by the Londoners, **as the** finest water in the universe—As to the intoxicating potion, sold for wine, it is a vile, unpalatable, and pernicious sophistication, balderdashed with cyder, corn-spirit, and the juice of sloes. In an action at law, laid against a carman for having staved a cask of port, it appeared from the evidence of the cooper, that there were not above five gallons of real wine in the whole pipe, which held above a hundred, and even that had been brewed and adulterated by the merchant at Oporto. The bread I eat in London, is a deleterious paste, mixed up with chalk, alum, and bone-ashes; insipid to the taste, and destructive to the constitution. The good people are not ignorant of this adulteration; but they prefer it to wholesome bread, because it is whiter than the meal of corn: thus they sacrifice their taste and their health, and the lives of their tender infants, to a most absurd gratification of a mis-judging eye; and the miller, or the baker, is obliged to poison them and their families, in order to live by his profession. The same monstrous depravity appears in their veal, which is bleached by repeated bleedings, and other villainous arts, till there is not a drop of juice left in the body, and the poor animal is paralytic before he dies; so void of all taste, nourishment, and savour, that a man might dine as comfortably on a white fricassee of kid-skin gloves; or chip hats from Leghorn.

As they have discharged the natural colour from their bread, their butchers-meat, and poultry, their cutlets, ragouts, fricassees and sauces of all kinds; so they insist upon having the complexion of their pot-herbs mended, even at the hazard of their lives. Perhaps, you will hardly believe they can be so mad as to boil their greens with brass halfpence in order to improve their colour; and yet nothing is more true—Indeed, without this improvement in the colour, they have no personal merit. They are produced in an artificial soil, and taste of nothing but the dunghills, from whence they spring. My cabbage, cauliflower, and 'sparagus in the country, are as much superior in flavour to those that are sold in Coventgarden, as my heath-mutton is to that of St. James's-market; which in fact, is neither lamb nor mutton, but something betwixt the two, gorged in the rank fens of Lincoln and Essex, pale, coarse, and frowzy—As for the pork, it is an abominable carnivorous animal, fed with horse-flesh and distillers' grains; and the poultry is all rotten, in consequence of a fever, occasioned by the infamous practice of sewing up the gut, that they may be the sooner fattened in coops, in consequence of this cruel retention.

Of the fish, I need say nothing in this hot weather, but that it comes sixty, seventy, fourscore, and a hundred miles by landcarriage; a circumstance sufficient without any comment, to turn a Dutchman's stomach, even if his nose was not saluted in every alley with the sweet flavour of *fresh* mackarel, selling by retail— This is not the season for oysters; nevertheless, it may not be amiss to mention, that the right Colchester are kept in slime-pits, occasionally overflowed by the sea; and that the green colour, so much admired by the voluptuaries of this metropolis, is occasioned by the vitriolic scum, which rises on the surface of the stagnant and stinking water—Our rabbits are bred and fed in the poulterer's cellar, where they have neither air nor exercise, consequently they must be firm in flesh, and delicious in flavour; and there is no game to be had for love or money.

It must be owned, the Covent-garden affords some good fruit; which, however, is always engrossed by a few individuals of overgrown fortune, at an exorbitant price; so that little else than the refuse of the market falls to the share of the community; and that is distributed by such filthy hands, as I cannot look at without loathing. It was but yesterday that I saw a dirty barrow-bunter in the street, cleaning her dusty fruit with her own spittle; and, who knows but some fine lady of St. James's parish might admit into her delicate mouth those very cherries, which had been rolled and moistened between the filthy, and, perhaps, ulcerated chops of a St. Giles's huckster—I need not dwell upon the pallid, contaminated mash, which they call strawberries; soiled and tossed by greasy paws through twenty baskets crusted with dirt; and then presented with the worst milk, thickened with the worst flour, into a bad likeness of cream: but the milk itself should not pass unanalysed, the produce of faded cabbage-leaves and sour draff, lowered with hot water, frothed with bruised snails, carried through the streets in open pails, exposed to foul rinsings, discharged from doors and windows, spittle, snot, and tobacco-quids from foot passengers, overflowings from mud carts, spatterings from coach wheels, dirt and trash chucked into it by roguish boys for the joke's sake, the spewings of infants, who have slabbered in the tin-measure, which is thrown back in that condition among the milk, for the benefit of the next customer; and, finally the vermin that drops from the rags of the nasty drab that vends this precious mixture, under the respectable denomination of milk-maid.

I shall conclude this catalogue of London dainties, with that table-beer, guiltless of hops and malt, vapid and nauseous; much fitter to facilitate the operation of a vomit, than to quench thirst and promote digestion; the tallowy rancid mass, called butter, manufactured with candle grease and kitchen stuff; and their fresh eggs, imported from France and Scotland.—Now, all these enormities might be remedied with a very little attention to the article of police, or civil regulation; but the wise patriots of London have taken it into their heads, that all regulation is inconsistent with liberty; and that every man ought to live in his own way, without restraint—Nay, as there is not sense enough left among them, to be discomposed by the nuisance I have mentioned, they may, for aught I care, wallow in the mire of their own pollution.

80.

William Cowper

THE POPLAR-FIELD [1784]

The poplars are fell'd, farewell to the shade
And the whispering sound of the cool colonnade,
The winds play no longer, and sing in the leaves,
Nor Ouse on his bosom their image receives.

Twelve years have elaps'd since I first took a view
Of my favourite field and the bank where they grew,
And now in the grass behold they are laid,
And the tree is my seat that once lent me a shade.

The blackbird has fled to another retreat
Where the hazels afford him a screen from the heat,
And the scene where his melody charm'd me before,
Resounds with his sweet-flowing ditty no more.

My fugitive years are all hasting away,
And I must ere long lie as lowly as they,
With a turf on my breast, and a stone at my head,
Ere another such grove shall arise in its stead.

'Tis a sight to engage me, if any thing can,
To muse on the perishing pleasures of man;
Though his life be a dream, his enjoyments, I see,
Have a being less durable even than he.

81.

Thomas Robert Malthus

From ESSAY ON THE PRINCIPLE OF POPULATION [1798]

[The pamphlet-length
Essay on the Principle of Population published by Malthus in 1798
has long since taken its place among the most influential writings
in history. The Malthusian doctrine dominated economic thought
for a century and helped give economics the name of the "dismal
science." The economic revolution of industrialization, which vastly
increased the productive power of society, seemed then for a time
to confute his conclusion that population would always outrun the
supply of the necessities of life, but, by the mid-twentieth century,
the change began to look rather more like only a temporary respite.]

I have read some
of the speculations on the perfectibility of man and of society with
great pleasure. I have been warmed and delighted with the enchanting picture which they hold forth. I ardently wish for such happy
improvements. But I see great, and, to my understanding, uncon-

querable difficulties in the way to them. These difficulties it is my present purpose to state, declaring, at the same time, that so far from exulting in them, as a cause of triumph over the friends of innovation, nothing would give me greater pleasure than to see them completely removed.

. . . .

In entering upon the argument I must premise that I put out of the question, at present, all mere conjectures, that is, all suppositions, the probable realization of which cannot be inferred upon any just philosophical grounds. A writer may tell me that he thinks man will ultimately become an ostrich. I cannot properly contradict him. But before he can expect to bring any reasonable person over to his opinion, he ought to show that the necks of mankind have been gradually elongating, that the lips have grown harder and more prominent, that the legs and feet are daily altering their shape, and that the hair is beginning to change into stubs of feathers. And till the probability of so wonderful a conversion can be shown, it is surely lost time and lost eloquence to expatiate on the happiness of man in such a state; to describe his powers, both of running and flying, to paint him in a condition where all narrow luxuries would be contemned, where he would be employed only in collecting the necessaries of life, and where, consequently, each man's share of labour would be light, and his portion of leisure ample.

I think I may fairly make two postulata.

First, that food is necessary to the existence of man.

Secondly, that the passion between the sexes is necessary and will remain nearly in its present state.

These two laws, ever since we have had any knowledge of mankind, appear to have been fixed laws of our nature, and, as we have not hitherto seen any alteration in them, we have no right to conclude that they will ever cease to be what they now are without an immediate act of power in that Being who first arranged the system of the universe, and for the advantage of his creatures, still executes, according to fixed laws, all its various operations.

. . . .

Assuming then, my postulata as granted, I say that the power of population is indefinitely greater than the power in the earth to produce subsistence for man.

Population, when unchecked, increases in a geometrical ratio. Subsistence increases only in an arithmetical ratio. A slight acquaintance with numbers will show the immensity of the first power in comparison of the second.

By that law of our nature which makes food necessary to the life of man, the effects of these two unequal powers must be kept equal.

This implies a strong and constantly operating check on population from the difficulty of subsistence. This difficulty must fall somewhere and must necessarily be severely felt by a large portion of mankind.

Through the animal and vegetable kingdoms, nature has scattered the seeds of life abroad with the most profuse and liberal hand. She has been comparatively sparing in the room and the nourishment necessary to rear them. The germs of existence contained in this spot of earth, with ample food, and ample room to expand in, would fill millions of worlds in the course of a few thousand years. Necessity, that imperious all-pervading law of nature, restrains them within the prescribed bounds. The race of plants and the race of animals shrink under this great restrictive law. And the race of man cannot, by any efforts of reason, escape from it. Among plants and animals its effects are waste of seed, sickness, and premature death; among mankind, misery and vice. The former, misery, is an absolutely necessary consequence of it. Vice is a highly probable consequence, and we therefore see it abundantly prevail, but it ought not, perhaps, to be called an absolutely necessary consequence. The ordeal of virtue is to resist all temptation to evil.

This natural inequality of the two powers of population and of production in the earth and that great law of our nature which must constantly keep their effects equal form the great difficulty that to me appears insurmountable in the way to the perfectibility of society. All other arguments are of slight and subordinate consideration in comparison of this. I see no way by which man can escape from the weight of this law, which pervades all animated nature. No fancied equality, no agrarian regulations in their utmost extent, could remove the pressure of it even for a single century. And it appears, therefore, to be decisive against the possible existence of a society all the members of which should live in ease, happiness, and comparative leisure, and feel no anxiety about providing the means of subsistence for themselves and families.

Consequently, if the premises are just, the argument is conclusive against the perfectibility of the mass of mankind.

82.

William Blake

From MILTON [1804]

And did those feet in ancient time
   Walk upon England's mountains green?
And was the holy Lamb of God
   On England's pleasant pastures seen?

And did the Countenance Divine
   Shine forth upon our clouded hills?
And was Jerusalem builded here
   Among these dark Satanic Mills?

Bring me my Bow of burning gold!
   Bring me my Arrows of desire!
Bring me my Spear! O clouds, unfold!
   Bring me my Chariot of fire!

I will not cease from Mental Fight,
   Nor shall my Sword sleep in my hand,
Till we have built Jerusalem
   In England's green and pleasant Land.

[The two qualities of
the American land that most struck early explorers and settlers
were, as we have seen, its richness and its seeming boundlessness.
The typical reaction was, understandably enough, prodigality in the
use of what nature had to offer. The day when America, like Europe,
would be completely domesticated was far, far off, and it was
virtually inconceivable to most Americans that they could ever face
shortages of natural resources. There were, nonetheless, perceptive
observers who quite early criticized thoughtless exploitation of the
land's wealth and warned that the future was much closer than it
appeared to be.]

83.

Peter Kalm [1753]

[Peter Kalm, an
outstanding Swedish naturalist, visited North America during 1748–
51 to study the flora and fauna of the New World. He also observed
the human inhabitants and was sharply critical of some of their
practices, as in this selection from his *Travels in North America*.]

Agriculture was in a
very bad state hereabouts. Formerly when a person had bought a
piece of land, which perhaps had never been plowed since Creation,

he cut down a part of the wood, tore up the roots, tilled the ground, sowed seed on it, and the first time he got an excellent crop.—But the same land after being cultivated for several years in succession, without being manured, finally loses its fertility of course. Its possessor then leaves it fallow and proceeds to another part of his land, which he treats in the same manner. Thus he goes on till he has changed a great part of his possessions into grain fields, and by that means deprived the ground of its fertility. He then returns to the first field, which now has pretty well recovered. This he tills again as long as it will afford him a good crop; but when its fertility is exhausted he leaves it fallow again and proceeds to the rest as before.

It being customary here to let the cattle go about the fields and in the woods both day and night, the people cannot collect much dung for manure. But by leaving the land fallow for several years a great quantity of weeds spring up in it, and get such strength that it requires a considerable time to extirpate them. This is the reason why the grain is always so mixed with the seed of weeds. The great richness of the soil which the first European colonists found here, and which had never been plowed before, has given rise to this neglect of agriculture, which is still observed by many of the inhabitants. But they do not consider that when the earth is quite exhausted a great space of time and an infinite deal of labor are necessary to bring it again into good condition, especially in these countries which are almost every summer scorched by the excessive heat and drought.

. . . .

All the old Swedes and Englishmen born in America whom I ever questioned asserted that there were not nearly so many edible birds at present as there used to be when they were children, and that their decrease was visible. They even said that they had heard the same complaint from their fathers who were born in this locality. In their youth the bays, rivers and brooks were quite covered with all sorts of water fowl, such as wild geese, ducks, and the like. But at present there was sometimes not a single bird upon them. About sixty or seventy years ago, a single person could kill eighty ducks in a morning; but at present you frequently waited in vain for a single one. A Swede above ninety years old assured me that he had in his youth killed twenty-three ducks at a shot (hunting party?). This good luck nobody is likely to have at present, as you are forced to ramble about for a whole day, without getting a sight of more than three or four. Cranes at that time came hither by hundreds in the spring: at present there are very few. The wild turkeys, and the birds which the Swedes in this country call partridges and hazelhens, were seen in large flocks in the woods. But at this time a person gets tired with walking before he can start a single bird.

The cause of this diminution is not difficult to find. Before the arrival of the Europeans, the country was uncultivated and full of great forests. The few Indians that lived here seldom disturbed the birds. They carried on no trade among themselves, iron and gun powder were unknown to them. One hundredth part of the fowl which at that time were so plentiful here, would have sufficed to feed the few inhabitants. And considering that they cultivated their small maize fields, caught fish, hunted stags, beavers, bears, wild cattle, and other animals whose flesh was delicious to them, it will soon appear how little they disturbed the birds. But since the arrival of great crowds of Europeans, things are greatly changed; the country is well peopled, and the woods are cut down. The people, increasing in this country, have by hunting and shooting in part extirpated the birds, in part frightened them away. In spring the people still steal eggs, mothers and young indifferently, because no regulations are made to the contrary. And if any had been made, the spirit of freedom which prevails in the country would not suffer them to be obeyed.

. . . .

The leaves which dropped last autumn had covered the ground three or four inches in depth. As this seemed to hinder the growth of the grass, it was customary to burn it in March, or at the end of that month (according to the old style), in order to give the grass the opportunity of growing up. I found several spots burnt in this manner to-day; but if it be useful one way, it does a great deal of damage in another. All the young shoots of several trees were burnt with the dead leaves, which diminishes the wood and timber considerably; and in places where the dead leaves had been burnt for several years in succession the old trees only were left, which being cut down, there remained nothing but a large field, and without any wood. At the same time all sorts of trees and plants were consumed by the fire, or at least deprived of their power of budding. Now, a great number of the plants and most of the grasses here are annuals; their seeds fall between the leaves, and by that means are burnt. This is another cause of universal complaint that grass is much scarcer at present in the woods than it was formerly. A great number of dry and hollow trees are burnt at the same time, though they could serve as fuel in the houses, and by that means spare part of the forests. The upper mould likewise burns away in part by that means, not to mention several other inconveniences with which this burning of the dead leaves is attended. To this purpose the government of Pennsylvania has lately published an edict which prohibits this burning; but every one does as he pleases and this prohibition meets with a general censure.

. . . .

The rye grows very poorly in most of the fields, which is chiefly owing to the carelessness in agriculture, and to the poorness of the fields, which are seldom or never manured. After the inhabitants have converted a tract of land into a tillable field, which has been a forest for many centuries, and which consequently has a very fine soil, the colonists use it as such as long as it will bear any crops; and when it ceases to bear any, they turn it into pastures for the cattle, and take new grain fields in another place, where a rich black soil can be found and where it has never been made use of. This kind of agriculture will do for a time; but it will afterwards have bad consequences, as every one may clearly see. A few of the inhabitants, however, treated their fields a little better: the English in general have carried agriculture to a higher degree of perfection than any other nation. But the depth and richness of the soil found here by the English settler (as they were preparing land for plowing, which had been covered with woods from times immemorial) misled them, and made them careless husbandmen. It is well known that the Indians lived in this country for several centuries before the Europeans came into it; but it is likewise known, that they lived chiefly by hunting and fishing, and had hardly any agriculture. They planted corn and some species of beans and pumpkins; and at the same time it is certain that a plantation of such vegetables as serve an Indian family during one year take up no more ground than a farmer in our country takes to plant cabbage for his family. At least, a farmer's cabbage and turnip ground, taken together, is always as extensive, if not more so, than all the corn fields and kitchen gardens of an Indian family. Therefore, the Indians could hardly subsist for one month upon the produce of their gardens and fields. Commonly, the little villages of Indians are about twelve or eighteen miles distant from each other. Hence one may judge how little ground was formerly employed for planting; and the rest was overgrown with large, tall trees. And though they cleared (as is yet usual) new ground, as soon as the old one had lost its fertility, such little pieces as they made use of were very inconsiderable, when compared to the vast forest which remained. Thus the upper fertile soil increased considerably, for centuries; and the Europeans coming to America found a rich, fine soil before them, lying as loose between the trees as the best bed in a garden. They had nothing to do but to cut down the wood, put it up in heaps, and to clear the dead leaves away. They could then immediately proceed to plowing, which in such loose ground is very easy; and having sown their grain, they got a most plentiful harvest. This easy method of getting a rich crop has spoiled the English and other European settlers, and induced them to adopt the same method of agriculture as the Indians; that is, to sow uncultivated grounds, as long as they will produce a crop without manuring, but to turn them into pastures as soon as they can bear no more, and to take on new spots of ground, covered since ancient times with woods, which have been spared by the fire or the hatchet ever since the Creation. This is likewise the reason why agriculture and its science is so imperfect here that one can travel several days and learn almost nothing about land, neither from the English, nor from the Swedes, Germans, Dutch and French; except that from their gross mistakes and carelessness of the future, one finds opportunities every day of making all sorts of observations, and of growing wise by their mistakes. In a word, the grain fields, the meadows, the forests, the cattle, etc. are treated with equal carelessness; and the characteristics of the English nation, so well skilled in these branches of husbandry, is scarcely recognizable here. We can hardly be more hostile toward our woods in Sweden and Finland than they are here: their eyes are fixed upon the present gain, and they are blind to the future. Their cattle grow poorer daily in quality and size because of hunger, as I have before mentioned. On my travels in this country I observed several plants, which the horses and cows preferred to all others. They were wild in this country and likewise grew well on the driest and poorest ground, where no other plants would succeed. But the inhabitants did not know how to turn this to their advantage, owing to the little account made of Natural History, that science being here (as in other parts of the world) looked upon as a mere trifle, and the pastime of fools. I am certain, and my certainty is founded upon experience, that by means of these plants, in the space of a few years, I should be able to turn the poorest ground, which would hardly afford food for a cow, into the richest and most fertile meadow, where great flocks of cattle would find superfluous food, and grow fat. I own that these useful plants are not to be found on the grounds of every planter: but with a small share of natural knowledge, a man could easily collect them in the places where they are to be had. I was astonished when I heard the country people complaining of the badness of the pastures; but I likewise perceived their negligence, and often saw excellent plants growing on their own grounds, which only required a little more attention and assistance from their unexperienced owner. I found everywhere the wisdom and goodness of the Creator; but too seldom saw any inclination to make use of them or adequate estimation of them, among men.

84.

Philip Vickers Fithian [1774]

[Philip Vickers Fithian was a teacher and later a clergyman in Virginia. The following journal entry is dated April 1, 1774.]

Towards Evening we rode home. I observed as I rode along People are universally plowing up their Land for planting Corn & for Tobacco. And in one field I saw several Women planting Corn. I think however, it is early even here—They raise no Flax, their Land in general being so poor that it will not produce it—And their method of farming is slovenly, without any regard to continue their Land in heart, for future Crops—They plant large Quantities of Land, without any Manure, & work it very hard to make the best of the Crop, and when the Crop comes off they take away the Fences to inclose another Piece of Land for the next years tillage, and leave this a common to be destroyed by Winter & Beasts till they stand in need of it again to plough—The Land most commonly too is of a light sandy soil, & produces in very great quantities shrubby *Savins & Pines*, unless in the Vallies, (for it is very hilly) & near the Potowmack where it is often vastly rich—Mr. Carter has been lately solicited & was to have gone this Day with a number of Gentlemen to Horn-Point on the River Ucomico, with an intention, if they think the Situation will be proper, to establish Ware-Houses, & form a small Town—It is however, in my opinion, a fruitless Scheme.

85.

Edgar Allan Poe

SONNET—TO SCIENCE [1829]

Science! true daughter of Old Time thou art!
    Who alterest all things with thy peering eyes.
Why preyest thou thus upon the poet's heart,
    Vulture, whose wings are dull realities?
How should he love thee? or how deem thee wise,
    Who wouldst not leave him in his wandering
To seek for treasure in the jewelled skies,
    Albeit he soared with an undaunted wing?
Hast thou not dragged Diana from her car,
    And driven the Hamadryad from the wood
To seek a shelter in some happier star?
    Hast thou not torn the Naiad from her flood,
The Elfin from the green grass, and from me
The summer dream beneath the tamarind tree?

86.

Thomas Cole

THE LAMENT OF THE FOREST [1841]

[Though known primarily
as a landscape painter, Thomas Cole was also a poet of minor note.
His verses, like his paintings, were strongly romantic. The following
comprises the last two-thirds of the poem "The Lament of the
Forest."]

"Mortal, whose love for our umbrageous realms
Exceeds the love of all the race of man;
Whom we have loved; for whom have opened wide
With welcome our innumerable arms;
Open thine ears! The voice that ne'er before
Was heard by living man, is lifted up,
And fills the air—the voice of our complaint.
Thousands of years!—yea, they have passed away
As drops of dew upon the sunlit rose,
Or silver vapors of the summer sea;
Thousands of years! like wind-strains on the harp,
Or like forgotten thoughts, have passed away
Unto the bourne of unremembered things.
Thousands of years! When the fresh earth first broke
Through chaos, swift in new-born joy even then
The stars of heaven beheld us waving high
Upon the mountains, slumbering in the vales:
Or yet the race of man had seen their light,
Before the virgin breast of earth was scarred
By steel, or granite masses rent from rocks
To build vast Thebes or old Persepolis,
Our arms were clasped around the hills, our locks
Shaded the streams that loved us, our green tops
Were resting places for the weary clouds.
Then all was harmony and peace; but MAN
Arose—he who now vaunts antiquity—
He the destroyer—and in the sacred shades
Of the far East began destruction's work.
Echo, whose voice had answered to the call

Of thunder or of winds, or to the cry
Of cataracts—sound of sylvan habitants
Or song of birds—uttered responses sharp
And dissonant; the axe unresting smote
Our reverend ranks, and crashing branches lashed
The ground, and mighty trunks, the pride of years,
Rolled on the groaning earth with all their umbrage.
Stronger than wintry blasts, and gathering strength,
Swept that tornado, stayless, till the Earth,
Our ancient mother, blasted lay and bare
Beneath the burning sun. The little streams
That oft had raised their voices in the breeze
In joyful unison with ours, did waste
And pine as if in grief that we were not.
Our trackless shades, our dim ubiquity,
In solemn garb of the primeval world,
Our glory, our magnificence, were gone;
And but on difficult places, marsh or steep,
The remnants of our failing race were left,
Like scattered clouds upon the mountain-top.
The vast Hyrcanian wood, and Lebanon's
Dark ranks of cedar were cut down like grass;
And man, whose poets sang our happy shades,
Whose sages taught that Innocence and Peace,
Daughters of Solitude, sojourned in us,
Held not his arm, until Necessity,
Stern master e'en of him, seized it and bound,
And from extinction saved our scanty tribes.

"Seasons there were, when man, at war with man,
Left us to raze proud cities, desolate
Old empires, and pour out his blood on soil
That once was all our own. When death has made
All silent, all secure, we have returned,
Twisted our roots around the prostrate shafts
And broken capitals, or struck them deep
Into the mould made richer by man's blood.
Such seasons were but brief: so soon as earth
Was sanctified again by shade and art,
Again resolved to nature, man came back,
And once more swept our feeble hosts away.

"Yet was there one bright, virgin continent
Remote, that Roman name had never reached,
Nor ancient dreams, in all their universe;
As inaccessible in primal time
To human eye and thought, as Uranus
Far in his secret void. For round it rolled
A troubled deep, whose everlasting roar

Echoed in every zone; whose drear expanse
Spread dark and trackless as the midnight sky;
And stories of vast whirlpools, stagnant seas,
Terrible monsters, that with horror struck
The mariner's soul, these held aloof full long
The roving race of Europe from that land,
The land of beauty and of many climes,
The land of mighty cataracts, where now
Our own proud eagle flaps his chainless wing.

"Thus guarded through long centuries, untouched
By man, save him, our native child, whose foot
Disdained the bleak and sun-beat soil, who loved
Our shafted halls, the covert of the deer,
We flourished, we rejoiced. From mountain top
To mountain top we gazed, and over vales
And glimmering plains we saw our banners green
Wide waving yet untorn. Gladly the Spring
On bloomy wing shed fragrance over us;
And Summer laughed beneath our verdant roof,
And Autumn sighed to leave our golden courts;
And when the crimson leaves were strewn in showers
Upon the ample lap of Oregon,
Or the great Huron's lake of lazuli,
Winter upraised his rude and stormy songs,
And we in a wild chorus answered him.
O peace primeval! would tho hadst remained!
What moved thee to unbar thine emerald gates,
O mighty Deep! when the destroyer came?
Strayed then thy blasts upon Olympus' air,
Or were they lulled to breezes round the brow
Of rich Granada's crafty conqueror,
When with strong wind they should have rushed upon
Our enemy, and smitten him, as when
The fleet of Xerxes on the Grecian coast
Was cast like foam and weed upon the rocks!

"But impotent the voice of our complaint:
He came! Few were his numbers first, but soon
The work of desolation was begun
Close by the heaving main; then on the banks
Of rivers inland far, our strength was shorn,
And fire and steel performed their office well.
No stay was there—no rest. The tiny cloud
Oft seen in torrid climes, at first sends forth
A faint light breeze; but gathering, as it moves,
Darkness and bulk, it spans the spacious sky
With lurid palm, and sweeps the stupendous o'er
The crashing world. And thus comes rushing on
This human hurricane, boundless as swift.

Our sanctuary, this secluded spot,
Which the stern rocks have guarded until now,
Our enemy has marked. This gentle lake
Shall lose our presence in its limpid breast,
And from the mountains we shall melt away,
Like wreaths of mist upon the winds of heaven.
Our doom is near: behold from east to west
The skies are darkened by ascending smoke;
Each hill and every valley is become
An alter unto Mammon, and the gods
Of man's idolatry—the victims we.
Missouri's floods are ruffled as by storm,
And Hudson's rugged hills at midnight glow
By light of man-projected meteors.
We feed ten thousand fires: in our short day
The woodland growth of centuries is consumed;
Our crackling limbs the ponderous hammer rouse
With fervent heat. Tormented by our flame,
Fierce vapors struggling hiss on every hand.
On Erie's shores, by dusky Arkansas,
Our ranks are falling like the heavy grain
In harvest-time on Wolga's distant banks.

"A few short years!—these valleys, greenly clad,
These slumbering mountains, resting in our arms,
Shall naked glare beneath the scorching sun,
And all their wimpling rivulets be dry.
No more the deer shall haunt these bosky glens,
Nor the pert squirrel chatter near his store.
A few short years!—our ancient race shall be,
Like Israels', scattered 'mong the tribes of men."

87.

Henry David Thoreau

SHOULD FISH FIGHT BACK? [1849]

Salmon, Shad, and
Alewives were formerly abundant here, and taken in weirs by the
Indians, who taught this method to the whites, by whom they were
used as food and as manure, until the dam and afterward the canal
at Billerica, and the factories at Lowell, put an end to their

migrations hitherward; though it is thought that a few more enterprising shad may still occasionally be seen in this part of the river.
It is said, to account for the destruction of the fishery, that those
who at that time represented the interests of the fishermen and
the fishes, remembering between what dates they were accustomed
to take the grown shad, stipulated that the dams should be left
open for that season only, and the fry, which go down a month
later, were consequently stopped and destroyed by myriads. Others
say that the fish-ways were not properly constructed. Perchance,
after a few thousands of years, if the fishes will be patient, and
pass their summers elsewhere meanwhile, nature will have leveled
the Billerica dam, and the Lowell factories, and the Grass-ground
River run clear again, to be explored by new migratory shoals, even
as far as the Hopkinton pond and Westborough swamp.

. . . .

Shad are still taken in the basin of Concord River, at Lowell,
where they are said to be a month earlier than the Merrimack
shad, on account of the warmth of the water. Still patiently,
almost pathetically, with instinct not to be discouraged, not to be
reasoned with, revisiting their old haunts, as if their stern fates
would relent, and still met by the Corporation with its dam. Poor
shad! where is thy redress? When Nature gave thee instinct, gave
she thee the heart to bear thy fate? Still wandering the sea in thy
scaly armor to inquire humbly at the mouths of rivers if man
has perchance left them free for thee to enter. By countless shoals
loitering uncertain meanwhile, merely stemming the tide there,
in danger from sea foes in spite of thy bright armor, awaiting new
instructions, until the sands, until the water itself, tell thee if it
be so or not. Thus by whole migrating nations, full of instinct,
which is thy faith, in this backward spring, turned adrift, and
perchance knowest not where men do *not* dwell, where there are
not factories, in these days. Armed with no sword, no electric shock,
but mere Shad, armed only with innocence and a just cause, with
tender dumb mouth only forward, and scales easy to be detached.
I for one am with thee, and who knows what may avail a crow-bar
against that Billerica dam?—Not despairing when whole myriads
have gone to feed those sea monsters during thy suspense, but still
brave, indifferent, on easy fin there, like shad reserved for higher
destinies. Willing to be decimated for man's behoof after the
spawning season. Away with the superficial and selfish phil-*anthropy*
of men,—who knows what admirable virtue of fishes may be below
low-water-mark, bearing up against a hard destiny, not admired by
that fellow-creature who alone can appreciate it! Who hears the
fishes when they cry? It will not be forgotten by some memory
that we were contemporaries. Thou shalt erelong have thy way up
the rivers, up all the rivers of the globe, if I am not mistaken. Yea,
even thy dull watery dream shall be more than realized. If it were
not so, but thou wert to be overlooked at first and at last, then

would not I take their heaven. Yes, I say so, who think I know better than thou canst. Keep a stiff fin, then, and stem all the tides thou mayst meet.

88.

Jones Very

THE LAMENT OF THE FLOWERS [ca. 1860]

I looked to find Spring's early flowers,
    In spots where they were wont to bloom;
But they had perished in their bowers;
    The haunts they loved had proved their tomb!

The alder, and the laurel green,
    Which sheltered them, had shared their fate;
And but the blackened ground was seen,
    Where hid their swelling buds of late.

From the bewildered, homeless bird,
    Whose half-built nest the flame destroys,
A low complaint of wrong I heard,
    Against the thoughtless, ruthless boys.

Sadly I heard its notes complain,
    And ask the young its haunts to spare;
Prophetic seemed the sorrowing strain,
    Sung o'er its home, but late so fair!

'No more with hues like ocean shell
    The delicate wind-flower here shall blow;
The spot that loved its form so well
    Shall ne'er again its beauty know.

'Or, if it bloom, like some pale ghost
    'T will haunt the black and shadeless dell,
Where once it bloomed a numerous host,
    Of its once pleasant bowers to tell.

'And coming years no more shall find
  The laurel green upon the hills;
The frequent fire leaves naught behind,
  But e'en the very roots it kills.

'No more upon the turnpike's side
  The rose shall shed its sweet perfume;
The traveler's joy, the summer's pride,
  Will share with them a common doom.

'No more shall these returning fling
  Round childhood's home a heavenly charm,
With song of bird in early spring,
  To glad the heart and save from harm.'

89.

[From *The Overland Monthly*]

SEA-ELEPHANT HUNTING [1870]

The mode of capturing
them, is, for the sailors to get between the herd and the water;
then, raising all possible noise by shouting, together with the
flourishing of clubs, guns, and lances, the party advance slowly
toward the rookery, when the animals will retreat, appearing in a
great state of alarm. Occasionally, an overgrown male will give
battle, or attempt to escape; but a ball from a musket, through his
brain, dispatches him, or some one, with a lance, checks his progress by thrusting it into the roof of the animal's mouth, which
causes it to settle on its haunches. Meanwhile, two men, with heavy
oaken clubs, give it repeated blows about the head, until it is
stunned or killed. After securing those that are disposed to show
resistance, the party rush on to the main body. The onslaught
creates such a panic among those harmless creatures, that, losing
all control of their actions, they will climb, roll, or tumble over
each other, when prevented from further retreat by the projecting
cliffs. We recollect, in one instance, where sixty-five were captured,
that several were found showing no signs of either being clubbed
or lanced, but were smothered by numbers of their kind heaped

upon them. The whole flock, when attacked, manifested alarm by their peculiar roar, the sound of which, among the largest males, is nearly as loud as the lowing of an ox, but more prolonged in one strain, accompanied by a rattling noise in the throat. The quantity of blood in this species of the seal tribe is supposed to be double that contained in a neat animal, in proportion to its size.

. . . .

Owing to the continual pursuit of the animals, they have become nearly, if not quite, extinct on the California coast, or the few remaining have fled to some unknown point for security.

Thus far, we have been writing of the Sea-Elephant and manner of capturing it on the islands and coasts of the Californias; and, although thousands of the animals, in past years, gathered upon the shores of the islands contiguous to the coast, as well as about the pebbly or sandy beaches of the peninsula, affording full cargoes to the oil-ships, yet their numbers were but few, when compared with the multitudes which once inhabited the remote, desolate islands, or places on the main, within the icy regions of the southern hemisphere.

. . . .

Notwithstanding the hardship and deprivations that are undergone to make a successful voyage, there is no lack of enterprising merchants ready to invest their capital in any adventure when there is a prospect of ultimate gain, and no ocean or sea which there is a possibility of navigating appears too perilous for the adventurous seamen to try their luck upon.

. . . .

The extent and value of the Sea-Elephant fishery, from its commencement up to the present date, is not definitely known, as the ships engaged in the enterprise when whaling and sealing was at its height in the Southern Ocean, were also in pursuit of the valuable fur-bearing animals, as well as the *cachalot* and the *baloena*; hence their cargoes were often made up of a variety of the oils of commerce.

We have reliable accounts, however, of the Sea-Elephant being taken for its oil as early as the beginning of the present century. At those islands, or upon the coasts on the main, where vessels could find secure shelter from all winds, the animals have long since been virtually annihilated; and now they are only sought after in the remote places we have mentioned, and these points are only accessible under the great difficulties that beset the mariner when sailing near the antipodes of the globe.

Enough data are at hand, nevertheless, to show that hundreds of thousands of the animals, yielding as many barrels of oil, have been taken from Desolation and Herd's Islands, by American ships, which have maintained a monopoly of the business for many years.

90.

Frederick Law Olmsted [1870]

[Frederick Law Olmsted
was the foremost landscape architect of his time. Central Park in
New York City, Fairmount Park in Philadelphia, and the Capitol
grounds in Washington are some of his many achievements. He was,
not surprisingly, also a leading advocate of parks and recreational
areas in cities.]

We have reason to
believe, then, that towns which of late have been increasing rapidly
on account of their commercial advantages, are likely to be still
more attractive to population in the future; that there will in
consequence soon be larger towns than any the world has yet
known, and that the further progress of civilization is to depend
mainly upon the influences by which men's minds and characters
will be affected while living in large towns.

Now, knowing that the average length of the life of mankind in
towns has been much less than in the country, and that the average
amount of disease and misery and of vice and crime has been much
greater in towns, this would be a very dark prospect for civilization, if it were not that modern Science has beyond all question
determined many of the causes of the special evils by which
men are afflicted in towns, and placed means in our hands for
guarding against them. It has shown, for example, that under
ordinary circumstances, in the interior parts of large and closely
built towns, a given quantity of air contains considerably less of
the elements which we require to receive through the lungs than
the air of the country or even of the outer and more open parts
of a town, and that instead of them it carries into the lungs highly
corrupt and irritating matters, the action of which tends strongly
to vitiate all our sources of vigor—how strongly may perhaps be
indicated in the shortest way by the statement that even metallic
plates and statues corrode and wear away under the atmospheric
influences which prevail in the midst of large towns, more rapidly
than in the country.

The irritation and waste of the physical powers which result from
the same cause, doubtless indirectly affect and very seriously affect
the mind and the moral strength; but there is a general impression
that a class of men are bred in towns whose peculiarities are not
perhaps adequately accounted for in this way. We may understand
these better if we consider that whenever we walk through the

denser part of a town, to merely avoid collision with those we meet and pass upon the sidewalks, we have constantly to watch, to foresee, and to guard against their movements. This involves a consideration of their intentions, a calculation of their strength and weakness, which is not so much for their benefit as our own. Our minds are thus brought into close dealings with other minds without any friendly flowing toward them, but rather a drawing from them. Much of the intercourse between men when engaged in the pursuits of commerce has the same tendency—a tendency to regard others in a hard if not always hardening way. Each detail of observation and of the process of thought required in this kind of intercourse or contact of minds is so slight and so common in the experience of towns-people that they are seldom conscious of it. It certainly involves some expenditure nevertheless. People from the country are even conscious of the effect on their nerves and minds of the street contact—often complaining that they feel confused by it; and if we had no relief from it at all during our waking hours, we should all be conscious of suffering from it. It is upon our opportunities of relief from it, therefore, that not only our comfort in town life, but our ability to maintain a temperate, good-natured, and healthy state of mind, depends. This is one of many ways in which it happens that men who have been brought up, as the saying is, in the streets, who have been most directly and completely affected by town influences, so generally show, along with a remarkable quickness of apprehension, a peculiarly hard sort of selfishness. Every day of their lives they have seen thousands of their fellow-men, have met them face to face, have brushed against them, and yet have had no experience of anything in common with them.

91.

Nathaniel S. Shaler

THE FLOODS OF THE MISSISSIPPI VALLEY [1883]

The Mississippi Valley differs in many ways from any other river valley with which our race has had to deal. In the first place, it is much larger than any of the valleys of Europe; it has a greater share of alluvial lands

along its several streams, and a more extensive delta at its mouth,
than any Old World rivers. The process of occupation by man, and
the change in the conditions which this occupation brings about,
have taken place with great rapidity, without allowing any time
for the readjustment of the physical conditions which the use of a
region by civilized men compels.

When our race came to occupy the Mississippi Valley, its conditions had already been modified by the action of his Indian predecessors to a considerable degree. Nearly all the region west of the
Mississippi, and a large portion of that to the north and west of
the Ohio, where now lie the States of Indiana, Illinois, and Wisconsin, were destitute of forests. In part, this absence of woods was
due to the original influence of climate; but in larger degree it was
owing to the Indian habit of burning the herbage, to foster the
growth of the fresh grasses which were so advantageous to the
buffalo and other large game.

. . . .

What the savages could not do with fire, their successors, more
skillful despoilers of the earth, have set about with the axe. A large
part of the forest coating of the Ohio Valley has disappeared, and
what remains is marked all over by the hand of man.

The first and most important result of this invasion of the forests
by civilization is that the rain-water flows more rapidly into the
streams, and thence to the sea, than it did before. We easily perceive
how this is brought about. In the old virgin forests, whose
wildnesses are known to few, the water had a long and slow
journey to the main streams. There was commonly a foot or more
of vegetable mould, porous as a sponge, and capable of retaining
a rainfall of several inches, which it yielded slowly to the streams.
This was overlaid in every direction by fallen trees, whose moulder-
ing frames made little dams across every depression, from which
the water would slowly filter down the drainage slopes. In the
torrential rains that flooded the surface of the wood, the action
of the flowing water heaped the decayed débris in every channel,
and served to bar its path to the main streams. When the flood had
found its way to the open brooks, it encountered the system of
beaver dams, which once existed in thousands along all the lesser
streams. . . . Each of these barriers held the waters imperfectly,
serving only to hinder the flood in its swift course; no one dam
would hold more than a few acres of water; but, with every little
"branch" full of them, the aggregate restraining effect on the current
was very great indeed. The floating ice and drift-wood would catch
on the barrier of the dam, and so increase its effect in holding
back the waters. . . .

Let us consider how man's interference has changed the behavior
of these floods. In the first place, the larger part of the forests have
utterly disappeared. Instead of the spongy mass of the forest bed
that never could be entirely closed by frost, and of the sheltering

woods that fenced the snow from the sun and from warm winds, we now have more than half the valley, with bare fields, compacted by tillage, open to sun and to the south wind, freezing to the hardness of stone, and from which the rains of the late winter flow away as speedily as they do from the house roofs.

Besides this, all the beaver-dammed, timber-obstructed streams are cleared out, in order that the lumberman may "run" his logs from the remnants of forests among the hills. All the alluvial lands along the streams are turned into open fields, so that the overflowing water has no longer to creep through a tangle of vegetation, as soon as it escapes from the channel, but may move swiftly, however wide its stream. If now, after a time of frost, there comes a general rain that exceeds two or three inches in total fall, the water from the most of the valleys is swiftly precipitated into the main ways, and it all hurries at the average rate of six or more miles an hour from the place where it falls to the earth to the great rivers. These main rivers speedily escape from their banks, and flood the fields and towns throughout the alluvial plains, carrying destruction all the way to the sea. For a time, the increasing volume of the flood waters that each year has brought has managed to make some compensation for itself. The main channels have been widened by cutting away the alluvial plain on either side. In this fashion the flood water way of the Ohio has widened by about one fifth since the settlement of the country began. But now, when many cities have grown on its banks, and the alluvial lands have come to be highly valued, means have been taken to keep the stream as far as possible within its bounds, and even to recover some part of its recent gains on its shores. So the waters are compelled to mount in height, and they rush onward in a swift tide that requires several days to pass any given point. As this flood, reinforced by every tributary, goes onward, it lengthens, but becomes less deep, and takes more hours to pass by. Thus a flood that will be dangerously high for only two days in the upper Ohio will be a week above the danger line on the Mississippi. It is impossible to estimate the loss by such a flood as that of February, 1883, on the Ohio. . . .

Bad as this is at the moment, the prospect for the future is yet more discouraging. The remaining forests of the Ohio Valley, which still cover something over one third of its surface, and serve to modify the floods, lie principally in the mountain districts about its head waters,—the head streams of the Tennessee, Cumberland, Kentucky, Licking, Sandy, Kanawha, Monongahela, etc. These forests clothe steep hillsides, whence the infinitely ramifying streams fall rapidly to the main rivers. The heaviest rainfall of the valley is in this district. As yet the lumberman has left much of this country unchanged; the flood water has there something of the slow escape that once marked its overflow in all the lower regions as well. Now, however, the changes arising from settlement is invading these valleys; the axe is stripping their hill-sides, turning them into bare roofs, from which soil and water flow away in swift

yellow torrents. The streams are using the old barriers of fallen
trees and the tangle of lodged drift-wood, that moderated the speed
of the current even after the beaver dams had disappeared. When
these mountain ridges have been thoroughly subjugated, a process
that will be complete within half a century, the disastrous power
of the flood will be greatly enhanced; for this region has the largest
rainfall of any part of the valley, and when stripped of its forests
will, on account of its steepness of surface, send its tide of water
with greater speed to the low countries than those regions which
now give the worst floods.

92.

Black Elk

THE WHITE MAN'S GREED [ca. 1880]

When I was older,
I learned what the fighting was about that winter and the next
summer. Up on the Madison Fork the Wasichus [white men] had
found much of the yellow metal that they worship and that makes
them crazy, and they wanted to have a road up through our country
to the place where the yellow metal was; but my people did not
want the road. It would scare the bison and make them go away,
and also it would let the other Wasichus come in like a river. They
told us that they wanted only to use a little land, as much as a
wagon would take between the wheels; but our people knew better.
And when you look about you now, you can see what it was they
wanted.

Once we were happy in our own country and we were seldom
hungry, for then the two-leggeds and the four-leggeds lived together
like relatives, and there was plenty for them and for us. But the
Wasichus came, and they have made little islands for us and other
little islands of the four-leggeds, and always these islands are
becoming smaller, for around them surges the gnawing flood of
the Wasichu; and it is dirty with lies and greed.

. . . .

As I told you, it was in the summer of my twentieth year (1883)
that I performed the ceremony of the elk. That fall, they say, the

last of the bison herds was slaughtered by the Wasichus. I can
remember when the bison were so many that they could not be
counted, but more and more Wasichus came to kill them until
there were only heaps of bones scattered where they used to be.
The Wasichus did not kill them to eat; they killed them for the
metal that makes them crazy, and they took only the hides to sell.
Sometimes they did not even take the hides, only the tongues;
and I have heard that fire-boats came down the Missouri River
loaded with dried bison tongues. You can see that the men who did
this were crazy. Sometimes they did not even take the tongues;
they just killed and killed because they liked to do that. When we
hunted bison, we killed only what we needed. And when there was
nothing left but heaps of bones, the Wasichus came and gathered
up even the bones and sold them.

93.

George Bird Grinnell

THE LAST OF THE BUFFALO [1892]

The early explorers
were constantly astonished by the multitudinous herds which they
met with, the regularity of their movements, and the deep roads
which they made in travelling from place to place. Many of the
earlier references are to territory east of the Mississippi, but even
within the last fifteen years buffalo were to be seen on the Western
plains in numbers so great that an entirely sober and truthful
account seems like fable. Describing the abundance of buffalo in
a certain region, an Indian once said to me, in the expressive sign
language of which all old frontiersmen have some knowledge, "The
country was one robe."

Much has been written about their enormous abundance in the
old days, but I have never read anything that I thought an exaggeration of their numbers as I have seen them. Only one who has
actually spent months in travelling among them in those old days
can credit the stories told about them. The trains of the Kansas
Pacific Railroad used frequently to be detained by herds which
were crossing the tracks in front of the engines, and in 1870, trains

on which I was travelling were twice so held, in one case for three hours. When railroad travel first began on this road, the engineers tried the experiment of running through these passing herds, but after their engines had been thrown from the tracks they learned wisdom, and gave the buffalo the right of way. Two or three years later, in the country between the Platte and Republican Rivers, I saw a closely massed herd of buffalo so vast that I dare not hazard a guess as to its numbers; and in later years I have travelled for weeks at a time, in northern Montana, without ever being out of sight of buffalo.

. . . .

The dismal story of the extermination of the buffalo for its hides has been so often told, that I may be spared the sickening details of the butchery which was carried on from the Mexican to the British boundary line in the struggle to obtain a few dollars by a most ignoble means. As soon as railroads penetrated the buffalo country, a market was opened for their hides. Men too lazy to work were not too lazy to hunt, and a good hunter could kill in the early days from thirty to seventy-five buffalo a day, the hides of which were worth from $1.50 to $4 each. This seemed an easy way to make money, and the market for hides was unlimited. Up to this time the trade in robes had been mainly confined to those dressed by the Indians, and these were for the most part taken from cows. The coming of the railroad made hides of all sorts marketable, and even those taken from naked old bulls found a sale at some price. The butchery of buffalo was now something stupendous. Thousands of hunters followed millions of buffalo and destroyed them wherever found and at all seasons of the year. They pursued them during the day, and at night camped at the watering places, and built lines of fires along the streams, to drive the buffalo back so that they could not drink. It took less than six years to destroy all the buffalo in Kansas, Nebraska, Indian Territory, and northern Texas. The few that were left of the southern herd retreated to the waterless plains of Texas, and there for a while had a brief respite. Even here the hunters followed them, but as the animals were few and the territory in which they ranged vast, they held out here for some years. It was in this country, and against the very last survivors of this southern herd, that "Buffalo Jones" made his very successful trips to capture calves.

The extirpation of the northern herd was longer delayed. No very terrible slaughter occurred until the completion of the Northern Pacific Railroad; then, however, the same scenes of butchery were enacted. Buffalo were shot down by tens of thousands, their hides stripped off, and the meat left to the wolves. The result of the crusade was soon seen, the last buffalo were killed in the Northwest near the boundary line in 1883, and that year may be said to have finished up the species, though some few were killed in 1884 to 1885.

After the slaughter had been begun, but years before it had been accomplished, the subject was brought to the attention of Congress, and legislation looking to the preservation of the species was urged upon that body. Little general interest was taken in the subject, but in 1874, after much discussion, Congress did pass an act providing for the protection of the buffalo. The bill, however, was never signed by the President.

. . . .

Of the millions of buffalo which even in our own time ranged the plains in freedom, none now remain. From the prairies which they used to darken, the wild herds, down to the last straggling bull, have disappeared. In the Yellowstone National Park, protected from destruction by United States troops, are the only wild buffalo which exist within the borders of the United States. These are mountain buffalo, and, from their habit of living in the thick timber and on the rough mountain sides, they are only now and then seen by visitors to the Park. . . .

On the great plains is still found the buffalo skull half buried in the soil and crumbling to decay. The deep trails once trodden by the marching hosts are grass-grown now, and fast filling up. When these most enduring relics of a vanished race shall have passed away, there will be found, in all the limitless domain once darkened by their feeding herds, not one trace of the American buffalo.

94.

Charles W. Dabney

WASTE IN THE WHEAT FIELDS [1902]

The wheat farmers say that it does not pay to take undue care of old machinery, that more money is lost in repairing and tinkering an old machine than would pay for a new one. The result is that new machinery is bought in very large quantities, used until it is worn out or cannot be repaired without considerable work, and then left in the fields to rust. Heaps of cast-iron can be seen already upon many of the large farms. Of course a great many extra parts are bought to take the place of those which break most frequently, and some men are always kept at work repairing machines in the field.

95.

Ambrose Bierce [1906]

[A journalist and author of a particularly sardonic stripe, Ambrose Bierce took great delight for many years in constructing word definitions ranging from facetious to outrageously cynical. He collected and published them in 1906 as *The Cynic's Word Book*, later called *The Devil's Dictionary*.]

GEOLOGY, *n*. The science of the earth's crust—to which, doubtless, will be added that of its interior whenever a man shall ccme up garrulous out of a well. The geological formations of the globe already noted are catalogued thus: The Primary, or lower one, consists of rocks, bones of mired mules, gas-pipes, miners' tools, antique statues minus the nose, Spanish doubloons and ancestors. The Secondary is largely made up of red worms and moles. The Tertiary comprises railway tracks, patent pavements, grass, snakes, mouldy boots, beer bottles, tomato cans, intoxicated citizens, garbage, anarchists, snap-dogs and fools.

MAN, *n*. An animal so lost in rapturous contemplation of what he thinks he is as to overlook what he indubitably ought to be. His chief occupation is extermination of other animals and his own species, which, however, multiplies with such insistent rapidity as to infest the whole habitable earth and Canada.

96.

Robinson Jeffers

SCIENCE [1925]

Man, introverted man, having crossed
In passage and but a little with the nature of things this latter
     century
Has begot giants; but being taken up
Like a maniac with self-love and inward conflicts cannot manage
     his hybrids.

Being used to deal with edgeless dreams,
Now he's bred knives on nature turns them also inward: they have
    thirsty points though.
His mind forebodes his own destruction;
Actæon who saw the goddess naked among leaves and his hounds
    tore him.
A little knowledge, a pebble from the shingle,
A drop from the oceans: who would have dreamed this infinitely
    little too much?

97.

Robert Frost

A BROOK IN THE CITY [1923]

The farmhouse lingers, though averse to square
With the new city street it has to wear
A number in. But what about the brook
That held the house as in an elbow-crook?
I ask as one who knew the brook, its strength
And impulse, having dipped a finger length
And made it leap my knuckle, having tossed
A flower to try its currents where they crossed.
The meadow grass could be cemented down
From growing under pavements of a town;
The apple trees be sent to hearthstone flame.
Is water wood to serve a brook the same?
How else dispose of an immortal force
No longer needed? Staunch it at its source
With cinder loads dumped down? The brook was thrown
Deep in a sewer dungeon under stone
In fetid darkness still to live and run—
And all for nothing it had ever done
Except forget to go in fear perhaps.
No one would know except for ancient maps
That such a brook ran water. But I wonder
If from its being kept forever under
The thoughts may not have risen that so keep
This new-built city from both work and sleep.

98.

Sigmund Freud

THE ARTIFICES OF SOCIETY [1930]

For various reasons, it is very far from my intention to express any opinion concerning the value of human civilization. I have endeavoured to guard myself against the enthusiastic partiality which believes our civilization to be the most precious thing that we possess or could acquire, and thinks it must inevitably lead us to undreamed-of heights of perfection. I can at any rate listen without taking umbrage to those critics who aver that when one surveys the aims of civilization and the means it employs, one is bound to conclude that the whole thing is not worth the effort and that in the end it can only produce a state of things which no individual will be able to bear. My impartiality is all the easier to me since I know very little about these things and am sure only of one thing, that the judgments of value made by mankind are immediately determined by their desires for happiness: in other words, that those judgments are attempts to prop up their illusions with arguments. I could understand it very well if anyone were to point to the inevitable nature of the process of cultural development and say, for instance, that the tendency to institute restrictions upon sexual life, or to carry humanitarian ideals into effect at the cost of natural selection, are developmental trends which it is impossible to avert or divert, and to which it is best for us to submit as though they were natural necessities. I know, too, the objection that can be raised against this: that tendencies such as these, which are believed to have insuperable power behind them, have often in the history of man been thrown aside and replaced by others. My courage fails me, therefore, at the thought of rising up as a prophet before my fellow-men, and I bow to their reproach that I have no consolation to offer them; for at bottom this is what they all demand—the frenzied revolutionary as passionately as the most pious believer.

The fateful question of the human species seems to me to be whether and to what extent the cultural process developed in it will succeed in mastering the derangements of communal life caused by the human instinct of aggression and self-destruction. In this connection, perhaps the phase through which we are at this moment passing deserves special interest. Men have brought their powers of subduing the forces of nature to such a pitch that by using them they could now very easily exterminate one another to the last man. They know this—hence arises a great part of their current unrest, their dejection, their mood of apprehension.

99.

Arthur Kallet and F. J. Schlink

POISON FRUIT [1933]

Six thousand poisonings, 70 deaths in England in the year 1900, from beer containing small quantities of arsenic. . . . Three hundred French sailors poisoned early in 1932 by wine contaminated with arsenic. . . . A girl, aged seven, killed by arsenic fumes from dye in moldy wall paper. . . . Six persons poisoned in California in 1931 by greens sprayed with lead arsenate. . . . A four-year-old Philadelphia girl dead, in August, 1932, from eating sprayed fruit. With a background of cases like these, are you willing to have even very small doses of arsenic, a deadly poison, administered to you and your children daily, perhaps several times daily? Willing or not, if you eat apples, pears, cherries and berries, celery, and other fruit and vegetables, you are also eating arsenic, and there is good reason to believe that it may be doing you serious, perhaps irreparable injury.

The source of this dangerous poison is the lead arsenate which is sprayed on fruits and on some vegetables to protect them from the coddling moth and other insects destructive to crops. It is extensively used, especially in the Western States, which produce our most attractive and unblemished fruits. A residue of arsenic and lead remains on the fruit, and when you wash your apple or pear under the faucet you remove only a small part of the poison. The fruit grower, however, can, under Government direction, remove the poison almost completely with a wash of dilute hydrochloric acid.

But the Federal Food and Drug Administration, proceeding on the unproved theory that arsenic in small quantities is not injurious to your health, permits the grower to market fruit and vegetables contaminated with 12/1000 of a grain of arsenic, in the form of arsenic trioxide, per pound of fruit.

Twelve-thousandths of a grain is today the legal limit, but with numerous fruit growers completely unequipped for removing the spray residue, with the staff of Government inspectors available for fruit inspection far too small to exercise more than a fraction of the necessary supervision, and with the Food and Drug Administration, in its usual fashion far more concerned about the economic interests of the growers than about the health of the public, one must be blind to suppose that a large part of the supply of apples and pears and many other fruits and vegetables is not contaminated with far more arsenic than is legally permitted. In the Northwest, after a dry season in which an unusual amount of spraying was necessary, apples were found to be contaminated with more than ten times the legal maximum of arsenic. Of four samples of California apples and pears purchased in New York City in August, 1932, three carried arsenic above the legal limit. Two carried twice the legal limit.

. . . .

Let it not be supposed that the removal of the arsenic residue from fruits is a difficult business requiring expensive equipment. As has already been stated, the cost of removing the residue from a bushel of fruit is less than five cents, in many sections of the country averaging about two or two and one-half cents. If the fruit grower cannot pay this cost, better that a Government grant should be made to have the work done efficiently and expertly, as a frank subsidy to fruit growers—and eaters—than to let the poison enter our food supply. If something of the sort is not done, it merely means that what the farmers and our government save we consumers shall all spend on medical care, and on antidotes for arsenic poisoning, many times over.

100.

Bernard De Voto

THE WEST: A PLUNDERED PROVINCE [1934]

It was a strange land, and all its strangeness came from the simple arithmetic of its rainfall. A grudging land—it gave reluctant crops only. A treacherous land—its thin rain might fail without reason or warning, and then there were no crops at all and the pioneer, who

had been ignorant of drouths, promptly starved. An inventive land
—besides drouth it had other unprepared-for plagues: armies of
locusts and beetles, rusts and fungi never encountered in the
forests, parasites that destroyed grains and cattle which had been
habituated to an Eastern climate. A poisoned land—it was var-
iously salted with strange earths which must be leached away
before seeds could germinate. And in the end as in the beginning,
a dry land—so that all problems returned to the master problem
of how to get enough water on land for which there could never
be water enough. In sum, conditions that made unavailing everything that the pioneers had learned, conditions that had to be
mastered from scratch if the last frontier was to be subdued.

And, therefore, the final strangeness of the West: it was the place
where the frontier culture broke down. The pioneer's tradition of
brawn and courage, initiative, individualism, and self-help was unavailing here. He could not conquer this land until history caught
up with him. He had, that is, to ally himself with the force which
our sentimental critics are sure he wanted to escape from: the
Industrial Revolution. . . .

The pioneer might cut sod or mold adobe bricks for a shanty,
but he could not fence his claim until industrialism brought him
barbed wire. The Plains Indians were better equipped than he for
the cavalry campaigns that had to be the West's warfare—so the
Industrial Revolution had to give him repeating rifles and repeating pistols, especially the latter. So far as the Winning of the West
was a war of conquest, victory waited upon the Spencer, the
Winchester, and especially the Colt. And always the first condition: to grow crops where there was not water enough. The
Revolution's railroads had to bring westward the Revolution's
contrivances for deep cultivation, bigger and tougher plows, new
kinds of harrows and surfacers and drills, and its contrivances for
large-scale operations, new harvesters and threshers, steam and
then gasoline group-machines which quadrupled cultivating power
and then quadrupled it again. Finally, the problem of the water
itself. The axe-awinging individualist had farmed his small claim
with methods not much different from those of Cain's time. The
Western pioneer could not farm at all until the Revolution gave
him practicable windmills, artesian wells, and the machinery that
made his dams possible. When he crossed the hundredth meridian,
in order to be Cain at all he had first to become Tubal-Cain.

. . . .

Meanwhile the government, the press, the whole nation were
expediting the rush of settlement. It was *Zeitgeist*, by God! The
continent had to be occupied—a bare spot on the map was an
affront to the eagle's children. The folk migration, now in its last
phase, was speeded up. Manifest destiny received the valuable
assistance of high-pressure publicity.

. . . .

The rainless country was the last frontier, and in its poisoned
areas, without dignity, the wayfaring Americans came to the end
of their story. Reclamation is a shining image of something or
other—aspiration, it may be, or futility. Confronted by the last
acres of the tradition and finding them incapable of producing,
the Americans wasted millions trying to enforce their will on the
desert. The impulse and the glory of the migration died hard but,
when the desert was conceded to be desert in spite of will-power,
they died at last, in something between pathos and farce. So here
ends ingloriously what began gloriously on the Atlantic littoral,
below the falls line; and the last phase of the westward wayfaring
has the appearance of a joke. Yet, this having always been a country of paradox, there is something more than a joke. Before that
ending the Westerner learned something. Implicit in the westward surge, both a product and a condition of it, was the sentiment that has been called, none too accurately, the American
dream. It is a complex sentiment not too easily to be phrased. The
plain evidence of the frontier movement, from the falls line on,
indicated that there could be no limit but the sky to what the Americans might do. The sublimate of our entire experience was just
this: here was a swamp and look! here is Chicago. Every decade
of expansion, every new district that was opened, backed up the
evidence till such an expectation was absolutely integral with the
national progress. There was no limit but the sky: American ingenuity, American will power, American energy could be stopped
by nothing whatever but would go on forever building Chicagos. It
was a dream that, in the nature of things, had to be wrecked on
reality sometime, but in actual fact the West was the first point
of impact. Just as the pioneer had to give up his axe and learn
mechanics when he crossed the hundredth meridian, just as he had
to abandon his traditional individualism, so he had to reconcile
himself to the iron determinism he faced. In the arid country just
so much is possible, and when that limit has been reached nothing
more can be done. The West was industry's stepchild, but it set a
boundary beyond which industrialism could not go. American ingenuity, will power, and energy were spectacular qualities but,
against the fact of rainfall, they simply didn't count. The mountains and the high plains, which had seen the end of the frontier
movement and had caused the collapse of the pioneer culture, thus
also set the first full stop to the American dream. Of the Americans, it was the Westerners who first understood that there are
other limits than the sky.

101.

Stuart Chase [1936]

[In reading—and perhaps rereading—this selection from Stuart Chase's *Rich Land, Poor Land*, it is well to keep in mind the date of its original publication; for, as you will see, it could as easily have been published today as in 1936.]

How does the continent look today after three hundred years of occupation? Suppose we climb into a metaphorical airplane and cruise about America, first observing the whole picture, then circling to examine this area and that, finally looking into conditions underground—with the help of whatever scientific instruments may be necessary.

The basic map has changed but little: a slit across the Isthmus of Panama, a few minor shifts in the coast line, small islands thrown up here and there or washed away, some river channels recut. But coming closer we find the cover enormously changed, as well as the denizens thereof. The old forest, the old grasslands have almost completely disappeared. Desert lands have broadened. A dust desert is forming east of the Rockies where firm grass once stood. Woodlands—and a spindly lot they are by comparison— cover only half the area the primeval forest once covered. Grazing areas are still immense but the old types of native grasses have largely gone.

On one-quarter of continental United States are new fields, bare in the winter, green with crops in the summer. Adjacent to these tilled fields are pasture lands, unknown before, of an almost equal area. On some of the old arid grasslands irrigation ditches now run, and between them is the green of crops. This is particularly noticeable around Salt Lake in Utah, in regions of the southwest, in the Imperial and Central valleys of California. Scattered about the continent, especially along the rivers and the sea coasts, are the black clusters of cities and the smaller dots of towns and villages. Linking them run a million miles and more of highways, railroads, the tracery of power lines, and pipe lines underground.

. . . .

We drop 10,000 feet and look closer still. If this be progress, it is bitter tonic. The continental soil, the center of vitality, is visibly and rapidly declining. The forest cover has been stripped and burned and steadily shrinks. The natural grass cover has been torn to ribbons by steel plows and the hooves of cattle and sheep. The skin of America has been laid open. Streams have lost their measured balance, and, heavy with silt, run wild in flood to the sea at certain seasons, to fall to miserable trickles in the drier months. This land may be bristling with tall chimneys and other evidences of progress, but it has lost its old stability.

The humus is going, and when it is gone natural life goes. Two powerful agents are destroying the soil: erosion and the loss of fertility due to mining the soil for crops. Soils which have been building steadily for 20,000 years since the last ice age now in a single century lose the benefits of several thousand years of accumulation. Corn yields in sections of Iowa have dropped from 50 to 25 bushels per acre within the lifetime of a man not yet old. This, remember, is the richest soil in America.

. . . .

One hundred million acres of formerly cultivated land has been essentially ruined by water erosion—an area equal to Illinois, Ohio, North Carolina and Maryland combined—the equivalent of 1,250,000 eighty-acre farms. In addition, this washing of sloping fields has stripped the greater part of the productive top soil from another 125 million acres now being cultivated. Erosion by wind and water is getting under way on another 100 million acres. More than 300 million acres—one-sixth of the country—is gone, going or beginning to go. This, we note, is on land orginally the most fertile.

Kansas farms are blowing through Nebraska at an accelerating rate. In the spring of 1934, the farms of the Dust Bowl—which includes western Oklahoma, western Kansas, eastern Colorado, the panhandle of Texas and parts of Wyoming—blew clear out to the Atlantic Ocean, 2,000 miles away. On a single day 300 million tons of rich top soil was lifted from the Great Plains, never to return, and planted in places where it would spread the maximum of damage and discomfort. Authentic desert sand dunes were laid down. People began to die of dust pneumonia. More than nine million acres of good land has been virtually destroyed by wind erosion, and serious damage is reported on nearly 80 million acres.

Taking the continent as a whole, it is reliably estimated that half of its original fertility has been dissipated by these various agents. The rate of loss tends to follow the laws of compound interest. The stricken areas grow cumulatively larger.

. . . .

From the packed earth of the crop lands, the bare-burned slopes of the devastated forests, the broken sods of the grasslands, rain and melting snow rush to the rivers in a fraction of the time they used to take. In some watersheds runoff which should require three months is carried down to the sea in a month. The rivers run red with mud where once they were clear. Reservoirs are filled,

power dams rendered increasingly impotent. Lower a bucket into
the Canadian River and allow it to settle. One-quarter of the water
turns out to be rich soil which the upstream owner paid for in
cash.

The baked earth of the tilled fields prevents the rain from perco-
lating into the artesian basins as it used to percolate through the
cover of forest and grass. We see the underground water table
falling all over the western half of the continent. In the Dakotas
and Iowa the drop is serious; in the Central Valley of California,
it is still more serious. Meanwhile pumping for irrigation helps to
exhaust the basins. The cool, dark reservoirs which once did so
much to equalize flood and drought are sinking. The same is happening with surface reservoirs. Marshes and swamps have been
drained in the hope of reclaiming good agricultural land. Sometimes the land is good and sometimes it is bad, unsuited for crops.
When it is bad, fires course through the dried underbrush, as in
the sterile Wisconsin and Minnesota marshes.

In the lower reaches of the rivers, the old natural side reservoirs
have been blocked off by levees. Here is rich farm land, to be sure,
but the rivers rise as the silt sinks, and the levees must rise higher
still. In New Orleans at flood crests, the Mississippi runs high
above the streets of the town. River channels are straightened and
further aid the rush to the ocean. Levees break; indeed the whole
levee system nears its breaking point as a practicable engineering
method for flood control.

Floods under these conditions must grow worse; droughts must
grow worse. The safeguards of nature have been stripped away.
In times of low water, the pollution of streams becomes an ominous menace. Each community in the watershed area dumps its
untreated sewage into the drinking supply of the town below.
When the river is low, sewage poisons remain unoxidized.

In uncounted streams, fish lie killed by the wastes of cities and
the black refuse of mine and factory. Pollution has destroyed more
fish than all the fishermen, and silt has killed more than pollution.
When the sun cannot get through because of the mud, the tiny
water plants die and fish lose their basic food supply. Oil wastes
strangle the fish fry when they come to the surface. Sewage com-
petes with marine life for a limited oxygen supply. Waxy sludge
coats the river bottoms and kills plants there. Our streams, according to Sears, have become watery deserts, inimical to life.
Simpletons try to restock them. "To release millions of fingerlings
into such an environment and expect them to live is like driving a
flock of yearlings into Death Valley."

. . . .

The last passenger pigeon died in the Cincinnati Zoo in 1914, the
sole survivor on earth of the "most abundant and the most beautiful
of all American game birds." Toward the end, a single season's
slaughter in Michigan accounted for five million of these creatures.

The last heath hen died on Martha's Vineyard in 1932. Recently Mr. William Finley, naturalist and wild-life photographer, exhibited two films of the lower Klamath region in Oregon. The first was taken in 1915 and showed a great watershed swarming with game birds and migratory waterfowl. The second was taken twenty years later and showed the same area despoiled by promoters, a biological desert devoid of water, food or cover and forsaken by the birds which once lived and nested there. Birds, it must never be forgotten, are the chief enemies of insects. Without their protection plant life and animal life are thrown out of equilibrium, while life for man speedily becomes unendurable.

. . . .

Besides the material and financial loss here represented, an environment lovely to the eye has been sacrificed. The most hideous spots are the environs of mines and the slums and industrial areas of great cities. Gashed earth, culm banks, dead trees and streams putrid with chemicals, refuse and coal dust distinguish the mines. Cities seem to pride themselves on turning their river banks or waterfronts into majestic privies. Here cluster smoking dumps high as Bunker Hill, gas works, sewer outlets, dilapidated coal sheds, switch yards, oil refineries, slaughterhouses, glue factories, tanneries which stun the nose and great barges laden down with garbage. Yet these waters determined the location of the city in the first place, and have often been its chief builder and nourisher. Can ingratitude go farther? European cities respect their waters and adorn their banks with parks, boulevards and public buildings. Latin-American countries do the same. Compare the waterfront of Havana with that of Brooklyn or Hoboken.

In place of green foliage and clear water, man has brought to the continent of America stinking rivers, charred forests, the incomparable filth of cities, the wretched shacks of tenant farmers along Tobacco Road.

. . . .

Suppose present trends were to be projected unaltered into the future. I have had an opportunity to look at that future, not with a magical electric eye but with my own. In a certain area these trends have been speeded up with the aid of chemistry, and the future now stands stark for all to see. The normal processes of erosion are mechanical and take longer in the working out. But the end is substantially the same. The hills of the country I am about to describe are as terrible as the man-killed hills of China, but they have been blasted by the sulphuric acid fumes of a copper smelter rather than by the stripping of forest and grass.

We left Knoxville, Tennessee, in a March snow squall and headed south along a broad concrete highway. Presently the sun came out and revealed the Great Smoky Mountains really smoking like

Popocatepetl. The road passed beside a muddy river, log cabins, rail fences, steep cornfields, some of them badly gullied. At the town of Benton we turned east, steering for a 4,000-foot pass in the mountains, close to the Georgia line. The road climbed steeply up the river valley and the mountainsides drew closer. Suddenly we came upon a large concrete dam and powerhouse, beside it a steam power plant and a tourist hotel, beset with notice boards. Behind the dam in the mountain gorge was a long narrow lake called the Ocoee reservoir, in which the water was very low. This, like the hotel, the powerhouse and the road belonged to a private power company—a big, costly development.

The scenery was wild and impressive: sheer precipices, deep ravines, tumbling cascades, the gray lake. Rocks lay on the road where they had fallen from cliffs above. It must require a considerable crew to clear this road of avalanches. We turn a bend and suddenly see a thing that belongs in no lake. It is a chocolate-colored tongue of shaking mud, half a mile long, and behind it are other tongues and trembling islands. These are deposits of silt, brought down by the water from the lands above. The formations are about six feet high, constantly caving in where the current strikes them. The whole upper end of the reservoir is full of them. The banks themselves have changed from good honest mud to this forbidding red-brown jelly.

We entered the narrow gorge with the river. There was hardly room for both of us. It was a river not of water but of boiling molasses. The whole stream bed, every rock, every log, every leaf of grass, was coated with silt. We passed another power plant. Across the gorge a wooden flume ran for four or five miles along the mountainside, leaping the side ravines on steel bridges. It seemed to be bearing water from some higher level. The trees about us were dead. Great charred logs thrust hideously out of the perpendicular slopes of the gorge. Mile upon mile had been blasted by fire.

Up, up, we went. Suddenly the mountain wall to the east dissolved and we looked over a broad expanse of bare rounded hills faintly green. They looked like the hills near San Francisco and seemed strangely out of place in Tennessee. Beyond the fire area were live trees again, some in their first spring raiment. Another mile and they began to die. It was not fire this time, but something still more unnatural.

We were among the rounded hills. There were bunches of withered grass on them and the occasional white skeleton of a tree. They were ribbed with cracks through which the red earth appeared. In some places terracing had been attempted to hold the soil, but the terraces had long since been breached with raw open gullies. Fences fell crazily into these gulfs. The earth was opening about us; the road seemed the only firm place. Grass remained but it was functionless, its holding power gone. I cannot tell you what it means to see and feel the power of the earth cover gone. Anything might happen. Here was no place for life or for man. The gullies grew wider and deeper—twenty feet, thirty feet down, a hundred feet across. The hills burst open like a skinless dry peach. Then even the dead grass disappeared. The desolation was monstrous and complete, like mountains on the moon.

Over a crest we saw a cloud of black smoke. The road curved around the crest and Ducktown rose before us—a little village and a huge dark smelter perched on a hill. In a great circle about the smelter, measuring perhaps ten miles in diameter, every living thing had been destroyed by the sulphur fumes. These were bad lands without the balance and natural composure of a desert. Here was a wall-sided red brick schoolhouse with ten-foot gullies of livid earth leading up to it. Here a lone house with a tiny green garden, protected by heaven knows what labor and what chemistry against the sulphur. We pass a sign, WELCOME TO DUCKTOWN, and enter a huddle of wretched houses crouched under the bleak walls of the gigantic smelter, the land rushing away from every doorstep.

Inside the town, the horror is momentarily shut out. Main Street as usual—drugstore, cinema, Masonic hall, A & P, filling station, garages, motorcars parked at proper angles against the curb, people talking, shopping, smiling. COME AGAIN TO DUCKTOWN.

We halt the car at a lookout on the far side of the hill beyond the houses. Across a blasted plain on the northeast we see the far horizon with hills and trees again. Thank God for trees! We head the car for those far woodlands.

People live in Ducktown. Main Street bustles as in Middletown. Incredible. But on second thought it is the most appropriate setting for Main Street. Ugliness matches ugliness, and desolation suits desolation. A raw commercial age merits such a background, where nature throws up her hands and the good earth runs bleeding to the sea. Before it finds the ocean, it chokes the power company's reservoir. This, too, is as it should be. The true spirit of individualism. The copper company ruins the reservoir; the power company seeks whom it may devour farther down the stream.

Ducktown. The symbol of the logical end of an undirected machine age. It supports the gas stations, billboards, schoolhouses and Masonic lodges of Main Street out of the bowels of the earth with good red copper. But in the process the land has gone. Presently silt will completely fill the reservoir and no more electric power will come over the lines to Ducktown. The mine elevators will stop. Ducktown will perish. Its subterranean workers will perish. Its shacks and garages will slide into fifty-foot gullies. The belching sulphur fumes will cease. Life has gone and man must now go. The years pass. The grass begins to creep back on the edges of the desert ten miles away. After the grass come pine seedlings and oak. They come slowly, for Nature has a great wound to heal. In a thousand years, perhaps, the humus will return, the streams will run clear, the great lateral cracks will be overgrown, the gullies will be filled, and earth creatures may live once more in Ducktown—where wild ducks lived before man came.

Here is the whole story of the future—"if present trends continue"—highly simplified and very clear. Metaphorically speaking, the smelter is industry, feeding on a declining resource. While that resource lasts, the people of Ducktown have jobs and automobiles. The world congratulates Ducktown on its high standard of living. Meanwhile the land crumbles away and the waters become wild and useless. This does not matter—for men without eyes—if other lands grow food and if copper keeps coming out of the mines to exchange for it. But no mine can be operated without power, and finally the outraged land and water cut off the power. What happens then? What happens when the copper runs out? What happens when other lands cease to grow crops, by virtue of Ducktowns of their own? What happens when a continent is one great Ducktown?

102.

William Carlos Williams

CLASSIC SCENE [1938]

A power-house
in the shape of
a red brick chair
90 feet high

on the seat of which
sit the figures
of two metal
stacks—aluminum—

commanding an area
of squalid shacks
side by side—
from one of which

buff smoke
streams while under
a grey sky
the other remains

passive today—

103.

John Steinbeck [1939]

[The advance of
cultivation into the dry areas of the southern and southwestern
plains destroyed the native grasses and the natural ground cover
that was perfectly adapted to holding the region's scant rainfall.
After an encouraging run of abnormally wet years, a disastrous
drought struck in the early 1930's. In the opening passage of *The
Grapes of Wrath* John Steinbeck described the coming of the Dust
Bowl.]

To the red country
and part of the gray country of Oklahoma, the last rains came
gently, and they did not cut the scarred earth. The plows crossed
and recrossed the rivulet marks. The last rains lifted the corn
quickly and scattered weed colonies and grass along the sides of the
roads so that the gray country and the dark red country began to
disappear under a green cover. In the last part of May the sky
grew pale and the clouds that had hung in high puffs for so long
in the spring were dissipated. The sun flared down on the growing
corn day after day until a line of brown spread along the edge of
each green bayonet. The clouds appeared, and went away, and in
a while they did not try any more. The weeds grew darker green
to protect themselves, and they did not spread any more. The
surface of the earth crusted, a thin hard crust, and as the sky became pale, so the earth became pale, pink in the red country and
white in the gray country.

In the water-cut gullies the earth dusted down in dry little
streams. Gophers and ant lions started small avalanches. And as
the sharp sun struck day after day, the leaves of the young corn
became less stiff and erect; they bent in a curve at first, and then,
as the central ribs of strength grew weak, each leaf tilted downward. Then it was June, and the sun shone more fiercely. The
brown lines on the corn leaves widened and moved in on the central
ribs. The weeds frayed and edged back toward their roots. The air
was thin and the sky more pale; and every day the earth paled.

In the roads where the teams moved, where the wheels milled
the ground and the hooves of the horses beat the ground, the dirt
crust broke and the dust formed. Every moving thing lifted the
dust into the air: a walking man lifted a thin layer as high as his
waist, and a wagon lifted the dust as high as the fence tops, and
an automobile boiled a cloud behind it. The dust was long in settling
back again.

When June was half gone, the big clouds moved up out of Texas and the Gulf, high heavy clouds, rain-heads. The men in the fields looked up at the clouds and sniffed at them and held wet fingers up to sense the wind. And the horses were nervous while the clouds were up. The rain-heads dropped a little spattering and hurried on to some other country. Behind them the sky was pale again and the sun flared. In the dust there were drop craters where the rain had fallen, and there were clean splashes on the corn, and that was all.

A gentle wind followed the rain clouds, driving them on northward, a wind that softly clashed the drying corn. A day went by and the wind increased, steady, unbroken by gusts. The dust from the roads fluffed up and spread out and fell on the weeds beside the fields, and fell into the fields a little way. Now the wind grew strong and hard and it worked at the rain crust in the corn fields. Little by little the sky was darkened by the mixing dust, and the wind felt over the earth, loosened the dust, and carried it away. The wind grew stronger. The rain crust broke and the dust lifted up out of the fields and drove gray plumes into the air like sluggish smoke. The corn threshed the wind and made a dry, rushing sound. The finest dust did not settle back to earth now, but disappeared into the darkening sky.

The wind grew stronger, whisked under stones, carried up straws and old leaves, and even little clods, marking its course as it sailed across the fields. The air and the sky darkened and through them the sun shone redly, and there was a raw sting in the air. During a night the wind raced faster over the land, dug cunningly among the rootlets of the corn, and the corn fought the wind with its weakened leaves until the roots were freed by the prying wind and then each stalk settled wearily sideways toward the earth and pointed the direction of the wind.

The dawn came, but no day. In the gray sky a red sun appeared, a dim red circle that gave a little light, like dusk; and as that day advanced, the dusk slipped back toward darkness, and the wind cried and whimpered over the fallen corn.

Men and women huddled in their houses, and they tied handkerchiefs over their noses when they went out, and wore goggles to protect their eyes.

When the night came again it was black night, for the stars could not pierce the dust to get down, and the window lights could not even spread beyond their own yards. Now the dust was evenly mixed with the air, an emulsion of dust and air. Houses were shut tight, and cloth wedged around doors and windows, but the dust came in so thinly that it could not be seen in the air, and it settled like pollen on the chairs and tables, on the dishes. The people brushed it from their shoulders. Little lines of dust lay at the door sills.

In the middle of that night the wind passed on and left the land quiet. The dust-filled air muffled sound more completely than fog

does. The people, lying in their beds, heard the wind stop. They
awakened when the rushing wind was gone. They lay quietly and
listened deep into the stillness. Then the roosters crowed, and their
voices were muffled, and the people stirred restlessly in their beds
and wanted the morning. They knew it would take a long time for
the dust to settle out of the air. In the morning the dust hung like
fog, and the sun was as red as ripe new blood. All day the dust
sifted down from the sky, and the next day it sifted down. An
even blanket covered the earth. It settled on the corn, piled up on
the tops of the fence posts, piled up on the wires; it settled on
roofs, blanketed the weeds and trees.

104.

E. E. Cummings

PITY THIS BUSY MONSTER, MANUNKIND [1944]

pity this busy monster, manunkind,

not. Progress is a comfortable disease:
your victim (death and life safely beyond)

plays with the bigness of his littleness
—electrons deify one razorblade
into a mountainrange;lenses extend

unwish through curving wherewhen till unwish
returns on its unself.
                  A world of made
is not a world of born—pity poor flesh

and trees,poor stars and stones,but never this
fine specimen of hypermagical

ultraomnipotence. We doctors know

a hopeless case if—listen:there's a hell
of a good universe next door;let's go

105.

Fairfield Osborn

IS MAN NECESSARY? [1948]

There is no risk in making the flat statement that in a world devoid of other living creatures, man himself would die. This fact—call it a theory if you will—is far more provable than the accepted theory of relativity. Involved in it is, in truth, another kind of principle of relativity— the relatedness of all living things.

As a somewhat extreme illustration, among many others, take that form of life that man likes the least—of which the unthinking person would at once say, "Kill them all." Insects. Of the extra-ordinary number of kinds of insects on the earth—about three quarters of a million different species have already been identified —a small minority are harmful to man, such as the anopheles mosquito, lice, the tsetse fly, and crop-destroying insects. On the other hand, innumerable kinds are beneficent and useful. Fruit trees and many crops are dependent upon insect life for pollina-tion or fertilization; soils are cultured and gain their productive qualities largely because of insect life. Human subsistence would, in fact, be imperiled were there no insects. On the other hand, insects, capable of incredibly rapid reproduction, have been freed by man himself of many natural controls such as those once pro-vided by birds, now so diminished in numbers, or by fish, once a potent factor in insect control, no longer existing in countless lakes, rivers and streams now so polluted that aquatic life has disap-peared. In attempting to find substitutes for natural controls man has resorted to the use of chemicals of increasing power. A few years ago arsenicals came into style—widely used in freeing fruit orchards of pests. So promising this method has seemed—but in-sidiously it sometimes results in destroying insect-eating birds; and after several seasons the ground itself, in many orchards, has become so impregnated with the poison that the trees are affected and their fruit-bearing capacity dwindles. More recently a power-ful chemical known as D.D.T. seems the cure-all. Some of the initial experiments with this insect killer have been withering to bird life as a result of birds eating the insects that have been impreg-nated with the chemical. The careless use of D.D.T. can also result in destroying fishes, frogs, and toads, all of which live on insects. This new chemical is deadly to many kinds of insects—no doubt of that. But what of the ultimate and net result to the life scheme of the earth? On another front man is blindly in conflict with nature, too often overlooking the fact that the animal life of the earth, its interrelationships, its preservation, are wrapped up directly with his own well-being. Will the day come when this is generally realized?

Here we come to a kind of paradox. It is apparent that many of the lower forms of animal life—ranging from protozoa up through the insects and other invertebrates even to the reptiles, fishes, birds and certain small mammals—play an essential part in the economy of nature. On the other hand, it is far from easy to prove that some of the higher orders or families of mammals are necessary to the life scheme of the earth, at least of this earth today, when human beings are so numerous and their demands for both space and subsistence so pressing.

106.

[From the *New York Times*]

KILLER SMOG [1948]

Donora, Pa., Oct. 30—
Eighteen persons died in this steel mill town of 15,000 today and health authorities said the deaths apparently were the indirect result of a smothering "smog." . . .

"It's very hard to breathe," said Rudy Schwerha, a member of the Board of Health. "It's impossible to determine just how many residents are sick, but the doctors and nurses can't keep up with the situation."

All of the deaths today occurred unexpectedly after a fog which has prevailed for several days became exceptionally heavy. Smoke from the industrial community mixed with it to create a thick smog.

"The deaths seem to have hit people who were suffering from cardiac or asthmatic conditions," Mr. Schwerha said. "There's no doubt the smog has been the cause."

*   *   *

Donora, Pa., Oct. 31—Several hundred asthma and cardiac sufferers remaining in this stricken town were evacuated to other areas tonight as a welcome rain helped to clear the air of a smog believed to have contributed to the deaths of twenty residents. The mysterious air-borne plague struck yesterday. . . .

Norbert Hochman, a chemist attached to the Pittsburgh Smoke Prevention Bureau, advanced the theory that there was definitely enough sulphur trioxide to be toxic in the air in Donora, particularly close to the zinc works of the American Steel and Wire Company, a United States Steel Corporation subsidiary. . . .

Doctors and emergency workers reported that patients showed similar symptoms, a gasping for air and complaints of unbearable chest pains.

*   *   *

Cleveland, Nov. 16 (UP)—The American Steel and Wire Company said today it was "certain" its zinc works at Donora, Pa., was not responsible for the smog linked to twenty deaths there last month.

The company, in a statement released here and carried as an advertisement in the Donora *Herald-American*, declared that "our conviction from the start has been that the zinc works was not the cause of the disaster."

"We are certain," it added, "that the principal offender in the tragedy was the unprecedentedly heavy fog which blanketed the borough for five consecutive days—a phenomenon which no resident could recall ever happening before."

107.

Friedrich Georg Juenger

THE PILLAGE OF THE EARTH [1949]

The impression we gain as we observe technical processes of any sort is not at all one of abundance. The sight of abundance and plenty give us joy: they are the signs of a fruitfulness which we revere as a life-giving force. Rooting, sprouting, budding, blooming, ripening, and fruition —the exuberance of the motions and forms of life—strengthen and refresh us. The human body and the human mind possess this power of bestowing strength. Both man and woman have it. But the machine organization gives nothing—it organizes need. The prospect of vineyard, orchard, or a blossoming landscape cheers us, not because these things yield profits, but because of the sensation of fertility, abundance, and gratuitous riches. The industrial scene, however, has lost its fruitfulness; it has become the scene of mechanical production. It conveys, above all, a sense of hungriness, particularly in the industrial cities which, in the metaphorical language of technological progress, are the homes of a flourishing industry. The machine gives a hungry impression. And this sensation of a growing, gnawing hunger, a hunger that becomes unbearable, emanates from everything in our entire technical arsenal.

. . . .

What is euphemistically called production is really consumption. The gigantic technical apparatus, that masterpiece of human ingenuity, could not reach perfection if technological thought were to be contained within an economic scheme, if the destructive power of technical progress were to be arrested. But this progress becomes all the more impetuous, the larger the resources at its disposal, and the more energetically it devours them. This is shown by the concentration of men and machines in the great mining centers where the mechanization of work and the organization of man are most advanced. The rationality of technology, so impressively displayed here, becomes intelligible only when one has understood the conditions on which it depends. Its concomitant is waste and contempt for all rationality in the exploitation of the resources on whose existence technology depends, as the lungs depend on air.

Where wastage begins, there begins desolation, and scenes of such desolation can be found even in the early days of our technology, in the era of the steam engine. These scenes are startling by the extraordinary ugliness and the Cyclopean power which are characteristic of them. The machine invades the landscape with destruction and transformation; it grows factories and whole manufacturing cities overnight, cities grotesquely hideous, where human misery is glaringly revealed; cities which, like Manchester, represent an entire stage of technology and which have become synonymous with hopeless dreariness. Technology darkens the air with smoke, poisons the water, destroys the plants and animals. It brings about a state in which nature has to be "preserved" from rationalized thinking, in which large tracts of land have to be set apart, fenced off, and placed under a taboo, like museum pieces. What all museum-like institutions make evident is, that preservation is needed. The extension of protected areas, therefore, is an indication that destructive processes are at work.

. . . .

The obverse side of technology is a pillage which becomes constantly better organized; this must not be overlooked when one speaks of technical progress. True, we have made a technical advance if by means of artificial fertilizers we succeed in squeezing uninterrupted crops out of our overburdened plough and pasture land. But this advance itself is at the same time the consequence of a calamitous deficiency, for if we did not have the fertilizer we should no longer be able to feed ourselves at all. Technical progress has deprived us of the free choice of nutriment which our ancestors possessed. A machine which trebles the output of a previous model constitutes a technical advance, for it is the result of a more rational design. But for this very reason it also possesses a more intense consuming and devouring power. Its hunger is sharper, and it consumes correspondingly more. In this way, the whole realm of the machine is full of a restless, devouring power that cannot be satisfied.

Closely linked to this is the rapid wear and tear the machine suffers. That most of our machines become junk so soon results from their design and purpose. Their durability, strength, and usability are lessened, restricted in the very degree to which technology approaches perfection. The consumption brought about by technology extends even to its own apparatus. The repairs and replacements these mechanisms constantly demand represent an immense amount of human labor. And the machine falls quickly into that state of disrepair in which we see it around us everywhere. Technical progress covers the earth, not alone with its machines and workshops, but also with junk and scrap. All this rusty tin, these twisted girders, these bent and broken machine parts and castaway tools—they remind the thoughtful observer of the fleeting impermanence of the process he witnesses. Perhaps they keep him from overestimating all this progress and help him to an understanding of what really goes on. Wear and tear is a form of consumption; it manifests itself pre-eminently where plundering goes on and so we find it in particular wherever technology is at work.

If two thousand years hence there should still be archaeologists —which is rather unlikely—who were to undertake excavations, say, in Manchester, Essen, or Pittsburgh, they would find but little. They would discover nothing as enduring as Egyptian burial chambers and classic temples. For the stuff with which the factory system works is not *aere perennius* ("more lasting than bronze"—Horace). These archaeologists might even be surprised at the paltriness of their discoveries. The earth-spanning power of technology is of an ephemeral kind—a fact easily overlooked by those engrossed in it. Everywhere it is threatened by decay, given over to decay, and decay follows upon its heels all the more insistently and closely, the faster it marches on towards new triumphs.

108.

Harrison Brown

THE FUTURE OF WATER [1954]

Tucson, Arizona, which receives an annual rainfall of only 11.5 inches, is pumping water from the ground at rates far greater than rates of replenishment. Overuse of ground water in the Los Angeles area has resulted in greatly lowered water tables, followed by encroachment of salt water from the ocean. In addition, land surfaces have sunk as much as 8 feet in some spots. In many arid and semi-arid regions one can see pump after pump bringing water to the surface for irrigation at rates that are far greater than rates of replenishment. As there is no hope of materially raising the level of ground water in most such areas, the alternatives are either to abandon the land eventually or to obtain water from distant points.

Only a small fraction of the water used for irrigation purposes can be re-used. Most of the water which is poured over the land is ultimately evaporated, and very little percolates through the soil and returns to the underground reservoirs. However, a large part of the water used for industrial purposes can be re-used, and indeed often is.

We have seen that a major industrial use of water is for cooling. When water is so used it is unaltered and can be used by another plant downstream for the same purpose. However, there is a limit to the extent to which such practices can be carried out without penalty, as was demonstrated recently when it was found that so many industries were using and re-using the water of the Mahoning River near Youngstown, Ohio, that it became too hot to be used for cooling.

On the average, cities and industries return as waste over 90 per cent of the water withdrawn. But frequently the returned water is accompanied by huge quantities of destructive chemicals, garbage, excreta, and many other elements of pollution. Virtually every industry contributes noxious stuff to streams for disposal, and the sewage of 30 million people is dumped into rivers without treatment. The net result of these practices is that the cities and industries downstream must purify the water before it can be re-used. Without treatment it is frequently too contaminated for human or livestock

consumption, and the impurities make it unsuitable for many industrial operations.

As the population of the United States increases and industrial
activity expands, problems of water supply and stream pollution
will become even more acute than they are at the present time.
Increasing efforts will have to be made to remove noxious materials,
to reclaim water once it has been used, to regulate the flow of
streams, to develop new ground-water reservoirs, to avoid con-
taminating ground water with noxious substances, and to recharge
existing reservoirs.

As time goes on we will see an ever expanding network of aqueducts, dams, reservoirs, sewage-treatment plants, and water-purify-
ing units. The penalties for the improvements will be greatly
increased cost of water and, above all, increased per capita expenditures of energy. Energy must be consumed to construct and
maintain water systems and to separate waste from water so that
it can be re-used.

As more areas begin programs of public health, extended agriculture, and industrialization, the world water situation will become
increasingly acute. Eventually, as the populations become larger
and larger, we may reach the time when practically no water that
falls on land will reach the oceans via streams. Every gallon will
be conserved, used, purified, and re-used, and the process will be
repeated again and again until nearly all has been evaporated.

109.

Leonard Hall

LUMBERING THE OZARKS [1958]

All in all, the
picture of land use in the Current River country for the past
hundred years has not been a happy one. It has been largely a
picture of land going downhill. Over-logging, overgrazing, poor
farming, and erosion have combined to seriously reduce the life-
carrying capacity of the region. As the good timber and forage
plants disappeared, their places were taken by others less commercially valuable and less palatable. Wildlife largely disappeared,
and fewer game fish grew in gravel-choked streams. This is Nature's

only means for healing a ruined landscape and is the means she always adopts when her resources are ruthlessly overexploited.

. . . .

The history of forest use in the Ozarks could hardly be demonstrated better than in the plateau area lying along Highway 32 between Possum Trot Farm and Salem. The first serious commercial timber cutting was done here in the late 1800's, and the method followed was what we know today as "high-grading." This simply means that the best and most easily marketed trees were taken first, without regard to damage to the remaining timber, tree reproduction, or any other consideration except to skim the cream for the quickest profit. Thus the readily salable pine was logged off and then, in successive waves of cutting, the various species of oak.

Little or no attention was paid in those times to trees with less commercial value, although eventually the walnut was harvested and then the hickory, which was used for farm-tool handles and wagon parts. In this particular area of the Ozarks, which was neither very rugged nor far from market, the remaining tree growth was now slashed clean to make charcoal. If this had been the end, the forest would somehow have started making a comeback. But the hill people looked at this cut-over land, no longer useful to the lumberman, and decided it would make pasture for their livestock. As the first step toward putting it to this use, they set fire to it, in the mistaken belief that this would permanently keep down the brushy second-growth trees and also make the grass grow. And for a short time this is what actually happened, since the ash from the burning slashes created a certain amount of available plant food. Some grass grew; most of this being short-lived annual species with low nutritive value which furnished, at best, a few weeks of poor grazing in early summer.

The long-range result of this treatment of the land, which included annual burning and grazing by far more cattle, goats, hogs, and horses than the range could carry, was disastrous; as it has been throughout history and on every continent. A deep layer of humus is created in a forest by decaying matter and by the annual fall of leaves. On the burned-out land this of course soon disappeared. The thin topsoil washed away down the hollows until there was little left but rocky chert, and the mountain streams became choked with gravel. Trampling feet of sharp-hoofed animals compacted the soil to speed still further the run-off from every rain. Now almost no water seeped into the earth to feed springs, streams, and the permanent underground reservoir. The cut-over forest lands of the Ozarks became, for all practical purposes, a biological desert. Starting with the soil fauna and flora which are essential to the processes of both growth and decay of plants, the land supported steadily less life. Game birds and wild animals disappeared because of lack of food and cover; and the fish population in every stream declined for the same reason. But still the hill folk burned each spring, then turned out their thin animals to forage, until the Ozarks became one of the depressed rural areas of America.

. . . .

Like such other Ozark customs as gigging fish, hunting out of season, and setting fires in the timber, "grandmawing" deserves an explanation. As in any forested country that is opened up to logging, most of the land surface of the Ozarks belonged to big lumber companies who bought the land outright for a few cents an acre or merely purchased the timber-cutting rights. The logging operations in their heyday employed most of the local population and even brought in other workers who, oftener than not, settled down on land contiguous to the forest. When the cutting and sawmilling was over, these people were left without means of support except to farm their barren acres, run some thin cattle and hogs in the cut-over woods, and salvage anything they could find in the way of saw logs. Being woods-runners by nature, they knew every nook and cranny of the forest, including the location of every marketable tree missed by the loggers as well as every young tree growing to marketable size.

The years went by, and the illegal harvesting of these trees from "company land" by natives who had formerly worked for these very timberland owners became a recognized hill-country occupation. The only difficulty lay in marketing the logs, and even this was readily solved. In order to maintain some semblance of legality in disposing of his logs, the logger is required to state at the sawmill just where this particular timber was cut—in terms of township, range, and section. The law has never been enforced very strictly, however, and in the Ozark hills until recently when you asked a woodsman where he had cut the logs he had just hauled to the mill, his answer was likely to be, "I cut 'em out on Grandmaw's place."

110.

Lorus J. Milne and Margery Milne

OYSTER VALLEY [1959]

This pattern of man-made changes in the little valley of the Oyster River is familiar all over the East. Only the dates for each locality differ slightly. We can walk from the here and now—our particular place and time—into a sort of universal early America merely by going the short distance to the edge of the river and sitting a while on a big rock from which we can watch in both directions. Only fifty years ago, residents of an earlier generation had a little rustic summerhouse bolted to this vantage point. At night they held parties in the frame mansion at the top of the hill, and guided their guests along the path to the summerhouse on the big rock by means of Japanese lanterns. Three hundred years ago, only the Indians knew the course the water followed—and they had no lamps to guide their feet in darkness. Now the summerhouse, the lanterns, and the Indians are gone.

Above the backwaters of the dam, the stream passes through a riffle with large moss-covered stones the Indians might have used as we do, in crossing to the other side. We balance, and jump, and are into the fringing alders. Pressing up the bank, we emerge into a bit of second- or third-growth woodland deep in fallen cones of hemlock and leather-brown leaves of beech. Gazing down at the dark water below the crossing place, it is easy to imagine how the countryside was when oaks now more than a century old were sprouting from the acorn.

Yet it is important to realize what changes have altered the valley since the Indians walked its trails. One of the most conspicuous is a swath through the forest past Beech Hill, cut and patrolled by people from the power company. Chemical sprays keep the oaks and birches from coming back. Most of the other alterations are the products of ax and saw, of dynamite stick and bulldozer, of cement mixer and paving machine. These devices have leveled most of the woodlands as well as many of the smaller hills. They have dammed some of the valley and filled various low places. Usually they have buried the rich forest soil, or hurried it as silt down the streams in flood time. They seem to have devastated the land much as did the great glaciers, although on a smaller scale. We wonder how important they actually are in the evolution of living things in the valley.

. . . .

No longer is there any chance that we might come face to face with an Indian, or that our path would take us into an acre of virgin forest left standing. Only the ghosts of Indians, of giant trees, of passenger pigeons and beaver families parade before us as we try to think back to an earlier scene in this selfsame place.

Which of the features in the present landscape would be visible a century hence, were our own ghosts to revisit the Oyster River valley? Would there still be orchards and beehives, and perhaps bears to raid them in the night? How the ponds and the river, the meadows and forests will fare if viewed "only" as esthetic assets, paying little tax to the town, depends upon the beliefs of the men who can control their fate.

The pace of change grows ever swifter. Automobiles now speed from all directions toward the White Mountains, that were explored at real risk three centuries ago by Darby Field. The hotel atop Mount Washington has celebrated a hundred years' use of the "carriage road" to the summit. But the wild creatures in the rising forests and flowing streams of every valley seem to ignore the rumble of trucks, the roar of bulldozers, and the thunder of jet aircraft overhead. Just as life has done for uncounted millions of years, it retains its resiliency. It waited out the Ice Ages, and waits now for man to rediscover how to share the earth.

III.

William O. Douglas [1961]

[Supreme Court Justice William O. Douglas has long been one of the nation's most prominent conservationists. An ardent backpacker and camper, he has visited virtually every wilderness area left in America. In the following selection from *My Wilderness: East to Katahdin,* he recounts his discoveries in one of them.]

On the entire trip we had seen the degradations committed by sheep. The trailways they had followed in getting into and out of the mountains were badly eroded. Too many sheep had been in here too frequently and for visits that were much too long. Broken turf had been evident along every trail. Lake basins, with some exceptions, were beginning to show the wear and tear. Alpine meadows were beginning to look moth-eaten. The pass above Fall Creek was symptomatic of the peril facing the Wind River range.

Most of the country we traveled was in the Bridger National Forest. It was a primitive area and since then has been classified as a wilderness area. The high meadows and passes under proper range management could be given a respite; in the long turn of a cycle, timothy and nut grass might return.

We discussed the problems of range management.

In a 1911 decision it was said that the grazing fees were fixed to "prevent excessive grazing and thereby protect the young growth, and native grasses, from destruction."

Yet the Forest Service fee for grazing a sheep is only ten cents a month. On Taylor grazing lands outside the forests, the fee is but half of that.

"That amount of 'rental is cheap—dirt cheap," Carroll stated. "A rancher can keep a sheep up here all Summer for thirty cents. That rental is so low that the owner does not worry about what his sheep are doing."

Olaus broke in to say, "It's practically free room and board."

"Right," said Carroll. "Free room and board at the expense of the people. This is public land. It belongs to everyone. Yet we let a few private interests exploit it."

"Either keep them all out or raise the rental," Carroll added. "If a man must pay only ten cents a month to graze a sheep, he's not going to be too particular about whether the animal has good grazing. If he has to pay a dollar a month, he's going to be sure he's getting his money's worth."

"Trouble is," said Olaus, "that a permittee who has the right to run sheep on public land pretty soon begins to think he owns the range. Take it away from him, or cut down on the number of sheep or cattle he can graze, or increase the rental, and he hollers as if his property has been confiscated."

"What about the cattle?" I asked, turning to Carroll.

"They are grazed lower down in these forests. The meadows like the ones we saw at Elkhart are called parks by our local people. They are grazed by permittees."

"Any problems there?" I inquired.

"Same as the sheep," said Carroll. "You see, the grazing fee for a cow is five times that for a sheep. Fifty cents a month is all the cattlemen have to pay."

"Too low?" I asked.

"Too low?" Carroll retorted. "It's not a fourth or a fifth or perhaps even a sixth of what it should be. Why should Uncle Sam rent me grazing land for fifty cents per cow per month when a private landowner would charge two dollars or three dollars a month? Why shouldn't Uncle Sam be a good businessman too? What right do cattlemen have to get this subsidy?"

"Especially when they help ruin the mountains, making mud-holes or dustbins out of our meadows," said Olaus, as he reminded us of the severely pounded grasslands we had seen at Elkhart Park, where cattle still grazed.

"It's all right to let cattle and sheep into the high country," Carroll added. "But let's set the grazing fees high enough so that the public gets a fair return on the value of this public property."

We kept coming back to this theme as we cooked supper. The sun came out briefly before it set and brought two camp robbers and several pink-sided juncos to our camp. Then new black clouds rolled in, bringing spits of snow. By the time we had dinner it was snowing in earnest.

"A big snow in prospect?" I asked.

Carroll did not answer until he had gone over to inspect the horses. "Not a big snow," he said. "The horses always get nervous and sometimes snort when a big snowstorm is on its way. Tonight they are quiet and settling down."

It was a light snow that came during the night. But the temperature dropped fast. In the morning the water in a cup I had left by my bedroll in my small Himalayan tent was frozen solid.

. . . .

Twenty years ago or more there were trappers in these mountains who stayed all Winter. We had seen remnants of old cabins which they had used. They trapped for marten, which then were plentiful.

"There are a few marten left," Olaus said, "but not many."

"What happened?" I inquired.

Olaus, usually soft-spoken, raised his voice to say, "Poison."

"Who and why?"

"You see," Olaus replied, "stockmen got the idea that the coyote was a bad predator. So they got the government to put out poisoned bait. They dropped it from planes all through this country."

"I'm a stockman," Carroll said. "I raise both cattle and sheep; and I value my herds as much as anyone. But actually in all my years here there are very few calves and very few sheep the coyote takes."

"John Muir once said," I interposed, "that the coyotes only sin was his love of mutton."

"A coyote will take a few, as Carroll says," Olaus replied, "but he's not the great killer he's made out to be."

"How about deer and antelope?" I asked.

"The coyote takes a few, but my studies show that the ones taken are usually the sick or the weak."

"Would you say that the coyote has ever caused wild-life population to drop greatly?" Carroll inquired.

"Absolutely not," said Olaus. "The great regulator of wild-life population is a food deficiency of one kind or another. Take our mountain sheep as an example. Predators don't eliminate them. Hunters take a few, not many. Real disaster hits those fine herds when sheepmen turn grass meadows into dust bowls."

"What relation does poisoning the coyote have to the decline in marten?" I asked.

"The poisoned bait dropped from planes killed everything that ate meat—coyotes, bears, fox, marten," Olaus answered. "They were mostly cleaned out of the Wind River."

"More that that," said Carroll, "birds that eat carrion died when they ate animals who had eaten the poisoned bait. That blasted poison almost wiped out our camp robbers."

"Any coyotes left?" I asked Olaus.

"None in these mountains. They were all poisoned out."

. . . .

One of our deepest conflicts is between the preservation of wild life and the profits of a few men. The coyote, with his wise, doglike face and his haunting call, is gone. Fox, marten, and bear have been sacrificed. Mountain sheep are doomed. Is there no place left for any life except man and his greed? Must we see our wild animals only in zoos? Is there no place left for mountain sheep and coyotes? The thought of their eradication was as dismal as the prospect that all trails would be paved, that man will go only where a machine will take him.

.   .   .   .

"Used to be lots of field mice here," Carroll said. "Field mice are good for the farmer because they help keep the soil porous. Ground squirrels help too. And mice and ground squirrels keep the badgers alive."

Stopping to emphasize his words, Carroll said, "Know what the federal men did? Poisoned the mice and squirrels."

He stopped to let that sink in and then asked, "Know what happened? The poison killed the blackbirds and the doves. Then what happened? The grasshoppers came in and got to be a real danger because they had no enemies. Know what the federal men did then?"

I shook my head, and Carroll added, "They used more spray to kill the grasshoppers."

Olaus took up the conversation to talk about the balance nature has provided and how dangerous it is to upset it. "Man and his sprays may be the end of us yet," Olaus added.

.   .   .   .

Man is crowding everything but himself out of the universe, I thought. Why must we be so destructive? What of people who want to hear the whir of sage grouse, who thrill at the white, saucy rump of the antelope as it makes its getaway? How about those who, wanting to fish, find the beaver a stout ally? What is to be said for people who love the sight of moose in willow? Must we sacrifice all of these for the almighty Dollar that goes into the pockets of a privileged few?

The official destruction committed in the sacred precincts of this massive range would be called vandalism if others had done it. The damage is vast, incredible, awful. The memory of these sights come back vividly every time I hear or read a speech or paper on "multiple" use. The national forests are designed by Congress for "multiple" use. That is the professed policy. I had long suspected that "multiple" use was semantics for making cattlemen, sheepmen, lumbermen, miners the main beneficiaries. After they gutted and ruined the forests, then the rest of us could use them—to find campsites among stumps, to look for fish in waters heavy with silt from erosion, to search for game on ridges pounded to dust by sheep. On Piñon Ridge, I realized that the pretense of "multiple" use as applied in this area in Wyoming was an awful wrong.

"Perhaps we should go to Pinedale next Friday," I told Carroll, "to hear what the federal men say about these spraying projects."

We went. Forest Service men, officials of the Bureau of Land Management, and the County Agent of the Department of Agriculture were present; and they spoke.

If a doctor had performed an operation for reasons as unfounded as we heard that night, his license would be revoked. If a lawyer had stood before a court, claiming national assets on behalf of a client and resting on such fanciful hypotheses, he would be ridiculed. The federal men we heard were not dishonest; they were merely spokesmen of interests that have Wyoming by the throat. They said the removal of sagebrush would increase grass, increase the water content of the soil, and decrease erosion. But as they talked it was plain they were not reciting facts. This was mere conjecture. Yes, they had a pilot plant of a few acres that they had sprayed. But what effect it will have over a period as short as five years, no one knew.

"What effect will it have on willows?" someone asked.

"We think the willow will come back."

"When?"

"Perhaps in a year, perhaps in five years."

"What will happen to antelope, to sage grouse, to moose in the meantime?"

No one knew. The only ounce of rational talk that night was supplied by Carroll Noble.

"Maybe willows and other browse will come back in time. But so will sagebrush. Then I suppose there will be another spraying program."

One federal agent reported that an elderly lady had asked him, "What effect will this spray have on wildflowers?" This seemed to me to be as relevant as Carroll's questions and Olaus's concern about the antelope, the beaver, the sage grouse, and the moose. But when the elderly lady's question about the wildflowers was reported, the federal man laughed. And that laughter marked for me a new low in American civilization.

112.

Lewis Mumford

THE PRICE OF TRAFFIC [1961]

Even where overcrowding of the land did not exist—for example in many of the smaller towns of midland America—the broad street or avenue was valued as a symbol of progress: so that it was laid out with an amplitude that bore no functional relation to its present or its potential use, though the excessive cost of paving and upkeep would be reflected in increased taxes on the abutting properties. The value of such street planning, a sort of belated caricature of the baroque enlargement of space as an expression of princely command, was largely decorative: it was a symbol of possible traffic, possible commercial opportunity, possible conversion from residence into more extensive business use. The street itself thus provided an extra excuse for the fantastic land values that were sometimes optimistically tacked in advance onto rural properties that stood in the path of the advancing city. . . .

All over the Western World during the nineteenth century, new cities were founded and old ones extended along the lines I have just described. The first sign of a boom would be the extension of skeleton streets, consisting of curbstone and standpipes for the water systems. The multiplication of these streets prematurely extended the city and added to the amount of expensive pavement, expensive sewers and water mains forcing growth to take place in the most costly fashion possible, by scattered individual houses, spotted at random in time and space, instead of in compact settlements, built within a limited time. For any purpose but speculation, this system was extremely wasteful, and the cost of such premature exploitation fell back on the rest of the city.

. . . .

With the invention of the cheap stage coach, the railroad, and finally the tramway, mass transportation came into existence for the first time in history. Walking distance no longer set the limits of city growth; and the whole pace of the city extension was hastened, since it was no longer avenue by avenue, or block by block, but railroad line by railroad line, and suburb by suburb, raying out in every direction from the central district. In some respects, these supplementary forms of transportation, following routes that did not always coincide with the street network, offset the worst weaknesses of the street system of circulation; and in an era of cheap fares, it gave the poorer paid workers a degree of mobility that placed them on a parity with those who could afford private vehicles.

Unfortunately, the provision of public transportation went on under the same canons of speculative profit that governed the rest of the city: traffic speculation and land speculation played into each other's hands, often in the person of the same enterpriser. At the very moment this took place, the perceptive Emerson, as early as 1836, identified the great potentiality of the new scale of time and space: that it would turn roads into streets, and transform the regions into neighborhoods. But the ideal consummation of this possibility through the use of the region as the unit of development remained unfulfilled, for the increase of range of traffic was utilized as a means of increasing the perimeter of cities already too big for human advantage. Rapid public transportation, instead of reducing the time required for reaching the place of work, continued to increase the distance and the cost with no gain in time whatever.

What holds true for the horizontal extension of the commercial city in the nineteenth century and later, holds true equally for its vertical expansion by means of the elevator. The latter was at first confined to the bigger cities of the New World. But the radical mistakes that were first made in the promotion of skyscrapers are now universal, partly through a relaxation of over-stringent controls, partly through commercial pressure, partly through fashionable imitation, partly through the architect's desire to exploit new technological facilities. All the mistakes first made in American cities are being repeated on an equally horrendous scale in Europe and Asia. If fast transportation made the horizon the limit for urban sprawl, the new methods of construction made the "sky the limit," as gamblers loved to say. Apart from any functions it might better serve by piling one floor upon another, the high rise building became a status symbol of 'modernity.'

The combination of these two methods of expansion and congestion, horizontal and vertical, produced the maximum opportunities for profit: that was in fact the principal motivating force. But this purely mechanical system of growth becomes in the end self-limiting; for the disadvantages of crawling traffic, moving through the city at half the speed of horse-drawn vehicles fifty years ago, are the direct results of inordinate increases of urban density, residential and business, as well as the increase in the number of private motor cars. And the lack of space to move in is not diminished by the dedication of ever larger areas of the city to widened avenues, expressways, viaducts, parking lots, and garages: for the time is approaching in many cities when there will be every facility for moving about the city and no possible reason for going there. Even now, the befouled and poisonous air, the constricted housing at three or four hundred residents per acre, the demoralized social life, teeming with violence and crime, have led to a general exodus from the central areas of cities. In this sense the disease is a self-limiting one; but only because it must eventually destroy the organism that harbors it.

. . . .

Under the present suburban regime, every urban function follows the example of the motor road: it devours space and consumes time with increasing friction and frustration, while, under the plausible pretext of increasing the range of speed and communication, it actually obstructs it and denies the possibility of easy meetings and encounters by scattering the fregments of a city at random over a whole region.

At the bottom of this miscarriage of modern technics lies a fallacy that goes to the very heart of the whole underlying ideology: the notion that power and speed are desirable for their own sake, and that the latest type of fast-moving vehicle must replace every other form of transportation. The fact is that speed in locomotion should be a function of human purpose. If one wants to meet and chat with people on an urban promenade, three miles an hour will be too fast; if a surgeon is being rushed to a patient a thousand miles away, three hundred miles an hour may be too slow. But what our experts in transportation are kept by their own stultifying axioms from realizing is that an adequate transportation system cannot be created in terms of any single limited means of locomotion however fast its theoretic speed.

What an effective network requires is the largest number of alternative modes of transportation, at varying speeds and volumes, for different functions and purposes. The fastest way to move a hundred thousand people within a limited urban area, say a half mile radius, is on foot: the slowest way of moving them would be to put them all into motor cars. The entire daytime population of historic Boston could assemble by foot on Boston Common, probably in less than an hour if the streets were clear of motor traffic. If they were transported by motor car, they would take many hours, and unless they abandoned their unparkable vehicles would never reach their destination.

Our highway engineers and our municipal authorities, hypnotized by the popularity of the private motor car, feeling an obligation to help General Motors to flourish, even if General Chaos results, have been in an open conspiracy to dismantle all the varied forms of transportation necessary to a good system, and have reduced our facilities to the private motor car (for pleasure, convenience, or trucking) and the airplane. They have even duplicated railroad routes and repeated all the errors of the early railroad engineers, while piling up in the terminal cities a population the private motor car cannot handle unless the city itself is wrecked to permit movement and storage of automobiles.

113.

Rachel Carson [1962]

[A noted marine biologist and a gifted nature writer, Rachel Carson provoked a national controversy in 1962 with the publication of *Silent Spring*, a scathing and scientifically documented attack on the indiscriminate use of pesticides. Although she died a short time later, her efforts bore fruit within a few years, with the banning of the use of DDT by several states and, finally, by the U.S. Department of Agriculture. It should be noted that the grebes, whose disappearance from Clear

Lake, California, in the middle 1950's is described in the last portion of this selection, have since returned to their former home. The essence of Rachel Carson's argument—that man, in applying heavy doses of exotic chemicals to control what he calls pests, is operating in the complete absence of knowledge of, and often in total disregard of, possible consequences—remains nonetheless valid.]

There was once a town in the heart of America where all life seemed to live in harmony with its surroundings. The town lay in the midst of a checkerboard of prosperous farms, with fields of grain and hillsides of orchards where, in spring, white clouds of bloom drifted above the green fields. In autumn, oak and maple and birch set up a blaze of color that flamed and flickered across a backdrop of pines. Then foxes barked in the hills and deer silently crossed the fields, half hidden in the mists of the fall mornings.

Along the roads, laurel, viburnum and alder, great ferns and wildflowers delighted the traveler's eye through much of the year. Even in winter the roadsides were places of beauty, where countless birds came to feed on the berries and on the seed heads of the dried weeds rising above the snow. The countryside was, in fact, famous for the abundance and variety of its bird life, and when the flood of migrants was pouring through in spring and fall people traveled from great distances to observe them. Others came to fish the streams, which flowed clear and cold out of the hills and contained shady pools where trout lay. So it had been from the days many years ago when the first settlers raised their houses, sank their wells, and built their barns.

Then a strange blight crept over the area and everything began to change. Some evil spell had settled on the community: mysterious maladies swept the flocks of chickens; the cattle and sheep sickened and died. Everywhere was a shadow of death. The farmers spoke of much illness among their families. In the town the doctors had become more and more puzzled by new kinds of sickness appearing among their patients. There had been several sudden and unexplained deaths, not only among adults but even among children, who would be stricken suddenly while at play and die within a few hours.

There was a strange stillness. The birds, for example—where had they gone? Many people spoke of them, puzzled and disturbed. The feeding stations in the backyards were deserted. The few birds seen anywhere were moribund; they trembled violently and could not fly. It was a spring without voices. On the mornings that had once throbbed with the dawn chorus of robins, catbirds, doves, jays, wrens, and scores of other bird voices there was now no sound; only silence lay over the fields and woods and marsh.

On the farms the hens brooded, but no chicks hatched. The farmers complained that they were unable to raise any pigs—the litters were small and the young survived only a few days. The apple trees were coming into bloom but no bees droned among the blossoms, so there was no pollination and there would be no fruit.

The roadsides, once so attractive, were now lined with browned and withered vegetation as though swept by fire. These, too, were silent, deserted by all living things. Even the streams were now lifeless. Anglers no longer visited them, for all the fish had died.

In the gutters under the eaves and between the shingles of the roofs, a white granular powder still showed a few patches; some weeks before it had fallen like snow upon the roofs and the lawns, the fields and streams.

No witchcraft, no enemy action had silenced the rebirth of new life in this stricken world. The people had done it themselves.

This town does not actually exist, but it might easily have a thousand counterparts in America or elsewhere in the world. I know of no community that has experienced all the misfortunes I describe. Yet every one of these disasters has actually happened somewhere, and many real communities have already suffered a substantial number of them. A grim specter has crept upon us almost unnoticed, and this imagined tragedy may easily become a stark reality we all shall know.

.   .   .   .

The history of life on earth has been a history of interaction between living things and their surroundings. To a large extent, the physical form and the habits of the earth's vegetation and its animal life have been molded by the environment. Considering the whole span of earthly time, the opposite effect, in which life actually modifies its surroundings, has been relatively slight. Only within the moment of time represented by the present century has one species—man—acquired significant power to alter the nature of his world.

During the past quarter century this power has not only increased to one of disturbing magnitude but it has changed in character. The most alarming of all man's assaults upon the environment is the contamination of air, earth, rivers, and sea with dangerous and even lethal materials. This pollution is for the most part irrecoverable; the chain of evil it initiates not only in the world that must support life but in living tissues is for the most part irreversible. In this now universal contamination of the environment, chemicals are the sinister and little-recognized partners of radiation in changing the very nature of the world—the very nature of its life. Strontium 90, released through nuclear explosions into the air, comes to earth in rain or drifts down as fallout, lodges in soil, enters into the grass or corn or wheat grown there, and in time takes up its abode in the bones of a human being, there to remain until his death. Similarly, chemicals sprayed on croplands or forests or gardens lie long in soil, entering into living organisms, passing from one to another in a chain of poisoning and death. Or they pass mysteriously by underground streams until they emerge and, through the alchemy of air and sunlight, combine into new forms that kill vegetation, sicken cattle, and work unknown harm on those who drink from once-pure wells. As Albert Schweitzer has said, "Man can hardly even recognize the devils of his own creation."

It took hundreds of millions of years to produce the life that now inhabits the earth—eons of time in which that developing and evolving and diversifying life reached a state of adjustment and balance with its surroundings. The environment, rigorously shaping and directing the life it supported, contained elements that were hostile as well as supporting. Certain rocks gave out dangerous radiation; even within the light of the sun, from which all life draws its energy, there were short-wave radiations with power to injure. Given time—time not in years but in millennia—life adjusts, and a balance has been reached. For time is the essential ingredient; but in the modern world there is no time.

The rapidity of change and the speed with which new situations are created follow the impetuous and heedless pace of man rather than the deliberate pace of nature. Radiation is no longer merely the background radiation of rocks, the bombardment of cosmic rays, the ultraviolet of the sun that have existed before there was any life on earth; radiation is now the unnatural creation of man's tampering with the atom. The chemicals to which life is asked to make its adjustment are no longer merely the calcium and silica and copper and all the rest of the minerals washed out of the rocks and carried in rivers to the sea; they are the synthetic creations of man's inventive mind, brewed in his laboratories, and having no counterparts in nature.

To adjust to these chemicals would require time on the scale that is nature's; it would require not merely the years of a man's life but the life of generations. And even this, were it by some miracle possible, would be futile, for the new chemicals come from our laboratories in an endless stream; almost five hundred annually find their way into actual use in the United States alone. The figure is staggering and its implications are not easily grasped—500 new chemicals to which the bodies of men and animals are required somehow to adapt each year, chemicals totally outside the limits of biologic experience.

Among them are many that are used in man's war against nature. Since the mid-1940's over 200 basic chemicals have been created for use in killing insects, weeds, rodents, and other organisms described in the modern vernacular as "pests"; and they are sold under several thousand different brand names.

These sprays, dusts, and aerosols are now applied almost universally to farms, gardens, forests, and homes—nonselective chemicals that have the power to kill every insect, the "good" and the "bad," to still the song of birds and the leaping of fish in the streams, to coat the leaves with a deadly film, and to linger on in soil—all this though the intended target may be only a few weeds or insects. Can anyone believe it is possible to lay down such a barrage of poisons on the surface of the earth without making it unfit for all life? They should not be called "insecticides," but "biocides."

. . . .

Water must also be thought of in terms of the chains of life it supports—from the small-as-dust green cells of the drifting plant plankton, through the minute water fleas to the fishes that strain plankton from the water and are in turn eaten by other fishes or by birds, mink, raccoons—in an endless cyclic transfer of materials from life to life. We know that the necessary minerals in the water are so passed from link to link of the food chains. Can we suppose that poisons we introduce into water will not also enter into these cycles of nature?

The answer is to be found in the amazing history of Clear Lake, California. Clear Lake lies in mountainous country some 90 miles north of San Francisco and has long been popular with anglers. The name is inappropriate, for actually it is a rather turbid lake because of the soft black ooze that covers its shallow bottom. Unfortunately for the fishermen and the resort dwellers on its shores, its waters have provided an ideal habitat for a small gnat, *Chaoborus astictopus*. Although closely related to mosquitoes, the gnat is not a bloodsucker and probably does not feed at all as an adult. However, human beings who shared its habitat found it annoying because of its sheer numbers. Efforts were made to control it but they were largely fruitless until, in the late 1940's, the chlorinated hydrocarbon insecticides offered new weapons. The chemical chosen for a fresh attack was DDD, a close relative of DDT but apparently offering fewer threats to fish life.

The new control measures undertaken in 1949 were carefully planned and few people would have supposed any harm could result. The lake was surveyed, its volume determined, and the insecticide applied in such great dilution that for every part of chemical there would be 70 million parts of water. Control of the gnats was at first good, but by 1954 the treatment had to be repeated, this time at the rate of 1 part of insecticide in 50 million parts of water. The destruction of the gnats was thought to be virtually complete.

The following winter months brought the first intimation that other life was affected: the western grebes on the lake began to die, and soon more than a hundred of them were reported dead. At Clear Lake the western grebe is a breeding bird and also a winter visitant, attracted by the abundant fish of the lake. It is a bird of spectacular appearance and beguiling habits, building its floating nests in shallow lakes of western United States and Canada. It is called the "swan grebe" with reason, for it glides with scarcely a ripple across the lake surface, the body riding low, white neck and shining black head held high. The newly hatched chick is clothed in soft gray down; in only a few hours it takes to the water and rides on the back of the father or mother, nestled under the parental wing coverts.

Following a third assault on the ever-resilient gnat population, in 1957, more grebes died. As had been true in 1954, no evidence of infectious disease could be discovered on examination of the dead birds. But when someone thought to analyze the fatty tissues of the grebes, they were found to be loaded with DDD in the extraordinary concentration of 1600 parts per million.

The maximum concentration applied to the water was 1/50 part per million. How could the chemical have built up to such prodigious levels in the grebes? These birds, of course, are fish eaters. When the fish of Clear Lake also were analyzed the picture began to take form—the poison being picked up by the smallest organisms, concentrated and passed on to the larger predators. Plankton organisms were found to contain about 5 parts per million of the insecticide (about 25 times the maximum concentration ever reached in the water itself); plant-eating fishes had built up accumulations ranging from 40 to 300 parts per million; carnivorous species had stored the most of all. One, a brown bullhead, had the astounding concentration of 2500 parts per million. It was a house-that-Jack-built sequence, in which the large carnivores had eaten the smaller carnivores, that had eaten the herbivores, that had eaten the plankton, that had absorbed the poison from the water.

Even more extraordinary discoveries were made later. No trace of DDD could be found in the water shortly after the last application of the chemical. But the poison had not really left the lake; it had merely gone into the fabric of the life the lake supports. Twenty-three months after the chemical treatment had ceased, the plankton still contained as much as 5.3 parts per million. In that interval of nearly two years, successive crops of plankton had flowered and faded away, but the poison, although no longer present in the water, had somehow passed from generation to generation. And it lived on in the animal life of the lake as well. All fish, birds, and frogs examined a year after the chemical applications had ceased still contained DDD. The amount found in the flesh always exceeded by many times the original concentration in the water. Among these living carriers were fish that had hatched nine months after the last DDD application, grebes, and California gulls that had built up concentrations of more than 2000 parts per million. Meanwhile, the nesting colonies of the grebes dwindled—from more than 1000 pairs before the first insecticide treatment to about 30 pairs in 1960. And even the thirty seem to have nested in vain, for no young grebes have been observed on the lake since the last DDD application.

114.

[From *Changing Times*]

AMERICA THE BEAUTIFUL—
HERITAGE OR HONKY-TONK? [1962]

What are they really like today, the places your kids read about in school and which you hope to show them sometime as the finest representations of the American spirit? In case you haven't looked lately, a shock is in store. Marvels like Yellowstone Park and Gettysburg battlefield are infested, often within their borders and almost always around the edges, by a spreading disease of our time—tourist blight.

It's more than a sickness of an era marked by mobility and leisure; the manufacture of tourist blight is also a lucrative business. Competition is keen among those who cater to and exploit the simplest expressions of public taste.

Now Coney Island is one thing. It serves a delightful purpose, aflutter with pennants and sideshows and mistaken for nothing else but itself. So does Atlantic City, for those who like to walk the Boardwalk and Steel Pier, feeling content in company of loud signs, loud noises and throngs of people. But this is hardly the atmosphere to spread from one coast to another, hardly an appropriate symbol to find at the gateway to, or within, a national shrine.

Of course, everyone is entitled to his own taste and should pursue it freely. But the public landscape, which all of us must live with, deserves farsighted care. And our national monuments should be more than an opportunity for promoters to make a fast buck.

Perhaps the surge of the last decade to lay waste to large sections of the countryside owes its inspiration to the success of Disneyland. Walt Disney built a synthetic thing, ballyhooed it on television and proved that millions of families would come running. Enterprising hopefuls copied some of the Disney image, playing up to public interest in history, the American West, nature, patriotism and religion. In almost every part of the country—often adjacent to a National Park or Monument drawing millions of visitors—are places bearing such names as Fantasyland, Six Gun City and even Bibleland.

But they lack Disney's greatest promotional advantage, the handy access to network television, and have to compensate in other ways. They resort to mammoth roadside billboards unashamedly representing their attractions as the "most outstanding," "foremost," "most historic," "most scenic" single spot in the state or nation. They harass with their signs, they demand attention, they cajole through appeals to children and parents until the poor family can hardly pass the place by without a guilty conscience.

.   .   .   .

Thomas Jefferson would hardly recognize the towering limestone arch that he once owned. He treasured the great bridge, carved by rushing mountain streams over the centuries, and described it as "the most sublime of Nature's works." He resisted suggestions for man-made changes and said the bridge should remain as nature left it.

Today the wide Bridge, 215 feet above Cedar Creek, supports Route 11, the main road down the Shenandoah Valley. But the view is blocked by a wooden fence, as though protecting the inside of a baseball park. Jefferson would be required, before gaining admission, to pay his fee of $1.50. But there would be no extra charge if he elected to visit during the evening to see the "soul stirring" performance of the "Drama of Creation," when the Bridge is illuminated with colored lights and voice recordings evoke various religious images. And after coming through the entrance, he could also stop at the swimming pool, skating rink and an enormous souvenir counter vending a multitude of trinkets and doodads.

A recent addition at Natural Bridge is the antique car collection known as the "Museum of Motoring Memories"; this kind of companion piece is now widely found together with money-making commercial tourist attractions. Natural Bridge is perhaps the pace-setter for Route 11, a once-beautiful route, now adorned from Winchester to Roanoke with unrestrained advertisements for motels, commercial caverns, a place called "Zoorama" (it failed after a short, unhappy life, but the signs remain) and some ill-maintained state roadside rests.

.   .   .   .

"Yes, it is amazing to see the long line of commercial attractions on the road out here," a prominent and responsible citizen of the Black Hills area told a visitor from the East last summer. "The number is growing each year, too. Of course, we receive many complaints from visitors that this sort of thing destroys the feeling for Rushmore. But it seems somebody is bent on trying a new gimmick on every piece of private land from Rapid City to Mount Rushmore."

The gimmicks are multifarious indeed. The 25-mile road to Rushmore is an obstacle course of commercial attractions, all seeking to divert a million visitors, heading for a famous shrine, into their

little crannies. The Reptile Gardens leads the way with the largest
number of signs. There are four separate self-professed natural
phenomena: Gravity Hill, Gravity Spot, Dizzyland, U.S.A. (Mysteries
of Gravity) and the Cosmos (the *Real* Nature's Mystery Area).
Then assorted caves and gold mines, and the usual Horseless
Carriage Museum and Fairyland's Bewitched Village.

At one point the tragic contrast between the shrine and the
commercial surroundings becomes most evident. A neat, small
green and white sign reads "Mount Rushmore Memorial, 3 miles,"
but this can hardly be seen for the much larger, garish signs
above and around it advertising mines, motels, caves and bars.

There is a novel little stunt in the Black Hills not seen elsewhere, a seal of approval at the entrance to many of these places.
This sign reads "Family Approved Attraction." Approved by *Parents' Magazine*? The Automobile Club? No, nothing as objective
as that. These tourist operators have their own organization,
the Black Hills, Badlands and Lakes Association, and simply approve each other.

The picture within the Memorial grounds has its dim side, too.
One would think the National Park Service would maintain the
vantage points facing the four presidential heads carved high on
the granite mountain. But one of the best spots is operated by
a commercial concessionaire as a kind of carnival.

The mammoth souvenir shop carries the feeblest assortment
of native handicrafts made by the Sioux Indians. The emphasis
is on merchandising such items as nylon flags of all nations,
Japanese-made plates bearing pictures of President and Mrs.
Kennedy and figurines of Jesus Christ.

The sorry truth is that federal officials sometimes contribute
to tourist blight, too. Despite the proud tradition and generally
high standards of the National Park Service, the core of Yellowstone, the nation's oldest and largest National Park, has deteriorated into a scandalous slum, the consequence of poor commercial management over a period of years and of soft and sloppy
administration by Park officials.

Park people concede this privately, often with grim humor.
"I heard my neighbor brushing his teeth this morning," says one
visiting Park man to another after spending a night at Canyon
Village Motor Lodge, the first new overnight accommodation
in the Park in 30 years. "That's nothing," his friend replies. "I
heard by neighbor *thinking* about brushing his teeth. When do
we leave?"

In short, 512-room Canyon Village, intended as a model in
commercially developed lodgings for the entire Park System, has
turned out to be a failure, faulty in design, faulty in construction, with poor heating, flimsy soundproofing and a multitude
of other shortcomings. Rooms are horribly overpriced ($13.50
for two, $18.50 for four), and the entire setting is incongruous
with the great Park, landscaped largely with black asphalt and

blinking lights over the cocktail lounge. The gift shop offers one of the worst assortments of trinkets in America, 8,000 separate items, principally cheap (but profitable) importations from the Far East, including imitation English Wedgewood, Spanish toreador figurines in several colors, bells of Sarna and bongo drums.

. . . .

Avoid the blight of Yellowstone? It is possible to a certain extent. You can find decent, clean and modern cabin and motel-type accommodations at the Grand Tetons, or well-kept campgrounds in surrounding areas. Look only at the thermal wonders, the wildlife and the marvels of a vast wilderness, shutting your eyes to all else. .

But this is exactly the trouble: thinking Americans have shut their eyes for too long while blight and mass vulgarization have swept over the landscape. The amusement parks, the souvenir stands, the roadside animals won't go away by themselves. But neither must they be accepted as being here forever.

The point isn't that such places are not interesting or entertaining or even, in some cases, in good taste. But, rather, do they belong where they are? What does Mother Goose have to do with the commemoration of a Civil War battlefield? What are commercial Biblical dioramas doing in the Great Smokies?

115.

Russell Baker

THE GREAT PAVER [1963]

The director of this tiny but immensely powerful group, whose tentacles reach even into the Mafia, is known only as The Great Paver.

His dream, which he would dismiss as implausible if concocted by one of Ian Fleming's villains, is to pave the entire United States with concrete and asphalt. He envisions a nation buried under six-lane, limited-access turnpikes. When the last blade of American grass is buried, he plans to go on to pave Europe. Then Asia. And on and on until the whole planet is coated in cement. Today America—tomorrow the world.

Accusations that The Great Paver is power mad are unfair. True, he has henchmen whose motives are not unselfish. We all know the motives of the oil cartel and the notorious auto repair syndicate whose goals correspond with The Great Paver's. The Great Paver, however, is utterly principled.

His philosophy is summed up in the sentence with which he refutes every attempt to stop him: "The world must move cars."

Seeing thousands of cars jammed up in the city's narrow arteries, he has thrown concrete over houses and shops and covered the parks with asphalt to let the traffic move. When human beings have protested, he has told them simply: "The world must move cars."

Now, of course, he has learned that new superexpressways pour more cars into more narrow arteries. He realizes, not entirely without sorrow, that there can be no end until the entire continent is utterly and completely paved.

The Great Paver has been especially active in Washington lately. He has laid concrete all over the beautiful Virginia hills across the Potomac and is busy pouring it through the lush Maryland valleys. With splendid highways now surrounding the capital, there is nothing to do but buy a car or two and get out and drive on them.

116.

Gene Marine

OUTRAGE ON BODEGA HEAD [1963]

About 500 people live in this little community. They don't count. A couple of million people in or near San Francisco, and about 15,000 more along the fifty-mile line between the two places, don't count either, but that's different. They don't know what's happening. The people in Bodega Bay do. They—and a few others who care about things like nuclear safety and conservation and the right of a populace to make its own decisions—are the only people who know what the Pacific Gas and Electric Company is up to.

In brief, P. G. & E. is going to build a nuclear-powered, steam-electric, generating plant. The plant will contain seventy-five tons of 2½ per cent enriched uranium fuel—375 pounds of pure uranium, or about 150 times as much fissionable material as the Hiroshima atomic bomb. It will be kept from blowing up by a new safety system which has never been completely tested.

The reactor will be about 333 yards—1,000 feet—from the line of San Andreas Fault, the same ever-active line of earth slippage that caused the 1906 San Francisco earthquake, as well as a few hundred lesser tremors before and since. (The one in 1906 turned over a locomotive just twenty miles from where the new reactor will be.)

Fantastic? We haven't begun. A 300-foot stack on the reactor plant will emit waste gases, including some charming stuff called iodine-131, which is radioactive. I-131 decays fairly rapidly, but since the plant will operate all the time, it will drop I-131 all the time. It will drop it, mostly, on Sonoma County dairy lands. This is an area which prides itself on the speed with which it gets milk to the market. It should be no trick at all for the Sonoma dairymen to get milk into California homes three or four days before half the I-131 has decayed.

The question, of course, is how much iodine-131? Nobody knows. Then wouldn't they try to find out before they build the plant? No.

The little town of Bodega Bay—two miles from the reactor site—pulls twice as much fish out of the ocean as does the publicized fishing fleet at San Francisco's Fishermen's Wharf. The Bodega fleet comes into the bay through a dredged channel, directly downwind from the 300-foot stack.

The bay itself is good for clamming, too—at the moment. But the plant is being built on Bodega Head, the peninsula that forms the harbor, and it's going to be a boiling-water reactor. That means picking up bay water, running it through the reactor, then discharging it, heated, into the ocean. Once in a while the water is recirculated—in effect, pushed back through. This will ruin whatever clamming hasn't already been destroyed by the road to the plant, which will run through clam-rich tidelands.

Nor is that all, though it ought to be enough. The existence of the reactor, playing its suck-and-spit game with the water, will very probably destroy a unique marine ecology which the University of California has been wanting to study for years.

Then there's Doran Park, a sandspit which, with Bodega Head, makes Bodega Bay one of the only five safe harbors along 300 miles of tortuous, treacherous Pacific Coast. Doran Park was turned over to Sonoma County by the State of California on condition that it be preserved as a park. At its *widest* point, it's less than 350 feet wide. P. G. & E. will run power lines down the center of the park; its easement is 180 feet wide. Why don't they put the wires underground? "Uneconomical." (P. G. & E. refers to its about-to-be-constructed facility as the "Bodega Bay Atomic Park"—a description we can let pass with a mildly derisive snort.)

117.

John F. Kennedy

ON THE NUCLEAR TEST-BAN TREATY [1963]

This treaty can be a step toward freeing the world from the fears and dangers of radioactive fallout. Our own atmospheric tests last year were conducted under conditions which restricted such fallout to an absolute minimum. But over the years the number and yield of weapons tested have rapidly increased—and so have the radioactive hazards from such testing. Continued unrestricted testing by the nuclear power, joined in time by other nations which may be less adept in limiting pollution, will increasingly contaminate the air that all of us must breathe.

Even then, the number of children and grandchildren with cancer in their bones, with leukemia in their blood or with poison in their lungs might seem statistically small to some, in comparison with natural health hazards. But this is not a natural health hazard—and it is not a statistical issue. The loss of even one human life, or the malformation of even one baby—who may be born long after we are gone—should be of concern to us all. Our children and grandchildren are not merely statistics toward which we can be indifferent.

Nor does this affect the nuclear powers alone. These tests befoul the air of all men and all nations, the committed and the uncommitted alike, without their knowledge and without their consent. That is why the continuation of atmospheric testing causes so many countries to regard all nuclear powers as equally evil; and we can hope that its prevention will enable those countries to see the world more clearly, while enabling all the world to breathe more easily.

118.

Edmund K. Faltermayer

THE HALF-FINISHED SOCIETY [1965]

Our American civilization
is only half built. From the standpoint of per capita consumption
of goods, home ownership, education, and social mobility, the U.S.
leads the world and the American Dream is now largely fulfilled.
But that dream, which spurred on frontiersmen clearing the wilderness and inspired immigrants to break out of the slums, was
never really a blueprint for a mature society. It emphasized the
individual's demands for material comfort, privacy, and the education needed to obtain them. But it largely ignored the other
half of civilized life: a whole spectrum of human needs that can
be met only through communal action.

The society we have built fulfills the lopsided American Dream
with a vengeance. Our immaculate homes are crowded with gleam-
ing appliances and our refrigerators are piled high with convenience foods. But beyond our doorsteps lies a shamefully neglected social and physical environment. Foreigners who come to
these shores expecting to find splendid countrysides and magnificent cities discover other things instead: noise, vandalism, polluted air, befouled streams, filthy streets, forests of ugly telegraph
poles and wires, decrepit mass-transit systems, and parks that
are unkempt and unsafe. They also see: a countryside being
devoured by housing subdivisions and by shopping centers whose
graceless buildings are little more than merchandise barns; highways splattered with enormous billboards and hideous drive-ins
that shreik for the passing motorist's attention; central cities that,
except for a rather insignificant amount of reconstruction at the
core, are sprawling wastelands of decayed speculative construction left over from yesteryear. The only places where Americans
have extensively beautified their country, visitors soon discover,
are certain upper-middle-class suburbs—fine for those who can
afford them—and some college campuses. Otherwise, there is
little relief from what the English magazine *Architectural Review*
a decade ago called "the mess that is man-made America."

The archvillain in the despoliation of our landscape, it sometimes seems, is American capitalism. To one returning here after

a long sojourn abroad, the impression gained is one of pathologically profit-minded enterprises striving to outdo each other in the creation of eyesores. You see the results everywhere: the exhausted gravel pit that was never replanted, the porcelain gasoline station that brutally shoulders up against the village church, the speculative office tower that has all the aesthetic appeal of a throwaway container, which is basically what it is in the eyes of its tax-motivated builders. A rather disturbing question naturally arises: is public ugliness the price America must pay for its incredibly high level of private consumption?

The answer is no. Western Europe is managing to retain its beauty amid rapidly rising consumption. Blaming it all on American capitalism is about as logical as criticizing plants for wanting to grow toward the sun. If there is chaos, it is the community's fault for failing to exercise its role as gardener. European countries, governed by men with a pride in appearances rarely encountered here, have never lost control of their environment. America has yet to *gain* control of its environment. Because of this the American free-enterprise system, whose efficiency and command of technology could have created the tidiest-looking country in the world, has tended to produce an overpowering disorder.

.   .   .   .

First, the American capitalist system, for all its efficiency, presents a rather shabby image to the outside world. "An important test of an economy is how it looks," says conservationist William H. Whyte, a former FORTUNE editor. Ours, for the most part, looks like hell. Reaching the moon will gain us little, in worldwide acclaim, if we cannot build habitable cities. Second, we are in an era of onrushing technological change. If we cannot create a more harmonious environment to mitigate the effects of this change, our nerves may get awfully taut.

Third, we are running out of living space. Superficially, this statement sounds absurd, for the urban portions of the forty-eight contiguous states use up only 2 percent of the total land area. But the best job opportunities today are in the major metropolitan regions, where the surrounding countryside is rapidly being gobbled up by haphazard real-estate development. In one region, the so-called "megalopolis" that stretches from Boston to Washington between the Appalachian ridges and the sea, the population density is already greater than in such crowded foreign lands as Britain and West Germany. The arc that extends from Pittsburgh through Chicago and Milwaukee is almost as densely peopled as Western Europe, and the corridor between San Francisco and San Diego will be before long. The vast national parks and wilderness areas in the hinterlands are of significance only during vacations; half of America's people spend most of their lives in crowded little "countries" like megalopolis. It is precisely in these areas that the coming population increase will be concentrated. In fifty years, President Johnson forecasts, America will have a population of 400 million, four-fifths of it urban. If we do not establish intelligent controls over land use, most Americans will soon be spending 95 percent of their lives in huge blighted zones, hundreds of miles long, that are neither city nor country, but one vast, dispiriting Nowhere.

It is profitable to look at what is going on in Western Europe. Traditionally, Europe has lagged behind the U.S. in social mobility and in the more commonly accepted yardsticks of a high living standard—e.g., gadgets and cars. But it has maintained an ordered environment and pioneered in social legislation. Now Europeans are getting more social mobility—technology provides an upward route that bypasses the class system—and plenty of gadgets as well. Meanwhile, slums have been eliminated in such areas as West Germany, Holland, and Scandinavia; the streets are safe at night and the average citizen is rarely more than ten minutes *by foot* from parks and attractive shopping areas. The European, in other words, is well on his way to having the best of both worlds. It would be ironic indeed if Western Europe, from which our ancestors fled in search of a better life, should beat us at our own game.

119.

C. W. Griffin, Jr.

AMERICA'S AIRBORNE GARBAGE [1965]

If we continue on our present course, such basic atmospheric contaminants as sulfur dioxide, carbon monoxide, and nitrogen oxides will increase to two to four times present counts within the next thirty or forty years, according to Vernon G. MacKenzie, chief of the Public Health Service air pollution division. Probably the nation's chief source of atmospheric poisons, the nation's 88,000,000 motor vehicles spew into the air the staggering total of 350,000 tons of carbon monoxide, hydrocarbons, and nitrogen dioxide gas daily. Proceeding at a rate more than double the rate of population increase, the sheer growth in automobiles and the spread of traffic jams throughout our metropolitan areas destroy any hope of adequately controlling automobile pollution by presently proposed methods. Even if unapproved pollution-abating engine modifications proposed for new automobiles in California fulfil their most hopeful promise and become mandatory for new automobiles throughout the nation, they can only keep a bad situation from degenerating into an impossible one. If we want to make our cities' air fit to breathe, we must consider ways of limiting automobile travel in large urban centers like New York, Los Angeles, Chicago, Detroit, and Washington, particularly during rush hours. The rush-hour traffic jam is more than a fantastically efficient way to squander commuter's time; it is civilization's most diabolical method of multiplying atmospheric poisons.

Los Angeles, of course, best illustrates the desperate struggle against smog. Forced into action by the sheer necessity of keeping the area habitable, Los Angeles County has pressed its control program several light-years ahead of any other U.S. city's. The country's air pollution control district has enforced regulations that limit pollutant emissions from power plants, petroleum refineries, organic solvent industries, home heating furnaces, and other stationary sources almost to the limit of present technology. As a consequence, motor vehicles now contribute at least four times as many pollutants to Los Angeles's air as all other sources combined. Despite the many successes of their anti-smog campaign, including a hard-won victory over backyard trash burners, Los Angeles smog control officials have abandoned the hope of attaining their original goal of restoring 1940 air quality. Pollutant levels from automobiles are now three and a half times the 1940 level. Under the most hopeful projection, with all new cars fitted with ideally maintained smog control devices, the pollutant levels in 1975 will still be nearly three times the 1940 level.

. . . .

The automobile is the most serious source of a changing style that, within the past two decades, has radically altered the nature of air pollution. As an inevitable by-product of burning, air pollution of some degree has been with us since Prometheus. Seneca reviled the "heavy air of Rome and the stench of its smoky chimneys," and Roman patricians complained about the soot that soiled their togas. During the Middle Ages the substitution of coal for Europe's dwindling timber supply created the smoke and soot that still plague some industrial cities. Coal smoke, fumes, and soot from iron smelters fouled the air of medieval London. Despite the grisly example of a fourteenth-century artificer hanged for violating a ban against the burning of sea coal, the gray pall over the city darkened. "Hell is a city much like London, a populous and smoky city," wrote Shelley at the beginning of the Industrial Revolution.

London's smog, a true smoke suspended in fog, is today's counterpart of traditional air pollution. It consists predominantly of sulfur compounds, notably sulfur dioxide gas, released in the burning of coal and low-grade heating oil, ore roasting, acid manufacture, and similar industrial processes. Because England has limited access to the high-grade oil and natural gas fuels that have brightened the air of cities like Pittsburgh and St. Louis, London retains the pollution of Blake's dark, satanic mills.

At the opposite extreme, Los Angeles's smog is the prototype of modern air pollution—a diabolical brew of irritant gases produced by complicated photochemical reaction. Almost all of Los Angeles's smog is gaseous; only 1 per cent by weight of Los Angeles's atmospheric contaminants is suspended particulates (solid particles so tiny that they literally float in the air). American cities lacking Los Angeles's rigorous control lie somewhere in the spectrum between London's smog and Los Angeles's. New York and Chicago record sulfur dioxide counts approaching London's. Only superior atmospheric ventilation spares these cities the catastrophic killer smogs that periodically kill hundreds, and sometimes thousands, of Londoners.

Of greater concern than the well-publicized but relatively infrequent killer smogs that have struck London, Donora, Pennsylvania, and the Meuse Valley in Belgium are the long-term health hazards. Some 120,000,000 Americans are exposed to perpetual attack from atmospheric poisons. Common sense suggests that pollutants capable of darkening white housepaint, disintegrating stone, corroding metal, dissolving nylon stockings, and embrittling rubber are less than beneficial to the delicate pink lung tissue, and common sense appears to be right. An accumulating file of circumstantial evidence, paralleling the evidence that convicted cigarettes, has linked air pollution with the common cold, asthma, pneumonia, tuberculosis, influenza, chronic bronchitis, pulmonary emphysema, lung cancer, and even Hodgkin's disease. At the latest National Conference on Air Pollution Control, in December 1962, the chairman of a panel of medical experts concluded: "The evidence that air pollution contributes to the pathogenesis of chronic respiratory disease is overwhelming." Seven medical experts on this panel unanimously agreed that air pollution is a cause of chronic respiratory disease. In the intervening two and a half years, the damning evidence has piled even higher. Beyond reasonable doubt, air pollution, like cigarettes, puts thousands of Americans into premature graves every year. Through its aggravation of diseases like chronic bronchitis and pulmonary emphysema, which entails a slow disintegration of the lungs' oxygen-absorption capacity, air pollution helps make the declining years of thousands of elderly city dwellers a perpetual struggle for breath. Breathing the air of cities like Birmingham, Alabama, exposes one to a lung cancer hazard equivalent to smoking two and a half packs of cigarettes a day. And against the proliferating, smog-borne poisons in the air, will power means nothing; the only possible protection is a gas mask.

120.

Richard S. Latham

THE ARTIFACT AS A CULTURAL CIPHER [1966]

Throughout history we find one thing common to all artifacts. They were used, they disappeared, and they were eventually replaced by new ones. Even while in use they were small enough to be ignored. They served man and fit into his environment without dominating it or him.

Before the Industrial Revolution the only permanent objects large and solid enough to persist and dominate the environment were architectural: cathedrals, pyramids, medieval towns, Roman aqueducts. Only these occasional large masses of stone and mortar remaining on the landscape had a permanent effect on man's aesthetic perceptions and measurement. The rest were eroded away or covered over by nature.

Since the Industrial Revolution things have changed radically. The machine has multiplied not only in size but in number, until it dominates our visual world as architecture once did and affects our senses twenty-four hours a day. Industry produces five to seven million artifacts yearly in the form of automobiles, and their size and number are now such that we cannot regard them as humble artifacts ready to disappear when their time is up. They line the streets, fill acres of parking lots, and later pile up in junkyards which in themselves are vast graveyards on an architectural scale; they encroach on our aesthetic sense from every side and dominate how we build, how we live and breathe, how cities grow or die. At the same time roads, signs, and power lines blot out the natural landscape and row houses swallow it up in unspeakable monotony. Still, we have not reached the ultimate machine-dominated environment. That can be visualized by visiting a SAC base or by spending a day (as many military people do) in the underground headquarters of Air Defense Command at Colorado Springs. Perhaps the totality is most easily observed at Cape Kennedy: a landscape that is one awesome endless artifact whose scale dwarfs any cathedral.

The physical aspects of our present Western culture, compared to previous Middle Eastern and Oriental cultures, seem almost anti-man. They are in a very real way anti-nature. Our artifacts are no better aesthetically than those produced by the Egyptian culture three thousand years before us. In many ways they are worse. In fact, man's relationship to his artifacts has not improved, but has grown worse in the past three hundred years. Man today, in our society, does not value or enjoy everyday objects at the level of his forefathers. He does not have a basic appreciation of their intrinsic beauty; he also appears to be losing his ability to sense and appreciate the same qualities in nature. He is not as "whole" a man as his ancestors were.

121.

Harry M. Caudill

PARADISE IS STRIPPED [1966]

Descendants of the people who settled in the shallow valley of the Green River founded a small hamlet called Paradise, Ky. It was well-named, for the countryside was green and pleasant and the stream teemed with fish. Game abounded and a man could live an unworried life, the tedium broken by an occasional visit to the country seat to listen to trials and swap yarns with friends from other parts of Muhlenberg County.

But times have changed. There is still a dot called Paradise on the map of Kentucky but last year Muhlenberg produced 17.6 million tons of coal—more than any other county in America—and the production record was achieved at a staggering cost. Paradise is isolated and shrunken, huddled in an appalling waste. Thousands of acres of earth are piled high into ghastly ridges, sometimes black with coal, sometimes brown with sulphur. The streams that wind through this dead landscape are devoid of life.

Here in western Kentucky, part of America's Eastern Interior coal field, the mineral lies near the surface, and the region has fallen prey to strip mining on an immense scale. Strip mining is as easy as it is ruthless. It simply tears the earth apart stratum by stratum in order to rip out the minerals. Conventional tunnel and pillar mining leaves the surface relatively undisturbed, but stripping totally disrupts the land and its ecology.

In a typical Appalachian operation the development may proceed in two or more seams of coal at different levels in a mountain. The uppermost seam may be laid bare by the violent expedient of blasting away the entire overlying crest—a process known to the industry as "casting the overburden." Lower down, the seam is exposed or "faced" by bulldozing and dynamiting the timber and soil away from the coal. The uprooted trees, loose dirt and shattered stone are pushed down the slope. The coal is loosened by light explosive charges, scooped up with power shovels and loaded onto giant trucks for hauling to the nearest railroad loading docks.

Where the terrain is level or gently rolling, the bulldozers and power shovels scrape away the dirt to expose the rock layer roofing the coal. The stone is then shattered with dynamite and lifted by immense shovels or draglines onto the spoil heaps, accumulations that sometimes rise almost sheer to a height of 200 feet. Several acres of the fuel may be bared in this manner before smaller shovels begin loading it onto the trucks.

One gigantic shovel owned by the Peabody Coal Company is as tall as a 17-story building and has become a major tourist attraction. Thousands of people drive out of their way to watch it devastate the American land.

. . . .

The Appalachian coal field extends through Pennsylvania, West Virginia, eastern Kentucky, western Virginia, eastern Tennessee and northern Alabama. This mountain range is one of the richest resource areas in the continent—rich with coal, oil, natural gas, sandstone, limestone, low-grade iron ore, water, timber-growing potential and marvelous scenery. The hunters and wilderness scouts who first penetrated the gaps never beheld a land more enchantingly beautiful than the wooded Appalachian hills and hollows on a misty morning.

With wise management of its resources, Appalachia could have been the richest part of America today. Instead, it has become synonymous with poverty of land and people. But Appalachian destitution did not occur by accident. It is the result of nearly a century of remorseless exploitation.

The timber stands were bought by Eastern lumber companies, and the forests were cut down, sawed up and shipped away in a barbarous manner which totally disregarded the capacity of the land to regenerate the stands. Few healthy seed trees were spared, and today the woods consist mainly of low-grade stock which the lumbermen have culled many times.

But the disastrous exploitation of timber never equaled that which characterized the coal interests. Traditionally, America's industrial muscle has rested on Appalachian coal seams, and mining has garnered huge fortunes for Philadelphia, Boston, Detroit, Cincinnati, New York and Chicago.

From the beginning, coal companies displayed a reckless contempt for the earth. Near their tipples they piled up tremendous culm heaps which they never troubled to vegetate. They poured—and continue to pour—immeasurable quantities of mine wastes into streams. Hundreds of them permitted the inhabitants of their towns to use waterways as dumping grounds for garbage and trash.

. . . .

The coal industry's lack of responsibility has culminated in today's strip mining. A flight along the Appalachian crest from Pennsylvania to Alabama reveals the awesome scope of the depredations. For hundreds of miles one passes over lands churned into darkening death.

In Pennsylvania alone, 250,000 acres have been left as bleak and barren as the Sahara. As the hills steepen to the southward, contour strip mining begins. In West Virginia and in eastern Kentucky, whole valleys have been wrecked. Gigantic cuts are made at the face of the coal seam, the "highwalls" sometimes rising 90 feet straight up. The broken timber, shattered rock and dirt are shoved over the steep slopes, to be carried by the rains into streams and onto farm lands.

In Ohio, 202,000 acres in a half-dozen counties have been churned by the machines. So complete is the devastation that in some areas once-valuable farmlands can now be bought for as little as 25 cents per acre.

. . . .

The blight of strip mining does not stop at the edge of the spoil banks. When freshly exposed, the soil is hot with sulphuric acid: for years nothing can grow on it. In the meantime, the sulphur and mud wash into streams, killing aquatic life and piling up in horrible weed-grown banks. The long-range cost of dredging the Mississippi and its tributaries of this coal-flecked debris will be astronomical—a burden all Federal taxpayers will share.

. . . .

Unless we act now our grandchildren may inherit vast man-made deserts, devoid of life, polluted with acids, hideous to the eye, baked by the sun and washed by the rains. If this is their heritage, they will curse us so long as the deserts remain to monumentalize our greed and folly.

122.

John Bird

OUR DYING WATERS [1966]

This is the story of a national disgrace.

We Americans were privileged to start our national life on a virtually unused, unspoiled continent. The country which became the United States was vast and beautiful, a landscape of moun-

tains, valleys and plains, all drained by one of the world's most
generous systems of waters: crystal-clear mountain brooks, meandering lowland creeks, great rolling rivers, massive fresh-water
lakes and salty bays and estuaries. Here was a primary source of
life, wealth and enjoyment beyond measure, it seemed to our forefathers—enough good water to meet a nation's needs for all time
to come. Yet, within a few generations we have fouled and degraded our beautiful waters. With destructive ignorance and vanda-
listic abandon we have clogged the capillaries and arteries of our
land with filth. Perhaps we were lulled in the early days by the
reassuring platitude that "running water purifies itself." Perhaps
we simply didn't care. In any case we have used our creeks, rivers
and lakes—the same ones from which we must draw much of our
drinking water—as handy, cheap sewers to carry away every
imaginable kind of waste.

We have filled our streams with raw excrement and garbage, laden
with disease. We have stained them with oil, coal dust, tar, dyes
and chemical "liquors" discharged by industries. We have burned
them with powerful acids which destroy all aquatic life except a
stringy, loathsome type of algae. We have turned them gray and
murky with silt and sludge, smothering shellfish and other forms
of bottom life. We have used them to dispose of residues containing
long-lasting poisons, some so powerful that less than one part per
billion in a stream can kill fish. And, as though to show our contempt for our natural scene, we have dumped billions of tons of
trash and offal in our once lovely waters: beer cans, worn-out tires,
old mattresses, rusty oil drums, refuse from hospitals, broken glass,
dead animals, junked automobiles.

It is a dismal fact that we now have seriously contaminated and
despoiled almost every creek, river, lake and bay in the entire
United States. An early colonist called the graceful Potomac "the
sweetest and greatest river I have seene," but in recent years a
sign on the river landing below the green slopes and white pillars
of Mount Vernon has warned visitors: Do Not Come Into Contact
With Polluted Water. Any tourist who might have the urge to
take a dip in the river George Washington loved so well would
run about the same risk as swimming in a cesspool; at times the
Potomac in this area is loaded with 100,000 fecal bacteria per 100
milliliters—about two jiggers—of liquid. In summer the tidal portion of the river often is in a state of decay.

At that, the Potomac is no worse than many of our waters.
Honeymooners at Niagara Falls sometimes find the atmosphere
less than romantic because the torrent of tainted water often fills
the air with a stench like that of rotten eggs. Lake Tahoe, high in
the Sierra Nevada mountains, one of the three clearest lakes in the
world—"so clear you can see a beer can thirty, forty feet down,"
boasts a local resident—is ominously threatened by inflows of silt
and sewage which may turn the crystalline water a murky green.
Chesapeake Bay, like most of our major bays, long has been a

receptacle for the combined pollution load of a number of dirty rivers, plus sewage and oily wastes from heavy ship traffic. Long ago the Chesapeake's once-clear waters became turbid, and its bottom life was choked by silt and sickened by toxic pollutants. Particularly hard-hit were the oysters, whose young depend on clean rocks or shell-bars to which to attach themselves. Fifty years ago the Chesapeake was the main harvest ground for the 10 to 12 million bushels of oysters that Maryland then produced. Now, despite advances in oyster culture, the harvest is only one tenth as much. Each year hundreds of thousands of acres of shellfish beds along the American shores are "uncertified" by health authorities; that is, they are found to be polluted by fecal-carrying water and cannot be harvested.

Or consider the mighty Hudson, first described in the log book of Henry Hudson's *Half Moon*. As the explorer sailed up the palisaded river in 1609, searching for the fabled Northwest Passage, he was disappointed as the water lost its salty taste and became fresh. In our times anyone tasting water from the river would be taking his life in his hands. The Hudson repeatedly is contaminated by raw sewage before it flows past New York City, where it receives another colossal discharge of the stuff, more than 400 million gallons a day. Sen. Robert Kennedy, when transferring from one boat to another in New York harbor, looked at the water and said, "If you fall in here you don't drown—you decay." Just how dangerous the Hudson has become was shown more than a year ago when some children found a watermelon floating in the river near 125th Street. They took it home, washed it off and ate it. Eight of them came down with typhoid fever.

Mark Twain called the Mississippi Basin "the body of the nation" and wrote lovingly of "the great Mississippi, the magnificent Mississippi, rolling its mile-wide tide, shining in the sun." Today pollution experts call this once-proud river "the colon of mid-America." Along its winding, 4,000-mile length the river suffers all the indignities a slovenly society can heap on it. Hundreds of towns and cities use it as a sewer. Thousands of manufacturers, packers, stockyards, refineries and mills drain their assortment of wastes into it: oils, phenols, toxic metals, slaughterhouse offal, pickling liquors, chicken feathers, garbage, chemical sludge and other horrors. Water birds and fish on the Mississippi have been killed by oil slicks. Spawning beds have been smothered by silt and sludge. Occasional slugs of dead water, robbed of its oxygen by decomposing organic wastes, have slaughtered countless migrating fish.

. . . .

Many other examples show how we have gone to the brink of disaster with our water supplies, but the point should be clear: *Our surface waters are in horrible shape.* Long ago the immense load of filth and poisons we dump in our streams overwhelmed their natural ability to purify themselves. At the same time, the volume of wastes discharged by our cities and factories is steadily increasing.

. . . .

By this time it should be abundantly clear that we can't save our water resources simply by passing a law or two. We also need goals and the means to reach them. And what is especially baffling to an ordinary citizen, such as this reporter, is the general low level of the goals. You seldom hear a politician, an industrial spokesman or, for that matter, even a water-quality official, say "Our streams and lakes should be the cleanest, best and most attractive in the world," or "Let's make sure that we are steadily *improving* our waters." Instead, they emphasize that pollution control costs money, that water can be of many different qualities, and there is no need to make it better than required for its major uses. Much of this worthy talk adds up to: *Let's do just enough to get by.*

American industries now are responsible for more than half of the pollution in our streams and lakes, and the wastes from their factories and mills are among the meanest, most complex and most difficult to clean up. Some heavy-industry streams are dead and gone as normal waterways. The bottom of Arthur Kill, a tidal connection between Newark Bay and Raritan Bay, has *no* living organisms; the bottom is covered by a thick mattress of oil, grease and chemical sludge. In the unlikely prospect that the water is cleaned up, the sludge will remain for many years.

Industry's attitude toward pollution control has been ambivalent, to say the least. Some companies have invested millions of dollars and the best engineering talent they can find to safeguard the streams they use. But others go merrily along, dumping their brines, acids and offal. "Most industries haven't lifted a finger to stop pollution unless the government forced them to," says one water-quality expert. "Big companies haven't hesitated to use political and economic pressure to avoid spending money on pollution control. They threaten to move out of an area, taking their payrolls with them, if regulations are enforced.

. . . .

If we continue to blunder along, setting our sights too low, worrying more about immediate costs than the future of our natural resources, may not much of the countryside become a disaster area, not by the year 2066, but by 1996 or 1986? Will children now being born be able to look upon our American earth and find it fair, inviting and secure? Or must they accept a despoiled land in which once-pleasant streams are open sewers, lakes and bays are cesspools, and beaches are places of peril instead of joy?

The key question still is: "Can we save our waters?" and as of now the answer, at best, is only "Maybe."

123.

A. Q. Mowbray

THE ASPHALT SHROUD [1969]

The measure of a modern, industrialized nation can be taken by observing the quality of its works in the two extremes of its environment—cities and wilderness. The quality of the city and of life within its borders bespeaks the attitudes of that nation toward the human being; the quality of a nation's wilderness bespeaks its attitude toward the living earth. The United States is swiftly destroying its cities and its wilderness with highways.

Americans are a restless, moving people. Before the land was ours, we leaped upon her virgin wealth to invade, rend, and devour her, expelling the hot energies of our youth against the raw wilderness. Now the frontiers have gone, but still we tear at the land with giant machines and thrust black tentacles of asphalt through the living flesh of our cities. We will not rest until the last remnants of wild spaces are open to the rubber tire, until the last clear mountain stream is bridged, until the last cathedral grove of redwoods is visible from the back seat of a Chevrolet.

The city was once envisioned as the place where a man could find his highest expression as a human being, where he could find rewarding labor, go to a concert, exchange philosophies in his neighborhood bar or on a park bench, grow in wisdom through exposure to human diversity, listen to the teachers at a great university, assuage his loneliness with crowds, and find protection from the iron forces of nature.

But the highest function of the city has become the efficient moving and storage of automobiles. The fine-grained, human-scale diversity of shops and homes and bars and parks and newsstands and shoeshine parlors is being wiped out by freeways, interchanges, boulevards, and parking lots. The bustle, the color, the friction, the exuberance of human contact are giving way to the sterile ooze of steel automata moving along the corridors between high-rise monuments to insurance companies and towering ghettos for their clerks, and marking their passage with the stench of fumed rubber and burned hydrocarbons. At night, the lights of the monumental city blaze down on streets empty of humanity, silent except for the whisper of rubber against asphalt, as the rear guard of the daytime clerks escape along the freeways to the suburbs.

. . . .

If the city was envisioned as the place where man could find his place among men, the wilderness and open spaces were believed to be the place where man could find his place in Nature. And the preservation of that wilderness should testify to man's reverence for the earth from which he comes and to which he will return. By his very act of preservation he acknowledges his humility before his creator. By staying his destructive hand, he disavows the arrogant notion that he is the be-all and the end-all of creation; he surrenders to the wolf and the lizard that which is rightfully theirs; and he preserves for future generations some unturned bits of earth far beyond road's end, beyond the ordered geometry of man's works, beyond the last outpost of man's concerns.

But land is money, and Americans are nothing if not commercially enterprising. In the "developer's" eyes, the way to make the wilderness more attractive for the sightseer is to improve it with hamburger stands, souvenir shops, motels, and barbered "scenic overlooks" complete with coin-operated binoculars. And the key to the success of all this endeavor is roads. Hiking is for the birdwatchers and other such nuts. "See the U.S.A. in your Chevrolet." If the developers have their way, it will some day be possible for Mom, Pop, Junior, and Sissie to spend two weeks touring the scenic spots of the United States without leaving the car except to drain and de-sludge their innards. Even the drive-in mortuary has come to pass.

124.

William O. Douglas

THE PUBLIC BE DAMMED [1969]

"The Army Corps of Engineers is public enemy number one." I spoke those words at the annual meeting of the Great Lakes Chapter of the Sierra Club, early in 1968; and that summary supplied an exclamation point to a long discussion of the manner in which various Federal agencies despoil the public domain.

It is not easy to pick out public enemy number one from among our Federal agencies, for many of them are notorious despoilers and the competition is great for that position. The Tennessee

Valley Authority, for example, like the Corps of Engineers, has an
obsession for building dams, whether needed or not. Its present
plan to wipe out the Little T River and its fertile valley is rampant
vandalism. TVA is also probably the biggest strip miner in the
country, using much coal for its stand-by steam plants. The sulphuric
acid that pours out of strip mines, ruining downstream waters,
is TVA acid.

The Bureau of Mines sits on its hands in Washington, D.C., pretty
much a captive agency of the coal-mine owners, and does precious
little about strip mining.

The Public Roads Administration has few conservation standards;
it goes mostly by engineering estimates of what is feasible and
of cost. In the Pacific Northwest, it has ruined 50 trout streams
through highway design. Everywhere—East and West—the Administration aims at the heart of parklands, because they need not
be condemned, and plays fast and loose with parts of the public
domain that were reserved for wildlife and outdoor recreation.

The list is long; and when the names of Federal agencies are
all in, the balloting for public enemy number one will not be
unanimous. But my choice of the Army Engineers has a powerful
case to support it.

. . . .

In the late Fifties, I was a member of a group of conservationists
fighting the Corps on the huge River Bend Dam on the Potomac
River. The dam was virtually useless as a power project and of no
value for flood control. Its justification was the creation of a head
of water that could be used to flush the polluted Potomac of
sewage. Some of the huge Federal agencies were silently opposed;
but none would speak up, for fear of losing the Corps' good will
and its research and development funds. We ended by getting an
independent engineering study that actually riddled the project.
That dam—which would have flooded 80 miles of river and shown
a drawdown of 35 vertical feet—would have been known in time
as the nation's greatest folly. It would have despoiled a historic
river; and the 35-foot vertical drawdown would have resulted in
several hundred yards of stinking mud flats exposed to public view.
Yet the Corps had the nerve to get a public-relations outfit to make
an estimate as to the millions of tourists who would be drawn to
this ugly mudhole from all over the East.

. . . .

I remember the Buffalo River in Arkansas and the Saline River
in the same state—both destined by the Army Engineers to be
destroyed as free-flowing rivers. The Buffalo I knew well, as I had
run it in canoes and fished for bass in shaded pools under its
limestone cliffs. Much of the land bordering the Buffalo is marginal
wood-lot acreage. Those who own that land were anxious to sell
it for a song to Uncle Sam. Chambers of commerce blew their

horns for "development" of the Buffalo. Bright pictures were drawn of motels built on the new reservoirs where fishing would abound and water-skiing would attract tourists.

The Corps had introduced Arkansas to at least 14 such river projects that buried free-flowing streams forever under muddy waters. The fishing is good for a few years. Then the silt covers the gravel bars where bass spawn and the gizzard shad—a notorious trash fish—takes over.

The people are left with the dead, muddy reservoirs. There is electric power, to be sure; but Arkansas already has many times the power that it can use. So why destroy the Buffalo? Why destroy the Saline?

· ·

The most alarming thing is the very number of dams proposed by the Corps. One of our wild, wild rivers is the Middle Fork of the Salmon in Idaho—a 100-mile sanctuary that should be preserved inviolate like the Liberty Bell. White sandspits make excellent campsites. The waters so abound with trout that barbless hooks should be used. Mountain sheep look down on the river from high embankments. Deer and elk frequent the open slopes. When I ran that scenic river and returned to Washington, I discovered that the Engineers had 19 dams planned for the Middle Fork.

125.

Jean Mayer

TOWARD A NON-MALTHUSIAN POPULATION POLICY
[1969]

Malthus was concerned with the steadily more widespread poverty that indefinite population growth would inevitably create. I am concerned about the areas of the globe where people are rapidly becoming richer. For rich people occupy much more space, consume more of each natural resource, disturb the ecology more, and create more land, air, water, chemical, thermal, and radioactive pollution than poor people. So it can be argued that from many viewpoints it is even more urgent to control the numbers of the rich than it is to control the numbers of the poor.

· ·

Our population is increasing faster than it ever has; our major nutrition problem is overweight, our major agricultural problem is our ever-mounting excess production. Does anyone seriously believe this means that we have no population problem? Our housing problems; our traffic problem; the insufficiency of the number of our hospitals, of community recreation facilities; our pollution problems, are all facets of our population problem. I may add that in this country we compound the population problem by the migratory habits of our people: from rural farm areas to urban areas and especially to "metropolitan" areas (212 such areas now have 84 per cent of our population); from low income areas to high income areas; from the East and Midwest to the South and Southwest; from all areas to the Pacific Coast; from the centers of cities to suburbs, which soon form gigantic conurbations, with circumstances everywhere pushing our Negroes into the deteriorating centers of large cities. All this has occurred without any master plan, and with public services continually lagging behind both growth and migrations.

Let us conclude with one specific example: 4 million students were enrolled in U.S. colleges and graduate schools in 1960; 6 million in 1965. The Bureau of the Census estimates that 8 million will seek admission or continued enrollment in 1970; 10 in 1975; 12 in 1980. No one questions our ability to feed these youngsters. But are we as a nation at all prepared for a near doubling of the size of our colleges and universities in 11 years?

Let us now examine the other argument, that in certain ways the rich countries are more immediately threatened by overpopulation. A corollary of this is that the earth as an economic system has more to fear from the rich than from the poor, even if one forgets for a moment the threat of atomic or chemical warfare.

Consider some data from our own country. We have already said that "crowding" is certainly one of the pictures we have in mind when we think of overpopulation. The increased crowding of our cities and our conurbations has been referred to, but what of the great outdoors? In 1930 the number of visitor-days at our national parks was of the order of 3 million (for a population of 122 million); by 1950 it was 33 million (for a population of 151 million); by 1960 it was 79 million (for a population of 179 million); by 1967, 140 million (for a population of 200 million). State parks tell the same story: a rise in visitor-days from 114 million in 1950 to 179 million in 1960, an increase in attendance of over 125 per cent for a rise in population of less than 20 per cent! Clearly, the increase in disposable income (and hence in means of transportation and in leisure) becomes a much more important factor in crowding and lack of privacy than the rise in population.

Not only does the countryside become more rapidly crowded when its inhabitants are rich, it also becomes rapidly uglier. With increasing income, people stop drinking water as much: as a result we spread 48 billion (rust proof) cans and 26 billion (non-degradable) bottles over our landscape every year. We produce 800 million pounds of trash a day, a great deal of which ends up in our fields, our parks, and our forests. Only one third of the billion pounds of paper we use every year is reclaimed. Nine million cars, trucks, and buses are abandoned every year, and while many of them are used as scrap, a large though undetermined number are left to disintegrate slowly in backyards, in fields and woods, and on the sides of highways. The eight billion pounds of plastics we use every year are nondegradable materials. And many of our states are threatened with an even more pressing shortage of water, not because of an increased consumption of drinking fluid by the increasing population, but because people are getting richer and using more water for air-conditioning, swimming pools, and vastly expanded metal and chemical industries.

That the air is getting crowded much more rapidly than the population is increasing is again an illustration that increase in the disposable income is perhaps more closely related to our own view of "overpopulation" than is the population itself. From 1940 to 1967 the number of miles flown has gone from 264 million to 3,334 billion (and the fuel consumed from 22 to 512 million gallons). The very air waves are crowded: the increase in citizen-licensees from 126 thousand to 848 thousand in the brief 1960-67 interval is again an excellent demonstration of the very secondary role of the population increase in the new overpopulation. I believe that as the disposable income rises throughout the world in general, the population pressure due to riches will become as apparent as that due to poverty.

I trust that I have demonstrated how dangerous it is to link constantly in the mind of the public the concept of overpopulation with that of undernutrition. I believe that it is dangerous to link it necessarily with poverty. It is absurd on the basis of any criterion of history, economics, or esthetics.

. . . .

The ecology of the earth—its streams, woods, animals—can accommodate itself better to a rising *poor* population than to a rising *rich* population. Indeed, to save the ecology the population will have to decrease as the disposable income increases. If we believe, like Plato and Aristotle, in trying for excellence rather than in rejoicing in numbers, we need a population policy now, for the rich as well as the poor. Excellent human beings will not be produced without abundance of cultural as well as material resources and, I believe, without sufficient space. We are likely to run out of certain metals before we run out of food; of paper before we run out of metals. And we are running out of clear streams, pure air, and the familiar sights of Nature while we still have the so-called "essentials" of life. Shall we continue to base the need for a population policy on a nutritional disaster to occur at some hypothetical date, when it is clear that the problem is here, now, for us as well as for others?

126.

Richard Curtis and Elizabeth Hogan

PERILS OF THE PEACEFUL ATOM [1969]

As most readers will recall, atomic reactors are designed to utilize the tremendous heat generated by splitting atoms. They are fueled with a concentrated form of uranium stored in long tubes bound together to form subassemblies. These are placed in the reactor's core, separated by rods which absorb radioactivity and thus control the chain reactions of splitting atoms. When the rods are withdrawn, the chain reactions intensify, producing enormous quantities of heat. Coolant circulated through the reactor core carries the heat away to heat exchange systems, where water is brought to a boil. The resultant steam is employed to turn electricity-generating turbines.

Stated in this condensed fashion, the process sounds innocuous enough. Unfortunately, however, heat is not the only form of energy produced by atomic fission. Another is radioactivity. During the course of separation the fuel assemblies and other components in the reactor's core become intensely radioactive. This irradiated material has been described as a million to a billion times more toxic than any known industrial agent. Some 200 radioactive isotopes are produced as by-products of reactor operation, and the amount of just one of them alone, strontium-90, contained in a reactor of even modest—100–200 megawatt—size is equal to that produced in the explosion of a bomb 190 times more powerful than the one dropped on Hiroshima.

Huge concentrations of radioactive material are also to be found in facilities that support atomic power plants. Because the intense radioactivity in a reactor core eventually interferes with the fuel's efficiency, the fuel assemblies must be removed from time to time and replaced by new, uncontaminated ones. The old ones are shipped to reprocessing plants where the contaminants are separated from the salvageable fuel. The ferociously radioactive liquid containing the contaminants must be neutralized, disposed of, or stored until it is no longer dangerous. Thus reprocessing plants and storage areas are immense repositories of "hot" and "dirty" material. Furthermore, transportation routes between power plants and re-processing facility and waste storage site, carry traffic bearing high quantities of that material.

Even from this glimpse it will be apparent that public and en-vironmental safety depend on the flawless containment of radio-activity every step of the way. For, owing to the incredible potency of this energy, even the slightest leakage is harmful—and a massive release would be catastrophic. The fundamental question, then, is how heavily can we rely on human wisdom, care and engineering to hold this peril under absolute control?

Abundant evidence points to the conclusion that we cannot rely on it at all.

. . . .

For one thing, all of us are familiar with technological disasters which occurred against fantastically high odds: the sinking of the "unsinkable" Titanic, or the collision of two big passenger planes over the enormity of the Grand Canyon. The November 9, 1965, "blackout" of the U.S. eastern seaboard illustrates how an "in-credible" event can occur in the electric utility field, most experts agreeing that the chain of circumstances which brought it about was so improbable that the odds against it defy calculation.

A disturbing number of reactor accidents have occurred—with sheer luck playing an important part in averting catastrophe— which seem to be the product of "incredible" coincidences. On October 10, 1957, for instance, the Number One Pile at the Wind-scale Works in England had a breakdown spewing fission products over so much territory that authorities had to seize all milk and growing food-stuffs in a 400-square-mile area around the plant.

A British report on the incident stated that all of the reactor's containment features had failed. It challenges credulity, but it happened. Much closer to home, a meltdown of fuel in the Fermi reactor in Lagoona Beach, Mich., in October, 1966, came within an ace of turning into a nuclear "runaway" eventuating in the explosive release of radioactive material.

. . . .

It has been estimated that a ton of processed fuel will produce from forty to several hundred gallons of waste. This substance is a violently lethal mixture of short- and long-lived isotopes. It would take five cubic miles of water to dilute the waste from just one ton of fuel to a safe concentration. Or, if we permitted it to decay naturally until it reached the safe level—and the word "safe" is used advisedly—just one of the isotopes, strontium-90, would still be too hot to handle 1000 years from now, when it will have only one seventeen-billionth of its current potency.

There is no known way to reduce the toxicity of these isotopes; they must decay naturally, meaning virtually perpetual containment.

Unfortunately, mankind has exhibited little skill in making

perpetual creations and procedures for handling radioactive wastes leave everything to be desired. The most common practice is to store the concentrates in large steel tanks shielded by earth and concrete. This method has been employed for some twenty years, and over 75 million gallons of waste is now in storage in about 200 tanks. This "liquor" generates so much heat it boils by itself for years.

Most of the inventory in these cauldrons is waste from weapons production, but as we approach the year 2000 the accumulation from commercial nuclear power will soar. Dr. Donald R. Chadwick, chief of the Division of Radiological Health of the US Public Health Service, estimated in 1963 that the accumulated volume would come to two billion gallons by 1995.

It is not just the volume that fills one with sickening apprehension, but the ugly disposition of this material. David Lilienthal put his finger on the crux of the matter when he stated: "These huge quantities of radioactive wastes must somehow be removed from the reactors, must—without mishap—be put into containers that will never rupture; then these vast quantities of poisonous stuff must be moved either to a burial ground or to reprocessing and concentration plants, handled again, and disposed of, by burial or otherwise, with a risk of human error at every step."

The burden that radioactive wastes place on future generations is cruel and may prove intolerable. Joel A. Snow, writing in "Scientists and Citizen," stated it well when he wrote: "Over periods of hundreds of years it is impossible to ensure that society will remain responsive to the problems created by the legacy of nuclear waste which we have left behind."

"Legacy" is one way of stating it, but "curse" seems far more appropriate, for at the very least we are saddling our children and their descendants with perpetual custodianship of our atomic refuse, and at worst may be dooming them to the same gruesome afflictions and agonizing deaths suffered by those who survived Hiroshima's fireball.

127.

Gordon Rattray Taylor

THE THREAT TO LIFE IN THE SEA [1970]

Thor Heyerdahl, of Kon-Tiki fame, has said that he and his companions, in journeying across the Atlantic in their reed boat, could not fill their tooth mugs from the ocean, hundreds of miles from the American coast, because of the filthy condition of the water.

The oceans are filling up with junk and assorted poisons. Man is dumping into the oceans, or into the rivers that flow into the oceans, many thousands of products, the biological effects of which are in most instances unknown. These include oil, chemical effluents, heavy metals, trace elements, dry-cleaning fluids, radio-active wastes, chemical warfare gases and irritants, detergents, pesticides, and innumerable other substances. In fact, practically everything we throw away in liquid form reaches the sea, except a few things that decompose rapidly, while much of what we discharge into the air also descends eventually into the sea. It is reckoned that we now add a half-million different substances to the sea.

Lead, which is pumped into the atmosphere by motor vehicles using fuels spiked with tetraethyl lead to raise the octane number, is now present in the Pacific—an area remote from those in which cars are mostly used—at about ten times the natural level. Even in the Arctic snows, lead is present at seven times the natural level. These levels have been rising ever since tetraethyl lead first was introduced forty-five years ago; by the end of the century they may double.

Pesticides, such as DDT and dieldrin, are accumulating in the sea, as are various curious by-products of industry, whose very names are mysterious to all but the initiated—polychlorinated biphenyls, for example.

Again, the highly poisonous substance mercury is reaching the sea in ever increasing quantities: About half the world's total production reaches the oceans. Already the coastal waters of the Baltic Sea are polluted by it, and it is accumulating in the fish to the point where they are uneatable. Here I wish only to draw attention to the way we are changing the composition of the shallower parts of the sea—areas where most fish live. More than half the world's population depends solely on fish for a supply of essential protein.

A more serious threat may be radioactive wastes. Already, radioactivity can be detected in any fifty-gallon sample of sea water taken anywhere in the world. The U.S. Atomic Energy Commission (AEC) has been mixing low-level wastes with cement in eighteen-gauge steel drums (little more than cans) and dropping them in the Atlantic. Recently Spain complained of such dumping taking place only 200 miles from the Spanish and Portuguese coastline. The British, more economically, run a pipeline a mere two miles out to sea and claim that it is safe to discharge up to 100,000 curies a month by this means. The basis of this claim is obscure.

. . . .

The late Dr. Lloyd Berkner, who was president of the Graduate Research Center of the Southwest, wrote a paper a few months before his death in 1966 drawing attention to the fact that the world's supply of oxygen comes largely from the diatoms, the small free-floating plants which form the basic food of most fish.

Earth's oxygen would be used up in 2,000 years if not replenished by the photosynthetic activities of plants—that is, the process by which they make sugars from carbon dioxide and water in the atmosphere, a reaction powered by sunlight, giving off oxygen which they have split from the carbon dioxide. Seventy per cent of the new oxygen comes from diatoms, the rest from land vegetation. "If our pesticides should be reducing our supply of diatoms or forcing evolution of less productive mutants," he pointed out, "we *might find ourselves running out of oxygen.*" (The italics are Berkner's, not mine.) Since we know that fish are loaded with pesticides, it is absolutely certain that the diatoms are also, for this is how they get into the fish.

128.

David R. Zimmerman

DEATH COMES TO THE PEREGRINE FALCON [1970]

Last November 7, a week before the Federal Government restricted DDT and similar persistent poisons—which for 24 growing seasons since 1946 had been sprayed abundantly on the land—a group of hawk experts met at Cornell to plan new research on American birds of prey. Their meeting turned out to be the post-mortem conference on *Falco peregrinus anatum*, the bold, baleful, free-flying peregrine falcon, or duck hawk, that once bred on cliffsides across America. In 23 breeding seasons since 1947, when the first sign of disaster was seen, but misdiagnosed, the peregrine has become all but extinct as a breeding bird, outside Alaska. DDT, unquestionably, caused its demise.

This spring, all peregrine eyries in the East and in the Upper Mississippi Valley, where once the bird flourished, were empty. In the Rocky Mountains and Far West, less than 10 per cent of the prepesticide breeding population remains; these survivors' days are believed numbered, for vast residues of DDT remain in the soil and water. In all the U.S., excepting Alaska, perhaps a dozen, and certainly no more than two or three dozen, peregrine families mated, laid eggs and hatched and fledged their young this year. A few itinerant nonbreeding birds remain; two recently were spotted in New England. Peregrines that nest as far north as the Arctic tundra in Canada and Alaska are threatened by pesticides picked up on southward migrations. In all North America, only birds living on islands out in the Pacific remain relatively unaffected. Peregrines in England and Europe have also been severely stricken.

The birds are gone. And the evidence is at last all in. At just the moment DDT use finally was limited, the hawk experts meeting in Ithaca were able to assemble a full, detailed and experimentally reproducible scientific proof that accounts, precisely, for how pesticide destroyed the peregrines.

What is important about the peregrine, aside from its loss—which is a disaster—is the fact that it is the first chemically killed American bird for which documentation of *how* and *why* it died has been provided. This documentation provides so-called *hard* scientific evidence, heretofore lacking, against which one may test industrial, agricultural and governmental claims for other pesticides, often glibly alleged to be safe if used according to directions on the package.

. . . .

Because peregrines are almost impossible to breed in captivity, a related, breedable species, the sparrow hawk, was used. The experimental birds were given sublethal doses of DDT and dieldrin. In the first, and much more clearly in the second generation, their reproduction was impaired. Dosed birds laid about the same number of eggs as clean birds, but their eggs were from 8–17 per cent thinner. These eggs tended to disappear from the nests before they could hatch. "Egg disappearance probably was due to breakage of thin-shelled eggs and to eating of eggs or newly hatched young by parent birds," Porter and Wiemeyer say. Reproductive failure from thin eggs, which Ratcliffe had found in the wild, now had been neatly reproduced in the research station. There was more to come.

Other Patuxent investigators, using mallard ducks, found the specific chemical that caused the damage. They fed different groups of ducks three different chemicals: Some got DDT. Some got a related pesticide, DDD. And a third group got DDE, the DDT breakdown product, which had been found in large amounts in wildlife, but had not been carefully studied in reproductive tests.

The DDD caused slight reproductive loss, but not eggshell damage. Low doses of DDT—comparable to amounts a duck might pick up in normal feeding—also failed to impair reproduction or eggshell thickness. But high DDT doses thinned the shells, 18 per cent of which cracked. It also cut by a third the survival rate among live-born ducklings.

Since the DDT fed to ducks in part broke down to DDE, it was the experiment with this metabolite alone that was of differential importance. Both at high doses, and at the low dose of 10 parts per million, the DDE "severely impaired reproductive success"; the eggshells were 13 per cent thinner than normal duck eggs—and of course cracked readily. Some 25 per cent cracked; many that did not crack nevertheless failed to match. In one generation, 10 parts per million of dietary DDE reduced mallard duck breeding success by 75 per cent.

· ·

DDT's stanch defender, the U.S. Department of Agriculture, still resists the evidence. The issue of a total ban on DDT now is before the United States Court of Appeals for the District of Columbia, in a suit brought by environmentalists against the Secretary of Agriculture. The suit demands that a ban be imposed. In a brief explaining why it declines to follow the court's order to do so, U.S.D.A. says: "There is information which *suggests* that it [DDT] is interfering with the reproduction of certain species of raptorial birds and *may be* a contributor, among other factors, to the decline of some of these species." [Emphasis added.]

Nonetheless, the case linking DDT and the fall of the peregrine as cause and effect finally had been made, according to stringent scientific criteria. As then-H.E.W. chief Robert Finch read his announcement that the U.S. would ban all "nonessential" use of long-acting chlorinated hydrocarbon pesticides, and some others, ecologist [Joseph] Hickey declared the just published DDE study in mallard ducks to be "the final paper in the whole mosaic of research." Summing up the situation as it emerged at the post-mortem conference at Cornell, Hickey added: "Research on [U.S.] peregrine populations is finished—because there is not much more that can be done for it."

129.

Tom Wicker

DUMPING NERVE GAS [1970]

In all the remarkable circumstances of the nerve-gas affair, the least of the evils may be the Army's operation of shipping 3,000 tons of the deadly stuff thru seven southern states, to dump it in the ocean 283 miles off Florida. Even so, the gross offensiveness and latent risks of the scheme suggest what a mess the nation has got itself into.

· ·

As near as anyone can tell, the manufacture of this ghastly concoction was undertaken so mindlessly that, once it existed, there was no way to disarm or neutralize it.

The defense establishment simply stockpiled tons of the stuff, waiting to see what would turn up. When there began to be leaks—of gas, on the one hand; to the press, on the other—the gas rockets were enclosed in concrete vaults which had the dual flaw of neither preventing leakage nor allowing anyone to get at the rockets safely even if a way to neutralize their contents had been developed.

Finally alerted after 15 years to the obvious dangers of the situation, the Army cast about for something to do with all that GB.

It does no good to say that the New Jersey dumping of some of the gas several years ago was not protested; since then, environmental dangers have made a deep if belated impression on many people. The State Department can dismiss U Thant's protest, for instance, on legal grounds; it cannot dismiss the impact he, and the dumping of the gas, will make on the people of the world—perhaps literally.

Nor is it convincing when scientists assure us there is no danger from the dumping. It is conceded that they cannot know what effect it may have on the plant and animal life of the seas, even if there is no present danger to humans. When will we learn that life is of a piece, a vast and mysterious entanglement of species, and that what endangers one must have its ultimate effect on others? Who thought there was any "danger" to humans in dumping a little mercury into some big lakes?

The most frequently suggested alternative—an underground nuclear explosion to destroy the gas—may seem more sensible and "scientific," but it could well prove more lethal, too, as at least one example suggests. The hard truth is that, in such matters, all the consequences never can be foreseen.

130.

John Noble Wilford

PESTICIDE DEATH [1970]

Pink Hill, N.C., August 19—
After he planted his nine acres of tobacco this spring, Clarence Lee Boyette came to a store here to buy pesticides. He wanted something to kill the worms that can riddle tobacco leaves—something like DDT, which he had used for more years than he could recollect.

The man at the store suggested parathion because DDT could not be used on tobacco if a farmer wanted to qualify for Government price supports. Parathion went by the local trade name of "Big Bad John," and all the farm experts said it was a "sure-fire killer."

And so it was. No budworms or hornworms "worried" his crop, Mr. Boyette said. But his youngest son, Daniel, 7 years old, is dead. Another son, 11-year-old Curtis, barely escaped death. They were poisoned by parathion.

Several dozen other cases of serious parathion poisoning, mostly among young people, have occurred across this tobacco-growing state this summer. Doctors at Duke University's Poison Control Center report five fatalities since late July. State health officials are sure that at least two of the deaths came from exposure in sprayed tobacco fields.

Although parathion poisoning is not new, the deadly outbreak this year represents a classic case of what can happen in an environment-conscious society when one pesticide is replaced by another, less familiar one, such as parathion or related organic phosphates.

The problem with DDT is its durability. Being an extremely stable chemical, it can pass from field to animals to humans sometimes becoming more dangerous as its residues accumulate along the food chain.

Parathion decomposes fairly fast, but presents a more immediate threat. It is 300 times more toxic than DDT, for it is a member of the same chemical family as the nerve gas that the Army dumped in the Atlantic Ocean earlier this week.

Dr. Martin P. Hines, director of the epidemiology division of the North Carolina Board of Health, who is investigating the deaths, commented: "Only one thing I'm ready to say now is that parathion is too deadly a pesticide to be distributed without any type of control on it."

131.

Edwin L. Dale, Jr.

THE ECONOMICS OF POLLUTION [1970]

We can count on the output of the average worker to continue to rise in the years ahead, as it has in the past. Nearly all current forecasts put this rise in productivity much closer to 3 per cent than to 2, and 3 per cent has been our average in the years since World War II. So without any change in the labor force at all, our national output will go on rising by some 3 per cent a year.

What does output mean?

It means electric power produced—and smoke produced.

It means cans and bottles produced.

It means steel produced—and, unless something is done about it, water and air polluted.

It means paper produced—with the same result as for steel.

And so on and on.

But that is not the end, for there will not be a static labor force. As noted, the force for the next 20 years is already born and it is going to grow year by year (with a caveat, to be described below).

Obviously, we want to offer these people employment opportunity. So, in addition to a 3 per cent productivity growth, there will be an added growth of at least 1 per cent a year in the number of workers. The result is that we are almost "condemned" to a rise in our total output of 4 per cent a year. The only escape, it seems, would be a national decision either to have high unemployment or to try to be less efficient. Both are absurd on their face.

The law of economic growth says, then, that we already know that the national output in 1980 will be, and almost must be, some 50 per cent higher than it is now. President Nixon has said so publicly, and he is right. That is the result of an annual rate of real growth of about 4 per cent, compounded. It is terrifying. If an economy of $900-billion in 1969 produces the pollution and clutter we are all familiar with, what will an economy half again as large produce?

.   .   .   .

It is a fair question to ask: Why weren't we bothered about pollution 12 or 15 years ago? In October, 1957, to pick a date, the Soviet Union sent the first earth satellite into orbit. The American economy had just begun a recession that was to send unemployment to 7 per cent of the labor force. The late George Magoffin Humphrey, who had just resigned as Secretary of the Treasury, was warning of what he saw as vast Government spending, at that time $77-billion, and saying it would bring "a depression that would curl your hair." There were plenty of things to think about.

But nobody was worried about pollution. Conservation groups were properly bothered about parts of the wilderness (the Hell's Canyon Dam in Idaho, for example), but that was an entirely different thing. That was an issue of esthetics, not health. Nobody seemed to mention air pollution or waste that might overwhelm the space in which to put it. In a peculiarly sad irony, the late Adlai E. Stevenson had fought and lost an election against Dwight D. Eisenhower in 1956 partially on a "pollution" issue—radiation in the atmosphere from the explosion of atomic weapons.

The question, to repeat: Why didn't we worry about pollution then? The answer is that, relatively speaking, there was no pollution. Yes, there were electric power plants then, too. Yes, there were paper mills polluting streams. Yes, there were tin cans and paper and bottles. Some snowflakes, though we didn't know it, were already a bit black, and Pittsburgh got national attention because it tried to do some cleaning up.

But here we come to the law of compound interest. In 1957 —*only 13 years ago*—our gross national product was $453-billion. In 1969, in constant dollars, it was $728-billion. That is an increase of nearly $300-billion in tin cans, electric power, automobiles, paper, chemicals and all the rest. It is an increase of 60 per cent.

So what? That was not the result of an unnaturally rapid growth rate, though a bit more rapid than in some periods of our past. The *so what* is this: in the preceding 13 years the growth had been *only $100-billion*. We were the same nation, with the same energy, in those preceding 13 years. We invested and we had a rise both in productivity and in our labor force. But in the first 13 years of this example our output rose $100-billion, and in the second 13 it rose $300-billion.

In the next 13 it will rise more than $500-billion.

That is the law of compound interest. These are not numbers; they are tin cans and smoke and auto exhaust. There is no visible escape from it. Applying the same percentage growth to a larger base every year, we have reached the point where our growth in one year is half the total output of Canada, fully adjusting for inflation. Another dizzying and rather horrifying way of putting it is that the real output of goods and services in the United States has grown as much since 1950 as it grew in the entire period from the landing of the Pilgrims in 1620 up to 1950.

Part Three

THE FLAMING SWORD

> Therefore the Lord God sent [them] forth from the Garden of Eden . . . and He placed at the east of the garden . . . a flaming sword which turned every way, to keep the way of the tree of life.

For centuries, while most men either were too dazzled by material progress to see or to care about the violence done to nature by man and machine or were more than eager to rationalize it away as the perhaps unfortunate but bearable price exacted for the riches of technology, only a few spoke out against the general trend. And, though their numbers slowly grew over the years, they remained for the most part criers in the wilderness: It was both easy and customary to dismiss them as crackpots, agrarian snobs, arch conservatives, and enemies of progress generally. Eventually, as the destruction of nature shifted from what was for the majority the rather remote problem of resources depletion to the immediate and impossible-to-ignore threat of pollution, the ranks of those who were already at least to question the wisdom of unbridled exploitation of the earth swelled until the "environmental crisis" became a popular cause.

*   *   *

Part III is divided into three sections. The first, comprising Selections 132 through 172, is concerned with the idea of conservation, which can be defined most broadly as the attempt to adjust the manner and pace of the exploitation of natural resources to very long-term needs. The readings in this section exhibit the development of conservation from reactions against single problems or abuses—soil depletion, overforesting, wildlife-slaughtering—to a conception of systematic national planning in the allocation of resources. What makes this development of more than usual interest is the presence of a large region of ambiguity (centering, in the working definition above, in the word "needs"), which gives rise naturally to disagreements among allies. The devil's-advocate selection in this section is number 152, in which George L. Knapp bluntly dismisses the entire topic of conservation as nonsense. It is followed by a group of readings (Selections 153–56) all revolving around the same issue—the damming of the Hetch-Hetchy Valley in California— and illustrating the internecine sniping that can result when conservationists discover that they have different ideas of what constitutes conservation. Despite some notable successes, such as game protection (Selection 135) and the establishment of national parks (Selection 142) and wilderness preserves (Selection 162), the history of conservation is a bit dispiriting, as R. H. Fuller (Selection 148) in particular, points out. The last few readings (Selections 164 through 172) are contemporary with, and in some cases products of, the lately sprung-up "save the environment" movement; they are placed in this section instead of the next because of their tendency to be oriented to a single problem or to a closely connected string of problems.

The second section of Part III deals with ecology, in both the technical and the popular sense. The section is fairly short, comprising only fifteen readings (Selections 173 through 187), because ecology has only comparatively recently come to signify more than any other subdiscipline of biology, and it is for this reason, too, that most of the readings are of quite recent origin. A brief passage from Alexander Pope (Selection 173) and two nineteenth-century suggestions of the ecological viewpoint (Selections 174 and 175) precede a jump into the middle of the twentieth century and the beginning of a gradual assimilation of at least the notion of ecology into the public's awareness.

The final section considers the question of a "land ethic," which represents a radical change in attitude that would replace the idea of man's dominion over nature with that of his participation in it. Comprising Selections 188 through 194, the section is unhappily but necessarily brief. If a book of this sort may be said to have a climax, however, it is here, in Selection 192 by Aldo Leopold.

One last note on Part III: The James Madison of Selection 136 is indeed the U.S. President, though by 1818 he had been out of office for over a year. The intelligence of this reading may surprise some who expect only libraries from ex-Presidents.

THE STOPGAP APPROACH

132.

Francis Bacon

OF GARDENS [1625]

God Almighty first planted a Garden. And indeed it is the purest of human pleasures. It is the greatest refreshment to the spirits of man; without which buildings and palaces are but gross handyworks: and a man shall ever see that when ages grow to civility and elegancy, men come to build stately sooner than to garden finely; as if gardening were the greater perfection.

133.

John Ruskin

AN IDEALIST'S ARRAIGNMENT OF THE AGE [ca. 1879]

There are three material things, not only useful, but essential to life. No one "knows how to live" till he has got them.

These are pure air, water, and earth.

. . . .

Heaven gives you the main elements of these. You can destroy them at your pleasure, or increase, almost without limit, the available quantities of them.

You can vitiate the air by your manner of life and of death to any extent. You might easily vitiate it so as to bring such a pestilence on the globe as would end all of you. You or your fellows, German and French, are at present vitiating it to the best of your power in every direction—chiefly at this moment with corpses and animal and vegetable ruin in war, changing men, horses, and garden-stuff into noxious gas. But everywhere, and all day long, you are vitiating it with foul chemical exhalations; and the horrible nests, which you call towns, are little more than laboratories for the distillation into heaven of venomous smokes and smells, mixed with effluvia from decaying animal matter and infectious miasmata from purulent disease. On the other hand, your power of purifying the air, by dealing properly and swiftly with all substances in corruption, by absolutely forbidding noxious manufactures, and by planting in all soils the trees which cleanse and invigorate earth and atmosphere, is literally infinite. You might make every breath of air you draw, food.

Secondly, your power over the rain and river-waters of the earth is infinite. You can bring rain where you will, by planting wisely and tending carefully; drought where you will, by ravage of woods and neglect of the soil. You might have the rivers of England as pure as the crystal of the rock; beautiful in falls, in lakes, in living pools; so full of fish that you might take them out with your hands instead of nets. Or you may do always as you have done now—turn every river of England into a common sewer, so that you cannot so much as baptize an English baby but with filth, unless you hold its face out in the rain; and even *that* falls dirty.

Then for the third, earth, meant to be nourishing for you and blossoming. You have learned about it that there is no such thing as a flower; and as far as your scientific hands and scientific brains, inventive of explosive and deathful instead of blossoming and life-giving dust, can contrive, you have turned the Mother Earth, Demeter, into the Avenger-Earth, Tisiphone—with the voice of your brother's blood crying out of it in one wild harmony round all its murderous sphere.

· ·

I am not rich (as people now estimate riches), and great part of what I have is already engaged in maintaining art-workmen, or for other objects more or less of public utility. The tenth of whatever is left to me, estimated as accurately as I can (you shall see the accounts), I will make over to you in perpetuity, with the best security that English law can give, on Christmas Day of this year, with engagement to add the tithe of whatever I earn afterwards. Who else will help, with little or much? The object of such fund being to begin, and gradually—no matter how slowly—to increase, the buying and securing of land in England, which shall not be built upon, but cultivated by Englishmen with their own hands and such help of force as they can find in wind and wave. I do not care with how many or how few this thing is begun, nor on what inconsiderable scale—if it be but in two or three poor men's gardens. So much, at least, I can buy, myself, and give them. If no help come, I have done and said what I could, and there will be an end. If any help come to me, it is to be on the following conditions:

We will try to make some small piece of English ground beautiful, peaceful, and fruitful. We will have no steam-engines upon it, and no railroads; we will have no untended or unthought-of creatures on it; none wretched but the sick; none idle but the dead. We will have no liberty upon it, but instant obedience to known law and appointed persons; no equality upon it, but recognition of every betterness that we can find, and reprobation of every worseness. When we want to go anywhere, we will go there quietly and safely, not at forty miles an hour in the risk of our lives; when we want to carry anything anywhere, we will carry it either on the backs of beasts or on our own, or in carts or boats. We will have plenty of flowers and vegetables in our gardens, plenty of corn and grass in our fields—and few bricks. We will have some music and poetry; the children shall learn to dance to it and sing it; perhaps some of the old people, in time, may also. We will have some art, moreover; we will at least try if, like the Greeks, we can't make some pots. The Greeks used to paint pictures of gods on their pots. We, probably, cannot do as much; but we may put some pictures of insects on them, and reptiles—butterflies and frogs, if nothing better. There was an excellent old potter in France who used to put frogs and vipers into his dishes, to the admiration of mankind; we can surely put something nicer than that. Little by little, some higher art and imagination may manifest themselves among us, and feeble rays of science may dawn for us—botany, though too dull to dispute the existence of flowers; and history, though too simple to question the nativity of men; nay, even perhaps an uncalculating and uncovetous wisdom, as of rude Magi presenting, at such nativity, gifts of gold and frankincense.

134.

Peter Kalm

IN PHILADELPHIA [1753]

The fences and pales are generally made here of wooden planks and posts. But a few good economists, having already thought of sparing the woods for future times, have begun to plant quick hedges round their fields; and for this purpose they take the above-mentioned privet, which they plant in a little bank that is thrown up for it. The soil everywhere hereabouts is a clay mixed with sand and of course very loose. The privet hedges, however, are only suitable for keeping out domestic cattle and other such animals here, for the hogs all have a triangular yoke about their necks, and the other cattle are not very unruly. But in places where the latter seek to break through the fences, hedges of this kind make but a poor defence. The people who live in the neighborhood of Philadelphia are obliged to keep their hogs enclosed.

135.

BIRD PROTECTION [1818]

[The following selection is from an act of the Massachusetts legislature entitled "An Act to prevent the destruction of certain useful Birds at unseasonable times of the year." Approved on February 12, 1818, it was the earliest such law in the United States.]

WHEREAS there are within the Commonwealth, many birds which are useful and profitable to the citizens, either as articles of food, or as instruments in the hands of Providence to destroy various noxious insects, grubs and caterpillars, which are prejudicial or destructive to vegetation, fruits and grain; and it is desirable to promote the increase and preservation of birds of the above description, and to prevent the wanton destruction of them at improper seasons:

SEC. 1. *BE it enacted by the Senate and House of Representatives, in General Court assembled, and by the authority of the same,* That hereafter it shall not be lawful for any person to take, kill or destroy, any of the birds called partridges and quails, at any time from the first day of March, to the first day of September in every year; and no person shall take, kill or destroy, any of the birds called woodcocks, snipes, larks and robins, at any time from the first day of March to the fourth day of July in each year; and if any person shall take or kill, or shall sell, buy or have in his possession after being killed, or taken, any of the birds aforesaid, within the times limited as aforesaid respectively, he shall forfeit and pay for each and every partridge, quail, or woodcock, so taken, killed or in his possession, two dollars; and for each and every snipe, lark or robin, so killed, taken, or in his possession, one dollar. . . .

SEC. 2. *Be it further enacted*, That if any person shall shoot at or kill any of the birds aforesaid, or any other birds, upon lands not owned or occupied by himself, without license from the owner or occupant of such lands, at any time from the first day of March to the fourth day of July in each year, such person shall forfeit and pay to the occupant or owner of such lands, where he may shoot at, or kill such birds, ten dollars, as a penalty in addition to all other actual damages, to be recovered by the party injured, by an action of trespass, in any court having jurisdiction of the amount demanded: *Provided however*, that nothing in this act shall be construed to prevent the killing of crows, blackbirds, owls, blue jays, and hawks, at any season of the year.

136.

James Madison

INTELLIGENT HUSBANDRY [1818]

I shall venture on the task, a task the least difficult, of pointing out some of the most prevalent errors in our husbandry, and which appear to be among those which may merit the attention of the society, and the instructive examples of its members.

I. The error first to be noticed is that of cultivating land, either naturally poor or impoverished by cultivation. This error, like many others, is the effect of habit, continued after the reason for it has failed. Whilst there was an abundance of fresh and fertile soil, it was the interest of the cultivator to spread his labor over as great a surface as he could. Land being cheap and labor dear, and the land co-operating powerfully with the labor, it was profitable to draw as much as possible from the land. Labor is now comparatively cheaper and land dearer. Where labor has risen in price fourfold land has increased tenfold. It might be profitable, therefore, now to contract the surface over which labor is spread, even if the soil retained its freshness and fertility. But this is not the case. Much of the fertile soil is exhausted, and unfertile soils are brought into cultivation; and both cooperating less with labor in producing the crop, it is necessary to consider how far labor can be profitably exerted on them; whether it ought not to be applied towards making them fertile, rather than in further impoverishing them, or whether it might not be more profitably applied to mechanical occupations, or to domestic manufactures?

In the old countries of Europe, where labor is cheap and land dear, the object is to augment labor, and contract the space on which it is employed. In the new settlements taking place in this country, the original practice here may be rationally pursued. In the old settlements, the reason for the practice in Europe is becoming daily less inapplicable; and we ought to yield to the change of circumstances, by forbearing to waste our labor on land which, besides not paying for it, is still more impoverished, and rendered more difficult to be made rich. The crop which is of least amount, gives the blow most mortal to the soil. It has not been a very rare thing to see land under the plough, not producing enough to feed the ploughman and his horse; and it is in such cases that the death blow is given. The goose is killed, without even obtaining the coveted egg.

There cannot be a more rational principle in the code of agriculture, than that every farm which is in good heart should be kept so; that every one not in good heart should be made so; and that what is right as to the farm, generally, is so as to every part of every farm. Any system therefore, or want of system, which tends to make a rich farm poor, or does not tend to make a poor farm rich, cannot be good for the owner; whatever it may be for the tenant or superintendent, who has transient interest only in it. The profit, where there is any, will not balance the loss of intrinsic value sustained by the land.

II. The evil of pressing too hard upon the land, has also been much increased by the bad mode of ploughing it. Shallow ploughing, and ploughing up and down hilly land, have, by exposing the loosened soil to be carried off by rains, hastened more than any thing else, the waste of its fertility. When the mere surface is pulverized, moderate rains on land but little uneven, if ploughed up and down, gradually wear it away. And heavy rains on hilly land, ploughed in that manner, soon produce a like effect, notwithstanding the improved practice of deeper ploughing. How have the beauty and value of this red ridge of country suffered from this cause? And how much is due to the happy improvement introduced by a member of this society, whom I need not name.* by a cultivation in horizontal drills with a plough adapted to it? Had the practice prevailed from the first settlement of the country, the general fertility would have been more than the double of what the

* Col. T. M. Randolph.

red hills, and indeed all other hilly lands, now possess; and the scars and sores now defacing them would no where be seen. — Happily, experience is proving that this remedy, aided by a more rational management in other respects, is adequate to the purpose of healing what has been wounded, as well as of preserving the health of what has escaped the calamity. It is truly gratifying to observe how fast the improvement is spreading from the parent example. The value of our red hills, under a mode of cultivation which guards their fertility against wasting rains, is probably exceeded by that of no uplands whatever; and without that advantage they are exceeded in value by almost all others. They are little more than a lease for years.

Besides the inestimable advantage from horizontal ploughing, in protecting the soil against the wasting effect of rains, there is a great one in its preventing the rains themselves from being lost to the crop. The Indian corn is the crop which most exposes the soil to be carried off by the rains; and it is at the same time the crop which most needs them. Where the land is not only hilly, but the soil thirsty, (as is the case particularly throughout this mountainous range,) the preservation of the rain as it falls, between the drilled ridges, is of peculiar importance; and its gradual settling downwards to the roots, is the best possible mode of supplying them with moisture. In the old method of ploughing shallow, with the furrows up and down, the rain as well as the soil was lost.

III. The neglect of manures is another error which claims particular notice. It may be traced to the same cause with our excessive cropping. In the early stages of our agriculture, it was more convenient, and more profitable, to bring new land into cultivation, than to improve exhausted land. The failure of new land has long called for the improvement of old land; but habit has kept us deaf to the call.

Nothing is more certain than that continual cropping without manure, deprives the soil of its fertility. It is equally certain that fertility may be preserved or restored, by giving to the earth animal or vegetable manure equivalent to the matter taken from it; and that a perpetual fertility is not, in itself, incompatible with an uninterrupted succession of crops. The Chinese, it is said, smile at the idea, that land needs rest, as if like animals it had a sense of fatigue. Their soil does not need rest, because an industrious use is made of every fertilizing particle that can contribute towards replacing what has been drawn from it. And this is the more practicable with them, as almost the whole of what is grown on their farms is consumed within them. That a restoration to the earth of all that annually grows on it, prevents its impoverishment, is sufficiently seen in our forests, where the annual exuviae of the trees and plants replace the fertility of which they deprive the earth. Where frequent fires destroy the leaves and whatever else is annually dropped on the earth, it is well known that the land becomes poorer: this destruction of the natural crop, having the same impoverishing effect, as a removal of a cultivated crop. A still stronger proof that an animal restoration to the earth of all its annual product will perpetuate its productiveness, is seen where our fields are left uncultivated and unpastured. In this case the soil, receiving from the decay of the spontaneous weeds and grasses more fertility than they extract from it, is for a time at least improved, not impoverished. Its improvement may be explained, by the fertilizing matter which the weeds and grasses derive from water and the atmosphere, which forms a net gain to the earth. At what point, or from what cause, the formation and accumulation of vegetable mould from this gain ceases, is not perhaps very easy to be explained. That it does cease, is proved by the stationary condition of the surface of the earth in old forests; and that the amount of the accumulation varies with the nature of the subjacent earth, is equally certain. It seems to depend also on the species of trees and plants which happen to contribute the materials for the vegetable mould.

But the most eligible mode of preserving the richness, and of enriching the poverty of a farm, is certainly that of applying to the soil a sufficiency of animal and vegetable matter in a putrified state or a state ready for putrefaction; in order to procure which, too much care cannot be observed in saving every material furnished by the farm. This resource was among the earliest discoveries of men living by agriculture; and a proper use of it has been made a test of good husbandry, in all countries, ancient and modern, where its principles and profits have been studied.

. . . .

With so many consumers of the fertility of the earth, and so little attention to the means of repairing their ravages, no one can be surprized at the impoverished face of the country; whilst every one ought to be desirous of aiding in the work of reformation.

The first main step towards it, is to make the thieves restore as much as possible of the stolen fertility. On this, with other improvements which may be made in our husbandry, we must depend for the rescue of our farms from their present degraded condition.

137.

George Catlin [1832]

[George Catlin, an author and painter who was deeply interested in the American Indian, spent the years 1832–39 traveling in the West. In the selection below, from his published notes, he makes a proposal that, though ignored at the time, eventually became part of the national conservation policy—but only after the Great Plains had been put to the plow.]

Many are the rudenesses and wilds in Nature's works, which are destined to fall before the deadly axe and desolating hands of cultivating man; and so amongst her ranks of *living*, of beast and human, we often find noble stamps, or beautiful colours, to which our admiration clings; and even in the overwhelming march of civilised improvements and refinements do we love to cherish their existence, and lend our efforts to preserve them in their primitive rudeness. Such of Nature's works are always worthy of our preservation and protection; and the further we become separated (and the face of the country) from that pristine wildness and beauty, the more pleasure does the mind of enlightened man feel in recurring to those scenes, when he can have them preserved for his eyes and his mind to dwell upon.

. . . .

This strip of country, which extends from the province of Mexico to Lake Winnipeg on the North, is almost one entire plain of grass, which is, and ever must be, useless to cultivating man. It is here, and here chiefly, that the buffaloes dwell; and with, and hovering about them, live and flourish the tribes of Indians, whom God made for the enjoyment of that fair land and its luxuries.

It is a melancholy contemplation for one who has travelled as I have, through these realms, and seen this noble animal in all its pride and glory, to contemplate it so rapidly wasting from the world, drawing the irresistible conclusion too, which one must do, that its species is soon to be extinguished, and with it the peace and happiness (if not the actual existence) of the tribes of Indians who are joint tenants with them, in the occupancy of these vast and idle plains.

And what a splendid contemplation too, when one (who has travelled these realms, and can duly appreciate them) imagines them as they *might* in future be seen (by some great protecting policy of government) preserved in their pristine beauty and wildness, in a *magnificent park*, where the world could see for ages to come, the native Indian in his classic attire, galloping his wild horse, with sinewy bow, and shield and lance, amid the fleeting herds of elks and buffaloes. What a beautiful and thrilling specimen for America to preserve and hold up to the view of her refined citizens and the world, in future ages! A *nation's Park*, containing man and beast, in all the wild and freshness of their nature's beauty!

I would ask no other monument to my memory, nor any other enrolment of my name amongst the famous dead, than the reputation of having been the founder of such an institution.

138.

SOIL PRESERVATION [1850]

[This brief selection is an editorial from the Milledgeville, Georgia, *Federal Union* of April 23, 1850.]

Two questions present themselves: one is, could this desolation have been prevented? and the other, can it be repaired or modified? A few days since, in common with the great mass of agriculturists in Georgia, we should have answered both of these questions in the negative. A recent visit, however, to our friend Gen. Tarver in Twiggs County, and a minute examination of his plantations in the vicinity of his residence, have materially changed our opinion. His lands there are as hilly and broken as any of the table lands of Georgia; yet upon none cleared within the last few years was there a single gully or red hill to be seen, and what is more, none will ever be seen, as long as his present system is practiced. He has not only succeeded in rendering secure and permanent his fresh land, but has also taken fields abandoned by their former owners, and which are trenched by gullies thirty and twenty feet wide and as many deep, and whose hillsides have been too poor to yield the poorest grasses, and he is resuscitating and restoring them to a condition in which they will again be productive, filling up the gullies, and by a process that is as simple and economical as it is successful.

All who know Gen. Tarver, know that he is one of the largest and most successful planters in the South. He indulges in no theory that will not by its practical results commend itself. The system by which he has perfected such wonders is simply in his fresh lands so to conduct the water by trenches as to prevent washing, and in his old land so to conduct it as to accomplish this end and at the same time to repair the washes occasioned by the former rush of the water. Before we had examined Gen. Tarver's plantation we had read much about and seen something of, hillside ditches and circular plowing, but had no conception of what could be accomplished by either the one or the other. His successful experiments have enlisted the admiration of his neighbors and all who have noticed them. He has demonstrated the truth and practicability of the theory that he has practiced; and if, as it has been said, he is a public benefactor, who can cause two straws to grow where before but one grew, Gen. Tarver is entitled to that epitaph. None can visit his Twiggs plantation without being forcibly struck with what Georgia would now be, had her lands been tilled by such agriculturists, or what she would yet be, were they under the control of men of his energy and practical skill.

139.

Henry David Thoreau [1851]

[A recurring theme among lovers of and writers about nature—and a corollary to their major point—has been the importance for each individual of maintaining or renewing direct contact with the natural world. In "Walking," an essay written for a Lyceum lecture, Thoreau broached an idea that the reader will encounter again and again in subsequent selections.]

The West of which I speak is but another name for the Wild; and what I have been preparing to say is, that in Wildness is the preservation of the World. Every tree sends its fibres forth in search of the Wild. The cities import it at any price. Men plow and sail for it. From the forest and wilderness came the tonics and barks which brace mankind. Our ancestors were savages. The story of Romulus and Remus being suckled by a wolf is not a meaningless fable. The founders of every state which has risen to eminence have drawn their nourishment and vigor from a similar wild source. It was because the children of the Empire were not suckled by the wolf that they were conquered and displaced by the children of the northern forests who were.

I believe in the forest, and in the meadow, and in the night in which the corn grows. We require an infusion of hemlock spruce or arborvitæ in our tea. There is a difference between eating and drinking for strength and from mere gluttony. The Hottentots eagerly devour the marrow of the koodoo and other antelopes raw, as a matter of course. Some of our northern Indians eat raw the marrow of the Arctic reindeer, as well as various other parts, including the summits of the antlers, as long as they are soft. And herein, perchance, they have stolen a march on the cooks of Paris. They get what usually goes to feed the fire. This is probably better than stall-fed beef and slaughter-house pork to make a man of. Give me a wildness whose glance no civilization can endure—as if we lived on the marrow of koodoos devoured raw.

There are some intervals which border the strain of the wood thrush, to which I would migrate—wild lands where no settler has squatted; to which, methinks, I am already acclimated.

The African hunter Cumming tells us that the skin of the eland, as well as that of most other antelopes just killed, emits the most delicious perfume of trees and grass. I would have every man so much like a wild antelope, so much a part and parcel of nature, that his very person should thus sweetly advertise our senses of his presence, and remind us of those parts of nature which he most haunts. I feel no disposition to be satirical, when the trapper's coat emits the odor of musquash even; it is a sweeter scent to me than that which commonly exhales from the merchant's or the scholar's garments. When I go into their wardrobes and handle their vestments, I am reminded of no grassy plains and flowery meads which they have frequented, but of dusty merchants' exchanges and libraries rather.

. . . .

Life consists with wildness. The most alive is the wildest. Not yet subdued to man, its presence refreshes him. One who pressed forward incessantly and never rested from his labors, who grew fast and made infinite demands on life, would always find himself in a new country or wilderness, and surrounded by the raw material of life. He would be climbing over the prostrate stems of primitive forest-trees.

140.

George Perkins Marsh [1864]

[George Perkins Marsh's *Man and Nature* (later retitled *The Earth as Modified by Human Action*) has been called the fountainhead of conservationism in America. Certainly it was alone in its time, and for some decades remained practically so, in offering a general view of man's effects on nature and of the need not only for remedal action but for a revision of outlook as well.]

In fine, in countries untrodden by man, the proportions and relative positions of land and water, the atmospheric precipitation and evaporation, the thermometric mean, and the distribution of vegetable and animal life, are subject to change only from geological influences so slow in their operation that the geographical conditions may be regarded as constant and immutable. These arrangements of nature it is, in most cases, highly desirable substantially to maintain, when such regions become the seat of organized commonwealths. It is, therefore, a matter of the first importance, that, in commencing the process of fitting them for permanent civilized occupation, the transforming operations should be so conducted as not unnecessarily to derange and destroy what, in too many cases, it is beyond the power of man to rectify or restore.

In reclaiming and reoccupying lands laid waste by human improvidence or malice, and abandoned by man, or occupied only by a nomade or thinly scattered population, the task of the pioneer settler is of a very different character. He is to become a co-worker with nature in the reconstruction of the damaged fabric which the negligence or the wantonness of former lodgers has rendered untenantable. He must aid her in reclothing the mountain slopes with forests and vegetable mould, thereby restoring the fountains which she provided to water them; in checking the devastating fury of torrents, and bringing back the surface drainage to its primitive narrow channels; and in drying deadly morasses by opening the natural sluices which have been choked up, and cutting new canals for drawing off their stagnant waters. He must thus, on the one hand, create new reservoirs, and, on the other, remove mischievous accumulations of moisture, thereby equalizing and regulating the sources of atmospheric humidity and of flowing water, both which are so essential to all vegetable growth, and, of course, to human and lower animal life.

.   .   .   .

The earth is fast becoming an unfit home for its noblest inhabitants, and another era of equal human crime and human improvidence, and of like duration with that through which traces of that crime and that improvidence extend, would reduce it to such a condition of impoverished productiveness, of shattered surface, of climatic excess, as to threaten the depravation, barbarism, and perhaps even extinction of the species.

True, there is a partial reverse to this picture. On narrow theatres, new forests have been planted; inundations of flowing streams restrained by heavy walls of masonry and other constructions; torrents compelled to aid, by depositing the slime with which they are charged, in filling up lowlands, and raising the level of morasses which their own overflows had created; ground submerged by the encroachments of the ocean, or exposed to be covered by its tides, has been rescued from its dominion by diking; swamps and even lakes have been drained, and their beds brought within the domain of agricultural industry; drifting coast dunes have been checked and made productive by plantation; seas and inland waters have been repeopled with fish, and even the sands of the Sahara have been fertilized by artesian fountains. These achievements are more glorious than the proudest triumphs of war, but, thus far, they give but faint hope that we shall yet make full atonement for our spendthrift waste of the bounties of nature.

It is, on the one hand, rash and unphilosophical to attempt to set limits to the ultimate power of man over inorganic nature, and it is unprofitable, on the other, to speculate on what may be accomplished by the discovery of now unknown and unimagined natural forces, or even by the invention of new arts and new processes. But since we have seen aerostation, the motive power of elastic vapors, the wonders of modern telegraphy, the destructive explosiveness of gunpowder, and even of a substance so harmless, unresisting, and inert as cotton, nothing in the way of mechanical achievement seems impossible, and it is hard to restrain the imagination from wandering forward a couple of generations to an epoch when our descendants shall have advanced as far beyond us in physical conquest, as we have marched beyond the trophies erected by our grandfathers.

. . . .

Could this old world, which man has overthrown, be rebuilded, could human cunning rescue its wasted hillsides and its deserted plains from solitude or mere nomade occupation, from barrenness, from nakedness, and from insalubrity, and restore the ancient fertility and healthfulness of the Etruscan sea coast, the Campagna and the Pontine marshes, of Calabria, of Sicily, of the Peloponnesus and insular and continental Greece, of Asia Minor, of the slopes of Lebanon and Hermon, of Palestine, of the Syrian desert, of Mesopotamia and the delta of the Euphrates, of the Cyrenaica, of Africa proper, Numidia, and Mauritania, the thronging millions of Europe might still find room on the Eastern continent, and the main current of emigration be turned toward the rising instead of the setting sun.

. . . .

Comparatively short as is the period through which the colonization of foreign lands by European emigrants extends, great, and, it is to be feared, sometimes irreparable, injury has been already done in the various processes by which man seeks to subjugate the virgin earth; and many provinces, first trodden by the *homo sapiens Europæ* within the last two centuries, begin to show signs of that melancholy dilapidation which is now driving so many of the peasantry of Europe from their native hearths. It is evidently a matter of great moment, not only to the population of the states where these symptoms are manifesting themselves, but to the general interests of humanity, that this decay should be arrested, and that the future operations of rural husbandry and of forest industry, in districts yet remaining substantially in their native condition, should be so conducted as to prevent the widespread mischiefs which have been elsewhere produced by thoughtless or wanton destruction of the natural safeguards of the soil. This can be done only by the diffusion of knowledge on this subject among the classes that, in earlier days, subdued and tilled ground in which they had no vested rights, but who, in our time, own their woods, their pastures, and their ploughlands as a perpetual possession for them and theirs, and have, therefore, a strong interest in the protection of their domain against deterioration.

141.

Frederick Law Olmsted

TREES IN TOWNS [1870]

It must be within the observation of most of us that where, in the city, wheel-ways originally twenty feet wide were with great difficulty and cost enlarged to thirty, the present width is already less nearly adequate to the present business than the former was to the former business; obstructions are more frequent, movements are slower and oftener arrested, and the liability to collision is greater. The same is true of sidewalks. Trees thus have been cut down, porches, bow-windows, and other encroachments removed, but every year the walk is less sufficient for the comfortable passing of those who wish to use it.

It is certain that as the distance from the interior to the circumference of towns shall increase with the enlargement of their population, the less sufficient relatively to the service to be performed will be any given space between buildings.

In like manner every evil to which men are specially liable when living in towns, is likely to be aggravated in the future, unless means are devised and adapted in advance to prevent it.

Let us proceed, then, to the question of means, and with a seriousness in some degree befitting a question, upon our dealing with which we know the misery or happiness of many millions of our fellow-beings will depend.

We will for the present set before our minds the two sources of wear and corruption which we have seen to be remediable and therefore preventible. We may admit that commerce requires that in some parts of a town there shall be an arrangement of buildings, and a character of streets and of traffic in them which will establish conditions of corruption and of irritation, physical and mental. But commerce does not require the same conditions to be maintained in all parts of a town.

Air is disinfected by sunlight and foliage. Foliage also acts mechanically to purify the air by screening it. Opportunity and inducement to escape at frequent intervals from the confined and vitiated air of the commercial quarter, and to supply the lungs with air screened and purified by trees, and recently acted upon by sunlight, together with opportunity and inducement to escape from conditions requiring vigilance, wariness, and activity toward other men,—if these could be supplied economically, our problem would be solved.

In the old days of walled towns all tradesmen lived under the roof of their shops, and their children and apprentices and servants sat together with them in the evening about the kitchen fire. But now that the dwelling is built by itself and there is greater room, the inmates have a parlor to spend their evenings in; they spread carpets on the floor to gain in quiet, and hang drapery in their windows and papers on their walls to gain in seclusion and beauty. Now that our towns are built without walls, and we can have all the room that we like, is there any good reason why we should not make some similar difference between parts which are likely to be dwelt in, and those which will be required exclusively for commerce?

Would trees, for seclusion and shade and beauty, be out of place, for instance, by the side of certain of our streets? It will, perhaps, appear to you that it is hardly necessary to ask such a question, as throughout the United States trees are commonly planted at the sides of streets. Unfortunately they are seldom so planted as to have fairly settled the question of the desirableness of systematically maintaining trees under these circumstances. In the first place, the streets are planned, wherever they are, essentially alike. Trees are planted in the space assigned for sidewalks, where at first, while they are saplings, and the vicinity is rural or suburban, they are not much in the way, but where, as they grow larger, and the vicinity becomes urban, they take up more and more space, while space is more and more required for passage. That is not all. Thousands and tens of thousands are planted every year in a manner and under conditions as nearly certain as possible either to kill them outright, or to so lessen their vitality as to prevent their natural and beautiful development, and to cause premature decrepitude. Often, too, as their lower limbs are found inconvenient, no space having been provided for trees in laying out the street, they are deformed by butcherly amputations. If by rare good fortune they are suffered to become beautiful, they still stand subject to be condemned to death at any time, as obstructions in the highway.

What I would ask is, whether we might not with economy make special provision in some of our streets—in a twentieth or a fiftieth part, if you please, of all—for trees to remain as a permanent furniture of the city? I mean, to make a place for them in which they would have room to grow naturally and gracefully. Even if the distance between the houses should have to be made half as much again as it is required to be in our commercial streets, could not the space be afforded? Out of town space is not costly when measures to secure it are taken early. The assessments for benefit where such streets were provided for, would, in nearly all cases, defray the cost of the land required. The strips of ground reserved for the trees, six, twelve, twenty feet wide, would cost nothing for paving or flagging.

The change both of scene and of air which would be obtained by people engaged for the most part in the necessarily confined interior commercial parts of the town, on passing into a street of this character after the trees had become stately and graceful, would be worth a good deal. If such streets were made still broader in some parts, with spacious malls, the advantage would be increased. If each of them were given the proper capacity, and laid out with laterals and connections in suitable directions to serve as a convenient trunk-line of communication between two large districts of the town or the business centre and the suburbs, a very great number of people might thus be placed every day under influences counteracting those with which we desire to contend.

142.

YELLOWSTONE NATIONAL PARK [1872]

[The Washburn-Doane expedition into the Yellowstone Valley in 1870 was followed by a publicity campaign that resulted in the creation of the first national park by means of the following act, passed by Congress on March 1, 1872.]

Be it enacted by the Senate and House of Representatives of the United States of America in Congress assembled, That the tract of land in the Territories of Montana and Wyoming, lying near the head-waters of the Yellowstone river, and described as follows, to wit, commencing at the junction of Gardiner's river with the Yellowstone river, and running east to the meridian passing ten miles to the eastward of the most eastern point of Yellowstone lake; thence south along said meridian to the parallel of latitude passing ten miles south of the most southern point of Yellowstone lake; thence west along said parallel to the meridian passing fifteen miles west of the most western point of Madison lake; thence north along said meridian to the latitude of the junction of the Yellowstone and Gardiner's rivers; thence east to the place of beginning, is hereby reserved and withdrawn from settlement, occupancy, or sale under the laws of the United States, and dedicated and set apart as a public park or pleasuring-ground for the benefit and enjoyment of the people; and all persons who shall locate or settle upon or occupy the same, or any part thereof, except as hereinafter provided, shall be considered trespassers and removed therefrom.

SEC. 2. That said public park shall be under the exclusive control of the Secretary of the Interior, whose duty it shall be, as soon as practicable, to make and publish such rules and regulations as he may deem necessary or proper for the care and management of the same. Such regulations shall provide for the preservation, from injury or spoliation, of all timber, mineral deposits, natural curiosities, or wonders within said park, and their retention in their natural condition. The secretary may in his discretion, grant leases for building purposes for terms not exceeding ten years, of small parcels of ground, at such places in said park as shall require the erection of buildings for the accommodation of visitors; all of the proceeds of said leases, and all other revenues that may be derived from any sources connected with said park, to be expended under his direction in the management of the same, and the construction of roads and bridle-paths therein. He shall provide against the wanton destruction of the fish and game found within said park, and guard against their capture or destruction for the purposes of merchandise or profit. He shall also cause all persons trespassing upon the same after the passage of this act to be removed therefrom, and generally shall be authorized to take all such measures as shall be necessary or proper to fully carry out the objects and purposes of this act.

143.

R. S. Elliott

FOREST TREES IN KANSAS [1873]

The present population of the State will soon consume all the timber in it. The same process is going on in other States. If we are to have no reproduction here and elsewhere, there must soon be a general want without supply. The natural increase of our people, and the immigration that will continue to come, will hasten the period of destitution.

Let any man in Kansas ask himself, where is the pine lumber of the future to be sought? The region of the lakes and the Upper Mississippi will be stripped before the babe of to-day will reach the age to vote. In the pineries of Missouri and Arkansas, where all was original wildness but a few years ago, the railroad is extending and the hum of the saw-mill is heard. The pineries of the States east and south-east tell the same tale. Not only must the pine lumber to supply Kansas come from distant points, with heavy freight charges, but distance and charges will increase, and it must also have the enhanced cost due to increasing scarcity where produced. The supplies cannot, to any considerable extent, come from the West. The forests of Wyoming and New Mexico are too distant. Colorado will soon need all her timber for agricultural and mining industries, which are rapidly extending, and for growing cities and multiplying railroads. Kansas must therefore grow her own pines, or substitutes for them, to save her people from a future drain of their earnings beyond computation.

. . . .

The thrifty farmer, by devoting a part of his land and labor to forest culture, if he can manage to plant but one acre a year, will be adding to the value of his estate, and establishing a source of future income beyond any estimate he is likely to make. He need not mortgage his farm, or borrow money on note of hand, in order to begin the work. A little extra exertion, a little vigorous effort, and he will have a beginning made. The honest pride which he and his family will feel as his trees grow, will coöperate with the certainty of profit to brace him up in further efforts in this direction.

Farmers having native wood on their land, can with profit imitate the landowners and foresters of Europe, by making it a rule to plant one or more trees for every one they remove. In France and Germany, the utmost care is taken to have continued succession of forest growth, and the same rule is observed in England and Scotland. The importance of this rule cannot be too strongly urged on the farmers of Kansas, particularly those on the edges of the prairie districts.

In Europe men of capital plant timber as an investment, assured that nothing will pay a better and more certain interest. In the United States the day has perhaps not yet arrived for this to be done on a large scale. Capital, especially in the West, is yet comparatively scarce and dear; and so many opportunities present themselves to realize immediate returns, that a smaller near profit is apt to be preferred to a greater remote one. Besides, the whole subject of forest culture is so new in our country, that we need not wonder that the attention of capital has not been turned to it. Scarce ten years have elapsed since the prospective exhaustion of the forests, and the consequent timber famine that impends over us, has become the subject of earnest discussion. Great movements require time to organize themselves, and so it is with forest-planting by monied men.

. . . .

In truth, forest culture has not yet so possessed the general mind as to have produced results of much consequence, so far as actual tree-planting is concerned. Compared with what ought to be done, the work so far accomplished is small; but compared with what had been done a few years ago, it is large. It is a great deal to have made a beginning, and we have learned much to aid future efforts.

144.

[*From Appleton's Journal*]

SPARE THE TREES [1876]

An immense field for useful effort in this direction is open for every local community, and for every individual landholder. With little effort, not only every village street but every highway might in a few years be bordered and shaded by trees. It was wise advice which the old

Laird of Dambiedikes gave to his son: "Be aye putting in a tree; it will be growing while ye are sleeping." This one sentence is said to have been worth millions to Scotland by turning the attention of landlords to the subject; and it is good advice here as well as there. Wherever on your farm is a rocky knoll, unavailable for plough or scythe, put in a tree and let it grow. Wherever on a hillside or by a spring there is a clump of trees, preserve them as the apple of your eye. A keen axe in a stout woodman's hand will in an hour destroy what it has taken a century to produce, and what a century cannot replace. A few cords of wood are indeed worth something; but not so much as an ever-flowing fountain.

In nearly every part of our settled states one of the most pressing needs is that of more trees. Plant them then in every spot not needed for other uses. Above all things, spare every fine tree now growing. Spare the trees! Not merely the one particular tree which sheltered you in childhood, and which you have so solemnly vowed to protect, but a great many other trees—every tree for the destruction of which you cannot show good and sufficient reason. Spare them not merely from the reason that a fine tree is one of the most beautiful works of Nature, although that is a good and valid reason; but also for the far higher reason of the duty which you owe posterity. Science is beginning to lift up her warning voice and tell us how manifold are the relations which forests bear to human welfare. History has taught us, and observation and experience are still teaching us, that our woodlands stand between the death and the life of a land; that their destruction surely, and by no means slowly, will bring about the decay of fertility, and the consequent desolation of the fairest portions of the earth's surface.

145.

Carl Schurz [1889]

[The following is from "The Need of a Rational Forest Policy," a speech delivered before the American Forestry Association and the Pennsylvania Forestry Association in Philadelphia on October 15, 1889.]

The gentleman who introduced me did me the honor of mentioning the attention I devoted to this subject years ago as Secretary of the Interior. When I entered upon that important office, having the public lands in charge, I considered it my first duty to look around me and to study the problems I had to deal with. Doing so I observed all the wanton waste and devastation I have described. I observed the notion that the public forests were everybody's property, to be taken and used or wasted as anybody pleased, everywhere in full operation. I observed enterprising timber thieves not merely stealing trees, but stealing whole forests. I observed hundreds of sawmills in full blast, devoted exclusively to the sawing up of timber stolen from the public lands.

I observed a most lively export trade going on from Gulf ports as well as Pacific ports, with fleets of vessels employed in carrying timber stolen from the public lands to be sold in foreign countries, immense tracts being devastated that some robbers might fill their pockets.

I thought that this sort of stealing was wrong, in this country no less than elsewhere. Moreover, it was against the spirit and letter of the law. I, therefore, deemed it my duty to arrest that audacious and destructive robbery. Not that I had intended to prevent the settler and the miner from taking from the public lands what they needed for their cabins, their fields or their mining shafts; but I deemed it my duty to stop at least the commercial depredations upon the property of the people. And to that end I used my best endeavors and the means at my disposal, scanty as they were.

What was the result? No sooner did my attempts in that direction become known, than I was pelted with telegraphic despatches from the regions most concerned, indignantly inquiring what it meant that an officer of the Government dared to interfere with the legitimate business of the country! Members of Congress came down upon me, some with wrath in their eyes, others pleading in a milder way, but all solemnly protesting against my disturbing their constituents in this peculiar pursuit of happiness. I persevered in the performance of my plain duty. But when I set forth my doings in my annual report and asked Congress for rational forestry legislation, you should have witnessed the sneers at the outlandish notions of this "foreigner" in the Interior Department; notions that, as was said, might do for a picayunish German principality, but were altogether contemptible when applied to this great and free country of ours. By the way, some of the gentlemen who sneered so greatly might learn some lessons from those picayunish German principalities, which would do them much good. I recently revisited my native land and saw again some of the forests I had known in my younger days—forests which in the meantime had yielded to their owners or to the Government large revenues from the timber cut, but were now nevertheless as stately as they had been before, because the cutting had been done upon rational principles and the forests had been steadily improved by scientific cultivation. I passed over a large tract I had known as a barren heath, the heath of Luneburg, which formerly, as the saying was, sustained only the "Heidschnucken," a species of sheep as little esteemed for their wool as their mutton—the same heath now covered with a dense growth of fine forest. Instead of sneering, our supercilious scoffers would do better for themselves as well as for the country if they devoted their time a little more to study-ing and learning the valuable lessons with which the experience of other countries abounds.

What the result of my appeals was at the time I am speaking of, you know. We succeeded in limiting somewhat the extent of the depredations upon the public forests, and in bringing some of the guilty parties to justice. A few hundred thousand dollars were recovered for timber stolen, but the recommendations of rational forestry legislation went for nothing. Some laws were indeed passed, but they appeared rather to favor the taking of timber from the public lands than to stop it. Still, I persevered, making appeal after appeal, in public and in private, but I found myself standing almost solitary and alone. Deaf was Congress, and deaf the people seemed to be. Only a few still voices rose up here and there in the press in favor of the policy I pursued.

Thank Heaven, the people appear to be deaf no longer. It is in a great measure owing to your wise and faithful efforts that the people begin to listen, and that in several States practical steps have already been taken in the right direction.

146.

Alpheus Hyatt

CITY PARKS [1891]

It is while this complex growth of a city is going on that sanitary precaution and a due regard for the health and recreation of an increasing popula-tion demand more and larger spaces in the forest of chimneys than those furnished by the playgrounds of the early days; and in due time these considerations become so pressing that more or less extensive parks are planned and laid out. Although the rivalry of cities or the generosity of individuals may sometimes lead to an early provision for such open spaces in our newer centres of population, the park is really one of the latest signs of civilization.

It is only after we have grown familiar with what museums can do that we arrive at any hearty appreciation of what Nature can also do for us, if we will wait upon her; and thus at last it comes about that no city can claim a high place until it has actually inclosed and guarded a good bit of the open country.

147.

John Muir

THE WILD PARKS AND FOREST RESERVATIONS OF THE WEST [1898]

The tendency nowadays to wander in wildernesses is delightful to see. Thousands of tired nerve-shaken, over-civilized people are beginning to find out that going to the mountains is going home; that wildness is a necessity; and that mountain parks and reservations are useful not only as fountains of timber and irrigating rivers, but as fountains of life. Awakening from the stupefying effects of the vice of over-industry and the deadly apathy of luxury, they are trying as best they can to mix and enrich their own little ongoings with those of Nature, and to get rid of rust and disease. Briskly venturing and roaming, some are washing off sins and cobweb cares of the devil's spinning in all-day storms on mountains; sauntering in rosiny pinewoods or in gentian meadows, brushing through chaparral, bending down and parting sweet, flowery sprays; tracing rivers to their sources, getting in touch with the nerves of Mother Earth; jumping from rock to rock, feeling the life of them, learning the songs of them, panting in whole-souled exercise and rejoicing in deep, long-drawn breaths of pure wildness. This is fine and natural and full of promise. And so also is the growing interest in the care and preservation of forests and wild places in general, and in the half-wild parks and gardens of towns. Even the scenery habit in its most artificial forms, mixed with spectacles, silliness, and kodaks; its devotees arrayed more gorgeously than scarlet tanagers, frightening the wild game with red umbrellas,—even this is encouraging, and may well be regarded as a hopeful sign of the times.

All the Western mountains are still rich in wildness, and by means of good roads are being brought nearer civilization every year. To the sane and free it will hardly seem necessary to cross the continent in search of wild beauty, however easy the way, for they find it in abundance wherever they chance to be. Like Thoreau they see forests in orchards and patches of huckleberry brush, and oceans in ponds and drops of dew. Few in these hot, dim, frictiony times are quite sane or free; choked with care like clocks full of dust, laboriously doing so much good and making so much money, —or so little,—they are no longer good themselves.

When, like a merchant taking a list of his goods, we take stock of our wildness, we are glad to see how much of even the most destructible kind is still unspoiled. Looking at our continent as scenery when it was all wild, lying between beautiful seas, the starry sky above it, the starry rocks beneath it, to compare its sides, the East and the West, would be like comparing the sides of a rainbow. But it is no longer equally beautiful. The rainbows of to-day are, I suppose, as bright as those that first spanned the sky; and some of our landscapes are growing more beautiful from year to year, notwithstanding the clearing, trampling work of civiliza-tion. New plants and animals are enriching woods and gardens, and many landscapes wholly new, with divine sculpture and architec-ture, are just now coming to the light of day as the mantling folds of creative glaciers are being withdrawn, and life in a thousand cheerful, beautiful forms is pushing into them, and new-born rivers are beginning to sing and shine in them. The old rivers, too, are growing longer like healthy trees, gaining new branches and lakes as the residual glaciers at their highest sources on the mountains recede, while their rootlike branches in their flat deltas are at the same time spreading farther and wider into the seas and making new lands. . . .

Man, too, is making many far-reaching changes. This most influen-tial half animal, half angel is rapidly multiplying and spreading, covering the seas and lakes with ships, the land with huts, hotels, cathedrals, and clustered city shops and homes, so that soon, it would seem, we may have to go farther than Nansen to find a good sound solitude. None of Nature's landscapes are ugly so long as they are wild; and much, we can say comfortingly, must always be in great part wild, particularly the sea and the sky, the floods of light from the stars, and the warm, unspoilable heart of the earth, infinitely beautiful, though only dimly visible to the eye of imagina-tion. The geysers, too, spouting from the hot underworld; the steady, long-lasting glaciers on the mountains, obedient only to the sun; Yosemite domes and the tremendous grandeur of rocky cañons and mountains in general,—these must always be wild, for man can change them and mar them hardly more than can the butterflies that hover above them.

. . . .

The wildest health and pleasure grounds accessible and available to tourists seeking escape from care and dust and early death are the parks and reservations of the West. There are four national parks,—the Yellowstone, Yosemite, General Grant, and Sequoia,—

all within easy reach, and thirty forest reservations, a magnificent realm of woods, most of which, by railroads and trails and open ridges, is also fairly accessible, not only to the determined traveler rejoicing in difficulties, but to those (may their tribe increase) who, not tired, not sick, just naturally take wing every summer in search of wildness. The forty million acres of these reserves are in the main unspoiled as yet, though sadly wasted and threatened on their more open margins by the axe and fire of the lumberman and prospector, and by hoofed locusts, which, like the winged ones, devour every leaf within reach, while the shepherds and owners set fires with the intention of making a blade of grass grow in the place of every tree, but with the result of killing both the grass and the trees.

. . . .

These grand reservations should draw thousands of admiring visitors at least in summer, yet they are neglected as if of no account, and spoilers are allowed to ruin them as fast as they like. A few peeled spars cut here were set up in London Philadelphia, and Chicago, where they excited wondering attention; but the countless hosts of living trees rejoicing at home on the mountains are scarce considered at all. Most travelers here are content with what they can see from car windows or the verandas of hotels, and in going from place to place cling to their precious trains and stages like wrecked sailors to rafts. When an excursion into the woods is proposed, all sorts of dangers are imagined,—snakes, bears, Indians. Yet it is far safer to wander in God's woods than to travel on black highways or to stay at home. The snake danger is so slight it is hardly worth mentioning. Bears are a peaceable people, and mind their own business, instead of going about like the devil seeking whom they may devour. Poor fellows, they have been poisoned, trapped, and shot at until they have lost confidence in brother man, and it is not now easy to make their acquaintance. As to Indians, most of them are dead or civilized into useless innocence. No American wilderness that I know of is so dangerous as a city home "with all the modern improvements." One should go to the woods for safety, if for nothing else.

148.

R. H. Fuller [1906]

[It is often thought that, once a conservation problem is recognized and public support is marshaled, the solution ought to follow rather simply. The episode in New York State outlined in this selection argues against such a view. Involving, as it does, vested interests as well as questions of morality, health, and aesthetics, the fight for conservation is more often than not a long and difficult battle of wits.]

It happened that for years the State had been a large owner of Adirondack land. Before the exhaustion of other sources of supply forced the lumber and pulp men to turn in that direction, these tracts were of so little value that many owners neglected to pay their taxes upon them, the lands were sold at tax sales, and the State brought them in. It became possessed in this way of hundreds of thousands of acres which it did not want, and which it disposed of as rapidly as possible to private owners. It was the custom of lumbermen to cut over a tract, and when they had taken what they wanted, to permit it to be sold for taxes. When the young trees had grown sufficiently to make them valuable, application would be made upon some pretense or technicality for a cancellation of the sale, which the State readily granted.

It was not until 1883 that the State was induced to adopt the policy of retaining all the lands that came into its possession, and it was the first State thus to undertake, although in an incomplete and tentative way, the preservation of its forests. Two years later a Forest Commission was placed in charge of the lands, and in 1890 the State had advanced so far that it began to make small appropriations for the purchase of additional tracts. By that time their value had been established and was increasing so rapidly that owners paid their taxes, and there was no longer any chance of acquiring new areas through tax sales. A State Forest Preserve was created to include all the lands belonging to the State in the Adirondack and Catskill counties, and it was made the duty of the Forest Commission "to maintain and protect the forests now on the forest preserve, and to promote as far as practicable the further growth of forests thereon."

There was comparatively little opposition at first to the new policy of the State. A supply of timber for the mills was still in sight. But as this supply rapidly dwindled, the lumber and pulp men began to covet the timber that was "going to waste" on the lands that the people had bought and paid for. They set about to get possession of this timber, and a struggle then began between the destroyers rendered desperate by the exhaustion of their raw material, and the people as represented by officials who, when not secretly enlisted as allies of the enemy, were often negligent or indifferent.

The lumbermen and the owners of the pulp mills wield great influence in the forest counties. They are usually men of wealth. Their great mills give employment to entire communities whose prosperity depends upon them. The native population is in sympathy with them. It looks upon the forests as its natural means of gaining a livelihood. It cannot understand why a tree should be allowed to grow after it is large enough for the saw or the pulp mill. It sees the mountain sides still clothed with forests, and it believes that it has a "vested right" to cut them, and that not even the State ought to forbid.

With this strong local support the lumber and pulp men went into politics. It is true that they were competitors among themselves, and that some of them were Republicans while others were Democrats; but to get at the forests they sunk their own rivalries and made common cause against the State. They sat in conventions and aided in nominating officials who would stretch a point of law in their favor. They sent their representatives to the Legislature and had them appointed upon the committees which frame the forestry laws. They bribed the men appointed by the State to protect the forest domain from them. What was probably worst of all, they began to urge the adoption of a system of "scientific forestry," based ostensibly upon the methods of the German states.

In the first enthusiasm for forest preservation, its advocates held out the hope that the State preserves might be farmed as they were in Germany, and thus be made to produce a constant revenue. The idea seemed reasonable. The Legislature passed a law in 1893 giving the Forest Commission power "to sell the standing spruce, tamarack, and poplar timber, the fallen timber, and the timber injured by blight or fire." The species named in the law were exactly the species that the pulp men wanted, and they congratulated themselves upon their foresight in sending representatives to the Legislature to look out for their interests. They became more earnest advocates of "scientific forestry" than ever.

Of course, under the law of 1893, they had no difficulty in buying State timber practically at their own prices; but a German forester would have been driven to despair at the way in which the supposed "scientific" principles of treatment were applied. The standing timber was sold under contract; the lumbermen came on and left behind them the usual devastated firetrap. The forest area continued to shrink.

Realizing at last that so long as they temporized with the destroyers they would continue to be tricked, swindled, and robbed, the people finally lost patience. Their real interest in the preservation of the forests was sentimental rather than commercial. They saw that "scientific forestry" as practiced by the lumber and pulp men and their allies was a sham, and they determined to raise a barrier which could not be evaded by faithless officials or dishonest lawmakers. So in 1894 they inserted in the Constitution of the State the following clause:

"The lands of the State, now owned or hereafter acquired, constituting teh forest preserve as now fixed by law, shall be forever kept as wild forest lands. They shall not be leased, sold, or exchanged, or be taken by any corporation, public or private, nor shall the timber thereon be sold, removed, or destroyed."

This prohibition seemed clear and explicit enough. It meant "Hands off!" to the lumber and pulp men. It meant that upon the lands of the State the forest should be permitted to grow as it grew before the *Half Moon* sailed up the Hudson, and that not so much as a twig, alive or dead, should be sold under any pretense or removed from the spot where nature had placed it. Let us see what happened.

The law provided that "trespassers" upon State forest lands—which means timber thieves—should be subject to a heavy money penalty for every tree cut by them and also to imprisonment. The State officials who were charged with the duty of enforcing this law and its penalties proceeded very much as though the forestry amendment to the Constitution never had been adopted. They arbitrarily adopted the policy of actually permitting the pulp men, as "trespassers," to remove the timber from lands that had been burned over, arguing that as the trees would die they might as well be put to some use. The pulp men were not slow to take the hint. They trespassed freely upon the State preserve and cheerfully compromised the penalties that they had incurred under the law by paying the market value of the timber, estimated by measurement of the stumps or of the logs themselves. The law directed the confiscation of stolen timber, but the officials evaded the necessity of enforcing this requirement by taking care not to find the trespass until the timber had been safely removed. It has been proved that at least some of the official protectors of the forests were in the pay of the pulp men, receiving a percentage of the value of the stolen property, very much as a policeman collects "graft" from the illegal gains of lawbreakers whom he protects.

It was the unconcealed practice of selling the State's timber from burned lands that caused the greatest injury to the forests. Fires became alarmingly frequent notwithstanding the elaborate precautions taken by the State to prevent them. The temptation was great. Imagine a hundred idle men living in a region where they knew they could get employment if there were only timber to be cut. They saw plenty of timber growing upon State land, but it could be cut from burned tracts only. It was no wonder that forest fires occurred. They burned over areas of sufficient size and value in some instances to warrant the pulp men in making formal contracts with lumbermen to cut over the burned State tracts and to deliver the logs. Winter camps were established and scores of men went to work. That was what the Constitution amounted to between the pulp men and the officials.

. . . .

The state had another experience with "scientific forestry," which did great harm because it engendered distrust of the system and helped to bring it into disrepute. The idea of managing the forests so as to make them yield a revenue at least sufficient to pay for their protection, appealed to many persons. It seemed inevitable that a definite plan of sylviculture must be adopted if the timber was to be preserved, but there were very few in this country who had studied European methods and knew how to do it. Therefore when the suggestion was made that the State ought to charter and support a School of Forestry as a part of Cornell University, it met with approval. Such an institution, it was urged, would graduate young men equipped with knowledge of how to preserve the forest lands and at the same time turn them to account.

Accordingly the Legislature of 1897 passed an act creating the New York State College of Forestry, and directed that a tract of thirty thousand acres should be purchased in the Adirondacks for its use. The college was made a part of the university, which, in the language of the act, was authorized to "conduct upon said land such experiments in forestry as it may deem advantageous to the interests of the State and the advancement of the science of forestry," and to "plant, raise, cut, and sell timber at such times, of such species and quantities, and in such manner as it may deem best, with a view to obtaining and imparting knowledge concerning the scientific management and use of the forests, their regulation and administration, the production, harvesting, and reproduction of wood crops and earning a revenue therefrom."

This seemed so praiseworthy a purpose that nobody thought of asking whether the law did not violate at least the spirit of the constitutional prohibition against the cutting of timber on lands purchased by the State within the forest preserve. The university selected a tract of 30,000 acres in the heart of the woods, and the Forest Preserve Board bought it for $165,000 out of an appropriation of $500,000 for the purchase of additional forest lands.

Unfortunately the director selected to conduct the college held radical theories. He was impatient of the German method of cutting only so much of the forest annually as the annual natural growth of the forest would replace. "There is no need to adhere to this principle," he said, "and to waste money and energy in finding out what the future growth will be. Let the next generation count the chickens for which we have secured the opportunity of development, favoring the better breeds." In accordance with these ideas, the director adopted the simple plan of cutting down all the trees, burning the land over to remove the *débris*, setting out seedlings and leaving them to grow up.

His first care was to find a market for the standing timber on the college tract. This he conceived to be "the pivotal point of the whole problem." The college, therefore, made a fifteen-year contract with the Brooklyn Cooperage Company, a concern formed to supply barrels to the Sugar Trust, under which the college bound itself to furnish the company each year a large amount of material at a stated price. The contract called for a clean sweep of the forest. The lumbermen and even the pulp men left something behind them, but the cooperage company used all the material above eight inches in diameter in making barrels, and what remained, down to a diameter of three inches, was utilized in producing wood alcohol!

This remarkable contract involved the denudation of much larger areas than the college could hope to replant. In effect, it was a simple agreement to sell to the cooperage company all the timber on the 30,000-acre tract. The result was that the forest was completely destroyed and the amount of replanting done was so insignificant as to be ridiculous. The records indicate the quality of the "science" of forestry inculcated by the college. One of the two serious fires that occurred in the woods in 1904 was started by the college manager. Two hundred acres had been cut over to supply the cooperage company with material. The dead treetops and branches had been permitted to remain where they fell. Early in May, when the law forbids the burning of brush in the woods, the manager set fire to the tract for the purpose of clearing it. The flames ran into the growing timber, and scores of men were required to subdue them. The manager was arrested and fined $200.

As soon as the State found out that the college was not only a dismal failure but that it was actually promoting the destruction that it had been created to prevent, appropriations for its support were cut off and it was suppressed. Legal proceedings were begun to break the agreement between the State and the university, so as to recover the 30,000-acre tract with what remained of the timber, and make it a part of the forest preserve. The cooperage company thereupon appealed to the courts to enforce its contract with the university and to permit it to continue cutting the timber. This suit is still pending.

149.

Theodore Roosevelt [1907]

[Theodore Roosevelt was the first U.S. President to take a position of active leadership in conservation. His interest in the cause had two quite different sources: As an avid outdoorsman, he had a deep love of wild, open country and a comprehension of the need to preserve some portion of it; at the same time, as an opponent of the concentration of unbridled power in huge business organizations, he fought their depredations on all fronts, including that of the natural environment. These selections are from his seventh annual message to Congress, delivered on December 3, 1907.]

The conservation of our natural resources and their proper use constitute the fundamental problem which underlies almost every other problem of our National life. We must maintain for our civilization the adequate material basis without which that civilization can not exist. We must show foresight, we must look ahead. As a nation we not only enjoy a wonderful measure of present prosperity but if this prosperity is used aright it is an earnest of future success such as no other nation will have. The reward of foresight for this Nation is great and easily foretold. But there must be the look ahead, there must be a realization of the fact that to waste, to destroy, our natural resources, to skin and exhaust the land instead of using it so as to increase its usefulness, will result in undermining in the days of our children the very prosperity which we ought by right to hand down to them amplified and developed. For the last few years, through several agencies, the Government has been endeavoring to get our people to look ahead and to substitute a planned and orderly development of our resources in place of a haphazard striving for immediate profit. . . .

Irrigation should be far more extensively developed than at present, not only in the States of the Great Plains and the Rocky Mountains, but in many others, as, for instance, in large portions of the South Atlantic and Gulf States, where it should go hand in hand with the reclamation of swamp land. The Federal Government should seriously devote itself to this task, realizing that utilization of waterways and water-power, forestry, irrigation, and the reclamation of lands threatened with overflow, are all interdependent parts of the same problem. The work of the Reclamation Service in developing the larger opportunities of the western half of our country for irrigation is more important than almost any other movement. The constant purpose of the Government in connection with the Reclamation Service has been to use the water resources of the public lands for the ultimate greatest good of the greatest number; in other words, to put upon the land permanent home-makers, to use and develop it for themselves and for their children and children's children. There has been, of course, opposition to this work; opposition from some interested men who desire to exhaust the land for their own immediate profit without regard to the welfare of the next generation, and opposition from honest and well-meaning men who did not fully understand the subject or who did not look far enough ahead. This opposition is, I think, dying away, and our people are understanding that it would be utterly wrong to allow a few individuals to exhaust for their own temporary personal profit the resources which ought to be developed through use so as to be conserved for the permanent common advantage of the people as a whole.

. . . .

Some such legislation as that proposed is essential in order to preserve the great stretches of public grazing land which are unfit for cultivation under present methods and are valuable only for the forage which they supply. These stretches amount in all to some 300,000,000 acres, and are open to the free grazing of cattle, sheep, horses and goats, without restriction. Such a system, or lack of system, means that the range is not so much used as wasted by abuse. As the West settles the range becomes more and more over-grazed. Much of it can not be used to advantage unless it is fenced, for fencing is the only way by which to keep in check the owners of nomad flocks which roam hither and thither, utterly destroying the pastures and leaving a waste behind so that their presence is incompatible with the presence of home-makers. . . .

Optimism is a good characteristic, but if carried to an excess it becomes foolishness. We are prone to speak of the resources of this country as inexhaustible; this is not so. The mineral wealth of the country, the coal, iron, oil, gas, and the like, does not reproduce itself, and therefore is certain to be exhausted ultimately; and wastefulness in dealing with it to-day means that our descendants will feel the exhaustion a generation or two before they otherwise would.

150.

THE NATIONAL CONSERVATION COMMISSION [1909]

[In 1908, as part of his conservation program, President Theodore Roosevelt called a governors' conference on the topic, one result of which was the appointment of the National Conservation Commission under the chairmanship of forestry expert Gifford Pinchot. The following selections are from the beginning of the Commission's report.]

The duty of man to man, on which the integrity of nations must rest, is no higher than the duty of each generation to the next; and the obligation of the nation to each actual citizen is no more sacred than the obligation to the citizen to be, who, in turn, must bear the nation's duties and responsibilities.

In this country, blessed with natural resources in unsurpassed profusion, the sense of responsibility to the future has been slow to awaken. Beginning without appreciation of the measure or the value of natural resources other than land with water for commercial uses, our forefathers pushed into the wilderness and, through a spirit of enterprise which is the glory of the nation, developed other great resources. Forests were cleared away as obstacles to the use of the land; iron and coal were discovered and developed, though for years their presence added nothing to the price of the land; and through the use of native woods and metals and fuels, manufacturing grew beyond all precedent, and the country became a power among the nations of the world.

Gradually the timber growing on the ground and the iron and coal within the ground came to have a market value and were bought and sold as sources of wealth. Meanwhile, vast holdings of these resources were acquired by those of greater foresight than their neighbors before it was generally realized that they possessed value in themselves; and in this way large interests, assuming monopolistic proportions, grew up, with greater enrichment to their holders than the world had seen before, and with the motive of immediate profit, with no concern for the future or thought of the permanent benefit of country and people, a wasteful and profligate use of the resources began and has continued.

The waters, at first recognized only as aids to commerce in supplying transportation routes, were largely neglected. In time this neglect began to be noticed, and along with it the destruction and approaching exhaustion of the forests. This, in turn, directed attention to the rapid depletion of the coal and iron deposits and the misuse of the land.

The public conscience became awakened. Seeing the increased value and noting the destructive consumption and waste of the natural resources, men began to realize that the permanent welfare of the country as well as the prosperity of their offspring were at stake.

. . . .

In the growth of the country and gradual development of the natural resources there have been three noteworthy stages. The first stage was that of individual enterprise for personal and family benefit. It led to the conquest of the wilderness.

The next stage was that of collective enterprise, either for the benefit of communities or for the profit of individuals forming the communities. It led to the development of cities and States, and too often to the growth of great monopolies.

The third stage is the one we are now entering. Within it the enterprise is collective and largely cooperative, and should be directed toward the larger benefit of communities, States, and the people generally.

In the first stage the resources received little thought. In the second they were wastefully used. In the stage which we are entering wise and beneficial uses are essential, and the checking of waste is absolutely demanded.

. . . .

The wastes which most urgently require checking vary widely in character and amount. The most reprehensible waste is that of destruction, as in forest fires, uncontrolled flow of gas and oil, soil wash, and abandonment of coal in the mines. This is attributable, for the most part, to ignorance, indifference, or false notions of economy, to rectify which is the business of the people collectively.

Nearly as reprehensible is the waste arising from misuse, as in the consumption of fuel in furnaces and engines of low efficiency, the loss of water in floods, the employment of ill-adapted structural materials, the growing of ill-chosen crops, and the perpetuation of inferior stocks of plants and animals, all of which may be remedied.

Reprehensible in less degree is the waste arising from nonuse. Since the utilization of any one resource is necessarily progressive and dependent on social and industrial conditions and the concurrent development of other resources, nonuse is sometimes unavoidable. It becomes reprehensible when it affects the common welfare and entails future injury. Then, it should be rectified in the general interest.

For the prevention of waste the most effective means will be found in the increase and diffusion of knowledge, from which is sure to result an aroused public sentiment demanding prevention. The people have the matter in their own hands. They may prevent or limit the destruction of resources and restrain misuse through the enactment and enforcement of appropriate state and federal laws.

At every stage in the growth of our country, strong men grew stronger through the exercise of nation building, and their intelligence and patriotism grew with their strength. The spirit and vigor of our people are the chief glory of the republic. Yet even as we have neglected our natural resources, so have we been thoughtless of life and health. Too long have we overlooked that grandest of our resources, human life. Natural resources are of no avail without men and women to develop them, and only a strong and sound citizenship can make a nation permanently great. We can not too soon enter on the duty of conserving our chief source of strength by the prevention of disease and the prolongation of life.

Wastes reduced and resources saved are the first but not the last objective of conservation. The material resources have an additional value when their preservation adds to the beauty and habitability of the land. Ours is a pleasant land in which to dwell. To increase its beauty and augment its fitness can not but multiply our pleasure in it and strengthen the bonds of our attachment.

151.

Gifford Pinchot [1910]

[If any man was more closely identified with the great conservation movement of the early 1900's than Theodore Roosevelt, it was Gifford Pinchot, chief of the Bureau of Forestry (later the Forest Service) and the President's principal adviser on conservation. Through his work,

his writings, and even the controversies he raised, he led the way
in awakening the country to the dangers it faced from the unwise
use of the land's resources. The following selection is from *The
Fight for Conservation.*]

The central thing for
which Conservation stands is to make this country the best possible place to live in, both for us and for our descendants. It
stands against the waste of the natural resources which cannot be
renewed, such as coal and iron; it stands for the perpetuation of
the resources which can be renewed, such as the food-producing
soils and the forests; and most of all it stands for an equal opportunity for every American citizen to get his fair share of benefit
from these resources, both now and hereafter.

Conservation stands for the same kind of practical common-sense
management of this country by the people that every business man
stands for in the handling of his own business. It believes in
prudence and foresight instead of reckless blindness; it holds that
resources now public property should not become the basis for
oppressive private monopoly; and it demands the complete and
orderly development of all our resources for the benefit of all the
people, instead of the partial exploitation of them for the benefit
of a few. It recognizes fully the right of the present generation to
use what it needs and all it needs of the natural resources now
available, but it recognizes equally our obligation so to use what
we need that our descendants shall not be deprived of what they
need.

Conservation has much to do with the welfare of the average
man of to-day. It proposes to secure a continuous and abundant
supply of the necessaries of life, which means a reasonable cost of
living and business stability. It advocates fairness in the distribution of the benefits which flow from the natural resources. It will
matter very little to the average citizen, when scarcity comes and
prices rise, whether he can not get what he needs because there is
none left or because he can not afford to pay for it. In both cases
the essential fact is that he can not get what he needs. Conservation holds that it is about as important to see that the people in
general get the benefit of our natural resources as to see that there
shall be natural resources left.

Conservation is the most democratic movement this country has
known for a generation. It holds that the people have not only the
right, but the duty to control the use of the natural resources, which
are the great sources of prosperity. And it regards the absorption
of these resources by the special interests, unless their operations
are under effective public control, as a moral wrong. Conservation
is the application of common-sense to the common problems for the
common good, and I believe it stands nearer to the desires, aspira-

tions, and purposes of the average man than any other policy now before the American people.

. . . .

We are beginning to realize that the Conservation question is a question of right and wrong, as any question must be which may involve the differences between prosperity and poverty, health and sickness, ignorance and education, well-being and misery, to hundreds of thousands of families. Seen from the point of view of human welfare and human progress, questions which begin as purely economic often end as moral issues. Conservation is a moral issue because it involves the rights and the duties of our people—their rights to prosperity and happiness, and their duties to themselves, to their descendants, and to the whole future progress and welfare of this Nation.

152.

George L. Knapp

ANOTHER VIEW [1910]

I propose to speak for those exiles in sin who hold that a large part of the present "conservation" movement is unadulterated humbug. That the modern Jeremiahs are as sincere as was the older one, I do not question. But I count their prophecies to be baseless vaporings, and their vaunted remedy worse than the fancied disease. I am one who can see no warrant of law, of justice, nor of necessity for that wholesale reversal of our traditional policy which the advocates of "conservation" demand. I am one who does not shiver for the future at the sight of a load of coal, nor view a steel-mill as the arch-robber of posterity. I am one who does not believe in a power trust, past, present or to come; and who, if he were a capitalist seeking to form such a trust, would ask nothing better than just the present conservation scheme to help him. I believe that a government bureau is the worst imaginable landlord; and that its essential nature is not changed by giving it a high-sounding name, and decking it with home-made haloes. I hold that the present forest policy ceases to be a nuisance only when it becomes a curse.

[Although the conservation movement that swept the United States at the beginning of the twentieth century grew so quickly as almost to be classed as a fad, it became apparent rather early that it was not a united front. The movement comprised two distinct schools of thought that, while they could agree and cooperate on very general principles, inevitably clashed at the brass-tack level. One—the "official" school of Roosevelt and Pinchot—was, as we have seen, dedicated to conservation in a narrow sense: conservation as a rationally programed use of resources and public development of power sites, mineral and timber lands, and potential agricultural areas. The other—better termed the "preservationist" school of John Muir—was principally interested in the saving of landscape and wildlife from all development, however and by whomever. The contest was between the scientifically managed tree farm and the wilderness preserve, between efficiency and aesthetics.

After several minor skirmishes, the conflict burst out in full-scale warfare over the Hetch-Hetchy Valley of Yosemite National Park. In 1906, after two earlier attempts had failed, the city of San Francisco again applied to the Department of the Interior for permission to dam Hetch-Hetchy and create a reservoir for the city's water supply system. The Department's approval aroused the preservationists, and they launched a publicity campaign for reversal. The developers joined the fray in the nation's journals, and the debate, more often than not vituperative, dragged on until the reservoir was finally approved by Congress and President Woodrow Wilson in 1913.

The following four selections, spanning almost five years of the controversy, are presented together in order to illustrate the kinds of argumentation a specific conservation-development conflict usually evokes and to underscore the fact that conservation is one of those topics about which honest men can and typically do disagree.]

153.

John Muir [1908]

[This selection is from a letter written by John Muir to President Theodore Roosevelt on April 21, 1908. The two had camped together in Yosemite five years earlier (a fact alluded to elsewhere in the letter), and Muir was confident that Roosevelt would stop the proposed dam. The President, personally torn by the schism in the conservation movement, reluctantly sided with Gifford Pinchot, however, and gave the go-ahead.]

I am anxious that the Yosemite National Park may be saved from all sorts of commercialism and marks of man's work other than the roads, hotels, etc., required to make its wonders and blessings available. For as far as I have seen there is not in all the wonderful Sierra, or indeed in the world, another so grand and wonderful and useful a block of Nature's mountain handiwork.

There is now under consideration, as doubtless you well know, an application of San Francisco supervisors for the use of the Hetch-Hetchy Valley and Lake Eleanor as storage reservoirs for a city water supply. This application should, I think, be denied, especially the Hetch-Hetchy part, for this Valley, as you will see by the inclosed description, is a counterpart of Yosemite, and one of the most sublime and beautiful and important features of the Park, and to dam and submerge it would be hardly less destructive and deplorable in its effect on the Park in general than would be the damming of Yosemite itself. For its falls and groves and delightful camp-grounds are surpassed or equaled only in Yosemite, and furthermore it is the hall of entrance to the grand Tuolumne Cañon, which opens a wonderful way to the magnificent Tuolumne Meadows, the focus of pleasure travel in the Park and the grand central camp-ground. If Hetch-Hetchy should be submerged, as proposed, to a depth of one hundred and seventy-five feet, not only would the Meadows be made utterly inaccessible along the Tuolumne, but this glorious cañon way to the High Sierra would be blocked.

I am heartily in favor of a Sierra or even a Tuolumne water supply for San Francisco, but all the water required can be obtained from sources outside the Park, leaving the twin valleys, Hetch-Hetchy and Yosemite, to the use they were intended for when the Park was established.

. . . .

These sacred mountain temples are the holiest ground that the heart of man has consecrated, and it behooves us all faithfully to do our part in seeing that our wild mountain parks are passed on unspoiled to those who come after us, for they are national properties in which every man has a right and interest.

154.

Lyman Abbott

SAVE YOSEMITE [1909]

Far be it from
The Outlook to say that San Francisco should not be given the
opportunity to wash and dress itself properly and drink a moderate
amount of pure water. The point we wish to make here is that if
its drinking water is to be kept pure, it means that the Hetch-
Hetchy Water Company must eventually be given practical supervision of at least half of the Yosemite National Park. We have
neither the knowledge nor the time to go into details of rainfall,
watershed topography, or bacteriological chemistry, but we do
know that if a municipal water-works is permitted to erect its
plant in the Hetch-Hetchy Valley, it means that the Yosemite Park
will become the back yard of a great municipal utility instead of a
recreation ground for all the people of the country.

The Outlook says this with full recognition of the fact that
Mr. Garfield, Secretary of the Interior, and Mr. Pinchot, the National Forester, men of the highest character, most unselfishly
devoted to National welfare on the highest plane, and experts in
the matter of National resources and National parks, have both
approved the project of turning the Hetch-Hetchy Valley into a
San Francisco reservoir. . . .

If this country were in danger of habitually ignoring utilitarian
practice for the sake of running after sentimental dreams and
aesthetic visions, we should advise it to cut down the California
big trees to shelter its citizens from the weather, and to dam the
Tuolumne River in order to instruct its citizens in the use of the
bathtub. But the danger is all the other way. The National habit
is to waste the beauty of nature and save the dollars of business.

155.

James D. Phelan

DAM HETCH-HETCHY [1909]

[James D. Phelan, a former mayor of San Francisco, understandably minimizes the aesthetic value of the valley and emphasizes the needs of the people of his city.]

The Hetch-Hetchy is one of a dozen mountain gorges, and, while beautiful, it is not unique. It is accessible over difficult trails about three months during the year, and few ever visit it. The Yosemite Valley satisfies every craving for large numbers of tourists, and the State of California, a few years ago, freely ceded this Valley to the Federal Government, and at the same time purchased a great redwood forest in the interest of forest preservation. California would not countenance the desecration of any of her scenery, and yet the State Legislature, now in session, has unanimously petitioned Congress to pass this bill. President Roosevelt, Secretary Garfield, Forester Pinchot, will yield to none in their love of nature; yet they strongly favor this bill. . . . The only question is, after all, the conversion of the Hetch-Hetchy Meadow into a crystal clear Lake —a natural object of indeed rare beauty. For the few hundred acres wanted by San Francisco on the floor of the Valley the city gives the Government the original camping-places taken up by the pioneers and until now held in private ownership. The patrol of the watershed will protect it for beauty and from fire loss and defilement. It will be made accessible by good roads, like the beautiful Lake Katrine—the water supply of Glasgow—and it will be a delight to visitors, while at the same time it serves a great and useful purpose. The people of San Francisco have entered into a solemn agreement, by an overwhelming vote, with the Government, by which Secretary Garfield has protected the public interests. There are eight hundred miles of wild mountain scenery in the Sierras, and, according to John Muir, "There are a dozen Yosemites;" then why deplore the loss of a mosquito meadow? . . .

By yielding their opposition, sincere lovers of nature will turn the prayers of a million people to praise for the gifts bestowed upon them by the God of Nature, whom they cannot worship in his temple, but must perforce live in the sweltering cities. A reduced death rate is a more vital consideration than the discussion of the relative beauties of a meadow or a lake.

156.

Martin Dies

DAMN HETCH-HETCHY [1913]

[During the final Congressional debate on Hetch-Hetchy, Representative Martin Dies of Texas rose to indict all who would restrict development, even the liberal conservationists of the Pinchot stripe.]

I am awfully glad my friends from California and elsewhere are getting tired of this conservation hobby, because, Mr. Chairman, I think it is one of the delusions of the age in which we live.

. . . .

I sympathize with my friends in California who want to take a part of the public domain now, notwithstanding all their declamations for conservation of resources. I am willing to let them have it. I am willing to let them have it when they take it in California and San Francisco for the public good.

That is what the great resources of this country are for. They are for the American people. I want them to open the coal mines in Alaska. I want them to open the reservations in this country. I am not for reservations and parks. I would have the great timber and mineral and coal resources of this country opened to the people, and I only want to say, Mr. Chairman, that your Pinchots and your conservationists generally are theorists who are not, in my humble judgment, making propaganda in the interest of the American people.

Let California have it, and let Alaska open her coal mines. God Almighty has located the resources of this country in such a form as that His children will not use them in disproportion, and your Pinchots will not be able to controvert and circumvent the laws of God Almighty.

[The Roosevelt era of conservationism passed, and, with World War I and the "roaring twenties," public interest in saving the land waned. A few people tried to keep the spark alive, and, indeed, there was a slow growth in the ranks of what has been called the "wilderness cult," but, except for a brief revival of interest in specific soil-, timber-, and water-conservation practices during the period of the Depression and the Dust Bowl, the general public remained largely apathetic until the 1960's.]

157.

Aldo Leopold

THE LAST STAND OF THE WILDERNESS [1925]

How many of those whole-hearted conservationists who berate the past generation for its short-sightedness in the use of natural resources have stopped to ask themselves for what new evils the next generation will berate us?

Has it ever occurred to us that we may unknowingly be just as short-sighted as our forefathers in assuming certain things to be inexhaustible, and becoming conscious of our error only after they have practically disappeared?

Today it is hard for us to understand why our prodigious waste of standing timber was allowed to go on—why the exhaustion of the supply was not earlier foreseen. Some even impute to the wasters a certain moral turpitude. We forget that for many generations the standing timber of America was in fact an encumbrance or even an enemy, and that the nation was simply unconscious of the possibility of its becoming exhausted. In fact, our tendency is not to call things resources until the supply runs short. When the end of the supply is in sight we "discover" that the thing is valuable.

.   .   .   .

Can not we for once use foresight, and provide for our needs in an orderly, ample, correlated, economical fashion?

The next resource, the exhaustion of which is due for "discovery," is the wilderness. The purpose of this article is to show why the wilderness is valuable, how close it is to exhaustion and why, and what can be done about it.

Wild places are the rock-bottom foundation of a good many different kinds of outdoor play, including pack and canoe trips in which hunting, fishing, or just exploring may furnish the flavoring matter. By "wild places" I mean wild regions big enough to absorb the average man's two weeks' vacation without getting him tangled up in his own back track. I also mean big areas wild enough to be free from motor roads, summer cottages, launches, or other manifestations of gasoline. Driving a pack train across or along a graded highway is distinctly not a pack trip—it is merely exercise, with about the same flavor as lifting dumbbells. Neither is canoeing in the wake of a motor launch or down a lane of summer cottages a canoe trip. That is paddling—and the supply is unlimited.

.   .   .   .

Right here I had better explain that motor roads, cottages, and launches do not necessarily destroy hunting and fishing, but they destroy the wilderness, which to certain tastes is quite as important.

Neither do I imply that motors, cottages, summer resorts, and dude ranches are not in themselves highly valuable recreational assets. Obviously they are. Only they are a different *kind* of recreation. We need to preserve as many different kinds as we possibly can. The civilized kinds tend to preserve themselves through the automatic operation of economic laws. But wilderness travel is a kind that tends to disappear under the automatic operation of economic laws, just as the site for a city park tends to disappear with the growth of a city. Unlike the city park, however, the wilderness can not be re-created when the need for it is determined by hindsight. The need for it must be determined by foresight, and the necessary areas segregated and preserved. Wilderness is the one kind of playground which mankind can not build to order.

.   .   .   .

In all the category of outdoor vocations and outdoor sports there is not one, save only the tilling of the soil, that bends and molds the human character like wilderness travel. Shall this fundamental instrument for building citizens be allowed to disappear from America, simply because we lack the vision to see its value? Would we rather have the few paltry dollars that could be extracted from our remaining wild places than the human values they can render in their wild condition?

A national policy for the establishment of wilderness recreation grounds would in some instances be easy to put into operation if we act at once. The National Forests and Parks still contain a few splendid areas of relatively low value for other purposes, which could be readily segregated as roadless playgrounds. Wilderness areas in the National Forests would serve especially the wilderness-hunter, since hunting is not and should not be allowed in the Parks. On the other hand, wilderness areas in the National Parks would serve all kinds of wilderness-lovers except the hunter. In general, I believe that both the Forest Service and the Park Service would be receptive to the wilderness idea, but neither can be expected to execute it with the vigor and despatch necessary to save the situation, unless they can point to a definite crystallized public demand for such action. The public being still largely unconscious that the end of the wild places is in sight, there is as yet no articulate public expression for or against the wilderness plan. Meanwhile the remaining wild areas in both the Forests and Parks are being pushed back by road construction at a very rapid rate,—so rapid that unless something is done, the large areas of wilderness will mostly disappear within the next decade.

. . . .

To urge that wilderness playgrounds are unnecessary because ample forest playgrounds of other kinds are already being established is just as idle as to urge that there is no need for public tennis courts because there are already public golf links. The two things represent differing needs of different people, each entitled to recognition in due proportion to their numbers and importance. The people in need of wilderness areas are numerous, and the preservation of their particular kind of contact with Mother Earth is a national problem of the first magnitude.

158.

Wallace Stevens

ANECDOTE OF THE JAR [1923]

I placed a jar in Tennessee,
And round it was, upon a hill.
It made the slovenly wilderness
Surround that hill.

The wilderness rose up to it,
And sprawled around, no longer wild.
The jar was round upon the ground
And tall and of a port in air.

It took dominion everywhere.
The jar was gray and bare.
It did not give of bird or bush,
Like nothing else in Tennessee.

159.

Robert Marshall

THE CASE FOR WILDERNESS [1937]

Wilderness skeptics in almost all arguments raise the question: "Why should we set aside a vast area for the enjoyment of a few hundred people when roads would make that area available for half a million? Aren't we obligated to consider what will bring the greatest good to the greatest number?"

The doctrine of the greatest good to the greatest number does not mean that this laudable relationship has to take place on every acre. If it did, we would be forced to change our metropolitan art galleries into metropolitan bowling alleys. Our state universities, which are used by a minor fraction of the population, would be converted into state circuses where hundreds could be exhilarated for every one person who may be either exhilarated or depressed now. The Library of Congress would become a national hot dog stand, and the new Supreme Court building would be converted into a gigantic garage where it could house a thousand people's autos instead of Nine Gentlemen of the Law.

Ridiculous as all of this sounds, it is no more ridiculous than the notion that every acre of land devoted to outdoor recreation should be administered in a way that will give the maximum volume of use. Quality as well as quantity must enter into any evaluation of competing types of recreation, because one really deep experience may be worth an infinite number of ordinary experiences. Therefore, it is preposterous to hold that the objective of outdoor recreational planning should be to enable the maximum number of people to enjoy every beautiful bit of the outdoors.

. . . .

Of course, non-primitive forms of recreation will continue to bring joy into the lives of multitudes to whom the true wilderness would be as unattainable as the canals of Mars. However, this should not mean that the minority that is able to enjoy the far greater elation of wilderness travel must have every primeval tract destroyed by routes of facile transportation. It would seem only reasonable that the available outdoors should be divided among both types of enjoyment. Each group should be tolerant enough to respect the variety of pleasure that the other desires. Similar tolerance is the accepted rule with most types of esthetic experience. The old lady who admires the postage stamp replica of Whistler's Mother does not demand that the original be destroyed. The person who prefers the jazzy strains of *Dancing Cheek to Cheek* to the *Unfinished Symphony* does not insist that the Philadelphia Orchestra should alter its program in order to appease his musical taste and wreck those of the symphony lovers'.

It would seem just as possible for the person who enjoys the outdoors by motor to obtain in ample extent his favorite recreation without extinguishing much more of the primitive. There are already about 3,500,000 miles of roads in the United States, enough at 50,000 miles a year to last a person 70 years, with the opportunity for building a large additional mileage of splendid scenic value without invading any important wilderness areas. America is big enough and rich enough for both primitive and non-primitive recreation, if there is some subordination of selfishness and rational, balanced planning.

160.

[Great Plains Committee Report]

THE FUTURE OF THE GREAT PLAINS [1937]

In 1934 and again in 1936 drought conditions in the Great Plains area of the United States became so severe that it was necessary for the Federal Government to take emergency steps to rescue dying cattle, relieve destitute families, and safeguard human life. The experience of the two tragic years made it evident that the drought had merely accentuated a situation which had been long developing. The agricultural economy of the Great Plains had a perilously narrow reserve. Its prosperity depended on favorable weather and markets, neither of which could be expected to be continuously present.

Droughts could not be prevented. They were admittedly part of a weather cycle which runs its course beyond the range of human interference. Agriculture must adapt itself to the cycle and make the most of what Nature has to offer. This it had largely failed to do. It became clear that unless there was a permanent change in the agricultural pattern of the Plains, relief always would have to be extended whenever the available rainfall was deficient. Current methods of cultivation were so injuring the land that large areas were decreasingly productive even in good years, while in bad years they tended more and more to lapse into desert. The water supply, which literally meant life or death to human activities in the Region, was being in part permitted to run to waste, in part put to uses which did not extract all its values.

. . . .

Nature has established a balance in the Great Plains by what in human terms would be called the method of trial and error. The white man has disturbed this balance; he must restore it or devise a new one of his own.

. . . .

The people of the Plains are finding their way toward an attitude of mind, deep-seated and not often brought out into the open, which will affect both their thinking and their doing. Many of the assumptions which the pioneers had found workable in other regions, under other conditions, have proved unworkable on the Plains. The Plainsman cannot assume that whatever is for his immediate good is also good for everybody—only of his long-run good is this true, and in the short run there must often be sacrifices; he cannot assume the right always to do with his own property as he likes—he may ruin another man's property if he does; he cannot assume that the individual action he can take on his own land will be sufficient, even for the conservation and best use of that land. He must realize that he cannot "conquer Nature"—he must live with her on her own terms, making use of and conserving resources which can no longer be considered inexhaustible.

161.

Henry Beetle Hough

OF TIME AND THE ECONOMY [1960]

The Federal Reserve Bank of Boston has issued "a projection of the New England economy over the next decade, described as potentially the greatest in the region's history." This is, of course, reassuring. "More investment, greater automation, higher productivity"—one hears the busy sound of machinery grinding past in the streets, heading for 1970.

. . . .

Granted the survival of our region, and granted the fulfillment of the reserve bank's prophecies as far as they go, would it not be well to hear from a poet, an artist, a naturalist, a humanist, based on considerations of the broadest and least tangible sort?

"More investment, greater automation, higher productivity"—but will the geese still fly north and south in season, will there be white sand for the surf to roll upon, will trees and wildflowers beckon from beyond the dooryard, will pinkletinks sound their peeping from the marshes in April? Will the world be as livable as we know it today, and will new generations be as free?

162.

THE WILDERNESS ACT [1964]

[The preservationist school won a major victory in 1964 with the passage of a bill establishing the National Wilderness Preservation System. By that time, conservation was again coming to public notice, but the emphasis was less on preservation or even the conservation of resources and more on the rapidly growing problems of pollution, which threatened not only landscape and wildlife but also the city and man himself.]

In order to assure that an increasing population, accompanied by expanding settlement and growing mechanization, does not occupy and modify all areas within the United States and its possessions, leaving no lands designated for preservation and protection in their natural condition, it is hereby declared to be the policy of the Congress to secure for the American people of present and future generations the benefits of an enduring resource of wilderness. For this purpose there is hereby established a National Wilderness Preservation System to be composed of federally owned areas designated by Congress as "wilderness areas," and these shall be administered for the use and enjoyment of the American people in such manner as will leave them unimpaired for future use and enjoyment as wilderness, and so as to provide for the protection of these areas, the preservation of their wilderness character, and for the gathering and dissemination of information regarding their use and enjoyment as wilderness; and no Federal lands shall be designated as "wilderness areas" except as provided for in this chapter or by a subsequent Act.

. . . .

A wilderness, in contrast with those areas where man and his own works dominate the landscape, is hereby recognized as an area where the earth and its community of life are untrammeled by man, where man himself is a visitor who does not remain. An area of wilderness is further defined to mean in this chapter an area of undeveloped Federal land retaining its primeval character and influence, without permanent improvements or human habitation, which is protected and managed so as to preserve its natural conditions and which (1) generally appears to have been affected primarily by the forces of nature, with the imprint of man's work substantially unnoticeable; (2) has outstanding opportunities for solitude or a primitive and unconfined type of recreation; (3) has at least five thousand acres of land or is of sufficient size as to make practicable its preservation and use in an unimpaired condition; and (4) may also contain ecological, geological, or other features of scientific, educational, scenic, or historical value.

163.

Kenneth E. Boulding [1966]

[The paper from which this selection is taken was presented on March 8, 1966, at the sixth forum of Resources for the Future, which had as its general theme "Environmental Quality in a Growing Economy." In the paper, Kenneth E. Boulding, an economist of a particularly reflective turn, used an image—that of "spaceship Earth"—that in subsequent years has become more and more relevant as it has been more and more often quoted.]

We are now in the middle of a long process of transition in the nature of the image which man has of himself and his environment. Primitive men, and to a large extent also men of the early civilizations, imagined themselves to be living on a virtually illimitable plane. There was almost always somewhere beyond the known limits of human habitation, and over a very large part of the time that man has been on earth, there has been something like a frontier. That is, there was always some place else to go when things got too difficult, either by reason of the deterioration of the natural environment or a deterioration of the social structure in places where people happened to live. The image of the frontier is probably one of the oldest images of mankind, and it is not surprising that we find it hard to get rid of.

Gradually, however, man has been accustoming himself to the notion of the spherical earth and a closed sphere of human activity. A few unusual spirits among the ancient Greeks perceived that the earth was a sphere. It was only with the circumnavigations and the geographical explorations of the fifteenth and sixteenth centuries, however, that the fact that the earh was a sphere became at all widely known and accepted. Even in the nineteenth century, the commonest map was Mercator's projection, which visualizes the earth as an illimitable cylinder, essentially a plane wrapped around the globe, and it was not until the Second World War and the development of the air age that the global nature of the planet really entered the popular imagination. Even now we are very far from having made the moral, political, and psychological adjustments which are implied in this transition from the illimitable plane to the closed sphere.

.   .   .   .

The closed earth of the future requires economic principles which are somewhat different from those of the open earth of the past. For the sake of picturesqueness, I am tempted to call the open economy the "cowboy economy," the cowboy being symbolic of the illimitable plains and also associated with reckless, exploitative, romantic, and violent behavior, which is characteristic of open societies. The closed economy of the future might similarly be called the "spaceman" economy, in which the earth has become a single spaceship, without unlimited reservoirs of anything, either for extraction or for pollution, and in which, therefore, man must find his place in a cyclical ecological system which is capable of continuous reproduction of material form even though it cannot escape having inputs of energy. The difference between the two types of economy becomes most apparent in the attitude towards consumption. In the cowboy economy, consumption is regarded as a good thing and production likewise; and the success of the economy is measured by the amount of the throughput from the "factors of production," a part of which, at any rate, is extracted from the reservoirs of raw materials and noneconomic objects, and another part of which is output into the reservoirs of pollution. If there are infinite reservoirs from which material can be obtained and into which effluvia can be deposited, then the throughput is at least a plausible measure of the success of the economy. . . .

By contrast, in the spaceman economy, throughput is by no means a desideratum, and is indeed to be regarded as something to be minimized rather than maximized. The essential measure of the success of the economy is not production and consumption at all, but the nature, extent, quality, and complexity of the total capital stock, including in this the state of the human bodies and minds included in the system. In the spaceman economy, what we are primarily concerned with is stock maintenance, and any technological change which results in the maintenance of a given total stock with a lessened throughput (that is, less production and consumption) is clearly a gain. This idea that both production and consumption are bad things rather than good things is very strange to economists, who have been obsessed with the income-flow concepts to the exclusion, almost, of capital-stock concepts.

. . . .

It may be said, of course, why worry about all this when the spaceman economy is still a good way off (at least beyond the lifetimes of any now living), so let us eat, drink, spend, extract and pollute, and be as merry as we can, and let posterity worry about the spaceship earth. It is always a little hard to find a convincing answer to the man who says, "What has posterity ever done for me?" and the conservationist has always had to fall back on rather vague ethical principles postulating identity of the individual with some human community or society which extends not only back into the past but forward into the future. Unless the individual identifies with some community of this kind, conservation is obviously "irrational." Why should we not maximize the welfare of this generation at the cost of posterity? *"Après nous, le déluge"* has been the motto of not insignificant numbers of human societies. The only answer to this, as far as I can see, is to point out that the welfare of the individual depends on the extent to which he can identify himself with others, and that the most satisfactory individual identity is that which identifies not only with a community in space but also with a community extending over time from the past into the future. If this kind of identity is recognized as desirable, then posterity has a voice, even if it does not have a vote; and in a sense, if its voice can influence votes, it has votes too. This whole problem is linked up with the much larger one of the determinants of the morale, legitimacy, and "nerve" of a society, and there is a great deal of historical evidence to suggest that a society which loses its identity with posterity and which loses its positive image of the future loses also its capacity to deal with present problems, and soon falls apart.

. . . .

All these considerations add some credence to the point of view which says that we should not worry about the spaceman economy at all, and that we should just go on increasing the GNP and indeed the gross world product, or GWP, in the expectation that the problems of the future can be left to the future, that when scarcities arise, whether this is of raw materials or of pollutable reservoirs, the needs of the then present will determine the solutions of the then present, and there is no use giving ourselves ulcers by worrying about problems that we really do not have to solve. There is even high ethical authority for this point of view in the New Testament, which advocates that we should take no thought for tomorrow and let the dead bury their dead. There has always been something rather refreshing in the view that we should live like the birds, and perhaps posterity is for the birds in more senses than one; so perhaps we should all call it a day and go out and pollute something cheerfully. As an old taker of thought for the morrow, however, I cannot quite accept this solution; and I would argue, furthermore, that tomorrow is not only very close, but in many respects it is already here. The shadow of the future spaceship, indeed, is already falling over our spendthrift merriment.

164.

[From *Time*]

THE AGE OF EFFLUENCE [1968]

What ever happened to America the Beautiful? While quite a bit of it is still visible, the recurring question reflects rising and spreading frustration over the nation's increasingly dirty air, filthy streets and malodorous rivers—the relentless degradation of a once virgin continent. This man-made pollution is bad enough in itself, but it reflects something even worse: a dangerous illusion that technological man can build bigger and bigger industrial societies with little regard for the iron laws of nature.

.   .   .   .

Finding effective antidotes will take a lot more alertness to ecological consequences. What cities sorely need is a systems approach to pollution: a computer analysis of everything that a total environment—greater Los Angeles, for example—is taking in and giving out via air, land, water. Only then can cities make cost-benefit choices and balance the system. Equally vital are economic incentives, such as taxing specific pollutants so that factories stop using them. Since local governments may be loath to levy effluence charges, fearing loss of industry, the obvious need is regional cooperation, such as interstate river-basin authorities to enforce scientific water use.

Similar "air shed" action is starting between some smog-bound states and is considered preferable to federally imposed air standards, which might not fit local climate conditions. Still, far greater federal action—especially money—is urgently needed to help cities build all kinds of waste-treating facilities. In fact, the Secretary of the Interior really ought to be the Secretary of the Environment. To unify federal leadership, he might well be given charge of the maze of rival federal agencies that now absurdly nibble only at their own slice of the pollution mess.

.   .   .   .

Above all, man should strive to parallel natural decay by recycling —reusing as much waste as possible. Resalvaging already keeps 80% of all mined copper in circulation. But U.S. city incinerators now destroy about 3,000,000 metric tons of other valuable metals a year; magnetic extractors could save the metal and reduce incineration by 10%. The packaging industry could do a profound service by switching to materials that rot—fast. The perfect container for mankind is the edible ice-cream cone. How about a beer container that is something like a pretzel? Or the soft-drink bottle that, when placed in the refrigerator, turns into a kind of tasty artificial ice? Soft drinks could also come in frozen form, as popsicles with edible sticks.

There are some real prospects of profit in reconstituting other waste. Take sulfur, for example, which is in short supply around the world. While 26 million tons are mined a year, smokestacks belch 28 million tons of wasted sulfur dioxide, which could easily be trapped in the stack and converted to sulfuric acid or even fertilizer. Standard Oil of California is already profitably recovering the refinery sulfur waste that pollutes streams.

To reduce smog over cities, one of the most visible and worst forms of pollution, smog-causing power plants might be eliminated from densely populated areas. Why not generate electricity at the fuel source—distant oil or coal fields— and then wire it to cities? On the other hand, industrialization must not be taken to distant places that can be better used for other purposes. Industrializing Appalachia, for example, would smogify a naturally hazy region that settlers aptly named the Smokies. The right business for Appalachia is recreation; federal money could spur a really sizable tourist industry.

Sometimes pollution can even help recreation. In flat northeastern Illinois, for instance, the handsomest recreation area will soon be Du Page County's fast-rising 118-ft. hill and 65-acre lake —artfully built on garbage fill. One form of pollution could even enhance—rather than spoil—water sports. Much of the nation's coastline is too cold for swimming; if marine life can be protected, why not use nuclear plant heat to warm the water? Or even create underwater national parks for scuba campers?

.   .   .   .

In the search for solutions, there is no point in attempting to take nature back to its pristine purity. The approach must look forward. There is no question that just as technology has polluted the country, it can also depollute it. The real question is whether enough citizens want action. The biggest need is for ordinary people to learn something about ecology, a humbling as well as fascinating way of viewing reality that ought to get more attention in schools and colleges. The trouble with modern man is that he tends to yawn at the news that pesticides are threatening remote penguins or pelicans; perhaps he could do with some of the humility toward animals that St. Francis tried to graft onto Christianity. The false assumption that nature exists only to serve man is at the root of an ecological crisis that ranges from the lowly litterbug to the lunacy of nuclear proliferation. At this hour, man's only choice is to live in harmony with nature, not conquer it.

165.

Paul R. Ehrlich

TOO MANY PEOPLE [1968]

I have understood the population explosion intellectually for a long time. I came to understand it emotionally one stinking hot night in Delhi a couple of years ago. My wife and daughter and I were returning to our hotel in an ancient taxi. The seats were hopping with fleas. The only functional gear was third. As we crawled through the city, we entered a crowded slum area. The temperature was well over 100, and the air was a haze of dust and smoke. The streets seemed alive with people. People eating, people washing, people sleeping. People visiting, arguing, and screaming. People thrusting their hands through the taxi window, begging. People defecating and urinating. People clinging to buses. People herding animals. People, people, people, people. As we moved slowly through the mob, hand horn squawking, the dust, noise, heat, and cooking fires gave the scene a hellish aspect. Would we ever get to our hotel? All three of us were, frankly, frightened. It seemed that anything could happen— but, of course, nothing did. Old India hands will laugh at our reaction. We were just some overprivileged tourists, unaccustomed to the sights and sounds of India. Perhaps, but since that night I've known the *feel* of overpopulation.

. . . .

I have just scratched the surface of the problem of environmental deterioration, but I hope that I have at least convinced you that subtle ecological effects may be much more important than the obvious features of the problem. The causal chain of the deterioration is easily followed to its source. Too many cars, too many factories, too much detergent, too much pesticide, multiplying contrails, inadequate sewage treatment plants, too little water, too much carbon dioxide—all can be traced easily to *too many people*.

166.

Lee A. DuBridge [1969]

[On September 9, 1969, Lee A. DuBridge, Science Adviser to President Nixon, made the following remarks to a symposium on public-policy aspects of the environmental problem. The symposium had been organized by the American Chemical Society.]

Clearly, the human being is the one form of life that is making the greatest inroads on the environment. In the industrial society which man has built he uses the natural resources of the earth at a colossal rate, and to a large extent converts these resources to unuseable forms, thus

producing vast quantities of waste materials which must go into
the atmosphere, into the water or onto or beneath the surface
of the land. In recent years the people of America have become
keenly and somewhat belatedly aware of the inroads which our
kind of living makes upon our environment. As we breathe polluted
air, as we observe and use polluted water, as we observe colossal
mountains of junk and waste, and as we see the rapid disappearance of open spaces and recreation areas, we have realized that
the earth's environmental resources are limited, and that the
further deterioration of the environment must be brought to a halt.

This, of course, is easier said than done. In order to live at all,
and especially to live in the way to which we have been accustomed, we must use oxygen and convert it into carbon dioxide
to maintain life and to provide, through combustion of fuels, the
energy that we require in such huge quantities for domestic and
industrial purposes.

We must also use water in huge quantities, and although we do
not normally destroy the molecules themselves, we contaminate
the water with all sorts of organic and inorganic waste materials.
Our civilization cannot get along without coal and oil and copper
and iron and a host of other materials which we extract in huge
quantities from the earth's crust. We must plant crops for food,
we must grow and cut trees, and we must, over an ever-larger
fraction of the earth's surface, replace the natural environment by
a man-made one.

To ask human beings to stop altering their environment or using
it, would be to ask them to cease living. Human beings evolved
because of the earth's environment, they live off the environment,
and in living they inevitably change it. The question, therefore, is
not how shall we cease to use or change our environment, but how
can we avoid despoiling and degrading it, and how can we reverse
those habits and procedures which now contaminate our air, our
water and our landscape. This is not a simple matter. . . .

Nevertheless, I do not wish to suggest that the problem is a
hopeless one. I do suggest that it will take the best resources of
science and technology and the best instruments of economics,
finance and government to slow down and eventually reverse the
processes which do degrade the environment.

. . . .

I can assure you that many major national problems are under
intensive study, and we hope as the months and years go by that
through research, through public opinion, through legislation at all
levels, this nation can begin to bring its environmental problems
under more adequate control.

At the same time, we must continuously emphasize that the
environment is everybody's business. Practically everyone drives a
car and everyone produces waste products which must be disposed
of. Millions of citizens still vote against bonds for improving

sewage treatment facilities or they protest an increase in taxes for the purposes of more effective disposal of garbage, junk and other solid wastes. We have always in the past adopted the cheapest method of disposing of wastes, discharging them into the atmosphere or the water, or strewing them on the surface of the land. The cheapest way is no longer the best way and no longer a tolerable way. Make no mistake about it, billions upon billions of dollars of private, municipal, state and federal funds will be required to cope fully with environmental problems.

167.

Peter Schrag

A LARGER VIEW [1969]

Who controls this environment? Pollution, pesticides, fallout. The world's experience with nuclear tests has begun to create a wholly new concept of civility and community. In a strange way pollution became a problem by analogy: we learned, for example, that the same ecological processes that concentrate strontium-90 in bones concentrate DDT in fish, that contamination in one place jeopardizes life in others. A bomb test in New Mexico kills infants in Mississippi and Alabama; pesticides on Michigan farms poison fish in distant lakes; sewage from Detroit fouls beaches in Ohio. One can respond cheaply by lamenting the fix that science and technology have gotten us into, but a bumper sticker proclaiming SAVE LAKE ERIE pasted barely a foot above a smoky automobile exhaust is more an illustration of the problem than a solution.

The burden of a moral compromise symbolized by Hiroshima and Nagasaki will not be lifted by building a new sewer system in Detroit, however necessary that system may be. Technological amelioration of one facet of environmental destruction can be no more than a surrogate for continued acceptance of its larger and more catastrophic forms. Can one take seriously an organization whose interest in conserving fish is unmatched by a position on the ABM?

The questions are backwards: how much civility can we afford after we have paid for Vietnam? For the car? For our missiles?

Can we sustain a decent welfare program despite the war? Can we clean the river without jeopardizing the profits of industry? Because we are trying to satisfy a new, though still unclear, sense of community with old priorities, evasion is inevitable. Which is to say that a professed commitment to protect an environment that ends with a squabble over sewer taxes is no commitment at all. The issue of pollution can produce a paranoid fanaticism just like every other; no one has died from swimming on a contaminated beach on Lake Erie or from drinking its water. Yet somehow, if we cannot distinguish between fanaticism on behalf of a distant generation and that which defends immediate returns and private ends we have simply lost our claim to live.

168.

Gene Marine

KILL A BABY THIS WEEK [1969]

There's a little island in the Pacific, not far from Guadalcanal of World War II fame, where they've got the biggest problem in the world all figured out.

By our standards, Tikopia isn't very big. You can stand there and look around and see that there's just so much land and that there are a certain number of people. The people who live there have a pretty strict patriarchal society: what the old man says, goes. And the old man controls all the land that the family has.

He is responsible, however, for making sure that everybody eats. So what he does is very simple: after a couple of his older sons have married and become fathers, he forbids the younger sons to marry. They still get to enjoy the island girls without anybody caring much about it, but impregnating them is strictly out. If somebody goofs, there's an abortion. And if a pregnancy somehow slips by, they simply kill the baby.

Westerners find this revolting. The restrictions on marriage they understand; the abortions many of them are willing to accept; but the cruelty of the calmly effected and cold-blooded infanticides, however rarely they occur, turns Western stomachs.

Possibly that is because Western stomachs are full.

This is the difference between the island you live on and the island of Tikopia: On your island the younger sons may marry and breed. Abortion is possible but generally frowned upon. And—even more cold-bloodedly than the Tikopians—on your island the *only* control is to kill the babies.

Of course we do not kill our babies as directly, or as quickly and mercifully, as the Tikopians do. We starve them to death—10,000 of them every day. It is true that some of them struggle, half-starved, into their twenties or even their thirties before they die. And it is true that we sometimes keep a few more babies alive for a while by killing older people instead. But the total is 10,000 people a day all the same. For, also unlike Tikopia, we have not solved our problem. Having omitted from our practice the essential factor of theirs, we have to kill more babies every day, and even so we can't keep up.

Yes, you have heard the population story before. They have it tough over there in India and down there in Latin America. We ought to give them all pills or something. And I guess we ought to cool it a little ourselves. I'll have to be sure to teach the kids about that.

Do. Please do.

169.

Frank M. Potter, Jr.

TAKING ACTION [1970]

It is difficult to find a newspaper today that doesn't have at least one story on environmental problems. People who read these stories react to them and, with increasing frequency, their reaction is sympathetic. Environmental concerns are no longer the private preserver of the birdwatchers: the same bell tolls for us all.

In 1969, the National Wildlife Federation commissioned two polling organizations to investigate American attitudes on environment. The polls reached the conclusion that most people are actively concerned about environmental problems and would prefer that a greater proportion of their taxes be devoted to the costs of solving them. The level of concern here rose with income and varied inversely with age. Over fifty per cent of those interviewed felt that the government was devoting insufficient attention to environmental problems and was providing insufficient funds to resolve them. Over eighty per cent felt a personal concern, and most of these registered "deep concern." What, then, keeps them from the barricades?

Apathy, one might think, but the surveys rule that out. The most significant inhibitor of action may be that we are too easily convinced of our own political impotence. The larger the grouping, the more difficult it is for any person to make a significant impact upon social decisions.

On the other hand, when they are really aroused, people can take and have taken effective action. For example, a coalition of citizens joined forces in 1969 to require a reluctant U.S. government to quadruple the amount of funds to be used for waste-water facilities. They did so by informing their elected representatives that this was a matter of specific, personal, and urgent priority; their representatives listened and responded. Again, a few years ago, a small group of citizens banded together against the largest utility in the United States, opposing plans to construct a major hydroelectric plant within fifty miles of New York City. They stopped the utility company in its tracks. That company was Consolidated Edison, the plant was the Storm King project. The Federal Power Commission, which must decide whether or not the plant should be built, has still not made its decision. The strong case made by the citizens depended in large measure on the fact that they were able to propose alternatives to the project and to support their case by a wealth of technical and engineering detail that showed New York's serious power problems could be met by less damaging methods. Although Con Edison has not yet given up the project, it has adopted the alternatives, and many sophisticated agency-watchers now consider it unlikely that the Storm King plant will ever be built.

Collective action, then, can make a difference. Individually or collectively, we are confronted with a clear option: Are we to live well only for a short period, or must we cut back economic growth in favor of long-term survival for the species? For the most part we appear to have adopted the former course of action, and it is by no means clear that we would act much differently if the choice were clearer. "Après moi, le déluge" is an attitude confined neither to France nor to the eighteenth century. As individuals, we tend to be somewhat ambivalent about the importance of what might be called an environmental conscience.

· ·

It is important to distinguish between the actions and attitudes of individuals and those of the citizen groups organized to consider environmental problems. The biggest problem faced by such groups is seldom a lack of motivation; it is financial. It is still rare for anyone whose economic interests are involved to oppose a polluter; this means that concerned citizens must themselves assume these costs, although the financial burdens of speaking out and working against a powerful and well-financed industry or government agency may be great. The costs of carrying on a major controversy may exceed five hundred thousand dollars. We cannot reasonably expect any private group to bear such a burden, nor should we as long as the group is acting to protect assets that are common and valuable to all of us.

. . . .

To look to private business for solutions to pollution may be futile. Its horizons are deliberately limited to those factors which are considered to be of immediate importance, principally economic, and the hidden costs to the society at large tend to be ignored. These costs still exist, however, and they must be borne by everyone if not by the industry which creates them. A classic example would be a pulp processing plant which emits fumes of hydrogen sulphide, causing foul air and peeling paint for miles downwind. The resulting inconvenience, possible health hazards, and certain increases in maintenance costs have not traditionally been imposed upon the agency which created them. Instead, they have been borne by our whole society, regardless of the capability or willingness of individual members to bear them.

To be sure, some private companies have taken steps to limit the anti-social consequences of their operations and have done so at considerable cost, quite beyond what they have been required to assume by law. But a voluntary approach to reducing environmental problems, it is clear, is just not good enough. For one thing, the forces of competition tend to minimize such voluntary efforts. Few men or companies, however public-spirited they may be, are prepared to expend large sums on the internalization of indirect costs. Nor can they do so without incurring the wrath of profit-seeking stockholders, who are even further removed from the environmental mischief they have indirectly created.

. . . .

The mechanics for balancing social costs against economic values, then, must be found outside the private institutions themselves, and they are—this is a major function of government. The laissez-faire philosophy which at one time characterized the attitude of American government toward American industry won't work today. It is also apparent that the government is likely to expand its program in this area. Public attention has already been focused on air and water pollution. But there are other areas in which governmental action must be anticipated—among them, noise, solid-waste disposal, and the by-products of energy transfer are mentioned with increasing frequency.

Governmental over-view, if impartially and reasonably imposed, need not be hostile to the private sector; it may even be in its interest, both short-termed and long-termed. The National Association of Manufacturers has never been known as a hotbed of social activists, yet members of N.A.M. operating committees have endorsed proposals for a strong federal body to oversee environmental issues. Businessmen have to breathe, too, and most of them are prepared to accommodate themselves to the ecological imperative—as long as their competitors are subject to the same rules. We cannot assume, however, that increased governmental concern will take place without some economic disruption. Marginal producers will feel the pinch most strongly, and some may not survive. Nevertheless, the important consideration is that the rules must be enforced fairly and impartially upon all parties.

170.

PEACE OR POWER [1970]

[A good example of citizens' concern and action on behalf of their threatened environment is the following selection from a pamphlet by the Berkshire-Litchfield Environmental Conservancy Council, an *ad hoc* local organization that sprang up in a rural section of New England when an electrical-power company applied to the U.S. Federal Power Commission for preliminary permits for an installation in the area.]

The proposed project would be among the largest pumped-storage installations in the world, a peaking power and stand-by facility capable of producing in the range of 1,000,000 to 2,000,000 kilowatts and presently estimated to cost up to $185,000,000.

As the Commission is aware, a closed cycle pumped-storage installation consists of adjacent upper and lower reservoirs. Electric power produced at other sources is used to pump water from the lower reservoir to the upper reservoir. Then, at times of peak or emergency demand in the utility company's service area, or when it can profitably sell power to other utilities, the water is allowed to flow back down through the generators to the lower reservoir. The water rises and falls through large tunnels connecting the two reservoirs and passing through an electric generating plant.

Pumped-storage plants thus must depend, for their reliability and economic operation, upon sufficient supplies of water and ready sources of low cost, off-peak power to fill their upper reservoirs whenever needed.

A pumped-storage installation does not, in its net effect, produce electricity, for it usually takes roughly three kilowatts of electricity to lift to the upper reservoir enough water to generate two kilowatts on its downward flow. The plant is, in reality, a giant electrical storage place, dependent for its usefulness upon outside sources of electricity generated by remote thermal, nuclear or other plants. It can be operated in its generating phase for only a relatively few hours before exhausting the store of water at its upper reservoir.

The *Sheffield* site, one alternative under consideration by Northeast Utilities for the proposed plant, is located about 27 miles southwest of Pittsfield, Massachusetts. It would consist of a lower reservoir in the valleys of Schenob Brook and Willard Brook and an upper reservoir, for storage of up to approximately 30,000 acre-feet of water, occupying the area where Plantain Pond in Mount Washington, Massachusetts, is now located. The surface areas of the lower and upper reservoirs would be about 2,300 acres and 275 acres, respectively, and the water levels would rise and fall about 175 feet in the upper reservoir and nearly 20 feet in the lower one, as the water is moved between the two.

The *Falls Village site,* the other alternative under consideration, is located about 15 miles northwest of Torrington, Connecticut. It would consist of a lower reservoir in the valley of Wangum Lake Brook and an upper reservoir, for storage of up to approximately 41,000 acre-feet of water, on Canaan Mountain near Wangum Lake. The surface areas of the lower and upper reservoirs would each be about 750 acres, and the water levels would each rise and fall about 80 feet.

The lower reservoirs would be formed by constructing high dikes —up to 200 feet high in some cases—to dam up the valleys. The upper reservoirs would also be formed by large dikes, sealing off depressions in the mountain summits.

In each case the generating plant would be located inside the mountain beneath the upper reservoir, if geological studies should prove this possible.

The two sites lie in one of the most unspoiled regions of lower New England. The Appalachian Trail, in one of its most frequented sections, winds past Plantain Pond. Schenob Brook is a famous trout stream. Canaan Mountain is considered a unique ecological area unmatched in New England for the variety of its vegetation. The valley of Wangum Lake Brook is thought by many to be one of the loveliest rural valleys in Connecticut.

Both Schenob Brook and Wangum Lake Brook are tributaries of the Housatonic River. They are clear streams which help importantly to dissipate the pollution of the Housatonic. The valley bottoms contain farmlands, extensive swamps and open fields, with many varieties of wildlife, waterfowl, plants and wildflowers. In the streams and swamps, beaver thrive and build their dams. In their upper regions, both sites include mountain streams falling over steep escarpments, extensive overlooks and broad undulating summits with grasslands, swamps, ponds, laurel thickets and stands of hemlock and hardwoods in climax forests.

Canaan Mountain, rising to a height of 1,962 feet, is the largest and most rugged and varied wilderness area in Connecticut, according to distinguished ecologists who have studied it for many years. A large portion of the Mountain is used for forest and ecological research by Great Mountain Forest, Yale University and other university ecologists. Housatonic State Forest land on Canaan Mountain (which would in part be flooded by the upper reservoir at the Falls Village site) has been managed as a Wilderness Area by the Connecticut Park and Forest Commission for over 40 years. The Advisory Committee appointed by the Governor of Connecticut under the State's recently enacted Natural Area Preserves Act has recommended that a part of the State Forest land on the Mountain be designated a "natural area preserve".

Plantain Pond is a mountain lake, located in the Taconic Range at an altitude of over 1,700 feet and ringed by mountains rising up to 2,600 feet in elevation. It is a part of the splendid panoramas that can be seen from nearby Mt. Race and Mt. Everett, two of the highest peaks in the southern Taconic Range. From Plantain Pond, a clear stream flows over the steep mountain face to form Bear Rock Falls, one of the finest falls in this region. On the shores of the Pond there has been for many years a YMCA camp which each year benefits more than 1,000 boys from urban Bridgeport.

These areas are within 2½ hours of New York City, 1½ hours of Hartford, 1¾ hours of New Haven and Bridgeport, 1 hour of Pittsfield, 2 hours of Springfield and 4 hours of Boston. There are no other areas, in this part of New England, which possess such scientific, educational and cultural worth. They are havens of natural beauty and wildlife in two small states that are among the most thickly populated in the country.

If the project of Northeast Utilities were to be carried out, the mountain top in Mount Washington or on Canaan Mountain would be scalped and converted into a giant reservoir, bordered by high dikes that destroy the beauty of the mountain skyline, in order to store water for the generation of power during hours of peak or emergency demand. The mountain itself would be blasted and disemboweled. The valley of Schenob Brook or of Wangum Lake Brook would become a barren area, surrounded by high, unsightly banks bare of vegetation, holding only a minimum of water except when the water on the mountain would be allowed to flow down to the turbines through tunnels in the mountain during the brief, intermittent periods of demand. This same water would then be pumped back up the mountain until the next time it is released.

The water would be used again and again, possessing only limited capacity to support life, fit for little else but the generation of electricity.*

Transmission lines with towers up to 80 feet high would fan out from a large and conspicuous switchyard. They would extend for miles along 350 foot wide rights of way, cutting destructive swaths across the countryside, to carry the 345,000 volt lines that would send the power throughout Massachusetts and Connecticut and into New York State.

Years of construction would be required for the project. The violence worked during this period by the blasting, the huge machines, the many hundreds of transient workers, the vast movements of earth and rock, would destroy and degrade the natural surroundings beyond repair. Life in the nearby communities would be drastically disrupted.

The inevitable and permanent environmental effects of these measures would be devastating. The ecological balance, vital for human, plant and animal life, would be seriously upset. All of this would be for the purpose of producing power for remote consumers—power that could be produced closer to the place of need.

. . . .

We do not believe that the Commission, exercising a basic concern for natural beauty and resources and giving effect to the national policy of maintaining environmental quality, could license the destruction of these mountains and valleys, with their ponds and brooks and meadows and swamps, as the price of producing peaking and emergency power in this particular way.

Both regions have already been selected and are in use for parks, forests and trails and for scientific and educational purposes. They should be protected forever from commercial or industrial use and preserved for the future benefit of all society. The wilderness that they represent is a public trust, to be appraised at its true value, not merely for the present generation but for the countless succeeding generations.

Good alternatives for the production of peaking power exist today, and more will come into existence.

The first pumped-storage project was constructed in the United States more than 40 years ago. One cannot doubt, in these closing years of the 20th century, when our technology performs miracles, that this same technology, if properly motivated and endowed, can within a short span of time fulfill many of the promises held by techniques that are in their experimental stages today.

* In the understated language of the industry's Northeast Regional Advisory Committee Report referred to below: "Pumped storage project reservoirs are not generally well adapted to recreation development because of the rapid fill and drawdown cycles that make them both unattractive and in some cases dangerous. This is particularly true of the upper reservoirs that usually have relatively small capacities and fluctuate from near-empty to full."

Northeast Utilities has applied for a preliminary permit to cover a period of *three years*, during which its efforts would be concentrated on the investigation of the proposed project. The cost of this investigation, as estimated by Northeast Utilities in its applications, would be an amount that is nearly *eight* times its total 1968 expenditures for research and development. If the applications are denied, Northeast Utilities will be led to concentrate instead on productive areas of research and development. Surely, it is possible for Northeast Utilities and the great industry to which it belongs to keep pace with the research efforts and accomplishments of other industries to ensure the proper protection of our environment.

. . . .

Traditionally, American enterprise has forged ahead with infinite ingenuity and unrestrained vigor to make life easier and happier for all of us. We now know that this ingenuity and vigor must be applied to existing means, and through research and inventive engineering must find new means, to meet growing demand for electric power without destroying precious natural resources.

171.

Gerald M. Weinberg

THE NATION AS A PARK [1970]

In but a few short years, public consciousness of the destruction of our environment has all but eliminated the formerly familiar attitude that conservationists were naïve children, unable to cope with the realities of "progress." Today, the conservationist is, in the public image, not simply kind and good, but, increasingly, wise. And, of all the conservationists, those whose external vigilance guards our national parks certainly occupy the highest ranks of wisdom.

But is there not a danger in occupying such a perfect and unassailable position that no fault—by definition—can ever be found with it? When teaching young engineers, I often admonish them to follow a simple rule of self-criticism: If you cannot think of at least three reasons why what you are proposing to do might produce exactly the opposite effect to that which you intend, you have not thought sufficiently about the problem. And so it happened that while reading a particularly glorious article in *National Parks & Conservation Magazine* I was struck with an idea of an almost tragic flaw in the scheme of the national park system.

Simply stated, the flaw is this: In accepting the idea of a park as a place to be preserved and protected against human destruction, we may be encouraging the idea that any place which is *not* a park may be abandoned to man's destructive impulses. We do not have far to look for illustrations of this peculiar psychology. In our road system, for example, we designate some roads as "parkways," which means that they are set aside to be beautiful—and also means that other roads are more or less expected to be ugly. In our cities, we set aside certain blocks as parks—which seems to diminish the care and attention that one gives blocks that have "only houses," and also seems to justify setting aside certain blocks as garbage dumps. In our national park system we set aside certain areas as parks—which evidently is interpreted to mean that once the park boundary is crossed, any kind of unsightly commercial establishment or land usage is permitted.

As Americans, perhaps we take this philosophy for granted—we have set aside beautiful places, so we have done our duty to man's esthetic sense; now let us get on with the business of America, which is, after all, business. For me, this attitude disappeared when I had the good fortune to live in Switzerland for two years, for the Swiss do not feel this way about their country.

I recall walking one day in the Parc des Eaux Vives in Geneva and stopping to view the numerous redwoods that had been grown there from seedlings brought from California over 100 years ago. As I stood there, a rather poor-looking man walked off the path to retrieve a newspaper lying among the giant trees. Stepping with utmost care among the tiny plants that grew there, he got the paper, folded it neatly, and carried it to an inconspicuous disposal can some distance away. All this had taken him some distance from his course, but he seemed undisturbed by the necessity for doing what was evidently his civic duty.

At the time—being newly arrived in the country—I saw this act as a fine example of the devotion that the Swiss had to their parks. Indeed, this devotion is so great that one rarely sees such an act performed, for there is rarely any litter lying about to be retrieved —at least, when tourists are not there. But the next time, and the next, and the next, that I saw a similar happening, it was *not in one of the parks*, but on some "ordinary" street.

. . . .

By the end of my stay in that Alpine wonderland, I came to realize that the Swiss do not think about their country the way Americans generally do. Although they have a "national park" (which need make no apologies to any in the United States), the general Swiss attitude is that their *entire country is a park!* Or possibly that it is not a park at all, but simply their home—and who throws trash on the floor at home? Or possibly it is a park *and* a home, for in a small country one cannot afford the luxury of fragmenting one's living space as we seem to do here.

But time grows short for us, for our country, too, grows smaller. (Indeed, the earth is growing smaller.) Perhaps it is impossible to keep our parkways free of litter *because* we have set them aside as parkways—and thus set aside every other road as a garbageway. Perhaps it is impossible to keep our streams free of chemicals *because* we have set aside some streams as nonpollutable and thus, in a backhanded way, authorized the pollution of all the others. Is it really worse to throw a soda bottle into Brilliant Pool at Yellowstone than into the Hudson River at Yonkers? Is it really worse to carve initials in a Muir Woods Sequoia than in a pitifully struggling little tree on Sixth Avenue? Does respect for our "temples not built with hands" precede or follow simple respect for the "houses built with hands" that happen to be the places where we spend most of our lives?

For me, the picture seems clear enough. By concentrating solely on the preservation of the national parks—by elevating them to the role of holy shrines above the dung heap in which we live most of our days—we may succeed in preserving them for a decade or two after the rest of our home is entirely destroyed, but then they too will surely fall. Only a nation with the concept of "the nation as a park" can hope to preserve our national parks in perpetuity—not as examples of beauty alone among man's ugliness but as examples of nature's grand untouched beauty as contrasted to the tiny beauties that man has managed to forge.

172.

Gladwin Hill

A NOT SO SILENT SPRING [1970]

[The rapid growth of public awareness of, and interest in, the problems of pollution became an explosion in 1970, when, unexpectedly, the subject was taken up as a cause on college campuses throughout the United States. Activity focused on "Earth Day," April 22, when millions of people participated in demonstrations, teach-ins, discussions, and other means of signifying their interest. It remained to be seen whether the day marked the momentous beginning of a great popular movement or its anticlimax.]

The environmental revolution is a sudden, remarkable, spontaneous rebellion not of one group against another so much as of everybody against the physical conditions to which two centuries of promiscuous "progress" have brought us—a world where ugliness is endemic, where corporeal hazards are rife, and where the issue of actual human survival suddenly has become poignantly explicit. And it is young people who are the vanguard of that revolution.

Humans, like all animals, display a remarkable, if often lamentable, capacity for adjusting themselves to their surroundings. That is what the adult world has done. But we now have a whole generation of young people under thirty, 100 million strong, who have the insight and perception to look around and appraise conditions objectively. And they have pronounced them appalling. They have said: "Look—the emperor has no clothes on."

. . . .

The youth crusade raises many questions. How substantial and enduring does it promise to be? Where does it stand in relation to that other high concern of young people, Vietnam, and our other murky overseas involvements? Is this another "generation backlash" or can young people find common cause with their sluggish elders in radically reshaping a polluted world?

The answers to these questions are emerging daily, and they are uniformly good. One only has to attend any sort of conservation or environmental meeting anywhere in the country to be reassured by young people's interest, perspicacity, and zeal. Blue jeans or gray flannels, they comport themselves maturely. Their sense of organization and effectiveness far surpasses that of the average fumbling, windy, all-adult gathering.

. . . .

The intrinsic power of the youth-sparked environmental revolution is its catholicism. Whatever your ideology, personality, or intellectual bent, the water is just as dirty, the air just as smoggy, the dangers of DDT-laden fish just as alarming.

On the campus the environmental cause is drawing out supporters who wouldn't have dreamed of attending a football rally. A conspicuous feature of every environmental gathering is the mixture of gray heads and young people. The atmosphere is one of community of interest.

. . . .

It's an encouraging and inspiring picture. At Santa Barbara's January observance of the first anniversary of the oil well blowout, a feature of the day was the promulgation of an "Environmental Bill of Rights" composed by a University of California professor, Roderick Nash. But he was upstaged, in the attention of observers, by his own eight-year-old daughter, a pig-tailed, outgoing little girl whose own painstakingly scrawled declaration in some ways outshone her father's lofty verbiage.

"The world I want," she wrote, "is like a lot of the world I saw last summer. We drank cold water from clear streams. We rode through big rapids. . . . I like fields where trees and flowers grow and forests where birds sing and chipmunks chatter.

"I would like to live in a world full of people who love it as much as I do. I hope my children's world is like that too."

THE QUINTESSENTIAL SCIENCE

[Conservation, whether conceived in the narrow sense of rationalized doling out of resources or in the broader one of reserving parks and wilderness areas for the recreation of nature buffs and urban escapees, does not at its core conflict with the conception of man as the master of nature. The entire range of controversy over conservation can be viewed as more or less friendly disagreement among allies over how man might best set about dominating the world.

A concomitant aspect of traditional conservationism is its tendency to treat the effects of man's ravaging of nature on a superficial level, as a series or complex of possibly related but functionally distinct problems. Such a fragmentation of nature into components —forests, soil, wildlife, air, water—is perhaps an understandable if illogical result of originally postulating the separation of man from nature.

An alternative viewpoint is that of ecology, a science (or, more broadly, simply an attitude) that attempts to see and understand nature, including man, as an integrated whole. To the ecologist, nature cannot be thought of as a collection of independent components; all are joined in a web of infinitely complex interrelationships. Like the notion of nature as a unity, the science of ecology is not new. It has, however, made but gradual headway against the tide of false pride.]

173.

Alexander Pope

NATURE'S CHAIN [1733–34]

See, through this air, this ocean, and this earth,
All matter quick, and bursting into birth.
Above, how high, progressive life may go!

Around, how wide! how deep extend below!
Vast chain of being! which from God began,
Natures ethereal, human, angel, man,
Beast, bird, fish, insect, what no eye can see,
No glass can reach; from infinite to thee,
From thee to nothing.—On superior pow'rs
Were we to press, inferior might on ours;
Or in the full creation leave a void,
Where, one step broken, the great scale's destroy'd:
From Nature's chain whatever link you strike,
Ten, or ten thousandth, breaks the chain alike.

    And, if each system in gradation roll
Alike essential to th' amazing whole,
The least confusion but in one, not all
That system only but the whole must fall.
Let earth unbalanc'd from her orbit fly,
Planets and suns run lawless through the sky;
Let ruling angels from their spheres be hurl'd,
Being on being wreck'd, and world on world;
Heaven's whole foundations to their centre nod,
And Nature tremble to the throne of God.
All this dread order break—for whom? for thee?
Vile worm!—Oh, madness! pride! impiety!

What if the foot, ordain'd the dust to tread,
Or, hand, to toil, aspir'd to be the head?
What if the head, the eye, or ear repin'd
To serve mere engines to the ruling mind?
Just as absurd for any part to claim
To be another, in this gen'ral frame,
Just as absurd, to mourn the tasks or pains,
The great directing Mind of all ordains.

    All are but parts of one stupendous whole,
Whose body Nature is, and God the soul;
That chang'd through all, and yet in all the same;
Great in the earth, as in th' ethereal frame;
Warms in the sun, refreshes in the breeze,
Glows in the stars, and blossoms in the trees,
Lives thro' all life, extends thro' all extent,
Spreads undivided, operates unspent;
Breathes in our soul, informs our mortal part,
As full, as perfect, in a hair as heart;
As full, as perfect, in vile man that mourns,
As the rapt seraph that adores and burns:
To him no high, no low, no great, no small;
He fills, he bounds, connects, and equals all.

174.

Ralph Waldo Emerson [1858]

[This brief passage is from an address entitled "The Man With the Hoe," delivered on September 28, 1858, and later published in *Society and Solitude* (1870).]

Science has shown the great circles in which Nature works; the manner in which marine plants balance the marine animals, as the land plants supply the oxygen which the animals consume, and the animals the carbon which the plants absorb. These activities are incessant. Nature works on a method of *all for each and each for all*. The strain that is made on one point bears on every arch and foundation of the structure. There is a perfect solidarity. You cannot detach an atom from its holdings, or strip off from it the electricity, gravitation, chemic affinity or the relation to light and heat and leave the atom bare. No, it brings with it its universal ties.

175.

George Perkins Marsh [1864]

[Although he maintained a station for man somewhat apart from, and slightly above, brute nature, George Perkins Marsh approached closely an ecological viewpoint in his thoughts on the interlocked harmonies among nature's creatures.]

Young trees in the native forest are sometimes girdled and killed by the smaller rodent quadrupeds, and their growth is checked by birds which feed on the terminal bud; but these animals, as we shall see, are generally found on the skirts of the wood only, not in its deeper recesses, and hence the mischief they do is not extensive. The insects which damage primitive forests by feeding upon products of trees essential to their growth, are not numerous, nor is their appearance, in destructive numbers, frequent; and those which perforate the stems and branches, to deposit and hatch their eggs, more commonly select dead trees for that purpose, though, unhappily, there are important exceptions to this latter remark. I do not know that we have any evidence of the destruction or serious injury of American forests by insects, before or even soon after the period of colonization; but since the white man has laid bare a vast proportion of the earth's surface, and thereby produced changes favorable, perhaps, to the multiplication of these pests, they have greatly increased in numbers, and, apparently, in voracity also. Not many years ago, the pines on thousands of acres of land in North Carolina, were destroyed by insects not known to have ever done serious injury to that tree before. In such cases as this and others of the like sort, there is good reason to believe that man is the indirect cause of an evil for which he pays so heavy a penalty. Insects increase whenever the birds which feed upon them disappear. Hence, in the wanton destruction of the robin and other insectivorous birds, the *bipes implumis*, the featherless biped, man, is not only exchanging the vocal orchestra which greets the rising sun for the drowsy beetle's evening drone, and depriving his groves and his fields of their fairest ornament, but he is waging a treacherous warfare on his natural allies.

. . . .

Man has too long forgotten that the earth was given to him for usufruct alone, not for consumption, still less for profligate waste. Nature has provided against the absolute destruction of any of her elementary matter, the raw material of her works; the thunderbolt and the tornado, the most convulsive throes of even the volcano and the earthquake, being only phenomena of decomposition and recomposition. But she has left it within the power of man irreparably to derange the combinations of inorganic matter and of organic life, which through the night of æons she had been proportioning and balancing, to prepare the earth for his habitation, when, in the fulness of time, his Creator should call him forth to enter into its possession.

Apart from the hostile influence of man, the organic and the inorganic world are, as I have remarked, bound together by such mutual relations and adaptations as secure, if not the absolute permanence and equilibrium of both, a long continuance of the established conditions of each at any given time and place, or at least, a very slow and gradual succession of changes in these conditions.

. . . .

Purely untutored humanity, it is true, interferes comparatively little with the arrangements of nature, and the destructive agency of man becomes more and more energetic and unsparing as he advances in civilization, until the impoverishment, with which his exhaustion of the natural resources of the soil is threatening him, at last awakens him to the necessity of preserving what is left, if not of restoring what has been wantonly wasted. The wandering savage grows no cultivated vegetable, fells no forest, and extirpates no useful plant, no noxious weed. If his skill in the chase enables him to entrap numbers of the animals on which he feeds, he compensates this loss by destroying also the lion, the tiger, the wolf, the otter, the seal, and the eagle, thus indirectly protecting the feebler quadrupeds and fish and fowls, which would otherwise become the booty of beasts and birds of prey. But with stationary life, or rather with the pastoral state, man at once commences an almost indiscriminate warfare upon all the forms of animal and vegetable existence around him, and as he advances in civilization, he gradually eradicates or transforms every spontaneous product of the soil he occupies.

.   .   .   .

The ravages committed by man subvert the relations and destroy the balance which nature had established between her organized and her inorganic creations; and she avenges herself upon the intruder, by letting loose upon her defaced provinces destructive energies hitherto kept in check by organic forces destined to be his best auxiliaries, but which he has unwisely dispersed and driven from the field of action. When the forest is gone, the great reservoir of moisture stored up in its vegetable mould is evaporated, and returns only in deluges of rain to wash away the parched dust into which that mould has been converted. The well-wooded and humid hills are turned to ridges of dry rock, which encumbers the low grounds and chokes the watercourses with its debris, and—except in countries favored with an equable distribution of rain through the seasons, and a moderate and regular inclination of surface— the whole earth, unless rescued by human art from the physical degradation to which it tends, becomes an assemblage of bald mountains, of barren, turfless hills, and of swampy and malarious plains.

176.

Fairfield Osborn

THE GRAND ILLUSION [1948]

There would seem to be no real hope for the future unless we are prepared to accept the concept that man, like all other living things, is a part of one great biological scheme. There are those who will deny this just as the leaders and peoples of vanished nations have failed to recognize this truth in the past. Today, almost every purpose and activity of modern life takes precedence over the one most basic purpose of all, namely that of conserving the living resources of the earth. There is a growing consciousness that all is not well, and a stirring and uneasiness in numerous countries where at least initial steps are being taken to cope with the problem. At best there is a mere beginning.

. . . .

The fact that more than 55 per cent of our population live in cities and towns results inevitably in our detachment from the land and apathy as to how our living resources are treated. As a result the majority of voters in the United States at this time neither know nor care about the problem that is facing us. As a consequence, elected representatives of the majority of our people are likewise apathetic.

This great section of our people, as well as large portions of our rural population, either do not realize what is going on or are lulled into a false sense of security by misleading reports regarding the status of our life-supporting resources that are inspired by groups having special interests in such properties as timberlands, cattle and water rights. Probably, however, the most potent soporific affecting popular opinion comes from the belief we all innately share these days to the effect that the marvels of modern technology can solve any of the riddles of life. The miraculous succession of modern inventions has so profoundly affected our thinking as well as our everyday life that it is difficult for us to conceive that the ingenuity of man will not be able to solve the final riddle— that of gaining a subsistence from the earth. The grand and ultimate illusion would be that man could provide a substitute for the elemental workings of nature.

177.

Scott Buchanan

REDISCOVERING NATURAL LAW [1962]

This split in our culture, between material and spiritual, between the materialist and the idealist, between the technical and the cultural, has peculiar consequences. The immediate direct judgment and enjoyment of natural things, both human and nonhuman, are sharply inhibited and redirected. We all note and some of us mourn the drainage of values from work and organization. Some of us used to accept the gray neutrality of means in the lively hope that a better world was in the making. The making of means was the building of the road to a better day; the postponement and projection of ends was required by progress. We had learned the right disciplines and sentiments from theology and economics. But the better day has been coming into view, and we now see that the deferred ends have themselves become means.

In a kind of despair we have increasingly turned to the fine arts where the bare data of nature are separated off from their sources in nature, are refined and transformed by artifice, combined and represented in theatre, museum, records, and camera for nothing but the immediate contemplation and enjoyment of their artificial surfaces. The fine artists and the critics join, not always happily, in cults and schools that imitate, sometimes deliberately, the lower practices of pagan and orthodox religions. They also identify the painting, the dance, or the symphony with the beatific vision of an unknown god. The technicians combine these cults and build them into a technical epiphenomenon, the entertainment that eases the surrender of men to the technical system itself. The sign that signifies the take-over of technics is the appearance of massive exploitation in the entertainment or show business, the exploitation of sentiment and frustration in the audience as well as of talent and ambition in the performers.

But there are other cults that organize themselves around isolated remnants of the kingdom of nature, the apostolic lines that originated with naturalists who had literary and artistic gifts, such as Goethe and Leonardo. These original deviants from the dogmas of exploitation have more or less worthy successors, like Ruskin,

Thoreau, Fabre, Kropotkin, Schweitzer, even Whitman, Tagore, and Tolstoi. Schweitzer is an interesting case, because he has deliberately made connection with those massive primitive and peasant cultures that survive like promontories from continents of tradition where the kingdom of nature has always been taken for granted without benefit of theoretical apology. Systems of medicine based on the Hindu, Chinese, and Malayan respect for life, which includes what we would call inanimate things, are extending our pharmacopeia as well as our psychiatric lore of images and symbols. These cultures are now passionately responding to the magnetism of the technics of exploitation, and it may be expected that a two-way osmosis between the old and the new kingdoms of nature will take place.

But I am not recommending the cults of the fine arts and the naturalists as methods of research in natural law; they are only occasions for reminding ourselves of lost insights. We presumably have learned the hard way that human beings should not be exploited even with their consent. We have learned that the farming that becomes the quarrying and exhaustion of the soil is not true farming; that the industries that pollute air and water and turn cities into slums are not true industries; that the cities that devastate the countryside and reduce it to desert are not true cities; that the nations that destroy forests to feed smelting furnaces, or a countryside to make roads, or even wildlife to make sport are not true polities; that even mining, the original occupation that established exploitation, if it exhausts natural resources, is not true mining. Such frustrated human arts do not belong to the kingdom of nature, no matter how well they may serve apparent human goods. The appeal to merely human ends and values does not justify or rationalize them.

We have had a rough history of learning some of these things. As long as our natural resources, so-called, were open to unlimited exploitation by free enterprise, we gradually came to realize not only that beauty was disappearing, but that we were using up resources. So there was the conservation movement. Gifford Pinchot and Theodore Roosevelt were able to isolate and establish national parks, and these have become monuments to the courage of their conviction that exploitation should be limited. But such conservation was relatively empty until it was discovered that the nursing care of national parks had high unintended uses, namely the increase in ground-water and the building of soil. Following this discovery, there now exist tree farms where industrial lumbermen have learned to care for trees and therefore to increase the lumber supply as they pursue the lumber business. This and other similar lessons have now led to long-term planning for the allocation of resources in which the aim of the prudent saving of resources for future use is always combined with the increase and enhancement of nature. Such thinking is perhaps best epitomized in the original act that established the TVA. Its stated purpose was to serve the welfare of the valley, and the purpose was carried out by planning forests, fertilizer plants, soil analysis, and flood control as well as electric power. The welfare of the valley obviously and necessarily includes concern for natural ends, non-human as well as human.

Out of this dialectical learning there has developed a new and somewhat mysterious science, ecology. As I understand it, ecology was originally an attempt to collate various lines of linear exploitive planning, such as an industrial firm might practice to make an integral pattern of the side-effects and unintended consequences of procurement, employment, and production. Industrial production in a complex city would present the acute problem. The result of the attempt led to another definition and posing of the problem, namely to conceive the plant as an organism with the city as the environment. Soon it was necessary to conceive the city as an organism with its environment. And so one might go on to national economies and to the world community. This is surreptitious teleological thinking, which, made explicit, would mean that everything in the situation would be viewed reciprocally with the others as means and ends. . . . The purpose of the city in the valley would be the enhancement of nature including human nature in the valley. Human beings would no longer be exploiting nature or themselves. They would be free citizens in a constitutional kingdom of nature.

178.

Aldous Huxley

THE POLITICS OF ECOLOGY [1963]

Ecology is the science of the mutual relations of organisms with their environment and with one another. Only when we get it into our collective head that the basic problem confronting twentieth-century man is an ecological problem will our politics improve and become realistic. How does the human race propose to survive and, if possible, improve the lot and the intrinsic quality of its individual members? Do we propose to live on this planet in symbiotic harmony with our environment? Or, preferring to be wantonly stupid, shall we choose to live like murderous and suicidal parasites that kill their host and so destroy themselves?

Committing that sin of overweening bumptiousness, which the Greeks called *hubris*, we behave as though we were not members of earth's ecological community, as though we were privileged and, in some sort, supernatural beings and could throw our weight around like gods. But in fact we are, among other things, animals —emergent parts of the natural order. If our politicians were realists, they would think rather less about missiles and the problem of landing a couple of astronauts on the moon, rather more about hunger and moral squalor and the problem of enabling three billion men, women, and children, who will soon be six billions, to lead a tolerably human existence without, in the process, ruining and befouling their planetary environment.

Animals have no souls; therefore, according to the most authoritative Christian theologians, they may be treated as though they were things. The truth, as we are now beginning to realize, is that even things ought not to be treated as *mere* things. They should be treated as though they were parts of a vast living organism. "Do as you would be done by." The Golden Rule applies to our dealings with nature no less than to our dealings with our fellowmen. If we hope to be well treated by nature, we must stop talking about "mere things" and start treating our planet with intelligence and consideration.

Power politics in the context of nationalism raises problems that, except by war, are practically insoluble. The problems of ecology, on the other hand, admit of a rational solution and can be tackled without the arousal of those violent passions always associated with dogmatic ideology and nationalistic idolatry. There may be arguments about the best way of raising wheat in a cold climate or of re-afforesting a denuded mountain. But such arguments never lead to organized slaughter.

.   .   .   .

Power politics, nationalism, and dogmatic ideology are luxuries that the human race can no longer afford. Nor, as a species, can we afford the luxury of ignoring man's ecological situation. By shifting our attention from the now completely irrelevant and anachronistic politics of nationalism and military power to the problems of the human species and the still inchoate politics of human ecology we shall be killing two birds with one stone—reducing the threat of sudden destruction by scientific war and at the same time reducing the threat of more gradual biological disaster.

179.

[Interior Department's Yearbook]

THE NEW CONSERVATION [1965]

Today we face the future with every sign urging us to reassess the material base on which we must support our exploding population. In an earlier period of our history we held it wise and necessary to wrest the riches from our surroundings. Later it behooved us to preserve, protect, even to hoard our natural resources. Today we find conservation challenging not our muscles, but our minds.

No longer can we afford to cluster our conservationists into clubs. The concept of conservation cannot be isolated on little islands of awareness. It must become universally accepted as a familiar, taken-for-granted part of everyday life. Only thus can the "golden days balance" we now enjoy be preserved.

The new direction conservation is taking has been defined as "applied ecology," which means living things and how they relate to their total environment. It means stretching our resources to cover the demands of a growing population and still observing the rightful claims of the inhabitants of many an obscure "ecological niche."

It means not just the setting aside of priceless and irreplaceable natural treasures and the wisest multiple use of renewable resources, but an honest attempt to understand the relationship of all creatures—from the tiniest organisms in the chain of life to the lords of creation which we fondly imagine to be ourselves. The integrity of this chain is becoming increasingly apparent. Our exalted position atop the pyramid of life is secure only if the base is allowed to remain broad and varied.

Thoughtfully and surely this Nation's caretakers are arriving at new programs designed not just to remedy our yesterdays, but to enhance our tomorrows.

The program of wise and prophetic stewardship being forged today is both careful and daring. Conceived on a truly national scale, it is deeper than soil conservation, broader than wildlife preservation, more penetrating than forest husbandry, more encompassing than control of air and water pollution.

. . . .

The boundaries of our task are suddenly universal. For quality cannot be contained within the confines of a wildlife preserve, any more than blight could be contained on the other side of the tracks. Our environment is truly "of a piece" today and no amount of smug superiority will protect one shining section of it against the rot that lurks in another corner of the environmental fabric.

180.

Marston Bates

THE HUMAN ECOSYSTEM [1968]

Ecologists find it convenient to use, as their unit of study, the *ecosystem* rather than only the biological community, thus taking into account both the living organisms and their physical environment, which together form an interacting system. Every organism is affected by the conditions of the world in which it lives, but every organism also has some effect on these conditions, however trivial. The kind of forest growing in a particular region is in part a consequence of the soil, climate, and water supply of that region; but the kind of soil is also in part a consequence of the type of forest—coniferous, hardwood, or other—and the presence of the forest has a measurable influence on local climatic conditions and water supply.

The reciprocal interactions between organisms and environment are particularly striking in the case of the human species. Our activities are influenced in many ways by the nature of the physical setting in which we live—coastal, inland, desert, mountain, or forest. But we are also capable of altering the environment with unprecedented speed and effect. We would do well, then, to think in terms not of modern man in dominant relationship with other biological communities but of the human ecosystem—of the man-altered landscape and its biological components.

Man's actions can be looked at as efforts to simplify the biological relationships within the ecosystem to his own advantage. By clearing land and planting crops or orchards a complex of mixed species of wild plants may be replaced by a single kind of plant, a monoculture, which may extend over a wide area. In living off grain or fruit or tubers, man functions as a first-order consumer.

In largely vegetarian societies he is, thus, a "key industry animal," which means that a large population can be supported—but he is also a dead end, not giving support in turn to the usual predators and scavengers. With modern medicine he has even largely defeated the parasites.

Man's food web, in such societies, is thus reduced to a simple producer-consumer interaction, often with the decomposer system greatly modified as plant growth is maintained by adding fertilizers to the soil. Man also tries as far as possible to reduce or eliminate competition, controlling the insect pests of the crops and attempting to eliminate vertebrate competitors, whether crows, rats, or raccoons.

As a meat-eater, man becomes a second-order consumer, growing grain for his chickens or hogs or pasture for his cattle and then eating the animals. Again there is an attempt to eliminate competition from hawks, weasels, big cats, or wolves; again there is a vastly simplified food relationship, unique to the human ecosystem.

. . . .

The danger in the simplified ecosystem is in its liability to catastrophe. . . . The most complex of natural ecosystems (in the sense of those including the largest numbers of different kinds of organisms) are the most stable in that they are the least liable to great fluctuations in number of individuals of a particular species from year to year. Greatest contrast observed is between complex biotas such as those of the tropical rain forest or coral reef and the relatively simple biotas of the arctic tundra or northern forests. Records of fluctuations in various tundra animals suggest either a cyclic Malthusian relationship with food supply or catastrophic physiological or psychological controls. Such cyclic fluctuations are unknown in the rain forest, where the complexity of relations makes for flexibility and results in a relatively steady state among limited populations of the many species there.

. . . .

Modern man, thus, depends on the simplified food relations of intensive agriculture, and modern technology has been efficient in developing methods of pest control. But the danger is always there—of a new pest, of immunity to chemical methods of control, and of environmental pollution from the pesticides. It would seem most prudent, therefore, to preserve as much of the natural diversity as possible, as is done in densely settled Europe with the hedgerows—at least until we understand the system well enough to foresee, guard against, and repair the consequences of possible oversimplification.

The aesthetic argument depends on the impression that a varied landscape is more pleasing, more satisfactory for living, than a monotonous one. This may be a matter for debate; and it carries over from landscapes to the general question of the value of diversity in styles of life, in ways of thinking and acting. From diversity comes the possibility of change, of adaptive response to new conditions, of development and evolution.

181.

Barry Commoner [1969]

[In the spring of 1969, Barry Commoner, noted biologist and director of the Center for the Biology of Natural Systems, made the following remarks before the Senate Subcommittee on Intergovernmental Relations.]

We are all aware that there is something very wrong with the relationship between technology and the environment—that there is an urgent lesson to be learned from the growing intensity of air pollution, from the continued deterioration of our surface waters, from the proliferating problems of the urban environment. What is less clear is what that lesson is.

A prevalent view is that environmental deterioration is a consequence of relatively minor faults in our technology—the lack of adequate scrubbers on smoke stacks, of insufficient treatment of sewage, of the absence of proper fume traps on automotive exhausts. If this view were sufficient to the problem, then the present efforts of the Congress and the government to deal with it would be adequate, given the necessary funds. . . .

However, there is strong evidence which shows that the environmental deterioration that we are now experiencing is not due to minor faults in our technology, but to major ones, and that the future productivity and quality of life that the Nation can hope to enjoy requires that these faults be corrected. I believe that our very survival is at stake.

. . . .

If we are to succeed as inhabitants of a world increasingly transformed by technology, we need to reassess our attitudes toward the natural world on which our technology intrudes. For in the eager search for the benefits of modern science and technology, we have become enticed into a nearly fatal illusion: that we have at last escaped from the dependence of man on the rest of nature.

The truth is tragically different. We have become, not less dependent on the balance of nature, but more dependent on it. Modern technology has so stressed the web of processes in the living environment at its most vulnerable points that there is little leeway left in the system. And time is short; we must begin, now, to learn how to make our technological power conform to the more powerful constraints of the living environment. To succeed we shall need to reexamine not only the nature of technology, but also its relation to our economic system.

I suggest that we must reverse the order of relationships which now connect economic need, technology, and the biology of the natural world. In the present scheme of things, relatively narrow economic needs dictate the aim of technology. But when this technology is intruded upon the natural world, a myriad of ecological and biological problems arise—and it is left to the biologists, physicians, and others concerned with the survival of living things, to cope with these hazards as best they can.

So long as the scale of technological intrusion into the environment remained small relative to the scale of the biosphere itself, this kind of haphazard arrangement could perhaps be tolerated. But that stage in the human occupancy of the earth has now come to an end. There is now simply not enough air, water, and soil on the earth to absorb the resultant man-made insults without effect. If we continue in our reckless way to destroy the living systems which support us, we threaten the stability of our systems of productivity. If it continues on a worldwide scale, this planet will before long become an unsuitable place for human habitation.

Instead, I suggest that we need learn how to *proceed from* an evaluation of human needs and desires, and the potential of a given environment to meet them. We must then determine what technological processes and economic resources are needed to accomplish these desires, in harmony with the demands of the whole natural system. And, finally, as the founders of the Republic did in their time, we need to develop economic, political, and social processes suitable to these purposes.

182.

David Perlman

THE EARTH FROM SPACE [1969]

This year, America took a firsthand look at the moon. But in years to come, 1969 may best be remembered as the year of our first long view of America the Beautiful and the rest of our earth. The Apollo capsules, invisible in the vastness of space, broadcasting television images back to American viewers, became mirrors in which we could see ourselves anew. It was a humbling experience.

From Apollo, the receding earth looked as lonely in space as the spacecraft seemed from earth. Suddenly, we could understand what Adlai Stevenson had said: "We travel together, passengers on a little spaceship; dependent on its vulnerable reserves of air and soil; all committed for our safety to its security and peace; preserved from annihilation only by the care, the work and . . . the love we give our fragile craft."

The earth was revealed as Apollo's twin: Spaceship Earth. Man on one spaceship radioed to man on the other: "The earth from here is a grand oasis in the . . . vastness of space!" An oasis: a fragile outpost of life in a lifeless pocket of the universe.

183.

William Murdoch and Joseph Connell

THE ROLE OF THE ECOLOGIST [1970]

The public's awakening to the environmental crisis over the past few years has been remarkable. A recent Gallup Poll showed that every other American was concerned about the population problem. A questionnaire sent to about five hundred University of California freshmen asked which of twenty-five topics should be included in a general biology course for non-majors. The top four positions were: Human Population Problems (85%), Pollution (79%), Genetics (71.3%), and Ecology (66%).

The average citizen is at least getting to know the word ecology, even though his basic understanding of it may not be significantly increased. Not more than five years ago, we had to explain at length what an ecologist was. Recently when we have described ourselves as ecologists, we have been met with respectful nods of recognition.

A change has also occurred among ecologists themselves. Until recently the meetings of ecologists we attended were concerned with the esoterica of a "pure science," but now ecologists are haranguing each other on the necessity for ecologists to become involved in the "real world." We can expect that peripatetic "ecological experts" will soon join the ranks of governmental consultants jetting back and forth to the Capitol—thereby adding their quota to the pollution of the atmosphere. However, that will be a small price to pay if they succeed in clearing the air of the political verbiage that still passes for an environmental policy in Washington.

Concern about environment, of course, is not limited to the United States. The ecological crisis, by its nature, is basically an international problem, so it seems likely that the ecologist as "expert" is here to stay. To some extent the present commotion about ecology arises from people climbing on the newest bandwagon. When the limits of ecological expertise become apparent, we must expect to lose a few passengers. But, if only because there is no alternative, the ecologist and the policymakers appear to be stuck with each other for some time to come.

While a growing awareness of the relevance of ecology must be welcomed, there are already misconceptions about it. Further, the traditional role of the expert in Washington predisposes the nation to a misuse of its ecologists. Take an example. A common lament of the socially conscious citizen is that though we have enough science and technology to put a man on the moon we cannot maintain a decent environment in the United States. The implicit premise here seems clear: the solution to our ecological crisis is technological. A logical extension of this argument is that, in this particular case, the ecologist is the appropriate "engineer" to resolve the crisis. This reflects the dominant American philosophy (which is sure to come up after every lecture on the environment) that the answer to most of our problems is technology and, in particular, that the answer to the problems raised by technology is more technology. Perhaps the most astounding example of this blind faith is the recent assurance issued by the government that the SST will not fly over the United States until the sonic boom problem is solved. The sonic boom "problem," of course, cannot be "solved." One job of the ecologist is to dispel this faith in technology.

. . . .

Even if we dispense with the idea that ecologists are some sort of environmental engineers and compare them to the pure physicists who provide scientific rules for engineers, do the tentative understandings we have outlined provide a sound basis for action by those who would manage the environment? It is self-evident that they do not.

. . . .

We submit that ecology as such probably cannot do what many people expect it to do; it cannot provide a set of "rules" of the kind needed to manage the environment. Nevertheless, ecologists have a great responsibility to help solve the crisis; the solution they offer should be founded on a basic "ecological attitude." Ecologists are likely to be aware of the consequences of environmental manipulation; possibly most important, they are ready to deal with the environmental problem since their basic ecological attitude is itself the solution to the problem. Interestingly enough, the supporting data do not generally come from our "abstract research" but from massive uncontrolled "experiments" done in the name of development.

. . . .

Tinkering with technology is essentially equivalent to oiling its wheels. The very act of making minor alterations, in order to placate the public, actually allows the general development of technology to proceed unhindered, only increasing the environmental problems it causes. This is what sociologists have called a "pseudo-event." That is, activities go on which give the appearance of tackling the problem; they will not, of course, solve it but only remove public pressure for a solution.

Tinkering also distracts the ecologist from his real job. It is the ecologist's job, as a general rule, to oppose growth and "progress." He cannot set about convincing the public of the correctness of this position if in the meantime he is putting his shoulder behind the wheel of technology. The political power system has a long tradition of buying off its critics, and the ecologist is liable to wind up perennially compromising his position, thereby merely slowing down slightly or redirecting the onslaught of technology.

. . . .

We do not believe that the ecologist has anything really new to say. His task, rather, is to inculcate in the government and the people basic ecological attitudes. The population must come, and very soon, to appreciate certain basic notions. For example: a finite world cannot support or withstand a continually expanding population and technology; there are limits to the capacity of environmental sinks; ecosystems are sets of interacting entities and there is no "treatment" which does not have "side effects" . . .; we cannot continually simplify systems and expect them to remain stable, and once they do become unstable there is a tendency for instability to increase with time. Each child should grow up knowing and understanding his place in the environment and the possible consequences of his interaction with it.

In short, the ecologist must convince the population that the only solution to the problem of growth is not to grow. This applies to population and, unless the population is declining, to its standard of living. It should be clear by now that "standard of living" is probably beginning to have an inverse relationship to the quality of life. An increase in the gross national product must be construed, from the ecological point of view, as disastrous. (The case of underdeveloped countries, of course, is different.)

We do not minimize the difficulties in changing the main driving force in life. The point of view of the ecologist, however, should be subversive; it has to be subversive or the ecologist will become merely subservient.

184.

Frank K. Kelly

THE NEW MAN [1970]

The landing on the moon confirmed the solidity of other worlds. Many of us expected to see what we saw; many accepted it with a shrug or a smile. To young people already aware of science fiction, it was a happening that had happened long before. But the sight of our little globe shining in space made us realize that we can be inside and outside at the same time.

In each of us, now that we know so much and know how little that is, there are two states of being, embracing and struggling: Mankind I and Mankind II. We are still attached to the earth, but our minds move in and out in a dizzying rhythm. We are changing so swiftly that we do not know what we are or what we may become.

Since Hiroshima, we have known that the old man must die. The man of devouring ambition, the consuming man, must give way to the new man, the learning man, the man of understanding, the servant of life. The future depends upon our opening of ourselves to the emergence of the servant.

185.

Hal Borland

SPRING, AND A TIME TO LISTEN [1970]

There's something about the vernal equinox that takes me right back to fundamentals. It reminds me, for one thing, that the year began with March, not January, before the Roman emperors began tinkering with the calendar. It makes me thankful that winter doesn't last six months instead of three. It reminds me that April is at hand—April, a teen-age girl with a bunch of daffodils in her hand, stars in her eyes, a taunt in her laughter, and an inclination to play practical jokes. And the equinox makes me glad I live where I do. Doubly glad this year.

Up here in the hills we know that we always have to earn spring by enduring January and February and sometimes March. This year, by the middle of February we began to think the price had been inflated a good deal more than the six per cent they concede for everything else. We had the snowiest December and the coldest January on record. Groundhog Day was dour and lowery, as usual, and spring didn't come early, also as usual. However, here is April, bought and paid for. April, with blue sky, an early thunderstorm, a late snowstorm, cursed with March's leftovers, blessed with a foretaste of May. April, yellow rocket and shadblow and dandelions, pink buds on the apple trees, purple leaves on the lilacs, peepers in the twilight, robins in the dawn.

And high time. It's much easier to listen to and believe the facts of conservation in April than in January, and the tide of environmental concern has been rising all winter. For years a handful of us have been warning that things were getting out of hand, but we were largely talking to a vacuum. The technologists, the industrial chemists, the public officials, and most of the general public, when they heard us at all, said, "Nonsense! Who cares about a little smog and smoke? They are signs of full employment. What does a little sewage and industrial waste matter in the rivers and lakes? Water is water, isn't it? And what if the miracle pesticides do kill a few songbirds? We are prosperous, the most prosperous nation in the world, with the highest standard of living in history. That's what really matters."

But finally even they began to choke on their own fumes and gag on their own water. And conservation became a popular cause.

. . . .

I am sure there are plenty of other writers and talkers to expatiate on the need for open space, breathing room, grass, trees, potable water, breathable air, and the lethal nature of biocides. Others undoubtedly will discuss our incredible mountains of trash and garbage, our billions of tons and gallons of industrial waste, our mad population growth.

But beyond the scientific fact that a tree is the best source of oxygen on earth is the fact that a tree is a tree. Not board feet of lumber, or gallons of turpentine, or rolls of newsprint. But a tree, a growing plant, a marvel of fiber and sap and bud and leaf and blossom. Shade in summer, and shelter for nesting birds. Nuts in autumn for hungry squirrels. And a beauty forever, with its haze of new leaves in the spring; its mass of green, fluttering in the breeze, pattering in the rain, casting shade, making life more pleasant in the summer; its color in the autumn, sheer beauty that not even the most enterprising chemist has yet been able to sell as a pigment or a flavor or a food. A tree, one of the most beautiful things on earth.

The land, of course, is a commodity. It is a building site, a field for corn or hay, a sand and gravel pit, a place to put a superhighway, or an airport, or a parking field. It is open space between houses, between towns. It is room for cities and suburbs to expand. But the land is also the only place where the fundamental green of the leaf grows. And that green is the fundamental sustenance of life. It manufactures the oxygen and it is the ultimate food of all of us, ant to elephant, horse to human being. That is the land. And when we want to have a piece of that land to stand on, to walk upon, to know intimately, it is more than mere acquisitiveness. It is fundamental with us, for we need to know and be in daily contact with the earth of our own origins. It's as simple as that. And we want some of the wild places preserved wild because that is where we can come close to the truth of life and the earth itself. We smell it when we plow a field in spring. We see it when we cut and cure hay in June. We taste it when we take in the garden crop in September. But we feel it, we are a part of it, when we go to a wilderness area at any time of the year.

. . . .

Perhaps you begin to understand. More than air and water and soil are at stake. Conservation and environment are not so simple. There are ways of life, and there are fundamentals of living, that also need conserving, if only as reminders of what is possible for man if he ever again is master of his own life. Not as an example of the antique or the historical, not Grandfather's way, but a simpler way of life possible even today without privation or hardship or flight from reality.

What I am talking about is receptivity. Perhaps that sounds pretentious, but it really isn't. It is understanding and a willingness to participate. I have heard someone speak of "appreciation," but that is too precious a term; it smacks of the esthetic, and this is a thoroughly practical matter. Perhaps that is why I said at the start that April is a better time to discuss such matters than January. In April the world around you, particularly here in the country, cannot be ignored. You are receptive, or you are deaf, dumb, and blind, and an utter clod to boot. And I am not talking about the traveler out to see how many miles he can cover in a weekend, or about the bird watcher out to accumulate a longer list than her neighbor down the street. I am talking about understanding what is all around you, not merely counting or identifying.

We keep hearing that population is the ultimate cause of all these environmental problems, and in many areas that is true. Certainly some way should be found to make 1980, or 2000, less of a terminal deadline for human survival. Maybe disease will take care of that, or famine, or a cataclysmic war. But I have less fear of the standing-room-only prophecies than I have of the tendency to emulate the ants. And of the sophisticated disdain for all things rural, coupled with blind legislative insistence, largely of urban origin, that all farmland be vacated and all country folk be taken to the cities. You don't conserve anything that way, and you certainly don't improve environments. It often seems that the urban majority of our population, now up around eighty per cent I believe, is afraid of the open country except when passed through safely inside a speeding automobile or high above it in a supersonic transport. Afraid of open spaces and distrustful of their relatively few inhabitants.

Why? Not simple agoraphobia, I am sure. And not wholly a matter of thinking everyone living five miles from a metropolitan center is an oaf or a dolt. I think we all know now that a city lunkhead is just as witless as a rural simpleton, and the averages don't vary much per thousand. Can it be because they have forgotten so many things that should be remembered?

Actually, we all once lived close to the soil, even here in America. Well over half of us were still there within the memory of men barely old enough for Social Security. The ways of the country are in our blood, if not in our hearts, as a nation. We turn our back on them at our peril, and we embrace the technologies that have done so much to destroy our environment. We listened too long to the factory whistles, thinking that more was better, and bigger was best of all. Bigger cities, bigger industry, bigger armament, bigger wars.

And that is what this is all about, this sudden surge of concern over the environment. That's what some of us have been saying for twenty years or more. And now it's another April, another spring, and maybe it will be easier to listen to what was said all this time. As I said just a few paragraphs back, in April you are receptive, you listen and try to understand, or you are deaf, dumb, and blind, and an utter clod to boot. Let's stand on that for now. Let this be the time to separate the men from the clods.

186.

Thomas W. Wilson, Jr.

THE SHAPE OF THE PREDICAMENT [1970]

Ideally construed, the perception of a unitary and finite biosphere, beyond national jurisdiction or political coloration, and on which all life depends, should be a powerful unifying force in human affairs. There is little doubt that environmental concerns will extend and strengthen the fabric of world community in some of its dimensions. It is even permissible to hope that the imperative of common custody of the common environment might some day provide man with a "moral equivalent for war."

It also is prudent to note that powerful traditions, stubborn conflicts, human obstinacy, and plain ignorance all serve as brakes on such an evolution. It is prudent to know, too, that the agencies of government at various levels are only in the most preliminary stages of attempting to adapt to or even perceive the shape of the whole predicament—and are a long way from having the knowledge, the institutional forms, the administrative techniques, or the philosophical insights which ultimately will be needed for effective management of the life-support system of Spaceship Earth and its lonely crew called Man. For a long time to come, there will be many more questions than answers.

187.

Gladwin Hill

AFTER EARTH DAY [1970]

Psychologists have long recognized a phenomenon called "the self-fulfilling prophecy." It has nothing to do with extra-sensory perception or witchcraft. It simply means that the more talk there is about something—be it a potential riot or the success of a fund drive—the more likely it is to actually happen because people's thoughts and actions are subconsciously attuned to accomplishing what is talked about.

This explains the extraordinary intensity of public interest in environmental reform that reached a crescendo in the April 22 observance of Earth Day—an event such as the world had never seen before. For the first time in history virtually an entire nation, including Congress, paused in its workaday activities to contemplate the deterioration of its physical surroundings and life-patterns.

"Can the enthusiasm of Earth Day be sustained?" Although this question has been asked a million times, it is the wrong question. It tends to put Earth Day in the role of *cause* rather than *effect*.

The exact extent of Earth Day activities probably will never be known. Environmental Action, the Washington-based group of young people which promoted the event, now estimates that at least 20 million people participated in 4,000 campus and community programs that ran the gamut from picking up litter to praying.

. . . .

How much of all this is sound and how much of it is substantial?

Anything as big as the environmental crisis and the environmental revolution is bound to involve both the sham and the real—as history itself does.

There is an immense amount of lip service, of political opportunism, of official trimming and tacking. There are still few effective Federal and state measures against such elementary evils as air and water pollution. But no one who attended the May 22 General Motors stockholders' meeting in Detroit could doubt that a new value-system is descending upon American industry. The reformers lost the vote-skirmish, but their thesis remained virtually unchallenged: A new dimension of public well-being, physical and aesthetic, has to be built into the profit-making structure.

As people examine the significance of the environmental upheaval, they almost inevitably end up like the blind men examining the elephant, drawing different conclusions from disparate parts. The whole is almost too big to conceive.

That is why we now have some people talking about litter in the streets, while others are talking about the no-growth economy; why the success of a bond issue in the state of Washington will be taken as evidence that "environment" is triumphing, while the mutterings of some super-patriots that ecology is communistic will be chronicled as "emergent backlash."

Obviously the peak of involvement and excitement that came on Earth Day cannot be sustained through the year. But to suggest conversely—with the American propensity for casting things in alternative extremes—that concern might vanish, is to categorize the life-and-death problems of environment with crab-grass or pornography. The only way people can escape facing up to environmental problems is for the world to stop and let them off.

The immensity of it all means there are many questions that may not be resolved soon. For example: How do we mesh antipollution efforts with equally important aspects of environment such as race relations, civil rights and poverty? It will be no use to have clean air if the breathers are stifled by rancor and inequity; neither will it be any use to solve sociological problems if, as solutions are achieved, everyone is gasping his last.

Where, then, do we go from here?

THE LAND ETHIC

[While the ecological attitude is vastly more relevant to the reality of nature than the fragmented view of traditional conservationism is, it can still be seen, at its lowest level of application, as merely another technique, albeit more subtle and sophisticated, by which man can assert his dominance over nature. To the solution of problems engendered by an essentially primitive technology, that is, conservationism represents a first approximation of which ecology is a further refinement.

But ecology holds within it a suggestion, and in its more reflective expressions an explicit statement, of a more radical shift of viewpoint. Perhaps man ought to forgo thoughts of dominion and think, rather, in terms of cooperation. This is a change in ends, not means, and the difference is an ethical one. Called sometimes the "ecological conscience," sometimes the "land ethic," such an outlook involves taking man's inseparability from the rest of nature as a prime datum and going on from that basis to contend that, as man has rights, so too do nature's other creatures.

In the selections that follow, the theme is rights, and the organization is intended to show a development of the notion of rights from those of the individual man to those of life itself.]

188.

William L. Finley

GAME RIGHTS [1914]

The last session of Congress not only took its first step toward protection of song and plume birds, but it took a step in game protection that was far-reaching in its effect.

Who would have thought twenty-five years ago that Uncle Sam would come to assume the right to regulate the shooting of wild birds? The killing of its own game has been regarded as one of the sacred privileges of the State. Several of the States had passed laws permitting their citizens to shoot ducks from September 1 to March 1, whether they were mallards or wood ducks. Uncle Sam has stepped in and said: "You can shoot mallards from October 1 to January 15, but you can't shoot a wood duck for a period of five years."

This is not a radical step. It is merely following to a logical conclusion the action taken by the State and acting on the policy of the greatest good for the greatest number.

Years ago the landowner thought he could kill the wild birds and animals which he found running at large on his own premises, or take the fish out of the stream that ran through his place, at any time of the year. He owned his own land and as an American citizen had inherent rights.

Who would dispute the homesteader in the mountains when he took the water from his own spring? The water bubbled out of the bowels of the earth on his own land and he was lord of it. Yet when he began to use this same water to irrigate his garden, he was often careless. He sometimes let it run to waste, depriving his neighbor next below of the use of the water to quench the thirst of his orchard. Then it was necessary for the State to step in between warring landowners and settle the dispute.

The same question arose with the bobwhite quail which were to-day on Mr. A's property and to-morrow about Mr. B's house. Mr. A desired to kill and eat all the quail, but Mr. B wished to have them about because they were his friends and were of economic and aesthetic value. The State took the position that the birds belonged not only to Mr. A and Mr. B, but also to Mr. C and Mr. D, and made strict laws in accordance therewith. The State was upheld by the Supreme Court of the United States.

A little later on the State took a more advanced view—that no citizen could hunt or kill wild birds or animals until he had paid for the privilege. At that time the Hunters' License Law was regarded as an infringement upon the rights of an American citizen; yet at the present time it is in force in almost every State in the Union. The money collected from these licenses is used for protecting and propagating wild birds and animals.

It happens that many wild birds migrate from North to South in the fall to pass the winter and return to their breeding-grounds in the spring. They are "citizens," not of one State, but of many. They belong, not to the people of one State, but to the people of the United States.

·   ·

Inasmuch as the State formerly regulated certain rights that the individual thought belonged solely to him, just so Uncle Sam has at last taken a logical step in bird protection by issuing rules for the migrating flocks that belong to the National Government and not to each State government. The only objection is a far-away echo of the howler for States' rights who says everything is being concentrated in Washington.

189.

E. F. Roberts

PLEAD THE NINTH AMENDMENT! [1970]

Suppose, for example, that a coke-manufacturing plant had been built in an American city during the late nineteenth century. The manufacturing technique of the time involved quenching the burning coal with water, a process that generated vast clouds of gases, smoke, and soot and rendered the neighborhood uninhabitable for gentlefolk. If the old-time residents turned to the law for help against the plant, they found a doctrine dating back to the reign of Henry II to the effect that no one should do things on his land that would disturb his neighbors' enjoyment of their land. Presumably, the homeowners in our hypothetical situation should have been able to obtain either an injunction to stop the polluting of their environment or a judgment for money damages commensurate with the depreciation in value inflicted upon their homes. In all likelihood, however, they would have gotten nothing, no satisfaction at all, because the law went through a convulsive period early in the nineteenth century.

During the Industrial Revolution rules were overhauled wholesale, and the values of the agrarian society evolved into a new *coda* compatible with commerce and manufacturing. . . .

In this restructuring process the law of nuisance was translated into the prevailing ideology of fault. Our hypothetical coke manufacturer was not at fault—in legal terms he was not negligent—because he followed the accepted procedures in the manufacture of coke. Equally manifest, he was not at fault in locating his plant in the city because capital, labor, raw materials, and transportation routes converged there to make large-scale manufacture possible. Therefore, the harm visited upon the city's residents had to be chalked up as an accidental by-product of progress.

. . . .

The energies released by the Industrial Revolution have been the undoing of the conventional wisdom of that phenomenon. The prospering factories that have coagulated in the cities, belching fumes and disgorging chemically exotic wastes, have created conditions whereby the chance occurrence of a weather inversion can turn a city into a death camp. The bankers, lawyers, advertisers, and executives associated with commerce and industry realize too well that they must work in the cities. The city-dwelling working class, increasingly cognizant of its power to disrupt, is no longer put off with nineteenth-century sophistries to justify its deteriorating environment. . . .

Should our hypothetical entrepreneur open his coke plant in an urbanized area today and shower pollutants upon his neighbors, the result would be different but, interestingly enough, not totally. Again, given the facts that the area was appropriate and that conventional manufacturing techniques were employed, the plant probably would be assessed with a judgment for money damages to offset declining values in the immediate neighborhood. In all likelihood, however, no injunction would be issued to close the plant. This halfway change in nuisance law aptly reflects today's conventional wisdom.

. . . .

Exercising their power to enjoin nuisances, the judges could shut down our hypothetical plant. This option, however, still gives the judges chance to pause. Increased production, more jobs, and more taxable enterprises are still basic ingredients in the accepted economic formula for relieving the plight of the poor. Shutting down plants would decrease employment opportunities and subtract from the number of taxable enterprises necessary to sustain current welfare programs. While judges have been willing to restructure the rules to accommodate the law to contemporary needs, they are unwilling to recast the law into a new mold until they are certain that society has rejected growth as the keystone of its value system.

The judges are saying, in effect, that the solutions to industrial pollution must be devised by the legislative branch of government. Whether the public is willing to pay the price for eliminating pollution is better ascertained through the ballot box than through the best hunches of the judiciary.

. . . .

In one famous case the Federal Power Commission (FPC) was reversed when, upon purely hard-headed economic considerations, it licensed a hydroelectric project that would have destroyed one of the most scenic sites along the Hudson River. The case was significant because it established the right of conservationists to sue. The case was decided against the FPC because the congressional statute that had created the agency had expressly instructed it to take environmental considerations into account, something the FPC had flagrantly neglected to do. What if the statute had not contained that instruction? What would the conservationists, once in court, have talked about? What "law" could they point to in order

to fault the agency for its failure to take seriously the environmental consequences of their decision?

. . . .

At this point some lawyers, including myself, conclude that the
only answer to this conundrum lies in the Bill of Rights. To put it
bluntly, there exists a constitutional right to a decent environment,
which mandates that every government agency—be it federal, state,
or local—cast its decisions so as not to contribute further to the
decline of today's environmental status quo. This decision would
only operate prospectively and would not extend retroactively. The
harm that has already been done can only be undone by legislative
action and not by words alone; words alone, however, when they
are constitutional law words, are able to ensure that past mistakes
will not be repeated.

From whence can this right be derived? This is a horse soon
curried. In *Griswold* v. *Connecticut*, for example, the Supreme
Court discovered a "right of privacy" inherent in the Bill of Rights,
even though that right was not there in so many words. In fact,
the long ignored ninth amendment warns us that the listing of
rights in the other amendments, such as those guaranteeing freedom of religion and speech, does not eliminate other rights "retained by the people." Manifestly, if the people have the freedom
to exercise free speech and to enjoy their privacy, they must also
have the right to a decent environment. Why is this clear? Because
if we do not have a right to a decent environment, the rest of our
rights will prove illusory. We cannot enjoy our other rights if we
are all dead. True, this right has never been articulated before, but
until the advent of a potentially lethal technological society there
was no need to insist upon such a right. Now that there is a potential for environmental disaster, the time has become propitious
for the Supreme Court, sensing the felt needs of the time, to implement within the system this fundamental right held by the
people.

190.

William O. Douglas

From A WILDERNESS BILL OF RIGHTS [1965]

Our Constitution not
only spells out the authority of the majority; it also places re-
straints on them. It protects minorities, placing their rights be-

yond the reach of the majority—unless the Constitution is itself amended. The unpopular can speak and write as they wish and worship even in an unorthodox way. The majority cannot deprive the most depraved person of counsel in a criminal trial. Even a despised one is entitled to bail; he may not be punished by a statute that has a retroactive reach, that is, by an *ex post facto* law; if he is to be punished, he is entitled to a judicial trial—a legislative condemnation (bill of attainder) not being permitted.

Wilderness values may not appeal to all Americans. But they make up a passionate cause for millions. They are, indeed, so basic to our national well-being that they must be honored by any free society that respects diversity. We deal not with transitory matters but with the very earth itself. We who come this way are merely short-term tenants. Our power in wilderness terms is only the power to destroy, not to create. Those who oppose wilderness values today may have sons and daughters who will honor wilderness values tomorrow. Our responsibility as life tenants is to make certain that there are wilderness values to honor after we have gone.

The Forest Service stands guard over 14½ million acres of wilderness and the National Park Service over about 22 million acres. Yet at the federal level there is no constitutional guarantee that we will have even an acre of wilderness left out of the vast public lands owned by the central government. At the state level, New York leads the way. As already noted, she gives a constitutional guarantee that the Adirondacks shall be "forever wild." But constitutions can be—and frequently are—changed. As we have seen, strenuous efforts have been made to amend New York's constitution so that the Adirondacks will no longer be "forever wild." To date those efforts have failed.

Since one function of a free society is to protect minority rights, we need to guarantee that large areas of the original America will be preserved in perpetuity. Those who love the wildness of the land and who find exhilaration in backpacking and sleeping on the ground may be idiosyncratic; but they represent values important in a free society. Wilderness people are at the opposite end of the spectrum from any standardized product of this machine age; yet they represent basic values when they protest against automation for the wilderness and for their grandchildren.

The preservation of wilderness values requires a Wilderness Bill of Rights, and its preamble (to paraphrase Helene B. Hart of the American Camping Association) would read as follows:

We believe in the right of children to an understanding of their place in nature's community, of which they are a part.

We believe in their right to acquire skills for living in the out-of-doors as part of their heritage as descendants of pioneers, to swim, to fish, to manage a canoe, to climb, to hike, to worship.

We believe in their right of discovery and adventure in nature's world, their right to pit their strength against the elements and in their right to a sense of achievement.

We believe in their right to friendly comradeship with someone older, likewise an adventure in the out-of-doors.

We believe in their need of the healing found in the wildness of nature.

We believe in their unfolding response to the warm earth, the friendly stars, the music of streams, the unknown life in the hidden places, great trees, sunsets and storms.

We believe that all these are pathways for them, and for us, to God, and that their language is universal.

191.

Paul R. Ehrlich

NEW RIGHTS [1968]

At no small risk of being considered a nut, you can do a lot of good by persuading your personal acquaintances that the crisis is here, that something must be done, and that they can help. What follows are some specific suggestions for arguments that may help in certain circumstances. They are classified on the basis of a target individual.

. . . .

TARGET SAYS THERE IS AN "INALIENABLE RIGHT" TO HAVE AS MANY CHILDREN AS ONE WANTS. Point out that as long as the invention of inalienable rights is in vogue, you've invented a few of your own. They are:

1. The right to limit our families.
2. The right to eat.
3. The right to eat meat.
4. The right to drink pure water.
5. The right to live uncrowded.
6. The right to avoid regimentation.
7. The right to hunt and fish.
8. The right to view natural beauty.
9. The right to breathe clean air.
10. The right to silence.

11. The right to avoid pesticide poisoning.
12. The right to be free of thermonuclear war.
13. The right to educate our children.
14. The right to have grandchildren.
15. The right to have great-grandchildren.

Since the price of having all these "inalienable rights" is giving up the right to irresponsible reproduction, you win 15 "rights" to one.

192.

Aldo Leopold [1949]

THE LAND ETHIC [1949]

[In his nearly twenty years with the U.S. Forest Service, Aldo Leopold had ample opportunity to observe, teach, and practise conservation and to discover its fatal weakness: It was wholly without force in the face of economic pressures. "In our attempt to make conservation easy," he wrote, "we have made it trivial," and he went on to show that the lip service it drew from nearly everyone was a poor substitute for what was urgently needed—intelligence, dedication, and sacrifice. What was necessary, he contended, was the replacement of the economic bias, which, however "enlightened," invariably worked to nature's detriment, with a radically different outlook grounded in what he called the "land ethic." In the concluding section of A Sand County Almanac Leopold sketched the history of ethics as an evolutionary sequence in which the development is one of increasing inclusiveness: After beginning as a code dealing with little more than property rights, ethics evolved, slowly and with great difficulty, to encompass the ideas of personal rights and dignity. In the next step, to be achieved with no less difficulty and little more speed, ethics would grow further to encompass the whole of the living community. In the context of the land ethic, man would relinquish the futile title of conqueror—as well as that of cost accountant—and resume his original role as a member of nature's community.]

It is inconceivable to me that an ethical relation to land can exist without love, respect, and admiration for land, and a high regard for its value.

By value, I of course mean something far broader than mere economic value; I mean value in the philosophical sense.

Perhaps the most serious obstacle impeding the evolution of a land ethic is the fact that our educational and economic system is headed away from, rather than toward, an intense consciousness of land. Your true modern is separated from the land by many middlemen, and by innumerable physical gadgets. He has no vital relation to it; to him it is the space between cities on which crops grow. Turn him loose for a day on the land, and if the spot does not happen to be a golf links or a 'scenic' area, he is bored stiff. If crops could be raised by hydroponics instead of farming, it would suit him very well. Synthetic substitutes for wood, leather, wool, and other natural land products suit him better than the originals. In short, land is something he has 'outgrown.'

Almost equally serious as an obstacle to a land ethic is the attitude of the farmer for whom the land is still an adversary, or a taskmaster that keeps him in slavery. Theoretically, the mechanization of farming ought to cut the farmer's chains, but whether it really does is debatable.

One of the requisites for an ecological comprehension of land is an understanding of ecology, and this is by no means co-extensive with 'education'; in fact, much higher education seems deliberately to avoid ecological concepts. An understanding of ecology does not necessarily originate in courses bearing ecological labels; it is quite as likely to be labeled geography, botany, agronomy, history, or economics. This is as it should be, but whatever the label, ecological training is scarce.

The case for a land ethic would appear hopeless but for the minority which is in obvious revolt against these 'modern' trends.

The 'key-log' which must be moved to release the evolutionary process for an ethic is simply this: quit thinking about decent land-use as solely an economic problem. Examine each question in terms of what is ethically and esthetically right, as well as what is economically expedient. A thing is right when it tends to preserve the integrity, stability, and beauty of the biotic community. It is wrong when it tends otherwise.

It of course goes without saying that economic feasibility limits the tether of what can or cannot be done for land. It always has and it always will. The fallacy the economic determinists have tied around our collective neck, and which we now need to cast off, is the belief that economics determines *all* land-use. This is simply not true. An innumerable host of actions and attitudes, comprising perhaps the bulk of all land relations, is determined by the land-users' tastes and predilections, rather than by his purse. The bulk of all land relations hinges on investments of time, forethought, skill, and faith rather than on investments of cash. As a land-user thinketh, so is he.

I have purposely presented the land ethic as a product of social evolution because nothing so important as an ethic is ever 'written.' Only the most superficial student of history supposes that Moses 'wrote' the Decalogue; it evolved in the minds of a thinking community, and Moses wrote a tentative summary of it for a 'seminar.' I say tentative because evolution never stops.

The evolution of a land ethic is an intellectual as well as emotional process. Conservation is paved with good intentions which prove to be futile, or even dangerous, because they are devoid of critical understanding either of the land, or of economic land-use. I think it is a truism that as the ethical frontier advances from the individual to the community, its intellectual content increases.

The mechanism of operation is the same for any ethic: social approbation for right actions: social disapproval for wrong actions.

By and large, our present problem is one of attitudes and implements. We are remodeling the Alhambra with a steamshovel, and we are proud of our yardage. We shall hardly relinquish the shovel, which after all has many good points, but we are in need of gentler and more objective criteria for its successful use.

193.

Thomas Merton

AS BEST WE CAN [1968]

An investigation of the wilderness mystique and of the contrary mystique of exploitation and power reveals the tragic depth of the conflict that now exists in the American mind. The ideal of freedom and creativity that has been celebrated with such optimism and self-assurance runs the risk of being turned completely inside out if the natural ecological balance, on which it depends for its vitality, is destroyed. Take away the space, the freshness, the rich spontaneity of a wildly flourishing nature, and what will become of the creative pioneer mystique? A pioneer in a suburb is a sick man tormenting himself with projects of virile conquest. In a ghetto he is a policeman shooting every black man who gives him a dirty look. Obviously, the frontier is a thing of the past, the bison has vanished, and only by some miracle have a few Indians managed to survive. There are still some forests and wilderness areas, but we are firmly established as an urban culture. Nevertheless, the problem of ecology exists in a most acute form. The danger of fallout and atomic waste is only one of the more spectacular ones.

. . . .

The tragedy that has been revealed in the ecological shambles created by business and war is a tragedy of ambivalence, aggression, and fear cloaked in virtuous ideas and justified by pseudo-Christian clichés. Or rather a tragedy of pseudo-creativity deeply impregnated with hatred, megalomania, and the need for domination. Its psychological root doubtless lies in the profound dehumanization and alienation of modern Western man, who has gradually come to mistake the artificial value of inert objects and abstractions (goods, money, property) for the power of life itself. Against this ethic Aldo Leopold laid down a basic principle of the ecological conscience: "A thing is right when it tends to preserve the integrity, stability, and beauty of the biotic community. It is wrong when it tends otherwise."

In the light of this principle, an examination of our social, economic, and political history in the last hundred years would be a moral nightmare, redeemed only by a few gestures of good will on the part of those who obscurely realize that there *is* a problem. Yet compared to the magnitude of the problem, their efforts are at best pitiful: and what is more, the same gestures are made with great earnestness by the very people who continue to ravage, destroy, and pollute the country. They honor the wilderness myth while they proceed to destroy nature.

Can Aldo Leopold's ecological conscience become effective in America today? The ecological conscience is also essentially a peace-making conscience. A country that seems to be more and more oriented to permanent hot or cold war-making does not give much promise of developing either one. But perhaps the very character of the war in Vietnam—with crop poisoning, the defoliation of forest trees, the incineration of villages and their inhabitants with napalm—presents a stark enough example to remind us of this most urgent moral need.

Meanwhile some of us are wearing the little yellow and red button "Celebrate Life!" and bearing witness as best we can to these tidings.

194.

Paul Lambert

TOWARD A NEW CITIZENSHIP [1971]

A seabird played at the water's edge last time you went to the beach; you didn't know what kind it was. Now there is one in your arms and you try to assure it that you are a friend. Using mineral oil and Q-tips,

you clean out its nostrils and eyes carefully until they are reason-
ably free of the hardening bunker oil. A hand comes down to steady
the bird; you accept help without question.

The individuality of populated areas is rapidly diminishing; a
drive across the United States can often be a boring experience
—most any highway or suburb looks like any other. These interchangeable parts are very efficient; they, however, lack any effective
links with each other. There are fewer communities and more
people. The governing bodies are either left-overs from the past
when a sense of community existed, or new "models" of efficiency,
usually a confused mixture of the two, with elements to satisfy
local pressure groups.

The collective direction of the community is frequently controlled
by persons in government and business who have no sympathy with
the real psychological and practical needs of the people. The "leading
civic groups" are little more than large lobbies concerned with
boosting their area as the "Best for industrialization and Investment." They simply wish to use the land, the people, the climate,
as resources for continued growth and profit. These governing
bodies do *not* represent the people; they only relieve a fragmented
population of the ability to direct their lives.

Most Americans, true to their cultural roots, are loath to join or
participate in any organization tainted with politics; they simply
desire to live their lives with as little interference as possible. But
the village elders have vanished along with the buffalo, and for
the same reasons.

Peter, this gas station attendant, in his oily stained jeans, grey
whiskered cheeks, looks up from the maze of paper slips spread
across his make-shift desk, propped up on boxes. He quickly assigns
trucks for pick-up and delivery throughout the city. "See if the bird
cages have arrived at Clemintina yet." Someone whose name he
doesn't know yet surveys the six-foot long list of volunteered
resources, and begins to dial a number.

As community and family ties fragmented, the responsibility for
the collective health and welfare was taken on by the government
and delegated to the "proper" agency; dependency on these social
services increases faster than population growth. But disasters of
an ecological nature—oil spills and smog alerts—demand a height-
ened motivation and flexibility that these bureaucracies do not have.
Imagination and intitiative, not the usual channelled thinking, must
be the response to new problems; red tape and bureaucratic thinking have added to our current state of ecological vulnerability.

Although the crash of the Arizona and Oregon Standards took
place at 2 a.m. Monday, January 18, 1971, it was hours, sometimes
days, before many "official" organizations began to deal with the
emergency. Established organizations performed efficiently only
when they channelled the energies of volunteers by adapting to their
collective structures and enthusiastic flow.

The only resource capable of dealing with a disaster of this type is the community that views itself as directly affected physically and psychologically. Aside from boat and waterfront property owners, the only segment of the *four million* population of the Bay area to turn out in defense of the beaches and wildfowl in large enough numbers to be called the *major* work and organization force was the young people. While the majority of the population commuted to work and spent their lives as if nothing had happened, thousands of college students, young workers, and drop-outs took time out of their lives to work for something outside of themselves. In responding with such dedication, they demonstrated their allegiance to a place, the San Francisco Bay, and their commitment to each other as part of the large Family of Man. Hundreds worked with little sleep and no pay throughout the entire crisis, ten days; thousands devoted all their spare time before and after work while government remained inactive. The willingness of seemingly unskilled students and "drop-outs" to take on such heavy responsibility under such pressure is indicative not of youthful exuberance, or belief in their abilities, but of a particular approach to problems.

Three o'clock, the first night, nine hours have already passed. Tension builds, the sun will soon rise and thousands of sea birds will start diving for food into swollen gobs of bunker oil, floating on the ocean like pus from an ancient disease "Galen, Galen, get these volunteers out of the lobby. Tell them what to do with the leaflets." Fifteen people have just come from Hayward Switchboard to help distribute the 20,000 broadsides on bird-care and handling. Soon more and more will arrive and the beaches will be ours, if only we can get enough supplies.

. . . .

The first few hours were devoted to recognizing the problem, while attempting to apprise the public of the situation. We began to coordinate activities on the air and through the use of telephones, directing volunteers to needed spots, soliciting donations from a list that grew in complexity as we understood the depth of the problem. None of us were professional organizers, though the educational level was high; none of us knew the first thing about oil spills or bird care, but we were dedicated to the preservation of our environment. So we learned. People volunteering were put to work answering phones, or making lists. They delegated to themselves their own duties, which usually presented itself as a problem for which there was no answer. The person who became aware of that question as a problem to be solved would usually conduct an investigation into totally unknown but very necessary territory. That person would become the "expert."

Thus, by 2 a.m. of the first day, we were an experienced cadre, ready to redefine our role to keep up with the emergency. The second day and night we set up bird cleaning stations, then redefined ourselves, once again, as a communications network, leaving the coordination of supplies and transportation to San Francisco

Switchboard which performed admirably in the crush of responsibility. Collecting, verifying, and transmitting vital information
occupied us for the next ten days.

   *The fire at the edge of the beach never really warms you, but the
sight is cheering, especially after working without any stop for
three, or is it four days now. "Could we get someone to do primary
first aid?" You get up, letting the blanket fall from your shoulders,
and walk back to the lean-to; someone else has put the blanket
around his cold shoulders.*

Part Four

PARADISE AND APOCALYPSE

And I saw a new heaven and a new earth: for the first heaven and the first earth were passed away. . . . And there shall be no more death, neither sorrow, nor crying, neither shall there be any more pain: for the former things are passed away.

I beheld the earth, and, lo, it was without form, and void; and the heavens, and they had no light. I beheld the mountains, and, lo, they trembled, and all the hills moved lightly. I beheld, and, lo, there was no man, and all the birds of the heavens were fled. I beheld, and, lo, the fruitful place was a wilderness, and all the cities thereof were broken down.

However firmly man is enmeshed in nature, part of him rises above it. To change the metaphor: He is immersed in it up to his neck while his mind surveys and contemplates it from above. And, with his mind, he considers himself—this is the self-consciousness that we have suggested is a mark of civilized man—and all his works. What more characteristic and what more seemly than that he should also take thought for the future?

Because man has bound himself, perhaps irretrievably, to a technology that sometimes seems to have a momentum of its own, speculations on things to come generally revolve around not just man and nature but man and nature and machine. And because, as we have seen, the machine holds within it the potential either for something like heaven on earth or for something like hell, such speculations tend to picture paradise on the one hand, apocalypse on the other.

*   *   *

Part IV is a kind of epilogue; it is that, perhaps paradoxically, by virtue of concerning itself with the future. Necessarily the readings are speculative, ranging from the soberly analytical to the flamboyantly imaginative, but they are in every case rooted in conditions of the real present. The part consists of seventeen selections, divided somewhat unevenly into two sections. The first (Selections 195 through 201) presents optimistic views of the future; the second (Selections 202 through 211), pessimistic views. The reader may note a similarity between this arrangement and that of Part II, and it is true, in a sense, that Part IV suggests what Part II might be like if it were compiled some decades—or centuries—from now.

Some of the readings included here (Selections 203 and 207) are from works of science fiction, an unconventional field of research but one that contains a great deal of plausible prophecy. It is seldom realized how much of today's world was foreseen in the science fiction of the past; one can only hope that the examples herein will turn out to be less accurate than many of their predecessors.

THE NEW GARDEN

195.

J. A. Etzler

A CALL TO PARADISE [1842]

Fellow Men! I
promise to show the means of creating a paradise within ten years,
where everything desirable for human life may be had by every
man in superabundance, without labor, and without pay; where
the whole face of nature shall be changed into the most beautiful
forms, and man may live in the most magnificent palaces, in all
imaginable refinements of luxury, and in the most delightful
gardens; where he may accomplish, without labor, in one year,
more than hitherto could be done in thousands of years; may level
mountains, sink valleys, create lakes, drain lakes and swamps, and
intersect the land everywhere with beautiful canals, and roads for
transporting heavy loads of many thousand tons, and for travelling
one thousand miles in twenty-four hours; may cover the ocean with
floating islands movable in any desired direction with immense
power and celerity, in perfect security, and with all comforts and
luxuries, bearing gardens and palaces, with thousands of families,
and provided with rivulets of sweet water; may explore the interior
of the globe, and travel from pole to pole in a fortnight; provide
himself with means, unheard of yet, for increasing his knowledge
of the world, and so his intelligence; lead a life of continual
happiness, of enjoyments yet unknown; free himself from almost
all the evils that afflict mankind, except death, and even put death
far beyond the common period of human life, and finally render
it less afflicting. Mankind may thus live in and enjoy a new world,
far superior to the present, and raise themselves far higher in the
scale of being.

. . . .

Any wilderness, even the most hideous and sterile, may be converted into the most fertile and delightful gardens. The most dismal swamps may be cleared of all their spontaneous growth, filled up and levelled, and intersected by canals, ditches and aqueducts, for draining them entirely. The soil, if required, may be meliorated, by covering or mixing it with rich soil taken from distant places, and the same be mouldered to fine dust, levelled, sifted from all roots, weeds and stones, and sowed and planted in the most beautiful order and symmetry, with fruit trees and vegetables of every kind that may stand the climate.

. . . .

Large and commodious vehicles, for carrying many thousand tons, running over peculiarly adapted level roads, at the rate of forty miles per hour, or one thousand miles per day, may transport men and things, small houses, and whatever may serve for comfort and ease, by land. Floating islands, constructed of logs, or of wooden-stuff prepared in a similar manner, as is to be done with stone, and of live trees, which may be reared so as to interlace one another, and strengthen the whole, may be covered with gardens and palaces, and propelled by powerful engines, so as to run at an equal rate through seas and oceans. Thus, man may move, with the celerity of a bird's flight, in terrestrial paradises, from one climate to another, and see the world in all its variety, exchanging, with distant nations, the surplus of productions. The journey from one pole to another may be performed in a fortnight; the visit to a transmarine country in a week or two; or a journey round the world in one or two months by land and water. And why pass a dreary winter every year while there is yet room enough on the globe where nature is blessed with a perpetual summer, and with a far greater variety and luxuriance of vegetation? More than one-half the surface of the globe has no winter. Men will have it in their power to remove and prevent all bad influences of climate, and to enjoy, perpetually, only that temperature which šuits their constitution and feeling best.

. . . .

There will be afforded the most enrapturing views to be fancied, out of the private apartments, from the galleries, from the roof, from its turrets and cupolas,—gardens as far as the eye can see, full of fruits and flowers, arranged in the most beautiful order, with walks, colonnades, aqueducts, canals, ponds, plains, amphitheatres, terraces, fountains, sculptural works, pavilions, gondolas, places for public amusement, etc., to delight the eye and fancy, the taste and smell.

196.

Edward Bellamy [1887]

[Edward Bellamy's *Looking Backward* is a polemical novel intended to illuminate the source of the evils of industrial society and point the way to a rational and humane solution in economic terms. The central figure, Julian West, is a Bostonian who in 1887 has fallen asleep and, through a series of circumstances, has remained in a state of suspended animation until awakened in the year 2000.]

'Very well,' replied my extraordinary host. 'Since I cannot convince you, you shall convince yourself. Are you strong enough to follow me upstairs?'

'I am as strong as I ever was,' I replied angrily, 'as I may have to prove if this jest is carried much farther.'

'I beg, sir,' was my companion's response, 'that you will not allow yourself to be too fully persuaded that you are the victim of a trick, lest the reaction, when you are convinced of the truth of my statements, should be too great.'

The tone of concern, mingled with commiseration, with which he said this, and the entire absence of any sign of resentment at my hot words, strangely daunted me, and I followed him from the room with an extraordinary mixture of emotions. He led the way up two flights of stairs and then up a shorter one, which landed us upon a belvedere on the house-top. 'Be pleased to look around you,' he said, as we reached the platform, 'and tell me if this is Boston of the nineteenth century.'

At my feet lay a great city. Miles of broad streets, shaded by trees and lined with fine buildings, for the most part not in continuous blocks but set in larger or smaller inclosures, stretched in every direction. Every quarter contained large open squares filled with trees, among which statues glistened and fountains flashed in the late afternoon sun. Public buildings of a colossal size and an architectural grandeur unparalleled in my day raised their stately piles on every side. Surely I had never seen this city nor one comparable to it before. Raising my eyes at last towards the horizon, I looked westward. That blue ribbon winding away to the sunset, was it not the sinuous Charles? I looked east; Boston harbor stretched before me within its headlands, not one of its green islets missing.

I knew then that I had been told the truth concerning the prodigious thing which had befallen me.

. . . .

'If you had told me,' I replied, profoundly awed, 'that a thousand years instead of a hundred had elapsed since I last looked on this city, I should now believe you.'

'Only a century has passed,' he answered, 'but many a millennium in the world's history has seen changes less extraordinary.'

'And now,' he added, extending his hand with an air of irresistible cordiality, 'let me give you a hearty welcome to the Boston of the twentieth century and to this house. My name is Leete, Dr. Leete they call me.'

. . . .

After Dr. Leete had responded to numerous questions on my part, as to the ancient landmarks I missed and the new ones which had replaced them, he asked me what point of the contrast between the new and the old city struck me most forcibly.

'To speak of small things before great,' I responded, 'I really think that the complete absence of chimneys and their smokes is the detail that first impressed me.'

'Ah!' ejaculated my companion with an air of much interest, 'I had forgotten the chimneys, it is so long since they went out of use. It is nearly a century since the crude method of combustion on which you depended for heat became obsolete.'

'In general,' I said, 'what impresses me most about the city is the material prosperity on the part of the people which its magnificence implies.'

'I would give a great deal for just one glimpse of the Boston of your day,' replied Dr. Leete. 'No doubt, as you imply, the cities of that period were rather shabby affairs. If you had the taste to make them splendid, which I would not be so rude as to question, the general poverty resulting from your extraordinary industrial system would not have given you the means. Moreover, the excessive individualism which then prevailed was inconsistent with much public spirit. What little wealth you had seems almost wholly to have been lavished in private luxury. Nowadays, on the contrary, there is no destination of the surplus wealth so popular as the adornment of the city, which all enjoy in equal degree.'

. . . .

'I should be interested, Mr. West, if you would give me a little more definite idea of the view which you and men of your grade of intellect took of the state and prospects of society in 1887. You must, at least, have realized that the widespread industrial and social troubles, and the underlying dissatisfaction of all classes with the inequalities of society, and the general misery of mankind, were portents of great changes of some sort.'

'We did, indeed, fully realize that,' I replied. 'We felt that society was dragging anchor and in danger of going adrift. Whither it would drift nobody could say, but all feared the rocks.'

'Nevertheless,' said Dr. Leete, 'the set of the current was perfectly perceptible if you had but taken pains to observe it, and it was not toward the rocks, but toward a deeper channel.'

'We had a popular proverb,' I replied, 'that "hindsight is better than foresight," the force of which I shall now, no doubt, appreciate more fully than ever. All I can say is, that the prospect was such when I went into that long sleep that I should not have been surprised had I looked down from your house-top to-day on a heap of charred and moss-grown ruins instead of this glorious city.'

197.

Charles R. Van Hise

THE FUTURE OF MAN IN AMERICA [1909]

How long shall this nation endure? Or, more exactly, how long shall human beings occupy this land? It is only within the past two centuries that the lands of the country have been subject to agriculture upon an extensive scale, and the main drafts upon the soil of this country have been within the last century. We should think, not of a hundred years, nor of a thousand years, but of hundreds of thousands, or of millions of years of development of the human race. There is no reason, from a geological point of view, why human beings may not live upon this earth for millions of years to come, perhaps many millions of years, and, so far as we are concerned, such periods are practically infinite.

These considerations impose upon us as our most fundamental duty the transmission of the heritage of our natural resources to our descendants as nearly intact as possible.

. . . .

We may hope that the scientific advance will help in reference to some of these resources, but we cannot hope that we shall be able to reverse the great law that energy is run down in transformation, or that we can re-use indefinitely the resources of nature without loss.

It would be interesting, but idle, to prophesy as to the changes in our social structure which will result when people begin to be pinched by meagre soil, by lack of sufficient coal and wood. The people of that time will doubtless solve their problems as best they may, and any speculations we might make at this time would certainly be far from future realization, but that the problem of pinching economy will confront our descendants is beyond all question; and, therefore, the paramount duty remains to us to transmit to our descendants the resources which nature has bequeathed to us as nearly undiminished in amount as is possible, consistent with living a rational and frugal life. Now that we have imposed upon us the responsibility of knowledge, to do less than this would be a base communal crime.

In a few thousand years man has risen from the level of the savage to the height of the great creations of science, literature, and art. The human mind has dared to ask the meaning of the universe, even to the extent of its own creation. These amazing accomplishments have taken place in the mere infancy of the human race. The most daring speculations that I might make as to human achievements would be poor and futile as compared with future realizations. It is in order that humanity itself may be given an opportunity to develop through millions of years to come, under the most advantageous conditions, that we should conserve our natural resources and thus make possible to billions of future human beings a godlike destiny.

198.

Arthur C. Clarke

FUTURE RESOURCES [1963]

Today, there can be little doubt that the long-term (and perhaps the short-term) answer to the fuel problem is nuclear energy. The weapons now stockpiled by the major powers could run all the machines on Earth for several years, if their energies could be used constructively. The warheads in the American arsenals alone are equivalent to thousands of millions of tons of oil or coal.

It is not likely that fission reactions (those involving such heavy elements as thorium, uranium and plutonium) will play more than a temporary role in terrestrial affairs. One hopes they will not, for fission is the dirtiest and most unpleasant method of releasing energy that man has ever discovered. Some of the radioisotopes from today's reactors will still be causing trouble, and perhaps injuring unwary archeologists, a thousand years from now.

But beyond fission lies fusion—the welding together of light atoms such as hydrogen and lithium. This is the reaction that drives the stars themselves; we have reproduced it on Earth, but have not yet tamed it. When we have done so, our power problems will have been solved forever—and there will be no poisonous byproducts, but only the clean ash of helium.

Controlled fusion is the supreme challenge of applied nuclear physics; some scientists believe it will be achieved in ten years, some in fifty. But almost all of them are sure that we will have fusion power long before our oil and coal run out, and will be able to draw fuel from the sea in virtually unlimited quantities.

. . . .

For most of our raw materials, as for our power sources, we have been living on capital. We have been exploiting the easily available resources—the high-grade ores, the rich lodes where natural forces have concentrated the metals and minerals we need. These processes took a billion years or more; in mere centuries, we have looted treasures stored up over aeons. When they are gone, our civilization cannot mark time for a few hundred million years until they are restored.

. . . .

Nevertheless, the great developments in chemical processing that have taken place in recent years—especially as a result of the atomic energy program, where it became necessary to extract very small amounts of isotopes from much larger quantities of other materials—suggest that we may be able to work the sea long before we exhaust the resources of the land. Once again, the problem is largely one of power—power for pumping, evaporation, electrolysis. Success may come as part of a combined operation; the efforts under way in many countries to obtain drinkable water from the sea will produce enriched brines as a byproduct, and these may be the raw materials for the processing plants.

One can imagine, perhaps before the end of this century, huge general-purpose factories using cheap power from thermonuclear reactors to extract pure water, salt, magnesium, bromine, strontium, rubidium, copper, and many other metals from the sea. A notable exception from the list would be iron, which is far rarer in the oceans than under the continents.

If mining the sea appears an unlikely project, it is worth remembering that for more than fifty years we have been mining the atmosphere. One of the big, but now forgotten, worries of the nineteenth century was the coming shortage of nitrates for fer-

tilizers; natural sources were running low, and it was essential
to find some way of "fixing" the nitrogen in the air. The atmosphere
contains some 4,000 million million tons of nitrogen, or more than
a million tons for every person on Earth, so if it could be utilized
directly there would never be any fear of further shortages.

. . . .

Now let us widen our horizons somewhat. So far, we have been
considering only *this* planet as a source of raw materials, but the
Earth contains only about three millionths of the total matter in
the solar system. It is true that more than 99.9 per cent of that
matter is in the Sun, where at first sight it would appear to be out
of reach, but the planets, satellites, and asteroids contain between
them the mass of four hundred and fifty Earths. By far the greatest
part of this is in Jupiter (318 times the mass of Earth) but Saturn,
Uranus, and Neptune also make sizable contributions (95, 15 and
17 Earths, respectively).

In view of the present astronomical cost of space travel (several
thousand dollars per pound of payload for even the simplest
orbital missions) it may seem fantastic to suggest that we will
ever be able to mine and ship megatons of raw materials across
the solar system. Even gold could hardly pay its way, and only
diamonds would show a profit.

This view, however, is colored by today's primitive state of the
art, which depends upon hopelessly inefficient techniques. It is
something of a shock to realize that, *if* we could use the energy
really effectively, it would require only some 25 cents' worth of
chemical fuel to lift a pound of payload completely clear of the
Earth—and perhaps one or two cents to carry it from Moon to
Earth. For a number of reasons, these figures represent unattainable
ideals; but they do indicate how much room there is for improvement. Some studies of nuclear propulsion systems suggest that,
even with techniques we can imagine today, space flight need be
no more expensive than jet transportation; as far as inanimate
cargoes are concerned, it may be very much cheaper.

199.

William E. Siri [1965]

[At the Sierra Club's
1965 Wilderness Conference, William E. Siri presented the paper
from which the following selections are taken. In it, he imagined
the keynote address at the Wilderness Conference in 2065.]

Twenty-five years have elapsed since the last Wilderness Conference. There has been no need for one in the intervening years. Even now it is held only to monitor the adequacy and stability of primitive lands and natural scenic and recreational resources called for in the constitutional amendment providing for the master plan on land and water use. We have come far in reconciling ancient conflicts on land and water use. Many related problems that plagued mankind a hundred years ago have been solved.

. . . .

What some men failed to realize a century ago was that new sources of energy and machines, along with better insight into themselves and the world about them, were in the end their salvation. They alone made it possible to enjoy the best of two worlds: one natural, to be enjoyed in its primitive state; the other mechanized, comfortable, and productive without effort. Only our advanced technology and sources of vast energy released us from the tedious labor that would otherwise be needed to survive and gave us the time and the means to pursue a creative life with a freedom and variety that were inconceivable a century ago. Such technology and energy also enabled 300 million people to live uncramped in a country formerly thought over-crowded with 200 million.

Most important in the context of today's discussion, energy and machines enabled man to restore vast regions of the country to their natural state and preserve them for his own enjoyment.

. . . .

Today great bands of natural lands and forests stretch across the country from coast to coast and from Mexico northward beyond the arctic circle. Large expanses of prairie, desert, and the hardwood forest of the midwest and east are restoring themselves. The ancient trees of the old Redwood National Park in Northern California are being joined by vigorous young trees spreading southward along the coast. The vast buffer zones of managed lands paralleling the wilderness bands provide the immediate daily recreational needs of the millions who live in the adjacent urban strips.

Decades ago our rivers and streams ceased to be fouled by the wastes of civilization. Our atmosphere has never been freer of contaminants since man first learned to use fire.

A hundred years ago some 800 species of animals faced extinction. Seventy-five succumbed, among them, the Indian rhinoceros, the Yeti, and the hydroelectric engineer.

The Bureau of Reclamation has for several decades conscientiously discharged its responsibility for restoring the land. The Bureau is now busily engaged in removing many of the long useless dams and other works that were once marvels of engineering achievement. Hoover Dam and a few others are preserved as historical monuments. But Glen Canyon Dam has been dismantled, as have other dams in the Colorado River.

200.

Ron M. Linton

THE CITY TOMORROW [1970]

The air is clear as the plane approaches the airport, and the New York skyline stands out sharply against the horizon. It is an electrifying sight. Below is a panorama of boats in both the lower and upper parts of the bay. It has become a pleasure to sail on the blue-green waters fed by a Hudson River where fishing and swimming are enjoyed.

There are two ways into Manhattan from the airport: a quick underground journey in sleek, clean subway trains or a twenty-minute surface trip in a cab or bus.

The streets are clean in Manhattan. Private cars are restricted to underground throughways, and commercial traffic moves at a steady pace. Moving-belt sidewalks are wide enough to accommodate both walkers and stationary riders. Crowds are large, but there is no sense of jamming.

The situation is the same in all major cities. Growth rates are managed, and new towns are created when necessary. Air and water quality is rigidly maintained at levels that make it a pleasure to live. Land is used to serve human needs. Waste disposal problems have been conquered, and nuclear power, carefully monitored, is bringing a bonanza to life.

This is the U.S.A. of tomorrow.

Utopia? Perhaps. But one thing is certain; the choice between the confused society and the clean one lies completely with man.

201.

Isaac Asimov

THE FOURTH REVOLUTION [1970]

Suppose the fourth [communications] revolution is established before civilization breaks down; what may we expect it to accomplish?

For one thing, the day of the individual television station, of which hundreds are needed today merely to cover the United States with their limited short-range beams, will be over. Signals can be bounced off the space relays direct to the home set. Indeed, person-to-person communication on a scale of massive freedom becomes thinkable.

With an unlimited number of voice and picture channels available, every man could have his portable phone and dial any number on Earth. No one with such a phone need ever be lost; if he is, an emergency button can send out a signal that can be traced from anywhere else on Earth.

. . . .

The Earth for the first time will be knit together on a personal and not a governmental level. There will be the kind of immediacy possible over all the world as had hitherto existed only at the level of the village. In fact, we will have what has been called the global village.

To know all your neighbors on the global level does not mean that you will automatically love them all; it does not, in and of itself, introduce a reign of peace and brotherhood. But to be potentially in touch with everybody at least makes fighting more uncomfortable. It becomes easier to argue instead.

. . . .

No one would need to be at any one particular spot to control affairs, and businessmen need not congregate in offices. Nor, with the advance of automation, need workingmen congregate in factories. Men can locate themselves at will and shift that location only when they wish to travel for fun. Which means that the cities will spread out and disappear. They won't even have to exist for cultural reasons in a day when a play acted anywhere can be reproduced electronically at any point on Earth—and a symphony, and an important news event, and any book in a library.

Every place on Earth will be "where it's at." The world of the fourth revolution will be a global village in actuality and not merely metaphorically speaking.

The benefits will be enormous. The greatest problems of the world of the third revolution arise, after all, from the fact of over-concentration, which many times multiplies the impact of overpopulation. It is the great cities that are the chief source of pollution and the chief deprivers of dignity. Let the same billions be spread out, and the condition will already be not so acute.

Further, let the same billions be educated into birth control and let their numbers slowly decrease; let the same billions learn to contact each other, know each other, and even understand each other; let the same billions come to live under a world government —and our present problems will no longer be insoluble.

That there will be problems inseparable from the world of the fourth revolution will be certain, but they can be handled in their turn by the generations who must face them—provided we first handle ours.

So the race is on, and by 2000 at the latest it will be decided: Either the world of the fourth revolution will be in full swing or it will not be. In the latter event, the world of the third revolution (and all mankind with it, probably) will be in its death throes.

THE NEW WILDERNESS

202.

Percy Bysshe Shelley

OZYMANDIAS [1817]

I met a traveler from an antique land
Who said: Two vast and trunkless legs of stone
Stand in the desert. Near them, on the sand,
Half sunk, a shattered visage lies, whose frown,
And wrinkled lip, and sneer of cold command,
Tell that its sculptor well those passions read
Which yet survive, stamped on these lifeless things,
The hand that mocked them and the heart that fed;
And on the pedestal these words appear:
"My name is Ozymandias, king of kings:
Look on my works, ye Mighty, and despair!"
Nothing beside remains. Round the decay
Of that colossal wreck, boundless and bare
The lone and level sands stretch far away.

203.

H. G. Wells [1895]

[In *The Time Machine,*
H. G. Wells has a time traveler visit the year 802,701. In this selection, he relates his hero's observations and reflections on the future evolution of mankind.]

"It seemed to me that I had happened upon humanity upon the wane. The ruddy sunset set me thinking of the sunset of mankind. For the first time I began to realize an odd consequence of the social effort in which we are at present engaged. And yet, come to think, it is a logical consequence enough. Strength is the outcome of need: security sets a premium on feebleness. The work of ameliorating the conditions of life—the true civilizing process that makes life more and more secure—had gone steadily on to a climax. One triumph of a united humanity over Nature had followed another. Things that are now mere dreams had become projects deliberately put in hand and carried forward. And the harvest was what I saw!

. . . .

"What, unless biological science is a mass of errors, is the cause of human intelligence and vigour? Hardship and freedom: conditions under which the active, strong, and subtle survive and the weaker go to the wall; conditions that put a premium upon the loyal alliance of capable men, upon self-restraint, patience, and decision. And the institution of the family, and the emotions that arise therein, the fierce jealousy, the tenderness for offspring, parental self-devotion, all found their justification and support in the imminent dangers of the young. *Now*, where are these imminent dangers? There is a sentiment arising, and it will grow, against connubial jealousy, against fierce maternity, against passion of all sorts; unnecessary things now, and things that make us uncomfortable, savage survivals, discords in a refined and pleasant life.

"I thought of the physical slightness of the people, their lack of intelligence, and those big abundant ruins, and it strengthened my belief in a perfect conquest of Nature. For after the battle comes Quiet. Humanity had been strong, energetic, and intelligent, and had used all its abundant vitality to alter the conditions under which it lived. And now came the reaction of the altered conditions.

. . . .

"Here was the new view. Plainly, this second species of Man was subterranean. . . .

"Beneath my feet then the earth must be tunnelled enormously, and these tunnellings were the habitat of the New Race. The presence of ventilating-shafts and wells along the hill slopes—everywhere, in fact, except along the river valley—showed how universal were its ramifications. What so natural, then, as to assume that it was in this artificial Underworld that such work as was necessary to the comfort of the daylight race was done? The notion was so plausible that I at once accepted it, and went on to assume the *how* of this splitting of the human species. I dare say you will anticipate the shape of my theory, though, for myself, I very soon felt that it fell far short of the truth.

"At first, proceeding from the problems of our own age, it seemed clear as daylight to me that the gradual widening of the present merely temporary and social difference between the Capitalist and the Labourer, was the key to the whole position. No doubt it will seem grotesque enough to you—and wildly incredible!—and yet even now there are existing circumstances to point that way. There is a tendency to utilize underground space for the less ornamental purposes of civilization; there is the Metropolitan Railway in London, for instance, there are new electric railways, there are subways, there are underground workrooms and restaurants, and they increase and multiply. Evidently, I thought, this tendency had increased till Industry had gradually lost its birthright in the sky. I mean that it had gone deeper and deeper into larger and ever larger underground factories, spending a still-increasing amount of its time therein, till, in the end——! Even now, does not an East-end worker live in such artificial conditions as practically to be cut off from the natural surface of the earth?

"Again, the exclusive tendency of richer people—due, no doubt, to the increasing refinement of their education, and the widening gulf between them and the rude violence of the poor—is already leading to the closing, in their interest, of considerable portions of the surface of the land. . . . So, in the end, above ground you must have the Haves, pursuing pleasure and comfort and beauty, and below ground the Have-nots; the Workers getting continually to the conditions of their labour. . . .

"The great triumph of Humanity I had dreamed of took a different shape in my mind. It had been no such triumph of moral education and general co-operation as I had imagined. Instead, I saw a real aristocracy, armed with a perfected science and working to a logical conclusion the industrial system of to-day. Its triumph had not been simply a triumph over nature, but a triumph over nature and the fellow-man.

. . . .

"I grieved to think how brief the dream of the human intellect had been. It had committed suicide. It had set itself steadfastly towards comfort and ease, a balanced society with security and permanency as its watchword, it had attained its hopes—to come to this at last. Once, life and property must have reached almost absolute safety. The rich had been assured of his wealth and comfort, the toiler assured of his life and work. No doubt in that perfect world there had been no unemployed problem, no social question left unsolved. And a great quiet had followed."

204.

Eugene Zamiatin [1924]

[Eugene Zamiatin, a Russian writer, was hounded from his homeland because of his critical attitude toward the Stalin regime. The regimented and machine-like future society that he describes in his novel *We* is a realistic prospect—and by no means only for a Communist nation.]

Soon I reached the road running along the Green Wall. From beyond the Wall, from the infinite ocean of green, there arose toward me an immense wave of roots, branches, flowers, leaves. It rose higher and higher; it seemed as though it would splash over me and that from a man, from the finest and most precise mechanism which I am, I would be transformed into . . . But fortunately there was the Green Wall between me and that wild green sea. Oh, how great and divinely limiting is the wisdom of walls and bars! This Green Wall is, I think, the greatest invention ever conceived. Man ceased to be a wild animal the day he built the first wall; man ceased to be a wild man only on the day when the Green Wall was completed, when by this wall we isolated our machine-like, perfect world from the irrational, ugly world of trees, birds, and beasts. . . .

The blunt snout of some unknown beast was to be seen dimly through the glass of the Wall; its yellow eyes kept repeating the same thought which remained incomprehensible to me. We looked into each other's eyes for a long while. Eyes are shafts which lead from the superficial world into a world which is beneath the surface. A thought awoke in me: "What if that yellow-eyed one, sitting there on that absurd dirty heap of leaves, is happier than I, in his life which cannot be calculated in figures!" I waved my hand. The yellow eyes twinkled, moved back, and disappeared in the foliage. What a pitiful being! How absurd the idea that he might be happier!

205.

Don Marquis

WHAT THE ANTS ARE SAYING [ca. 1925]

dear boss i was talking with an ant
the other day
and he handed me a lot of
gossip which ants the world around
are chewing over among themselves

i pass it on to you
in the hope that you may relay it to other
human beings and hurt their feelings with it
no insect likes human beings
and if you think you can see why
the only reason i tolerate you is because
you seem less human to me than most of them
here is what the ants are saying

it wont be long now it wont be long
man is making deserts of the earth
it wont be long now
before man will have used it up
so that nothing but ants
and centipedes and scorpions
can find a living on it
man has oppressed us for a million years
but he goes on steadily
cutting the ground from under
his own feet making deserts deserts deserts

. . . .

america was once a paradise
of timberland and stream
but it is dying because of the greed
and money lust of a thousand little kings
who slashed the timber all to hell
and would not be controlled
and changed the climate

and stole the rainfall from posterity
and it wont be long now
it wont be long
till everything is desert
from the alleghenies to the rockies
the deserts are coming
the deserts are spreading
the springs and streams are drying up
one day the mississippi itself
will be a bed of sand
ants and scorpions and centipedes
shall inherit the earth

men talk of money and industry
of hard times and recoveries
of finance and economics
but the ants wait and the scorpions wait
for while men talk they are making deserts all the time
getting the world ready for the conquering ant
drought and erosion and desert
because men cannot learn

. . . .

it wont be long now it won't be long
till earth is barren as the moon
and sapless as a mumbled bone

dear boss i relay this information
without any fear that humanity
will take warning and reform
                                        archy

206.

Charles Galton Darwin

POWER AND FOOD IN THE FUTURE [1952]

A very great change
in world economics is inevitable when the accumulated stocks of
coal and oil are exhausted. In the scale of human lives this will
of course be a gradual process, marked by their slowly growing

rarer, but on the scale of a million years the crisis is practically with us already. We shall have spent the capital accumulations of hundreds of millions of years, and after that we shall have to live on our income.

. . . .

To provide energy on the sort of scale to which we are accustomed will call for a very elaborate organization, a great many machines, and a great many people to mind those machines. In view of the shortsightedness and unreliability of human nature, it seems rather unlikely that any process of this kind could be made to work on a world-wide scale for century after century. But it does seem very possible that some part of the plan should be carried out, so that there should be a considerable supplementation to the large amount of energy we already get from water-power, which does of course provide energy out of income.

The general picture of the economic condition of the world then is that the chief centres of power production, and so of the most elaborate civilization, will be the regions where there is water-power, that is speaking rather loosely, mountainous regions. . . . It may be guessed that it will be what I may call the mountaineers, who possess the most readily available energy, who will become dominant; through their wealth they will tend to have the highest culture, since culture most easily comes from the leisure created by wealth. It will be they who will tend to rule the world on account of their economic advantages, and to judge by most past experience they will be hated by the others for it.

There will be the same sort of contest of interests between the mountaineers and the plain-dwelling agriculturists, as there is even now between town and country. Most of the time the mountaineer will have the advantage, but the farmer being the food producer is bound to have the advantage in times of famine, which will not be infrequent. And there will be parts of the world that relapse frankly into barbarism; they will be the less fertile regions which could not produce much food, so that the more civilized people would get no advantage from exploiting them. But there will be other regions which also relapse into barbarism, though the fertility of the soil could support a greater population than it in fact bears. It is to be expected that such a state of affairs will not usually be tolerated by the civilized countries, who will conquer them, and export their own starving margins to fill up the vacant places. . . .

It is quite safe to say that there will always be rich and poor. Wealth will be the mark of success, and so the abler people will tend to be found among the wealthy, but there will always be many among them of a far less estimable character. These are the people who are interested not in the work, but only in the reward, and they will all too often succeed in gaining it in a variety of discreditable ways, such as by currying favour with an autocrat.

As to the less successful members, the standard of living of any community living on its real earnings, as the communities of the future will have to do, is inevitably lower than that of one rapidly spending the savings of hundreds of millions of years as we are doing now. There will also be the frequent threat of starvation, which will operate against the least efficient members of every community with special force, so that it may be expected that the conditions of their work will be much more severe than at present. Even now we see that a low standard of living in one country has the advantage in competing against a high standard in another. If there is work to be done, and, of two men of equal quality, one is willing to do it for less pay than the other, in the long run it will be he who gets the work to do. Those who find the bad conditions supportable will be willing to work harder and for less reward; in a broad sense of the term they are more efficient than the others, because they get more done for less pay. There are of course many exceptions, for real skill will get its reward, but in the long run it is inevitable that the lower types of labour will have an exceedingly precarious life. One of the triumphs of our own golden age has been that slavery has been abolished over a great part of the earth. It is difficult to see how this condition can be maintained in the hard world of the future with its starving margins, and it is to be feared that all too often a fraction of humanity will have to live in a state which, whatever it may be called, will be indistinguishable from slavery.

207.

Frederik Pohl and C. M. Kornbluth

CONSERVATIONIST UNDERGROUND [1952]

Schocken was speaking again. "There's one thing you'll have to watch out for: the lunatic fringe. This is the kind of project that's bound to bring them out. Every crackpot organization on the list, from the Consies to the G.O.P., is going to come out for or against it. Make sure they're all for; they swing weight."

"Even the Consies?" I squeaked.

"Well, no. I didn't mean that; they'd be more of a liability." His white hair glinted as he nodded thoughtfully. "Mm. Maybe you could spread the word that spaceflight and Conservationism are diametrically opposed. It uses up too many raw materials, hurts the living standard—you know. Bring in the fact that the fuel uses organic material that the Consies think should be made into fertilizer—"

I like to watch an expert at work. Fowler Schocken laid down a whole subcampaign for me right there; all I had to do was fill in the details. The Conservationists were fair game, those wild-eyed zealots who pretended modern civilization was in some way "plundering" our planet. Preposterous stuff. Science is *always* a step ahead of the failure of natural resources. After all, when real meat got scarce, we had soyaburgers ready. When oil ran low, technology developed the pedicab.

I had been exposed to Consie sentiment in my time, and the arguments had all come down to one thing: Nature's way of living was the *right* way of living. Silly. If "Nature" had intended us to eat fresh vegetables, it wouldn't have given us niacin or ascorbic acid.

. . . .

His words were noble, even in such a cause. I hated the twisted minds who had done such a thing to a fine consumer like Gus. It was something like murder. He could have played his part in the world, buying and using and making work and profits for his brothers all around the globe, ever increasing his wants and needs, ever increasing everybody's work and profits in the circle of consumption, raising children to be consumers in turn. It hurt to see him perverted into a sterile zealot.

I resolved to do what I could for him when I blew off the lid. The fault did not lie with him. It was the people who had soured him on the world who should pay. Surely there must be some sort of remedial treatment for Consies like Gus who were only dupes. I would ask—no; it would be better not to ask. People would jump to conclusions. I could hear them now: "I don't say Mitch isn't sound, but it was a pretty far-fetched idea." "Yeah. Once a Consie, always a Consie." "Everybody knows that. I don't say Mitch isn't sound, mind you, but—"

The hell with Herrera. He could take his chances like everybody else. Anybody who sets out to turn the world upside down has no right to complain if he gets caught in its gears.

208.

Harrison Brown

MAGGOTS [1954]

There are, of course, physical limitations of some sort which will determine the maximum number of human beings who can live on the earth's surface. But at the present time we are far from the ultimate limit of the number of persons who could be provided for. If we were willing to be crowded together closely enough, to eat foods which would bear little resemblance to the foods we eat today, and to be deprived of simple but satisfying luxuries such as fireplaces, gardens, and lawns, a world population of 50 billion persons would not be out of the question. And if we really put our minds to the problem we could construct floating islands where people might live and where algae farms could function, and perhaps 100 billion persons could be provided for. If we set strict limits to physical activities so that caloric requirements could be kept at very low levels, perhaps we could provide for 200 billion persons.

At this point the reader is probably saying to himself that he would have little desire to live in such a world, and he can rest assured that the author is thinking exactly the same thing. But a substantial fraction of humanity today is behaving as if it would like to create such a world. It is behaving as if it were engaged in a contest to test nature's willingness to support humanity and, if it had its way, it would not rest content until the earth is covered completely and to a considerable depth with a writhing mass of human beings, much as a dead cow is covered with a pulsating mass of maggots.

209.

Harrison Brown and James Real

BACK TO THE CAVE [1960]

If the arms race continues, as it probably will, its future pattern seems clear in broad outline. As a result of the emergence of the current tremendous capabilities for killing and destroying, programs will be started aimed at the evacuation of cities, the construction of fallout shelters in regions outside the major metropolitan areas, and the construction of limited underground shelters. Increased offensive capabilities will then emerge which will to some extent neutralize these efforts. Larger bombs will be compressed into sufficiently small packages to be carried by ICBM's. Very large bombs (about 1,000 megatons) will be built which, when exploded at an altitude of about 300 miles, could sear six Western states.

The new developments will cause people to burrow more deeply into the ground. Factories will be built in caves, as will apartment houses and stores. Eventually most human life will be underground, confronted by arsenals capable of destroying all life over the land areas of the earth. Deep under the ground people will be relatively safe—at least until such time as we learn how to make explosives capable of pulverizing the earth to great depths.

. . . .

Once the people are convinced that they can survive the present state of the art of killing, a broad and significant new habit pattern will have been introduced and accepted, one grotesquely different from any we have known for thousands of years—that of adjusting ourselves to the idea of living in holes. From that time onward it will be simple to adjust ourselves to living in *deeper* holes.

Tens of thousands of years ago our Mousterian and Aurignacian ancestors lived in caves. The vast knowledge which we have accumulated during the intervening millenia will have brought us full cycle. The epic of man's journey upward into the light will have ended.

210.

Paul R. Ehrlich [1969]

[In this frightening scenario of the near and all too possible future, biologist Paul Ehrlich outlines some of the likely results of certain nonsensical policies and practices currently in vogue.]

The end of the ocean came late in the summer of 1979, and it came even more rapidly than the biologists had expected. There had been signs for more than a decade, commencing with the discovery in 1968 that DDT slows down photosynthesis in marine plant life. It was announced in a short paper in the technical journal, Science, but to ecologists it smacked of doomsday. They knew that all life in the sea depends on photosynthesis, the chemical process by which green plants bind the sun's energy and make it available to living things. And they knew that DDT and similar chlorinated hydrocarbons had polluted the entire surface of the earth, including the sea.

But that was only the first of many signs. There had been the final gasp of the whaling industry in 1973, and the end of the Peruvian anchovy fishery in 1975. Indeed, a score of other fisheries had disappeared quietly from over-exploitation and various eco-catastrophes by 1977. The term "eco-catastrophe" was coined by a California ecologist in 1969 to describe the most spectacular of man's attacks on the systems which sustain his life. He drew his inspiration from the Santa Barbara offshore oil disaster of that year, and from the news which spread among naturalists that virtually all of the Golden State's seashore bird life was doomed because of chlorinated hydrocarbon interference with its reproduction. Eco-catastrophes in the sea became increasingly common in the early 1970's. Mysterious "blooms" of previously rare micro-organisms began to appear in offshore waters. Red tides—killer outbreaks of a minute single-celled plant—returned to the Florida Gulf coast and were sometimes accompanied by tides of other exotic hues.

It was clear by 1975 that the entire ecology of the ocean was changing. A few types of phytoplankton were becoming resistant to chlorinated hydrocarbons and were gaining the upper hand. Changes in the phytoplankton community led inevitably to changes in the community of zooplankton, the tiny animals which eat the phytoplankton. These changes were passed on up the chains of life in the ocean to the herring, plaice, cod and tuna. As the diversity of life in the ocean diminished, its stability also decreased.

Other changes had taken place by 1975. Most ocean fishes that returned to fresh water to breed, like the salmon, had become extinct, their breeding streams so dammed up and polluted that their powerful homing instinct only resulted in suicide. Many fishes and shellfishes that bred in restricted areas along the coasts followed them as onshore pollution escalated.

By 1977 the annual yield of fish from the sea was down to 30 million metric tons, less than one-half the per capita catch of a decade earlier. This helped malnutrition to escalate sharply in a world where an estimated 50 million people per year were already dying of starvation. The United Nations attempted to get all chlorinated hydrocarbon insecticides banned on a worldwide basis, but the move was defeated by the United States. This opposition was generated primarily by the American petrochemical industry, operating hand in glove with its subsidiary, the United States Department of Agriculture. Together they persuaded the government to oppose the U.N. move—which was not difficult since most Americans believed that Russia and China were more in need of fish products than was the United States. The United Nations also attempted to get fishing nations to adopt strict and enforced catch limits to preserve dwindling stocks. This move was blocked by Russia, who, with the most modern electronic equipment, was in the best position to glean what was left in the sea. It was, curiously, on the very day in 1977 when the Soviet Union announced its refusal that another ominous article appeared in Science. It announced that incident solar radiation had been so reduced by worldwide air pollution that serious effects on the world's vegetation could be expected.

. . . .

It became apparent in the early '70s that the "Green Revolution" was more talk than substance. Distribution of high yield "miracle" grain seeds had caused temporary local spurts in agricultural products. Simultaneously, excellent weather had produced record harvests. The combination permitted bureaucrats, especially in the United States Department of Agriculture and the Agency for International Development (AID), to reverse their previous pessimism and indulge in an outburst of optimistic propaganda about staving off famine. They raved about the approaching transformation of agriculture in the underdeveloped countries (UDCs). The reason for the propaganda reversal was never made clear. Most historians agree that a combination of utter ignorance of ecology, a desire to justify past errors, and pressure from agro-industry (which was eager to sell pesticides, fertilizers, and farm machinery to the UDCs and agencies helping the UDCs) was behind the campaign. Whatever the motivation, the results were clear. Many concerned people, lacking the expertise to see through the Green Revolution drivel, relaxed. The population-food crisis was "solved."

But reality was not long in showing itself. Local famine persisted in northern India even after good weather brought an end to the ghastly Bihar famine of the mid-'60s. East Pakistan was next, followed by a resurgence of general famine in northern India. Other foci of famine rapidly developed in Indonesia, the Philippines, Malawi, the Congo, Egypt, Colombia, Ecuador, Honduras, the Dominican Republic, and Mexico.

Everywhere hard realities destroyed the illusion of the Green Revolution. Yields dropped as the progressive farmers who had first accepted the new seeds found that their higher yields brought lower prices—effective demand (hunger plus cash) was not sufficient in poor countries to keep prices up. Less progressive farmers, observing this, refused to make the extra effort required to cultivate the "miracle" grains. Transport systems proved inadequate to bring the necessary fertilizer to the fields where the new and extremely fertilizer-sensitive grains were being grown. The same systems were also inadequate to move produce to markets. Fertilizer plants were not built fast enough, and most of the underdeveloped countries could not scrape together funds to purchase supplies, even on concessional terms. Finally, the inevitable happened, and pests began to reduce yields in even the most carefully cultivated fields. Among the first were the famous "miracle rats" which invaded Philippine "miracle rice" fields early in 1969. They were quickly followed by many insects and viruses, thriving on the relatively pest-susceptible new grains, encouraged by the vast and dense plantings, and rapidly acquiring resistance to the chemicals used against them. As chaos spread until even the most obtuse agriculturists and economists realized that the Green Revolution had turned brown, the Russians stepped in.

In retrospect it seems incredible that the Russians, with the American mistakes known to them, could launch an even more incompetent program of aid to the underdeveloped world. Indeed, in the early 1970's there were cynics in the United States who claimed that outdoing the stupidity of American foreign aid would be physically impossible. Those critics were, however, obviously unaware that the Russians had been busily destroying their own environment for many years. The virtual disappearance of sturgeon from Russian rivers caused a great shortage of caviar by 1970. A standard joke among Russian scientists at that time was that they had created an artificial caviar which was indistinguishable from the real thing—except by taste. At any rate the Soviet Union, observing with interest the progressive deterioration of relations between the UDCs and the United States, came up with a solution. It had recently developed what it claimed was the ideal insecticide, a highly lethal chlorinated hydrocarbon complexed with a special agent for penetrating the external skeletal armor of insects. Announcing that the new pesticide, called Thanodrin, would truly produce a Green

Revolution, the Soviets entered into negotiations with various UDCs for the construction of massive Thanodrin factories. The USSR would bear all the costs; all it wanted in return were certain trade and military concessions.

It is interesting now, with the perspective of years, to examine in some detail the reasons why the UDCs welcomed the Thanodrin plan with such open arms. Government officials in these countries ignored the protests of their own scientists that Thanodrin would not solve the problems which plagued them. The governments now knew that the basic cause of their problems was overpopulation, and that these problems had been exacerbated by the dullness, day-dreaming, and cupidity endemic to all governments. They knew that only population control and limited development aimed primarily at agriculture could have spared them the horrors they now faced. They knew it, but they were not about to admit it. How much easier it was simply to accuse the Americans of failing to give them proper aid; how much simpler to accept the Russian panacea.

. . . .

Air pollution continued to be the most obvious manifestation of environmental deterioration. It was, by 1972, quite literally in the eyes of all Americans. The year 1973 saw not only the New York and Los Angeles smog disasters, but also the publication of the Surgeon General's massive report on air pollution and health. The public had been partially prepared for the worst by the publicity given to the U.N. pollution conference held in 1972. Deaths in the late '60s caused by smog were well known to scientists, but the public had ignored them because they mostly involved the early demise of the old and sick rather than people dropping dead on the freeways. But suddenly our citizens were faced with nearly 200,000 corpses and massive documentation that they could be the next to die from respiratory disease. They were not ready for that scale of disaster. After all, the U.N. conference had not predicted that accumulated air pollution would make the planet uninhabitable until almost 1990. The population was terrorized as TV screens became filled with scenes of horror from the disaster areas. Especially vivid was NBC's coverage of hundreds of unattended people choking out their lives outside of New York's hospitals. Terms like nitrogen oxide, acute bronchitis and cardiac arrest began to have real meaning for most Americans.

The ultimate horror was the announcement that chlorinated hydrocarbons were now a major constituent of air pollution in all American cities. Autopsies of smog disaster victims revealed an average chlorinated hydrocarbon load in fatty tissue equivalent to 26 parts per million of DDT. In October, 1973, the Department of Health, Education and Welfare announced studies which showed unequivocally that increasing death rates from hypertension, cirrhosis of the liver, liver cancer and a series of other diseases had resulted from the chlorinated hydrocarbon load. They estimated that Americans born since 1946 (when DDT usage began) now had a life expectancy of only 49 years, and predicted that if current patterns continued, this expectancy would reach 42 years by 1980, when it might level out. Plunging insurance stocks triggered a stock market panic. . . . Giants of the petrochemical industry, attempting to dispute the indisputable evidence, launched a massive pressure campaign on Congress to force HEW to "get out of agriculture's business." They were aided by the agro-chemical journals, which had decades of experience in misleading the public about the benefits and dangers of pesticides. But by now the public realized that it had been duped. . . . The year 1973 was the year in which Americans finally came to understand the direct threat to their existence posed by environmental deterioration.

And 1973 was also the year in which most people finally comprehended the indirect threat. Even the president of Union Oil Company and several other industrialists publicly stated their concern over the reduction of bird populations which had resulted from pollution by DDT and other chlorinated hydrocarbons. Inspect populations boomed because they were resistant to most pesticides and had been freed, by the incompetent use of those pesticides, from most of their natural enemies. Rodents swarmed over crops, multiplying rapidly in the absence of predatory birds. The effect of pests on the wheat crop was especially disastrous in the summer of 1973, since that was also the year of the great drought. Most of us can remember the shock which greeted the announcement by atmospheric physicists that the shift of the jet stream which had caused the drought was probably permanent. It signalled the birth of the Midwestern desert. Man's air-polluting activities had by then caused gross changes in climatic patterns.

. . . .

At first Thanodrin seemed to offer excellent control of many pests. True, there was a rash of human fatalities from improper use of the lethal chemical, but, as Russian technical advisors were prone to note, these were more than compensated for by increased yields. Thanodrin use skyrocketed throughout the underdeveloped world. The Mikoyan design group developed a dependable, cheap agricultural aircraft which the Soviets donated to the effort in large numbers. MIG sprayers became even more common in UDCs than MIG interceptors.

Then the troubles began. Insect strains with cuticles resistant to Thanodrin penetration began to appear. And as streams, rivers, fish culture ponds and onshore waters became rich in Thanodrin, more fisheries began to disappear. Bird populations were decimated. The sequence of events was standard for broadcast use of a synthetic pesticide: great success at first, followed by removal of natural enemies and development of resistance by the pest. Populations of crop-eating insects in areas treated with Thanodrin made steady comebacks and soon became more abundant than ever. Yields

plunged, while farmers in their desperation increased the Thanodrin dose and shortened the time between treatments. Death from
Thanodrin poisoning became common. The first violent incident occurred in the Canete Valley of Peru, where farmers had suffered a
similar chlorinated hydrocarbon disaster in the mid-'50s. A Russian
advisor serving as an agricultural pilot was assaulted and killed by
a mob of enraged farmers in January, 1978. Trouble spread rapidly
during 1978, especially after the word got out that two years earlier
Russia herself had banned the use of Thanodrin at home because
of its serious effects on ecological systems. Suddenly Russia, and
not the United States, was the *bête noir* in the UDCs. "Thanodrin
parties" became epidemic, with farmers, in their ignorance, dumping carloads of Thanodrin concentrate into the sea. Russian advisors fled, and four of the Thanodrin plants were leveled to the
ground. Destruction of the plants in Rio and Calcutta led to hundreds of thousands of gallons of Thanodrin concentrate being
dumped directly into the sea.

. . . .

It was in January, 1979, that huge blooms of a previously unknown variety of diatom were reported off the coast of Peru. The
blooms were accompanied by a massive die-off of sea life and of
the pathetic remainder of the birds which had once feasted on the
anchovies of the area. Almost immediately another huge bloom was
reported in the Indian ocean, centering around the Seychelles, and
then a third in the South Atlantic off the African coast. Both of
these were accompanied by spectacular die-offs of marine animals.
Even more ominous were growing reports of fish and bird kills at
oceanic points where there were no spectacular blooms. Biologists
were soon able to explain the phenomena: the diatom had evolved
an enzyme which broke down Thanodrin; that enzyme also produced a breakdown product which interfered with the transmission of nerve impulses, and was therefore lethal to animals. Unfortunately, the biologists could suggest no way of repressing the
poisonous bloom in time. By September, 1979, all important animal
life in the sea was extinct. Large areas of coastline had to be evacuated, as windrows of dead fish created a monumental stench.

211.

Mark Van Doren

SO FAIR A WORLD IT WAS [1969]

So fair a world it was,
So far away in the dark, the dark,
Yet lighted, oh, so well, so well:
Water and land,
So clear, so sweet;
So fair, it should have been forever.

And would have been, and would have been,
If—what?
Be still. But what?
Keep quiet, child. So fair it was,
The memory is like a death
That dies again; that dies again.

INDEX OF AUTHORS

Authors whose work is represented in this book are listed here alphabetically, along with bibliographic information on the sources of the selections. Figures in boldface type are selection numbers. Where a title has been changed, the original is clearly noted. Bibliographic information covers original publication and, when different, editions actually used in preparing this volume, except in the cases of poems and other works widely anthologized or available in numerous reprint editions.

INDEX OF ANONYMOUS SELECTIONS

(arranged alphabetically by title)